Recycled Reads
APL Bookstore

The War Within

The War Within

America's Battle over Vietnam

TOM WELLS

With a Foreword by Todd Gitlin

University of California Press

BERKELEY   LOS ANGELES   LONDON

The publisher gratefully acknowledges the contribution provided by the General Endowment Fund of the Associates of the University of California Press.

To Lisa and my mother, Alma Wells

University of California Press
Berkeley and Los Angeles, California

University of California Press, Ltd.
London, England

© 1994 by
The Regents of the University of California

Library of Congress Cataloging-in-Publication Data

Wells, Tom, 1955–
  The war within : America's battle over Vietnam / Tom Wells ; with a foreword by Todd Gitlin.
      p.   cm.
  Includes bibliographical references and index.
  ISBN 0-520-08367-9 (alk. paper)
  1. Vietnamese Conflict, 1961–1975—Protest movements—United States.   2. United States—Politics and government—1963–1969.   3. United States—Politics and government—1969–1974.   I. Title.
DS559.6.W45   1994
959.704'3373—dc20   93-28460

Printed in the United States of America
9 8 7 6 5 4 3 2 1

The paper used in this publication meets the minimum requirements of American National Standard for Information Sciences—Permanence of Paper for Printed Library Materials, ANSI Z39.48-1984. ∞

Contents

Photographs following page 286

Acknowledgments

I wish to thank first of all those people who agreed to be interviewed for this book. Their contribution was immense. Without them, the book would have been of much less value and considerably less interesting to read. Extra thanks to those who provided photographs.

I am very grateful to the following people for reading and commenting on parts or all of the manuscript: Ted Alden, Bob Blauner, Ken Bock, Lisa Bryant, Joe Burros, Todd Gitlin, Paul Joseph, Richard Leo, Staughton Lynd, Roger Morris, Carl Oglesby, Michael Rogin, Skip Schick, and Lois West. Todd Gitlin was my principal adviser on my Ph.D. dissertation, which consisted of the first half of this book, and a formative influence on the entire project. His advice and insight were invaluable.

I had the good fortune to receive the assistance of many archivists, archives technicians, and curators. They included: Jacquie Demsky, Linda Hanson, David Humphrey, E. Philip Scott, and Steve Yount of the Lyndon Baines Johnson Library; James Hastings, Joan Howard, Richard McNeill, Byron Parham, and Karl Weissenbach of the Nixon Project; Wendy Chmielewski of the Swarthmore College Peace Collection; and Andy Kraushaar of the State Historical Society of Wisconsin. Thanks also to Jeffrey Blankfort and Henry Wilhelm for digging up old photographs.

I wish to thank the staff of University of California Press, particularly Naomi Schneider, for all of their help in bringing the book to fruition. The same goes for my copy editor, Peter Dreyer.

I received financial support from a number of sources, including: an Institute on Global Conflict and Cooperation dissertation fellowship, an Institute for the Study of World Politics dissertation fellowship, a National Science Foundation dissertation grant, a University of California Chancellor's Patent Fund grant, a University of California Regents fellowship, and a University of California research fellowship.

Most of all, I wish to thank my wife, Lisa Bryant, for her steadying support, patient ear, and wise advice, not to mention tolerance of my fixations and self-absorption. Without her, the writing of this book would have been much less enjoyable, and the result would have substantially less merit.

Foreword
By Todd Gitlin

The 1992 presidential campaign made clear that the agony of the Vietnam war remains a live issue in American politics—as well it deserves to be. To be sure, the polarization is not as sharp as before. Despite the labors of Republican sleuths to find the youthful antiwar demonstrator Bill Clinton guilty of trickery, Clinton—a draft evader who at the time wrote of his moral revulsion against "killing or dying" (note the order of the verbs) in Vietnam—was elected president of the United States. Even Ross Perot, who had fervently supported the Vietnam war while it was happening, defended candidate Clinton's right to his youthful views against a reproachful George Bush. A certain gray consensus has built up in the passage of time that the war was terrible, and that, whether it was "well-intentioned" or "fundamentally wrong and immoral," the country would have been better off not fighting it. The common culture believes in putting history behind us, especially when war goes badly. In January 1993, on the twentieth anniversary of the Paris peace agreement that formally ended the American phase of the war, one poll had 68 percent saying it had been "a mistake" to send troops to Vietnam. Earlier polls give even larger majorities.

Still, the war left a gash in the heart of America. When President Bill Clinton appeared at the memorial wall early in his administration to take his boos and cheers, he did not—he could not—pretend that gash into oblivion. Neither could his predecessor, George Bush, who in the wake of the Persian Gulf war declared wishfully that America had "kicked the Vietnam syndrome once and for all"; nor could *his* predecessor, Ronald Reagan, who declared it a "noble cause." The war remains a watershed in American history. On one side of that history, America, whatever its rights and wrongs, stands triumphant, its glorious destiny manifest. On the other, America knows defeat, even shame. That is why Maya Lin's brilliant, black, unconsoling wall is like no other monument in Washington. It is the most beautiful of all scars, neither above ground nor below, but sunk into a green place where death inhabits life and defeat is in the nature of things. Far into the twenty-first century, Americans may well go on debating the meaning of that war, just as in parts of the Old South, one hundred twenty-five years after Appomattox, they still fight over the flying of the Confederate Stars and Bars. They are fighting over the racial identity of the Old South—over whose Old South it was. And we, throughout America, are still fighting, and may go on for decades fighting—and *should* be fighting—over the meaning of the longest war in American history.

Time does not heal all wounds, though it does impose fresh ones that require attention. Still, even now that the Cold War is finished, there are many reasons why the history of the Vietnam war should remain fresh and the effort to grasp both the war and the antiwar opposition remains important. In Southeast Asia there are, of course, the millions of Vietnamese, Cambodian, and Laotian dead, who have no monument. The Vietnamese have always been either demonized, sentimentalized, or rendered invisible. The most reputable *conservative* calculation, in Guenter Lewy's *America in Vietnam*, estimates that 400,000 civilians were killed in the course of the war, as were 850,000 North Vietnamese Army and Viet Cong combatants. If we add a likely equivalent number of Saigon army dead, the *Vietnamese* death toll rises above two million—not including the Laotians and Cambodians. For most Americans—and for official America— they still do not exist, they are still nameless.

Vietnam, an actual place and a brutalized people, is not "Vietnam," the label for a policy or a "syndrome." The actual war of napalm and phosphorus, B-52s and land mines, cluster bombs and punji sticks and Agent Orange is still inscribed in the skins and bones of the wounded. And so the story of the war itself has the power and scale of all deep tragedy. It is a case of history at the boiling point: the product of bad thinking yoked to the modern superstate's power to inflict vast bodily harm. But because there was also a "war within," the story of the Vietnam war is more than a horrible chapter in the barbaric history of the twentieth century. It is here that Tom Wells's exemplary history has the greatest importance. The premise of his book is that the history of the war without is inseparable from that of the war within. Together they *are* America. Understand the two in relation to one another and you understand not only the disasters of war but the limits and possibilities of American democracy. The two together express the tangled nature of America.

The Vietnam war is, of course, an episode in military history. It is also, certainly, an episode in the sorry history of the Cold War and of decolonization. It has frequently been analyzed from the angle of political strategy. But if, with Tom Wells, we trace the two together, we see that the war and the antiwar were inseparable, and then we can also approach this history as one of the phenomenal episodes in the history of democracy—and I mean democracy on a world scale, democracy as an idea that has defined political life, by attraction and by repulsion, for more than two centuries.

In this light, the movement against the Vietnam war was one of the triumphs of democratic history. Over many years, resisting illegitimate authority—in the language of one of its clarion calls—the movement defended the Constitution against a war that lacked constitutional warrant. For democracy is not simply the rule of a majority. Majority rule, if unrestricted, may lead to one episode of demagogic authoritarianism after another. No, democracy is also to be measured by the vitality of the common life. It is a quality not of the state alone, but of the populace. Democratic society is both more than and different from democratic government; it requires the engagement of a whole population and, if need be, the exercise of popular sovereignty. One of its prerequisites is that it afforded minorities the opportunity to become, or to amalgamate into, majorities. This opportunity comes not only through periodic elections; it also comes through all the measures of popular argument, assembly, mobilization, and countermobilization. But opportunity is only a door; the point is to walk through it. The society must also take advantage of the opportunity. Minorities must not only seek to make themselves into majorities, they must find, or create, the means to achieve the popular will. Democracy is not for bad nerves or ancestor worship. That is why, in Carl Oglesby's words, democracy is nothing if it is not dangerous.

In the conduct of foreign policy, America's rulers during the Vietnam war were (as Arthur Schlesinger, Jr., wrote) imperial. Whatever one concludes from the recent debate about John F. Kennedy's intentions in his last months, it is clear that at least in his early years he pursued the war with his customary vigor. "Special operations" like those of the Green Berets expressed his passion for guerrilla maneuver as well as the logic of his commitment to the "long, twilight struggle" against Communism. The deepening commitment to war proved largely uncontroversial within his administration. Those who dissented resigned (like Assistant Secretary of State Roger Hilsman) or were ignored (like Undersecretary of State George Ball). "Our greatest mistake was Vietnam," replied McGeorge Bundy to a question I posed at a Berkeley luncheon in 1992. "I wish we had quit [Vietnam] when I was there. It would have taken bravery."

Whatever Kennedy might have done if he had lived, it is plain that after his assassination and for more than a decade beyond, Lyndon Johnson and Richard Nixon were hell-bent on winning—or at least, as Daniel Ellsberg has argued, refusing to lose—a war with no constitutional warrant. Informed debate was not their interest. They tried to outflank debate by lying and lying again and lying about their lies. They used the immense powers of the modern executive to create "facts on the ground." They brandished thousands of American casualties (the Vietnamese, of course, didn't count in their calculus) as arguments for tens of thousands more American casualties. They deceived, discouraged, and tried to disrupt and suppress the usually legal opposition of their countrymen and -women. Eventually they were discredited and defeated by their own recklessness—and by the extraordinary resolve and organization of an enemy fighting on its home ground, an enemy they did not begin to understand. However fervently they tried to bomb and lie what Johnson called "this damn little piss-ant country" into submission, however devoutly Henry Kissinger refused to "believe that a fourth-rate power like North Vietnam doesn't have a breaking point," they were unable to win. And winning, for them as for Vince Lombardi, was not the main thing, it was the only thing.

Because they staked so much for so long on their arrogance, by the late 1960s they faced a political dilemma that offered no good solution. Lyndon Johnson had plunged deeply into the war, multiplying the American expeditionary force from some twenty-five thousand in 1963, at the time of Kennedy's assassination, to more than half a million in 1968. To keep up American morale, he had to produce victories—or the image of victories. To convey that image, he sent more troops, dropped more bombs, killed more people, and made more insupportable claims about how successful this all was. This inflammable combination was bad for morale. It aroused yet more opposition everywhere in America. Johnson's fundamental blunders helped wreck the Democratic Party for the next quarter-century and converted a potentially great (in the lowercase sense) society into a moral wasteland and a political swamp.

What had started as a rivulet, the protest of a few, grew into the torrent of a vast and representative majority—probably the largest and most effective antiwar movement in history. In his remarkable study, Wells shows in detail that from the moment Richard Nixon took office in 1969, he was obsessed with the antiwar movement. Most of the movement, in turn, misread the signs from the White House; they took at face value the administration's insistence that the movement was impotent. After carefully sifting the documentary evidence and conducting his own methodical interviews with many administration officials, Tom Wells concludes that for all its miscalculations and deep divisions, *and yet without understanding its own strength,* the movement kept Nixon at crucial junctures from ratcheting up the war. It functioned as a veto force. Nixon feared that the opposition would prevent him from governing. To defeat the movement, he phased out the draft, "Vietnamized" the ground war (or, as the movement used to say, changed the color of the bodies), and succeeded in moving the carnage off television. But these adroit maneuvers weren't enough. He cranked up the superstate's punitive apparatus. His administration's obsession with an implacable opposition drove him to overreach. In fact, it was the obsessive quality of his fear—that is, his ignorance and his lack of faith in democracy—that brought him down. The measures he took to suppress opposition boomeranged. The resulting authoritarian blunders will forever be known as Watergate.

Nixon was more insecure, and therefore more erratic, than other recent chief executives. But his idiosyncrasies also have an ancient lineage. Even more than Lyndon Johnson, Nixon played out one classic motif in the history of failed rule: contempt for the governed. One of the fundamental truths about these men and their inner circles is that they were not democrats. Their temper was "can-do." They were whiz kids (Democrats) or advertising executives (Republicans) or grandiose would-be architects of world order (Kissinger). All of them prized secrecy. They failed abysmally at one of the prerequisites of leadership in a democratic society: curiosity. For all their denunciations of the antiwar movement for its "negativism," they refused to understand the depth and breadth of the antiwar movement and failed to grasp even how badly they misunderstood it. As Tom Wells tells us, President Richard Nixon's speechwriter Raymond Price thought the antiwarriors were lost in "an orgy of right-brain indulgence." Nixon's chief of staff, H. R. Haldeman, thought of protesters as "people who want to get excited about something, and they don't really give much of a darn what it is they're excited about."

With the apparatchik's contempt for democracy, Haldeman failed to grasp the essence of a working democracy: that a good many people do indeed "want to get excited about something," and even find many public issues worth getting excited about, because they have the audacity to think the government is theirs. Haldeman's view was a bad caricature of something real. What was developing was the spirit, if not the program, of a general radical movement. The longer the war went on, the more the radical wing of the antiwar movement felt in its bones that there were deep, not just transient, reasons why the national leadership was unable or unwilling to call it quits. The war had to be more than a mistake, it was a crime; or even more than a crime, it had to be symptomatic of a rotten system or even an irredeemably monstrous civilization. The radical wing came to think that the war had been produced not simply by one single branch of the political establishment or even by two branches, but by the poisoned roots of American society as a whole. Because the war pitted a technologically superior, white-led juggernaut against a largely peasant Asian society, growing numbers of opponents came to see it as a racist war—the foreign component of a seamless economic and cultural system characterized by white supremacy, murderous technology, and irresponsible central power devoid of justice. And if established America refused to relinquish the Vietnam war, if it *needed* the war, then it seemed to follow that America needed more than an antiwar movement. It needed a radical revolt, or what growing numbers of activists came to call a revolution.

The radical conclusion built on the experience and sensibility of the first great 1960s movement—the civil rights movement. There the young rebels of the New Left had first acquired a taste for direct action and a distaste for the euphemisms of power. There too for many years the mechanisms of constitutional democracy were evidently broken, and students had learned to resort to unconventional means, to "go into the streets," to arouse the collective conscience. Eventually, to increasing numbers of activists, unreason did not seem unreasonable either. Because of the deadly combination of government repression and their own fecklessness, there was no significant Old Left of elders to lead the movement. The young radicals were available. As the SDS organizer Robb Burlage said (drawing on the American critic Van Wyck Brooks), they—we—were "spiritually unemployed." The New Left could hardly believe in the Cold War, the only other absorbing political crusade America had to offer. So the young radicals played an immense part in the antiwar movement. And the government kept ham-handedly, thick-headedly making the case for a radical shift not only in foreign policy but in the national ethos as well.

Because the warmakers failed to grasp that the problem was their war—an unjust and (if that were not bad enough for a good American pragmatist) unwinnable war—the war ended up testing the resilience of virtually every American institution, not least the antiwar movement itself. What for many organizers started out as an antiwar movement pure and simple rapidly became more than that. It was a seedbed of organized and not-so-organized political and cultural opposition. Because the warmakers, America's chief authorities, were smug and entrenched and apparently obdurate, many of the antiwarriors shed their faith in authority overall. They shed their respect for authority, even their knowledge of authority, and eventually their acknowledgment of authority altogether. They elevated themselves into the only authority they would recognize—an alluring but dangerous political principle. They went their own cultural and political way. Because such radical self-reliance is psychologically difficult, they eventually constructed fantasies about revolutionary leaders abroad—Ho Chi Minh, Mao Tse-tung, Che Guevara, Fidel Castro. They created their own institutions and even, finally, thought they would create their own revolution. Never mind that this was a contradiction in terms, since a revolution cannot be the exclusive property of any group. With their rigid designs, some sectarians conjured their own hypothetical populace, their own moment in history, into an abstract self-aggrandizement. Militancy became recklessness, even self-immolation. For the most part, this wildness in the streets played into the hands of the White House. (As Wells tells us, Haldeman's notes from a 1971 meeting with Nixon put it memorably: "Smear the liberals with the left—and keep at it.") Other sectarians, especially those of the Socialist Workers Party, woodenly repeated their formulas for decorous politics when more audacious action might have intervened more effectively. From today's vantage point after the Cold War, the story Wells tells of the internecine battles within the top antiwar organizations may seem merely arcane, a question of how many factions can dance on the edge of a precipice, but it is an important cautionary tale.

And yet, for all its sins and stupidity, the movement, especially at the grass roots, proved ingenious—a marvel of popular inventiveness. For every prominent leader or celebrity there were thousands of Bill Clintons involved in a Vietnam Moratorium or a local march, thousands of soldiers, sailors, Marines, nurses, and airmen rebelling against the war. Tom Wells reminds us of the amazing scope and intricacy of the antiwar movement. He gives African American organizers and religious groupings like Clergy and Laymen Concerned About Vietnam their due. He notes the rehabilitation work undertaken by Quakers in Vietnam itself. He points to the antiwar influence of the wives and children of powerful officials. He has opened his ears to many unsung heroes—though not all, of course; there were far too many for one book, even one long book.

The War Within is an indispensable account of that indispensable movement, and I hope it is read by students as well as scholars and journalists and truth-seekers in general. Today, I get the impression that many students and other young people who want to change the world believe that they face an absolute either/or. Pragmatic to the core, they want results. They identify the 1960s with sound and fury but no results—or bad results. They are inclined to think that, whatever the 1960s' movements might have achieved, the world was left more miserable, more disappointing than before. True, as a would-be revolution, the militant wing was a catastrophic failure. But as an antiwar movement, the whole was a considerable if limited success. It restricted the most awesome prerogative of the chief executive: the power to deal death and destruction. It saved lives, limbs, and minds. It shortened the subsequent wars that did take place. Two decades later, many of those limits are still in force.

In telling his story, Wells is not misled by the distorting lens of the media, which at the time often preferred the garish and gaudy if unrepresentative images—the bandannas, the occasional burning of flags—and today keep the photogenic images in circulation as cheap mementos to electrify otherwise mediocre documentary reminiscences. Collective memory is warped by the disproportionate weight of events that were theatrical enough to be recorded by cameras and passed down through the decades as honest-to-goodness "history." Lights! Camera! Cops! Dissolve to Viet Cong flags flapping in the breeze to the soundtrack of "Street Fighting Man"! Wells knows that flashy images left to themselves are distortions.

Wells contributes more than an absorbing saga. He shows that the movement was not the simple, self-indulgent spasm of lawlessness flogged by right-wing commentators. He has a keen eye for the dramatic collisions in what was, finally, a fight for the soul of America. He subtly probes the thinking on both sides, moving fluidly from the warmakers to the antiwarriors and back again. He has done the most careful analysis yet of the movement's impact. He puts the lie to the canard that blames antiwar students for trying to sneak out of the draft by pointing out (as SDS did in 1967) that it was the Selective Service System itself that decided to "channel" college students into protected professions by exempting them from the draft. Dr. Wells, younger than most movement participants, brings a valuable distance to the fervent disputes of the time. In compiling and weighing evidence, he is thorough and scrupulous. His partisanship is frequently clear—better clear than disguised—but he is fair, and his scholarship is lucid: he offers evidence against which his own conclusions can be tested. He does not pretend to a more general "theory" of social movements than his material warrants, nor does he make the error of thinking that either "conditions" or "grievances" or "resources" are the authors of history.

The warmakers and the antiwarriors, entangled with each other, were at odds not only over the destiny of Southeast Asia but also over the destiny of the United States. Theirs is a momentous story, a great human drama, and thanks to Tom Wells's fine work, it is here in full for subsequent generations.

Introduction

This is the story of a protracted contest between two political camps in the United States during the Vietnam War: ordinary citizens, armed mainly with only their bodies and minds, who actively opposed their government's military intervention in Vietnam, and America's top government officials, commanders of the most powerful military machine on the face of the earth. It was a clash unprecedented in American affairs—never before had so many U.S. citizens defied their leaders during wartime.

What dialogue there was between these two opposing camps was frustrating, often excruciating, and sometimes violent. It was marked by considerable mutual contempt and misperception. Participants on both sides regarded their antagonists as either villains or fools. It was also largely a mediated dialogue, with the debaters isolated from each other and communicating mainly through the media. I have sought in this book to bring these debaters together, if not in the same room, then at least in the same pages.

The first camp was less a unified army than a bountiful mix of political notions and visions that brought together teenagers and senior citizens, Democratic Party lobbyists and Maoist revolutionaries, pacifists and street fighters, letter writers and draft resisters, healers and bomb makers. The story attempts to capture this camp's tremendous political and social richness, for it was in this richness that its power ultimately resided. It explores protesters' multifarious reasons for undertaking particular types of antiwar activity, including legal demonstrations, civil disobedience, electoral challenges, grass-roots organizing, fasts, and political violence. I have tried to bring both the thinking and actions of peace activists to life, to allow the reader to *feel* the antiwar movement's inner life and vitality as well as comprehend them. The protesters' thoughts are expressed largely in their own words, both in written documents and in interviews.

Deciding which antiwar activities to pursue was, of course, an ongoing task

1

for protesters. They were forever asking themselves, "What do we do next?" Shaping their decisions were perceptions of what had worked in the past. Whether a particular antiwar tactic had already netted apparent political returns colored its appeal. Accordingly, this narrative examines peace activists' perceptions of their political effectiveness during the course of the war. For many, the antiwar fight brought mounting and profound political frustration. Despite the movement's steady expansion, they observed, the bloodletting in Vietnam only increased. The White House seemed heedless of public protest, its occupants amoral. There was apparently no telling how far the U.S. government would go to impose its designs on the peasantry of Southeast Asia: even World War III was possible. Public support for U.S. policies compounded activists' distress. The building frustration in the movement bred feelings of desperation in many circles. For some protesters, the desperation even begot self-sacrifice. "What more can we possibly do?" was a common cry in the movement. The frustration was greatest amongst youth. And it was particularly pronounced in periods following large national demonstrations, when, despite the dissent, little if anything seemed to change. Few activists fully appreciated the considerable political power they possessed.

This story tracks the mounting political frustration experienced by protesters and analyzes its effect on the movement. One of my theses is that thwarted political hopes were the main (but by no means the only) impetus behind escalations in antiwar tactics. Frustrated hopes were the principal reason for the growing militancy in the movement, including the use of political violence. The only way to stop the war, many protesters concluded, was to make America ungovernable. Others simply sought existential satisfaction; still others sought vengeance. The frustration also nourished revolutionary sentiment. And it goes a long way toward explaining the rise and actions of the ultraleft youth group who called themselves the Weathermen.

The story argues that activists' failure to appreciate their actual political power hurt their cause. That failure spawned defections from the movement. It bred lethargy, stagnation, and despair in the movement's ranks, impeding the organization of protests and the maintenance of antiwar groups. It fostered antipathy to traditional legal demonstrations, hindering the public display of antiwar sentiment. It hampered efforts to sustain outpourings of dissent, particularly in the early 1970s, when, amid Richard Nixon's escalations of the war, cynicism about the efficacy of antiwar protest was especially widespread. Not least important, it aggravated dissension over strategies and tactics among activists, thereby depleting energies, hardening internal divisions, and reducing the movement's capacity for coordinated action. Moreover, some Americans never protested because they felt it was futile.

The story also explores what inspired activists, what gave them hope and kept them going in the face of the war's horrors. For despite the building frustration among them, the antiwar movement repeatedly showed its staying power and remained a weighty political force.

Political diversity proved to be a double-edged sword. Although it compounded the movement's numbers, it engendered fierce and enduring disputes among protesters that tore peace organizations apart. Often, participants at antiwar meetings could agree on little more than their opposition to U.S. intervention in Vietnam. Both the student and adult national antiwar coalitions split bitterly into opposing factions. Internal strife also destroyed Students for a Democratic Society (SDS), the dominant radical youth group. The tendency of many protesters to combat each other rather than the war wreaked tremendous damage. It sapped energy from the movement that could otherwise have gone into building it. The strife also turned off recruits, alienated the public, demoralized activists, created personal enemies, and led protesters to drop out. Moreover, it stalled antiwar planning and hampered nationally coordinated peace activity. And splits in antiwar groups not only weakened the movement but stoked perceptions of powerlessness. The Trotskyist Socialist Workers Party (SWP) was the most divisive force; its zealous attempts to control the movement and rigid insistence on taking the "correct line" poisoned the atmosphere of countless antiwar meetings. Indeed, the SWP must bear the primary blame for the splits in the national antiwar coalitions, as its political rigidity and gladiatorial approach to coalition work left little room for compromise.

The U.S. government greatly aggravated the antiwar movement's internal divisions. Through the use of dirty tricks and agents provocateurs, government bodies fanned the strife. The movement's schisms were not totally self-generated. But the main responsibility for the combat must lie with the combatants themselves. It was they who chose to pick up the sword, and they who could have put it down.

This book also examines voices of hindsight from the peace movement. Based on interviews with leading antiwar activists scattered across the country, it explores how these activists later felt about political choices they made. Many were regretful. Some of those most deeply involved in the movement's internal strife, in fact, remembered it with embarrassed disbelief. Contrary to press reports, however, many had remained politically active.

The U.S. government took the antiwar movement quite seriously. If many protesters failed to appreciate their political clout, officials in the Johnson and Nixon administrations did not. They considered the movement a nagging sign of domestic dissatisfaction with the war, a threat to their base of domestic support, a menace to American social stability, and a source of encouragement to the Vietnamese enemy. Officials recognized that protesters were, in fact, the cutting edge of domestic antiwar sentiment as a whole. Washington consequently followed the movement's activities closely, nervously, relentlessly. Officials at the highest levels paid keen attention to them. Presidents Johnson and Nixon both took an active interest in the movement's doings. The intelligence reports they requested and received on protests exhibited marked detail. Nixon, whose White House craved intelligence on all of its political enemies, received multiple reports per day on some demonstrations.

This study explores Washington's concern about particular antiwar protests and the policies it employed to try to blunt them. It pays considerable attention to the steps officials took to counteract the peace movement's political influence in the United States. The story chronicles an American government increasingly restive over the antiwar force rising in its domestic rear and logging long hours devising schemes to contain it. "The youth problem" was the subject of more than a few White House memos and meetings. The story also examines officials' perceptions of how they were faring in the battle for American hearts and minds.

Yet despite the close attention they paid to the antiwar movement, these pages show, both the Johnson and Nixon administrations seriously misunderstood their antagonists. Officials attributed the wellsprings of dissent more to emotionalism, character flaws, and sinister external forces than reasoned judgments. Indeed, both Lyndon Johnson and Richard Nixon, and many of their aides, were convinced that foreign communists were behind the dissent.

This book also considers the peace movement's painful personal consequences for U.S. officials. Protesters disrupted officials' lives by restricting their public appearances and travel in the United States. Moreover, the movement infiltrated officials' social circles and—most agonizing of all—their immediate families. More than a few had sons or daughters on the other side of the barricades. In a very real sense, the movement spelled personal torment for many government officials. Such torment sapped some officials' strength for the war.

Finally, this study explores the actual effect of the movement on U.S. policy in Vietnam. It contends that the movement played a major role in constraining, de-escalating, and ending the war. The movement inhibited both U.S. air and ground activity in Indochina during the Johnson administration. It fed the mounting unease with the conflict of key administration officials in late 1967 and early 1968. The movement fueled Eugene McCarthy's presidential bid, which shaped official perceptions in 1968 that the public had turned against the war. It had a significant effect on the influential private Johnson advisers known as the Wise Men. And it was the most important manifestation of the domestic antiwar mood that forced the Johnson administration to reverse course in Vietnam in 1968.

The peace movement also exerted a substantial impact on the Nixon administration's policies in Vietnam. It fueled U.S. troop withdrawals from Vietnam.

It continued to inhibit both the U.S. air and ground wars in Indochina. It exerted a critical influence on Nixon's decision not to carry out his 1969 threat to Hanoi of a massive military blow. It shaped his determination to prematurely withdraw U.S. forces from Cambodia in 1970. The movement nourished the deterioration in U.S. troop discipline and morale in Vietnam, which provided additional impetus to U.S. troop withdrawals. It put pressure on the administration to negotiate a settlement of the war. And it gave impetus to congressional legislation that cut off U.S. funds for the war.

What's more, the movement promoted the Watergate scandal, which ultimately played a pivotal role in ending the war. It influenced Nixon's decisions to bomb Cambodia secretly and then to lie to Congress about it, a consideration in the subsequent proceedings to impeach him. Public exposure of the bombing prompted the administration's illegal wiretaps of officials and reporters, which were among the "White House horrors" later revealed to the public. The movement, particularly its militant wing, and Nixon's conviction that foreign communists were behind the dissent, engendered the infamous Huston Plan, another White House horror and consideration in the Watergate inquiries. Peace activists inspired Daniel Ellsberg, who made the Pentagon Papers public, giving rise to the Plumbers, whose illegal activities (burglarizing Ellsberg's psychiatrist's office among them) were also a major factor in the impeachment proceedings. Ellsberg's leak further inspired a White House plot to break in to the Brookings Institution, yet another "White House horror." And the evidence that the Pentagon Papers provided of high-level duplicity fed domestic skepticism of Nixon during the Watergate hearings. The movement also fed the White House's paranoia about its political enemies, which played no small part in hatching the Watergate break-in itself. And the Watergate revelations undermined Nixon's authority in Congress and thus his ability to wage war.

The antiwar movement accomplished none of these feats alone. Its power was always tied to broader political forces. It was simply, as officials realized, the cutting edge of domestic antiwar sentiment as a whole. In fact, the movement's *precise* impact on U.S. policies is impossible to pin down. Yet, this study demonstrates, that impact was clearly substantial. In addition, the movement nurtured broad antiwar sentiment in the United States. It provoked doubts about the war's merits among the American public and elites, including in Congress and the media, who, in turn, influenced other Americans. The threat the movement apparently posed to domestic social stability also fostered public and elite discontent with the war.

All in all, the movement was very effective. And it was effective despite an intensive, sustained, and well-financed effort by the U.S. government to disrupt, divide, and blunt it by every means officials could think up.

What if there had been no antiwar movement? What would the war have looked like then? The questions are unanswerable, but speculation is possible. Public distaste for the war would surely have developed without vocal dissent, so Washington would not have been given a free rein in Indochina. But that distaste would neither have developed as soon nor been as strong. And without vocal dissent, Americans' disquiet would have been more easily contained and manipulated by official propaganda. Washington would also not have had to fear for domestic social stability—the war would not have come home. Consequently, the domestic political constraints on the war would have been considerably weaker. The likely results: a much harsher bombing campaign over both North and South Vietnam, more U.S. troop deployments, a wider ground war in Indochina, and countless more deaths, particularly Vietnamese ones. The United States might well eventually have pummeled Hanoi into submission—if not, as protesters feared, sparked World War III.

As successful as the antiwar movement was, however, it could have been even more effective. The unrealistic expectations and political impatience of many activists, and the resulting frustration among them, served to limit the size, frequency, and scope of antiwar protest. So did the movement's internal strife. Perceptions that the war was inexorably ending in the late 1960s and early 1970s further weakened the movement; many felt protest was no longer pressing or even necessary. A larger, stronger movement would have imprinted the war's unpopularity and cost in domestic peace even more forcefully on governmental minds. It would have also exerted greater influence on the public. Consequently, the domestic political restraints on the war would have been still greater. More American and Vietnamese lives could have been saved as a result.

This study draws on numerous sources. Aside from interviewing antiwar activists, I examined thousands of pages of peace movement documents at the State Historical Society of Wisconsin archives in Madison and the University of California's Bancroft Library in Berkeley. These documents included meeting notes, letters, leaflets, pamphlets, and position papers. I also read many articles in antiwar periodicals, as well as most secondary literature on the movement. The main sources for my investigation of governmental attitudes and policies toward protesters are also interviews and primary documents. I conducted over three dozen interviews with senior officials in the Johnson and Nixon administrations. I also examined small mountains of government documents at the Lyndon Baines Johnson Library in Austin, Texas, and the Nixon Project archives in Alexandria, Virginia. These documents included internal memoranda, meeting notes, official essays on protest, and "talking papers." For the Nixon administration, such documents are especially abundant (so abundant, in fact, that many of the administration's machinations against the antiwar movement could not be included in this book). The Pentagon Papers shed valuable additional light on the Johnson administration's decision making. Officials' memoirs were helpful, too. In addition, I interviewed a number of prominent people who were not members of the Johnson and Nixon administrations to assist my analysis of the peace movement's influence on domestic attitudes toward the war. And the *New York Times, Washington Post,* and *Guardian* (New York) newsweekly proved to be valuable sources of information on the activities of both protesters and officials.

I was not active in the antiwar movement. I was nine years old when the first U.S. ground combat units entered Vietnam and a fresh high school graduate when the last ones left. The war was essentially a sporadic series of television images for me; I gave it little thought. The social pressures of adolescence, schoolwork, and sports were more pressing than Vietnam. What politics I had were not well considered. Raised in a nominally Republican household, I harbored a vague perception that it was George McGovern, not Richard Nixon, who was the chronic liar during the 1972 presidential campaign, but the issues scarcely registered. By the mid 1970s, with a year of college under my belt, however, I had come to share the peace movement's opposition to U.S. intervention in Vietnam. It is a sentiment I continue to hold; I have made no effort to conceal it in these pages. Nonetheless, I have striven to provide no less accurate an account of governmental sentiment and actions than of those of the antiwar movement.

This book had its origins in my Ph.D. dissertation at the University of California, Berkeley. I began my more than ten years of work on it with the aim of comparing antiwar activists' perceptions of their political power with their actual power. During the course of my research, several trips around the country conducting interviews and several more to archives, I came to realize that, surprisingly, a worthy *history* of the antiwar movement had not yet been written. I thus elected to expand my study to provide a relatively comprehensive account of the movement as well. As my access to former government officials and White House documents grew, I also decided to explore official thinking and policies toward the movement further. The result is a more ambitious work than I had originally envisioned, but one that, I would like to believe, sheds additional light on this turbulent period of America's past.

ONE   # 1965

War on the Edge

Operation 34-A proceeded in earnest in the summer of 1964. Under the cover of night, squads of South Vietnamese saboteurs parachuted into North Vietnam to blow up bridges, railroads, munitions depots, waterworks. Propagandists rained leaflets from the sky and engineered radio broadcasts from ships offshore. South Vietnamese agents kidnapped citizens of North Vietnam to extract intelligence. American-made Swift boats manned by South Vietnamese commandos peppered North Vietnamese coastal and island installations with cannon and machine-gun fire.

According to Marshall Green, a senior U.S. State Department official at the time, Operation 34-A was "a fiasco. . . . A *terrible* disappointment. Nothing seemed to work." Despite receiving unbridled American support and guidance, the South Vietnamese obviously "had no capability to strike against the North, even in a subversive way like this." They "just didn't have the stuff." Jittery South Vietnamese paratroopers failed to report for their missions. Their officers periodically showed up in drunken stupors designed to render them unfit for service. Those guerrillas who did make it into North Vietnam would often "never show up again"; they were "like sitting ducks."[1]

In Washington, one option took center stage. Bomb. Convinced that the mushrooming revolution in South Vietnam was manufactured in Hanoi, the Johnson administration prepared a plan for graduated air strikes against the North, culminating in sharp blows. The State Department's Walt Rostow, inspired by his experience picking bombing targets during World War II (Rostow *knew* bombing) and persuaded that peasant revolutions could be squelched by cutting off their external sources of support, joined the Joint Chiefs of Staff (JCS) in calling for decisive strikes.

Most administration principals were reluctant to move toward overt escalation, however. It might arouse China and the Soviet Union, they feared, and worry America's allies. It might also prompt the enemy to step up his attacks on the shaky Saigon government. Not least forbidding, it would probably evoke consternation at home; short months before the presidential election, this was a poor time to upset the public. Some politicking was necessary before asking the American people to join a crusade.

At a high-level strategy conference in June, securing a supportive congressional resolution "prior to wider U.S. action" was a key concern. Secretary of State Dean Rusk argued that public opinion on U.S. policy was "badly divided" and that President Johnson therefore required "an affirmation of support." Assistant Secretary of State for East Asian and Pacific Affairs William Bundy stressed the need for an "urgent" public relations campaign "to get at the basic doubts of the value of Southeast Asia and the importance of our stake there." With Johnson's apparent encouragement, the State Department began assembling information for answering "prevalent public questions" on the war. Officials dispensed a steady stream of leaks to the press professing America's intention to stand up to "aggression" in Vietnam.[2]

Then came the Tonkin Gulf incidents. In the early morning hours of July 31, 1964, four Swift boats under the direction of General William Westmoreland, commander of U.S. forces in Vietnam, attacked two small North Vietnamese islands. While the attacks were occurring, the U.S. destroyer *Maddox* was steaming menacingly toward the area. The next day, and again on August 2, T-28 bombers deposited their payloads on North Vietnamese villages near the Laotian border.

On the afternoon of August 2, the enemy struck back. Three North Vietnamese torpedo boats launched a high-speed run at the *Maddox*. One of the boats was knocked dead in the water by jets from a U.S. aircraft carrier nearby, and the others were disabled. Hours later President Johnson ordered the U.S. destroyer *C. Turner Joy* to join the *Maddox* in its muscular patrol of the gulf. "The other side got a sting out of this," Rusk told reporters. "If they do it again, they'll get another sting."[3] That seemed to be the intention. On the night of August 3, the United States orchestrated two more Swift boat raids against North Vietnam. Both American destroyers had been informed of the raids in advance.

The next evening, the *Maddox's* radar detected what appeared to be rapidly closing targets. Over twenty times, the ship's sonarman shouted "Torpedoes in the water," causing the *Maddox* and *Turner Joy* to cut erratically across the sea. Although the *Turner Joy* repeatedly reported the ranges of the targets at which it was firing, the *Maddox's* radar could discern nothing since the first readings. The *Maddox* was, in fact, even having difficulty locating the *Turner Joy*.[4]

Near midnight, the *Maddox's* gun director was given a range reading of the "firmest target we've had all night." "It was a damned big one, right on us," he said later. "No doubt about this one." Just as he was about to squeeze the firing key, however, the gun director realized something was seriously wrong. "'Where is the *Turner Joy?*'" he shouted. "There was a lot of yelling of 'Goddamn' back and forth, with the bridge telling me to 'fire before we lose contact,' and me yelling right back at them," the gun director recalled. "I finally told them, 'I'm not opening fire until I know where the *Turner Joy* is." The bridge directed the *Turner Joy* to turn on its lights. "Sure enough, there she was, right in the cross hairs. I had six five-inch guns [aimed] right at the *Turner Joy*. . . . If I had fired, it would have blown it clean out of the water. In fact, I could have been shot for *not* squeezing the trigger."[5]

At 11 A.M. Washington time, Navy authorities in the Pacific sent the Pentagon a FLASH message indicating the two destroyers were engaged in combat. Several hours later, President Johnson ordered Operation Pierce Arrow "reprisal" strikes against four North Vietnamese torpedo boat bases and an oil-storage depot. While rejecting pleas from the JCS to "clobber" Hanoi,[6] he dispatched air assault forces to Southeast Asia capable of initiating a sustained bombing campaign against the North. He also decided to immediately seek a congressional resolution declaring war.

Late that afternoon, Admiral Ulysses S. Grant Sharp, commander in chief, Pacific (CINCPAC), conveyed some disquieting news to Secretary of Defense Robert McNamara. It was unclear to officers on the spot whether the two U.S. ships had actually been attacked. Before Sharp could get back to him with confirming evidence, McNamara gave the formal execute order for the reprisal strikes. It is now apparent that the attacks never took place. In early 1965, Johnson offered the episode as an example of "what I have to put up with" at the Pentagon. "For all I know, our Navy was shooting at whales out there," he said.[7]

On August 7, Congress passed the Southeast Asia Resolution granting Johnson the considerable power to "take all necessary measures to repel any armed attacks against the forces of the United States and to prevent further aggression." Only two senators—Wayne Morse (D-Oreg.) and Ernest Gruening (D-Alas.)—voted against it. The House of Representatives was even more compliant: it passed the resolution unanimously.

Following the Gulf of Tonkin affair, Johnson's popularity in the Harris poll catapulted from 42 to 72 percent overnight; support for his Vietnam policies increased from 58 to 85 percent.[8] Despite the opposition of Morse and Gruening, the questioning of a few other senators, and a handful of small peace demonstrations, the administration's domestic rear guard appeared safe after all.

Yet officials were taking few chances. The FBI collected the names of citizens who telegrammed Morse in support of his stand. The senator and his secretaries soon noticed suspicious "humming and clicking sounds" on their office phone system. When Morse directed the FBI to sweep the office for bugs the next year, the bureau's agents "would never let us watch as they searched," his receptionist recalled. "I always thought that letting the FBI into our office was letting the fox inside the chicken coop." David Hartsough, a conscientious objector (CO) to the war performing alternative service with the Friends Committee on National Legislation (FCNL) at the time, encountered obstacles when he tried to "dig out the facts" about the Tonkin Gulf incidents:

> I kept making these calls to the Pentagon, and I would keep getting referred to someone else. This happened for two days. I mean, I must have made forty calls. Finally, I got referred to a general. . . . And the general said, "Wait a minute. Let me put you on hold." So he put me on hold, and then he called this other general. He said [to the other general], "This man Hartsough has been calling the Pentagon for the last two days asking all these questions, and his questions are of more than just *passing* interest. If I had anything to say about it, I'd draft him and send him over to Vietnam immediately." And I could hear this while I was on hold. . . . He got back on and said, "We're not going to answer your questions." . . . About a week later, the FCNL was notified that COs could no longer do alternative service work with them.[9]

The government was in no mood for open dialogue with its Vietnamese foes either. In an interview with Eric Sevareid published in *Look* magazine the following year, Adlai Stevenson, U.S. ambassador to the United Nations, revealed that the administration had rebuffed an offer from Hanoi to negotiate a settlement of the war shortly after the Tonkin Gulf affair. When the article appeared, Sevareid recalled, "Johnson *chewed me out*." The president's venom didn't daunt the newsman, though. "He could chew you out but you always knew you could see him again," Sevareid said. President Kennedy, on the other hand, "was a grudge fighter. He was unforgiving."[10]

Throughout the fall of 1964, Johnson assured the public he had no intention of "committing a good many American boys to fighting a war that I think ought to be fought by the boys of Asia." The United States would help the South Vietnamese ward off aggression, but it was not America's war, and he was appalled at the reckless threats of his ultrahawkish presidential opponent, Senator Barry Goldwater (R-Ariz.), to blow North Vietnam to bits. But Johnson's private agenda was rather different. In September, administration principals concluded that, to prevent Saigon's fall, systematic air strikes would probably have to be launched against North Vietnam by early 1965. On November 3—the date of Johnson's lopsided reelection as the "peace candidate"—planning for the strikes began "in earnest."[11]

During the remainder of the year, doubts about the public's stomach for war continued to plague the administration. To make the case for communist belligerence, officials began feeding the press evidence of mounting "infiltration" of North Vietnamese troops into the South. General Westmoreland argued for a "people-to-people program to get the American people emotionally involved" in the war and infuse them with "a greater understanding of what it was all about." William Bundy advocated getting key congressional leaders on board before escalating; he also suggested that the U.S. Information Agency and CIA assemble the "right kind of materials" for foreign distribution. The administration opted against releasing a report on Hanoi's responsibility for the war in the South for fear it might elicit "undesirable speculation."[12]

Seeds of a Movement

In late December, members of the Young Socialist Alliance (YSA), youth group of the Socialist Workers Party, met in Chicago for their national convention. The YSA and SWP would come to play major roles in the anti–Vietnam War movement in the years ahead. At this time, however, the YSA "paid no special attention to Vietnam." It would continue to emphasize "general socialist education" focused on, as the YSA leader Lew Jones later remembered, "whatever issue we could get our hands on."[13] Many of the conventioneers knew little about the war in any event. Some may not even have known where Vietnam was.

Simultaneously, the National Council (NC) of the Students for a Democratic Society, a politically diverse left-leaning organization, was gathered in the venerable meeting hall of the Cloakmakers' Union in New York. Before getting to the tasks at hand, the SDSers seized a large portrait of Lyndon Johnson gawking at them from a wall and turned it around. It was late afternoon by the time Todd Gitlin, SDS's co–point man on international issues with Paul Booth, proposed that the organization write and circulate a "We Won't Go" antidraft statement to protest the growing U.S. intervention in Vietnam. The war was not the main political issue on Gitlin's mind at this time (he was more concerned with U.S. funding of South African apartheid), but he felt *something* had to be done about it, and he and Booth had even invited the progressive journalist I. F. Stone to speak to the NC the evening before to rouse indignation over the issue.[14]

Gitlin's proposal failed to take hold, as did another to send medical supplies to the National Liberation Front (NLF) in South Vietnam. They seemed a bit too radical to some, even pro-communist. Jim Brook, a liberal SDSer, weighed in with a proposal to hold an April march against the war in Washington. The objections came fast and steady. Despite the fact that they were licking their wounds from a sobering summer in the ghettos, the many SDSers then bent on building "community unions" of the urban poor argued vehemently that antiwar protest was too centered on a single issue and not where the radical action was. Furthermore, it might alienate their constituents, more than a few of whom seemed hawkish on Vietnam. SDSers also opposed Brook's proposal on tactical grounds. Impressed by the grass-roots organizing in the South of the Student Nonviolent Coordinating Committee (SNCC), many felt large marches tended to stall local political motion, usurp inordinate amounts of time, energy, and resources, leave no lasting impact on their participants, and bring paltry political returns. "The past few years . . . have shown the government to be increasingly unresponsive to public mass protest," wrote two SDSers. "Even when concessions in legislation or public policy are granted, the concessions are generally sufficient to make the marcher, but not the grievances or problems, go away." The result, often enough, was "demoralization." SDSers also maintained that national marches tended to target specific government policies without challenging the "undemocratic" manner in which those policies were made. As Clark Kissinger, who was then SDS's national secretary, would recall, "There was a tendency to write national marches off on the basis of just the nature of the tactic alone without coming to grips with the political content of them and the role that they can play if they're done right." The 1963 March on Washington for Jobs and Freedom led by the Reverend Martin Luther King, Jr., was responsible for much of the antimarch sentiment inside SDS. It seemed to many activists to have been little more than an Establishment-led legislative exercise that had derailed local civil rights activity. "There was a real bad taste coming off the 1963 march," Kissinger said.[15]

Come late evening, during a lull in the NC debate—and when a number of community organizers were out of the room—Brook's proposal squeaked by.[16] The march's public appeal, the NC decided, would be gut-level: "SDS advocates that the U.S. get out of Vietnam for the following reasons: (a) the war hurts the Vietnamese people, (b) the war hurts the American people, (c) SDS is concerned about the Vietnamese and American people."[17] SDS would be the event's sole organizational sponsor, but any group was welcome to participate. The first national action against the war was now in the works.

Carl Oglesby was a newcomer to SDS at the time of the group's meeting. When I met him years later, he was a free-lance writer in Cambridge, Massachusetts. A slender, bespectacled man with gray-brown hair, a rough complexion, and a short beard, he looked younger than his fifty-one years. He spoke eloquently and effusively. In the fall of 1964, Oglesby was running the technical publications department of a major military contractor in Ann Arbor, Michigan. He commanded a sizable army of workers and was leading "a very high-powered bourgeois life-style." "I had a little red car, and my wife had a little blue car, and we jollied around town," Oglesby recalled. That November, an open letter he had written beseeching a newly elected local congressman to denounce the war was published in the University of Michigan's literary magazine. It quickly caught the alert eyes of local SDSers. Wondering why they had never heard of this guy Oglesby before, this articulate critic of the war living smack dab in their own backyard (surely they knew all the radicals around), they called him up. Two SDSers then "came out on a motorcycle in a couple of minutes and we wound up rapping the whole evening about SDS and change and politics and the country," Oglesby remembered. "I right away felt a real kinship with SDS people."[18]

Oglesby was turned on by these "whippersnapper middle-class white kids" and decided to go to an SDS meeting. He was impressed by what he observed there:

> That was the best debate I ever heard. . . . That was an amazing meeting. I had never been around a bunch of people who were so smart and who were so sincere, in the sense that they listened to each other and they actually tried to meet one another's points. You could even see people have their minds changed because somebody showed them a reason or a fact that they hadn't known about. . . . And I was personally persuaded at that meeting, by that debate, that instead of coming into SDS as a director of research or some such thing, I should come into SDS as a community organizer and come with my wife and kids to live in Boston, in Roxbury, where we had a project.[19]

Why community organizing? The "analysis," as Oglesby reconstructed it, was relatively simple. Since the path to change was through the Democratic Party, argued Tom Hayden and other SDSers, student activists had to build a base inside the party by organizing a new constituency. The urban poor were a logical target group for radicals inspired by SNCC's work among the downtrodden, particularly those convinced that economic trends would soon bloat the ranks of the poor. If impoverished whites and blacks could be mobilized together, the theory went, they would overcome the racial anxieties and hostilities then restraining the growth of a powerful "interracial movement of the poor." Many SDSers contended that such a movement was the only vehicle capable of wielding the political clout necessary to stop the war. SDS would halt "the seventh war from now," one offered.[20]

Ghetto organizing also had romantic appeal. Many SDSers sentimentalized poverty. Whenever a community organizer would rise from his indigent element and drift into a meeting—soiled t-shirt, jeans, work boots, Marlboros, and all—"there would always be 'ooohhhs' and 'aaahhhs' and great deference, as though we were being visited by royalty," Oglesby recalled. "'Hey, a real person is coming in.' . . . You could tell he was real, he pinched all the girls' asses, and the girls would put up with it from the working-class guy because they knew he didn't know any better, right, whereas from their true class brothers they would never tolerate this kind of behavior." SDS's "cult of the ghetto" was "slightly sick," one SDSer deduced.[21]

According to the community organizers, then, SDS had to leave the campuses behind. Oglesby:

> The Tom Hayden program . . . meant students are not really that important. Students are debaters and debate is not important. Tom always is an anti-intellectual. He is now and he was then. He never had respect for the academic situation as such. To him it was in certain respects a necessary way station—you had to go there, you had to pass through it—but if you were going to grow as a person and mature as a political figure you had to put it behind you. You couldn't play around in the sandbox. . . . [Hayden] wanted to get students to drop out of school and go off to some ghetto in a big city far from home, live with cockroaches and racial torment and the agonies of poverty, and in that way try to blend into the community—in which they would, in fact, stand out like so many sore thumbs.[22]

Although poised to mingle with cockroaches, Oglesby was a bit skeptical about the returns. The poor's "alienation" from the American political process struck him as more of an "obstacle" than a spur to political action. "They weren't people who tended to think of themselves as involved anyway," he said. "It wasn't their city, it wasn't their state, it wasn't their America—it was somebody else's." But middle-class people, Oglesby thought, "identified with the state or the government, they saw it as theirs, they felt like it should be responsive to them." Their expectations seemed to him "a powerful source of resistance to an administration that lied and deceived."[23]

SDS's veteran community organizers were by then pessimistic themselves. During gloomy meetings in early January, they conceded that no interracial movement of the poor was going to arise soon. By late summer SDS's community organizing venture had proven "a failure."[24]

Preparations for the spring peace march began immediately after the December NC meeting. Most SDSers were not expecting an earthshaking event. Kissinger remembered that when he took the liberty of chartering a train to transport people to Washington "everybody else on the national committee almost had a fit, because they thought we'd be paying it off for the rest of our lives." Two to three thousand might show up if things went well. Todd Gitlin was feeling "doomed." Given the government's "enormous commitment to the war" and "so little opposition to it," he brooded, the fighting in Vietnam would probably drag on "for a very long time." "It felt to me simply a matter of existential ethics to do what you could [to stop the war], but without any great expectations," he recalled.[25]

SDS sent out letters inviting all progressive political organizations to join the march. Most hedged. America's prominent peace groups—SANE, Student Peace Union, Women's International League for Peace and Freedom, Turn Toward Peace, Committee for Nonviolent Action, War Resisters League, Fellowship of Reconciliation—simply ignored this bid to protest their government's violence in Vietnam. They were irritated that SDS had assumed sole sponsorship and failed to offer alternative U.S. policies in Vietnam. Most disturbing, its nonexclusionary policy meant that communists would be on the scene (including the Communist Party's youth group, the Du Bois Clubs, whose name sounded so much like the Boys Club that the vigilant Richard Nixon called it "an almost classic example of communist deception and duplicity"); amid continuing Cold War fever at home, the antiwar groups perceived, cavorting with communists would be the peace movement's "kiss of death."[26] The Du Bois Clubs and May 2nd Movement immediately expressed interest in the march, however. So did the Socialist Workers Party—in more ways than one.

Peter Camejo was then a major SWP leader. In 1986, when I met him, he was the president of Progressive Asset Management, a broker-dealership in Oakland, California, specializing in "socially responsible" investments. He had remained a radical and was still active in various political causes. Camejo left the SWP in 1981 after a nearly thirty-year association because of growing "sectarian" and "dogmatic" behavior by the organization. "I began to have doubts about our ability to work with anybody," he told me, likening his SWP days to living in a religious sect. "I *totally* believed that the SWP had all the answers to all questions. I was a *cultist* of the SWP." Camejo said SDS's call for the April peace march was the "decisive turning point" in the SWP's political trajectory during the war. The SWP promptly began flooding existing local antiwar committees and organizing new ones. "Our position was to go into the antiwar committees . . . and propose that they declare against both the Democrats and Republicans," Camejo remembered. "This was very sectarian, because that wasn't the issue—the issue was to unite people who opposed the war."[27]

The SWP sensed that a national movement might take hold and wanted to build it not only for the purpose of stopping the war but also to radicalize the American people as a stepping-stone on the path to socialist revolution, its ultimate goal. Since the Democratic and Republican parties were both "parties of the ruling class" that sold the capitalist system to the public, according to the SWP, they had to be attacked. A national movement would also be fertile ground for recruiting new SWP members. "You know, we can build an organization of eight hundred to a thousand people off of this," Camejo told himself, gazing out a window in the SWP's national office in New York and licking his chops over the march's enlistment possibilities. ("That's how small we were thinking at the time," he would exclaim years later.) In Clark Kissinger's words, the SWP "perceived immediately when we said we were willing to do [the march] on a nonexclusionary basis that this was their big opportunity."[28]

The SWPers' naked recruitment goals would soon anger large segments of the peace movement and fuel internal tensions. "They clearly put the recruiting of members above the issue of ending the war," the War Resisters League leader David McReynolds recalled.[29]

Several months later, the SWP dropped its insistence that local antiwar committees denounce America's two bourgeois parties. Instead, they should simply demand "U.S. Out of Vietnam Now!" More significant, the SWP decided that by far the most effective antiwar activity was organizing large, legal demonstrations. Since most Americans were more likely to join a legal demonstration than more militant forms of protest, the SWP reasoned, that tactic would maximize the movement's size. "Our whole approach was focused on trying to find forms of activity that could be understood by the average working person and would seem possible for them to participate in when they reached the point of beginning to question the war," the later YSA leader Don Gurewitz remembered.[30]

The SWP also believed that large demonstrations would be most likely to convince silent skeptics about the war that they were not alone; many would then voice their concerns. "Most people hear the media and think, 'I'm the only one who's doubting,' or, 'There's very few of us,'" Camejo explained. "And people in governmental power, from Johnson all the way to Nixon, continuously tried to emphasize that the opposition was a tiny minority. Our theory was that if a million people went into the streets that you would break that." The SWP also felt the government was more likely to respond to large protests than small ones. They demonstrated broader public opposition and threatened widespread upheaval. With small protests, officials "don't feel the pressure," Camejo said.[31]

The SWP's robotlike promotion of mass demonstrations was to become its main badge of identity in the peace movement. Inside the SWP, the position assumed divine truth. Camejo remembered:

> It became like fundamental religious dogma that you were for single-
> issue, peaceful, legal demonstrations. And there were very few ques-
> tioning it. We would pound away at this inside the SWP. Because,
> you see, it was the cutting edge. When new people came around to
> be in the Vietnam War movement in general, SWPers would explain
> why this is the key, and on that basis they would recruit. . . . So that
> was a, b, c, d. I mean, that was pounded away over and over and over
> again. . . . You wouldn't join the SWP unless you agreed with that.
> It was sort of like a definition of membership.[32]

It was a definition other activists would come to know all too well.

Quiet Escalation

In late 1964 and on into 1965, the ground beneath the wobbly South Vietnamese government (GVN) continued to crumble. On November 1, the National Liberation Front moved on the Bien Hoa airfield, killing five Americans and wounding seventy-two. Two months later the South Vietnamese Army (ARVN) suffered a conspicuous defeat at Binh Gia; two of its battalions were virtually obliterated. NLF victory loomed as a real possibility.[33]

On January 6, 1965, a worried William Bundy urged "*some* stronger action"; supplementing the more than twenty-one thousand U.S. "advisers" then stationed in the South with a "limited" number of U.S. ground troops and bombing North Vietnam "has great appeal to many of us," Bundy and other State Department officials wrote Dean Rusk. William's brother, National Security Adviser McGeorge Bundy, advised Johnson to abandon America's "essentially passive role" in Vietnam; "our current policy can lead only to disastrous defeat," he warned. Ominously, Robert McNamara advocated clearing U.S. dependents out of Vietnam. "React promptly and firmly to next reprisal opportunity," he admonished.[34]

On February 6, the opportunity arrived. NLF troops attacked the U.S. military advisers' compound at Pleiku and an army helicopter base nearby. Nine Americans were killed, over a hundred wounded. Fourteen hours later, forty-nine U.S. Navy jets pierced dense monsoon cloud cover to drop their bombs on a North Vietnamese training garrison. That night, an excited Walt Rostow "wandered around the White House clapping Air Force officers on the back, asking about the weather, reminding them that he had once picked targets, and he knew that weather was important."[35]

McGeorge Bundy was in South Vietnam when the assault at Pleiku occurred. Flying back to Washington the next day, he composed one of the most revealing memos of the Vietnam War. Bundy was distressed. "The prospect in Vietnam is grim," he informed President Johnson. "The energy and persistence of the Viet Cong [i.e., NLF] are astonishing. They can appear anywhere—and at almost any time. They have accepted extraordinary losses and they come back for more. . . . At its very best, the struggle in Vietnam will be long." Bundy argued that the most promising course of action was to unleash the sustained bombing campaign against North Vietnam that had long tantalized officials. It would rectify the "one grave weakness in our posture in Vietnam which is within our own power to fix—and that is a widespread belief that we do not have the will and force and patience and determination to take the necessary action and stay the course." Bundy conceded that the policy might turn out to be a bust, but even so it would "be worth it." Not only would it answer foreign and domestic charges that "we did not do all that we could" in Vietnam, he wrote, but, "to the extent that it demonstrates U.S. willingness to employ this new norm in counter-insurgency," it would "set a higher price for the future upon all adventures of guerrilla warfare."[36]

Bundy may have also had retribution on his mind. When he visited wounded American soldiers in Pleiku following the attack there, his aides were surprised by "the intensity of his feeling." The normally self-controlled official had seemingly "blown his cool." The United States couldn't sit idly by while its boys were "dying in their tents," Bundy retorted to anyone who questioned the wisdom of bombing North Vietnam in the weeks ahead. The president was "fascinated" by Bundy's emotional state. "Well, they made a believer out of you, didn't they?" he later ribbed him. "A little fire will do that." Bundy was acting like a prudish preacher's son who had gone to a whorehouse, Johnson delightedly told others.[37]

On February 13, the president ordered Operation Rolling Thunder, the program of sustained air strikes against North Vietnam. Officials said the strikes were a response to Pleiku. However, a later, unguarded remark by Bundy was closer to the mark. "Pleikus are like streetcars," he said.[38] In other words, they will always come along.

The public again rallied behind their commander in chief: 83 percent supported the bombing. But the war's critics were growing in number. Hundreds of small protests erupted across the United States. On February 11, three hundred Women Strike for Peace (WSP) and Women's International League for Peace and Freedom (WILPF) activists picketed the White House. Eight days later, fourteen people were arrested for blocking the entrances to the U.S. Mission to the UN. On February 20, four hundred SDSers and others demonstrated in Washington; hundreds marched in at least nine additional cities. Antiwar ads appeared in major newspapers. The White House received more than a thousand telegrams denouncing the bombing. The *New York Times* pressed for negotiations.[39]

The administration was well aware of these stirrings. "We have an education problem that bears close watching and more work," McGeorge Bundy told Johnson. Persuaded that most college students were opposed to the bombing, Bundy's aide Kevin Delaney cautioned, "We cannot afford to have campus attitudes . . . [be] overwhelmingly one-sided." Delaney suggested coaxing Senator Robert Kennedy (D-N.Y.) and Vice President Hubert Humphrey to hit the campuses to talk sense to students.[40]

U.S. officials were not the only ones vexed by the war's critics. On many campuses, right-wing students harassed antiwar demonstrators. At one university in Ohio, a small group of protesters were assaulted by more than a hundred prowar students. The campus police stood passively by, refusing to intervene. The school was Kent State University.[41]

To bolster support for its bombing policy, the administration released a lengthy White Paper on February 27. The paper accused North Vietnam of plotting to conquer "a sovereign people" in South Vietnam through a "totally new brand of aggression"—"concealed aggression." It summarized "massive evidence" for this claim. [42]

The White Paper received many credits at home. The *Washington Post* bought its thesis hook, line, and sinker, stating that the administration's data were "incontrovertible." Senators Mike Mansfield (D-Mont.) and Russell Long (D-La.) also praised the paper; Long urged preparation for war with China or the Soviet Union if Hanoi did not cease its aggression. Vocal critics of the document emerged as well, however, shattering its propaganda value and embarrassing the administration. Senator Wayne Morse exclaimed that the White Paper was so full of holes it resembled "Swiss cheese" and wondered why "we get excited" about North Vietnamese troops in the South when the United States had sent thousands of its own. "Why shouldn't they?" he reasoned. In his *Weekly*, I. F. Stone showed that the paper was "incomplete where it was not inaccurate, misleading where it was not dishonest, and contrary in its broad argument to every informed history of the war." The "striking thing" about the document was "how little" Northern support for the NLF it could prove, Stone marveled. The journalist's criticisms were reprinted widely in the media. William Bundy later said the White Paper was "a disaster." [43]

As Washington strove to justify bombing North Vietnam, General William Westmoreland worried about the policy's main consequence for the war in the South. U.S. air bases had become prime targets for NLF raids and mortar attacks. On February 22, Westmoreland requested thirty-five hundred Marines to protect the giant U.S. air complex at Danang. President Johnson granted the request four days later, despite the prophetic forebodings of General Maxwell Taylor, U.S. ambassador to South Vietnam. Taylor feared the policy would open the door to further U.S. troop deployments and questioned whether the "white-faced soldier" was a "suitable guerrilla fighter for Asian forest and jungles." Taylor also feared diminished ARVN initiative and wondered "how [a] foreign soldier would distinguish between a VC and a friendly Vietnamese farmer." [44]

On the morning of March 8, the first of two Marine battalions splashed ashore at Danang. Under forewarned American news cameras, the soldiers were greeted by pretty local schoolgirls in long white dresses doling out orchid leis. One company then proceeded to march gallantly off to capture a nearby hill, only to encounter rock apes—"gorillas instead of guerrillas," the joke went. [45]

Now, while the troop-hungry Westmoreland optimistically interpreted the Marine landing as "the beginning of greater things to come," other officials saw it as "a one shot affair to meet a specific situation." They hoped Rolling Thunder would stabilize the war in South Vietnam and lead to a favorable negotiated settlement. However, after a month of bombing elicited no response from Hanoi, the hope ebbed and frustration set in. Dispatching U.S. Army Chief of Staff General Harold Johnson to Vietnam to get to the heart of the problem, a concerned President Johnson "thrust an index finger in his breastbone, leaned his face close, and said, 'You get things bubbling, General.'"[46]

At administration strategy sessions in early April, the prospect of a major U.S. and allied troop deployment to Vietnam dominated discussion. Officials knew the NLF was gearing up for a big summer offensive and doubted ARVN could hold the fort. Johnson rejected a petition from the JCS for more than a hundred thousand men, agreeing to only about a fifth that number. Significantly, he also granted Westmoreland's request to allow the troops to engage in offensive operations rather than merely guard base areas. Stealth was the watchword. "Premature publicity" on Johnson's decisions was to "be avoided by all possible precautions," wrote McGeorge Bundy in a highly sensitive memorandum. "The President's desire is that these movements and changes should be understood as being gradual and wholly consistent with existing policy." Johnson was determined to conduct the war as quietly as possible, Westmoreland said later, "to avoid getting the American public aroused."[47]

The administration was, in fact, sensitive to perceptions it was engaged in a war at all. Admiral Thomas Moorer, commander in chief of the Pacific Fleet in early 1965, remembered giving a luncheon address in Honolulu then in which he used the phrase "this dirty little war." Before Moorer could even get back to his office, Assistant Secretary of Defense for Public Affairs Arthur Sylvester got him on the phone and barked, "You're not to use the word *war*. This is not a war." Disgusted with the administration's soft-pedaling and its curbs on U.S. firepower, Moorer allegedly shot back, "Well, the people out here think it's a war. If you fellows come out here, I'll show you what a war is like."[48]

McGeorge Bundy subsequently acknowledged that "the president was trying to have the thing happen with as little political debate as possible. That was a difference between him and me, but that's what he wanted." Bundy suspected Johnson was mainly concerned with limiting congressional debate on Vietnam. The president feared the war would undermine his "Great Society" social legislation. "Johnson didn't want Doctor Great Society to become Doctor Win-the-War," White House Counsel Harry McPherson recalled. "He didn't want the tremendous momentum . . . in domestic legislation . . . aborted by a sudden sense that the president's whole mind and the mind of his government and the attention of the country ought to be on the South Vietnam War."[49]

Johnson's political antennae were also picking up broader signals. He worried that the country as a whole would not rally behind the war. The president "was profoundly convinced from the beginning of the unpopularity of the war," McPherson observed. Johnson knew that support for U.S. intervention in Vietnam was wide but not deep, and he feared that if the American people were asked to sacrifice their lives and money to any great extent, they would turn on him. Other officials shared Johnson's concern. "You always had to be conscious that there was a fuse of public opinion support," William Bundy remembered. The many officials who keenly recalled the progressive decline of public backing for the Korean War "instinctively" understood that the Vietnam War had "a time limit on it," Bundy said. That McGeorge Bundy, Under Secretary of State George Ball, and Johnson's adviser Clark Clifford, among others, were predicting that the war would be lengthy under the best of circumstances heightened officials' concern about whether they could carry the public with them.⁵⁰

Johnson's decision to conceal the Marines' change of mission only made Americans more uneasy, however. It was readily apparent to journalists in Vietnam that the Marines were not just sitting in foxholes minding their own business until attacked, and their press reports elicited curious official denials. When a State Department briefing officer inadvertently revealed the policy shift two months later, vastly compounding the administration's credibility problems, Johnson "went into one of his wildest rages."⁵¹

"This Is No Longer a Casual Form of Campus Spring Fever"

Three weeks before the Marines were turned loose, thirty faculty members at the University of Michigan gathered to plan an expression of opposition to the war. Present were many familiar faces, "veterans of a string of advertisements for the test ban, for a fair housing ordinance, for the election of Lyndon B. Johnson." They felt "betrayed." Their peace candidate, the man who had promised no wider war, had blood all over his hands. And they felt desperate. Despite preparing countless newspaper advertisements and letters to government officials protesting the bombings, the horror in Vietnam had only mounted. The State Department had had the gall to treat them like children: it answered their letters with pamphlets explaining the diabolical nature of communism illustrated by a leering Khrushchev.⁵²

The sociology professor William Gamson rose to speak. The situation in Vietnam was too grave to continue treading the old tired ground, he said. Ads and letters just wouldn't do anymore. Gamson proposed that the group organize a one-day faculty moratorium on teaching-as-usual and transform the university into a massive classroom on the war. Nearly fifty faculty members signed a petition supporting the plan.⁵³

On March 16, a group of nervous signers met to reconsider. Michigan's faculty senate was discussing censure, deans were up in arms, the governor and legislators were hollering for disciplinary action. The anthropologist Marshall Sahlins suggested that, instead of holding a strike, teachers conduct their classes during the day and hold sessions on the war at night—all night. The Michigan organizers ultimately agreed on the all-night format, although some believed "that we were making a very bad mistake." The detractors felt that the time for polite academic give-and-take was gone; to them the move reeked of retreat. Worse, they thought few would show up for a nocturnal educational experience. "We thought, 'Sure, a few hundred, that would be good,'" Carl Oglesby recalled. With the switch to the evening design, however, university administrators, relieved that the brouhaha was over, virtually began promoting the event. "They fell all over themselves trying to cooperate with us," Oglesby remembered.[54] Faculty and student interest skyrocketed.

On the evening of March 24, over three thousand people showed up on the Ann Arbor campus for the nation's first "teach-in" on the war. Lectures and debates ran until 8 A.M., despite a midnight bomb threat that temporarily forced people outside into 20° F weather (where they held a rally). Exchanges were both reasoned and passionate. "Facts were demanded and assumptions were exposed," one participant wrote. "On that night, people who really cared talked of things that really mattered." Hierarchical relations between faculty and students received a stiff jolt; students locked horns with professors whose classes they had hardly spoken in. Opponents of the war gained valuable social support, inciting many to plan future protests. Prowar participants were asked to explain their positions; some began questioning their allegiances. "It was such a powerful event," Oglesby fervently recalled. The campus was now alive with debate on Vietnam. It was impossible to avoid the controversy whether one wanted to or not.[55]

During the rest of the spring, teach-ins spread like wildfire across America's campuses. Over a hundred took place. The "stroke of genius out there in Michigan . . . put the debate on the map for the whole academic community," Oglesby said. "And you could not be an intellectual after those teach-ins and not think a lot and express yourself and defend your ideas about Vietnam." With the surprising success of the Michigan teach-in, his own "faith in students and the academic situation and the importance of directly organizing on Vietnam was switched back, it came alive again, and from that time on there was never any real thought of my . . . coming to Boston to do community organizing."[56]

The grandest of the teach-ins took place at the University of California in Berkeley. Two graduate students, Jerry Rubin and Barbara Gullahorn, had initially proposed the event to Stephen Smale, a mathematics professor and teachers' union activist. "The idea was to do something really big and exciting and very exceptional," Smale would recall. "To make it a very memorable kind of event." More than thirty thousand people participated in the 36-hour marathon, perhaps twelve thousand at one time. Some barely missed a beat. "I arrived there at the beginning and didn't leave until it was over," Marilyn Milligan recounted. "I was just totally taken by that teach-in, totally engaged. . . . I just didn't want to leave at all. We were there and that was it." Before wearily trudging home, Milligan signed up to work with the teach-in's sponsor, the Vietnam Day Committee. She would shortly assume a leadership role in that organization.[57]

The escalation of the war also fueled interest in the April SDS march. Besieged with requests for information on it, SDS organizers shifted into high gear. "We just rolled over the whole antiwar movement," Paul Booth said afterward—"they had never seen anything like this." Even activists with the old peace groups expressed interest. Estimates of attendance surged toward fifteen thousand.[58]

The White House was less enthusiastic about the protest. Thousands of peaceniks parading around Washington would hardly keep the war out of the public spotlight, officials knew. The march might also give the North Vietnamese the wrong impression about the American public's enthusiasm for the war, thereby encouraging them. On April 14, McGeorge Bundy mentioned the upcoming "left-wing student protest" to Johnson and counseled, "A strong peaceloving statement tomorrow or Friday might help cool them off ahead of time."[59] No statement was forthcoming.

April 17 was a gorgeous spring day. By early afternoon, twenty thousand people were gathered at the Washington Monument. Most were students. There were also many adults, including Communist Party members marching under their own banner for the first time since the birth of McCarthyism. The highlight of the afternoon was a moving closing speech by SDS's 25-year-old president, Paul Potter. The war, Potter declared, "has provided the razor, the terrifying sharp cutting edge that has finally severed the last vestige of illusion that morality and democracy are the guiding principles of American foreign policy." "What kind of system" allowed "good men" to work such evil, he asked? "We must name that system. We must name it, describe it, analyze it, understand it and change it." Despite pleas from the crowd to go ahead and name that system, Potter abstained. SDS's leaders feared that using the word *capitalism* would provoke more red-baiting and had earlier decided "to leave it as a mystery as to whether or not there was a capitalist system in the United States," Booth wryly recalled.[60]

Not everyone in the crowd was enraptured by Potter's testimony. In fact, not everyone was there to protest the war. The sun was shining, the cherry trees were blossoming—love was in the air. Daniel Ellsberg, a Defense Department official, arrived on the scene with his attention focused on one Patricia Marx. Ellsberg had been admiring Marx for some time now and several days earlier had gathered the fortitude to call her up to ask for a date. He was thinking about Saturday, he had said, the first Saturday he would have off since starting work at the Pentagon the previous August. Unfortunately, Marx responded, she already had plans to go to the SDS demonstration, partly because she opposed the war, but also to conduct interviews for her public radio program in New York. She had plans to interview I. F. Stone, for instance. But she would be pleased if he would accompany her. Ellsberg suddenly felt a little dizzy. He *supported* America's "commitment" in Vietnam and had even helped produce the White Paper that Stone had so mercilessly demolished. "You *can't* ask me to take my first day off from the Pentagon to go to an antiwar rally!" he stammered, incredulously. Yes, she could. Ellsberg donned marching shoes. He even lugged Marx's bulky tape recorder around for the day. Ellsberg later made no bones that he "never would have gone" to the demonstration had it not been for the lure of romance. He married Marx in 1970.[61]

Following Potter's speech, the crowd swept down the mall toward the Capitol. Youths wearing gas masks led the charge. Despite SDS's dislike of marches as a pressure tactic, the protesters planned to deliver Congress a petition demanding an end to the war. Along the way, their exuberant mood began to hint of "something darker." Reaching a wall of police near the Capitol steps, a barrier through which only a few were ticketed to pass, a chorus of voices rang out, "Let's all go. LET'S ALL GO." According to one marcher, "it seemed that the great mass of people would simply flow on through and over the marble buildings, that our forward motion was irresistibly strong, and that even had some been shot or arrested nothing could have stopped that crowd from taking possession of its government."[62]

But it was not to be. No more than several hundred demonstrators proceeded up the Capitol steps. Many went home frustrated. The war makers would not heed legal demonstrations, they believed; militant civil disobedience was required to move murderers.

The feeling would grow.

Lyndon Johnson avoided the protest by spending the weekend at his ranch in Texas. In the face of a 400-strong picket led by SDSers at the front gate, he undoubtedly took solace from an earlier note from an aide, Marvin Watson, that twenty-two Secret Service agents would be on hand to protect him from the "so-called demonstrators."[63]

The sudden outpouring of antiwar protest in the spring of 1965 struck a nerve in the American Establishment. James Reston, that titan of U.S. journalism, complained that many teach-ins had rejected "serious intellectual inquiry" for "propaganda of the most vicious nature. . . . This is no longer a casual form of campus spring fever." C. L. Sulzberger, a foreign affairs columnist for the *New*

York Times, detected "a strange lemming instinct" among the protesters; they "refuse," he lamented, "to see the struggle in its true meaning as advertised quite openly by the Communists themselves: a showdown with global implications." In the early fall, Senator Thomas Dodd (D-Conn.) apprised the nation that the peace movement was under the control of "pseudo-Americans," soldiers in a "massive psychological warfare attack" on the war by the global "Communist apparatus." Dodd expressed the hope that his revelations would "assist loyal critics of Administration policy to purge their ranks of the Communists and crypto-Communists" so that debate on Vietnam could be restricted to "honest men."[64]

Administration officials were the most agitated. On April 23, Dean Rusk abruptly departed from a prepared speech to take a shot at the war's opponents. "I continue to hear and see nonsense about the nature of the struggle" in Vietnam, commented the secretary of state. "I sometimes wonder at the gullibility of educated men and the stubborn disregard of plain facts by men who are supposed to be helping our young to learn." When a group of religious demonstrators publicly voiced their dissatisfaction with a meeting they'd held with Robert McNamara, Assistant Secretary Arthur Sylvester muttered angrily, "Only church people would do what you are doing." Johnson hit the roof when the poet Robert Lowell announced in early June that he was boycotting the White House Festival of the Arts to protest the war. "The roar in the Oval Office could be heard all the way into the East Wing," one White House staffer recorded. After other prominent American writers and artists declared their support for Lowell's stand, the president ranted about the "sonsofbitches" who had turned his perfectly decent cultural celebration into a goddamn platform on Vietnam. "None of us realized . . . the tawdry lengths that some people would go to in impoliteness and incivility," Jack Valenti, a White House aide, remarked later. Valenti exclaimed that he'd "never met a man with less civility, with less sense of good judgment about how you handle yourself when you're a guest in somebody's house" than the writer Dwight MacDonald, who circulated an antiwar petition at the festival. MacDonald, he gibed, "needed to gargle with Lavoris."[65] Following the festival, Johnson determined that all future White House guests would have to receive FBI clearances. This type of thing led the presidential aides Richard Goodwin and Bill Moyers to conclude in alarm that Johnson was literally suffering from "paranoid distintegration." The war, public opposition to it and other developments seemingly out of Johnson's control were triggering frequent "irrational outbursts" and "unacceptable orders," Goodwin recalled. Listening to one bizarre tirade from the president, Moyers "felt weird, almost felt as if he wasn't really talking to a human being at all."[66]

McGeorge Bundy, a former Harvard dean, exhibited an icy disdain for antiwar academics. "I cannot honestly tell you that I think your letter reflects great credit on its authors, either as a piece of propaganda or as a serious effort to engage in discussion," he told one correspondent from the teach-in movement. "If your letter came to me for grading as a professor of government, I would not be able to give it high marks." To a critic from the *Harvard Crimson*, Bundy acidly commented, "No useful purpose is served by assuming that Dr. Strangelove is in charge here."[67]

Years later Bundy was a professor of history at New York University, having received his professorship in 1979 over the objection of two dozen professors there that he had helped prosecute a war of "genocide" against the Vietnamese people. He subsequently said "I wish we had quit" the war before he left the government in 1966. A haughty man of privileged lineage, with a flint-sharp mind, caustic tongue, and little patience for lesser beings, Bundy could be particularly frosty on the subject of Vietnam, often refusing even to discuss the issue (although one journalist who interviewed him on the arms race, forewarned that he wouldn't touch Vietnam, got him talking about it after "a couple of tall Scotches"). When I interviewed him, Bundy was visibly defensive about the war, answering many queries with curt statements of little substantive content. He also exhibited remarkably persistent memory lapses. When asked about his expectations in early 1965 about future domestic opposition to the war, however, Bundy acted like a man eager to make an admission. He acknowledged that the spring upsurge in antiwar sentiment caught the administration off guard:

> I think that we were not paying a great deal of attention to what one thinks of now, looking back on it, as the "protest," or the people who were against the war from the beginning, largely out of their own perceptions of who were the good guys and who were the bad guys. And I think we underestimated the degree to which there had been a revival of what called itself the "New Left." So I think we weren't thinking very much about that. And I remember myself being somewhat surprised by the level of student and academic protest in the spring and summer of 1965. . . .
>
> My own encounter with direct opposition to the war came in [two teach-ins in June]. . . . It was all very sober and careful and well-behaved on both sides, but it did represent a kind of opposition that, even then was, I think, stronger than I would have predicted six months earlier. And in that sense . . . I think we were not fully alert to the way the country was going to see the matter.[68]

William Bundy emphasized that administration officials were "very definitely . . . concerned about" the spring antiwar protests. Sitting in a barren room at the Council on Foreign Relations' New York office, the tall, drawn, proud Bundy recalled, "What the arguments of that period revealed—and we should have acted on it much sooner than we did—was how much of the past history was understood in . . . a misleading fashion." For example, teach-in speakers were claiming that the United States had reneged on the 1954 Geneva Peace Accords on the war by refusing to implement their provision for democratic elections in South Vietnam in 1956; Bundy and other officials knew the United States had only *pledged* to uphold the Accords, however, not actually signed them. The protesters were also arguing that the revolution in South Vietnam was home-grown; but Bundy and his colleagues were persuaded by intelligence reports that Hanoi was pulling the strings. And the protesters were alleging that Ngo Dinh Diem, the mystic whom the United States installed as president of South Vietnam in 1954 after it assumed France's colonial role in Vietnam and who died in a U.S.-backed coup in 1963, was "a terrible character," Bundy derisively recalled, who had tortured and killed his political opponents; yet officials had no doubt worse nastiness would be in store if the communists took over. "A great deal of arguments that we had long known existed and discarded and never thought needed to be reargued suddenly came to the surface," Bundy said. The White Paper and other administration propaganda just "hadn't made the case" for the war, he lamented. "We discovered tremendous weaknesses in the way the thing was understood. People really hadn't focused on it before we started the bombing. An awful lot of people hadn't been paying any attention and hadn't seen how critical the situation was becoming. This was true of somebody like Arthur Schlesinger, for example, who spent 1964 and 1965 writing his book on Kennedy and, as it were, came out of the cave and looked around and said, 'Gee whiz, look what happened'—and turned into an opponent of the war."[69]

Feeble or not, however, realized officials, the protesters' arguments were influencing others. "Articulate critics" of the war from the universities and churches "have stimulated extensive worry and inquiry in the nation as a whole," McGeorge Bundy apprised Johnson in June. Dean Rusk was concerned the protests might be affecting Congress. Something had to be done to stem the onslaught. "We simply aren't doing our propaganda job right in this country," Jack Valenti told the president in April.[70]

In early May, the government dispatched a four-person "truth team" to six midwestern universities to discuss "the facts of life in Vietnam" (as one official put it). The team included "young, articulate" representatives of the State Department, Agency for International Development, and U.S. Army, all "just back from Vietnam," Valenti informed Johnson. Although the officials evoked much sympathy from their audiences, they typically ended up on the defensive, with some forums turning into "hooting sessions" when students felt their intelligence had been insulted.[71]

The University of Wisconsin in Madison was the scene of a particularly trying encounter for the administration's propagandists. Students laughed at the truth-team leader Thomas Conlon's assertion that the United States was fighting to defend South Vietnam's freedom. When he denied the United States "runs the show" there, shouts erupted from all over the room, "Aw c'mon. Let's be honest." Conlon's angry directives to students to "Sit down!" and mail their questions to Washington did nothing to boost his popularity. As the official was leaving the wreckage, Arnold Lochlin, a biochemistry student, blocked his path. "Get this straight, sweetie," Lochlin taunted. "We're not going to fight your filthy fascist war. Go fight it yourself."[72]

Other government spokesmen tried a different tack. Daniel Ellsberg was among the "bright young men" (as Valenti called them) that the administration sent out to campuses to explain the facts of life in Vietnam when requests for speakers came in. He used a "soft-sell" approach when talking to teach-in audiences:

> I conceded a great deal of the opponent's position. For instance, if they started telling me about Diem, I would say, "I'm not here to talk about Diem. Diem is everything you say. Diem is dead. That was two years ago." And that was totally disarming, see, because they were all there prepared to talk about the GVN. . . . They were so amazed to hear a government official knock Diem that they didn't know what to say next. And my general case was not unlike that: "The GVN has its faults, but let's look at the VC. . . . Are we sure to win? No. But should we quit without trying?" . . . And I really talked about negotiations right then.

Ellsberg's teach-in career was not a long one, however. He was privy to the "inside story" of the U.S. invasion of the Dominican Republic in late April and wasn't eager to face opponents of the action in a public forum. "We were 100 percent lying about what we were doing in the Dominican Republic," he recalled. Although Johnson claimed the invasion was necessary to fend off another spate of communist aggression, Ellsberg knew the Dominican Republic was "one of the few communist-free environments in the whole world. And so the explanation of why you were sending twenty thousand Marines was a little difficult." Ellsberg called the government office responsible for scheduling officials' appearances on campuses and demanded, "Take me off the list *now*. I ain't going out there to face questions about the Dominican Republic. You can screw that."[73]

As the government's truth teams were taking to the road, the Inter-University Committee for a Public Hearing on Vietnam (IUCPHV), a national antiwar body, was planning a national teach-in in Washington, D.C., on May 15–16. Many IUCPHV organizers lusted for a "confrontation" with a senior government official. They felt it would discredit the administration's justifications for the war in front of a wide audience. Other organizers argued that supporters of the war should not be part of the program; officials already had ready access to podiums for expressing their nonsense, they asserted, and the teach-ins' value lay in surfacing antiwar sentiment. The IUCPHV eventually decided on a confrontation. It solicited McGeorge Bundy's participation.[74]

Bundy agreed to do battle—but only under certain conditions. He vetoed the IUCPHV's choice of Hans Morgenthau, a famous political scientist, as his main debating foe, citing "personal reasons." Bundy found Senator Wayne Morse unsuitable for that role as well. The national security adviser and his aides also required that the moderator of the teach-in establish a "high tone of discussion . . . ruling out of order any heckling, rudeness, or other unseemly conduct"; he would have to field questions alternately from pro- and antiwar audience members "to inhibit a stream of hostile questioning," and questioners could not make "speeches." In short, Bundy's presence required that the teach-in be conducted on a "non-emotional level." In addition, neither Bundy nor other officials would participate in a closing session on alternative policies in Vietnam. As the White House aide Chester Cooper warned Bundy, the IUCPHV organizers planned to issue "a climactic call for a Congressional investigation" of the war at the session, which might facilitate a "psychological victory" by the peace movement.[75]

Bundy got his way on these points and signed on the dotted line. The administration's advance men then swung into action. State Department researchers prepared detailed analyses of the views the obviously feared Morgenthau (accepted as one of three antiwar panelists) had held on the war from 1962 on (he had been "essentially consistent," they reported). William Bundy and other officials briefed pro-administration participants in, according to Cooper, a "thorough and effective" manner. "There are excellent possibilities that our speakers, who have been doing their homework, will prevail in rational debate" with the "highly emotional" antiwar panelists, Cooper wrote Bundy. The White House snatched up a thousand tickets to the event (out of an audience capacity of five thousand) and made "a careful distribution" of them to ensure that "knowledgeable" questioners would be present. One hundred tickets were channeled to the Young Democrats, "who," Cooper knew, were "quite interested in supporting the President." The administration rented a nearby hotel room to house researchers in case the need for rapid-fire responses to troubling disclosures arose. Cooper advised Bundy that he had "underplayed the nature and extent of our advance preparations" in discussions with the media.[76]

Based on his contacts with "alienated and semi-alienated" academics, James Thomson, a National Security Council staffer, counseled Bundy on appropriate behavior. The "growing and potentially dangerous chasm" between many ("often naive") professors and the government could "be bridged," analyzed Thomson, if Bundy demonstrated "reasonableness, good humor, patience, warmth," and "concern" for his critics at the teach-in. This would help "discredit" protesters' "caricature" of officials as "computerized, hard-nosed monsters," a chief reason for the chasm between them. Although "silliness and ignorance and fraud" should not "go unchallenged," Thomson recommended, "the education of our critics" was best considered "a secondary objective" at the event; it was a "less promising" one anyway. "In sum, if you do nothing more on Saturday than convey a clear image of the humaneness, reasonableness, and intelligence of top policy-makers—whatever the provocation—you will do much to begin to bridge the chasm."[77]

As curtain time approached, the government's star performer abruptly pulled out of the production. Tight-lipped officials initially refused to explain Bundy's absence. They later stated that Johnson had whisked him off to deal with the crisis in the Dominican Republic. Bundy subsequently explained that he "had a lot of difference with the president" over whether he should participate in the teach-in. "He felt I shouldn't go and there shouldn't be any such encounter between the administration and [its critics]. He may well have been right. But I had undertaken to have a debate—and then I got sent to the Dominican Republic." Johnson evidently threatened to fire him for "disloyalty." Bundy released a written apology to the teach-in that reflected his contempt for protesters. When it was read, many in the audience of several thousand groaned.[78]

A speech by Arthur Schlesinger, Jr., whom Bundy had asked to serve as his replacement, also irked many at the teach-in. Schlesinger advocated sending more troops to Vietnam, cutting back on Rolling Thunder, and negotiating. He also maintained that the United States was fighting partly to preserve Americans' right to free speech. When Schlesinger finished his remarks, audience members, "bursting with impatience," queued up to give him a piece of their minds. By the time he had stepped down from the stage, Schlesinger was badly shaken. "What kind of audience is this?" he murmured. Two decades later Schlesinger called his recommendation of additional troops "a mistake I regret" and said that he was "quite rightly" attacked at the teach-in.[79]

As a holding action, Walt Rostow wrote Dean Rusk afterward, the administration's participation in the event was "a good idea. . . . On a one-shot basis it de-fused quite a lot of tension on our flank." Rostow opined that "the only truly objectionable feature of the occasion was the sanctimonious assumption of higher virtue among the critics"—a curious statement coming from a man known among his colleagues for an unhealthy attachment to his own ideas. Rostow was not eager to set up additional encounters with the IUCPHV, though. "We should not encourage a regular relation between this group and the U.S. government," he advised.[80]

Nagged by his hasty trip to the Dominican Republic, however, Bundy arranged to participate in two public "debates" on the war in June. He and his staff again secured favorable formats. With CBS, they planned a televised "dialogue" on June 21 moderated by their "preferred choice," Eric Sevareid. Believing the "rigid procedures of a debate . . . in which participants are primarily interested in attacking, defending or scoring debaters' points" a "poor" arrangement for gaining "acceptance and support of present policies," Bundy and his aides insisted the event have an "informal" and "'reasoning together'" tone. Sevareid should concentrate on "keeping the discussion moving and pertinent" rather than mediating between sides. The administration knew the IUCPHV would be "less than pleased" with this format; "as a sop," it agreed to accept Morgenthau as Bundy's opponent.[81]

During the CBS dialogue, Sevareid posed four questions central to the government's case on Vietnam. The questions allowed a scholarly looking Bundy, dipping heavily into classified material, to lay out the administration's arguments with studied precision (nonetheless many viewers found his performance arrogant and shallow). Morgenthau weakly advocated peace "with honor." When Bundy attacked Morgenthau's "pessimism" on the war by noting mistaken political forecasts he had made in the past, the political scientist responded, "I admire the efficiency of Mr. Bundy's office." "I do my own [research]," Bundy lied. For teach-in activists, it was an agonizingly placid affair.[82]

Over that spring and summer, the Johnson administration took other measures to counteract the growing peace movement. Following a talk with the president, who had "no doubt" that communists were behind the dissent, J. Edgar Hoover directed the FBI to prepare a memorandum linking SDS with communism. FBI agents infiltrated SDS chapters. Administration officials drafted speeches with the protesters' criticisms "in mind" and provided propaganda "kits" to friendly nongovernmental speakers. They recruited supportive students to tour the country and flew thirty such students to Vietnam to advance their expertise on the war. The administration suggested prowar youth come to Washington ("at their own expense") to meet officials, thereby receiving a few stimulative strokes ("it wouldn't take too much massaging to do the trick," predicted Cooper in advocating the visits). Compliant South Vietnamese intellectuals were flown to the United States to further educate Americans. The administration moved to get the Young Democrats "into the picture" too. And it shot a film entitled *Why Vietnam?* that was later distributed to the Army. Vietnam veteran David Cortright recalled that the film began with a southern Army officer wailing, "Whhhyyy Veeetnam?" followed by "five minutes of bullshit," followed by another "Whhhyyy Veeetnam?" then five more minutes of bullshit, and so on. "This was at basic training, and people were hooting and hollering," Cortright amusedly recounted. The film evoked "mixed feelings" inside the administration.[83]

Johnson expressed his interest in peace. On April 7, he told a Johns Hopkins

University audience that he was ready to enter into "unconditional discussions." The White House press secretary George Reedy later recalled the speech as "a response to the teach-ins." A month later, the president temporarily halted the bombing of North Vietnam, although he realized Hanoi was quite unlikely to respond.[84]

Chester Cooper organized official support for the American Friends of Vietnam (AFV). Formed in the 1950s, the AFV was, as Cooper put it, a private "people-to-people program" designed to "engage the American people generally, and university students in particular, in the Vietnam struggle." The administration's first task was (in Cooper's words) to "put the bite on" sympathetic citizens to secure some $25,000 in seed money for reviving the then-stalled organization. To attract contributions and "counteract . . . hostile sentiment" on campuses, the AFV held a kick-off rally at Michigan State University (home of the AFV's chairman, Dr. Wesley Fischel) on June 1. Cooper lined up Vice President Hubert Humphrey and USIA Director Carl Rowan, "eminent Government spokesmen who enjoy the unquestioned confidence of the university sector," as the featured speakers. Cooper reckoned the black Rowan's presence would weaken the "tie-in" between the civil rights and antiwar movements in the country. Dean Rusk may have appreciated Cooper's analysis; he remembered observing the civil rights movement being "transformed into the antiwar movement . . . around 1965."[85]

The AFV's "practical and exciting" projects (as Cooper described them) included collecting books and clothes for publicized shipments to "the people of Vietnam"; publishing a journal; running a speakers' bureau; and passing out literature on campuses. The White House did its work behind the scenes. "While we have been careful to keep our hand fairly hidden," Cooper told other officials, "we have, in fact, spent a lot of time on [the AFV] and have been able to find them some money" ("much money," according to the later White House official Charles Colson). If the AFV became "too closely identified with" the government, Cooper recognized, its "credibility" would be "badly affected." By August, the White House's relations with the AFV had become so cozy that Cooper could brag to other officials, "We have an instrument for public information on Vietnam." Another White House aide boasted to a prospective heavyweight AFV board member that the group's honorary chairman was "working directly from the White House."[86]

Continuing to act on the belief that "the basic task" of countering the war's opponents "must be accomplished through unofficial channels," as Cooper wrote Valenti, the administration helped organize another prowar group later that summer. The Committee for an Effective and Durable Peace in Asia was chaired by the veteran diplomat Arthur Dean and included David Rockefeller, Dean Acheson, and Walter Annenberg among its many prominent supporters. The committee surfaced on September 8 with a prowar statement in numerous newspapers. McGeorge Bundy, the White House's "monitor" of the committee, assured Johnson that Dean "knows this is not a one-shot job but one which will have to be kept up with sustained energy."[87]

Many officials were then puzzled by the anxiety and protest the war was causing at home. Why didn't more Americans share their zeal for so honorable an undertaking, they wondered? An August 3 "Dinner Meeting on the Information Problem" was a searching experience for those gathered around the White House mess table. Douglass Cater, a presidential aide, complained, "We don't seem to have the newscasting we once had . . . to quieten us and to give us perspective." A perception that Johnson thought "of nothing else but Vietnam" hurt the administration, the State Department's Jim Greenfield opined. "It is not a healthy image." Greenfield also noted that "we do not have the highest quality military spokesmen in Vietnam" and that the government was "involved in too many cliches. . . . We should look again at 'Our country's honor is at stake,'" since "one day we may be sorry that we are tied too closely to this stand." That the war was "different from anything we've seen and . . . we are all groping for ways to understand it" also contributed to the information problem, Greenfield added. It would help if the South Vietnamese government finally got around to appointing an ambassador to the United States, Cooper remarked. Voice of America Director John Chancellor (formerly and later with NBC News) agreed with Greenfield that Vietnam was "an entirely different kind of war," submitting, "perhaps we have, for the first time in our experience, a non-packageable commodity." Chancellor suggested that telling Americans "'we are a world power and are stuck with this sort of thing'" would bring them "greater comfort." According to Joseph Califano, another presidential aide, there was "great merit in repetition"; officials "should keep repeating the same facts again and again," he said. After one discussant argued that the public needed "specifics" on "how we got into Vietnam in the first place," McGeorge Bundy responded that "this particular piece of exposition might simply not be manageable. Our best posture may be to say simply that somehow we are there and that we have to stay."[88]

"At the President's direction," the administration formed a committee for coordinating its domestic propaganda operations on Vietnam in August. It also apparently concluded that official participation in the teach-ins had produced more opponents of the war than supporters. In future, the administration decided, it would only explain the facts of life in Vietnam at "responsible" forums.[89]

The first half of 1965 was an electric time for peace activists. Observing the proliferation of teach-ins around the country, they sensed that history was on their side. Marilyn Milligan was convinced that the many famous speakers at the Berkeley teach-in (including Dr. Benjamin Spock, Dave Dellinger, Senator Ernest Gruening, I. F. Stone, and the comedian Dick Gregory) were turning listeners against the war. "I saw that we could really have an impact," she would recall. "It seemed as though we could reach a wide range of people. . . . The teach-in definitely was a very hopeful event." Stephen Smale remembered feeling inspirited merely because Americans were becoming "more conscious of the war" and "starting to question it more," although most still basically supported it. Doug Dowd, a Cornell University professor and teach-in organizer, remembered the thrill of seeing people "changing their minds in your sight. You'd see this guy who has been a real turkey on something all of a sudden saying, 'Maybe,' and then . . . very quickly he'd say, 'Sure.' Once somebody began to open their eyes they just kept them open. It was real quick-change sort of stuff going on." SDS's Paul Booth wrote in early May: "The war has proven to be a subject on which debate could easily be awakened—we are really penetrating and moving liberals to actions in large numbers. . . . One Senatorial assistant (whose boss is against the war) says the march was a tremendous boon, opening up the Senate to a challenge of the bombings of the North."[90]

Collective action was itself exhilarating. "There was so much more going on than politics," Milligan remembered. "For me, so much of it was that feeling of being with thousands of people, thousands of kindred spirits. You know, how often do we feel that in life?" Dowd recalled experiencing a "wonderful camaraderie that I hadn't seen before on the left. . . . And you can't help but get hopeful when that sort of thing happens. It was really kind of like being high."[91]

Later a professor of economics at San Jose State University and a lecturer on international economics at Johns Hopkins University's School in Advanced International Studies in Bologna, Italy, Dowd was a political pessimist by nature; one friend with whom he worked during the war remembered him perennially predicting a large-scale clash with China or the Soviet Union. "What do you do when you live in a nation of infants?" he would remark sadly of Ross Perot's sudden popularity in 1992. Dowd recalled other reasons for his uncharacteristic political optimism in 1965. Like other older radical organizers who had gone through the political deep-freeze of McCarthyism, he was basking in the warmer political climate:

> All of a sudden it seemed to me that what I had always thought
> would be impossible—namely, a large-scale movement against a war
> that your country was in—began obviously to take hold. It seemed
> to me that that was absolutely amazing. . . . I was teaching at Berke-
> ley during the Korean War. Jesus Christ, you couldn't get *anybody*
> to say *anything* against the Korean War. . . . Everybody was scared
> shitless to identify themselves with being against that war because it
> meant, quite obviously, that you must be a ranking member of the

Communist Party. In fact, I was accused of exactly that. So to me, ten, twelve years later and the anti-Vietnam thing, all of a sudden it just seemed obvious that something was happening that was absolutely brand-new. . . . And I began to feel very different about the possibilities of politics in the mid 1960s. I really can remember that. It was as though spring had arrived after a very, very long fucking winter.[92]

Dowd noticed that the *quality* of protesters had also improved since the 1950s. There was a refreshing "liveliness" to these young activists:

All of my experience had been with the Old Left. Never as a member of anything, but always if you were going to do anything in the thirties and forties you had to do it with the CP [Communist Party]—or against the CP. And I always worked with the CP. I always thought they were a bunch of assholes in many ways, but they were the only assholes around, they were the only people that were doing anything. And there was a kind of tiredness to this whole thing of the CP and the Trots and so on. So all of a sudden you get all of these young guys. And, oh, a lot of it was fraudulent and a lot of it was, in fact, self-defeating. Nevertheless [their exuberance] . . . got itself into everybody's spirit. It was a time of real anger, but also of real hope.[93]

Dowd and other left-wing academics who had toiled through the oppressive and lonely 1950s were inspirited by yet another development. Their colleagues now took them more seriously. Dowd:

By the time the mid sixties came along, I'd been at Cornell for a dozen years or more, and had been very, very unpopular there. Because I was sort of outspoken. I used to give a lecture on why socialism was necessary in the United States every year [laughs]. . . . And everybody thought I was kind of a looney. . . . All of a sudden at Cornell by the mid sixties I was no longer a strange person. I was either someone who was being involved with a lot of other people moving in that direction, or I was a hated person.[94]

The sense of promise and accomplishment then invigorating the antiwar movement was warranted. As Carl Oglesby recalled, activists had awakened large segments of the academic community to the war. Many professors and students took their first public steps against it after attending teach-ins. Some peace movement leaders emerged, people whose dedication and resilience would help fuel the antiwar fire in less sanguine times ahead. As I. F. Stone observed, the government had been "put on the defensive."[95] Forced to explain its policies publicly more than it wanted, the administration ended up pouring kerosene on the flames. Johnson's dream of a quiet little war went up in smoke. As Mc-George Bundy told the president, the protests had increased doubts about U.S. policy off the campuses as well. Many Americans had been skeptical of the war before the spring outpouring; they now realized that their misgivings were hardly unique. Also, criticisms of the war advanced at teach-ins sometimes found receptive audiences in Congress, many of whose members were dubious of U.S. policy themselves; rising concern in their home districts exacerbated legislators' doubts. The movement probably prodded Senators Morse and Gruening to take noisier stands against the war than they would have otherwise. And the campus protests energized peace activists organizing in their own communities.

Not everyone in the antiwar movement was in an upbeat mood, however. Some judged the pace of public outreach too slow or were too pained by the war's violence to experience more than fleeting moments of joy. Todd Gitlin "had a feeling—which I had very often in the sixties—that we had done so much *and yet* there was so much more to do that it was almost unmanageable." Oglesby exclaimed to Paul Booth in May, "We're talking of building up the movement to stop the war just as if the war could really be stopped. . . . What gives you hope gives me bitterness." Another SDSer, Carl Davidson, remembered being so overwhelmed by the size of the April march that the next day he "ran down to get the newspaper. I was convinced I was going to read on the front page that the war was over, that Johnson had seen all those people and would start to pull the troops out. I really believed it."[96] From his lofty perch as SDS vice president, Davidson would soon be proclaiming the need for revolution.

"This Is Really War"

Three days after the SDS protest, senior administration officials and military leaders met in Honolulu to plan an expanded war.[97] Although the NLF had been "unusually inactive" of late, they knew this was "nothing but the lull before the storm." Intelligence reported that the enemy was quietly extending his influence throughout South Vietnam and recruiting more troops than he was losing. The conferees recommended doubling U.S. troop deployments to eighty-two thousand.[98]

As Johnson pondered this advice, the storm broke in all its fury. NLF forces overran a South Vietnamese provincial capital and its U.S. advisory compound, inflicting heavy casualties. They also "decimated" two ARVN battalions in other fighting. Ominously, senior ARVN commanders exhibited "tactical stupidity and cowardice." ARVN seemed on the brink of collapse.[99]

On June 7, General Westmoreland sent CINCPAC an unsettling message. "There are indications that the conflict in Southeast Asia is in the process of moving to a higher level," he reported. North Vietnamese Army (NVA) divisions had crept into South Vietnam, and the NLF was now "capable of mounting regimental-size operations." "ARVN forces on the other hand are already experiencing difficulty in coping with this increased VC capability," Westmoreland wrote. "Desertion rates are inordinately high. . . . ARVN troops are beginning to show signs of reluctance to assume the offensive and in some cases their steadfastness under fire is coming into doubt." Westmoreland requested a hundred and fifty thousand additional U.S. troops "as rapidly as is practicable."[100]

One week later the NLF attacked a Special Forces camp and an adjoining district headquarters. ARVN reinforcements rushed to the scene were "devoured." The battle marked, in the words of the Pentagon Papers historian, "the bitterest fighting of the war to date."[101]

The unstable political situation in Saigon continued to torment the administration. Following a series of coups and countercoups, a veritable gangster grabbed a share of the power. New prime minister Nguyen Cao Ky, a flashy dresser fond of Adolf Hitler, "drinking, gambling and chasing women," and his corrupt co-ruler, Nguyen Van Thieu, "seemed to all of us the bottom of the barrel, absolutely the bottom of the barrel," William Bundy remembered.[102]

Westmoreland's message and ARVN's deterioration "stirred up a veritable hornet's nest in Washington." Officials intent on leaving Vietnam triumphant now had to confront head on the prospect of large-scale U.S. involvement in ground combat. "Temperatures rose rapidly . . . and the debate was acrimonious and not without its casualties."[103]

Under Secretary of State George Ball launched an early salvo. Although a major infusion of U.S. troops might turn the tide, Ball wrote on June 18, the odds were not good. "Before we commit an endless flow of forces to South Viet-Nam we must have more evidence than we now have that our troops will not bog down in the jungles and rice paddies—while we slowly blow the country to pieces." Ball advised Johnson to make a "controlled commitment" of a hundred thousand troops "for a trial period of three months." He also suggested developing plans "for cutting losses and eventually disengaging from an untenable situation."[104]

Secretary of Defense Robert McNamara wanted to go for broke. In a memo circulated on June 26, McNamara advocated increasing U.S. and ARVN forces to *whatever* level was necessary to convince the NLF that it could not win. McNamara also urged an embargo on the movement of war matériel into North Vietnam, mining North Vietnam's harbors, destroying its rail lines to China, and wiping out all of its airfields, surface-to-air missile sites, and war-making supplies. Although confident his program would bring victory, McNamara cautioned Johnson, presciently, "the test of endurance may be as much in the US as in Vietnam."[105]

McGeorge Bundy found McNamara's agenda "rash to the point of folly." "If we need 200 thousand men now for these quite limited missions," he queried the secretary of defense, "may we not need 400 thousand later? . . . Is there any real prospect that US regular forces can conduct the anti-guerrilla operations which would probably remain the central problem in South Vietnam?" Bundy also questioned whether going for North Vietnam's jugular would affect the fighting in the South. Still, Bundy pressed for a "scaled down" version of McNamara's plan. [106]

Walt Rostow was not only hawkish but effusively optimistic. He maintained that a "clear-cut" military victory was "nearer our grasp than we . . . may think." The United States could force an end to the war, argued Rostow, if it struck hard at North Vietnam's industrial base. [107]

Like most other officials, William Bundy found himself occupying the middle ground of the debate. Although in favor of selectively escalating Rolling Thunder, he opposed increasing U.S. forces beyond the seventy-five thousand men Johnson had by then approved. Bundy doubted a major troop deployment would significantly aid the U.S. war effort. He was also apprehensive about the domestic response. Johnson, Bundy warned, needed to "reckon the Congressional and public opinion problems of embarking now on what might appear clearly to be an open-ended ground commitment. . . . We might be readily accepted if we moved gradually; but arouse the worst fears and adverse reactions if we move fast." [108]

Yet Bundy was of two minds on domestic opinion. He was aware that hawkish senators and other Americans wanted the United States to "really go in and do the job" in Vietnam. These people would be among those turning on the administration, Bundy suspected, if the nation got "mired down in a long, inconclusive war." Thus, he felt anti-escalation sentiment was "balanced" by demands for progress. "The most basic judgment of public opinion that we had to make," Bundy recalled, was, "'How much would the country object to violent methods, as compared to how much it would object if you got bogged down—which you might conceivably avoid by violent methods?'" [109]

Convinced another infusion of U.S. troops was required to prevent a humiliating U.S. defeat in Vietnam, Johnson elected in July to deploy roughly a hundred thousand additional men. He also implicitly agreed to send Westmoreland whatever forces might be needed later. The president opted against an all-out bombing campaign against the North in favor of gradual escalation. The previous month, he had unleashed the potent B-52 bombers for saturation strikes in the South.

With the administration moving sharply into an open-ended involvement in Vietnam, some advisers urged Johnson to mobilize the country behind him. McNamara and the JCS advocated calling up more than two hundred thousand National Guard and reserve troops, asking Congress for a tax increase, and declaring a state of national emergency. The president was tempted. To test the political waters, he and McNamara hinted at press conferences that a reserve call-up was likely. Daniel Ellsberg wrote a "trumpet call" speech for McNamara announcing national mobilization, which "raised our sights toward the containment of China," a more "suitable adversary" in a major war than "little North Vietnam." The speech was cleared by McNamara, Rusk, and McGeorge Bundy, and all of the military service chiefs were "expecting to mobilize," Secretary of the Army Stanley Resor later remembered.[110] In the end, however, Johnson decided against doing so.

Dean Rusk was at the center of the action. Years later he was a professor of international law at the University of Georgia. The small Rusk Center, sitting unobtrusively near the north edge of the sprawling Athens campus, was not a familiar landmark: none of the first three students I asked for directions had even heard of it. Rusk was a friendly man with a moonish face, large ears, and glasses as thick as Coke bottles. Despite suffering health problems, he chain-smoked cigarettes. When asked about Johnson's verdict, Rusk pointed after a long pause to a fear that domestic appetites for the war might grow too strong:

> The limited use of force is very difficult. It's difficult for the men and women in uniform who are carrying the battle, and it's difficult on the home front. We made a deliberate decision not to stir up war fever among the American people. You didn't see troop units parading through cities, you didn't see beautiful movie stars out at factories raising money for war bonds and things of that sort, as we'd done during World War II. One reason for that is that we felt that in a nuclear world it's just too dangerous for an entire people to become too angry. That that might push the situation beyond the point of no return.[111]

Johnson did indeed fear an avalanche from the right. "He felt if he mobilized and said, 'Now we're going to clean the bastards up,' . . . [it would] unleash all kinds of forces which would make it necessary for him to do things that he didn't want to do militarily," Rostow remembered. The president was well aware that influential Senate hawks opposed a reserve call-up unless it was accompanied by a greatly intensified bombing campaign against the North. He also understood that opening the floodgates on the right might engender a resurgence of McCarthyism. But even more disconcerting to Johnson was the specter of accelerating *opposition* to the war. Aware that the public's support for U.S. policy had shallow roots, Johnson was afraid mobilization would demand greater sacrifices than many Americans would tolerate. "He knew that was going to cause a ruckus because it was going to take people away from their jobs and that causes all kinds of domestic turmoil," the CIA's Richard Helms recalled. "These things fan out immediately." The policy would have jarred the lives not only of the men called up but also of their wives, employers, associates, parents, and other relatives. The president "instantly" foresaw this "ripple effect" of mobilization, Helms said. "I mean, if there was a political animal in the American twentieth century, it was Lyndon Johnson." Johnson remembered the unpopularity and evident wastefulness of President Kennedy's mobilization in 1961 during the Berlin crisis. After being called up in the Air Force reserve, Johnson's future son-in law, Patrick Nugent, "apparently became an annoyance to the president because he was always hanging around the White House and he didn't have anything to do," Westmoreland related. Johnson knew that a tax increase would greatly magnify the public's discontent. Suddenly "the war would have become *a war* rather than a dim event that everybody was *sort of* for because they were against communism," noted Paul Warnke, a later Pentagon official. "The price would have become too heavy." Johnson "saw nothing but domestic turmoil" in both measures, Helms thought, "and that's why he avoided them."[112]

The president recognized that Congress would be a key source of the turmoil. True, he had forgotten neither legislators' submissiveness during the Tonkin Gulf episode nor their nearly blanket approval of his politically motivated request for $700 million in extra funds for the war in May. As Senator Eugene McCarthy (D-Minn.) recalled, Congress was then behaving "like a garden society—just bring up a resolution and we pass it." But Johnson realized that members of Congress were uneasy about Vietnam. Senate Majority Leader Mike Mansfield had written him on June 9 that Congress's one-sided votes on the war hid "grave doubts" and "much trepidation." The following month, Mansfield told Johnson that Congress and the public supported him because he was president, not because they were enamored with his policies. There was "full agreement" among Senate leaders with whom he had recently spoken, said Mansfield, that the country was "deeply enmeshed in a place we ought not to be . . . and that every effort should be made to extricate ourselves." Johnson feared that congressional debate over mobilization would hamper passage of his Great Society legislation.[113]

The emerging peace movement surely also shaped the president's view that mobilization would not sit well at home. He knew students, professors, and others would fuel the domestic tumult over the policy. The dissections of the war performed at the teach-ins had warned the administration that mid 1965 was an "unpromising time to ask the country to join a crusade," Daniel Ellsberg later observed. For several months, campus and other audiences had been hearing unrelenting criticism of U.S. policy and getting a candid look at the South Vietnamese government. They had learned that the allegedly "democratic" friends of the United States in South Vietnam were corrupt, had little legitimacy among their own people, and stood no great chance of success. Most agonizing to officials, the whole notion that the war was a product of aggression from the

North had been seriously damaged. And though the administration remained convinced that the protesters' research on the war was shoddy, it recognized that "proving they were wrong was very difficult," Ellsberg recalled. "They had a good 'case' in front of the 'court of public opinion.' You could see that they were rather plausible." With mobilization, "people would be asking the wrong questions," Ellsberg said. "So it is better not to have a debate." It was "much better to tell them, 'Ah, we're making a very limited effort here to help out a friend in pursuit of our commitments. . . . Don't worry about it, don't worry about it, it will go away soon—and it ain't going to cost much.'"[114]

Officials had other arguments against mobilization. Some felt that most National Guard and reserve forces should be held back for use in other trouble spots. Mobilization was also expensive, and it might rile China and the Soviet Union.[115]

The president directed his staff to implement his escalatory policies in a "low-keyed manner . . . to avoid undue concern and excitement" at home and overseas. His press conference of July 28 rammed home the point. Johnson announced that he was increasing U.S. forces by fifty thousand, or half the actual figure. Among other officials, Ellsberg, who had recorded an increase twice that size in his "trumpet call" speech, was dumbfounded. "What's this?" he would remember asking his boss, Assistant Secretary of Defense for International Security Affairs John McNaughton:

> "Fifty thousand? Has he changed his mind?" And McNaughton's answer was, "Well, not that I know of. You'd better look into it."
> So . . . I called McNamara's office, I called somebody on the Joint Staff. I spoke to them. "What's going on here? Have they changed the figure?" And they said, "No, no, it's 100,000." I said, "Well, the President just said 50,000." "Well, we don't know about that. . . ."

In August, the administration apparently decided to tell people who questioned Johnson's honesty that he was tallying troops "as they arrive in Vietnam and not as they are alerted." It was a tale Dean Rusk continued to tell over twenty years later.[116]

Also to avoid undue concern and excitement, Johnson and McNamara misled Congress about the war's likely economic costs. Subsequent years also witnessed understated projections. The budgetary and inflationary problems that eventually set in largely as a result of this chicanery and Johnson's reluctance to seek a tax increase would come to haunt the administration.

For the moment, however, Johnson's maneuvers served him well. He had successfully presented himself as a man of restraint; most observers breathed "a sigh of relief." The president seemed intent on avoiding a wider war without giving in to the communists. "Few Americans will quarrel with President Johnson's determined conclusion to hold on in Vietnam," John Oakes's *New York Times* editorial page declared. As Oakes later recalled his own thinking, while escalating the war seemed "a great mistake . . . it was something else again to say that we should beat a retreat." The world's most powerful nation couldn't just "turn tail and pull out."[117]

"A Colossal Blunder"

Following the April peace march, many protesters looked to SDS for guidance. It was now the apparent leader of a rapidly growing movement begging for national coordination. Rather than using its authority, however, SDS committed, in the words of Paul Booth, "a colossal blunder." Acting out what Booth called "the chronicle of a bunch of intelligent people who were confused," SDS elected not to concentrate on Vietnam.[118] In fact, it would never again initiate a significant national antiwar action.

Events immediately following the march suggested a different course. For three days, SDSers, ecstatic over their "monster" demonstration, discussed possible follow-up activity. They decided to expand their grass-roots organizing on Vietnam. Some began building a May 3–8 "National Vietnam Week" of local actions; others pressed for a "national civil disobedience threat" in June.[119] The most hotly debated antiwar proposal came from SDS's national secretary, Clark Kissinger. In violation of the 1917 Espionage Act, he suggested that the organization urge young men not to register for the draft, report for induction, or serve in the armed forces.

In 1986 Kissinger was a leader of the Revolutionary Communist Party U.S.A. A short, genial man with muttonchop sideburns and a fondness for Lenin-style caps, Kissinger wore his revolutionary mettle on his sleeve. "It is only a small number of us who came through that [Vietnam] period actually more determined than we were then to put an end to this motherfucker [i.e., capitalism]," this former math teacher said earnestly. "I think that the largest single failing that we made during that whole period of time was not sending a contingent to North Vietnam to fight on the North Vietnamese side. For example, to man antiaircraft gun emplacements around Hanoi." The political effects in the United States would have been "very sharp," he conjectured.[120]

Following the April demonstration, Kissinger was unexcited about holding more marches in Washington. SDS had had its fling with ephemeral, liberal pressure activity, he reasoned. Although Kissinger judged grass-roots organizing important, he sensed that outright resistance to the war would rouse the public and government much faster. "I felt it was significantly important for the movement to take on more of a treasonous edge," he recalled. "I wanted to up the ante of the struggle politically." Kissinger remembered the "Manifesto of 121" signed by prominent French intellectuals in 1960 that advocated "insubordination" to France's colonial war in Algeria. The manifesto was "a real shock" in France that "caused people to think," Kissinger perceived. "I really dug it. . . . I wanted to repeat that situation in the United States as much as possible. I thought it could do more to move the antiwar movement than almost anything else." Since his "Kamikaze Plan" was blatantly illegal, Kissinger figured it would put the government "on the spot. If they let us get away with it, that's fine, we could continue to propagate and develop it." If the government "came down on us," there would be a messy political trial, with SDS defending itself on the basis of the Nuremberg Doctrine. "I looked at it as a 'heads we win, tails they lose' kind of tactic," he recalled. "Whichever way the goverment responded, it would read down to our support."[121]

"I certainly cannot say that I had it all thought out," Kissinger conceded. "It was much more of a gut feeling . . . that that's the direction that things had to go, had to have that treasonous edge on it." Along with many other antiwar organizers, he was "just grasping for anything that could become a vehicle" for a mass movement.[122]

Kissinger's proposal was considered too strong by most SDSers and was shelved. Nonetheless, the dominant feeling inside the organization was that something good was happening around Vietnam in the United States and that SDS should help propel it along. If only it could come up with the right vehicle.

Then, in June, at SDS's fateful national convention at Camp Kewadin in Michigan, a new breed of SDSers swept into the organization. Unintellectual and anarchistic, they emphasized action over strategic planning and resisted all attempts to formulate national programs. Marijuana was more important to them than political theory. SDS's ghetto organizers were also flexing their muscles at Kewadin, and they remained opposed to projects that might hinder their effort to build a poor people's movement. Tom Hayden acted "quite bemused by the whole idea of peace activity," Todd Gitlin remembered. "Just simply not interested." If SDS assumed the leadership of the antiwar movement, Hayden and others asked, where would it be when peace came?[123]

SDS failed to move on Vietnam at Kewadin. Although the sentiments of the new cadre and the ghetto organizers were largely responsible, the causes went beyond them. Many SDSers were disoriented by the antiwar movement's sudden birth. They had little sense of what shape a mass American peace movement might take; there were no historical precedents to enlighten them on how to guide it along. But they did know local organizing on domestic issues. "Basically what we were saying was, 'Well, for several years what we were doing seemed to turn out pretty well,'" Booth later analyzed. "'So let's keep developing along the track that we're most comfortable with and not pay any attention to this cataclysmic development that's going on around us. Because we haven't figured out how to handle it. . . .' Not a bad thing to do when you get involved in something and you can't quite figure it out—fall back on the things that you do understand."[124]

Many SDSers shared Kissinger's lack of ardor for holding another national *march*, the most obvious next step in building the antiwar movement. The standard antimarch reasoning was in the air, but there was something else there as well. "Have you ever organized . . . something like that?" asked Carl Oglesby, who was elected SDS president at Kewadin. "So you know how alienating it is. People just got bored with it. . . . Nobody wanted to do it. . . . See, people would never feel this way out of mere ideological reasoning. There was something in the seat of their pants that told them that this was a bummer not to be gone into again."[125]

Yet bummers can be borne if they seem to bear fruit. Souring more than a few SDSers on peace activity was deepening gloom about their ability to stop the war. Oglesby's and Gitlin's pessimism had by now grown to the point where they could open their guidelines for discussion of foreign policy issues at Kewadin with, "Diagnosis of US foreign policy may smack these days of just slightly premature world autopsy." Moving in their direction were other SDSers who had emerged from their postmarch euphoria only to examine the situation in Vietnam and see nothing new—except greater bloodletting. Even Booth, who in May had been exultant over spreading opposition to the war in the United States, was developing serious doubts about the peace movement's clout. He had always been skeptical about activists' ability to influence the foreign policies of what he and other SDSers considered an "authoritarian" federal government. But the spring protests had gotten his Vietnam juices flowing. The problem was that, when the smoke had cleared, the Johnson administration seemed unimpressed. "Nothing that we had done had had any visible impact on policy," he remembered. This was "particularly annoying and disheartening" to veteran SDSers like himself, Booth said, because

> an important part of our political education had been learned through experience in the civil rights and other movements where, when you did something, there was a reaction which allowed you to judge, (a) whether what you had done had been effective, and (b) what to do next. And you were in a very lively relationship to city hall or the sheriff or to . . . whatever the target was. You learned about politics because your actions had a reaction. And I must say that was a great political education. Irreplaceable. We developed a very sensitive understanding of how change is possible in the United States and how politics worked between the years 1961 and 1965. So we were completely disoriented by the phenomenon of mass protest and no reaction. Basically, we lost our bearings.[126]

Booth's frustration would grow over the summer, impelling him to collaborate with Lee Webb, a fellow SDSer, on a widely circulated call to transform the peace movement into a radical multi-issue movement. The level of political impatience that the October call expressed is, in retrospect, astonishing. U.S.

policy in Vietnam "is impervious to pressure placed directly on it," Booth and Webb maintained. "This is beginning to emerge with clarity." Furthermore, the antiwar movement "cannot involve masses of people here in the United States" because "few do or will see the issue of Vietnam as critical to their lives." "If we leave Vietnam," predicted the young strategists, "it will be a reflection of LBJ's tactical wisdom, not of our political force." Booth later observed of this call:

> It's an embarrassment to me. . . . There's certainly no historical basis for what we said. It was a product simply of our ability to say, "Well, we've been doing this so far and it hasn't succeeded. Therefore, it must be wrong." Which is an error of the first magnitude. What's more embarrassing about it is I'm quite sure that people pointed out the shallowness of the argument to us and made no impact on us. And we thought we were providing this great theoretical guidance to everybody. [127]

There was another factor in SDS's abdication of the peace movement's leadership. Many SDSers believed the movement would continue to develop regardless of their own political priorities. "The feeling was, 'If a thing is real, then people will pick it up and go with it, and you don't need to keep hammering away at it,'" Oglesby remembered. [128]

SDS exhibited acute strategic confusion for months after Kewadin. No political programs were in the mix, and the national office—infested with anti-organization anarchists—was a shambles. "There was nobody running the store," Gitlin recalled. Nevertheless, hundreds of SDSers across the country decided to pick up and go with the war issue on their own. That summer and fall, they leafleted draft induction centers urging youth to apply for CO status and "clog" the draft system with year-long appeals. They also confronted military recruiters on campuses. Some took their antiwar message door-to-door. In September, after Booth was drafted by other veteran SDSers to serve as acting national secretary, the national office even proposed a countrywide antidraft program. The initiative was partly a response to local SDSers' thirst for antiwar protest, Booth said, but more to "this intellectual disease that we had to do something more [to stop the war] because whatever else was being done wasn't enough." Antidraft protest "seemed to be an escalation." Although Booth offered SDSers all sorts of intricate strategic reasons for the program, they were merely "rationalization," he subsequently conceded. "We never indulged in saying, 'We're doing this because it makes us feel better.' That would have been frowned upon." [129]

SDS's rejection of the antiwar movement's stewardship provided temporary relief for the Johnson administration. Since most peace activists did not immediately comprehend what had transpired at Kewadin and believed SDS would still assume the initiative, planning for nationally coordinated actions proceeded tentatively. Also, SDS then had broader appeal among antiwar activists than any other political organization in the United States; had it chosen to organize another national peace march in the fall, the turnout would have been larger than that for the marches that did take place. Moreover, the leadership void left by SDS quickly attracted the keen attention of those bitter Old Left rivals the Socialist Workers Party and the Communist Party, whose unimaginative brands of Marxism-Leninism and incessant skirmishing were poorly received by many peace activists. The two groups' frenzied pushes for power diminished interest in national planning.

While the peace movement remained nationally leaderless, however, there was widespread action at the grass roots. Slowly, quietly, often imperceptibly, antiwar organizers were broadening their base. None were busier than the dogged women of Women Strike for Peace.

Carrying On

Largely middle-class housewives, WSPers were in perpetual motion against the war. They set up coffee klatches to discuss Vietnam with their neighbors, handed out leaflets door-to-door, on downtown street corners, and in suburban shopping malls, and organized synchronous demonstrations in cities across the country. WSPers also protested the sale of war toys at department stores, arranged speaking appearances for Senators Morse and Gruening, and rented billboard space for antiwar ads. Some picketed draft boards; others raised humanitarian aid for Vietnamese war victims. Alice Hertz, an 82-year-old activist with both WSP and WILPF (a common dual affiliation), even burned herself to death on a Detroit street. WSPers partook in virtually "anything that would bring the knowledge of the war home to the American people," WSP's Alice Hamburg remembered. "There was nothing too bizarre. . . . [We were] always trying to think of something that would arouse the people to what was going on."[130]

WSP was primarily focused on arousing other women. As Donna Allen, a leading WSP activist in Washington, D.C., recalled:

> We had this belief that only women are going to stop this war. And I
> don't think it's far wrong. If we had stayed home and played bridge, it
> might still be going on. . . . We just felt that, even though there
> were a lot of men and boys who felt strongly [opposed to the war],
> that there were too many of them who also felt warlike, or loved to
> fight—or whatever it is—so that if the women weren't in there very
> strong and solid you wouldn't end the war.

Only a minority of WSPers considered themselves feminists, though. "I never was one, really, to go out and fight for the women's cause," WSP's co-founder Dagmar Wilson said. "I wanted the women to fight for the human cause."[131]

WSPers were also a nettlesome source of direct pressure on U.S. officials. They organized a campaign to flood the White House and Capitol Hill with antiwar letters. ("There is some possibility that many 'Mother letters' are not legitimate and may represent a subtle attempt to influence Government action," one Johnson aide finally concluded.) "Inundate, swamp the powers that be with your mail," WSP's newsletter exhorted. WSPers kept White House switchboard operators busy during a nationwide phone-the-president campaign. Many picketed the White House, sometimes dressed in black to symbolize death. Although their repeated attempts to meet with Johnson were unsuccessful, WSPers gained hearings with his aides. The women were not easily cowed. "I must confess that my own experience with representatives of Women Strike for Peace has not been very satisfactory," Chester Cooper tersely wrote New York WSPers in July. After "literally three hours of discussion" with a group of them one Saturday afternoon, he complained, "I was told that, since the Administration and Government officials produced lies and propaganda, nothing I said or indeed anything anyone in the Government said could be taken seriously." It was the "first and only" time he had met with political activists "when I felt it pointless to proceed with any further discussion," Cooper conveyed.[132]

Although their tactics were diverse, most WSPers shied away from civil disobedience. They believed other American women would be turned off by illegalities and avoid protests that risked arrests. Further, as the New York WSP leader Cora Weiss remembered:

> We were all young women with children and families, and we had to
> go home at night and feed our kids and feed our husbands. This was
> before the age of what might be called "liberation." And many
> women were doing this without their husbands' full approval. And
> those women who had their husbands' full approval still had the
> marriage, the social contract [to consider]: "It's okay to go out and
> demonstrate, it's okay to go out and write leaflets, and it's okay to go
> see the president of the United States—but be home for dinner."[133]

In July, ten WSPers traveled to Indonesia for a "peaceful confrontation" with six women from the North Vietnamese government and three from the NLF. "In spite of the fact that our country was in a war with Vietnam, we said, 'The women of America will get together with the women of Vietnam and we will discuss what we can do to stop our countries from fighting each other,'" recalled the diminutive, animated Wilson. The Vietnamese women graphically described the effects of America's fragmentation bombs; the bombs' tiny pellets burrowed painfully into their victims' bloodstreams and were impossible to remove. "It was a rather shocking experience," Wilson said. The encounter strengthened the Americans' resolve.[134]

Activists with other peace groups were also speaking out against the war then. In many cities, local antiwar committees held vigils and picketed federal buildings and military bases. On May 12, following morning worship, some eight hundred protesters from the Interreligious Committee on Vietnam marched silently from a Washington church to the Pentagon; they lined up in single rows facing three of the building's entrances and stood silently for six hours. Nine leaders of the vigil had a "vigorous" meeting with Robert McNamara inside. Three days later, in New York, pacifists from the Committee for Non-violent Action (CNVA) sat down on the pavement in front of an Armed Forces Day parade. "Kick their brains in," some spectators shouted. Nearly thirty protesters were hauled away by police. On the evening of June 8, seventeen thousand people turned out for a SANE-sponsored rally at Madison Square Garden. The next week, CNVAers undertook a "sequel to and extension of" the spring teach-ins by distributing more than fifty thousand antiwar leaflets inside the Pentagon and giving extemporaneous speeches to Pentagon employ-ees. The demonstrators set up a literature table in the building's main concourse. Five had a trying meeting with McNamara. [135]

In Berkeley, Vietnam Day Committee activists were canvassing against the war in surrounding communities, mainly among poor blacks, "primarily be-cause those are the folks who . . . didn't slam their doors in our faces," Marilyn Milligan recalled. Several painted a pickup truck an official-looking gray, erected flashing lights and a yellow sign on its back warning, "Danger, Napalm Bombs Ahead," and conspicuously tailed trucks transporting locally produced napalm on Bay Area roads. VDCers also organized a picket against an appearance by General Maxwell Taylor in San Francisco. Demonstrators hurled a pile of flyers in Taylor's face bearing his picture and the declaration, "Wanted For War Crimes." They later chased the general up a hotel stairway, forcing him to take cover in the office of the hotel's manager. [136]

But what most caught the imaginations of VDCers at the time were attempts to blockade trains carrying U.S. soldiers bound for Vietnam. Promoted by VDC leaders mainly as a way to attract media attention to the movement and reach GIs, the troop-train demonstrations had a more basic appeal to many activists: they seemed a particularly fitting expression of their soaring moral outrage over the war. The protesters would not be good Germans. "To oppose the immoral war in Vietnam and to block the war machine is moral; to take orders from an immoral state is immoral," one VDC leaflet declared. By all accounts, the dem-onstrations were exhilarating experiences. With multi-ton loads bearing down on them, protesters scrambled off the tracks at the last second. "I could have wiped my nose on the side as it went by," one exclaimed after a close encounter with a train. Others were slammed aside by police. The soldiers on the trains didn't appear sympathetic; nor were any trains stopped or direct discussions with troops secured (except during brief forays on board). But the actions gen-erated reams of newsprint, and the demonstrators had left no doubt about where they stood. "I loved that," Milligan reminisced. "That seemed to be a clear expression of how I felt." At each of the four blockades that August, Milligan "felt I might die, and that would be okay. . . . Not that I *wanted* to do that, but I felt, 'If it happens, well, it is certainly morally correct.'" She could remember the shiver that shot down her spine after a cop knocked her off the track short feet from an oncoming train. "I don't know if I would have stood there and let the train mow me down, but . . . the front of the train looked enormous so it must have been pretty close. I was shocked. . . . 'Gee, maybe I really would have let myself get run down.'" Milligan's brush with death didn't quell her desire to put her body on the line for her political principles, though. Marching against many of the Reagan administration's foreign and domestic policies in 1986, "the only thing I could think of—all the way—that I wanted to do was go and lie down on the tracks in front of where they bring the missiles out of the factories," she recalled. "See, my mind goes immediately to that."[137]

Cooperation or Combat? The International Days, the National Coordinating Committee, and the SANE March

During the troop-train demonstrations, the VDC was also trying to rally support for a plan to organize antiwar protests overseas and in the United States on October 15–16. It was unwilling to wait for SDS to pick up the ball on Vietnam, although it did assume that SDS would take the lead in promoting the actions in America.[138] In early August, the VDC leader Jerry Rubin flew to Washington to propose the "International Days of Protest" at a gathering of political activists known as the Assembly of Unrepresented People (AUP).

The AUP had been organized largely by prominent radical pacifists to hold a series of workshops on domestic issues and a "Congress of Unrepresented People" (COUP) inside the Capitol building to protest the war. Two thousand people participated in the four-day event. On August 8, thirty-six were arrested for blocking all the entrances to the White House. The next day, police busted over three hundred at the foot of Capitol Hill, thwarting the attempted COUP. It was the largest roundup of peace demonstrators in Washington history. Some of those attending the AUP met with officials at the White House; among them were "some very limp young men," two aides reported to McGeorge Bundy.[139]

Rubin arranged a workshop at the AUP to discuss the International Days. The conferees agreed to help organize the protests. They also formed a coalition called the National Coordinating Committee to End the War in Vietnam (NCC). They would meet again in November to plan future national antiwar activity, the participants decided. The first step toward achieving countrywide coordination of the peace movement had been taken.

To many activists, it was not a big step. The NCC was considered more of an "accidental" than a representative national antiwar body at this point, and a member of the small Communist Party had been selected as its coordinator. But to the Socialist Workers Party, it was a gigantic step. Control of the antiwar movement was up for grabs, and the SWP wanted to make sure its particular brand of socialist politics was well represented at the top. It wasn't about to let the CP run the show, that was for damn sure. The SWP and its youth group, the YSA, hastily issued a call to their troops to accelerate their involvement in local antiwar committees, representatives of which would be attending the November NCC convention. "The norm should be that every member of the YSA should belong to an antiwar committee and the main thrust of local work should be antiwar work," the YSA's director of peace activity declared. "As long as the antiwar movement is ascending, it is better to err on the side of overinvolvement if we must err at all."[140]

More bodies were good for the peace movement, of course, and SWP bodies were sometimes the finest antiwar bodies around. They labored with the utmost determination, working phone lines until their voices gave out, spinning off leaflets for hours on end, pounding miles of pavement to convert other bodies to the cause of peace. They were professionals at making waves and relentless to boot. But there was also something a little *too* driven about these bodies. It wasn't just their insatiable hunger for recruits to their political party or mechanistic promotion of legal demonstrations that raised eyebrows. They seemed to have a difficult time compromising on any issue their organization had developed a position on, and they spent more time at meetings trying to peddle their ideological wares than searching for common points of departure. Their group-thinkitis was a little scary. The SWP's rigidity and propensity for political combat swiftly left their marks on planning for the International Days. Unfortunately, not everyone understood the source of the marks.

Preparation for the Days was undertaken mainly by the VDC and local ad hoc committees around the country. The largest local committee was New York's Fifth Avenue Peace Parade Committee led by Norma Becker, a veteran of the southern civil rights movement. Years later, Becker, a New York schoolteacher, lived in a compact, 21st-floor Greenwich Village cooperative with a breathtaking panorama of Manhattan. Her capacity for juggling umpteen tasks simultaneously while keeping her wits about her, and doing it day after day after day, was put to the supreme test during the Vietnam War. Besides teaching full-time and raising two daughters, she coordinated the Parade Committee, attended national antiwar planning conferences, and chaired a citywide teachers' peace organization. That she was able to bear the load—and bear it for nearly ten years—is truly remarkable. "I'll tell you, when I look back on it, I don't see how," Becker reflected. "It was adrenaline, it was a force . . . over and beyond personal volition. Probably whatever the chemistry is that enables individuals to accomplish unbelievable feats, like moving a piano out of a burning building. . . . They don't make a decision to do that: they just feel compelled to do it." How did she find time to relax? "How do you relax when they're killing people?"[141]

Becker called a meeting over Labor Day weekend and proposed that activists organize a march down Fifth Avenue on October 16. The more ordinary folks, the better. "I felt that the Vietnam protest was mainly a fringe element at that point and that we needed to be a little bit more daring and shoot for something that was more mainstream," Becker recalled. The meeting quickly degenerated into a swirling dispute over—amazingly—acceptable slogans for marchers' placards. Becker remembered:

> It seemed as if the meeting was going to blow. I was really
> astounded. . . . I could not believe the passion with which people
> were insisting upon a particular phrase. It didn't seem to me to mat-
> ter that much. There was intense feeling, and unyieldingness. So at
> one point . . . I just said . . . that if the people in that room can't
> agree, then we will get some other people and organize this march
> without any slogans if necessary. And then Abner Grunauer of
> SANE—there was a heavy silence then— . . . suggested that we
> agree to march behind one slogan, just "Stop the War [in Vietnam
> Now]." And people agreed to do that.

But they did so only after the skillful intervention of A. J. Muste, a widely respected older radical pacifist. Were it not for Muste's conciliatory effort, the meeting might well have broken up.[142]

Although the reasons for the distemper were many, the SWP was much to blame. It was adamant that the march's official slogan call for "immediate withdrawal" rather than "negotiations," the most prominent alternative. The SWP argued that the United States had no right to be in Vietnam and that its departure was nonnegotiable. Less openly, it was "afraid that the NLF was going to sell out if they got to the negotiating table," Lew Jones recalled. Even more alarming to SWP sensibilities was the specter of mass Democratic Party—that is, "ruling class"—involvement in the peace movement. The SWP felt that "immediate withdrawal" was the only slogan that "could not be coopted by the ruling class," Jones said. "Negotiations," on the other hand, were quite accept-able to most Democrats. If the Democratic Party exerted significant influence in the peace movement, the SWP feared, the movement's revolutionary potential would plummet. The SWP "was scared to death of the Democratic Party . . . taking over" the movement, Jones emphasized. And not only was the despised CP pushing "negotiations," but its entire political agenda assumed a coalition with the Democrats.[143]

The CP was also partly to blame for the fracas. It genuinely believed that the war would inevitably end through negotiations, and that activists should therefore call for them. But, as the CP student leader Bettina Aptheker recalled, the "real reason" the CP supported that slogan was "because the Trots [i.e., SWPers] were for the other one. . . ." The CP was bent on combat as well. Aptheker remembered her father, the CP theoretician Herbert Aptheker, "thundering about" the importance of demanding negotiations. "Yes, Daddy, that's right" was her weary response.[144]

The same fight over antiwar slogans was then erupting in other peace committees around the country as well. The participants were not limited to the Old Left (e.g., SANE was also firmly set on "negotiations"), but the hatred between the SWP and CP was largely responsible for the spiteful tone of discussions. The results were agonizingly long meetings, sapped energies, frayed nerves, stalled planning, and disillusionment with antiwar organizing. Most activists found it distasteful to work with people more intent on pummeling each other than on stopping the war. Some ceased active participation in the movement. Aptheker later readily granted that the "insanity" of the warfare between the CP and SWP "really, really hurt" the movement:

> When I look back at that, I think, "My God, we were crazy!" That's
> what I think the divisions [in the movement] came from. . . . Be-
> cause when I look back at that retrospectively what I see is a lot of
> people who used to come to those meetings from the community
> that weren't affiliated with anybody, that came because they were op-
> posed to the war. . . . But what happened in those meetings was that
> you had a struggle between the CP and the SWP for hegemony of
> the movement. And that struggle manifested itself over concrete is-
> sues, but independent people who came in couldn't understand what
> the debates were about and why they were so acrimonious, because
> they didn't have an awareness or understanding that this person was
> a Trot and this one was a CPer and that's what they were *really*
> fighting about. . . . I remember Jack [her husband then] and I at
> the time just sort of sitting there over the kitchen table looking at
> each other and saying, "This is crazy, this is just crazy." . . . It
> was supposed to be a peace movement and we were tearing each
> other apart. . . . We just raked each other up one side and down the
> other.[145]

Aptheker is not the only combatant who subsequently came to her senses. "The SWP was simply dogmatically and mechanically laying out to everyone that's around it, 'Either agree with us or fuck you,'" Peter Camejo spat. An environmental activist and also an SWP refugee, Lew Jones observed that the SWP's opposition to "negotiations" was "ridiculous. . . . The NLF were our people, and if they say they want to have negotiations we ought to support them. . . . And it was also important to get the U.S. to the damn bargaining table and away from the bombers, for Christ's sake." Jones's speech at a forum in Ann Arbor on a national tour to promote "immediate withdrawal" in 1965 "went over like the proverbial turd in the punchbowl." His fellow panelist Herbert Aptheker "just ignored me. To his credit. . . . I'm glad he did that."[146]

Why didn't the SWP and CP agree to disagree and organize mutually acceptable activity? There were substantial obstacles to cooperation between them. They had been bitter political enemies for decades. Moreover, since each group saw itself as the vanguard of a future American revolution, they were competing for political recruits. Also, the historical isolation of the political left in the United States had created few previous opportunities for the SWP and CP to work together in large coalitions; consequently, neither was well trained in the art of compromise. This same political history had failed to produce radical leadership of a stature capable of convincing the two groups to seek common ground. Camejo ardently described the weight the past exerted on the Old Left:

> Talking to each other as *humans* who want to end the war, who have something *in common* but don't agree on strategy, and acting *rational* so as to be most effective . . . was beyond us. That would have required a different type of person which history hadn't created in the American left. It would have required a Malcolm X type, a Fidel Castro type, a [Sandinista] Tomás Borge type. We didn't have those types. We were all petty. . . . The SWP leadership was petty, the CP leadership was petty. No one had the broader view. . . . We were mechanical. Even when we were right, we were mechanical.

Finally, since the late 1940s, the FBI had been exploiting the rivalry between the SWP and CP through assorted dirty tricks. The most common dirty trick was the anonymous letter. For example, the FBI sent a Milwaukee CP leader a poem accusing him of drinking excessively and abandoning "militant action" in the hope that he would conclude that a local SWP leader, an accomplished poet, had composed it. Sure enough, the CPer rose to the bait, firing off his own insulting poem to the SWPer. "Dizzy with its success in the use of the verse, the [FBI] field office drafted plans to exacerbate the quarrel through satirical cartoons," Frank Donner writes.[147]

Meanwhile, Johnson administration officials were pondering the damage the International Days of Protest could do to their war policies. The protests might increase public concern about Vietnam and hearten the enemy, they worried. As early as August, officials requested information from the FBI that could be used to link protest organizers to communism. The administration also began developing plans to "counteract" the actions with "positive publicity" on the war. "A television program for release prior to October 15 and featuring students, professors and other Americans who have visited Vietnam and are favorable to Administration policy will be looked into," the government's Vietnam propaganda group agreed on August 30. Two weeks later, it discussed orchestrating "a major peace-type announcement timed to the . . . Days of Protest," with the launching of a fund-raising drive for the prowar American–Southeast Asian Foundation "one possibility." On September 29, McGeorge Bundy advised Johnson to make a statement about "the non-military element of our Vietnam effort" at a forthcoming press conference "in view of the world opinion and forthcoming student demonstrations." He also suggested that the president undertake a television and radio campaign to deflect attention from the protests.[148]

Officials recognized that the civil disobedience protesters planned at military installations on October 15–16 would create its share of undesirable publicity. The Armed Forces aide to the president inquired of the secretary of the Air Force whether he had the authority to "preclude or interfere in the planning, organizing or conduct of" actions at Air Force bases. The aide received a negative reply. On the eve of the Days, Joseph Califano cautioned Johnson that there was "every expectation of some serious problems in connection with the . . . demonstrations." The "most likely place of trouble," he reported, was "the San Francisco area," home of the VDC, which was preparing to "pacify" the Oakland Army Terminal by directing a teach-in to the troops and urging them to refuse service in Vietnam. Clashes between soldiers and protesters, sure to attract media scrutiny, were to be eschewed: the Pentagon ordered all military commanders to "avoid direct physical contact with demonstrators who attempt to get on their bases," leaving the "handling" of the rabble to state and local police. Attorney General Nicholas Katzenbach braced for arrests; he ordered all U.S. attorneys to remain on duty throughout the weekend of the Days. Califano assured Johnson he was "keeping in close touch with" Katzenbach and Deputy Defense Secretary Cyrus Vance about the protests.[149]

State officials were not taking the International Days lightly either. California's attorney general, Thomas Lynch, warned the director of the U.S. Secret Service, James Rowley, that the Secret Service would have its work cut out for it during a scheduled appearance by President Johnson in Los Angeles on October 15. "It is not my intention to be unduly alarming, but I do want to advise you that those individuals planning to demonstrate are well-schooled and well-organized," Lynch wrote. "In recent weeks they have shown a growing militancy and antagonism toward all established law and order."[150]

Some Johnson administration officials may have responded in another way to the Days. Members of the American Legion, Veterans of Foreign Wars, and New York City Council were then planning a prowar parade in Manhattan on October 30. Given evidence of substantial administration assistance to organizers of subsequent prowar parades and official consideration of such assistance to counteract a peace demonstration in November, it seems likely that the government had a hand in this effort. On October 30, more than twenty thousand people "counted to cadence" as they stepped crisply down Fifth Avenue. As Paul Warnke recalled, this and the many other prowar demonstrations held during the war were "quite ineffective" in mustering public support for U.S. policy.[151]

On October 15–16, antagonists of law and order mobilized around a hundred thousand people for protests in several dozen cities across the United States. In New York, where twenty-five thousand marched, a clean-cut, athletic-looking young Catholic pacifist named David Miller burned his draft card in bold defiance of a recently enacted federal law. The remains of the card were quickly snatched up by a watchful FBI agent and later used to send Miller to prison for two years. In Berkeley, fifteen thousand held a teach-in and then headed off without a parade permit toward the Oakland Army Terminal; the nine leaders of the march were accompanied by bodyguards to protect them from right-wing thugs who had recently slashed the car tires of VDCers and physically threatened them. "There was a lot of paranoia about snipers," Marilyn Milligan remembered. The demonstrators were stopped at the Oakland border by a wall of helmeted police; after a heated debate, they voted to turn back, disappointing many. Near Madison, eleven protesters were arrested when they attempted to make a "citizen's arrest" of the commander of a local Air Force base. In Ann Arbor, three dozen youths (including one Bill Ayers) sat in at their local draft board. The protest begot a wave of bad publicity for the Johnson administration when the Selective Service System's director, General Lewis Hershey, his dander aroused by the youths' intemperance, revoked the student deferments of thirteen of the male protesters. This would place them, Hershey boasted, on "the belt that runs toward the induction station." The *Los Angeles Times*, CBS, and NBC all ran stories denouncing this policy. Some White House officials also questioned it. Press Secretary George Reedy wrote Johnson that it was difficult to claim it was done in the national interest when student deferments were also claimed to be in the national interest. Hershey was apparently unfazed by his critics, virtually taunting, "I'm one of those old-fashioned fathers who never let pity interfere with a spanking."[152]

The fall antiwar protests sent Establishment denunciations of the peace movement soaring to new heights. Ex-President Dwight Eisenhower expressed dismay over the "moral deterioration" of America's youth. J. Edgar Hoover labeled the demonstrators "halfway citizens who are neither morally, mentally nor emotionally mature." Yale University's president, Kingman Brewster, spoke of the "tragedy" of "college rebels" who "hurt their own cause when they demonstrate first and think about it later." Senator Robert Byrd (D-W. Va.) said the protests were "senseless, diabolical, abominable, disgraceful, hurtful." The columnists Rowland Evans and Robert Novak accused SDS of concocting a

"master plan" to "sabotage" the war; SDS's promotion of conscientious objection was "particularly malicious," asserted the journalists, since this struck at
the "soft underbelly of the draft machinery." Attorney General Katzenbach
announced that the government was closely monitoring the movement's impulse "in the direction of treason." "There are some Communists in it and we
may have to investigate," Katzenbach stated. "We may very well have some
prosecutions." (When another administration official forwarded Katzenbach a
VDC leaflet urging U.S. soldiers to refuse to fight in Vietnam and offered that
it was "pretty close to seditious material," however, no prosecutions resulted.)
Hubert Humphrey was the odd man out. The fall protests apparently made
little impression on him. The vice president apprised Johnson of a "rising tide
of support . . . among the college students."[153]

In early November, the antiwar movement took a stunning turn. Tormented
by a seemingly unstoppable war, Norman Morrison, a Quaker, sat down at the
river entrance to the Pentagon late one afternoon, not far from Robert Mc-
Namara's window. He covered himself with kerosene and lit a match. The flame
shot twelve feet in the air, sounding, some said, like the "whoosh of small rocket
fire." Seconds after Pentagon guards reported "a small fire of undetermined
origin," scores of horrified office workers—and Morrison's infant daughter, Emily, whom he had released from his arms at the last second—witnessed orange
flames engulfing his motionless torso. A man in uniform attempted to put them
out with his coat, but he could not prevent their fatal result. McNamara, who
witnessed medics covering either Morrison's body or Emily in blankets, later
called the immolation "a personal tragedy for me." The following week the
Catholic pacifist Roger LaPorte replicated Morrison's deed outside the UN building in New York. He died after being conscious, lucid, and assertedly free of
pain for many hours. Rumors circulated that a "suicide club" of pacifists
planned a self-immolation a week until the war was over.[154]

During November, Old Left divisions continued to hamper antiwar organizing. Among Parade Committee activists, members of the SWP and CP were
still pointing out each other's political sins to anyone who would care to listen,
at any time they would care to listen, which was not often. David McReynolds,
for his part, was adamantly opposed to working with either of the two groups,
particularly the CP. The War Resisters League leader explained:

> You would really have to be my age or a very imaginative scholar . . .
> in order to go back in time and understand the hostility and bitter-
> ness between the CP and those like myself who were in the Socialist
> Party, and the Trotskyists. . . . And that bitterness included the fact
> that we were called agents of the CIA by the CP, not only in public
> but in private. We resented this rather deeply. It also goes back to
> things like their breaking up our meetings physically in the thirties.

Also, they shot a lot of our people in Eastern Europe. For a variety of reasons, feelings were much more intense then than is easy to see now. You can read about it, but it seems a strange world. . . .

It's a problem of people feeling it's okay to lie to you because you're "bourgeois" and you don't count, you're not part of the revolutionary process. You go through that a few times and you say, "Okay, I don't want to work with you. Period."

McReynolds opposed continuation of the Parade Committee if the CP and SWP were allowed to remain in it. His position was rejected, and McReynolds effectively dropped out of the committee. "I was wrong," he reflected years later. "I wasn't judging the historical situation correctly."[155]

Over Thanksgiving weekend, the National Coordinating Committee held its first convention. The gathering consisted, in Lew Jones's words, of "three days of just all-out factional warfare." Disturbed by CP influence in the NCC's national office, the SWP had flooded the convention with its troops, primed to play hardball. "They were acting so sectarian and manipulative," Dave Dellinger, who chaired many of the convention's meetings, recalled. "They just really tried to take the whole thing by storm. . . . People would pull maneuvers under Robert's Rules of Order." During the opening plenary session, Jones unilaterally decreed that a workshop had been added to the conference agenda to discuss the formation of a national organization of the various "independent" local antiwar committees around the country, many of which were controlled by the SWP. "That just blew the whole thing up, because it was on the face of it an uncooperative act," Jones said. While the audience looked on in disbelief, the NCC coordinator and CPer Frank Emspak and the normally mild-mannered Jones engaged in an awkward tug-of-war over the microphone. Fistfights between CP and SWP activists nearly broke out numerous times at the convention. "It ended up essentially with the forces around the CP and the forces around the SWP whacking it out," reminisced the SWP leader Fred Halstead. "And the 1,500-odd ordinary folks who were there got lost in the shuffle."[156]

That they did. Marilyn Milligan remembered that she and the many other activists who had traveled to the convention hoping to join in a warm antiwar community experienced an abrupt political awakening. They had attended the meeting mainly because

> there were going to be antiwar people from all over the country there. . . . There were a few people who had political goals in mind, but most of us didn't. And most of us were totally shocked that this is what it turned into. . . . I had no idea until that convention that certain people in the VDC here in Berkeley were members of those political organizations. . . . They all came out of the woodwork. And they stayed up all night fighting about trivia as far as we were con-

cerned. . . . I still feel angry about it. . . . I was *terribly* disillusioned. . . .

It was demoralizing to the whole antiwar movement. Anybody
who came to that convention who was just an ordinary person like
myself and not a member of one of those political groups was totally
demoralized. . . . I talked to lots of folks there. In fact, that's all we
had to do, because what happened was all these people closeted themselves out of reach. . . . All night these people were holed up in hotel
rooms. And we had no idea [why]: "How come I drove all the way
across the country for this?"

Milligan added, "It was a big waste of time and energy and money—which we
didn't have a lot of." The Old Left's internecine feuding at the convention shaped
Milligan's decision to drop out of the antiwar movement the following year.[157]

Jones and Halstead, two of the SWP's heaviest hitters at the convention, came
to regret their performances there. "People tried to set up a conference and the
SWP walks in and tries to *re*organize the conference," Jones said with loathing.
"The SWP was heavy-handed. . . . From the very beginning the SWP had an
attitude of distrust and worry that the CP was going to do something. I just
think a far better tactic would have been to try to work with Emspak." A year
before he succumbed to cancer in 1988, still a member of the SWP, the amiable,
pajama-clad, chain-smoking Halstead smiled:

I have thought back on that NCC convention at some length. I'm not
totally convinced [that] walking into it I wouldn't have had to make
some kind of fight for what I believed in, but I do know . . . that
maybe there were fifteen hundred people there—and a thousand of
them never showed up again for anything. And maybe there were
two hundred who knew what was going on. That's a problem
[laughs]. . . . I would go into a thing like that well aware that that
could be a problem.

Halstead added, "We now know that if we're going to accomplish anything
we've got to do it together, so let's not have a war about it among ourselves."[158]

The combatants at the NCC convention laid down their arms long enough
to agree to call for two more International Days of Protest on March 25–26.
But the organization had suffered serious injury. As Dellinger remembered,
many peace activists were "very down on the Marxist left" even before the
conference, and now they had more reason than ever for their animosity. They
were not about to participate in a political arena dominated by Old Left game-
playing. Dellinger, who insisted that both the CP and SWP "had a contribution
to make" to the peace movement but that they "not make it in the Old Left
manner," was "constantly besieged by people badmouthing the NCC and telling
me not to be putting so much effort into it."[159] By the following summer the
NCC was out of the national antiwar picture.

Also giving pause to activists at this time was rising skepticism about their effectiveness. "Perhaps the most immediate and serious general problem facing antiwar activity on campuses is a feeling of demoralization," reported the workshop on student action at the NCC convention. "Are we really having an effect on the U.S. government's policy in Vietnam?" Wrote Paul Booth and Lee Webb: "Many activists have lost their confidence in the ability of the movement to involve large numbers of people. They feel that the movement will always be in a minority and unsuccessful." Some were "losing their grip," another SDSer observed. "There was this tremendous amount of pressure building and we were all running around behaving like all this pressure didn't mean anything to anybody," Booth later lamented.[160]

Prior to the NCC convention, SANE had called for an antiwar march in Washington on November 27. SANE organizers wanted no part of either the Old or New Left and announced that "kooks, communists or draft-dodgers" would be unwelcome. "They saw the possibility that we would drag everything much too far to the left . . . and get the right-wing waked up in a way that they ordinarily wouldn't get waked up," SDS's Carl Oglesby remembered. "You know, liberals are always trying to tiptoe around fascism." Yet SANE also realized that if SDS helped build the march it would attract many less distasteful youths to the event. It thus invited SDS's participation. Although unexcited about another national march and repulsed by SANE's anticommunism, SDS faced a real dilemma. It could "either," in Oglesby's words, "sit on the sidelines and let the march fail and give Johnson and his crowd the opportunity to crow over the death of the peace movement, or else go in there and try to make it work." Oglesby chose to enter into discussions with SANE organizers, including over the "momentous issue" of acceptable slogans. Relations were often tense. "They just wanted to utter pieties about 'peace' and 'understanding' and 'international brotherhood'—crap!" Oglesby recalled. The SDS president had "a huge fight" one afternoon with the SANE leader Sanford Gottlieb over the slogan "Vietnam for the Vietnamese." "I thought that was a pretty normal thing for people to say and there was no problem with it, but he saw it as . . . an implicit endorsement of the communist side," Oglesby said. "That was the kind of thing I was up against."[161] SANE ultimately agreed to let Oglesby speak at the demonstration.

Amidst the haggling, the Johnson administration prepared its game plan for the protest. It would feign disregard. McGeorge Bundy stated at a November 1 meeting of the government's Vietnam propaganda group that officials would "not attempt to counter the [demonstration] with pro-Administration rallies; any impression of an overly worried reaction is to be avoided." One week later, the same group agreed that a "mass presentation of pro-Administration student petitions on November 27" was "out of keeping with our tactic of reacting to the prospective Washington march in low key. This policy of not permitting the protesters to dictate the time and nature of our actions was re-affirmed." Quietly, officials coaxed notables to sign a prowar statement sponsored by Freedom House. The statement argued that the "national consensus" behind the war "must not be obscured by a small segment of our population." It surfaced in newspapers across the United States two days after the demonstration. Government security forces devised plans to snuff out any burning protesters. Secretary of State Dean Rusk told march organizers to address their concerns to Hanoi (which they had already done). The same month, officials assisted a cross-country train trip by prowar students and Jaycees designed to "solicit material contributions for Vietnam, inspire rallies and receive petitions of support at each stop." They also arranged national television appearances for five South Vietnamese "student leaders."[162]

On November 27, despite chilly temperatures and a threat of rain, thirty thousand people demonstrated in Washington. When it came time for Oglesby to speak, the sun was down and many of the protesters had retreated to the warmth indoors. Aware that he would be "on a liberal stage . . . filled with liberal half-ass ideas," Oglesby had composed a biting attack on the imperialistic side of traditional American liberalism. Ears cocked and eyes froze during his oration.

> The original commitment in Vietnam was made by President Truman, a mainstream liberal. It was seconded by President Eisenhower, a moderate liberal. It was intensified by the late President Kennedy, a flaming liberal. Think of the men who now engineer that war. . . .
> They are not moral monsters.
> They are all honorable men.
> They are all liberals.

America, declared Oglesby, had lost its desire for human equality and become "a nation of young, bright-eyed, hard-hearted, slim-waisted, bullet-headed make-out artists. A nation—may I say it?—of beardless liberals."[163]

When he finished, the applause was deafening.

A Christmas Bombing Pause

While the November protest told the Johnson administration that "the peace movement cannot be written off" (as Gottlieb remarked afterward), the Vietnamese enemy was demonstrating that he could not be written off either. Despite a gradual intensification of Rolling Thunder, Hanoi seemed as determined as ever. Washington's belief that pounding North Vietnam from the sky would coerce Hanoi into calling it quits had proven "a colossal misjudgment." Moreover, the NLF and NVA were increasing their troop strength much faster than U.S. intelligence had foreseen. The ramifications of this buildup were made "abundantly clear" by the gory fighting that broke out in the Ia Drang Valley in mid-month.[164]

This first big battle of the war brought U.S. and ARVN forces into heavy contact with enemy troops. Much of the fighting was hand to hand. U.S. commanders unleashed B-52 bombers for a series of punishing strikes and deployed tactical air sorties and artillery. More than two hundred U.S. soldiers perished in the protracted engagement; the NLF and NVA lost over twelve hundred.[165]

On November 23, General Westmoreland requested one hundred and fifty-four thousand additional U.S. troops. Three weeks later, he asked for a total of four hundred and forty-three thousand men by the end of 1966. Neither Westmoreland's requests nor President Johnson's approvals of them were publicly disclosed.[166]

Faced with the need for continued escalation of the war, officials contemplated the public's likely response. There were favorable signs. Fifty-seven percent of Americans supported the president's policies in Vietnam, and only 24 percent felt U.S. entry into the war had been a mistake. A quarter judged antiwar protesters "tools of the Communists" and a third believed they had "no right to demonstrate" (leading one White House aide to conclude that the public was "highly suspicious of the demonstrations"). Some union leaders seemed to be almost enjoying the war. "I would rather fight the Communists in South Vietnam than fight them down here in the Chesapeake Bay, when they are landing on our own shores," snorted the AFL-CIO's George Meany. The labor czar derided antiwar professors as "intellectual jitterbugs" and cried, "God help our children if we can't do a little better with these fellows." As George Christian, who joined the White House the following year, recalled with a laugh, Johnson "could talk to somebody like George Meany or Lane Kirkland . . . and he'd get an infusion of hawkism pretty quick."[167]

Yet officials realized the public was becoming increasingly impatient with the war. White House Counsel Harry McPherson remembered Johnson musing that if the fighting persisted for another year many of his supporters in Congress would lose their seats. "So he understood in late 1965 that the war had no public support to speak of," McPherson said. Chester Cooper told McGeorge Bundy that he suspected public backing of U.S. policy was "more superficial than . . . deep and committed (many people probably do not even understand what it is that they are supporting)." Cooper also fretted that "confused" antiwar liberals from Harvard, the National Council of Churches, and other institutions were giving "prestige and respectability" to the "hard-core left-cum-kooks" in the streets. By January nearly three-quarters of Americans would report feeling "deeply concerned" about the war.[168]

Domestic doubts about Vietnam were hitting at least one official quite close to home. One evening in November or December, Robert McNamara received a phone call from his only son, Craig, aged fifteen, a student at an elite New Hampshire prep school. Craig had attended a forum against the war at his school a day or so earlier organized by several of his closest friends. "I found that to be devastating," Craig recalled. "I found it to be really difficult to comprehend. . . . What [the speakers] said made sense." "Is this right?" Craig anxiously asked his father about the war while fidgeting in a phone booth. "Send me some information so I can better verse myself on this." Part of Craig yearned to be convinced that the speakers and his friends were mistaken. "I didn't want to believe that what my dad was doing was wrong," he said. The elder McNamara did send his son some literature on the war, but it was unpersuasive. Shortly after the forum it became "quite clear" to Craig "that what we were doing in Vietnam was absolutely wrong."[169] The fissure in the McNamara family would widen into a chasm in the years ahead, causing indescribable pain to the secretary of defense.

Some administration officials contended that a pause in Rolling Thunder would whet the public's appetite for further escalation of the war. McNamara wrote the president on November 30:

> It is my belief that there should be a three- or four-week pause in the
> program of bombing the North before we either greatly increase our
> troop deployments to Vietnam or intensify our strikes against the
> North. The reasons for this belief are, first, that we must lay a foun-
> dation in the mind of the American public and in world opinion for
> such an enlarged phase of the war and, second, we should give North
> Vietnam a face-saving chance to stop the aggression.[170]

Johnson ordered the bombing halted on December 24. The administration then orchestrated a ballyhooed "peace offensive," with officials waltzing between overseas capitals to communicate U.S. interest in negotiations. It was a show worthy of Hollywood. "We do not, quite frankly, anticipate that Hanoi will respond in any significant way," Dean Rusk cabled U.S. Ambassador Henry Cabot Lodge in Saigon on December 26. "There is only the slimmest of chances that suspension of bombing will be occasion for basic change of objective by other side." But, Rusk noted, the public would appreciate the policy. "The prospect of large-scale reinforcement in men and defense budget increases of some twenty billions for the next eighteen month period requires solid preparation of the American public. A crucial element will be clear demonstration that we have explored fully every alternative but that aggressor has left us no choice."[171]

On December 28, three American opponents of the war flew to North Vietnam in defiance of State Department regulations. During their nine-day stay, Herbert Aptheker, Staughton Lynd, and Tom Hayden were struck by the total determination of the North Vietnamese and NLF. "No gimmick, no diplomatic skill . . . no amount of military power can bring this dreadful war to an end," Lynd wrote. "The 'other side' wants one thing, and they will fight to the death for it: America must decide to withdraw."[172] The North Vietnamese hosts emphasized to their visitors the importance they placed on the peace movement in the United States. The Americans listened as their chief interpreter sang a song lauding Norman Morrison, already a national hero in North Vietnam.

TWO   1966

Antsy Senators, Angry Buddhists, Concerned Clergy

Johnson had initially planned to resume the bombing of North Vietnam in early January. However, domestic political considerations prompted a reassessment. Members of Congress returning to Washington after Christmas vacation told the White House tales of substantial unease over Vietnam among their constituents. Some reinforced Johnson's fear that Democrats would suffer at the polls if the war wasn't wound down. Many prominent lawmakers, including Senators Mike Mansfield, George Aiken (R-Vt.), J. William Fulbright (D-Ark.), and John Sherman Cooper (R-Ky.), publicly urged the president to maintain the pause. The politically savvy Johnson was undoubtedly aware that their sentiment was widely shared on Capitol Hill.[1]

Antiwar activists bolstered legislators' disquiet. With the help of Union Theological Seminary students, a group of prominent New York clergymen organized a campaign to express public support for the bombing halt. Clergy Concerned About Vietnam and its supporters held press conferences and besieged congressmen with letters backing the pause. Women Strike for Peace activists conducted "intensive" lobbying with legislators in their electoral districts. In Washington, members of Congress encountered a WSP "Lobby-by-Proxy" operation moving at top speed. WSPers handed the legislators antiwar statements signed by their constituents back home, and offered comments like "She can't come—she's busy ironing." Employed by WSP throughout the war, this proxy system of lobbying meant that "wherever [legislators] were they were confronted by the women with the same darn message," the WSP leader Dagmar Wilson recalled. "They couldn't escape us. It reminds me of the tortoise and the hare. It's the same approach." The proxy system also allowed WSPers living in Washington to pester members of Congress despite having no U.S. representatives of their own then. "I thought [it] was very clever," Donna Allen said.[2]

Johnson maintained the bombing pause until January 31.

The president was irked by his congressional critics and petulantly told them his policies were informed by the Southeast Asia Resolution they had signed in 1964. Most irksome to him was Fulbright. Johnson's former friend had burned his bridges to the White House by criticizing the U.S. invasion of the Dominican Republic in September, and now Fulbright's Senate Foreign Relations Committee was conducting nationally televised hearings on the war. On January 28, the opening day of the hearings, Fulbright suggested to Dean Rusk, who was there as an administration witness, that the antiwar movement had influenced his decision to hold them. "I do not recall any issue about which there is so much apprehension about a military involvement, and this is a reason, I think, why some public discussion of it at this time is appropriate," he said. "Something, it seems to me, is wrong or there would not be such a great dissent, that is evidenced by teach-ins and articles and speeches by various responsible people."[3]

Running through February 18, the Fulbright hearings were an eye-opener to the millions of Americans who watched them. They convinced many that opposing the war and patriotism were compatible. Americans heard Lieutenant General James Gavin and former Ambassador George Kennan, author of the Cold War "containment" doctrine, challenge the administration's justifications for the war. "If we were not already involved as we are today in Vietnam, I would know of no reason why we should wish to become so involved, and I could think of several reasons why we should wish not to," Kennan said. A U.S. military victory could only be achieved, he argued, "at the cost of a degree of damage to civilian life and of civilian suffering, generally, for which I would not like to see this country responsible." Witness General Maxwell Taylor dismayed some listeners with his callous disregard for the war's civilian victims. "I would doubt if we would find many of the [B-52 strikes] hitting exactly where we would like them to . . . but the over-all effect has been very helpful," he breezily testified. Taylor shrugged off America's napalming of Vietnamese babies as merely an "unhappy concomitant" of the air war. Taylor continued to display an appalling insensitivity to the war's human toll years later. Standing in a barbecue line at a holiday picnic at Clark Clifford's home in the 1970s, he remarked to Eric Sevareid, "Believe me, fifty thousand dead? We kill that many every year on the *highways*." The statement "really shook" Sevareid. "I never tried to talk to him again," he said.[4]

Anthony Lake, a State Department staff assistant, helped compose Rusk's briefing papers in preparation for his testimony in the Fulbright hearings. Although Lake was restive about U.S. policy, the hearings fortified his essential commitment to the war, and he believed they strengthened the resolve of other officials as well. Lake remembered getting "very testy" at the time with his father and wife, both of whom opposed the war. At the end of an argument at a restaurant, his father rose to his feet and shouted "so that the whole restaurant heard it, humiliating me, 'You sound just like Dean Rusk!'"[5]

By the end of the hearings, Fulbright's office had received ten thousand responses from concerned Americans. They ran seventeen-to-one in favor of Fulbright and his activity. Most officials, however, probably viewed the Fulbright hearings as a serious threat to the war's domestic rear guard. That prominent senators were challenging U.S. policy on national television must have been disconcerting to the administration. In fact, to deflect public attention from the proceedings, Johnson hastily arranged a star-studded conference on Vietnam in Honolulu. The president also moved to tarnish the reputations of Fulbright and other members of the Senate Foreign Relations Committee. He directed the FBI to monitor the hearings in order to document similarities between the senators' statements and "the Communist Party line." Johnson took an interest in the logs of FBI wiretaps of the Soviet Embassy, hoping to discover friendly conversations between the legislators and the Soviet ambassador. He noticed that his main critics in Congress had all either dined at the embassy or met privately with the ambassador before becoming outspoken on Vietnam. Johnson perceived that Fulbright and Wayne Morse were "definitely under control of the Soviet Embassy." The president and other officials privately derided Fulbright as "Senator Halfbright." On March 3, "Deke" DeLoach, the FBI official "most trusted" by Johnson, approved an FBI letter to the White House discussing Senator Morse. Although the letter's contents remain censored, released FBI memos of the same month document interest in Morse's personal finances, particularly money he garnered from speaking appearances. A March 26 FBI memo theorized that the "only reason" for Morse's opposition to the war was to ensure that "his services as a speaker would be in large demand." In July, Johnson ordered the FBI to seek out derogatory information on ninety-three of Morse's supporters in Oregon. At least one FBI official was nervous about the mission. "It would be extremely embarrassing to the Bureau if word leaked out that certain individuals who had criticized our Vietnam policy had been identified as communist by the Bureau," he warned his superiors. Six months later, an FBI report discussed possible subversive influences on Morse and two colleagues.[6]

As the Fulbright hearings were getting under way, administration officials were responding to another annoying outburst of Establishment opposition to the war. In late January, the "Lawyers Committee on American Policy Toward Vietnam," claiming four thousand members, released a letter to the press challenging the legality of U.S. intervention in Vietnam. The administration asked Professor Neill Alford, Jr., of the University of Virginia Law School to prepare a contrary statement and attract co-signers. Released on February 23, the prowar letter boasted all of five signatures. "I just don't know how we can gain attention for this letter; it's hard to generate interest in a 'pro' position," Harry McPherson complained to White House Press Secretary Bill Moyers. "Do you have any ideas?" Unenthusiastic about the war himself, Moyers answered weakly, "I'm afraid I don't."[7]

The results of a public opinion survey undertaken in late February and early March could not have assuaged officials' concern. More Americans "worried" about the war than about crime, race relations, and the cost of living, the survey showed. Contrary to previous press reports, opponents of U.S. policy were more likely to be "doves" than "hawks." Blacks were the most dovish social group. (The civil rights organization SNCC had recently become the first group outside the antiwar movement to endorse draft resistance.) The study found that a majority of Americans favored free elections in South Vietnam even if the NLF won. That these findings received national publicity and were inserted into the *Congressional Record* probably further upset the administration, since they might thereby spark additional doubts about the war.[8]

Despite the public's growing disquiet, many Americans remained averse to antiwar protesters. After a pack of high school students assaulted four draft resisters in Boston, a city police captain remarked, "Anyone foolish enough to commit such an unpatriotic gesture in South Boston can only expect what these people got." At Texas A&M, campus police arrested students handing out antiwar flyers and drove them eighty miles away under orders not to return.[9]

During March, officials tracked protesters' plans for the second International Days of Protest. D. W. Ropa, an aide at the White House, was hopeful that attendance at them would be unimpressive, although he was anxious about the probable media attention. "The reports I have indicate that the protest organizers will fall short of their expectations," he wrote Moyers. "My contacts tell me that a 'psychological deflation' has set in on many campuses following the Fulbright hearings, and this is giving the protest organizers some difficulty in whipping up enthusiasm for another round of demonstrations." Ropa's prediction was largely accurate, as in many U.S. cities the turnout for the March 25–26 protests disappointed antiwar organizers. Only seven hundred marched in Boston, for example, and thirty-five hundred in San Francisco. But despite continuing sharp tension in New York's Parade Committee over acceptable antiwar slogans, the turnout in Manhattan was great indeed. Fifty thousand people—double the October number—marched down Fifth Avenue. The breadth of participation had increased as well. "The marchers this time seemed to represent much more of a cross section of Americans," observed the *New York Herald Tribune*. This probably came as no surprise to George Reedy, who had told Johnson in late January that antiwar protesters were not simply "beatniks" or "radicals."[10]

Events in South Vietnam continued to distress officials. During a long dinner conversation with Robert McNamara in January, Arthur Schlesinger got the distinct impression that the defense secretary was "very concerned about the way things were going and very reluctant to resume bombing." McNamara warned the president on January 24 that, even with the more than four hundred thousand U.S. troops already earmarked for Vietnam, "the odds are about even that . . . we will be faced in early 1967 with a military stand-off at a much higher level, with pacification *hardly underway and with the requirement for the deployment of still more U.S. forces.*" Citing poor ARVN performance, a "moribund" GVN, and increasing enemy troop strength, John McNaughton wrote on January 18, "We . . . have in Vietnam the ingredients of an enormous miscalculation." General William Westmoreland was shocked when told that one ARVN officer "would only contemplate battle if so advised by his astrologer."[11] McGeorge Bundy apparently decided that he'd had it with the war. On February 28, he resigned from the administration.

The situation in South Vietnam deteriorated dramatically in March. Demonstrations initiated by Buddhist monks and joined by students, labor activists, and factions within ARVN broke out in Hue, Danang, and Saigon. Many denounced the American presence in Vietnam. In Hue, an irate mob torched the U.S. Consulate; firemen refused to put out the blaze. The demonstrations received considerable publicity in America, leading many previous supporters of the war to wonder why the United States was trying to help people who didn't want its help.[12]

Worried officials weighed their options. Informed by a recent visitor to South Vietnam that the place was an "unholy mess," McNaughton submitted that the United States might have to negotiate an end to the war. After South Vietnamese Prime Minister Nguyen Cao Ky crushed the rebellion with armed might, however, President Johnson "categorically thrust aside the withdrawal option," William Bundy recalled, and "we all relaxed."[13]

McNamara apparently did not, though. According to one observer that spring, his face was graying, his hair thinning, and his voice tended to go hoarse when he got emotionally riled. "Bob appears tired," commented U.S. Congressman Melvin Laird (R-Wis.). "He's getting a little testy. He should take off and get some rest." By now, Craig McNamara remembered, his father was so bothered by the war that he would "come home at night and walk around the house adjusting the paintings on the wall, just kind of pacing, working off tension." At dinner McNamara "did *not* want to talk about . . . Vietnam." Some nights his private war prevented sleep. Johnson ordered his troubled defense secretary to take a vacation.[14]

In April, antiwar activists organized demonstrations to express solidarity with the Buddhist-sparked uprising in South Vietnam. Nearly five thousand protesters ringed Times Square in New York. Despite being unable to obtain a demonstration permit, the Vietnam Day Committee attracted four thousand people to Berkeley's Telegraph Avenue. The writer Paul Goodman, Peter Camejo, and others spoke to the crowd from a fire escape outside a second-story apartment while police tried to stop the demonstration. The orators were later indicted on criminal charges, only to have the charges dropped when a defense attorney discovered that the date of the protest was listed incorrectly in the indictment. "None of my defendants were even *on* Telegraph Avenue on that date," he pleaded to the judge. "Case dismissed," the judge disgustedly replied.[15]

On April 10, a 20-year-old Boston University senior demonstrated his opposition to the war in a more dramatic way. "I'm going to burn in front of the White House," Arthur Zinner informed a Washington news station over the phone. "If you want any pictures, you'd better get there right away." Twenty-five minutes later, the quiet, slender government major, wearing a raincoat and tennis shoes, walked amid a crowd of Easter tourists toward the northwest White House gate, lifted two plastic jugs and began sloshing himself with gasoline. As Zinner was trying to strike two matches on the sidewalk, forewarned lawmen pounced on him, then led him away.[16]

Four days later, six American peace activists traveled to Saigon. Brad Lyttle of the Committee for Nonviolent Action had suggested the trip to A. J. Muste the previous year after Nguyen Cao Ky issued an edict prescribing summary execution as a potential penalty for advocating peace. Lyttle felt that openly challenging the edict would help expose the undemocratic nature of America's ally and inspire other peace activists. The elderly Muste was very receptive to the idea. "I think he just sort of felt that that was a good way to go out if he was going to go out, to be executed by Premier Ky," Lyttle chuckled. "That indicates the quality and the kind of person he was. I mean, at eighty years old most people are just about gone, if not gone, but here he was acting like a teenager . . . who's going out to beard the beast." The Americans met many of Vietnam's Buddhist dissidents during their week-long stay. "Johnson can send people all over the world to talk about peace, but if we talk about peace here we're accused of being communists," one remarked. The visitors were not harmed, but their press conference was broken up by agents of the GVN, and police spirited them off to the airport when they tried to demonstrate at the U.S. Embassy.[17]

As Buddhists were taking to the streets in Vietnam, religious opposition to the war was growing in the United States as well. The founders of Clergy Concerned About Vietnam had perceived the need for an ongoing national organization to channel trepidation about the war effectively within the American religious community. In April, building on a network of four hundred war dissenters they had established through their January campaign to continue the bombing pause, they hired a young minister and former civil rights activist named Richard Fernandez to direct and nurture Clergy and Laymen Concerned About Vietnam (CALCAV), as the group was renamed. He turned out to be a wise choice.

Twenty years later, Fernandez was the director of the Northwest Interfaith Movement, a progressive religious organization in Philadelphia. He bore a noticeable physical resemblance to the baseball player Pete Rose (a circumstance he had utilized to his amusement). Fernandez was an outspoken, driven man with a seemingly endless supply of energy. The antiwar leader Sam Brown said, "Dick Fernandez is the type of guy you can tell, 'You have to speak in San Francisco in the morning, L.A. in the afternoon, Albuquerque in the evening, San Antonio the next morning, Chicago that afternoon and New York at night,' and he'll say, 'No problem.'" Fernandez was also a skillful political mediator. Convinced that "in God's creation you'd better let a thousand flowers bloom or else they'll each put one another out," he distanced himself from the infighting among peace activists and continually asked the question, "What are the practical things that we can do together?" Fernandez became one of the movement's most prolific fund-raisers.[18]

When he assumed the reins of CALCAV, Fernandez started at "square one. There was nothing," he remembered. He was given office space in the headquarters of the National Council of Churches in New York and use of its bookkeeping services. The Council also passed a resolution supporting CALCAV, which allowed the new group to accept tax-exempt donations. But CALCAV was then a national organization in name only. All Fernandez had to work with was a stack of four hundred index cards bearing the names of the people involved in the bombing pause campaign. With no previous experience working in a national office, he was a little nervous. "I didn't know tit from tat," Fernandez recalled. Yet the minister did know from his past political experience that he had to have "a blank check to travel on. That if we didn't get out around the country we could very easily become a New York group of distinguished clergy." Fernandez understood that most people were disinclined to respond to mimeographed letters from national offices, but that they would reply to others who took the time and trouble to meet with them directly. He also felt personal encounters were necessary to convince people that they were "part of a larger picture" and a powerful whole. Fernandez successfully petitioned the CALCAV executive committee for unlimited travel funds. "I think that inclination in me [to get out among the public] was probably the most important one thing I brought to the group." Taking off across the country, he discovered something

> I don't think *anybody* understood. . . . In towns and cities across America, there were three Methodists, four Unitarians, two Catholics and five Jews who were outraged about the war, and they had no place—as religious people—to do anything about it. . . . When Clergy and Laity came around in 1966, we gave religious people an

[opportunity], *without changing their allegiance*, to, in a sense, join a para-religious organization. . . . These people didn't think they were doing anything different than going to the Methodist church on Sunday: this is just the way they acted out their religious convictions. It was not like asking them to join SANE or WILPF or some other secular group, which was a whole different thing than their church. . . . So there was a lot of naturalness to that.[19]

Fernandez also discovered that his association with CALCAV's famous founders (including the Yale chaplain Rev. William Sloane Coffin, Union Theological Seminary's President Dr. John Bennett, and Rabbi Abraham Heschel of the Jewish Theological Seminary) gave him instant credibility with many ministers across the country. "Half the clergy I would talk to had studied with these luminaries," Fernandez recalled. "My little letterhead with all these names . . . opened every door in every city I wanted to go to." That their former mentors had stuck their necks out against the war inspired some of these clergymen to do so too. The political "cover" that CALCAV gave them made their decisions easier. As Fernandez said, "It's very hard for the board of deacons and the trustees to come after you real hard if your national church or fifty religious leaders have already [spoken out] and you just say, 'Look . . . I'm not the only one saying these things.'" Fernandez was less than awestruck by CALCAV's founders himself, and thus it took him a while to accept working in their shadows. "I didn't want to be anybody's pimp or puppet," he said.[20]

Touring the country in 1966, Fernandez believed U.S. policy could be most effectively challenged by spurring *grass-roots* antiwar activity. Big national protests were important, he thought, but they would have to come later. "I always used to think of large rallies . . . as kind of an ecumenical service where the already committed came," he remembered. "I thought they very rarely drew brand-new people. Most people, when they take their first step, they take it locally. By the time they're ready to come to San Francisco, L.A., or Washington, they're into their third, fourth or fifth step." The specific forms of local protest that sprouted up did not concern Fernandez. "I saw my role as an enabler/facilitator of just a huge spectrum of activity," he recalled. Reflecting on CALCAV's entire history during the war, Fernandez said:

There was for us really nothing that was beyond the pale. . . . We were trying, with other movement groups, all the time, to create this theater. And everything was usable. [We felt] that our theater was finally going to beat the policymakers. That we would get people's attention, willy-nilly, no matter where they went, what they did. . . . That they would not be able to avoid just the rising sense that we ought to get out of that damn country.

Fernandez felt formal CALCAV chapters were necessary to sustain the local motion. "Chapters are what count," he said firmly. "Because that says staying power, tenacity, maybe a staff person, a little budget, doing things month after month."[21]

Fernandez saw Congress as the ultimate target of this activity. Aware of Congress's control of the war's purse strings, he also believed that President Johnson was isolated from public sentiment and thus would not respond to opinion alone. Congress had to exercise its authority. "I don't care who the president is or why he is isolated, they never know what the hell is happening," Fernandez argued. "And then if they surround themselves with a pack of liars they never know what the hell is going down. I don't think most of the presidents in my lifetime were nearly as bad as their isolation made them. You know, it's real hard to govern when you look in the mirror and you only see yourself." Fernandez thought most senators and representatives, on the other hand, "could be led on this issue. Often they, for me at least, typified people having kind of a chocolate eclair for a backbone. I thought they could be had by pressure and public opinion."[22]

It was slow going. Although anxious about the war, most religious Americans were not ready to protest it in 1966, Fernandez discovered. CALCAV's entry onto the political scene did exacerbate some doubts, though. CALCAV also transformed invisible and fragmented antiwar sentiment into organized pockets of motion. By the end of the year there were sixty-eight CALCAV chapters across the United States.[23] From such seeds would a thriving antiwar tree grow.

"There Is Nothing You Can Teach a Dog That You Cannot Teach a Congressman"

Richard Fernandez was not the only peace activist with an eye on Congress in 1966. Legislators were demonstrably educable. ("There is nothing you can teach a dog that you cannot teach a congressman," one activist would note later.) SANE was spearheading a nationwide "Voter's Pledge" campaign that asked citizens to support only those candidates for Congress who agreed to work "vigorously" to end the war. WSP played a major role in building the campaign while keeping up its own pressure. "I think it always has to come back down to the Congress," Dagmar Wilson said intently. "I mean, you've got to work on those birds!"[24] A coalition called the National Conference for New Politics fielded, raised money, and canvassed for peace candidates. In Washington, Quakers were an influential presence.

David Hartsough, a soft-spoken man with an unassuming personality, was the Quakers' Vietnam point man on Capitol Hill. As with other religious pacifists, Hartsough's gentle demeanor masked fierce political determination. In January 1966, he had just completed his master's degree at Columbia University and was hitchhiking to California. Upon arriving, he received an "urgent message" from the Friends Committee on National Legislation, which he had worked for earlier, requesting that he call its Washington office "any time of day or night." Hartsough phoned to discover that the FCNL wanted him to direct an "Emergency Project" to end the war. The organization was "going to dip into its reserves and was just going to pull out all the stops" to get Congress to cut off funds for the war, he was told. The effort was projected to last a grand total of three months. Hartsough served as director of it for nearly five years. The project itself continued until the end of the war.[25]

When Hartsough began work in February, one of his initial endeavors was to set up a "Wednesdays in Washington" program. He and other FCNL activists brought primarily church people to Washington, first, to receive information on the war and Vietnam legislation, and, second, to talk to their legislators. Through the program, Hartsough hoped to advance religious Americans' understanding of the war and incite them to greater action. As he recalled, "Many of the church lobbies . . . didn't even see themselves as lobbies at that time. They just saw themselves as informational: they would let their churches know what was happening in Washington. So we were, in a sense, educating them and encouraging them to begin to stick their own necks out, so [that] it wasn't just Friends putting pressure on Congress."[26]

The FCNL also held presentations on the war at least once a month for congressmen and their aides. Many of the speakers were AFSCers or others who had been to Vietnam and observed the war directly. Hartsough and his co-workers met informally with legislators and their staff members as well. The immediate goal of these encounters was to counteract the Johnson administration's propaganda on the war. "The papers were still full of lies," Hartsough remembered. "I mean, anything the administration said would get printed as truth. That's what Congress reads. And at hearings, that's who comes and testifies. . . . So in a sense what we were doing was setting up an alternative source of information." Hartsough also met with regional AFSC "Peace Education" leaders to keep them abreast of events on Capitol Hill. He hoped thereby to focus local pressure on Congress in advantageous ways.[27]

For Hartsough, 1966 was in many ways a frustrating year. "It was very slow at the beginning," he recalled, echoing Fernandez. Fewer people came to Washington to talk with their legislators than he had hoped: "Very little was happening compared to what needed to happen." Further, despite their doubts about the war, members of Congress were not shy about funding it: in March they approved $13.1 billion in supplemental appropriations. Yet various church groups did accelerate their activity in Washington "at our strong encouragement," Hartsough remembered. "We'd hold their hand." The FCNL also educated its visitors and prodded some local organizers to intensify their congressional pressure work. Some legislators were now hearing series of tough questions from their constituents for the first time. In addition, as Hartsough pointed out, just having the truth told in Washington to members of Congress and their staffs . . . was a first step. It hadn't been told before that; people were living in an unreal world. . . . So I think the opportunities that we provided for . . . them to really hear firsthand reports of what was going on was real important. . . . I'd say particularly on the Congressional staff level that you could tell that there were people that understood that "this is madness and we've got to turn this thing around," and who would then be very open to meeting with further people that had been over there, just to confirm some of the stuff they were beginning to suspect. Some of them were writing speeches for their members of Congress that would begin raising these questions. . . . So you'd see some of these speeches, or hear them.[28]

Among the senators whom Hartsough himself was meeting with were Eugene McCarthy and George McGovern (D-S. Dak.). He got to know both of them personally. He was also in touch with Senator Robert Kennedy and his aides. Hartsough believed that the information the FCNL gave these senators on the war increased their misgivings about it and made them "very receptive" to further critical reports. It nurtured their eventual outspoken opposition to the war. Did the FCNL's activity shape McCarthy's explosive decision to challenge Johnson for the presidency the next year? "I certainly wouldn't want to say that because of us McCarthy decided to run," Hartsough carefully replied. "But I think we began the process, at which [point] he was just questioning what was a national religion, that led to him deciding to run."[29]

As Hartsough observed, many peace activists were unexcited about congressional pressure work in 1966. "For the first two or three years of the war I don't think people paid much attention to it," the draft resister Michael Ferber recalled. To many it seemed like drudgery. It certainly wasn't as thrilling as street protests. "Most of us, being young and student-types, were temperamentally not lobbyists," Ferber pointed out. "We were more demonstrators and public speakers." Some protesters had had bad experiences with it in the past. "It wasn't my cup of tea, it never has been, it never will be," Doug Dowd commented. "I'd been involved in electoral politics and every time I got involved I felt like a horse's ass. . . . It's always turned into some kind of a circus joke." Many radical activists had written off the Democratic Party two years earlier when it refused to seat delegates of the Mississippi Freedom Democratic Party at its national convention. Their aversion to the Democratic Party increased as they watched a Democratic president lead the fight in Vietnam. Moreover, Congress seemed irrevocably wedded to the war. "Johnson commanded the votes," Ferber remembered. "So it seemed as though Congress was hopeless."[30]

Some activists felt lobbying was useful for keeping the heat on legislators, but expected few tangible returns until the public had turned against the war. Mobilizing the American people took precedence in their eyes. As the antiwar leader Sidney Peck subsequently theorized:

> When you're trying to build a mass movement, what you have to do is to isolate your opposition, to politically isolate them. So the focus is on those primarily involved in executing the policy. . . . Once you have isolated the Executive [branch] . . . and [its] military and political lieutenants, then . . . in a parliamentary society you've got to go after the parliament, because . . . eventually the funding has got to get cut off. . . . You isolate your opposition, you build a majority movement. You also build up resistance to that isolated and illegitimate authority. And then you get your parliament to act.[31]

The Socialist Workers Party considered lobbying Congress a complete "dead end." Since legislators were members of the American ruling class with an "objective" interest in crushing the Vietnamese revolution, talking to them would achieve nothing. Fred Halstead:

> We had no confidence at all that the governmental people or the people in Congress . . . would do *anything* for good reason. They would have to be forced to do anything decent. . . . The concept of government officials in this society in either the Democratic or Republican party having even an *ounce* of decency about them was something we just totally rejected to begin with. I don't mean that there isn't a decent individual here and there. But whether they are decent individual human beings or not on one level or another has nothing to do with it—they follow the orders of the ruling class. . . . And if there's an occasional aberration, that's what it is, an aberration. It's not going to get very far.[32]

Activists who argued against concentrating on Congress in 1966 had valid points. As Hartsough later granted, it was naïve of him to have hoped that Congress would come out against the war before the public did. "One of the things that I feel I learned in my five years or so working [in Washington] was that Congress is not going to stick its neck out until they feel the winds are blowing pretty strong in [a supportive] direction," he observed, while conceding that he failed to adequately appreciate the "real problem" of "a Democratic member of Congress not wanting to challenge a Democratic president." He didn't begin his congressional work "feeling the limitations" of it, Hartsough said. "I think I went into it feeling, 'Well, if these people can just understand the truth . . . they're going to change the policy.' That it was a question of deception. . . . 'And we'll do our darndest.'" Hartsough added: "The appealing thing about going directly to Congress is that it seems like a shortcut. I mean, to try to educate and mobilize millions of people seemed like a long haul. They said three months, you know! But I don't think there was a shortcut, given the enormity of the commitment on the part of the administration."[33]

Activists who targeted Congress in 1966 did achieve important gains, however. They advanced legislators' understanding of the war, decreasing their receptivity to administration handouts. They heightened congressional awareness of public unease over the conflict. By holding protests on Capitol Hill, outside legislators' home offices and in other locations, they also helped keep the issue of Vietnam in front of the American people. Thus, as Peter Camejo readily admitted to me, the SWP's blanket opposition to lobbying Congress was simply "*wrong.*" The SDS leader Greg Calvert came to regard the tendency of radical activists like himself to renounce electoral political activity generally as "one of our biggest failures."[34]

Debates over the value of congressional pressure work were often fierce. Rather than accepting political diversity and respecting those with other views, many opponents of legislative activity were in combative moods. Needless to say, SWPers were especially feisty. To the SWP, a lot was at stake. It felt lobbying Congress harmed the movement by taking protesters out of the streets and perpetuating dangerous illusions about Congress's class character. SWPers ridiculed lobbyers, quoting Trotsky to the effect that they were, shamefully, "crossing the class line." Disputes over legislative activity raised political and personal tensions within the movement, making coordinated activity even more difficult. They also spawned additional dropouts.

One of the most explosive conflicts over congressional work occurred in Berkeley's Vietnam Day Committee. The strife was so severe it contributed to the death of the organization.

"A Leftist Wrecking Crew"

Following the October 1965 International Days of Protest, the VDC had stagnated. One reason was uncertainty about its political clout. Not only had the war continued to escalate, but local supporters of the conflict seemed immovable. Opposition to the war in the Bay Area "has not grown appreciably since mid-October," the VDC's International Committee mourned in January.[35] A few VDCers had consequently left the organization; others had shifted into low gear, unsure what to do next.

Quarrels over antiwar tactics were also stalling the VDC. Stephen Smale and other militants were unhappy with what they considered the growing "moderation" of the group. They were particularly bothered by the VDC's decisions to discontinue the troop-train demonstrations and to turn the October march around at the Oakland border. Marilyn Milligan said the October retreat was "demoralizing" to numerous VDCers "because that was the first time that we'd ever been turned back."[36] Smale left the VDC—and the antiwar movement as a whole—shortly afterward.

The strife at the National Coordinating Committee convention in late November landed like a ton of bricks on many VDCers. The group "was never the same after that," Milligan remembered sadly. "That was a shocker."[37]

As the VDC reeled, Robert Scheer, an editor of *Ramparts* magazine and the author of a popular pamphlet on the war, announced he was going to run for Congress in the local district. Scheer was a radical, no-holds-barred critic of the war. His opponent in the June Democratic primary was Congressman Jeffrey Cohelan, a liberal supporter of U.S. policy. VDCers immediately launched into interminable debates over the merits of Scheer's candidacy.

Many were enthusiastic. The campaign would not only spread the antiwar message widely, they argued, but promote radical social change. "The question for me is whether or not our beautiful movement is ready now to begin the task of constructing nonviolent revolution," proclaimed Jerry Rubin, a Scheer advocate. More than a few VDCers hoped Scheer's candidacy would prepare the groundwork for continued radical action after the war ended. Milligan said she "accepted the talk that I heard that many groups that are organized around single issues die as soon as that issue is over with." The VDC "seemed like such a wonderful organization, in terms of involving so many people and having lots of good ideas and having a lot of fun," that she wanted "to try to keep [it] going beyond the Vietnam War." The VDC's problems were also on Milligan's mind. Scheer's candidacy "was the only thing happening at the time, because the VDC seemed to be going downhill," she recalled. "It seemed like maybe the Scheer campaign would give some life to the antiwar movement."[38] Other activists feared Scheer's bid would derail efforts to organize antiwar demonstrations. Many also opposed working inside the Democratic Party. SWPers were vitriolic critics of the campaign.

The VDC ultimately endorsed it by a narrow margin. The road leading to the verdict was littered with bodies. Scheer's candidacy "split the movement in half in this area," remembered one VDCer. The discord spread salt on wounds that were already festering and opened new ones as well. By the early spring of 1966, attendance at VDC meetings had dwindled dramatically. "When you say, 'Come to organization meetings and hear some infighting for four weeks in a row,' [people] won't come," Camejo, a VDC participant, observed.[39] The VDC would never again play a significant role in the peace movement.

Life in the Scheer campaign also disillusioned many VDCers. "Once I went to the meetings I was sorry that we were involved," Milligan recalled. Scheer's moderate supporters "wanted to soften everything that the VDC had to say." Some even claimed "that we dressed incorrectly—it got that bad. . . . I remember that as being really a low point, when we ended up at this meeting with all of these so-called high-powered people saying that the people in the VDC 'don't look right.' At that point I thought, 'This is not the place for me.' . . . They treated us like children." The campaign "did not hold people's interest at all in the VDC," Milligan said. [40]

It did hold the Establishment's interest, however. Columnists Rowland Evans and Robert Novak informed Americans that Cohelan was the "first target" of an "alarming" and "sinister" plot, hatched by "a leftist wrecking crew" at a "secret meeting" in Chicago, to "intimidate" President Johnson's congressional allies "by running leftists against them." The article seemed so ludicrous to Scheer organizers that they distributed it to voters. With Johnson's blessing, Postmaster General Lawrence O'Brien helped organize a testimonial dinner for Cohelan, and Senators Mansfield, Fulbright, and Robert Kennedy endorsed him. Cohelan claimed to have the support of Rev. Martin Luther King, Jr., too, but this proved fraudulent. Hubert Humphrey also stepped forward to offer his assistance, but was turned down, probably for the same reason Cohelan was uninterested in Johnson's backing. "A lot of people in this district don't like President Johnson," Cohelan said. "People are warm and friendly here, but when they get around to Johnson they begin to snarl." [41]

Scheer's campaign snowballed. Tapping and building widespread opposition to the war, it tore like a buzzsaw into Cohelan's constituency. By May, Cohelan feared for his political life. "I'm really on the rack now," he grumbled. Cohelan confided that the race was "no fun," and that he was "plain outraged" by the challenge of an "arrogant kid" after years of being a "good congressman." The White House was not taking the contest lightly either, as it knew the media would label a Scheer victory a repudiation of the war. On election night, Bill Moyers reportedly called the Alameda County Courthouse three times to see how Cohelan was faring. [42]

Cohelan narrowly defeated Scheer in the end. As an antiwar vehicle, however, the campaign had proven a resounding success. Scheer garnered 45 percent of the vote against an incumbent congressman, although six months earlier few had predicted he would receive more than 25 percent. Scheer appropriately gave the VDC's 1965 antiwar protests partial credit for the result:

> They forced the issue on Vietnam. They made the dissent about the war public and visible. The average person in the community, you know, would watch these people protesting on television. All right, but at the same time they couldn't understand what these [people] were all about. They knew that something was going on, that these people cared a lot, but what they were doing was so alien to their normal style that they turned against it with great hatred.
> . . . We capitalized on this interest. We came without the picket signs. I personally always dressed as conservatively as possible, and

we came with the rational arguments. . . . And above all, the campaign was doing something very traditional—I was a candidate.[43]

The antiwar movement's many other "peace candidates" attracted considerably fewer votes in the congressional primary elections than did Scheer. "We just didn't have any bite at all," Doug Dowd recalled. John Roche, a White House political adviser, agreed, telling Johnson that the election results showed that "the extreme peaceniks cannot mobilize any effective *political* leverage. They are off in a corner talking to themselves." By giving antiwar views wider play, however, the peace campaigns did make small inroads on the war's domestic base. Also, as Scheer commented, the participation of activists in a traditional political arena had increased the peace movement's credibility. And the campaigns nudged some congressmen leftward. The rattled Cohelan soon began growing dove's wings.[44]

Inflammatory Educational Reform: A, B, C, D, and Nam

Meanwhile, student protest was growing. In February the Johnson administration threw gasoline on the smoldering antiwar coals on campuses. Selective Service System Director Lewis Hershey announced that, for the first time, local draft boards could induct students who were in the lower levels of their classes. Two criteria would determine students' class level: their course grades and their performance on a special aptitude examination in May. (Although the exam was geared to tap general intelligence, Hershey conceded that it was "cocked over toward the mathematical, because it's easier to grade for one thing.")[45] Suddenly, students were being told that they could be carted off to die in the jungles of Vietnam. The shock on campuses was palpable.

SDS leaders put on their thinking caps and debated how to respond. They decided to give a "counter-exam" on the same day that the SSS gave its test at as many of the SSS test sites as possible. The "National Vietnam Examination," SDS determined, would "raise questions in students' minds about the war, the morality of America's position, the deception of the American government, and the authoritarian nature of the draft." SDS President Carl Oglesby told students, "You will be asked to 'grade' yourself—and decide whether you know enough about the Vietnamese to take some day the personal responsibility for their death."[46]

Acting SDS National Secretary Paul Booth was the administrative mover and shaker behind the counter-exam, which was held primarily to take advantage of the clustering of students at SSS exam locations across the country. "We wanted to raise the war issue in a public way in places where we hadn't reached people before—*lots* of them," Booth, later a union official, recalled. "We wanted to make our scope of action unlimited as far as college-aged people were concerned. . . . We perceived that our message was real powerful and we wanted to give it some life in all of these outposts around the country. Reach everybody." Booth also hoped to build SDS. "This was a means to expand the formal membership and affiliation of people dramatically," he said. Booth conceded that he harbored no great strategic vision at the time. He and other SDS leaders were still floundering in a sea of political strategies; although reluctant to abandon antiwar activity and its many student proponents, they were increasingly doubtful of its ability to stop the war or to engender a radical social movement. As with all of SDS's other programmatic initiatives, the decision to undertake the counter-exam "was made with a certain tentativeness: 'Let's try this and see where it goes, and then after we're done with it we'll figure out what to do after that.' I'm sure that you can find in the [SDS] literature some people who spelled out a series of steps, but this was all in the imagination."[47]

SDSers distributed the counter-exam on May 14 at some nine hundred SSS test sites. The activity took place quietly at most locations, although spirited protests were held at a few schools. Through the project SDS made further encroachments on the political allegiances of America's youth. It was a truly educative exercise. Written by Todd Gitlin and Mike Locker, the counter-exam laid waste to standard government propaganda on the war. The following question was typical: "The war in South Vietnam is supposed to be part of our policy to contain Communist Chinese aggression. How many Communist Chinese troops are actively engaged in combat in Vietnam? (A) None (B) 1,000 (C) 50,000 (D) 100,000 (E) 500,000." The answer: (A).[48]

Hershey's announcement provoked a different response from more militant antiwar activists in the United States. Students moved to stop class ranking at many universities. Disruptive actions, including sit-ins, broke out on more than a dozen campuses. The sharpest confrontation occurred at the University of Chicago. Some 350 students occupied the school's administration building for three days, attracting national media attention. Although university officials did not make a single concession to the invaders and vowed to react harshly to future sit-ins, they were badly shaken. The president of the University of Chicago, Edward Levi, later confided to Father Theodore Hesburgh of Notre Dame that, to survive the strain, "I just got up every morning and said, 'What's the worst thing I could do today?'—and I didn't do it."[49]

More powerful authorities were also worried about the spring antirank protests. Joseph Califano sent President Johnson progress reports on them. Two days into the Chicago sit-in, Califano warned his boss, "This could create some problems for Selective Service. We are looking into this to make certain Hershey does not aggravate the situation and can still operate even if this movement spreads." Jack Valenti was walking around the White House with egg on his face during the protests, having informed Johnson on May 1 that the "Vietnam debate is about over."[50]

The government's new induction policy had repercussions beyond the spring protests. The draft was thrust even more electrically into campus debates on the war, nourishing the full-fledged draft resistance movement that would emerge the following year. Conscription for the war became a hot issue throughout society as a whole. Two national commissions were set up to probe the causes of the campus disturbances, and politicians, looking to rack up political brownie points, fell all over themselves proposing solutions. The debate over class ranking heated to the point where the SSS discarded the practice within a year. What's more, the antirank protests heightened students' awareness of universities' complicity in the war and convinced many that their schools were vulnerable to "direct action" tactics. As Kirkpatrick Sale records, "Campus protest begins now in earnest."[51]

Napalm Protests and Medical Aid

Opposition to other forms of institutional complicity with the war was growing in the spring of 1966 as well. Many activists targeted the producers and distributors of napalm. Rained routinely from the sky by U.S. bombers in Vietnam, napalm is a petroleum jelly that sticks to its victims and devours them with flames. A housewife who visited South Vietnam in the fall of 1966 described its frightful toll to readers of the *Ladies Home Journal*:

> Before I went to Saigon, I had heard and read that napalm melts the flesh, and I thought that's nonsense, because I can put a roast in the oven and the fat will melt but the meat stays there. Well, I went and saw these children burned by napalm and it is absolutely true. The chemical reaction of this napalm does melt the flesh, and the flesh runs right down their faces onto their chests and it sits there and it grows there. . . . These children can't turn their heads, they were so thick with flesh. . . . And when gangrene sets in, they cut off their hands or fingers or their feet; the only thing they cannot cut off is their head.

Humiliated by their looks, some horribly disfigured napalm victims crawled off to live in caves.[52]

Protests against napalm assumed many forms. Activists organized a nationwide boycott of Saran Wrap and other consumer products of the Dow Chemical Company, the foremost producer of napalm in the United States. They also distributed leaflets and carried signs bearing graphic photos of napalm's young civilian victims.[53] Women were generally at the center of this activity. As WSP's Donna Allen recalled, mothers were uniquely sensitive to the war's toll on Vietnamese children, and napalm seemed a "particularly horrible" weapon to use on kids. An angry WSP speaker exclaimed at one rally, "Robert McNamara would not go out in the street and pour acid on a little child. . . . He would be horrified at the very thought of it. And yet he can let his airplanes go out there and pour it on these Vietnamese children!" Women were also particularly attuned to napalm's links to household goods, including Saran Wrap. In Cora Weiss's words, "The guys who made napalm in Vietnam made something that you used in your kitchen everyday. So you could understand it. And what makes it stick to food is what makes it stick to babies."[54]

In late May, four middle-class housewives in San Jose, California, blocked trucks loaded with napalm bombs for seven hours outside a trucking company. When they returned to the same location the next day, a truck driver confided to the women that the company had decided not to bring napalm through there anymore. Pleased at their accomplishment but unwilling to rest on their laurels, the women then moved on to an enormous napalm bomb storage facility in the nearby town of Alviso. There the bombs were poised to be loaded on barges for transportation to Port Chicago, the main West Coast arms shipping point. After scurrying up a steep hill, the women prevented a forklift from loading napalm onto a barge for over an hour. To maximize their public influence, they were dressed as reputably as possible, wearing high heels, stockings, gloves, and pearls. "We played the ladies to the hilt," Joyce McLean, one of the protesters, vigorously recalled. "We purposely wanted to appear as middle-class house-wives." The women learned afterward that their action and tidal conditions had prohibited the barge from leaving until the next day.[55]

The "napalm ladies" (as the media dubbed them) were arrested and put briefly in the slammer. Obviously new to the world of incarceration, they were treated "very delicately" by jail officials, save for one "very officious" nurse who "really hated us," McLean remembered. Clipboard in hand, she sarcastically sniped at the women, "And are you *fasting?*" The experience did nothing to deflate the women's spirits: Lisa Kalvelage, the only one who was not a member of WILPF, joined that organization while sharing an atrocious baloney lunch in jail. The women received suspended sentences.[56]

The Alviso protest had both local and national effects. It influenced Alviso officials to revoke the storage company's permit to stock the weapon. More significant, the ladies' audacity impressed the young Washington bureau chief of the *New York Times*, altering his attitude toward the war. The journalist's name was Tom Wicker.

Two decades later, Wicker was a political columnist for the *Times*. Plump with reddish hair, a ruddy face, and a native North Carolinian twang, he seemed unimpressed with his elevated station in life. He recalled that he had not questioned the war much before 1966. "I count myself fundamentally of the World War II generation, and the World War II generation learned the lesson . . . that you've got to stop 'aggression' before it starts," he said. "I took the general view that we were attempting to stop a communist aggression out there." Wicker did wonder whether the threat to South Vietnam warranted such a large U.S. military involvement, though, and whether the war could be won. In the spring of 1966 Wicker was traversing the country covering the congressional campaigns of peace candidates. His travels brought him to the San Francisco Bay Area to investigate Robert Scheer's candidacy. Following Scheer and a contingent of protesters on a march to a napalm manufacturing plant in Redwood City one day in late May, Wicker was approached by Joyce McLean. Dressed again as an all-American, middle-class mother, McLean told Wicker about the women's protest in Alviso a day or so earlier. The journalist innocently remarked, "Hey, you may go to jail." "Yes, of course," McLean replied. "We've thought about this for a long time." Wicker was visibly moved by the women's courage. He would recall:

> They had a very profound impact on me. Because these were very ordinary women. I mean, they may be remarkable for all I know, but they weren't government officials or anything like that, or big entrepreneurs. They were housewives. And that they were willing to go to jail, with all that that entailed for housewives—and they had children and families and everything—because they'd stopped those trucks from moving . . . struck me very forcefully. I said, "There's something going on in this country when people will do that." And I had tended up to that point to take peace activists to be more like Bob Scheer was then. You know, kind of academic lefties who were not very practical and so forth. But when I really began to get a look at people like that I saw that [the antiwar movement] was quite a different thing from what I had imagined. . . . By getting out and getting into those campaigns . . . I began to get a look at the actual composition of the peace movement, and saw that it was a very, very broad spectrum of the public, even by 1966.[57]

Wicker started listening more closely to protesters' arguments that the war was not only impractical but morally unjust. He soon came to conclude that its articulate opponents "knew what they were talking about," at least insofar as they criticized the United States rather than extolling the virtues of the North Vietnamese and NLF. The need to "think for myself" that accompanied Wicker's appointment as a regular columnist for the *Times* that summer also pushed him leftward. By the end of 1966, he had concluded that the United States "really had no business mixing into" the war. Peace activists continued to affect his views in later years, when his thrice-weekly columns touched frequently on Vietnam, shaping the opinions of many Americans. He felt challenged by the protesters to take his criticisms of the war further and to defend his lingering Cold War assumptions. Overall, the peace movement was "quite a strong factor" in the dovish evolution of his views.[58] Wicker's relationship to antiwar activists, as we shall see, was not unique among journalists.

As the four San Jose women were obstructing the shipment of napalm, another housewife was laying plans to provide medical care in the United States for the weapon's young Vietnamese victims. Helen Frumin of Scarsdale, New York, felt Americans were morally obligated to treat burned Vietnamese children. "Only the United States is using this weapon, and it is fitting that we should provide the care for the mutilated children," she said. Frumin helped form the Committee of Responsibility for Treatment in the United States of War-Burned Vietnamese Children (COR). By the late fall, the COR had secured promises of hospital beds and convalescent care from many medical professionals and lay people in the United States. Three hundred doctors offered their services. To bring Vietnamese children to the United States, however, the COR needed U.S. government assistance, including space on military planes and permission to enter the country. The State Department was unresponsive to its requests. Wary of the program's propaganda value to the peace movement, officials contended that Vietnamese children could be better treated in their home environments—conveniently ignoring both the obliteration of many Vietnamese home environments and the glaring deficiencies in South Vietnam's medical system. The government eventually discovered some extra space on military planes while throwing up every bureaucratic hurdle it could think of to keep the children from getting to the airport (e.g., the COR had to fill out "a thousand forms," one COR activist remembered, and get the approval of assorted U.S. Army divisions and three or four Vietnamese doctors—most of whom were "always across town"—before a child could leave Vietnam). The COR was only able to bring some eighty-seven children to the United States. The number would have been well in the hundreds had there been even a modicum of government cooperation.[59]

Through talks and films on the war's young victims, COR activists touched a strong moral chord in many people otherwise skeptical of antiwar activity. Yet the program had its costs. Although the American families who provided convalescent care for the Vietnamese children understood that the children would have to return to Vietnam after their treatment ended, "there wasn't a . . . foster family who had those kids for more than one day who didn't begin plotting to keep them," COR activist Madeline Duckles recalled. The departure of the little Vietnamese girl, Twee, who stayed with Duckles's family was painful for all whose lives Twee had touched. Although the girl's mouth had been disfigured by a grenade ("they had fixed it up so that it was functional, but it was a bad mouth," Duckles said softly) and she was missing several fingers on one hand, Twee was an animated, adorable child. When he arrived home after seeing Twee off at the airport, Duckles's 15-year-old son Jeremy "went into her room and said, 'My God, what a mess!' and shut the door—and I knew he was crying," Duckles remembered. The psychiatrist who treated Twee in the United States "just had to take six weeks off. He was a wreck, he just loved that little girl so."[60]

The revulsion COR activists felt for napalm was not shared by many Americans, of course. Some even applauded the weapon. The novelist John Steinbeck, a winner of the Nobel Prize, went so far as to suggest to the Johnson administration how napalm could be employed in a novel way in Vietnam. As Jack Valenti told Robert McNamara, Steinbeck, who wrote him "from time to time," was a "fascinating man" with an "imaginative flair for war and its weaponry." In a January 1966 letter to Valenti, Steinbeck followed recommendations for a "colossal strike" on North Vietnam ("if bombs are indicated") and use of 10-gauge automatic shotguns in the South (for those who "are man enough") with an idea that, he said,

> has been bugging me for some time. I think the most terrifying modern weapon is the napalm bomb. People who will charge rifle fire won't go through flames. The hand grenade is pretty good but the necessary weight of metal for fragmenting makes it hard to throw and limits its range. Did you ever throw one with a bent arm? It will put your shoulder out for a week.
>
> What I suggest is a napalm grenade, packed in a heavy plastic sphere almost the exact size and weight of a baseball. The detonator could be of very low power—just enough to break the plastic shell and ignite the inflammable. If the napalm is packed under pressure, it will spread itself when the case breaks. The detonator (a contact cap) should be carried separately and inserted or screwed in just before throwing. This would allow a man to carry a sack full of balls without danger to himself. Now we probably have developed some fine riflemen, sharp shooters, etc., but there isn't an American boy over 13 who can't peg a baseball from infield to home plate with accuracy. And a grown man with sandlot experience can do much better. It is the natural weapon for the Americans. Six good men could ring an area with either napalm or white phosphorus faster than you could throw a magazine into an automatic or a machine gun. And an enemy with a bit of flame on his clothes or even in front of him is out of combat. This weapon would also be valuable for cleaning out tunnels and foxholes where the grenade has to make contact. Mounted as a rifle grenade, the Steinbeck super ball would also be valuable for burning off cover of extra ambush country or of tree borne sniper fire.[61]

It is unknown whether the "Steinbeck super ball" was ever employed in Vietnam.

Peace activists' concern for Vietnamese civilian victims of the war also led them to provide humanitarian aid to the Vietnamese in their own country. In the spring of 1966, the AFSCers David and Mary Stickney traveled to South Vietnam to establish a project to alleviate the plight of the war's more than one million refugees. They chose to work in Quang Ngai province, which held nearly a hundred thousand refugees, who were receiving less help than refugees in other provinces. Off and running by late September, the program included a day-care center and classes in hygiene, nutrition, and sewing. The Stickneys recruited a Vietnamese staff to run it.[62]

The American Friends Service Committee was also exploring channels for funneling medical aid to civilian war victims in North Vietnam. The AFSC applied for a license to send aid through the North Vietnamese Red Cross. It was rebuffed. According to the U.S. Treasury Department, since the Red Cross in Hanoi was not supervised by the International Committee of the Red Cross, there were no guarantees that the assistance would reach only civilians. This reasoning led one Quaker to comment, "The government can't prove that their bombs go only to soldiers, either."[63]

The AFSC was reluctant to send medical supplies to North Vietnam without government permission, knowing that this risked criminal charges under the Trading with the Enemy Act, which carried maximum penalties of a 10-year prison term and $10,000 fine. Plus it might endanger the AFSC's other programs. Some youthful Quakers decided to organize a medical aid campaign on their own. Their Quaker Action Group (QAG) encouraged people to send aid to the Canadian Friends Service Committee (CFSC), which would, in turn, mail it to North Vietnam. The campaign proved popular with many AFSCers in the United States.[64]

David Hartsough worked with a QAG chapter in Washington, D.C. One day in 1966, he and twenty other people marched to that city's main post office carrying packages of medical supplies addressed to the CFSC. The postal employees showed them a government memo prohibiting the post office from accepting anything addressed to the CFSC. Hartsough responded, nonchalantly, "I have this friend up in Philadelphia that is going up there [to Canada] next week. So we'll just send it to him." The protesters then crossed out the CFSC's address on the packages and replaced it with that of Hartsough's friend. Illegally, the post office still refused to accept the packages. Some Quakers subsequently transported them to Philadelphia by car. "It's like the underground railroad," Hartsough said with a smile. "You get the stuff there one way or another."[65]

The Johnson administration's net for constricting subversive medical assistance stretched widely. In April, when some Quakers in New York were inadvertently allowed, in front of alerted reporters, to send the CFSC parcels containing medical supplies and three checks, the U.S. departments of Commerce and Treasury swung into action. While Commerce swooped down to try to intercept the packages in mid-flight, Treasury directed the Federal Reserve Board to "alert all banks in the New York area to be on the lookout for these three checks and not to honor them if they are returned for payment." It also attempted to "ascertain the location of the Quaker group's bank accounts in order to give specific instructions to such banks not to honor the checks." Within a year the government had frozen at least two QAG accounts.[66]

Administration officials realized they were treading on shaky ground, though. "This looks like a nasty situation," Under Secretary of the Treasury Joseph Barr wrote White House Counsel Harry McPherson about the New York developments. Barr told President Johnson that he was

> reluctant to recommend prosecution until we have had an opportunity to demonstrate to the country that we have given the Quakers every chance. For this reason . . . I propose that I personally go to New York and make a further attempt to induce the Quaker group to reverse the operation. I may very well be unsuccessful . . . but, in dealing with such an extremely sensitive issue, I feel strongly that we should establish a record which indicates that we have taken this problem to the very highest levels of our Government. I know of no other way to counteract what could be a spate of very nasty news stories.[67]

Barr's powers of persuasion were indeed deficient. The QAG's efforts to channel medical aid to North Vietnam through Canada continued unabated. What's more, Quakers began needling the government with related projects.

Some prepared to transport medical supplies to North Vietnam themselves. That December they stocked a boat named the *Phoenix* with $10,000 worth of supplies for treating victims of American-made fragmentation bombs. Although the government warned the *Phoenix*'s crew that their action risked arrests, the crew ignored the threat. The *Phoenix* delivered its cargo in March of 1967. It later made a second trip to North Vietnam.[68]

Pushed by QAG activists, the AFSC reassessed its earlier timidity. "Do we let the United States government tell us to whom we will ship or not ship?" it asked itself. The answer was no. But before the AFSC sent any medical supplies to Hanoi, its executive secretary, Bronson Clark, and the chairman of its board, Gilbert White, paid a visit to Assistant Secretary of State William Bundy in Washington. Clark remembered:

> We were going to tell him what we were going to do, but we weren't going to ask his permission. . . . Gilbert White explained that we had gone through a process of decision making, and we were united. We'd been giving medical help to the South, and we felt that we should be giving medical help to the North. And they'd asked for penicillin, and we were going to ship penicillin to their Red Cross. And they'd indicated that they would use it with civilians. . . . William Bundy, he said, "Oh, well, you're going to do that in *spite* of what we say." And Gilbert said, "Yeah, as a matter of fact, we are."

Without a license, the AFSC shipped several thousand dollars worth of propane penicillin to the Red Cross in Hanoi. It also sent money to the CFSC and the International Committee of the Red Cross in Geneva for the provision of other medical supplies to both North and South Vietnam.[69]

Finally, QAGers held vigils in front of post offices across the country at noon every Wednesday. "Our question was, 'Why does the post office have to be involved in committing war?'" Hartsough recalled. The vigils continued until the end of the conflict.[70]

Getting Together

In the spring of 1966, activists associated with the Inter-University Committee for Debate on Foreign Policy (IUCDFP) moved to give the peace movement the national direction that the distrusted and moribund National Coordinating Committee could not supply. They had played central roles in organizing the campus teach-ins of the previous year but questioned the value of holding additional teach-ins. Protest now had to take precedence over discussion, they believed. IUCDFP President Doug Dowd recalled one reason why:

> What was happening by 1966 was that our natural foils—the State Department and the Pentagon—wouldn't have anything to do with us, because they just kept losing. . . . By the time that had gone on for a year or so the State Department didn't want to send people out any more. The teach-in really got its energy from the clash. That's what made us look good, was the other guys. . . . So we realized that . . . the teach-ins really couldn't go on anymore, that it took two to tango. . . . It really was getting damn hard to find anybody to go against you. What we needed always was government people. You could get another professor to go against you, but most people didn't care about that.

Dowd would "never forget" how governmental participation in one teach-in had aided the peace movement. As the IUCDFP's representative at the event, Dowd had debated "one of the big mucky-mucks" in the State Department. During the contest he kept poking holes in his opponent's positions "with the information that was easily obtainable," visibly agitating the official. Afterward a Marine in the audience approached Dowd. "Goddamn you," he said. "I'm on my third tour in Nam now, and you're not 100 percent right, but you're at least 75 percent right. Goddamn you, I'll hate you for the rest of my life." Observed Dowd, "I wasn't the one who taught him anything. It was this fucking State Department man who taught him what was going on. Here he was over there believing all this bullshit all these years, and this guy admitted it, admitted it, admitted it, admitted it."[71]

By 1966 many IUCDFP activists had also concluded that holding teach-ins "just wasn't enough." More was needed to stop the mounting war. Dowd analyzed this evolution in activists' thinking and the initiation of the first national "Mobilization" committee in Cleveland that July that resulted from it:

> I don't think any of us—certainly not I—were conscious of the fact that we were on a ladder or a path. We were just doing the teach-in stuff. And then all of a sudden it became quite clear to all of us that the teach-in thing was no longer the way to go. And out of that came the Mobe. It just sort of naturally evolved. . . . I remember when we got together in Cleveland to start the Mobe that it was just taken for granted by everybody that we had to do something more than just getting up in an auditorium with some speeches. I can't remember even talking about it. It was as though you'd been sort of petting around, necking with somebody, and all of a sudden you begin to fuck, you know. You don't say, "Let's do it." It just happens. That's how the Mobe came to be.[72]

Sidney Peck, a Western Reserve University sociology professor, was one of the main organizers of the July meeting in Cleveland. When I interviewed him in 1986, Peck was living in Cambridge, Massachusetts. He was a short, stocky man with curly gray hair and reserved demeanor. His piercing eyes reflected both deep self-confidence and circumspectness toward others (he initially responded to my request for an interview by asking whether I was "with the government"). Although Peck received less public recognition than many fellow national antiwar leaders, his contributions to the peace movement rank among the greatest. His political clarity and judgment were widely respected. Peck was a master fund-raiser, and his commitment to the antiwar cause knew no bounds; at one time he was co-chairing five separate national, regional, and local antiwar bodies while also running Western Reserve's sociology department, teaching full-time, and supervising graduate research. How did Peck survive the physical and psychic strain? "I look back on that period and I don't know," he reflected, shaking his head. "It was unreal. . . . It was impossible. As impossible," he concurred with Norma Becker, "as lifting a piano out of a house when a fire comes."[73]

Unlike Richard Fernandez, Peck felt the peace movement's most pressing task in 1966 was to organize a large national demonstration. "We are convinced that now is the time for a meeting of national leaders to consider a common project to mobilize the anti-war sentiments of the American people on a truly massive scale," he wrote as head of the University Circle Teach-in Committee in July. "We have in mind an event of the scope and character of the 1963 Civil Rights March for Jobs and Freedom." Sitting in a lounge on the Harvard University campus many years later, Peck explained the reasoning behind his proposal:

> Up to that point I felt that we [the peace movement] had begun to move off the campuses. And I felt that the Days of Protest had been

successful, certainly on both coasts, but even within the country more and more people were beginning to come out into the streets. . . . So on the basis of our spreading out into the community and securing more and more community support, my sense of it was that we were beginning to make an impact on the thinking of people. And that's why I could say that most people who voted for Johnson in 1964 were beginning to be dissatisfied, and that that dissatisfaction within the base of his political support had to be surfaced. In other words, we had to surface the dissent [among those people] that Johnson claimed as the basis for his own legitimacy.

Peck felt a massive national demonstration would show the government and public "that the opposition to the war was not limited to . . . students or kooks or freaks. . . . That basically this was a division of opinion in the mainstream of American politics."[74]

As Peck knew, the movement's inroads on public opinion were then going unappreciated by many activists. With the war continuing to expand, they wondered whether all their work meant anything. "We are profoundly discouraged," the writer Susan Sontag remarked to an antiwar gathering in February. "Most of us have been deploring this wicked war, in public and private, for at least a year, some of us for much longer. But things go from bad to worse, from crime to greater crime." In July, New York Fifth Avenue Peace Parade Committee leaders wrote other activists, "We have paraded, we have picketed, we have petitioned our government, we have fasted, we have 'sat-in'—yet for over two years American military intervention in Vietnam has escalated relentlessly. Many of us are filled with a growing sense of weariness and despair." As another antiwar organizer observed, feelings of "impotence" were causing some protesters to "withdraw to private concerns." Peck hoped that a gigantic national demonstration would rejuvenate discouraged activists. "The flow of optimism . . . is from the national to the local level, and not in the reverse direction," he wrote. "Given a massive demonstration of its own resources and strength, it will be apparent to all that in the long run the anti-war movement will prevail."[75]

On July 22, some thirty people, representing fifteen major peace organizations, gathered in Cleveland to plan national antiwar activity. "Pessimism and futility were the pervasive moods of the conference," one participant recorded. Doug Dowd offered the gloomy assessment that the war might instigate a direct clash with China. His argument that future protest should focus on domestic issues as well as the war reflected, in part, his pessimistic attitude. "I didn't think that you could stop the war . . . unless you could cause the society to change in some basic sense," he remembered. Dowd's position reflected a noteworthy shift in his political perspective; only a year earlier he had believed that if protesters "could just get the people to see the truth about the war," they would be well on their way to stopping it. Dowd also advocated focusing on domestic issues in order to enlarge the movement's political base.[76]

Stoking the despair of many of the conferees was the Johnson administration's decision to begin bombing North Vietnam's petroleum, oil, and lubricant (POL) storage facilities on June 29. The facilities were located in the densely populated Hanoi and Haiphong areas, and the strikes were thus killing many innocent civilians. The conferees also recognized that the bombing hazarded Chinese and Soviet interventions. Officials' bald-faced lies about the strikes (e.g., Under Secretary of State George Ball had declared three days before the bombs started falling that no such bombs would fall) further vexed activists already chafing from official duplicity. President Johnson was himself fearful that the strikes would incite China and the Soviet Union. The evening of June 29, his daughter Luci noticed that he looked "tired and deeply worried." McNamara had just informed him that the bombers had taken off to drop the first of their payloads, the president told her. "Your daddy may go down in history as having started World War III," he said, incredibly. Shortly before midnight, the disturbed pair went to St. Dominic's church in Washington to, as Luci later put it, see "my little monks." The president and his daughter "knelt and prayed for some time."[77]

Much time at the Cleveland conference was spent wrangling over which political organizations should help organize the next national antiwar protest. Some activists continued to oppose working with the Old Left. Dowd recalled arguing that the American left as a whole "had been beating itself up in one way or another ever since I had been around it—which is from the mid thirties on—and that this [group] had to be a coalition. None of us could function alone. . . . And the coalition had to have as its principle, 'Nobody is excluded, *nobody* is excluded, *nobody* is excluded.'" Dowd added, "And we had Trots there, we had CP there, we had SDS there, we had SNCC there, we had all kinds of people—all of whom hated each other." A. J. Muste's support for this nonexclusionary policy was largely responsible for the group's ultimate agreement on it. "Muste was very, very important. Because in some sense everyone there was either disinclined or afraid to go against him. He had a real presence." The policy, in turn, was crucial to the group's continuation. "If the principle of nonexclusion hadn't been accepted," Dowd said, "there would have been no Mobe."[78]

The conferees could agree on little else. They did decide, however, that whatever protest they organized "was not going to be directed to Johnson." "We had no illusions any more about changing Johnson's mind," the minutes of the meeting read. "We were going to talk to the American people. Therefore, everyone agreed that this action would be multi-issue."[79] They also elected to meet again.

In September, more than a hundred antiwar leaders from around the country gathered in Cleveland. Painfully aware of their internal divisions and thus barriers to planning national activity of any sort, they decided simply to call for four days of locally determined forms of protest during the November election period. This way they could "keep the issue of the war central to the election," Peck remembered thinking, and gain enough mutual trust to work together on a large national demonstration in the spring. The decision of the November 5–8 Mobilization Committee (as the group named itself) to emphasize local rather than national antiwar protest also reflected a growing sense among activists that it would take long-range grass-roots organizing to stop the war.[80]

The unity at the conference was fragile. As Fred Halstead recalled, it was only activists' "desperation" over the continuing escalation of the war and the efforts of respected movement leaders like Muste, Peck, and the Chicago organizer Sidney Lens that "kept it together as much as it was kept together."[81] Moreover, two national antiwar organizations had not sent representatives to the meeting. SANE still viewed communists as political lepers and refused to rub elbows with them in Cleveland. SDS had loftier goals than stopping the war.

A Revolutionary SDS

Carl Davidson was SDS's vice president at the time of the Cleveland conference, having been elected to that post at SDS's national convention in Iowa ten days earlier. Years later, Davidson was running an alternative news service called "Insight" in Chicago and working on other "Networking for Democracy" projects aimed at making media and computer services available to grass-roots political organizations. Raised in Pennsylvania steel country, Davidson was a friendly, rugged-looking man; swigging coffee with the author in a blue-collar Chicago hamburger joint, jukebox blaring in the background, his jean-jacket collar turned upward, he appeared much at home. Davidson was not keen on organizing national antiwar activity in the late summer of 1966. He had his heart set on a "student syndicalist movement." By organizing students around the issue of student control of universities, he wrote in an influential essay distributed at the SDS convention, activists could build a "mass radical base" in the United States for waging "the *real* struggle yet to come against the administration." Revolution, not reform, was the watchword.[82]

Davidson's participation in a civil rights march through Mississippi in June that popularized the slogan "black power" strongly influenced his essay. He believed students needed to seize control of their lives just as blacks did. "While the blacks were doing their thing, we had to do our thing, and that way the two movements could form a revolutionary alliance," Davidson reasoned. His faith that fighting for student governance of universities would revolutionize students "came out of some anarchist views that we had . . . that the real radicalizing issue was control—control over your own life, against institutionalization." Davidson's witness to racist official brutality in Mississippi had diminished his faith that radical social change could occur nonviolently:

> We saw the limitations of nonviolence and peaceful struggle in a very immediate sense in the civil rights struggle in the South. A lot of us went to Mississippi believing in pacifism and legal change and nonviolence and all that sort of thing—and came back revolutionaries. I know that's where I changed my views on all that. I learned it from the Ku Klux Klan and the Mississippi Highway Patrol, that you needed revolution, and that there wasn't any other way.[83]

The persistent escalation of the war also entered Davidson's calculations. "We wanted to stop [it] and the traditional reform levers were not functioning," he recalled. "More and more people kept dying, more and more people kept getting slaughtered. So . . . we saw revolution as a necessity." Liberal compliance with the war increased the revolution's appeal. "One of the main things was the bankruptcy of liberalism and the Democratic Party and social democracy. Here you had . . . all these social democrats . . . complicit with the war in Vietnam. They refused to take a stand for the immediate withdrawal of U.S. troops. . . . In a way we saw them as the left wing of imperialism. . . . So we saw their bankruptcy." Davidson subsequently admitted that his view that the war could not be halted without a revolution involved "a lot of immaturity."[84]

Davidson's revolutionary aspirations were shared by many other SDSers, including, significantly, the newly appointed SDS national secretary, Greg Calvert. In a notable report to the SDS membership that fall, Calvert described SDS as revolutionary for the first time. Sitting in the Oregon home he owned with his gay lover (a Vietnam draft resister) many years later, Calvert expressed regret over this report. The product of two generations of radical union activists avowed that mention of his "revolutionary fantasizing" during the 1960s struck "a raw, raw nerve" in his psychological system:

> Because I regard the rise of revolutionary rhetoric as one of the most disastrous things that happened in the movement of the sixties, I regard whatever I did around raising the rhetoric as a real mistake. . . . So I've spent a lot of time trying to go back and figure out where that got into my vocabulary. And actually one of the things that I discovered is that I really picked a lot of that up from the radical pacifists. I was very influenced by the people around *Liberation* magazine . . . and their language of nonviolent revolution. Now . . . I believe . . . that that vision was really misleading, and that though I think in many ways that the radical pacifist section of the movement contributed some of the sanest, soundest and most brilliant leadership, that this vision of nonviolent revolution—which was very

much in the head of my friend Staughton Lynd, and my friend Dave Dellinger—created a misleading sense of strategy, and was part of what contributed to the debacle of [Chicago] 1968. Because if you believed in mobilizing larger and larger numbers of people and you had a rhetoric of nonviolent revolution, then you began to mobilize in a way as though you were going to overthrow *something*. And the riot in Chicago, with that kind of perspective—and you're going to get as many people there as possible, and you've got a few Jerry Rubins and some other self-serving folks on hand—you have a recipe for disaster. And that's what 1968 was. And I think most people in the know think it was one step from the summer of 1968 to the Days of Rage [organized by Weatherman in 1969]. That was just a little more rhetoric and a little more militancy, but the formula was all there. . . .

I think that it was a mistake to use the word *revolution* to characterize [a movement for radical change], that it conjured up people's most romantic and irresponsible selves. . . . What I'm sorry for is that at points like in that national secretary's report I used language that I think I hadn't thought through the implications of. [85]

The consensus at SDS's national convention in Iowa was that the group would agitate for student control of universities and thereby revolutionize other students. This syndicalist approach displeased veteran SDSers like Paul Booth and Clark Kissinger, but their objections proved futile. Booth was a much disliked person in the organization by this point, partly on personality grounds but mainly because of his vehement opposition to the anarchistic organizational style infecting the SDS national office. "My major preoccupation was, 'Let's have a structure, let's develop leadership, let's have chapters, let's have study groups, turn out literature, when people write us let's answer their letters, if they call us let's call them back,'" Booth remembered. His crusade sparked "a tremendous amount of political backbiting" against him and he was "losing the battle." Booth was also "very tired physically" and ready to step aside. After writing a series of discussion papers "which weren't really on point," Booth resigned from SDS that fall and concentrated on building the National Conference for New Politics. Kissinger made a self-described "detour back to the right." Impressed by the Scheer campaign, he too headed off in the direction of electoral politics, forming a political group in Chicago. Kissinger ran unsuccessfully for city alderman the next spring. [86]

Enemy Resolve, Public Doubt

As SDS was aspiring to build a second American revolution, the Johnson administration continued to pursue its counterrevolutionary hopes in Vietnam. Throughout the summer Operation Rolling Thunder focused its awesome firepower on North Vietnam's POL system. The word coming down from the Oval Office was that the first priority of the U.S. air war was the complete "strangulation" of that system. Although officials publicly maintained the strikes were a success, Washington was sweating. "What became clearer and clearer as the summer wore on was that while we had destroyed a major portion of North Vietnam's storage capacity," the Pentagon Papers historian writes, "she retained enough dispersed capacity, supplemented by continuing imports . . . to meet her on-going requirements." Further, while the United States was sacrificing men, munitions, fuel, and aircraft in distressing numbers, the flow of enemy troops and supplies down the Ho Chi Minh trail continued "undiminished." By late summer it was "clear" to officials "that the POL strikes had been a failure." Robert McNamara made no attempt to hide his chagrin and lambasted U.S. military leaders for offering misleading predictions. Souring on Rolling Thunder as a whole, McNamara turned his attention to alternative ways of checking enemy infiltration and ending the war.[87]

Late that August, a group of American scientists advised the administration to construct an anti-infiltration barrier across the demilitarized zone separating North and South Vietnam. The barrier would consist mainly of gravel mines, noisy button bomblets, wire, sensors, artillery, men, planes, and cluster bombs. McNamara was enthralled with the concept and ordered it speedily implemented. However, after estimates of the barrier's final cost mushroomed, the military's opposition to it hardened, enemy troops attacked people building it, and technical tests went awry (e.g., five thousand button bomblets were scattered on Florida beaches, forcing evacuation of ten thousand bewildered Sunday sunbathers), it was junked. Other hairbrained schemes for limiting North Vietnam's warmaking capacity met the same fate, including ones to drop containers of Budweiser beer (a brand U.S. intelligence concluded was favored by the enemy) along the Ho Chi Minh trail in order to "slow down" Vietnamese troops heading south, and to train flocks of (apparently ideology-distinguishing) pigeons to deposit bomblets on enemy vehicles.[88]

On August 5, the Joint Chiefs of Staff asked McNamara for 542,588 U.S. troops by the end of 1967, 100,000 more than were already ticketed for Vietnam. The secretary of defense directed the JCS to provide him with "a detailed, line-by-line analysis" of their latest request to verify that it was "truly essential" to U.S. policy. For the first time, McNamara was refusing to give U.S. military leaders carte blanche on troop deployments to Vietnam. The JCS's analysis failed to satisfy the secretary. In October, he took off on a trip to South Vietnam to get a better read on the war.[89]

The trip was an upsetting one for McNamara, not least of all because he had been targeted by an NLF assassination squad, which was discovered shortly before his arrival. McNamara bluntly informed the president upon returning to

Washington that there was *"no reasonable way to bring the war to an end soon."* The enemy was growing and *"pacification has if anything gone backward."* Rolling Thunder, he observed, was simply not doing the job. McNamara stressed that, despite suffering high losses, the enemy remained as determined as ever. "I never thought it would go on like this," he confided to an acquaintance around this time. "I didn't think these people had the capacity to fight this way. If I had thought they could take this punishment and fight this well, could enjoy fighting like this, I would have thought differently at the start." (McNamara's confession was duplicated by other senior policymakers after they had lost the war. Dean Rusk and William Westmoreland both volunteered to the author that they misgauged the enemy's tenacity during the conflict. "I think we in the United States leadership underestimated the toughness of the North Vietnamese," Westmoreland conceded.)[90]

Domestic opposition to the war was also weighing heavily on McNamara. Aware that the conflict would be lengthy at best, he doubted the public would stick it out. The secretary wrote Johnson in mid October that Rolling Thunder would only bring significant returns if undertaken with a ferocity "which would not be stomached either by our own people or by world opinion" and that risked war with China. An "endless" stream of troop deployments to Vietnam was also "not likely to be acceptable in the U.S.," he argued.[91]

The war's domestic rear guard was indeed wavering. "*Nobody* I talked to was affirmative about Vietnam," Harry McPherson reported to Bill Moyers upon returning from a late July vacation he had spent with well-educated, middle-income Republicans. "It is an extremely unpopular war, to judge by all I heard." McPherson lamented that his vacation companions could not believe "that we are there to 'defend the freedom of South Vietnam.'" Support from people of their social cast "is vital," the White House counsel wrote, "and we don't have much of it now." Although the public had expressed overwhelming support for the POL strikes in July, by October—when it had become apparent that the bombing had brought the conflict no closer to an end—only 38 percent gave Johnson high marks on his handling of the war.[92]

Less disturbing to the administration but disturbing nonetheless was an announcement by three Army privates that they were refusing the government's orders to serve in Vietnam. "We want no part of a war of extermination," the Fort Hood Three declared on June 30. The GIs also stated that they were filing a lawsuit challenging their orders on the grounds that the war was illegal. Their insubordination received considerable media attention. Within several days, federal agents had contacted each of the privates' families in an effort to get them to back down; authorities promised one's parents their son would receive an Army discharge if he recanted and dropped the suit. Plainclothes agents tailed the three GIs everywhere. On July 7, as they were on their way to a public meeting, military police intercepted the soldiers and whisked them off to the stockade at Fort Dix, New Jersey, where they were held incommunicado. The Fort Hood Three were tried by a military court typically unsympathetic to troublemakers (an admiral on one military court summed up the prevailing judicial attitude in the armed forces when he offered unguardedly, "Anyone sent up here for trial must be guilty of something"). They spent two years behind bars.[93]

To the peace movement, the Fort Hood Three were cause for celebration. Now soldiers were resisting. The privates' stance inspired many discouraged demonstrators.[94] Activists held rallies and distributed leaflets supporting the Fort Hood Three, convincing other protesters that GIs were an important constituency. The Army doctor Howard Levy's much-publicized refusal in October to train Green Beret medics also inspirited activists.

Public anxiety over the war forced Johnson to pace the halls of the White House like a caged animal that fall. He had made plans to campaign for Democratic congressmen up for reelection only to discover that many legislators were wary of close association with a war-making president. Intent on avoiding the issue of Vietnam, they knew that a visit by Johnson would also elicit noisy demonstrations. The president pursued a journey of another sort. In late October he embarked on a seventeen-day tour of East Asian and Pacific countries designed to grab headlines immediately before the elections. Antiwar protesters greeted him in these countries, however; Lady Bird Johnson recalled seeing placards bearing the "now-familiar" accusation that her husband was a child killer. Johnson cut short or canceled several speeches because of protests. In Canberra, three thousand partying Aussies waited fruitlessly outside a hotel for Johnson while "drinking beers and singing songs and exchanging good-natured banter with the cops and asking the milling reporters what the hell had happened to the bloody cowboy."[95]

Dissent continued to build on America's campuses. Antidraft activists were quietly organizing "We Won't Go" groups at many universities. Direct action against class ranking, Selective Service testing, and military recruiters was widespread. Students were giving hostile greetings to administration officials who made the mistake of venturing onto campuses, unwilling to accept that times had changed since the spring of 1965 and that students were now much less willing to listen passively to government spokesmen propagandize. Robert McNamara was the most rudely received official of all.

On November 7, McNamara was scheduled to address a select group of fifty students at Harvard. Unhappy with this arrangement, SDS suggested Harvard demonstrate its commitment to free speech by setting up a forum through which McNamara's views could be discussed more widely. The university refused, guaranteeing fireworks. McNamara's talk went off as planned, but as he attempted to leave the scene in a police car on a back street, events took a nasty turn. SDS was running "a James Bond-type operation, with walkie-talkie equipped spotters on all sides of the building." A dozen SDSers sat down around the police car while the head spotter, Jared Israel, screamed at the top of his lungs, "Maac-Naa . . . m . . . a . . . a . . . ra!" Suddenly nearly a thousand protesters were sprinting toward the startled official. "Within moments he was surrounded by what must have looked to him like a mob of howling beatniks; they were actually normal Harvard people . . . delighted to have trapped the Secretary." McNamara the quarry was *"mad,"* Israel recounted. "He was like a cornered bull." Demonstrating his deep-seated affinity for toughness ("Ho Chi Minh is a tough old SOB," McNamara once told his staffers, and "I'm as tough as he is"), the coiled official got out of the police car and mounted the hood of a nearby convertible. After grabbing a bullhorn and agreeing to field questions, he shouted, "I spent four of the happiest years on the Berkeley campus doing some of the same things you're doing here. But there was one important difference: I was both tougher and more courteous." Following laughter and taunts, McNamara persisted, voice even louder, "I was tougher then and I'm tougher now!"

> The audience loved it. Mac was blowing his cool—unable to handle himself, quite possibly scared. The first question was about the origins of the Vietnamese war. "It started in '54–'55 when a million North Vietnamese flooded into South Vietnam," McNamara said. "Goin' home!" someone shouted. Mac countered "Why don't you guys get up here since you seem to know all the answers?" The next question asked for the number of civilian casualties in the South. "We don't know," Mac said. "Why not? Don't you care?" came the shouts. "The number of civilian casualties . . ." Mac began, but was drowned out by cries of *"Civilian! Civilian!* Napalm victims!" A few PL-types in front were jumping up and down screaming "Murderer! Fascist!" Mac tried to regain his composure and said, "Look fellas, we had an agreement . . ." A girl shrieked "What about your agreement to hold elections in 1956?"

At about this juncture the police rescued McNamara from the horde. Years afterward, McNamara, who characteristically dove into his office and remained there "for a long time" following confrontations with demonstrators, granted that the experience was "pretty rough."[96]

Hounded Public Servants

The secretary of defense's encounter with antiwar protesters was unique only in its high drama. In scores of other locations, other Johnson administration officials found themselves the prey of demonstrators. By this time virtually any senior official who spoke in public drew an angry crowd, forcing officials to restrict their outside appearances. The next year the crowds grew even larger and more clamorous. It became "almost a game" to limit prior notice of President Johnson's public engagements so that "the Students for a Democratic Society and other campus militants did not have time to organize a protest," George Christian writes. Such confrontations "were to be avoided at all costs." Some officials urged Johnson to venture out of the White House more, claiming that clashes with demonstrators would benefit him, but the Secret Service wouldn't permit it—it was too perilous. Christian said that it never ceased to amaze him how antiwar organizers could mobilize large numbers of people for a protest in a short period of time. "It surprised me that there was that much venom," he recalled, although he "got accustomed to it after a while." The peace movement's organizational skills impressed other officials as well. In November 1967, the White House ordered the FBI to "discreetly" determine "how and why demonstrators are so well organized and so efficient in getting to locations where the President is speaking and whether there is any proof that there is a prearranged policy to prevent the President from speaking." Officials hoped to produce "some kind of magazine article" on the problem. The same month a CIA study of the peace movement observed that the "performance" of its "tireless" leaders was "impressive."[97]

Administration officials also had to contend with protesters close to home. Their houses were picketed and even vandalized. Walt Rostow's mother-in-law received a telephoned death threat intended for him. Opponents of the war intruded on officials' vacations. One summer the mother of the liberal journalist Jonathan Schell organized a tennis boycott of the Bundys and McNamaras, "forcing the two families to play only with each other." McNamara frequently attracted the attention of demonstrators while vacationing in Colorado. Some rocked his ski lift; one woman came up to him in a lodge and yelled that she hoped that catsup on his hamburger reminded him of blood. Another protester stuck a sign in the front yard of a glass house he was renting there that warned, "People who live in glass houses shouldn't drop bombs." Others set fire to a house he later owned in Colorado. That an outspokenly antiwar senator lived just down the street from him in Washington was "a real thorn" in McNamara's side, his son Craig remembered. Johnson had difficulty attending church in Washington without hazarding exposure to an antiwar sermon. After McNamara left office, a young man even tried to throw him off a ferry at night, repeatedly hitting him and pinning him against the railing.[98]

The badgering officials suffered at the hands of protesters and the limitations this placed on their public activity vexed them. Rather than receiving the red-carpet treatment allegedly due high-level "public servants," they were treated as criminals. But did these chilly receptions influence their policies in Vietnam?

Dean Rusk and Walt Rostow denied that their prescriptions for the war were affected. "I went around making many speeches, and sometimes . . . before I spoke I would spend an hour or so with these fellows, talking things over with them," Rusk recalled. "And I've autographed a number of signs saying 'Rusk Go Home' at the request of the young person carrying the sign. And that scene was not difficult." Rusk conceded, however, that when television directed its spotlight on his tormenters, he did not take them lightly:

> When the television cameras arrived the scene changed. They'd ball up their fists and start screaming, because that was the way you got on television. . . . On several occasions these fellows would set up their cameras in a place where I was supposed to enter so that their cameras would show me with the protesters in the background. Well, sometimes I would walk around behind the cameras and go into the building behind the cameras, and they would get furious. That would be sort of a game.

Rusk worried that the protesters were having some effect on public opinion using the "powerful instrument" of television. [99]

Harry McPherson and Pentagon officials Paul Warnke and Morton Halperin thought Rusk and Rostow were indeed unmoved by antiwar harassment. Warming to the subject during an interview in his sparkling, glass-walled Washington law office, peering out from behind tortoise-shelled glasses, the East Texas-bred McPherson drawled:

> One could have endured all of that and felt almost kindly and under-standing about it [if you believed the protesters] were young and they simply didn't understand, and we of the postwar generation . . . had to be the parents: "The kids want to smoke pot and eat ice cream, but the parents say, 'The family will do this.' And it has to be that way. . . . Don't trust anybody over thirty? Fine, we're over thirty and we are taking responsibility for the country, as we must do or one of these days we'll look up and say, 'Holy God, we lost all of Asia!'" . . . That's how I would have preferred to look at it. And I think that's how Walt Rostow did, and how Rusk did. [100]

William Bundy doubted that the "battering" protesters inflicted on officials influenced U.S. policy in Vietnam:

> We used to go to Martha's Vineyard, which was a liberal hotbed. And they made life very miserable for [the State Department's] Nick Katzenbach there after his statement that the Tonkin Gulf resolution was the functional equivalent of a declaration of war. The social at-mosphere on Martha's Vineyard was extremely intense and very un-pleasant. But I don't think that affected him. And I don't think it af-

fected me. As for going out and speaking, I kind of relished that—I might shock some people by saying I relished it—because I thought there was something to say, that one *had* to say, that people hadn't taken in. And there was a great deal of plain erroneous historical argument and so on in the debate that it seemed to me imperative to rebut, however you finally came out. . . . An awful lot of people . . . were just plain operating on a purely emotional basis, which I didn't think was the way you run a country. So it didn't get to me.[101]

George Christian took a different view. Christian joined the White House in the spring of 1966 and was appointed press secretary that December. Years later, he was a political consultant in Austin, Texas—a self-effacing man with a hearty, contagious laugh, a relaxed, forthright manner, and a certain air of machismo. "The Democratic Party is basically an undisciplined mob. That's why I like being a Democrat—I like mobs," he roared. Christian was convinced that peace activists' incessant pestering of officials weakened their resolve to remain in Vietnam:

When a cabinet officer went out to make a speech, he got the same type of demonstrations that the president did. And it came home to you pretty [fast]. I went to Chicago one day, in 1967 I guess it was, to make a speech . . . and I was shocked to find that there had been some minor demonstrations in Chicago just because the paper had run an article that I was coming to town. . . . They had broke some windows and did some other things. And I remember questioning the guy who had picked me up. He told me that there had been a few demonstrations. And I said, "About what?" And he said, "About you coming out here to be in Chicago." I said, "Good Lord, I ain't got that kind of profile in this thing. Why would anyone be concerned about me?" He said that anybody from the administration was always subject to that when they came into Chicago. And I think that's probably right for a lot of people. . . . It shocked me. I'm a fairly low profile person—I didn't know that anybody would want to throw rocks at me [laughs]. I didn't have anything to do with war policy. . . . They saw me on TV sometime and decided I was the enemy.

The security problems became so intense. You couldn't very well reconcile yourself to demonstrations and potential demonstrations and things when the intelligence reports and the police reports that we were getting indicated there was a violent streak in all this stuff, and that there was actually a danger of bodily harm, for the president in particular and for his surrogates in some cases. So it was pretty serious business. . . . And I'm sure the effect was worse on some others than it was on the president. Not that they were afraid of getting hurt or anything like that, but I mean just the signs of what was going on, the evidence that the country was torn up. . . . The cabinet officers and others who traveled around a lot . . . probably saw a heck of a lot more of it than those of us in the White House did. . . . The wear and tear on the will of the government to carry on with the policy was not just wear and tear on the president.

Christian said that Johnson's "general view" was that "'they may wear everybody else down, but I'm going to be the last one up here to go under.'" Yet Christian believed that the president's "inability to move about the country freely without having demonstrations" contributed to his momentous March 1968 partial bombing halt over North Vietnam and decision not to run for reelection. [102]

The protests that greeted Johnson administration officials most everywhere they turned did indeed weaken official resolve. The influence of this activity on U.S. policy in Vietnam was felt mainly in 1967 and 1968 as Washington pondered the likely domestic reaction to further escalation of the war. That issue will be discussed in chapters on those years. Here we shall consider why the harassment entered into officials' calculations at all. First, it was a nagging and glaring reminder of public opposition to the war. That Johnson was compelled to "sneak . . . around the country from one air base to another" in order to "dodge all these people meeting him wherever he arrived and shouting, 'Hey, hey, LBJ, how many boys have you killed today?'" as James Reston asserted, "undoubtedly had some influence on an old politician who, after all, knew very well that politicians live and die by public opinion, and if they can't carry the people with them, they're in trouble." Second, tumultuous encounters with protesters fed officials' perceptions that the war threatened American social stability. In Christian's words, they were "evidence that the country was torn up." Third, officials worried that the constant demonstrations were eroding the public's resolve. Not only were some Americans being influenced by the protesters' arguments, but others were simply wearying of the domestic clamor over the war. "You had a bad public relations situation," Christian recalled. Officials were also concerned that the protests were shaping opinion by demeaning the presidency in the public's eyes. "It ain't good for a president to go and be booed and to have eggs or, as in Australia, red paint thrown at his car and such things," Harry McPherson said evenly. The hounding "was *bad*," he remembered. Hearing people call Johnson a baby killer in front of the White House was "very disturbing," McPherson revealed. Fourth, officials simply lost strength for facing hostile and possibly harmful people wherever they went. "Presidents want to be loved," Paul Warnke said. "They don't want to hear people shouting, 'Hey, hey, LBJ, how many kids did you kill today?' That gets to them." McPherson admitted, "You didn't want to be conducting something that had stirred such a fierce opposition." Officials' privileged lifestyles made the onslaught all the more grating. "These were powerful men who were used to going anywhere they wanted," as the antiwar leader Linda Morse observed. "It had to have some effect on them." Among other officials, McNamara found it especially wearing to be denied access to the nation's elite universities, the most likely trouble spots of all. More than other schools they housed "intellectuals whose credentials the secretary of defense respected." Craig McNamara had no doubt that the antiwar badgering influenced his father. "Eventually it's *got* to," he argued. "I don't think there's anyone who could resist that." Asked whether this pestering and the physical security problems it posed to officials amounted to "a war of attrition at home" that "just got to be too much," CIA Director Richard Helms glared impatiently at me as if the answer was obvious. "All of this is true," he said matter-of-factly.[103]

Trouble with the Relatives

The peace movement was disrupting officials' lives in other ways as well. Many of their friends were turning against the war. William Bundy said "very many" officials had friends who joined the movement. "They caused you personal pain," he recalled. Washington cocktail parties were often unpleasant affairs, particularly after a few drinks had oiled the guests' tongues. Some of McNamara's numerous liberal friends began getting the willies around him. It must have been particularly trying for him to watch his friend Robert Kennedy becoming more critical of the war in 1966. As noted earlier, the social climate could turn cold on officials' vacations. In December 1966, it got positively icy for McNamara. The secretary of defense and his family were staying at a small inn in Aspen, Colorado, called the Mountain Chalet. It was run by the Melvilles, a clan of eight or nine who were friendly with the McNamaras. Craig McNamara would remember helping the Melvilles with various chores around the inn, tiling bathrooms, doing whatever needed to be done. "It was fun," he said. "It was a bunch of families, friends, that stayed there." During this particular stay, however, one of those families—the pacific Stickneys who had set up the AFSC's refugee project in South Vietnam—poisoned the atmosphere by holding forums at night against the war in the lodge. "The tension was thick as ice," Craig said. "Obviously there was tremendous friction between my father and this man [David Stickney]." Craig remembered his dad avoiding the forums.[104]

Officials also had to watch their close relatives suffer public condemnation as a result of their association with the war. Walt Rostow's son told him that the late 1960s were "the worst period of his life." William Bundy's son, an undergraduate at Harvard, left academia "more or less to get out of . . . my firing line," Bundy recalled. "It was terribly hard on him personally." Bundy said wives of officials were frequently accosted by family friends who opposed the war. Bundy's own wife, who eventually concluded that the war was "hopeless," found the Vietnam period "very painful." So did Marge McNamara, who developed a serious ulcer that required her hospitalization in 1967; it lasted until the day she died fourteen years later. Craig believed his mom's ulcer was a result of her concern for her distraught husband. "I'm sure that she was pulled apart by [the war], torn by it, but in no way manifested that outwardly," he said. Robert McNamara attributed her death to the war. General Westmoreland's daughter Stevie was visiting a friend at Harvard in early 1967 when she spied what looked like a campus bonfire. Only years afterward did she tell her father that the blaze was actually his body burning in effigy.[105]

Perhaps most painful of all to officials was the strife the war bred inside their families. George Reedy and George Christian both recalled knowing of wives of senior policymakers who opposed U.S. policy and unequivocally expressed that sentiment to their husbands (Reedy's own wife among them). Many sons and daughters of officials doubted or opposed the war. Dean Rusk recognized that his son, Richard, a student at Cornell, disagreed with his policies, despite then serving in the Marine Reserve. "Caught between love for my father and the growing horror of Vietnam," Richard Rusk would ultimately suffer a nervous breakdown. Numerous children of officials participated in the famous "Confrontation with the Warmakers" at the Pentagon in October 1967. No fewer than three of the senior Pentagon official Paul Nitze's four kids were part of that menacing crowd. Nitze was the government's self-described "mastermind of the planning of the defense of the Pentagon" for the demonstration. One of Nitze's kids hobnobbed with the radical leadership of Columbia University's SDS chapter. Paul Warnke's daughter, a student at Harvard, attended at least one demonstration in Washington while staying overnight (with fellow protesters) at the Warnke home. Secretary of the Army Stanley Resor had two sons and Under Secretary of the Army Ted Beal a daughter who, by the end of the decade, were committed antiwar organizers. Resor remembered having "big discussions" with his son John and John's friends when they came to Washington for protests, sleeping overnight at the Resor household. Nicholas Katzenbach's son Chris strongly opposed the war. Katzenbach's aide Anthony Lake recalled going to dinner at his boss's house and "hearing his kids really mau-mau him" on Vietnam. "His back would be against the wall," Lake related. "Of course, they were right and he was wrong, in retrospect." Chris Katzenbach later became an ardent peace activist at Stanford. Remembered one senior Pentagon official, "Like most of my friends, my evenings, when I did get home, were spent listening to my wife and children screaming about how awful the war was." McGeorge Bundy eventually found himself estranged from at least one of his four sons because of sharp disagreement on Vietnam. "His children were very upset by the position that he took," recalled Arthur Schlesinger, Jr., a family friend. Catherine Colby, daughter of the senior CIA official William Colby, died in 1973 of epilepsy and anorexia nervosa after suffering emotional problems for some time. According to an enduring rumor, Catherine was a "psychological casualty" of Vietnam. William Bundy said, "I won't go into names, of course, but fairly close relatives of mine were alienated from me for periods of time." Such estrangement "caused personal pain," he admitted.[106]

And then there were Robert McNamara and his son Craig. Nowhere was the split between father and child wider and the hurt greater. "That was a very painful one," recalled Resor, whose own son Eddie was a "good friend" and prep school classmate of Craig's and who knew the McNamara family "very well. . . . I'm sure it was awful."[107]

When I met him, Craig McNamara was a walnut farmer outside Davis, California. He and his dad were financial "partners" in the 265-acre operation (they owned another 255 acres, which they rented out to tomato growers). Craig, a trim, well-proportioned man with short, sandy brown hair and the trademark McNamara wire-rimmed glasses, did "all of the farming and bud-geting." As others have observed, he looked like a gentler version of his father. Craig lived in an old farmhouse with his wife Julie and their three children; roaming around their yard, surrounded by symmetrical rows of walnut trees, were cats and rabbits. A large portrait of Robert McNamara hanging just inside the front door of the farmhouse signified the change Craig's relationship with his father had undergone since the war. "We have a very mature and caring friendship and respect for one another right now," Craig said. "Which is won-derful. We're very close." Robert McNamara's emergence as an antinuclear weapons spokesman in the 1980s helped their relationship immensely. Craig recalled feeling "so *proud of him*" after one of his dad's talks on television against the arms race.[108]

During 1966, Craig's previous doubts about the war turned into outright opposition. Astonishingly for the son of a senior U.S. policymaker, he tacked a small NLF flag that his father had brought back from Vietnam onto one wall of his bedroom in his parents' Washington home. On the opposite wall, he hung an American flag—turned upside down. His dad was furious. "It must have just really hurt my folks," Craig reflected. "It must have been devastating." Thanks to his dad's travels to Vietnam, Craig was able to add to his room decorations some punji sticks—sharpened bamboo stakes the NLF concealed in the grass to slash the feet and legs of U.S. and ARVN soldiers. The sticks were also "a thorn in the side of my folks," Craig surmised.[109]

Craig felt emotionally split by the war. He loved his father but abhorred his father's policies in Vietnam. An incident in Colorado in the summer of 1966 illustrated the polarity. While his family was resting inside a friend's home in Aspen, sixty picketers appeared outside. Craig went out to meet them. "It wasn't . . . just to talk to them, to shoot the breeze or to offer them a cup of coffee," he recalled. "I definitely was sympathetic to them." He also "felt that it was necessary to have some communication with them: they had come for a purpose and somebody should address them." But Craig "felt torn." He hoped his visit would "soften the situation" for his dad. "I . . . felt like, 'Here is my father who obviously needs some mental space and relaxation and vacation. I understand why you're picketing him about the Vietnam War, but give him a chance, too.'" One of the picketers, the internationally known artist Thomas Hart Benton, gave Craig an autographed silkscreen of a dove on a black background, which he kept for many years. "I remember that protest as hurting a lot," he said pensively. "It hurt me a lot."[110]

Not surprisingly, Craig's emotional turmoil over the war affected his studies at prep school. He had dyslexia, a learning disability, but his counseled repetition of the tenth grade during the 1966–67 academic year was also a product of "the Vietnam saga and the frustration and upsetness that I was going through," he believed. In 1967, Craig's turmoil exhibited painful physical symptoms as well. At the relatively tender age of 17, he, too, suffered "a *very* excruciating ulcer." As Craig said, "You needn't look too far as to why."[111]

Craig's trauma was compounded by his inability to discuss the war with his father. "We never talked about it," he revealed. Years afterward, they still hadn't. Craig explained: "It's not that we are polarized. It's just that he has a private part of his life which we [Craig and his two sisters] are included in, and we are not included in his public, or his career, life. Never have been, never will be." Craig's first public mention of details of his complex relationship with his father appeared in a 1984 article in *Mother Jones* magazine. The elder McNamara was not pleased. Among Craig's quoted remarks were, "There has got to be a lot of guilt and depression inside my father about Vietnam." Craig recalled:

> He called up and said, "Craig, did you really talk with the person who wrote the article? Were those your quotes?" And I said, "Yeah, they were." And I knew they were going to hurt him. . . . But, you know, in rereading that article back then, I had many pangs or many feelings, but there were no regrets. . . . Everything that was said there were all things that I feel. They were all things that I've never said to my father. And maybe it's unfortunate that he read them in print and not hear them from me, but the problem is, he's not receptive to hearing them from me.

Craig is not the only person Robert McNamara refused to talk about Vietnam with. He invariably turned down requests for interviews on the subject. McNamara explained his refusal to be interviewed to me curiously: "Instead, I arranged for the preparation of the Pentagon Papers to assist scholars such as yourself." The Pentagon Papers, it should be noted, are a top-secret study of U.S. decision-making in Vietnam that McNamara commissioned in 1967. The study was probably never intended for public perusal. "Those papers would never have seen the light of day if I hadn't leaked them!" commented Daniel Ellsberg, who passed them to the *New York Times* in 1971. Indeed, the summer the *Times* ran excerpts from the study, his daughter Kathy recalled, McNamara, then the president of the World Bank, "got the shingles. And it wasn't the World Bank that was giving him the shingles."[112]

Although Craig McNamara didn't press his father to discuss the war, one of his best friends (Craig would even name his second son after the friend) did. The occasion was a Georgetown dinner party at the home of the parents of Craig's friend, Graham, also a prep school classmate. The McNamaras knew the family quite well. "Graham couldn't contain himself any longer on the issue of Vietnam," Craig remembered, "and at the dinner party just cornered my dad at the end of the table . . . and started to let go." The exchange "got very pointed." Although Craig bit his tongue during Graham's assault, "it was clear that I supported him." Sam Brown, invited to the McNamara home by Kathy McNamara (who also opposed the war), had a similarly heated exchange about Vietnam with McNamara over dinner.[113]

When Craig entered Stanford University in 1969, he began actively participating in the peace movement. The pressure he felt as a McNamara to be a spokesperson made him uncomfortable. Shy, Craig felt ill at ease in front of a crowd. And in quickly terminated exchanges about Vietnam, his dad had questioned his adequacy as a critic. "I had him saying, 'You don't know enough. Have you read this? Have you read that?'" Craig recalled. "That intimidated me in a certain way." But not enough to prevent him from protesting the war virtually full-time. "Pretty much the time at Stanford was occupied with anti-Vietnam and Cambodia demonstrations," Craig said. Some of them were not tranquil affairs. Once, an angry crowd of 15,000 put Richard Nixon on trial for war crimes. "It didn't take the verdict long to come in." Following the guilty decree, Craig and the other jurors tore through the streets, breaking windows. "I remember the rage setting in on me, and the frustration that we all felt because we couldn't stop the war," Craig said afterward. "What was in my mind . . . was rage, pure rage. . . ." Among Craig's fellow protesters at Stanford was one Susan Haldeman, the daughter of Nixon's powerful White House chief of staff, H. R. Haldeman.[114]

It took many years for the rift between the McNamaras to heal. The ponytailed Craig put on his leather pants, hopped on his motorcycle, and left Stanford in the spring of 1971 to journey to Chile. He wanted to see Marxist President Salvador Allende's socialist experiment firsthand and to get out of the belly of the imperialist beast. "I felt an enormous sense of frustration with my family, with my country," Craig remembered. "I felt there was nothing I could do to change my father. And so I left the country." Craig started a dairy cooperative on Easter Island. When his dad, then the president of the World Bank, came to Santiago in 1972 to extract concessions from Allende under the threat of cutting off the bank's loans to Chile, Craig did not try to contact him, although he then lived only a mile away. His father did not try to make contact either. After McNamara's World Bank did cut off Chile's loans (only to reextend them later to the Pinochet regime), Craig was livid. "I was really upset by that," he recalled. "That was hard to mend."[115]

Years later, Craig still seemed both loving and leery of his father. In one breath he'd say about the war, "Nobody else was telling the truth." In another, it was, "What I ask is, 'He had the facts, my father had the facts, and they were glaring. . . . So how long can you go on massaging the facts or manipulating the facts?'" Craig advised: "You've got to question authority. You've got to question everything that comes down the pipe."[116]

How much impact did rebellious relatives have on Johnson administration officials? Cautiously, Craig McNamara said he doubted he swayed his dad's opinions while his father was in the government. He was too young to wield that kind of weight, Craig suspected. "I think in subsequent years . . . I definitely have," he quickly added. "I think I have influenced some of his decisions." Other observers of the McNamaras disagree with Craig's view of the war period. A woman who worked with the secretary of defense in the Pentagon, an acquaintance of his oldest daughter, once remarked to Craig, "You don't know how much you influenced your father." Paul Warnke said of Robert McNamara, "I'm quite sure that the strong opposition of his own children to the war had a very definite impact on him. I think Craig in particular. He was very opposed to the war and very disapproving of his father. If you ever have sons that are of the age of reason, you will find that their opinion is very important to you. *Very* important."[117]

Paul Nitze and Dean Rusk denied that their children's views influenced them. "It didn't affect me at all," Nitze asserted of his kids' participation in the 1967 Pentagon demonstration. "I'd have been annoyed with them if they hadn't been part of their generation." They were "not . . . really that much against the government" anyway but merely "wanted to see what all the excitement was about," Nitze suggested. "They were Washington kids—why not be part of what's going on?" Like "most" of the marchers that day, his children were "good people," he said, in contrast to the "really dedicated" few who "had passed the point of no return." The war "wasn't an emotional issue within my family at all," Nitze recalled. "They understood me and I understood them. There wasn't any problem." William Bundy offered: "I have to say with all respect to my dear relatives . . . I don't honestly think I was affected [by them]. That's a personal matter." Bundy said the main reason he was unpersuaded was "because I thought they represented a strand of public opinion which seemed to me to be in a minority."[118]

Yet it seems likely that antiwar relatives did have some influence on officials.

Suffering the disapproval of those dear to them surely contributed to the acute sense of besiegement most came to feel by late 1967 and may even have altered their perceptions of the war's merits. "I think that if you have a close relative, particularly a child, who feels that the policy is incorrect, any responsive parent has to give some thought to it," Warnke argued. "If you're a good parent, you don't just automatically figure that you know best."[119] At the very least, opposition to the war inside officials' families heightened their awareness of public antagonism as a whole.

Endless War?

Two days after McNamara toughed it out with antiwar protesters at Harvard, the American people went to the polls. Lyndon Johnson could not have been pleased with the results. Democrats lost forty-seven seats in the House of Representatives and three in the Senate. Dissatisfied with U.S. policies in Vietnam and their economic repercussions at home (e.g., inflation), observers analyzed, many voters had decided to rid themselves of the administration's congressional supporters. In Oregon, the liberal Republican Mark Hatfield was elected to the Senate on a strong antiwar platform. The president, it will be remembered, had predicted such partisan political fallout from Vietnam a year earlier.[120]

Residents of Dearborn, Michigan, a white suburb of Detroit, participated in a referendum on the war. "Are you in favor of an immediate cease fire and withdrawal of United States troops from Vietnam so that the Vietnamese people can settle their own problems?" they were asked. Forty-one percent answered yes. Clear-cut antiwar sentiment was spreading. Later research found it was inversely associated with citizens' socioeconomic level, with blue-collar workers more disapproving of the war than professionals and managers.[121]

The November 5–8 protests called by the recently formed national Mobilization Committee were diffuse and "not particularly successful," the Mobe activist Linda Morse remembered. "There weren't as many things in fact happening in the community as we had hoped." The only sizable protest took place in New York, where some fifteen thousand marched. Weak planning and poor weather contributed to the low turnout nationwide. So did mounting pessimism among activists about their ability to stop the war. "The limited successes we have achieved—mobilizing impressive protests and demonstrations, opening up a national debate on the issue, smashing the myth of a Johnson consensus, etc.—have not been wasted efforts. But neither have they succeeded in stopping the continuous escalation of the war—leaving all of us with a profound sense of frustration and despair," wrote Parade Committee organizers. The frustration was reaching "near-hysterical" proportions, others observed. An SWPer reported upon returning from an October organizing trip, "The general attitude on the campuses seems to be heavily loaded with pessimism. . . . Because of the lack of success of the anti-war movement in ending the war with a demonstration or two the weakest forces have taken to defeatism, pot smoking, LSD and the like. A lot, surprising numbers in fact, of the antiwar people of the last two years have dropped out of activity." Dave Dellinger recalled that although the "floods" of new people joining the movement partially masked the problem, "a lot of us . . . were very aware of the defections because they were people we knew and had worked with."[122]

Movement leaders tried to buck up the dejected. The sage A. J. Muste appealed to activists' pride. "The feeling of let-down, of hopelessness . . . is in the final analysis something to be ashamed of," he asserted. "Did we really think the job would be easy?" But even those who were publicly optimistic felt disheartened by the war's steady climb. "There was a lot of anguish felt by all of us," Dellinger remembered, including "the terrible feeling that we weren't doing enough." WSP's Madeline Duckles recalled playing the role of "the elderly pom-pom girl in charge of school spirit" to depressed activists—while thinking to herself, "Boy, what a fraud I am. If they only knew how discouraged I was." The SWP leader Fred Halstead remembered, "All of us were in the same boat. We were all frustrated. . . . You get up your false hopes even if you know damn well that they [U.S. officials] aren't worth anything."[123]

The rising frustration helped convince Norma Becker that a "MASSIVE" civil disobedience protest was tenable. She sensed that many activists previously unsympathetic to risking arrest were now despairing and angry enough to take that step. In mid November, Becker and other Parade Committee activists formulated a plan to blockade the entrance of Manhattan's Whitehall induction center following the next major escalation of the war. They judged this escalation to be "imminent."[124]

On November 26, the Mobilization Committee gathered again in Cleveland. Nearly half of the one hundred and fifty registered delegates were SWP activists, which did not go unnoticed by non-SWPers, irritating most and aggravating a sharp debate over the value of mass demonstrations (the SWP's answer to all questions) relative to local organizing. The delegates eventually agreed to organize national demonstrations in New York and San Francisco on April 15, 1967. "A rallying of forces is needed which is quantitatively so much more impressive than any previous effort so as to constitute a qualitatively new development in the stop the war movement," Muste wrote. The delegates also agreed to stimulate local antiwar activity geared toward broadening the movement. The committee formally reconstituted itself as the Spring Mobilization Committee.[125]

In early December, President Johnson authorized air strikes on Hanoi. The bombing was quickly assailed overseas for causing substantial civilian casualties. On December 15, Becker and her co-workers activated their plan for blockading

Whitehall. Fifty-two people were arrested, including Fred Halstead and several others who "six months or a year [earlier] would have found it unthinkable," Becker said. The protest was much smaller than Becker had envisioned, though: "wishful thinking," she reflected. "The groundswell just wasn't there."[126]

The year ended on "a sour note" for Johnson. On December 25, Harrison Salisbury, senior editor of the *New York Times*, filed the first of a long series of articles from Hanoi. They revealed that America's bombs had indeed inflicted massive civilian casualties. Salisbury's dispatches stimulated "an explosive debate" about the bombing in the United States. Among those affected by them was Robert McNamara. While his spokesmen at the Pentagon "violently attacked" the articles, the secretary "was fascinated by them and followed them closely." Several of his close associates later agreed that it was around this time that McNamara fully came to understand the extent to which his policies were ravaging the innocent in Vietnam.[127]

THREE

1967: Part I

Broadening Opposition

On December 28–30, 1966, more than two hundred young opponents of the war from thirty states gathered in Chicago. The meeting had been called by Bettina Aptheker, a member of the Communist Party. During the previous nine months she had fired off "a huge number of letters" and talked to activists "all over the country" about organizing a national student strike against the war in the spring. She hoped the conferees would take on the project.[1]

Years later, Aptheker taught in the women's studies department at the University of California, Santa Cruz. She left the Communist Party in 1981 after a twenty-year association when its publishing company refused to print a book she had written on the grounds that it was "too feminist" (her lesbianism also influenced the company's decision, she believed). Aptheker said the notion of organizing a student strike first occurred to her in the fall of 1965 while researching her senior thesis in history at Berkeley on the American student peace movement of the 1930s. Sifting through the school's archives, she discovered that her predecessors at Berkeley had helped organize a national student strike. "I got inspired by that," she recalled. "I thought that was a fantastic idea." Aptheker sensed that a student strike would be a good way to surface the swelling opposition to the war on campuses. As a "dramatic" action that hadn't been undertaken yet, she mused, a strike might also energize faltering student activists. "We were all trying to dream up things to try to keep interest going," Aptheker remembered. Not least appealing, a strike might "catch on" with people who "really had power"— that is, workers. "My point of view was that if the Longshoremen refused to unload ships or load ships, if workers would pull work stoppages, that that was the most directly effective and powerful mechanism that you had," Aptheker said. Her vision was not unique. The possibility of a general strike against the war "was always in the back of our heads," Sidney Peck recalled.[2]

Aptheker's proposal received scant consideration at the conference. Virtually all of the participants felt there was insufficient time to build a strike by the spring. Moreover, the April 15 demonstrations called by the Spring Mobilization Committee had become the main focus of the peace movement. The students agreed to work on the demonstrations and local campus antiwar activity during the preceding week. They named themselves the Student Mobilization Committee (SMC). The first national student antiwar coalition had been born.[3]

Two weeks later, the working committee of the Spring Mobe met to discuss the April demonstrations. Rev. James Bevel of the Southern Christian Leadership Conference (SCLC), whom Dave Dellinger had suggested be the Mobe's director, addressed the gathering. The fiery preacher's talk was peculiar. Bevel began with what listener Fred Halstead "could only assume was some sort of allegory that I was not equipped to understand. It was a long, rambling story involving someone he spoke to in his cellar during recent long periods of meditation. Perhaps he meant God, but I don't really know." During his encounters in the cellar, Bevel said, he had experienced a revelation that the war could be stopped if a large group of peacemakers sailed to Vietnam to place their bodies between the combatants. He also suggested the Mobe train protesters in "love for Johnson." "It was in fact one of the strangest meetings I have ever attended," Halstead writes. Yet when all was said and done the discussants spiritedly agreed to hire Bevel as the Mobe's director. For with Bevel on board they would be more likely to attract the participation of Rev. Martin Luther King, Jr., a colleague of Bevel's in the SCLC. Mobe leaders believed that if the influential King joined their ranks, he would bring with him many other blacks, vastly augmenting the peace movement's political power. "Everybody thought it was *the* next stage for the antiwar movement to get this national hero to come in," Dellinger remembered. They also felt King's involvement would help build a multi-issue movement for domestic change.[4]

King was no easy catch. For two years antiwar leaders had been trying to "get him to come all the way out against the war," as Dellinger recalled, but to no avail.[5] King felt that demonstrating against U.S. policy would undermine his civil rights activity. Yet the minister knew as well that he was losing authority in the civil rights movement to militant black leaders who questioned his silence on the war when blacks were dying in disproportionate numbers in Vietnam. These leaders were also challenging his steadfast promotion of nonviolence in the face of continued racist brutalities and explosive ghetto uprisings in the United States. And with domestic opposition to the war growing daily, King understood, the political risks of speaking out were declining.

On January 14, King was at the Miami airport with a colleague preparing to fly to Jamaica for a month of solitude. While leafing through some magazines at the airport restaurant, he "froze." In front of King lay an article in the January *Ramparts* on Vietnamese children burned by napalm. Depicted in color photographs, many of the children had been horribly disfigured. King's colleague "never forgot" the minister's reaction. "Martin just pushed the plate of food away from him. I looked up and said, 'Doesn't it taste any good?' and he answered, 'Nothing will ever taste any good for me until I do everything I can to end that war.' . . . . That's when the decision was made. Martin had known about the war before then, of course, and had spoken out against it. But it was then that he decided to commit himself to oppose it."[6]

In beautiful Jamaica, King ruminated on bloodshed in Vietnam. When he returned to the United States in mid February, the war was "the uppermost subject in his mind." Later that month he told a Los Angeles audience that U.S. policy in Vietnam reflected both "our paranoid anti-Communism" and "the deadly western arrogance that has poisoned the international atmosphere for so long." In March, King declared that the war had left America "standing before the world glutted by our own barbarity." The same month he agreed to speak at the April Mobe demonstration in New York.[7]

But not without preconditions. King insisted that the Mobe remove all communists from its letterhead. The Mobe refused, and he dropped the demand. King later insisted it rescind an invitation to the militant SNCC leader Stokely Carmichael to speak at the demonstration too. During a long telephone conference call between King, the SCLC's Ralph Abernathy, King's aide Andrew Young, Dellinger, Bevel, and the actor Harry Belafonte, the first three men argued that if King appeared with Carmichael, it would cost him political and financial support. "I remember thinking a couple of times, 'Well, this is the end as far as I'm concerned, but I'm going to say it anyway,'" Dellinger later recounted, "and I really laid it out and attacked [that] position." Dellinger maintained "that the Mobilization was going to be a tremendous success with or without [King], and that he was in danger of letting history pass him by." At key junctures in the conversation "all of a sudden Harry would say, 'Well, Dave's right.' And then he'd go on and take [the argument] further, or at least as far but in his own way." Goaded by Dellinger and Belafonte, King agreed to tolerate Carmichael's presence.[8]

As King was coming out against the war, thousands of "respectable" students and professors were sending letters to Washington critical of the war as well. Many of the letters were published as full-page ads in major newspapers. "The effect was a public impression of spreading protest reaching every section of the country," Thomas Powers writes. More than eight hundred former Peace Corps volunteers signed a letter to Johnson emphasizing "the erosion of trust in our

Government" the war was causing. As one of their leaders, John McAuliff, remembered, many of the signatories had entered the Peace Corps without strong feelings on the war, only to conclude through working in other Third World settings that it was contrary to the interests of ordinary Vietnamese peasants. "Spending two years working with Peruvian peasants in the mountain valleys just seemed to make it all a lot clearer," McAuliff said of his own education. [9]

Antiwar organizers were heartened by the outpouring of letters. The recipients of the letters, however, were unhappy. George Christian recalled that administration officials judged antiwar statements signed by numerous professors telling indicators of the trend of public opinion as a whole. Dean Rusk admitted that officials considered these statements influential at home, as well as encouraging to the North Vietnamese. [10]

Of course, some officials sniffed at such communications. In January, after the *New York Times* printed a letter to Johnson signed by a hundred student body presidents and campus newspaper editors questioning U.S. policy, the White House adviser John Roche counseled him that a "direct response" to it "would be a mistake." "All letters with 100 signatures . . . are, of course, put-up jobs," wrote Roche, the key player in an elaborate White House put-up job later in 1967. [11] "There is nothing un-American about a put-up job, but I think it would be unwise to exaggerate the impact on a pretty knowledgeable public of a letter 5 kids probably composed and 95 signed to get their names in the *Times* as 'leaders of their generation.'" [12] Other officials apparently disagreed, as the administration decided Rusk should personally meet with the students.

The January 31 meeting was an eye-opener to most of the forty-three students who attended. Seated at the head of a table in the spacious State Department conference room, smoking and fingering an uninterrupted series of cigarettes, flanked by eight plainclothes security guards, Rusk "briefed" the students on "the Vietnamese situation." According to one, "his manner showed that he clearly assumed this was something we should be grateful to get." Rusk then fielded questions. His performance was apparently unsatisfactory. By the end of the meeting, he had "alienated everybody." Greg Craig, president of the Harvard Undergraduate Council, remembered:

> I think the Secretary of State misread entirely who this group of students was. . . . I think he thought everybody there had made up their mind already that the war was wrong, and so he was dealing, he thought, with critics. There were certainly people there who had made up their mind but there were many people there who had a completely open mind, and there were those who were inclined to support the war. . . . They were captains of football teams, they were fraternity presidents, they were mainstream kids. They were not radicals or revolutionaries by any stretch of the imagination.

Craig said he would "never forget" when Michigan State's student body president asked, "Mr. Secretary . . . what happens if we continue the policy that you've outlined . . . this continued gradual escalation until the other side capitulates . . . up to and including nuclear war, and the other side doesn't capitulate?" Rusk leaned back in his chair, exhaled a long stream of tobacco smoke, and solemnly replied, "Well, somebody's going to get hurt." According to Rick Weidman, a participant, "You could have heard a pin drop in that room. You had some really stunned people. And Rusk had no idea that [his answer] had had that kind of impact. And we just looked at each other around the table and said, 'My God, the Secretary of State of the United States is crazy. This guy has lost it.'" Said another student, "Everyone who walked out of that room was convinced that they really ought to do something more than they had done before against the war." Standing on the front steps of the State Department afterward, Stanford's brash and hairy student body president David Harris cracked to a fellow campus leader, "The man has no fucking shame. Only a whore would spout that kind of garbage."[13]

Many years later, Rusk was noticeably bothered by memory of the meeting. He complained that the students arrived "with a preprepared statement" expressing their dissatisfaction with the discussion, which they released to the press "within minutes after the close of the meeting." Rusk suspected that the Reform Democrat Allard Lowenstein, the students' "coach" and the coordinator of their letter to Johnson, was "largely responsible" for this statement. Rusk was also annoyed that Lowenstein "did not identify himself at that meeting. He just came in and sat in on it, in the back row, without making known his presence." Expressing a pet recollection, Rusk offered: "I remember the then-president of the Harvard student body made a little speech about 'We are doing the fighting, we are doing the fighting,' along that line. I said, 'By the way, what is your draft status?' He said, 'I have a student deferment.' I said, 'Well, aren't you being a little dramatic in saying that *'we* are doing the fighting?'" Rusk recalled that he "didn't feel that that meeting was very helpful to either side."[14] Weidman was right: the secretary *didn't* understand the education he gave the students.

The same day another impelling event transpired. Some twenty-four hundred clerics from across the United States gathered in Washington for an "Education-Action Mobilization" organized by Clergy and Laymen Concerned About Vietnam. The clerics paced silently back and forth in front of the White House in a "vigil for peace." Eyebrows rose when the veteran right-wing counterdemonstrator Joseph Mlot-Mroz chained himself to the White House fence and lifted a sign declaring "Communism is Jewish" (he was carted off to a paddy wagon singing "God Bless America"). The clerics spent the afternoon on Capitol Hill visiting their representatives. Their presence did not go unappreciated. Senator Henry Jackson (D-Wash.) "just couldn't believe" that eighty-five clerics

had rented a plane out of Seattle to come see their legislators. Other congressmen expressed a sense of powerlessness over the war. Some of the clerics met
with Walt Rostow, the president's national security adviser, in the White House.
One of Rostow's aides had earlier advised him that the visiting ministers were
"not irresponsible agitators" and that "to ignore them might hurt our public
relations." The mobilization incited many of the clerics to accelerate their antiwar activity upon returning home. "That was a great boon," the FCNL's David
Hartsough, who was then trying to rally religious Americans, remembered.
"That was fantastic. . . . It was hard not to just feel, 'My God, this is the crying
issue of the century.' I think that just really invigorated and encouraged a lot of
these people to go back to their churches and really start fires going. I mean,
that was real key."[15]

Among those impressed was Eugene McCarthy. Though doubtful about the
war, the senator had not previously forcefully criticized it. His reasons were
numerous, but prominent among them was an awareness that such criticism
would not sit well with many of his constituents in Minnesota. McCarthy's
concern waned during CALCAV's mobilization. Richard Fernandez, CALCAV's
director, recalled that though the protesting clergy had been

> counseled by the Friends Committee on National Legislation to be
> polite and all this, these are people who had come all the way across
> the country, and the idea of being polite, even for nice clergy, was the
> farthest thing [from their minds]. And I can still remember going by
> the doorway of Gene McCarthy's office. And he hadn't made up his
> mind about the war at that time. . . . I could hear the noise. I mean,
> it was like a football rally. There were about sixty Minnesotans in
> there. And so I kind of went in. And they were *screaming* at him.
> And the next day he was to deliver an address to us—and he came
> out against the war that day. He had written it on the back of an
> envelope, left the envelope in the pulpit of this big church, and we
> got called about three hours later: "Where is Gene's speech? We
> didn't know that he was going to do this . . ." That was his first
> statement about the war. And I'm sure to this day it was because the
> people screamed at him. All these people came in from his state. And
> he didn't know, he didn't understand, how outraged people were. Re-
> spectable people, you know—it wasn't just kids. And the respectable
> people wouldn't have been there except for the kids. There's a chain.

The senator's February 1 talk was indeed, as McCarthy later acknowledged, "the
first . . . really public statement that I made against the war." Although unwilling to condemn U.S. policy in toto, he argued that those concerned with
moral issues "must be prepared to pass a harsh moral judgment" on aspects
of it.[16]

The angry Minnesotans who invaded McCarthy's office may well have influenced his speech. In any event, it is clear that the CALCAV gathering as a whole registered profoundly with McCarthy. For months he had been considering running in the 1968 Democratic presidential primaries on an antiwar platform, but was wary of getting thrashed. Until CALCAV's mobilization, McCarthy hadn't noticed "much really serious public opposition" to the war, he recalled, only "fringe opposition," including a multitude of "undirected" students who were "protesters for the sake of protest." The country's antiwar forces were too small and woolly to be "achieving very much," he perceived. There certainly weren't any peace groups around that he could "rely on" to help mount a respectable campaign. But CALCAV's action seemed to McCarthy "a significant expression of a widening new judgment" on the war. "That was the first . . . organized group or identifiable group that the administration couldn't brush off as pacifists or freaks or agitators," he remembered. "The numbers weren't great, but what they represented was something the administration couldn't very easily ignore." The CALCAV gathering provided McCarthy with "some assurance" that "there was some solid base upon which to oppose the war." He "felt better knowing that there was this kind of opposition," he said.[17] McCarthy's subsequent decision to enter the presidential race would have consequence for U.S. involvement in Vietnam.

Shortly before CALCAV's mobilization a minister from St. Louis had flown to New York to meet with the group's executive committee. "He comes to me and says he has this brilliant idea," Fernandez amusedly recounted. The minister wanted to call for a nationwide fast against the war at the mobilization. "The last syllable wasn't out of his mouth and Bill Coffin says, 'It's a stupid idea.' So, enough. We had this discussion and we weren't going to do it." Then "Coffin gets up there at the closing session [of the mobilization] and says, 'There's going to be a fast.'" It would begin, Coffin declared, on Ash Wednesday the next week.[18]

Fernandez was driving from the Minneapolis airport to Collegeville, Minnesota, to give a speech at St. John's University then. He was skeptical that the fast would take off. And he was hungry. "I debated about whether I'd have lunch before I got to this place . . . or whether I'd go there and see if I could get something to eat," he remembered. "So I waited, and I went into this Catholic institution—they were all fasting. And I turned on the radio and the fast was all over the country. Little Quaker boarding homes in Roanoke, Virginia, were fasting. Everybody was. . . . I couldn't believe it got picked up like that. I mean, it just went zippo." Hundreds of thousands of Americans participated in the three-day "Fast for Renewal of Compassion."[19]

Why protest the war by fasting? To many, fasting seems an oddly quiet way to make a political statement. Some activists felt it would demonstrate the depth of their convictions to others and thereby advance public questioning of the war. But for most the primary motivations were more personal. "If someone had said, 'There's no chance in hell that this will change a thing,'" Fernandez recalled, he would have fasted anyway. "In the first instance it's a time for renewal and reflection," he explained. Fasting gave Fernandez and other activists an opportunity to catch their breath. It also allowed them to evaluate their work in a calmer mental state. Fernandez remembered how he "began to look at things a little differently" during a later fast:

> One of the things I read during that ten-day period was this incredible three- or four-page essay by [the philosopher] Karl Jaspers on German guilt during World War II. And I can't tell if the essay was so brilliant or my fasting had put me in such a vulnerable position, but I have used that essay probably a hundred times since then. There's a tendency in America to distance ourselves from the "good Germans." We'd rather think of Dietrich Bonhoeffer [a prominent theologian executed for opposing Hitler]. And the fact is, most of us, day in and day out, represent good Germans far more than we do any one other thing. Very few of us have a Dietrich Bonhoeffer running around inside of us. And I know the four of us [who fasted] stayed up one night just talking about that essay. And if I had read that at some other point I think I would have been trying to distance myself: "I'm doing something about the war. Look at all these little people." But the fact is, in that setting, it was much more of a feeling of, "What have we *not* done? How could we watch this stuff on TV? I mean, the Germans had no television, and yet we watch . . . American citizens dropping bombs, on the basis of a grid, on people they've never even seen, much less have any certainty that they have ever picked up a gun. . . . Is that worse or not worse than maybe thinking some Jews went to an oven?" And I can remember . . . right after that I was on some trip and I was on a radio program. And I'm sure if I hadn't read that essay I would never have said it. Someone said on the radio, "Are you saying that Richard Nixon is like Adolph Hitler?" And I said, "No, no, no. Not at all—he may be worse. . . . And that makes us, as citizens, worse than the good Germans."

Many activists also considered fasting a form of religious obedience. "We will fast first and primarily because that is what we believe our Lord would have us do during these days," one CALCAV leaflet stated.[20]

Two weeks after CALCAV's mobilization, Washington witnessed another noteworthy display of public opposition to the war. Some twenty-five hundred mainly well-dressed, middle-class women mobilized by Women Strike for Peace "stormed" the Pentagon. The ladies carried large blue shopping bags with bold green letters stating, "Mothers Say Stop the War in Vietnam"; a few hoisted placards urging, "Drop Rusk and McNamara, Not the Bomb." Although they had earlier made appointments to visit Pentagon officials inside, the women found the doors of the massive structure locked. Since this was not the first time that Defense Department authorities had given WSPers the runaround ("They're not reliable!" WSP leader Dagmar Wilson exclaimed, stomping her foot. "They are the weasels if ever there were any"), the women were "really angry." Several took off their shoes and banged the heels on one of the Pentagon's doors. Another tried to hand a general a black wreath, but he refused to touch it and it fell to the ground. "McNamara Come Out!" the women shouted repeatedly under the secretary of defense's window. He declined, however, to see them. Many of the women were accompanied by their children. "Some people take their children to churches," Wilson said later. "We take ours to marches." One protester told her five-year-old within earshot of a reporter, "Now you'll really have something for Show 'n Tell in school."[21]

The women vexed the Johnson administration with their well-publicized act of defiance. On March 2, Robert Kennedy rocked it. The New York senator called for an indefinite halt to the bombing of North Vietnam and the start of peace talks. It was his strongest statement against the war to date. Coming from a political leader of widespread influence—and one Johnson suspected would run for president in 1968—the speech resonated loudly inside the Oval Office. George Christian remembered Johnson working himself into a lather going over press clippings chronicling Kennedy's shifts in position on Vietnam. "He didn't like fellows that would be hawkish one year and dovish the next without any visible reason for the change," Christian smiled. "He used to resent that."[22]

The results of national opinion polls were also troubling Johnson. Shaken by the war's cost in American lives and resources, skeptical that it could ever be won, unsettled by the peace movement's nonstop criticism of the conflict, and tiring of the domestic strife Vietnam was breeding, the public were losing heart in growing numbers. "By 1967," pollster Louis Harris writes, Johnson "no longer cited public opinion poll results supporting him, for there simply were none to be found. The White House no longer called to inquire about the latest poll results. Visitors to the Oval Office came back and reported that the president had said, 'It's a time we have to honker over and take it on the haid.'" During the first quarter of 1967 the number of Americans supporting U.S. policies in Vietnam hovered below the 40 percent mark. Again blacks were especially disapproving, as were women.[23]

Johnson kept close tabs on his personal popularity ratings. He knew they were intimately tied to public attitudes on Vietnam. One day in early 1967, while digesting the news reports spewing out of two "ticker" machines in the White House, the president remarked over his shoulder to a nearby Walt Rostow, "I think [my grandchildren] will be proud of two things. What I did for the Negro and seeing it through in Vietnam for all of Asia. The Negro cost me 15 points in the polls and Vietnam cost me 20." Approximately 47 percent of the American people then approved of the way Johnson was "handling his job as president," as opposed to 67 percent two years earlier when the war began in earnest.[24]

"Murderers Do Not Respond to Reason"

Over the winter and spring of 1967, dark clouds of outright resistance to the war were gathering. By March there were some two dozen "We Won't Go" groups on college campuses, members of which pledged to refuse service in Vietnam. Counseling centers on conscientious objection run by the AFSC and other pacifist groups were attracting thousands of youths. Many black youths were rejecting induction orders. The draft was simply "white people sending black people to make war on yellow people in order to defend the land they stole from red people," SNCC's Stokely Carmichael observed. A number of white youths had also refused induction or publicly destroyed their draft cards.[25]

The National Council of SDS adopted a resolution encouraging draft resistance. "We sat down and purposely read all the laws around the draft so that we could violate every single one of them," SDS Vice President Carl Davidson, the main author of the resolution, humorously remembered. "We wanted to . . . come up with a program that was *totally* illegal." To many SDSers at the meeting, it was unnecessary to put the resolution up for a formal vote. "After going back and forth on the legality of this question," Davidson said, "finally after seventeen hours we decided, if this was so illegal, why did we need a resolution passed in order to support it? We should just go out and do it. We sort of took our anarchism to its logical conclusion."[26]

Activists at Cornell University began planning a national draft-card burning. Veterans of a lively anti-rank sit-in in the spring of 1966, they had formed one of the country's first We Won't Go groups early that fall. The group emphasized slow, grass-roots organizing over public protest. By December one of its leading members, 19-year-old Cornell SDS President Bruce Dancis, had become impatient with that approach. Dancis decided to up the ante for draft protesters at Cornell. At a campus rally, he read a letter he had written his draft board announcing that he was severing his ties to the SSS. Under the watchful eyes of TV news cameras—and FBI agents—Dancis placed the letter in an envelope, ripped his draft card into four pieces, stuffed the mutilated document inside and deposited the envelope in a nearby mailbox. Three months later, incited by his action, five Cornellians called for other youths to burn their draft cards in New York at the April 15 Spring Mobe demonstration if at least five hundred did so. "I sort of pushed all the events faster," Dancis recalled.[27]

Three thousand miles away, a national organization of draft resisters was independently taking shape. Early on the morning of March 8, David Harris, who had earlier returned to the government several draft cards bearing his name, met with his friend Dennis Sweeney and the Berkeley antiwar activists Steve Hamilton and Lennie Heller. Sitting in the rickety communal house Harris and Sweeney shared with a handful of others in East Palo Alto, California, smoking "a lot of dope," the four youths talked of holding a national draft-card turn-in in the fall. Hamilton and Heller had come prepared for serious organizing. They handed Harris and Sweeney some literature with the name "The Resistance" printed on it. This prospective name for their new group pointed to the resistance in Europe to Nazi occupation during World War II. Hamilton and Heller felt the war would soon bring fascistic political conditions to the United States. They were not alone. As Bettina Aptheker remembered, in 1967 "when you said the word *resistance*, it was with a capital *R*, and you meant the resistance to fascism in Europe. . . . People had a sense of very great repression in this country. . . . People felt like fascism was creeping in on us from a lot of different directions." Inspirited by hearty conversation, the four young activists decided to move. The following month they announced the Resistance's formation and their plan to hold a national draft-card turn-in on October 16.[28]

The upsurge in antidraft activity in early 1967 had strikingly diverse causes. Many young people had come to conclude that the whole draft system, particularly its provision for student deferments, had an unacceptable class bias. Also, signs were emerging with shocking lucidity that student deferments were oppressive themselves. *Ramparts* and *New Left Notes* publicized a memo written by SSS Director Lewis Hershey on the *real* reason for the draft system. According to Hershey, procuring manpower for the military was "not much of an administrative or financial challenge. It is in dealing with the other millions of registrants that the System is heavily occupied, developing more effective human beings in the national interest." Threatened by the "club of induction," students were being "channeled," they learned, into training and jobs deemed "essential" to the country's welfare by the same government that was waging the war. Hershey bragged:

> Many young men would not have pursued a higher education if there had not been a program of student deferment. Many young scientists, engineers, tool and die makers, and other possessors of scarce skills would not remain in their jobs in the defense effort if it were not for a program of occupational deferments.
> . . . From the individual's viewpoint, he is standing in a room

which has been made uncomfortably warm. Several doors are open, but they all lead to various forms of recognized, patriotic service to the Nation.

The growth in public opposition to the war had also enhanced draft resistance's appeal. Many youth perceived that it would now elicit a substantial popular response. And with draft calls skyrocketing and class ranking continuing, more than a few students feared losing their deferments and receiving a one-way ticket to Vietnam. By resisting the draft they might save their skins. Conscription "was perceived as a life or death question," Carl Davidson recalled. Students felt "if they don't pass, get a good grade on this test, maybe they'll flunk out—and then they'll die."[29]

But the single most important reason for heightened fascination with anti-draft activity in 1967 was the perception that previous peace protests had exerted insufficient influence on the war. If the government would not heed legal protest, many young people reasoned, it was time to take their opposition to a deeper level. Dancis remembered feeling

> that the antiwar movement had to become much more serious. That the days of writing postcards to congressmen and taking part in demonstrations [were] already growing short. That is, we were frustrated by the lack of action [by the government]. Even as the antiwar movement was growing very rapidly, we were having *no* effect on U.S. policy. The escalation was going further and further every day. There'd be ten thousand, fifty thousand more troops, more bombing and all that. So we thought we had to up the ante.
> . . . Like most young, inexperienced, naïve radicals in the sixties, we thought things were going to happen a lot faster than they did. . . . We never really understood the power of the United States government.

The call for the April 15 draft-card burning dramatically captured the frustration of young people over the mounting war: "We have argued and demonstrated to stop this destruction. We have not succeeded. Murderers do not respond to reason. Powerful resistance is now demanded: radical, illegal, unpleasant, sustained."[30]

For virtually all draft resisters, upping the ante was partly personal moral expression. For David Harris, personal morality was the bottom line. Sitting in the basement office of his woodsy, spacious California home years later, sweating from a freshly completed workout on his exercise machine, the bald, strapping, wild-eyed Harris stressed that he "didn't know what difference" draft resistance "was going to make in the end" for the war. That wasn't the crux of the matter. "I was in the antiwar movement because we were *right*," Harris said firmly between drags on a post-exertion cigarette. "And even if the government went ahead and did everything they had in mind, I wanted to be on public record as being as far against that policy as you could be—which I think I succeeded at." He elaborated:

> The way I came to the position of noncooperation is the same way I came to my position about the war—which was from the perspective of somebody who was supposed to fight it. . . . I was supposed to go kill people. Theoretically, I can accept the notion that there are circumstances in which you have to kill people. I could not accept the notion that Vietnam was one of those circumstances. And to me that left the option of either sitting by and watching what was an enormous injustice, perhaps the greatest injustice that a human being can do to another—killing them for no good reason—watch that be perpetrated, or find some way to commit myself against it. And the position that I felt comfortable with in committing myself against it was total noncooperation—I was not going to be part of the machine. And first and foremost as an isolated moral individual. Whether nobody joined me or not, I was going to do what I was doing. And if people joined me and we had a much larger effect, all the better. And I set out to organize that larger effect. But if we had been totally unsuccessful I would have still done what I did, because I felt that anybody with the morality that I claimed to have was obliged to do so.[31]

Yet even Harris envisioned political returns from draft resistance. Few who took that step were concerned solely with exorcising their personal demons. Resistance organizers claimed they were waging a multidimensional assault on the war. As noncooperation caught on among draft-age youth, they argued, it would expand exponentially, forcing the government to undertake mass prosecutions of resisters to maintain its legitimacy. But the courts and prisons would be unable to absorb the onslaught of lawbreakers, they contended, and the resulting bureaucratic knots would coerce the government to end the war.

Resisters also maintained that noncooperation would increase protesters' credibility with the public. By challenging the government to send them to jail, resisters asserted, they were demonstrating that their opposition to the war sprang not from cowardice or youthful frivolity—as supporters of the war often alleged—but from unyielding moral convictions. Since most students came from middle-class backgrounds, the Resistance's message was directed predominately at this community. Harris explained:

> The question in the antiwar movement was how to talk to new people, how to break yourself into new audiences, and quite specifically for college students, how to bring the question of the war home

to the segment of the population that they represented, which was also the principal power base of the government: the white middle class. That's where wars are made and wars are stopped. And we all came from it. I felt that in order to speak clearly to that group of people (which included my own parents, for example), it was necessary to put your body where your mouth was. You know, there was a lot of cheap talk going on in the antiwar movement: "We're against the war, we're against the war"—and then taking special privileges. And one of the first things that opponents of the antiwar movement pointed to was, "Hey, look, our young men are over in Vietnam dying, and these guys are sitting around smoking dope." I felt that in order for the antiwar movement to be effective speaking to that larger audience, it had to pay its own prices and make its own sacrifices and put itself in a position of vulnerability. Because I thought they were right, the critics were. I thought there were a lot of SDS members in Berkeley who were sitting around being tourists in the movement, myself. I don't care how radical they talked—they weren't paying any prices. When it came down to whether they would even [refuse to] carry a draft card in their pocket, they were chickenshit. The biggest problem we had when we set out organizing was with SDS, not with the government. Because there were a lot of armchair radicals who wanted to go scream "Off the pig!" at the rally and then go hide behind their student deferments. Oh, I don't blame the rest of the public for looking down on that kind of activity. *I* look down on that kind of activity. . . . Propagandizing by example, as it were, was the only way to be taken seriously as far as I was concerned.

Through making themselves just as susceptible to the draft as poor and working-class youths, noncooperators hoped to increase their credibility among these groups as well.[32]

Resistance organizers expected that mass prosecutions of noncooperators would also promote public debate on the war. Not only would Americans be impressed by their courage, but the war would simply become such an intrusion in people's lives that they couldn't avoid weighing its merits. Michael Ferber said he and other Resistance activists "did a lot of thinking about" the likely "ripple effects" of noncooperation throughout society:

One young man gets indicted and goes to prison. Well, there's his family, there's his friends, there's his school, there's his church. We were talking about these widening constituencies of support. . . . We were aware that some of the guys we'd get would be ruling-class kids, at least Ivy League kids, and that they had influential connections. And we were aware that when we got people like that we would start splitting the country in the place that it hadn't been split.[33]

Resisters further believed that many Americans—including government officials—would lose enthusiasm for the war because of the "turmoil" draft resistance was wreaking in the United States. Even if the criminal justice system could process the host of lawbreakers, they maintained, their wholesale defiance of the law would suggest a society splitting at the seams. "We were going to make the country so torn about this," Ferber remembered. "The universities were going to be a mess, the churches were going to be mobilized. We just felt we'd make enough trouble." The government "couldn't tolerate this kind of resistance . . . very long," he thought.[34]

Resistance organizers hoped their courage would inspire greater commitment from the rest of the antiwar movement as well. "We were aware also that we would be a kind of spearhead," Ferber said, sparking "a lot of other groups to do less kamikaze sorts of things." If widespread prison sentences resulted, all the better. "Many of our fellows on the campus and in the community at large will then be moved to action by a fresh instance of that repression which is becoming an increasingly important factor of American life," one Resistance flyer predicted.[35]

Finally, some resisters anticipated restricting the supply of American soldiers available for deployment to Vietnam. "Our ultimate strategy was to deny the government the troops with which to wage the war," Harris recalled.[36]

The Spring Mobilization

On April 4, one month after the Resistance's birth, Rev. Martin Luther King, Jr., delivered his weightiest statement on the war yet. U.S. intervention in Vietnam, he cried to an overflow crowd of three thousand in New York's Riverside Church, was extracting resources from America's poor "like some demonic, destructive suction tube." Blacks were dying "in extraordinarily high proportions relative to the rest of the population . . . to guarantee liberties in Southeast Asia which they had not found in Southwest Georgia and East Harlem." The minister called the U.S. government "the greatest purveyor of violence in the world today." After the speech, King was "in a buoyant mood," David Garrow writes, "pleased that he had finally made the moral declaration he had felt obligated to deliver ever since that January day when he saw the photos in *Ramparts*."[37]

Many influential liberals were in foul moods. *Washington Post* editorialists informed the nation that King's speech was "not a sober and responsible comment on the war" but "filled with bitter and damaging allegations and inferences that he did not and could not document." King, they asserted, had inflicted "grave injury" on both himself and his "natural allies" in the civil rights movement. "And this is a great tragedy." The editorial staff of the *New York Times* warned that King's attempt to link "his personal opposition to the war . . . with the cause of Negro equality" could be "disastrous" to the pursuit of both peace in Vietnam and racial justice. "There are no simple or easy answers" to either issue, the *Times* declared. "Linking these hard, complex problems will lead not to solutions but to deeper confusion."[38]

Other Americans—including one *New York Times* journalist—attained greater political clarity listening to King, however. Tom Wicker remembered being impressed by King's observation that blacks were dying in Vietnam at a disproportionate rate relative to whites. "That had a considerable effect on me," Wicker said. "That was an insight that I hadn't had."[39] Hardly a "disastrous" outcome for those concerned with ending the war.

The day after King's speech, John Roche sent President Johnson an EYES ONLY memo on it. The White House adviser claimed King was in dire straits. Roche wrote:

> Yesterday's speech by Nobel Laureate Martin Luther King was quite an item. To me it indicates that King—in desperate search of a con-stituency—has thrown in with the commies.
>
> As you know, the civil rights movement is shot—disorganized and broke. King, who is inordinately ambitious and quite stupid (a bad combination), is thus looking back to a promising future.
>
> The Communist-oriented "peace" types have played him (and his driving wife) like trout. They have—in effect—guaranteed him ideo-logical valet service. There will always be a crowd to applaud, money to keep up his standard of living, etc.
>
> In my judgment, however, his recruitment to "peace" will cut two ways: he will become the folk-hero of the alienated whites, but lose his Negro support *both* among "black nationalists" (who see him as a threat to their operations) and among the great bulk of the Negro community (who are solid, sensible supporters of the Administration).
>
> In short, King is destroying his reputation as a "Negro leader" for a mess of "Charlies'" pottage. He is painting himself into a corner with a bunch of losers.

Most of Roche's colleagues in the administration were not so sanguine. They knew King's transformation into an antiwar spokesman would advance domestic opposition to the conflict, as well as erect bridges between civil rights and peace activists. Asked to describe his reaction to King's spring offensive against the war, the White House Counsel Harry McPherson groused, "Bad. I mean, I was disturbed. And not a little angered." McPherson realized it would strengthen the peace movement. On April 8, George Christian contacted the black colum-nist Carl Rowan (a former USIA director), apparently to prod him to criticize King's stand. Rowan didn't need much prodding. He told Christian he was "exploring the Martin Luther King matter" and wanted to "take out after King" because he felt the minister had "hurt the Civil Rights movement with his statements." A few days later, Rowan revealed to the country that King was taking advice from an extremist aide "who is clearly more interested in embarrassing the United States than in the plight of either the Negro or the war-weary people of Vietnam." The FBI found King's words even more alarming. J. Edgar Hoover wrote Johnson, "Based on King's recent activities and public utterances, it is clear that he is an instrument in the hands of subversive forces seeking to undermine our nation."[40]

King was not, of course, the subversive threat the FBI imagined. Around the time of his Riverside Church speech, he threatened to pull out of the Spring Mobilization because several of his financial backers said they would withhold $20,000 if he didn't. That evening Dave Dellinger, Andrew Young, the Mobe organizer Robert Greenblatt, James Bevel, and several others gathered in a hotel room. Dellinger would remember "Greenblatt and I telling Andy Young that we were going to have so many people there that we didn't need King anyway. If he didn't come, he was going to be left behind." King reboarded the peace train. "I always felt that that was the key thing," Dellinger said. "That Andy Young became convinced that King was going to be . . . abandoned" if he didn't join the demonstration.[41]

King had another concern about the Spring Mobilization that was shared by many Mobe leaders themselves: the draft-card burning planned by Bruce Dancis and his friends. "We had major fights with the Mobe about this," Dancis recalled. "They got very upset." Some Mobe activists worried that burning draft cards would prevent the demonstration from projecting a "respectable" tone (to which the Mobe's David McReynolds annoyedly retorted, "Fuck it, this *is* respectable, this is the American tradition! We are acting within the framework of everything that built this country!"). Dancis remembered that "at one point the Mobe executive committee *chartered* a plane and flew down around seven of us from Cornell for a big meeting, where they tried to dissuade us from doing it. And we refused to go along with [them]." Intent on holding the Mobe together, Sidney Peck and other coalition leaders convinced its nervous members to permit the draft-card burning without granting it Mobe sponsorship. Competitive with Dellinger generally, Peck unsuccessfully motioned that Dellinger be replaced as Mobe chair for approving the burning before discussing it inside the Mobe.[42]

The U.S. government was also anxious about the draft-card burning. Dancis recalled that he and other Cornell organizers were "so naive in those days" that they sent out the calls for it through the regular mail. "We found out later a lot of them never got through," he said. Compliments of federal authorities, "we got tons of them returned to us." About ten days before the protest, Dancis was indicted for tearing up his draft card the previous December. When he obtained his bulky FBI file years later, Dancis discovered a memo from J. Edgar Hoover to the U.S. attorney's and FBI offices in upstate New York stating, "It's very important that you indict Dancis before April 15 action." Dancis contended that the Justice Department figured it could hinder the growth of the draft resistance movement by going after its leaders. "It was very clear that, in indicting me before the action, the goal was to scare people off," he said. "My file really takes off . . . once I tore up my draft card and we started organizing the draft-card burning. I mean, there's a massive amount of information [in it]. They were following me wherever I went. Every speech I made is recorded in there. They were very concerned."[43]

Yet Dancis gives the government too much credit. Ramsey Clark, who was U.S. attorney general then, later convincingly denied that the Justice Department had "a national policy of hitting leaders" of the draft resistance movement. "We had ninety-three federal judicial districts, but we had no real central oversight," Clark said. "Each U.S. attorney would be sitting out there in Denver or someplace doing his thing." These attorneys "instinctively" went after antidraft leaders, Clark surmised. Leaders' acts were more noticeable than those of other activists, picking off a leader provided a greater sense of accomplishment, and the attorneys could express their feelings toward protesters generally by picking off antiwar spokespeople. Leaders were most likely to "evoke some animus" from the attorneys too. "We had a lot of that," Clark irritatedly recalled. "I had a hard time controlling U.S. attorneys when I would put out policies on these things." Some "would simply *defy* your decisions not to prosecute." For his part, J. Edgar Hoover "had a very low level of interest in something like this," Clark believed. "I don't know how to explain that letter [urging timely indictment of Dancis], but my strong impression about the way the FBI was functioning and the way Hoover was functioning is that if you had asked him the day after that letter was signed who that person was, he wouldn't have known. I'm almost sure of that. . . . The idea that he was following campuses and student leaders across the country with a personal interest and knowledge I think is far removed from the actual reality." Perhaps "some special agent in charge up there generated some activity that led an assistant director to cause a letter like that" to be written, Clark suggested. "One of the bad things that happens when you have a personality cult like that [around Hoover] is that you've got people who are ambitious, who want to appeal to the boss, so they do things that they think he will like, and he may not even have a feeling about it."[44]

April 15 was a cold, gray day in New York. Despite light rain, demonstrators surged into Sheep Meadow in Central Park throughout the morning. They would eventually total more than three hundred thousand. It was the largest demonstration in U.S. history. In Fred Halstead's words, "It was a hugey."[45]

The crowd spanned a wide cross section of American society. Youth predominated, some sporting long hair and jeans, others tweed coats and ties. Also present were middle-aged businessmen in dark suits, housewives in dresses and nylons, bespectacled high school science teachers, and doctors in long white coats. There were nuns and priests outfitted in robes and collars and professors adorned with tassels, mortarboards, and gowns. Hundreds of medal-decorated war veterans with blue hats marked "Veterans for Peace" perched on their heads were gathered at the southern end of the park. Nearby stood a contingent of American Indians in native attire. Entire families dotted the crowd.[46]

Many were protesting for the first time. A housewife from New Jersey told a reporter, "So many of us are frustrated. We want to criticize this war because we think it's wrong but we want to do it in the framework of loyalty. I hope this demonstration won't encourage the North Vietnamese. . . . Maybe the President's right and we don't know what we're talking about. Maybe we shouldn't be protesting. . . . Oh, but this war. . . ." One study of the marchers' traits found that 43 percent of the 531 people who arrived by train from Cleveland had never attended a demonstration before.[47]

Observers were impressed by the mass of humanity. As the demonstrators waited in Central Park for the march to begin, a maintenance man on his lunch hour peered at them. "It makes you think," he murmured. "It makes you think who's right, *who is right?*"[48] That the demonstration was endorsed by Harry Belafonte, Linus Pauling, Norman Mailer, and television's "Man from Uncle," Robert Vaughn, enhanced its legitimacy among the public. Some citizens questioned an event that not a single congressman had endorsed, however.

At 11 A.M., on an outcropping of rock in the southeastern corner of Sheep Meadow, sixty young men prepared to burn their draft cards. The organizers of the burning had known for days that they would fall far short of their original goal of five hundred resisters, "but clearly the momentum was such and people had gotten to the point where we knew we were going to go through with it," Dancis remembered. A chain of supporters encircled the youths to keep hostile onlookers and reporters away. "We had very little regard for the media at the time," Dancis lamented. "Like a lot of people in the New Left, we were suspicious of it. . . . I refused interviews with the press. . . . Looking back on it, [that] was stupid. We could have articulated what we were trying to do much more effectively had we been willing to be interviewed." The resisters hoped to make "a very dignified statement." Following a speech by one of their leaders, they had earlier decided, each would give a brief explanation of why he was burning his draft card. But the crush of spectators was so great that "the whole thing collapsed." Youths huddled together around cigarette lighters and matches;

some passed their cards to the proud holder of a flaming coffee can. Cries of "Resist! Resist!" rose up from the crowd as the white cards caught fire. Scores of young men spontaneously rushed forward from the fringes to add their cards to the flaming tin. The protesters were startled when a burly blond youth wearing a Green Beret uniform and a solemn expression on his face stepped into the middle of the crowd. To the surprise of most, Army reservist Gary Rader pulled his draft card out of his wallet and set it on fire.[49]

New York Red Squad and FBI agents swarmed around the area like bees around a hive. At one point two plainclothesmen edged into the center of the crowd. One snatched a burning piece of paper from the coffee can and began to examine it. As the crowd closed in on him, the other ran away. "Go get him," yelled the first agent. The protesters turned to look at the fleeing figure. His partner then sauntered off, "the paper in his pocket, a smile on his face."[50]

The draft-card burning was the largest to date. About a hundred and seventy young men destroyed their cards. Their courage inspired others to resist the draft in the months ahead and strengthened the resolve of antiwar activists far and wide. "We call ourselves CADRE," wrote Rader of the Chicago Area Draft Resistance group that summer. "We speak of squads, escalation, campaigns. The terminology is no accident—it fits our attitude. We are no longer interested in merely protesting the war; we are out to stop it."[51]

At 12:20 P.M. the marchers began inching out of Central Park. At the head of the monstrous assemblage, arms linked, were King, Belafonte, Dr. Benjamin Spock, Stokely Carmichael, and other civil rights and peace leaders. Slogans on the protesters' placards included "No Vietnamese Ever Called Me 'Nigger.'" When the demonstrators reached the UN building they began spilling into side streets and alleys, creating pedestrian gridlock. The Mobe's Fred Halstead tried to convince New York Police Department official Sanford Garelik to move some police barricades to provide more room. Gerelik became agitated and snapped, "Look, you made your point! There's a lot of people against this war. Why don't you just go home?" Right-wing counterdemonstrators gathered across the street from the UN shared Garelik's wish; they taunted the marchers, recited the "Pledge of Allegiance," and denounced watchful cops as "Cossacks" and "Commies." The rally ended shortly after 5 P.M. when a downpour soaked the UN plaza. A few thoroughly drenched marchers continued to trickle in, though.[52]

The same day, sixty thousand demonstrated amidst periodic rain in San Francisco. The Santa Clara County Labor Council's endorsement of the protest and the participation of thousands of trade union members were marked signs of the peace movement's continuing growth.

As Sidney Peck wrote later, the April 15 demonstrations were "successful beyond all expectations."[53] They showed the Johnson administration and public that the antiwar movement had carved out a large political base in the United States. No longer could peace activists be discarded as a tiny minority of crazies.

To minimize the political damage inflicted by the Spring Mobilization, U.S. officials characterized it as the work of sinister forces. "I have no doubt at all that the Communist apparatus is very busy indeed in these operations all over the world and in our own country," Secretary of State Dean Rusk commented on NBC's *Meet the Press* on April 16. Asked if he had any evidence to support this charge, Rusk replied with a slight grin, "I am giving you my responsible personal view that the Communist apparatus is working very hard on it." Press Secretary George Christian announced that the FBI was keeping a close watch on "antiwar activity."[54]

The Spring Mobilization was derided by others as well. "The war in Vietnam is not a simple bedtime story between heroes and villains," the *New York Times* asserted. In calling for unilateral U.S. withdrawal from Vietnam, argued the *Times*, the Mobe was guilty of "romantic posturing." William F. Buckley, Jr., regarded the massive crowd in New York and spat in his typically arrogant style, "There are a lot of people in the zoo, too."[55]

Among those marching in New York were Committee for Nonviolent Action members undertaking a "Boston-to-Pentagon Walk for Peace." They paused in New York only long enough to demonstrate and catch a short rest. When they arrived in Virginia, the long-distance marchers launched a small, quiet, mannerly, yet unflinching human piercing of the Pentagon. "For about two days people just tried to walk into the War Room," the CNVA leader Brad Lyttle amusedly recounted. "They were these inoffensive pacifist types, and they would stand around there in the corridor of the Pentagon . . . chatting with the officers and security people. And pretty soon these folks would lose interest in the guarding—they didn't feel there was any threat. And then our people would just walk in after a general into the War Room. That got them a little bit upset." The guards grabbed the intruders, hauled them outside, and deposited them on the lawn. But the pacifists "kept getting up and walking back into the Pentagon." Finally the authorities "just arrested everybody they could see," Lyttle recalled.[56]

Liberal Stirrings

Nine days after the Spring Mobilization, the peace movement gained influential new recruits. A group of prominent liberals announced a campaign to collect one million signatures on a petition urging the Johnson administration to stop bombing North Vietnam and asking Hanoi and the NLF to join in a cease-fire. "Negotiations Now" included Victor Reuther of the United Automobile Workers, University of California President Clark Kerr, Joseph Rauh of Americans for Democratic Action, and the former Kennedy administration officials John Kenneth Galbraith and Arthur Schlesinger, Jr.

In 1986 Schlesinger was Albert Schweitzer Professor of the Humanities at the City University of New York. He was a friendly, dapper man with calm, mournful eyes, thick-rimmed glasses, a downturned mouth and a creased brow; his thinning gray hair fell to one side. Schlesinger characteristically sported a bow tie. Situated high above Manhattan's busy Forty-second Street, his roomy, book-filled office provided a tranquil perspective on the multitudes below.

Schlesinger had traveled a leftward political path between early 1965 and the birth of Negotiations Now. His journey was in many ways typical of those of other liberals during this period. Prior to the entry of U.S. ground forces into Vietnam in the spring of 1965, Schlesinger recalled, he had not paid "a great deal of attention to" the war. "In fact, I now repent," he smiled. After urging further U.S. troop deployments at the national teach-in that May, Schlesinger became increasingly apprehensive about the war. He thought the massive infusion of U.S. troops in late July overdone. By the end of the year, Schlesinger felt that continued escalation was "a great mistake." His misgivings intensified in 1966. Although a call for U.S. withdrawal from Vietnam was not worthy of "serious" Americans, Schlesinger wrote that fall, the United States should cut back Rolling Thunder to entice the enemy to negotiate. He described U.S. policy in Vietnam as "intellectual indolence" the following January. In joining Negotiation Now's campaign for a cease-fire in 1967, Schlesinger was advocating a step he had rejected only months earlier as "possibly very dangerous."[57]

What accounts for the professor's dovish journey? Schlesinger had come to feel that militarily Vietnam was "a hopeless situation. . . . That to win the war would require destruction and savagery out of all proportion to anything we stood to gain in the area." Schlesinger was also troubled that the conflict was "destroying the Great Society." The criticisms of U.S. policy voiced by Robert Kennedy, George McGovern, Eugene McCarthy, J. William Fulbright, and Walter Lippmann, among others, fed Schlesinger's discontent.[58]

So did antiwar activists. Schlesinger came to suspect that the views his "old friend" Hans Morgenthau advanced at the national teach-in in 1965 had a "long-run impact" on his opinions. Although "not terribly impressed by the intellectual arguments" of street demonstrators and "not happy about" their "excesses," the cost in domestic social peace they were exacting for the war weighed heavily on Schlesinger. "I suppose it must have had considerable effect," he later reflected. Writing in the second half of 1966 about this "frightful" price of the war, Schlesinger lamented such "ugly side-effects" as "protest," "indignation," and "angry divisions within our national community." "Above all," argued Schlesinger, the war "has estranged us from the future. For the future of all countries, developed or underdeveloped, depends on their youth. . . . These were exactly the young men and women who at the start of the sixties were beginning to look on the United States as the hope of the world; exactly those today who watch our course in Vietnam with perplexity, loathing and despair."[59]

Among the disgruntled young people on Schlesinger's mind were four of his own children. Three were college students during the 1960s, and the fourth was in VISTA. "All of them were opposed to the war," Schlesinger recalled. "They were all sort of active, but not fanatic in their participation in antiwar protests and so on." He reasoned that since his children's opposition to the war evolved "somewhat ahead of mine," their views "probably . . . had some impact on me."[60]

During the late 1960s the domestic strife the war was breeding continued to fuel Schlesinger's desire for peace in Vietnam. The war "was leading to all kinds of disruptions and concerns which were very alarming" and "causing general trouble," he remembered. Partly as a result, Schlesinger would conclude by the end of the decade that unilateral U.S. withdrawal was not only fit for consideration by serious people but the "only sensible position" to take on the war. "That's the position that I should have taken from the start," he avowed.[61]

The birth of Negotiations Now in the spring of 1967 nudged other liberals leftward. It fortified their doubts about the war and suggested that it was politically acceptable to speak out. John Oakes, the editor of the *New York Times's* editorial page, recalled that "Negotiations Now was something that I felt quite strongly about. . . . Certainly I would have been influenced by . . . that." Oakes had "a lot of respect for" Clark Kerr of Negotiations Now and was "an admirer of what he was doing."[62]

Former Federal Reserve Board Chairman Marriner S. Eccles was active in Negotiations Now. In late May, Eccles and more than three hundred other business executives signed an open letter to President Johnson asking him to "stop the war" for "moral" and "practical" reasons. The statement was printed in the *New York Times, Washington Post,* and *Wall Street Journal.* By September nearly six hundred business executives had signed it.[63]

The businessmen were worried about the war's impact on the economy. Afraid of advancing public opposition to the conflict, the reader will recall, Johnson had decided in 1965 to try to fund both it and his Great Society program without raising taxes or imposing economic controls. He and Robert McNamara had also deliberately understated the war's cost to Congress. The results were heavy deficit spending and booming inflation. By 1967 expenditures on Vietnam were creating a serious international balance-of-payments problem as well. Many businessmen feared that continued escalation would bring more bad economic news. Ralph Lazarus, the president of Federated Department Stores and a member of the Business Council, complained at a press conference in May that the war's cost in fiscal year 1968 would exceed the official estimate by five billion dollars. (Lazarus was immediately telephoned by U.S. Supreme Court

Justice Abe Fortas, a Johnson crony, who told him that he had upset no less than the president of the United States with his faulty estimate, and would he mind lowering it. The war's actual cost would surpass even Lazarus's projection, however.)[64]

The day before Negotiations Now sprang up, peace activists unveiled another new antiwar campaign. Rev. Martin Luther King, Jr., Dr. Benjamin Spock, and Robert Scheer stated at a packed press conference that "Vietnam Summer," a national community organizing project, was geared toward reaching the many "silent Americans" who were "deeply worried about the war." Vietnam Summer was endorsed by John Kenneth Galbraith and Wayne Morse.[65] Its creator was a former State Department and congressional aide named Gar Alperovitz.

Alperovitz felt the time was ripe for the project. For months he had suspected there was greater public antiwar sentiment than peace activists were tapping. A national canvassing effort, the Harvard research fellow thought, might significantly augment their returns. Not only was canvassing "sufficiently simple and replicable" to "permit large numbers of people to engage large numbers of people" in discussion of the war, but through such dialogue critics of the war would realize "they were not alone" and could speak out without fear of public censure. What's more, these critics would realize they were numerous enough to influence their government. Alperovitz felt many Americans were silent on the war because they believed opposing it was futile. The "dominant" public attitude at the time was that

> "nothing can be done. You can have a protest but that isn't going to change anything. The establishment's too powerful. . . ." You look in retrospect, there was a movement that built up. But at the time it didn't seem like power was building. It just seemed like an occasional protest. . . . [Johnson] was steadily escalating. Everyone in Congress, with a few exceptions, was voting for [the war]. The media was for it. The major labor unions were for it. Every major institution of this system was committed. . . . All the decisions are going the other way.[66]

Alperovitz expected that antiwar canvassers would prod silent Americans to start taking "little steps" against the war. They might sign a petition, for example. "My theory of that was, if they engaged at one level, they'd pretty soon find that they had to do something more," Alperovitz recalled. "They'd climb up the ladder. But let them take the first step to the level that they're comfortable with." With any luck, new local peace groups would take root. Alperovitz was unconcerned about the specific types of antiwar activities that sprouted up. "The idea was that 'this organization is mobilizing opposition to the war indiscriminately,'" he remembered. "We were not taking a position on who should do what. It was . . . 'different strokes for different folks, any place, everywhere, break down ideological barriers and go see the people.'" Alperovitz did hope for a major increase in grass-roots pressure on U.S. legislators, though. "Congressmen are like weather vanes," his previous work on Capitol Hill had convinced him. "If there is a lot of wind blowing from [their constituents], they move."[67]

Alperovitz understood that Vietnam Summer would have to be a *summer* project. It would rely heavily upon campus activists who were only available full-time during the summer. Also, funding a longer project would be difficult. But most compelling to Alperovitz were the "enormous rivalries" between the national peace organizations:

> This was an organization that came out of nowhere. . . . We just invented it. And the existing barons in the peace movement didn't like it until it was made clear that it did not intend to become an ongoing organization. . . . There was nervousness that some new organization of unknowns was encroaching on their territory. You know, it was a typical problem. And we thought that the existing peace organizations weren't reaching [many people], but we also weren't interested in having a big fight. We were interested in fighting the war rather than the peace organizations.[68]

Yet the movement's internal strife would soon infect Vietnam Summer itself.

Shortly after the April press conference, Alperovitz persuaded CALCAV's Richard Fernandez and the veteran SDSer Lee Webb to co-direct Vietnam Summer. By mid June more than three thousand project volunteers were active in communities as diverse as Laramie, Wyoming, and Roxbury, Massachusetts.[69]

On May 18–20, Vietnam Summer spokesmen King and Spock joined Sidney Peck and other Spring Mobe leaders for a vigil in front of the White House. They demanded that Johnson end the war in the name of the people who had demonstrated on April 15. The president declined their invitation to meet with them or speak at an immediately following Mobe conference. "Obviously we will regret," aide Marvin Watson wrote Johnson in forwarding him the Mobe's offer. J. Edgar Hoover sent the White House a report on the rabble parading outside the mansion. As was his wont, the FBI director smeared the protesters with a red brush. The Mobe included "members of the Communist Party and the Socialist Workers Party," Hoover stressed, "both of which have been designated as subversive by the Attorney General." Peck's most telling attribute was that he was "a former member of the Communist Party."[70] Hoover's smearing of protesters would continue in the months and years ahead, impeding rather than advancing the White House's understanding of its antagonists.

Dissenting Veterans and War Crimes

On June 1, another new peace organization was born. Although tiny, Vietnam Veterans Against the War (VVAW) would ultimately exert a powerful impact on the American psyche. Its founder, Jan Barry, was a lean, big-boned, 24-year-old veteran who had dropped out of West Point in 1965 so that he could publicly criticize a war that "made no sense whatsoever." Since then he had been "looking for the peace movement." Barry had noticed various antiwar demonstrations, but, as someone without political experience or contacts, he didn't know who to get in touch with about joining a peace group. He was also a bit queasy about marching in the street. "I was looking for something a little bit more responsible," Barry would recall. He had even moved to New York to aid his search for an acceptable point of entry into the peace movement. In the early spring of 1967, Barry got wind of the April 15 Mobe demonstration planned for Manhattan. Not only did it promise to be broader-based than previous protests, but Veterans for Peace had placed an ad in the New York Times asking veterans to participate in it. The prospect of meeting other veterans interested Barry. For two years he had been hearing that "there were a lot of bitter, bitter, bitter people coming back" from Vietnam, but he had been unable to find them. "They just disappeared into the woodwork," Barry remembered. On the morning of April 15, he and some friends headed off to Central Park. They "had no idea what to expect."[71]

Barry was impressed by the "enormous mob of people" in Sheep Meadow and "this great big contingent" of Veterans for Peace activists at the southern end of the park. As he approached the contingent, Barry heard someone say, "Vietnam veterans, go to the front." He thought, "Fine, I'm going to go join whoever that is." Reaching the front of the now moving procession, Barry saw someone dressed in a suit, tie, and raincoat hoisting a banner reading, "Vietnam Veterans Against the War." Marching next to the man were a handful of other Vietnam veterans. Barry felt uncomfortable. There seemed to be an awful lot of space between this small group, the dignitaries leading the parade, and the Veterans for Peace contingent behind the group. "We felt really naked," he recounted. "I said, 'Oh, shit, the snipers. And all these buildings . . .'" It seemed to Barry that the Vietnam veterans were "walking point" just as some had in the jungles of Vietnam. His anxiety grew when some right-wing counterdemonstrators started screaming at the dignitaries in the front. But the counterdemonstrators "shut up" when they saw signs denoting veterans. "And then they started screaming at the next group of people." It was an enlightening experience for Barry.[72]

Shortly after the demonstration, Barry attended a meeting of Veterans for Peace. To his disappointment, the group did not include any veterans of Vietnam. "They had hoped that some Vietnam veterans would come [to the demonstration], so they made a banner," Barry recalled. "And up until that time they had met one Vietnam veteran active in the peace movement. So I found this one Vietnam veteran and I proposed that we start our own organization." Members of Veterans for Peace were unhappy with Barry's plan. They "would have preferred that we stay under their umbrella," he said. "But I felt that we would be losing that direct ability for us to say, 'We've been there. This is the experience.' . . . I [also] didn't think we would get very many Vietnam veterans to join something just called 'Veterans for Peace.'" And that group's opposition to the war seemed weakly stated.[73]

After Barry and five other Vietnam veterans formally established VVAW on June 1, they "just started reaching out. If anybody'd heard of a Vietnam veteran, or if we saw somebody interviewed in the newspaper, we would track the guy down. Piece by piece we put together a national network, consisting of a very small number of people." The VVAWers spoke at rallies, distributed leaflets, collected signatures on petitions, and appeared on local radio and television. At first the sky seemed the limit of their political influence. "I literally felt at the time that if they would put me on national television for one half an hour that the war would end," Barry remembered. The veterans experienced a rude awakening. "You'd go to Times Square and people would scream at you. . . . People would come and interview us from the news media, and soon the interviewer started hollering and yelling at us. . . . It was a real fight." Wearing faded military fatigues and very nonmilitary hairdos, the veterans were merely "a curiousity" to some. Barry eventually "had a dream in which I had a meeting with LBJ. Here I am in the same room with him, and I give him my spiel—and he couldn't care less."[74]

But the small army of VVAWers was not ineffective. The veterans' experiences in Vietnam gave them unique credibility on the war. Occasionally they would debate government spokesmen. The veterans gave the officials a rough go. "We did our homework," Barry said. "We weren't just dumb GIs." Although soldiers were often their most vitriolic critics, the VVAWers found that spending a few hours with GIs could produce new allies. They also convinced other protesters to reach out to soldiers rather than berate them, thereby advancing antiwar sentiment inside the U.S. military. "When we would meet other people in the peace movement we constantly said to them, 'Stop screaming at the GIs! Talk to them. Listen to them. They might really agree with you,'" Barry recalled. "That's exactly what started to happen."[75]

The veterans also made an impact on J. Edgar Hoover. By September the FBI was investigating VVAW to see if the group was controlled by the Communist Party.[76]

Several years later VVAW would hold poignant hearings on U.S. war crimes in Vietnam. In May 1967, England's Bertrand Russell Peace Foundation conducted similar hearings in Sweden. Based on extensive research, the foundation's "International War Crimes Tribunal" accused the U.S. government of "aggression, civilian bombardment, the use of experimental weapons, the torture and mutilation of prisoners and genocide involving forced labour, mass burial, concentration camps and saturation bombing of unparallelled intensity." Testimony at the tribunal was gut-wrenching. Witnesses brought scarred victims of white phosphorous and napalm bombs before its members and described the grisly toll of antipersonnel bombs. "It got to you," remembered Carl Oglesby, one of three American members of the tribunal.[77]

The tribunal repeatedly invited U.S. officials to testify in defense of their policies. The Johnson administration was not about to lend legitimacy to the project and spurned the offers. Referring to Bertrand Russell, Dean Rusk told reporters that he had no intention of "playing games with a 94-year-old Briton." Jean-Paul Sartre, the tribunal's executive president, found Rusk's remark curious, coming as it did from "a mediocre American official." "I do not know if Mr. Rusk, confronted with Lord Russell, would play games with him, or if rather it might not be Russell who would play games with the wretched arguments with which Mr. Rusk has the habit of regaling the Press," Sartre commented.[78]

Following additional testimony in November, the tribunal issued a straightforward verdict: guilty on all counts. Russell remarked during his closing address, "The term genocide truly encompasses the enormity of American crimes in Vietnam. . . . The catalogue of horrors which we have witnessed . . . is nightmarish in its dimensions and vividness; we shall never forget it."[79]

The tribunal had little if any influence on opinion toward the war in the United States, however. According to a hostile American press, it was a political circus orchestrated by left-wing nuts. Morley Safer of CBS News called the tribunal a "farce" whose members were "not interested in peace." CBS's Eric Sevareid denounced the "anti-American propaganda ploy" unfolding in Sweden, writing, "If the Vietnam War is an affront to reason, for many people Lord Russell's brand of opposition is a mutilation of reason." A *New York Times Magazine* article trashed the tribunal before it began.[80]

Johnson administration officials delightedly scrutinized the media's scoldings. "The biased and propagandistic nature of this project has been fully documented in the press, so there is no reason for statements to this effect to be attributed to U.S. officials, either for the record or on background," directed a May 8 State Department telegram sent to U.S. embassies overseas. The telegram characterized the tribunal as "primarily . . . a front and outlet for outspokenly hostile propaganda supporting the communist cause." Walt Rostow forwarded Johnson a USIA summary of European press reaction to the tribunal in the expectation that the president would be "interested—and a little cheered by" antagonistic foreign commentary on "the shenanigans in Stockholm."[81]

Officials did not consider the tribunal merely a harmless joke, though. The State Department also sent U.S. overseas embassies six pages of propaganda on it "to draw on . . . if asked about the tribunal." The U.S. Embassy in Stockholm cabled Rusk on May 7, "Our private satisfaction at fumbles, troubles and bad press of Russell group in Sweden is tempered considerably by knowledge that from organizer's standpoint only two main facts are important: a) sessions held in Western democracy, b) final report of session will therefore hopefully become a basic document for all of world except most sophisticated and most honest."[82]

The Government Counterattacks

Meanwhile, Johnson administration officials debated how to counteract growing domestic opposition to the war. Many held that the majority of Americans, although anxious, still supported U.S. involvement in Vietnam and would publicly express their support if the proper inducements were employed. Without skillful persuasion, they worried, antiwar activists would ultimately win the battle for American hearts and minds. The veteran Johnson political adviser James Rowe expressed this view in a memo to the president on May 17:

> It is elementary that this is an unpopular war. Even though the bulk of the country presently supports the President's policies it is clear there is restlessness on the subject of the Vietnam struggle. This is particularly true among the "intellectuals"—the universities, the columnists and the large city "intellectuals." Not only is it fashionable for them to be against the war, it is *un*fashionable to be for it.
>
> The common people, in the form of the American Legion, the labor unions, the boiler makers and the bartenders, may parade down Fifth Avenue to "support the boys" in Vietnam.[83] Yet the "opinion makers" in the press, on the magazines and in the universities are more and more attacking the Vietnam policy. Eventually these "opinion makers" may convert the people, particularly if unopposed. Inevitably, their widely publicized, noisy and loud point of view will have the effect of a war of attrition against those who would support the Vietnam policy.
>
> Here and there . . . among the "opinion makers" are a number of people who think the policy is correct. But more and more these people feel they are outnumbered, that they have no allies, there is no place to turn and their own doubts are beginning to creep in. If everyone is against them, they may feel perhaps they themselves are wrong.
>
> The only individuals that these potential allies and supporters ever see replying to the "doves" are the President, the Secretary of State, and occasionally the Secretary of Defense. No one else appears to be raising his voice.
>
> . . . Should there not be some rallying ground for these supporters?[84]

Harry McPherson thought so. On April 20, five days after the Spring Mobilization, the White House counsel and speechwriter relayed Johnson "an interesting idea" a California businessman had submitted to him that morning. "Concerned about the noisiness of the anti-Vietnam Left, and the relative inertness of the majority that supports our effort there," the entrepreneur advised the White House to form a committee that would ask Americans to send prowar telegrams to the Pentagon. The telegrams would be "on the order of 'We pledge our support to our brave men in Vietnam,'" McPherson told Johnson. They would be forwarded—"with publicity"—to U.S. soldiers in Vietnam. The committee, "perhaps chaired by Eisenhower and Truman," would seek free advertising time and space from the media and "ask business and labor leaders to bring the campaign to the attention of their employees and members." The committee's director should be "a public relations specialist," McPherson wrote, "perhaps someone from the networks." He would "background the press that he hopes for at least as many signatories as marched last Saturday" in the Mobilization. McPherson told the president that, "with an aggressive campaign," the committee "should be able to hit half a million or more" signatures. There would have to be limits to the campaign's aggressiveness, however. *"There should be no overt White House involvement in this,"* McPherson emphasized to his boss. He noted that his fellow officials Jack Valenti, John Roche, and Nicholas Katzenbach all supported the idea. "The whole thing would be done within 10 days, if possible—so as to be completed *by Loyalty Day, May 1.*"[85] No telegram-generating committee was forthcoming.

On April 29, the Veterans of Foreign Wars sponsored prowar parades in Brooklyn and Manhattan. Although the group had predicted 150,000 people would turn out, a paltry 7,850 did. Wounded, the government helped organize a "Support Our Boys in Vietnam" parade in New York on May 13. It developed publicity for the event and coaxed endorsements out of labor leaders, businessmen, and members of Congress. McPherson and Roche served as the administration's point men with the main planners of the parade. The government's effort paid dividends. Twenty thousand people, "stirred by martial music," filed through the streets of Manhattan to affirm their support for the war. Especially spirited marchers paused to assault bystanders carrying peace signs on numerous occasions. One spectator uninvolved in the peace movement was tarred and feathered by a mob of thirty people who didn't appreciate his long hair and sandals. Although administration officials denied assisting with the march, its principal architect, Charles Wiley, wrote McPherson on May 25, "Many thanks to those on the White House staff, with whom I dealt so frequently by telephone, during the preparations for our parade."[86]

Secretary of the Navy Paul Nitze had an interesting prescription for deflating the peace movement. "I was redheaded about the idea of getting the draft deferment business changed, making it equitable," Nitze later remembered. He believed that the system of student deferments was not only placing a disproportionate burden of the fighting in Vietnam on those unable to attend college, but giving the antiwar movement a shot in the arm. Students "felt guilty," Nitze perceived, "that they had avoided the dangers that the others had taken" and realized they "couldn't really easily defend themselves against" charges of possessing "a yellow streak." To convince both themselves and others of "their manhood," the secretary deduced, students were "taking enormous risks," such as occupying "the front line of the protests, getting themselves arrested and so forth." The result was "an opposition which was radical and forceful in its radicalism." Such attempts by students to show "they weren't scared," Nitze believed, formed "the real strength of the protest movement."[87]

Nitze's social psychological skills were appreciated by Robert McNamara, who not only agreed with Nitze's analysis, but, at Nitze's instigation, "enthusiastically" proposed to Johnson a corresponding change in draft policy. All males at age eighteen should be equally liable to the draft regardless of their educational status, McNamara advised the president. Furthermore, young men who had previously been granted student deferments should be more susceptible to the draft than others when their deferments ended. Johnson "took a dim view of" McNamara's recommendations, however. "He thought that the scheme of transitioning from the current bad situation to one that would be better still involved undue consideration for what he called the 'Eastern Establishment'— for the graduate students at Harvard . . . the graduate students at Berkeley and so on and so forth," Nitze recalled. Johnson knew that many young men who had already been granted educational exemptions would still be able to escape the draft. The president felt that "all" students who had received deferments "ought to go into the army right away," Nitze said. "He wanted a much stricter thing. And he kept talking about the Eastern Establishment."[88]

Yet Nitze is only telling part of the story—and probably not the most important part. Although in early March a national commission on draft reform had also urged abolishing most student deferments, Johnson had strong *political* reasons for not taking that step. As the Washington insider James Reston divulged, there was a "genuine fear" "high in the Administration" that ending most deferments would provoke "massive defiance" of the draft among college undergraduates. According to one administration estimate, "as many as 25 per cent of them might refuse to serve." Officials worried that the policy "might inflame opposition on the university campuses into a national crisis," Reston wrote. The resistance to major draft reform of Congressman L. Mendel Rivers (D-S.C.), the powerful chairman of the House Armed Services Committee, also influenced Johnson.[89] In June, Rivers helped push through Congress an extension of the draft law that retained undergraduate (but not most graduate) deferments.

John Roche was also scheming to deflate the peace movement. "I have been busily working to get my trade-union friends to turn off the tap to various anti-Administration organizations," Roche reported to President Johnson in an EYES ONLY memo on April 27. He noted that the liberal Stern Family Fund had given the Southern Christian Leadership Conference and the antiwar Institute for Policy Studies—"a real Vietnik operation"—$60,000 and $50,000, respectively. "You might suggest to Secretary [of Labor Willard] Wirtz—a member of the Board of the 'Stern Family Fund'—that he read grant requests a bit more carefully," Roche advised.[90]

Since late 1966 Roche had been trying to pull together a group of prowar "experts" on Southeast Asia for the purpose of issuing a favorable public statement on U.S. policy. Roche hoped the statement would neutralize articulate liberal criticism of the war. On March 21, he proudly told Johnson that "the wheels are now moving" on the project. Days earlier Roche had persuaded the conservative Berkeley political science professor Robert Scalapino to convene a "small" but "serious" conference of "distinguished scholars" on "the future of freedom in Asia." He had also convinced Leo Cherne of Freedom House to raise money for the conference. "In return," Roche wrote an interested Walt Rostow, "Freedom House collects brownie points as sponsor." Roche assured Johnson that he and Scalapino had "selected the participants very carefully—not to eliminate 'dissent' but to insure that they all . . . share the same fundamental outlook." The conferees would "meet without publicity and—hopefully—prepare a report which can then be used as . . . fortification for our bewildered friends who listen to [the historian Henry Steele] Commager, [Arthur] Schlesinger, *et al.*, and have no basis for argument." Roche promised Johnson that he would "keep an eye on" Scalapino and Cherne's progress and "spur it along if necessary."[91]

The seeds of Roche's scheme germinated nine months later. On December 19, fourteen "leading political scientists and historians" released a report defending the war. "We are trying to get maximum publicity for it," Roche wrote the president's aide Marvin Watson.[92] That the *New York Times* found a prowar declaration of a mere fourteen intellectuals worthy of page-one coverage was probably partly due to official prodding.

Under Secretary of Agriculture John Schnittker did not share Roche's zeal for rallying prowar scholars to engage critics of the war in public debate. On June 9, two weeks after a discussion with President Johnson on the subject, Schnittker wrote Harry McPherson that conversations he had just had with numerous professors, deans, and other former associates at Kansas State University during a visit there suggested there were serious limits to that strategy. "Not one of the people I talked with supports present policies in Viet Nam," Schnittker submitted. Moreover, "no one with whom I talked would admit that any significant element in the University community would support present policies." Ominously, Schnittker conveyed that his contacts in Kansas felt the public was "beginning to turn the same corner on this subject that intellectuals turned some months ago."[93]

Throughout the month of May, James Rowe, McPherson, Roche, Rostow, and other officials had kept alive the idea of organizing a national prowar committee. They kept Johnson abreast of their deliberations, telling him they wished to set up a "citizens committee" with no visible government connection, along the lines of the Committee for an Effective and Durable Peace in Asia the administration had helped organize in 1965. In his May 17 memo to the president, Rowe offered Johnson a detailed description of what the new committee might look like. It should be led by "Great Names," he wrote, "preferably members of the Republican Party" to avoid accusations of partisanship:

> They should be articulate and ready to reply on their own. They should have sufficient connections with the Administration that they can get factual information supplied quickly to them when and if they wish to answer the [John Kenneth] Galbraiths, the Schlesingers, the [Senator Charles] Percys, the Fulbrights and the McGoverns.
>
> They should, when properly organized, have letterwriting squads who are able and willing to sign letters (carefully prepared by staff men) to the letter columns of various newspapers attacking and disagreeing with the editorial policies of those papers.

Members of the committee should include prowar academics, "tough-minded liberals," and representatives of "the 'Establishment.'" "Lots of people are still influenced by the 'Establishment,'" Rowe counseled Johnson. "In this particular battle of public opinion, it has been silent. It has not joined the intellectuals but it certainly is not breaking its back for the Administration." The committee should also include the "right kinds" of blacks, women, and young people. Rowe impressed upon Johnson his special role in launching the committee. "It will take the President to get some of the people that should head it up. It would also take the President to make it clear that the government should cooperate with this *independent* group . . . in terms of material and arguments."[94]

Two days later, in another EYES ONLY memo to Johnson, Roche exhorted, "This has been under discussion for a year and I believe that the time has come to stop holding meetings about organizing it—and organize the damned thing." Roche boasted that he was a veteran co-organizer "since 1947" of "perhaps twenty" proadministration committees. He also addressed Johnson's apparent concern that the committee's ties to the administration might be discovered. "Once it is started, there are bound to be accusations that it is a White House 'front.' (This is one reason why New York would be a better headquarters than Washington.) I will leave no tracks—for a man of my bulk, I can be remarkably invisible."[95]

In yet another EYES ONLY memo on May 26, Roche asked Johnson whether he should "move on this project." Johnson gave him the green light. But the president was nervous. Adjacent to his check mark of approval, he scrawled, "But don't get surfaced."[96]

Over the summer, administration officials surreptitiously moved to get the "Citizens Committee for Peace with Freedom in Vietnam" off the ground. Roche registered it as a nonprofit educational organization to allow for tax-deductible contributions—in possible violation of U.S. law. He and others also tried to line up heavyweight supporters. Although Roche informed Johnson that the committee was "moving along," progress was slow. Many influential people were unwilling to endorse a prowar organization when public opinion was turning against the war. Officials also had to act carefully to avoid being found out. "I would like to move it more rapidly, but the risks are too great," Roche told Johnson. The president received a steady stream of progress reports on the committee.[97]

By October, the administration had prodded Eisenhower, Truman, Dean Acheson, former Senator Paul Douglas, the television commentator Howard K. Smith, the author Ralph Ellison, General Omar Bradley, George Meany, and ninety-four others to join the committee. Douglas and Bradley agreed to co-chair it. Roche was jubilant when Eisenhower took it upon himself to mention the formation of this new people's committee to the press. "General Eisenhower's remarks about the National Committee for Peace with Freedom in Vietnam were a gift from God," Roche gushed to Johnson on October 7. "For him to surface the enterprise automatically takes suspicion off the White House and provides an aura of solid non-partisanship." Two weeks later, Roche wrote Johnson, "It has worked out extremely well." State and Defense "will quietly co-operate to the fullest possible extent" with plans to formally announce the committee on October 25, he transmitted. The government continued to take precautions to ensure that its ties to the organization would go undetected. "If necessary in response to questions: 'The President had nothing to do with the formation of the group,'" Roche directed Press Secretary George Christian on October 24. "'Up to now, everything the President knows about the committee he has read in the newspapers.'" A subsequent State Department telegram from Dean Rusk "to all diplomatic posts" instructed: "In any discussion of new committee, we should make clear it has no rpt [repeat] no official status or affiliation with USG [U.S. government]. In words of organizing chairman, former Senator Paul Douglas, quote We have no ties to anyone or anything except our own consciences. Unquote." At a Washington press conference on October 25, Douglas said that the idea for the committee was his alone.[98]

Walt Rostow had earlier urged Johnson to "mount a major information campaign to inform both the US electorate and world opinion of the realities in

Vietnam." The principal "reality" the administration should publicize, asserted Rostow, was "victory is near." In August Christian and a colleague seconded Rostow's motion to form a "Vietnam Information Group" (VIG) for coordinating the administration's domestic propaganda on the war.[99] "We are not making the most effective use of the information coming in from Vietnam to put out our position over here at home," Christian apprised the president. "As one result, the American people and the American press are skeptical, cynical, and—more often than not—uninformed." Christian projected the VIG as a "quick reaction team" that would enable the government to answer critics' charges *"before* we are thrown—as we so frequently are—on the defensive." Johnson approved the group's formation. Public awareness of this latest plan for educating the American people was to be avoided. One memo outlining the VIG's structure was marked "CONFIDENTIAL—LIMITED DISTRIBUTION (Please!)."[100]

Christian felt one of the VIG's tasks should be garnering favorable data on the war that officials could "regularly" leak to the media. This was not a new practice for the administration. Throughout the spring and summer of 1967—indeed, throughout its existence—the administration had been feeding the press background material designed to elicit public support for the war. On May 2, Roche advised Johnson that "it would be in the national interest (as I see it)" to pass a "responsible" journalist record of the government's peace efforts. One month later, Roche advocated "a *covert political warfare* attack" on Ho Chi Minh's legitimacy. "This would be a form of escalation and would have to be done with great care," he cautioned Johnson in a SECRET memo. "The fundamental line should be 'Save the D.R.V. [North Vietnam] from the insane military adventurism of Ho and his clique.' By implication, it could be suggested that Ho is a Chinese stooge." Johnson himself was a heavy leaker of pro-administration propaganda to the press. He did not have the exercise down to a science, however. Roche remembered Johnson becoming enraged once over a leak to a prominent columnist about a secret mission to Vietnam by an administration official. The president wanted to ferret out the leaker and punish him. Roche gingerly explained that he, Johnson, had delivered the leak himself only twenty-four hours earlier to demonstrate the government's unceasing peace effort.[101]

For months Harry McPherson had believed that the administration's standard public rationale for the war was partly responsible for its failure to rouse the American people. He felt that many Americans doubted the United States was really fighting to preserve "freedom" in South Vietnam. In August, McPherson counseled Johnson that contending the United States was waging "a small war" in Vietnam to prevent a much larger war—that is, "World War III"—might marshal greater public support. The president agreed.[102]

The same month the administration took legal action to mitigate the peace movement's threat to both its political legitimacy and its physical security. Following a lengthy internal debate, it banned protests of more than one hundred people in front of the White House and those of more than five hundred in Lafayette Park across the street. In addition, permits would now be required for smaller demonstrations in either location. Some hard-line officials had advocated an absolute prohibition on protests near the White House. "Even a small group may have a malicious intent and constitute a security risk" or hold "'lie-ins' and other repugnant activities which are not in keeping with the dignity of the White House area," they maintained. But other officials feared the political fallout of stifling dissent too much and of appearing frightened of even small clusters of protesters. [103]

"There May Be a Limit beyond Which Many Americans . . . Will Not Permit the United States to Go"

As officials strove to turn the tide in the political battle at home, a fierce struggle was being fought inside the administration over U.S. strategy in Vietnam. U.S. military leaders were exhorting Johnson to go for broke. Admiral Ulysses S. Grant Sharp, commander in chief, Pacific, continued to press for a "relentless application of force" against the North. Sharp lusted to wipe out North Vietnam's military and industrial facilities in the Hanoi and Haiphong areas. He also wished to undertake selective attacks on its dams and dikes, close its ports through aerial mining and bombing, and destroy its rail lines to China. General William Westmoreland's attention was "riveted" on South Vietnam's borders and the enemy's "sanctuaries" in Laos and Cambodia. Westmoreland was concerned about the buildup of enemy troops in these areas. He knew NVA commanders considered the rugged Central Highlands border region a "killing zone" for American soldiers unskilled in jungle warfare. In March, Westmoreland requested a "minimum" of 100,000 more troops "as soon as possible" but no later than July 1968. Without them, he reported, "it will be nip and tuck to oppose the reinforcements the enemy is capable of providing." The general also petitioned for an "optimum" force increase of 200,000 men. It was allegedly necessary to destroy the enemy's main units and bases in South Vietnam, invade the sanctuaries and the southern portion of North Vietnam, and provide a "shield" for "pacification." Fulfilling the optimum request would mean increasing U.S. troop strength from the already-approved level of 470,366 to 671,616 by 1969. Significantly, it would require calling up U.S. reserves. On April 20, the Joint Chiefs of Staff relayed Secretary of Defense McNamara their endorsement of Westmoreland's requests. They too recommended mining North Vietnam's ports. [104]

Walt Rostow heartily agreed that the war should be substantially escalated. On April 27, he urged Johnson to give Westmoreland authority to invade North

Vietnam. Standing aside a map in the Cabinet Room of the White House, the short, thickset Rostow explained to the president that the policy might force an end to the war. He expressed deep concern with faltering public support for U.S. policy. Rostow was "haunted" by a prediction North Vietnamese Premier Pham Van Dong had ventured in the early 1960s. "Americans don't like long, inconclusive wars," Dong had said. "This will be long and inconclusive. There-fore, we shall win." Rostow even kept a copy of Dong's statement in his White House office. There was "no question" in Rostow's mind that most Americans were hawks and would support a bold attempt to win the war. "They'd have backed anything," he said years later with a wave of the hand. "You know, 'bomb the hell out of them, mine the harbors—get moving.'" Rostow passion-ately exhorted the president, "The country can't stand more of the same! We've got to be decisive." Of the gradualist military approach pursued by the United States in Vietnam, Rostow later griped, "It was a hell of a way to fight a war. . . . War is too serious to fight that way."[105]

Rostow's performance in the Cabinet Room was a unique one. During the "searching reappraisal" of U.S. policy that followed the JCS's April 20 recom-mendation, he was the only senior civilian official to advocate substantial inten-sification of the war.[106] For the first time, Johnson was bombarded with advice to stabilize or deescalate U.S. involvement in Vietnam.

The president responded by steering a middle course. He slowly expanded Rolling Thunder in a "salami-slice" pattern throughout the spring, placing new targets on Admiral Sharp's hit list on a piecemeal basis. He continued with his policy of "a 'little' escalation" during June and July. Johnson refused to mine the ports. On August 4, the president disclosed plans to send from forty-five to fifty thousand additional U.S. troops to Vietnam—far fewer than Westmore-land wanted. He elected neither to call up U.S. reserves nor to invade North Vietnam, Laos, or Cambodia.[107]

Why didn't the administration pull out the stops and shoot for military vic-tory? The factors are numerous and specific to the type of military activity vetoed. But important among them was domestic opposition to the war. Offi-cials worried that stronger measures in Southeast Asia would worsen their public opinion problems. The discussion that follows considers the role of the domestic political climate and other factors in restraining the administration's activity in three areas: troop deployments, ground operations outside South Vietnam, and Rolling Thunder.

Immediately upon receipt of Westmoreland's troop request, Assistant Secretary of Defense for Systems Analysis Alain Enthoven ordered his staff to prepare a detailed response. Their memorandum argued that additional troops would be unlikely to raise enemy losses to a level intolerable to the NVA and NLF. Such deployments would also inhibit South Vietnam's political development and damage its economy. Moreover, they would increase the war's "cost" at home, the staffers stressed, "further degrading public opinion and preventing expansion of critical domestic programs. They would present the prospect of unending escalation, splitting the American public even more openly and seriously."[108]

Enthoven sent Robert McNamara a memo on May 1 that repeated these arguments, with added emphasis on escalation's political price in both the United States and South Vietnam. Enthoven wrote of the domestic situation, "Our escalation is designed to put pressure on the North Vietnamese. But they may be more resolved to withstand it than the United States electorate is." Granting Westmoreland's request would continue the "ominous history of unending escalation" and end up "increasing internal opposition to the war," Enthoven asserted. He conceded that North Vietnam's belief that domestic dissatisfaction with the conflict would eventually force the United States to withdraw might be realistic: "I think we're up against an enemy who just may have found a dangerously clever strategy for licking the United States."[109]

Enthoven discovered upon meeting with McNamara that the defense secretary was "thinking along the same lines." In fact, McNamara had already asked Assistant Secretary of Defense for International Security Affairs (ISA) John McNaughton to prepare a draft presidential memorandum (DPM) advancing "the same basic political arguments." McNamara presented McNaughton's May 19 memo to Johnson under his signature. It contended that sending two hundred thousand more troops to Vietnam would not make "a meaningful military difference" in the "stalemated" war. The DPM's "appraisal of the current situation dwelled on the unpopular nature of the Vietnam war in the country," as the Pentagon Papers historian writes. It observed that the war was becoming

> increasingly unpopular as it escalates—causing more American casu-
> alties, more fear of its growing into a wider war, more privation of
> the domestic sector, and more distress at the amount of suffering be-
> ing visited on the non-combatants in Vietnam, South and North.
> Most Americans do not know how we got where we are, and most,
> without knowing why, but taking advantage of hindsight, are con-
> vinced that somehow we should not have gotten this deeply in. All
> want the war ended and expect their President to end it. Successfully,
> or else.

The DPM recommended limiting U.S. force deployments to thirty thousand. It supplied "the catalyst" for Johnson's August troop decision.[110]

According to the Pentagon Papers analyst, the DPM understated McNaughton's anxiety over domestic opposition to U.S. policy in Vietnam. The former Harvard law professor was "very deeply concerned about the breadth and the intensity of public unrest and dissatisfaction with the war. To him the draft paper underplayed a bit the unpopularity of the conflict especially with young people, the underprivileged, the intelligentsia, and the women." In a May 6 memo to McNamara, McNaughton had written:

> A feeling is widely and strongly held that "the Establishment" is out of its mind. The feeling is that we are trying to impose some US image on distant peoples we cannot understand (anymore than we can the younger generation here at home), and that we are carrying the thing to absurd lengths. Related to this feeling is the increased polarization that is taking place in the United States with seeds of the worst split in our people in more than a century.

Still, McNaughton doubted that, "barring escalation of the 'external' war," a major U.S. troop increase would "polarize opinion to the extent that the 'doves' in the US will get out of hand—massive refusals to serve, or to fight, or to cooperate, or worse."[111]

We have seen that President Johnson opted against calling up U.S. reserve forces in 1965 largely out of concern that it would increase domestic opposition to the war. He and other officials continued to dread mobilization's "horrible baggage" in 1967. Not only would it raise the war's costs to an intolerable level for many Americans, but antiwar activists would protest even louder, advancing still further domestic antagonism to the war. The Pentagon Papers historian argues that the "limits" of Johnson's August troop deployment "can be traced to one primary factor—that of mobilization" for "a war which was becoming increasingly distasteful and intolerable to the public."[112]

The president remained sensitive to congressional opposition to a reserve call-up. In fact, he now perceived that Congress would refuse to grant him authority to undertake the policy. When McNamara proposed calling up reserves in order to replenish the supply of "reinforcement" troops available for emergencies, Johnson flatly rebuffed him. "You know," the president lectured, "when I go up and ask for authority to call up the reserves, the debate will not be on that issue. The debate will be on whether or not we ought to be in Vietnam. And we'll lose that vote. And therefore there's no point in trying to get it."[113]

The president's refusal to grant Westmoreland's troop request was thus largely a result of perceptions that a major U.S. force increase would fuel domestic opposition to the war while failing to bring the conflict closer to an end—a forbidding combination indeed. There were additional factors in his decision. The president and other officials remained anxious in 1967 about opening the floodgates to ultrahawkish political pressures. Johnson understood that powerful congressional hawks would fight a large troop increase if he didn't unleash the bombers. Officials also believed that calling up reserves risked increased Soviet and Chinese involvement in the war, heightened tension with the USSR on other international issues, diminished ARVN initiative, and greater economic problems at home. And the domestic debate over mobilization would convey political weakness to Hanoi.[114]

President Johnson's troop decision provided Westmoreland with less manpower than he deemed necessary to fight the enemy in South Vietnam *and* invade North Vietnam, Laos, or Cambodia. The considerations outlined above thus also help explain the administration's decision not to undertake major ground operations outside South Vietnam. But the policy also had separate motivations. The president feared invading North Vietnam would provoke direct Chinese military involvement in the conflict. "Johnson was constantly concerned about whether or not the Chinese might come into the war," CIA Director Richard Helms remembered. "He had a vision that maybe the Chinese would pour over the Vietnam border the way they did in North Korea" after U.S. troops crossed the Yalu River during the Korean War. Officials judged it "axiomatic" that Chinese intervention, in turn, meant a much more costly war. Recalled Dean Rusk, "There was a military memorandum at one point suggesting that we consider occupying North Vietnam. And in this memorandum it said, 'We do not think that this would bring in the Chinese, but if it should bring in the Chinese that would require the use of nuclear weapons.' Now, in this military memorandum that was like a piece of fine print. But for a president that sentence just popped out of the page."[115]

Trepidation about swarming Chinese troops may be sufficient explanation for Johnson's decision not to invade North Vietnam. But his determination was surely buttressed by an awareness that the operation would incite a storm of indignation at home. Asked why Johnson spurned later advice from Rostow to invade the North, Harry McPherson responded that the president was probably "concerned that he would be labeled a 'warmonger'" and suffer "a lot of heavy criticism." McPherson thought the policy "might have appealed to him" were it not for the likely domestic outcry. In their May 19 memo to the president, McNaughton and McNamara intimated that launching major ground actions outside South Vietnam would spark "massive civil disobedience." Lawrence Eagleburger, who was then special assistant to the under secretary of state, opined that concern over "how the body politic in the U.S. would react was probably as overwhelming a factor as any" in the president's refusal to invade North Vietnam.[116]

Officials had other arguments against invading the North. To do so might, they believed, provoke a major confrontation with the Soviet Union, as well as draw strong criticism from other foreign governments and publics. If the invasion stopped short of toppling the Hanoi government, it would also harden the enemy's resolve. And William Bundy thought the action would bring at least temporary political stability to China, which was then in the grip of the Cultural Revolution.[117]

The main reasons Johnson did not invade Laos or Cambodia were skepticism that it would shorten the war and fear of angry outbursts at home and abroad. "That it would tend to increase the opposition and tend to shorten the fuse [of public support] was certainly argued in some of the papers," Bundy recalled. Leaders of the violated countries would be among those upset.[118]

The limitations the Johnson administration placed on Rolling Thunder are less apparent than those it placed on the ground war. Hundreds of thousands of people were killed or maimed by U.S. bombs in North Vietnam (some 80 percent of them civilians); countless Vietnamese watched their homes go up in flames. Yet the administration's bombing campaign could have been even harsher. One need only look to President Nixon's 1972 "Christmas bombing" of Hanoi and Haiphong for evidence. Dean Rusk was telling the truth when he said, "Had we set out to destroy Hanoi and Haiphong, we could have done so with conventional bombing—and there wouldn't have been a Hanoi for Jane Fonda, Ramsey Clark and others to visit."[119]

The main reason for the administration's restraint was a belief that substantially escalating Rolling Thunder would have little consequence for the fighting in the South. "On the ineffectiveness of the bombing as a means to end the war, I think the evidence is plain," McGeorge Bundy, a key figure in launching Rolling Thunder, wrote Johnson in May. "Ho Chi Minh and his colleagues simply are not going to change their policy on the basis of losses from the air in North Vietnam. No intelligence estimate that I have seen in the last two years has ever claimed that the bombing would have this effect." Officials also feared that an intensified bombing campaign would incite China and the Soviet Union.[120]

Domestic opposition to the war was also a significant factor in Johnson's decision to restrict Rolling Thunder. The president was "extremely sensitive" to charges by antiwar critics that he was a "barbarian" who was "bombing a bunch of defenseless Asians," George Christian recalled. According to McPherson, "He didn't want to be the fellow who was caricatured by [the cartoonist] David Levine or others as the gun-toting, arrogant, unfeeling Texan who didn't have any sense of the necessary limits of the war." In their May 19 DPM, McNaughton and McNamara advised Johnson that an "important" cost to be considered before intensifying Rolling Thunder was "domestic and world opinion." Heavy bombing "creates a backfire of revulsion and opposition by killing civilians," they noted, starkly warning the president:

> There may be a limit beyond which many Americans and much of the world will not permit the United States to go. The picture of the world's greatest superpower killing or seriously injuring 1000 noncombatants a week, while trying to pound a tiny backward nation

into submission on an issue whose merits are hotly disputed, is not a pretty one. It could conceivably produce a costly distortion in the American national consciousness and in the world image of the United States—especially if the damage to North Vietnam is complete enough to be "successful."

In arguing against Rolling Thunder's expansion, McGeorge Bundy urged Johnson to weigh the program's "distinctly marginal impact" on the war against "the fact that strategic bombing does tend to divide the U.S . . . and to accentuate the unease and distemper which surround the war . . . both at home and abroad." In a June DPM, McNaughton contended that mining North Vietnam's ports would be "very costly in domestic and world support." William Bundy judged these ports, dams, and dikes "extremely sensitive targets" in that regard. General Westmoreland recalled, "When the air war was escalated, the antiwar activists took to the streets. And there was therefore a political tendency to pull back." William Bundy said there is "no question" but that administration officials recognized that

> a large and significant segment of the country would be put off by the application of large-scale force against a small and apparently defenseless country. . . . This was a war where you felt from the beginning that there would be sensitivity to . . . the methods of warfare. . . . And obviously anybody could see that you'd have a much more effective bombing campaign if you hit command centers in Hanoi, but that . . . you would [also] enlarge the segment of the public that was very turned off by the thing. . . . Certainly, public opinion [was] . . . very much there in the background on that general issue of methods of war.[121]

Bundy makes an important observation on the subtle manner in which domestic political attitudes influenced some officials. To the especially hard-nosed managers of America's national security, trained to make "the tough decisions" in a tough world, convinced that the making of foreign policy was beyond the masses' comprehension, the public's likely reaction to a harsher air war may indeed have been only a *background* consideration. Their immediate concerns were military efficacy and the responses of foreign governments. They couldn't be bothered by political flutters at home—they were statesmen, not politicians. Some officials even had difficulty admitting to themselves that domestic opposition to the war conditioned their views, since doing so threatened their senses of masculinity and professionalism. Many officials saw antiwar protesters as "so uninformed, so ill-dressed, so uncouth in their mannerisms" that it would have been "quite an admission," even "a failure of nerve," for them to acknowledge that they were being "influenced by such a mob," Daniel Ellsberg argued. Before warming to the subject of antiwar protest, William Bundy puffed out his chest in my direction and declared, "I stuck cotton in my ears when it came to domestic opinion."[122]

But whether in the background or at the fore, judgments of what the domestic political climate would sustain colored the recommendations of virtually all officials. Lawrence Eagleburger:

> No matter how much you think course A is the right course, you can't help but be impressed, subliminally most of the time, about the inability to carry out the policy [if you believe] the public support simply isn't there. . . . You inevitably end up cutting at the edges and making it a little less noisome as a public policy than it would have been otherwise. . . . There's always a tendency to say, "Well, maybe if we don't do X but do Y, the reaction won't be quite so bad." And usually it's just as bad. . . .

Eagleburger believed that domestic attitudes on the war exerted "a very large impact on the determination to use a gradualist approach" to Rolling Thunder during the Johnson administration.[123]

That Johnson himself *intuitively* grasped the domestic political hazards of concentrated air attacks on North Vietnam has been recorded by David Halberstam. In late 1966, Halberstam writes, U.S. military leaders had tried to convince Johnson that pulverizing Hanoi and Haiphong would save lives, since it promised to end the war sooner than would occur otherwise. To help illustrate this point a senior officer explained that some of the "bright young men" in the Defense Department had calculated that dropping the atomic bomb during World War II had spared seven hundred and fifty thousand American lives. Intrigued, Johnson asked the officer how they had arrived at this figure. It seems that the Pentagon's golden boys had simply plugged information on previous military invasions and battles into their computer, and the number had, miraculously, popped out. The president asked to meet with these young geniuses. When they were finally able to see him, Johnson acted impressed with their work for awhile. Then he barked, "I have one more problem for your computer—will you feed into it how long it will take five hundred thousand angry Americans to climb that White House wall out there and lynch their President if he does something like that?"[124]

The country's apparent intolerance of intense air strikes against North Vietnam sorely frustrated some officials. They were conducting a *war* in Vietnam, they maintained, not a tea party. Richard Helms vexedly asserted:

> This idea that we mustn't bomb the dikes because that will kill a lot of innocent civilians, we mustn't do this because [it] may kill innocent civilians, we mustn't mine harbors because that will kill innocent civilians—this whole idea is one of the reasons I believe history will

find that we were unsuccessful in the war. . . . *Wars are not pleasant affairs.* If you are going to embark on a war, the idea is to win it, not to have a draw or to lose it. . . . And therefore you use whatever devices you have at hand to win. And the gradualist approach was obviously unsuccessful.[125]

The administration had other reasons for restricting Rolling Thunder. Many officials *did* want to limit civilian casualties in Vietnam. Granted, it is difficult to appreciate the moral fiber of men responsible for at least one million Vietnamese deaths. That they had access to intelligence reports documenting this death toll as it mounted makes the task harder still. Yet most officials felt that granting Admiral Sharp's more destructive wishes was just plain beyond the ethical pale. Both Johnson and McNamara (who was becoming emotionally unsettled by civilian suffering in Vietnam) typically asked the Joint Chiefs of Staff how many noncombatants would be killed before approving particular bombing targets. Some officials also worried that a heavy bombing campaign would cost too many U.S. planes and pilots. It might bring political stability to China, too. Johnson weighed yet another factor in choosing bombing targets: whether the Holy Ghost approved. "He comes to me about 2 o'clock in the morning—when I have to give the word to the boys and I get the word from God whether to bomb or not," the president of the United States revealed.[126]

Is Anybody Listening?

The American peace movement was thus one factor in the Johnson administration's decision not to go for broke in Vietnam. It would vociferously protest that step, officials recognized, thereby advancing already widespread public disenchantment with the war. By contributing to the public's war weariness at the time, it had also promoted the disrelish for substantial escalation of everyday citizens. Yet many antiwar activists were painfully unaware that they were helping to restrain the administration. Young American men were still being sent off to die. More bombs were falling. The war's violence was so gruesome it was hard to imagine worse, and the policymakers seemed committed to drawing the thing out to the last drop of blood. "I never had a sense that there was great debate going on within the Johnson administration," Bruce Dancis would recall. Frustration over the movement's apparent inability to inhibit the war was "*very widespread*" among activists by the summer of 1967, Dancis remembered. Even the massive Spring Mobilizations had failed to deter officials. It was mindboggling that the administration could ignore *that* sea of humanity. "Despair became a cliche among young white radicals," one writes. "Many of us in Berkeley talked incessantly about political impotence. . . . Anti-war activity seemed purposeless." The draft protester Michael Ferber recalled his own frustration over the mounting war:

We were doing everything right in terms of organizing people, at least as far as making people speak out. I think there wasn't a lot of effective organizing for lobbying [Congress] . . . but as far as marches go, petitions, advertisements in newspapers, and public speak-outs of various kinds, and teach-ins, all of that was being done—and done very well—all across the country. . . . We were getting the people steadily. For three years or so all the demonstrations were getting bigger and bigger, and they were getting colossal in New York. So I didn't think we were doing anything wrong so much as it just wasn't enough. . . . We were always feeling kind of desperate.[127]

The summer's blues reflected a broader historical pattern. Perceptions of powerlessness were especially prevalent among antiwar activists in the weeks after big national protests. "You would pump a lot of adrenaline, so to speak, mobilize a lot of stuff, there's a big outpouring—and then nothing changes," Bettina Aptheker explained. Frayed nerves often made things worse. "To do a demonstration rubs an awful lot of feelings very raw," John McAuliff said. "It requires an immense amount of sacrifice of people's time and resources and lots of very painful discussions. . . . There was a need after any of the big mobilizations to back off, to let things cool down." Some activists were disheartened by the White House statements that perennially followed national demonstrations denying any influence of the peace movement on U.S. policy.[128]

Compounding activists' anguish in the spring and summer of 1967 was a rumor that Johnson *was* going to drastically escalate the war. According to several sources, the United States was poised to invade North Vietnam and level Haiphong, possibly with nuclear weapons. Some protesters feared the escalation would lead not only to war with China but to massive political repression in America. "When national solidarity becomes of paramount importance to those waging the war, they will not tolerate internal dissent—about anything," Carl Oglesby, Tom Hayden, and others warned. Backed by the SDS National Council, these activists advocated organizing a "large-scale" act of civil disobedience before the escalation occurred. While it was unlikely that Johnson could be forced to back down, they argued, "through the crises of arrests, a spirit could be generated to lift people out of their lethargy" and expunge the "feelings of impotence" then threatening to "immobilize potential organizers."[129] The escalation didn't materialize, but the specter of a dangerously expanded war haunted many protesters until nearly the end of the conflict.

Growing doubts about the movement's effectiveness aggravated arguments over strategies and tactics. SDS's Paul Booth:

Every time anybody said, "It's obvious that such and such that we've been doing doesn't work, therefore we've got to do . . . something different," all of that discussion was based on [our failure to see] that the system was actually working in all kinds of ways. . . . So there were all of these people outside thinking that they didn't have any impact and conducting interminable arguments about "Should we or should we not keep silent when we vigil? Should we or should we not carry the NLF flag? Should we or should we not have mass demonstrations? Should we or should we not engage in electoral politics? . . . Should the slogan be 'negotiations' or 'withdrawal'?" In hindsight, none of it made a goddamn bit of difference. And all of that discussion was born in our lack of ability to see what was actually going on. . . . The debates about what we should be spending our time and energy on were much more demented and difficult to resolve because of this. . . . We just weren't very sophisticated about politics.[130]

The peace movement's failure to visibly affect the war continued to lead some people to abandon antiwar activity. The inflated arguments resulting from that failure lengthened already long antiwar meetings, sapping additional energy from the movement. The many hours Madeline Duckles logged at meetings led her to remark later, "Now I'm at the point where I'll do anything for my country but go to another meeting."[131]

Despite the growing despair among activists, however, the peace movement pressed relentlessly on. Most antiwar organizers continued to ply their trade, working phone trees, raising money, leafleting, picketing, rallying. For all was not gloomy. There were reasons for hope, there were rewards in their work. Some activists had always suspected that stopping the war would take time. They knew it would only end when much of the public turned against it, and that inducing this would not be easy. When David Harris and several of his friends in Palo Alto, California, began preaching draft resistance in 1966, Harris recalled, "we didn't start with the notion, 'Here we are . . . in California and we're going to change the government.' . . . Where we started was, 'Here we are in California, we're going to see if we can change our friends, and see if we can maybe change their friends.' We were starting from the bottom and working up." Harris said he felt their work was successful because the ranks of draft resisters grew. And he was

not convinced one way or another how much effect we were having on the government, other than that the government knew that we were there, because they were fucking watching us all the time, and that they weren't terribly pleased with what we were doing, because they every now and then denounced us. . . . And I suspect we probably didn't have an effect on people who were determined to plunge forward with the policy. Nor did we expect to. I didn't . . . think McGeorge Bundy was going to convert to our position. What I expected was that we were going to make McGeorge Bundy irrelevant. We were going to cut Johnson's and whoever else's political base out from under them so that they couldn't wage the war. . . .

You know, politics is like living inside a pinball machine—whatever you do takes five or six bounces before it hits something. And that was always my premise. All you can do is keep pushing at it and seeing what pops up at the other end. And what was popping up at the other end was that the government was having a lot of trouble.[132]

Many activists shared Harris's gratification with the antiwar movement's continuing growth. For every person who left the movement, another two or three joined up. "That was inspiring," the YSA leader Lew Jones remembered. "My feeling throughout . . . is that we could beat the bastards, just given enough time and organizing." An awareness that the movement was helping to "prevent the development of a war hysteria" in the United States encouraged some. So did growing congressional criticism of the conflict. Reports of antiwar sentiment among American GIs also lifted activists' spirits. Increasing media criticism of the war was encouraging, too. Some protesters considered the government's attacks on them another sign of their clout. Spreading opposition to the war overseas was inspiriting as well.[133]

There were also rewards in managing the nuts and bolts of antiwar activities. If a demonstration went off according to plan, Brad Lyttle said, there was a good turnout, no one got hurt, the press covered it, and sufficient funds were raised,

you're happy, you feel you've done something. . . . I guess it's all of these secondary benefits that made you feel optimistic. Because a lot of people felt optimistic in the movement simply because of the support they were getting. Take a person like [CALCAV leader] Dick Fernandez. . . . He ended up getting a contribution of one and a half million dollars. Well, that would make one feel fairly successful if he were an organizer—no matter what Johnson was doing. Johnson may be pouring napalm on the Vietnamese, but you're obviously being successful in some respect. And that was to a certain extent the way everybody felt in the anti–Vietnam War movement. . . . These specific concrete gains . . . always gave you a sense of success for your efforts, even though you didn't seem to be affecting the government's policy very much.[134]

Many peace activists also received sustenance from the lengthening membership rolls of their own political organizations. Peter Camejo admitted that a major reason why he rarely despaired over the escalating war was because he equated the expansion of the SWP with political success. "As long as the SWP was growing, all questions were being solved," he said.[135]

Why were some activists too impatient to take heart from the antiwar movement's building domestic resonance, while others were sanguine and determined? Age is one clue to the puzzle. Youthful protesters were particularly prone to impatience. Those from privileged backgrounds may have been more prone to it than others. Raised in homes that provided for their material needs, many expected their political demands to be rapidly granted as well. Carl Oglesby argued later that the "enormous amount of impatience" of many SDSers was a product of "their upper-middle-class attitude. Which was, 'Hey, I want it. If I want it, I should get it. And if I don't get it, I'm going to pitch a bitch.' That's finally what politics came down to for a lot of these kids. It was bitch pitching, as though they were dealing with their parents. And they never got it through their heads that they weren't talking to their parents about this." Also, many youthful and other protesters without previous political experience had little understanding of the amount of hard work required to bring about political change. Hence "there was all of this quick disillusionment," Doug Dowd recalled. He added: "In the United States we've got such a screwy notion of what constitutes success. For one thing, success has got to be dramatic and quick and so on. We don't see success as making progress toward something. . . . We've got this goddamn 'instant this, instant that' attitude."[136]

Some activists were taught forbearance by the Vietnamese. Those who met with them directly were counseled that stopping the war would take time. "They would talk about what they'd been doing for hundreds of years, trying to gain their independence and fight off imperialists," Dave Dellinger remembered. "I think that helped me and some other people to have a little perspective." The Vietnamese also stressed how important antiwar activity in the United States was to them.[137]

The Vietnamese strengthened the resolve of American activists by way of immediate example, too. Their implacable determination and buoyant spirits in the face of the U.S. onslaught were contagious. After returning from a trip to North Vietnam, Dowd was "so high on those people. To walk down the streets of Hanoi and see those little kids . . . Jesus Christ, it makes you weep with joy for the species." The human suffering Dowd observed the United States wreaking in Vietnam also fueled his determination. "One of the incurable hatreds I will have for the rest of my life is [toward] the U.S. government for what they did to those people," he later fumed. "To meet with the Vietnamese and . . . to get a sense of what kinds of things they were trying to do, and the kinds of sacrifices they were making to do it, and the kind of commitment they had to a decent society—and to see what we did to that society. . . . Just absolutely *incredible* savagery that this country [practiced]. Everybody in this country should be deadly ashamed of it!" Donna Allen said of trips to Vietnam, "When you come back, you've dedicated your life."[138]

Many peace activists were also fortified by a trust that the Vietnamese revolution would ultimately prove victorious. Despite the persistent escalation of the war, the United States was fighting an enemy that would never give up. WSP's Dagmar Wilson remembered the boost she gained from a stay in North Vietnam in the late summer of 1967:

> We saw how well the children and the villagers were prepared, how the whole country was united. . . . The war effort was so widely dispersed throughout the countryside that it would have been impossible, really, to win that war without just laying waste to the whole darn country. And this was so apparent when you were there—in no time at all we knew—that the American authorities must also have known. . . .
>
> The strength and the unity of the Vietnamese people . . . was inspiring. And I said, "This is what it must have been like to have lived in the United States when they were fighting their revolutionary war, when they were trying to get the darn British off their back." . . .
>
> Once we'd been to Vietnam we knew that the Vietnamese were winning that war and that . . . there was no way we would win it. No matter what General Curtis LeMay said about bombing them back to the Stone Age. I mean, there was just no way that was ever going to happen.[139]

The Vietnamese bolstered the resolve of antiwar leaders more than that of rank-and-file activists, however. Few of the latter traveled to Vietnam or met with the Vietnamese in other locations. This helps explain why antiwar leaders generally exhibited greater persistence.[140]

There were additional reasons for activists' determination. The sense of community that movement life offered was invigorating. It contrasted starkly with the loneliness often experienced in everyday life. By protesting the war, friends could be made, sex obtained, and love exchanged. For some people, the social rewards of movement life overshadowed the political ones.

Most important of all, many protesters persisted simply because their moral principles would allow nothing else. "It was like breathing or like feeding your children," WSPer Alice Hamburg reflected. "We didn't think that there was any alternative." So morally driven were some activists that questions of political effectiveness were almost irrelevant. Asked about her sense of the movement's efficacy during Johnson's steady escalation of the war, Bettina Aptheker responded, "I never looked at it that way. . . . I don't expect to have an effect. I never have. . . . I thought that you protested something because it was wrong. Even if nobody listened. . . . I just kept doing it because the war was wrong." Considerations of political effectiveness received particularly short thrift from some religious pacifists. Protesting the war was first and foremost a way to remain faithful to their religious beliefs. The antiwar leader Sam Brown went so far as to assert that pacifists found it "very easy" to bear the Johnson administration's apparent indifference to their activities. "I mean, after all they have a several-hundred-year history of just getting the shit kicked out of them on a regular basis and coming back for more. So they didn't really expect that the world was going to come around to their point of view."[141]

FOUR

1967: Part II

Rehabilitating Broken Vietnamese Bodies

Personal morality was the engine that propelled a group of Quakers to mend civilian victims of the war in South Vietnam. Their heroic work constitutes a little known but remarkable chapter in the American peace movement. After the AFSC's David and Mary Stickney (Robert McNamara's vacation antagonists) had set up a refugee-assistance project in Quang Ngai province in 1966, they had discovered another urgent human need there. Of the hundreds of wounded civilians convalescing in hospitals, most were receiving little physical therapy and rehabilitation, with the result that many of them suffered complete or partial loss of the use of their limbs. On the Stickneys' advice, the AFSC established a rehabilitation center in Quang Ngai in 1967.[1]

Dot Weller was the center's first professional therapist. She arrived in Quang Ngai that July, joining a staff of three or four. "At that point we had nothing," Weller remembered. "No building, no plans. . . . Just the concept of what we were going to do." To help determine the concrete need for rehabilitation services in the province, Weller went over to the provincial hospital. Her experience was

> pretty damn discouraging. Because things were in a horrible, horrible condition. And we found that a large majority of the Vietnamese medical community . . . were not very well qualified. Number two, I think their attitudes were so heavily overlaid with the need to survive that protection of themselves and their families became more important than anything else. . . . Survival was the first issue in everybody's mind. Patients were way down the line in priority.
>
> Hygienic conditions were just undescribable. One of the things we first saw was a pile in the back of the hospital that was literally undulating with maggots and worms and . . . castoff dressings and ampu-

tated parts . . . right next to a well. In a shed in the back, bodies were stacked up like cordwood. And there wasn't enough of anything. Bandages were worn for weeks and finally just turned over because there were no new bandages. In essence, the patients . . . really were getting very, very little treatment. . . . If they survived, probably it was 10 percent due to medical care and 90 percent due to luck.[2]

The Quakers constructed a small brick building in which to house their program. They also taught Vietnamese trainees therapy methods and how to make splints, exercise aids, and prostheses. They emphasized use of local supplies to pave the way for an entirely Vietnamese-run operation and to minimize shopping trips to Hong Kong on U.S. military flights, a distasteful but frequently unavoidable way to travel.[3] The AFSCers were amazed at the ingenuity of their Vietnamese trainees. "We found out that they were head and shoulders above us already with improvisation," Weller recalled. "All we'd have to do was show them a picture or explain to them what we wanted and they would come up with something *very* quickly. They were great people for improvising, because they'd been doing it for years in other ways." Sandbags were used to construct exercise aids, frozen juice cans and metal drums to make splints, and bamboo to fashion prostheses. In November the Quakers hauled into their compound the surviving wing of a CIA airplane that had been shot down by NLF forces while trying to land at Quang Ngai airport. They then cut it up to make splints and parts of prostheses.[4]

Although most of their work consisted of teaching therapy skills to the Vietnamese, the Quakers sometimes helped out on the emergency ward of the provincial hospital. Their experiences there were not easily forgotten. In a letter to the AFSC's national office, the prosthetist Roger Marshall described one such shift as "the worst experience I have ever had in my life":

I arrived at the casualty department just after Marge, Dot, and Joe. I looked around. There seemed to be shattered bodies everywhere. I stepped across stretchers on the floor and saw two women with severe back wounds suckling their babies. An old man had been shot in the throat. There was every conceivable wound one could think of to be seen. Flesh and bones had been ripped by shrapnel or cannon fire.

I hadn't been there more than a few minutes when an open jeep ambulance backed up to the steps. It would be impossible to describe clearly what I saw inside. It was like looking through a hole into Hell. I saw a number of small children inside, their feet sticking out over the tail board. A smell of blood, urine, and feces drifted into my nostrils. I honestly did not want to see what came out of that ambulance.

We brought them in. There were five of them. Their ages ranged from about 3 yrs. to eight. I worked opposite Dot on a young boy about four or five years old. As we washed the sand and blood off him, we found bullet or shrapnel wounds in his cheek and stomach. One bullet had gone into his stomach and out through his left buttock just above his rectum. Blood, feces and bone chippings oozed out as we turned him over from the gaping hole where the bullet had emerged. There were other holes in his body also. He was so cold, and he kept looking at me in a puzzled sort of way. He didn't utter a sound.

An anguished Weller wrote back home, "What are we 'saving them from' that could be any worse than what they endure now??!!"[5]

Weller recalled that working in Quang Ngai was "very hard on most of us emotionally." She described the coping mechanisms the Quakers employed:

Probably we thrived a lot on crisis. There was so much need, there was so much to be done, that it just kind of kept us going. . . . We really needed each other. We found out a lot of times when each one of us was ready to fall apart . . . somebody else was looking to us for support. So you . . . sort of had to pull yourself up by your bootstraps and then carry on. So we kind of kept each other buoyed up. . . . A lot of times we were really appalled at ourselves, we were developing a tremendously gallows sense of humor. It was just gross and we were ashamed of ourselves, but I think this was all part and parcel . . . of trying to keep ourselves put together. You had to laugh at it.

The strain ultimately caught up with Weller, though. The heart problems that forced her to leave Quang Ngai in 1971 were "purely stress," she said.[6]

The Quaker rehabilitation project in Quang Ngai did more than repair war-ravaged Vietnamese bodies. It nourished opposition to the war in the United States. The Quakers' direct observations of the human suffering wrought by the conflict intensified the antagonism of the AFSC as a whole to the war and strengthened its members' commitments to stopping it. The manager of the physical and occupational therapy department of a California hospital, Weller recalled that working in Quang Ngai

pushed me a little further to the left. I think when I went over [to Vietnam] basically I was pretty much a liberal. . . . I was beginning to feel that the United States was making a mistake, but I was on the fence: "Maybe they know more than I do. . . ." But I hadn't been there very long before it just pushed me all the way over on the other side of the fence. I became very, very bitter about the American government and what they were doing over there. And I don't know that I've ever trusted our government since.

The Quakers also provided information critical of U.S. policies to American journalists and directed journalists to other people who possessed such information. Further, AFSCers gave speeches and distributed literature across the United States on Quang Ngai that focused on the pain of common Vietnamese peasants and eschewed ideological analysis. These communications often touched Americans unsympathetic to "political" antiwar propaganda. And by emphasizing the cost of the war to the Vietnamese, the Quakers fueled peace activity in 1973–75 after U.S. troops had left Vietnam. They heightened other activists' sensitivity to the continuing suffering of the Vietnamese under the Saigon regime and thus the need to halt U.S. economic and political support for the war as well.[7]

An Educational (Vietnam) Summer

The summer of 1967 witnessed considerable grass-roots antiwar activity in the United States. Vietnam Summer was responsible for much of this activity. Five hundred paid Vietnam Summer staffers and more than twenty-six thousand volunteers organized hundreds of local antiwar projects. Some were in locations that had previously experienced little or no antiwar protest. In West Virginia, for example, Vietnam Summer set up peace groups on quiet college campuses and distributed a newsletter door-to-door.[8]

As Gar Alperovitz had hoped, Vietnam Summer spawned many new protesters. "Half of the volunteers have never worked actively in the peace movement," Vietnam Summer Co-Director Lee Webb estimated. The project also provided activists with valuable training in door-to-door organizing. "At that moment the canvassing idea was a breakthrough, it was like a big invention," Alperovitz recalled. Many protesters had previously been reluctant to ring doorbells. "Some of the WSP women were willing to go down and march back and forth in front of the White House, but they wouldn't talk to their neighbors over the back fence. Because . . . it's very, very difficult to talk to someone who thinks you must be a commie," said WSP's Donna Allen. But with Vietnam Summer activists "went out in the public" and "opened things up."[9]

Sam Brown was among those who gained profitable canvassing experience through Vietnam Summer. "I know the first time that I ever went and knocked on somebody's door and waited for them to answer so that I could tell them that I wanted to talk to them about the war was *not* an easy moment," Brown recalled. He and many other Vietnam Summer activists subsequently applied their new skills organizing support for Eugene McCarthy's 1968 presidential bid. Brown headed Youth for McCarthy. "To some extent the McCarthy campaign couldn't have happened without that," he said of the training Vietnam Summer provided activists. Brown and others would use their skills to organize the important Vietnam Moratorium in 1969 as well.[10]

Through Vietnam Summer, its co-director, Richard Fernandez, gained insight valuable to his work as director of CALCAV:

> I learned by doing what the value was of putting money out all over
> the country for local organizers. And without that experience I prob-
> ably would have dragged my feet a couple more years . . . about the
> money issue. But after that summer I came back [to the CALCAV
> national office in New York] and said, "We have to put 25 percent of
> our resources into the field, and more if we can, but we have to kind
> of make a commitment so people around the country know what to
> expect. And heavy amounts of it should go into the South. And in
> the Ann Arbors and Detroits and Clevelands and Chicagos it should
> be more of a symbol"—you know, if you can't raise money in Ann
> Arbor, for Christ's sake, you shouldn't be around. So that helped to
> spawn, over about a two- or three-year period, a field network of
> about forty full- and part-time organizers. And that, you can imag-
> ine, just did geometrical good for the organization. [11]

Despite Vietnam Summer's accomplishments, however, many of its organizers were dissatisfied. They wondered whether they were achieving anything.
"Anti-war organizing proved exceedingly difficult," one lamented. Alperovitz
found gauging Vietnam Summer's success baffling:

> I remember feeling totally unable to assess it. . . . We knew we had
> all these activities out there in the field. There were WATS lines,
> there were people saying they did things, there was *Vietnam Sum-
> mer News* reporting stuff. But I all of a sudden knew what business-
> men meant about not really knowing what was happening. I didn't
> know. So I felt frustrated. . . . I knew in the areas where I had some
> direct experience that it had been a major catalyst [to antiwar ac-
> tivity]. No doubt about it. . . . You could see it. I remember we had
> a big summer fair on the Cambridge Common which brought in
> thousands of non-antiwar people. . . . And we kept getting reports
> that things like this were happening elsewhere. But the truth is we
> didn't know. No one *really* knew what the impact was. [12]

Alperovitz had another reason to feel discontented. Political infighting inside
Vietnam Summer had, to some degree, hampered its activity. Many liberals
"could not handle being in the same umbrella with the Resistance," he recalled.
"That got people uptight." Whether Vietnam Summer should promote draft
resistance was "very controversial. And I felt like if the organization was going
to carry on it . . . might split on that issue. Because the SANE-types were
getting *very*, very nervous." The political differences among Vietnam Summer
activists would not, in fact, have allowed the organization to continue much past
September. [13] Again, protesters' inability to get along had hurt their cause, as an

ongoing national canvassing campaign would have well complemented the militant demonstrations that erupted that fall.

"You Guys Are Just Going to Martyr Yourselves"

Resistance activists were then organizing for their national draft-card turn-in on October 16. Working existing antidraft groups, Lennie Heller emphasized the existential necessity of noncooperation. It was, Heller claimed, a way to "get your shit together" and "be free." It was also a way for males to prove their manhood. Those unwilling to return their draft cards to the government simply "had no balls," he said. More than a little of Heller's virility was addressed to women. Michael Ferber remembered that when he spoke in Boston, Heller "practically" declared to the females present, "If you girls want to sleep with me, you can form a line over there."[14]

Heller's brash style alienated many potential resisters. But it also turned some on. Although "half disgusted by" Heller's attempts to "pick up every girl he could find," the shy Ferber "half envied" them as well. Heller's manly swagger "was certainly better than the kind of 'wimpy' Quaker style that we were more used to," Ferber recalled. And Ferber was "quite excited" by Heller's bold talk on the turn-in. When the call for the action had been issued in April, Ferber had been somewhat skeptical of its success, given the stiff penalties for noncooperation. But Heller's braggadocio "made it sound as if we were really going to do it . . . out of sheer strength, out of pizzazz." And Heller "was serious."[15]

David Harris and Dennis Sweeney were building Resistance chapters from the ground up. "We did it in unfriendly turf," Harris recalled. "We were working places that weren't automatics by any means." Harris and Sweeney tried to get to know the youth they met personally, "playing guitar and dropping acid besides talking politics." They knew it would be difficult to face a possible five-year prison sentence and $10,000 fine without a social support system. Two or three kids "out there in Chico trying to be the only draft resisters in town . . . ain't going to last long," Harris observed, without "some sense of connection." Harris and Sweeney also attempted to make sure that those who agreed to join the turn-in were deeply committed to resistance and understood its consequences. "We quite consciously stayed away from trying to generate numbers right off the bat, by insisting that people be serious," Harris remembered. "We didn't say, 'Here, come do this, come do this, this is the latest gig that everybody should get in on.' We said, 'Think it over. . . . If you're going to do it, you're going to have to back it up, and when you back it up, it ain't going to be easy, it's going to be you by yourself backing it up.'" Harris tried to avoid "big ideological discussions." He felt other antiwar activists were spending "too much time sitting around saying, 'Are we being effective?' . . . too much time worrying, and not enough time going out and doing."[16]

Progress was slow. More than thirty Resistance chapters dotted the American political landscape by September. Noncooperation was being excitedly discussed among wide circles of youth. But few were willing to commit themselves to the action. Several hundred would be a good turnout on October 16, Resistance organizers ruminated.[17]

One reason for their low success rate was the scorn heaped upon the Resistance by other antiwar activists. The group was measuring the value of noncooperation more by individual moral standards of conduct than political ones, many SDSers sniffed. Returning a draft card to the government might make one feel good, but would any political benefit come of it? SDSers doubted enough young men would join the crusade to make a difference. "You guys are just going to martyr yourselves," Harvard SDS's Progressive Labor Party (PL) members sneered. According to PL, noncooperators were a bunch of "bourgeois moralists" who "didn't believe in struggle."[18]

Such charges that the Resistance was promoting apolitical moral witness made its organizers' blood boil. Ferber recalled feeling "a lot of scorn" for PL. "I thought, 'What the hell is wrong with bourgeois moralism? I can't help being bourgeois.'" And was moral behavior a problem? Furthermore, he certainly did believe in struggle. "I thought I was struggling pretty hard, but I guess I wasn't struggling their type," Ferber smiled. "We felt the strategy and the morality were the exact same thing," said Harris, who scoffed that SDSers were "a bunch of white kids playing Black Panther" who ultimately exerted "jackshit strategic impact."[19]

SDSers also deprecated the Resistance for organizing middle-class rather than working-class opposition to the war. PLers exhorted other activists to join them on the assembly lines that summer to talk to real, live toilers about the war. Most Resistance activists considered PL's push into the factories a joke. Typically adorned with wrinkled blue work shirts and short hair so as to look like the workers they were not, PL's mainly student cadres stuck out on the assembly lines like so many sore thumbs. Most of their fellow laborers thought they were nuts. Ferber remembered he and other Resistance organizers thinking "that they may have been full of all kinds of theoretical arguments, but they weren't doing shit, except organizing students, and not the working class at all." And while the official PL line was to enter the army if drafted and organize GIs, "I noticed none of them were doing that." Ferber and his friends eventually "just said, 'Fuck 'em. Idiots. They're probably all police agents.'" Ferber added, "Some of them turned out to be police agents."[20]

By midsummer the ex-PLer and Resistance co-founder Steve Hamilton had joined the ranks of the Resistance's detractors. After publicly condemning its "middle-class liberal" thrust, Hamilton and several other Berkeley radicals moved to a poor section of a nearby town to bring revolutionary consciousness to its citizens. Among other organizing tactics, they "went to a lot of country bars," Hamilton would later laugh. The young revolutionaries also distributed copies of their newspaper, subtly titled *Today's Pig Is Tomorrow's Bacon*. In response to a 23-year-old policeman's fatal collision with a street lamp, the front page of the paper's introductory issue blared, 23 YEARS IS TOO LONG FOR ONE PIG TO LIVE! Hamilton and his comrades later formed the Revolutionary Union (RU), a small Maoist organization headed by Bob Avakian. Hamilton subsequently said that the RU was a product of "Avakian and I having a few too many beers." He avowed that his leap toward working-class organizing resulted from "mechanical Marxism."[21]

Far from resisting the draft, some antiwar activists dared officials to put them in an army uniform. Clark Kissinger, the former national secretary of SDS, sent his draft board a picture of himself standing next to a junior minister of the North Vietnamese government with a note attached to it reading, "Please put this in my file." Kissinger also related that he had mailed his draft card to the NLF's office in Czechoslovakia. When asked at his draft board hearing, "Are you willing to fight in Vietnam?" Kissinger responded genially, "Sure I am— just not on your side." After receiving an induction order anyway, Kissinger held a festive "draft acceptance ceremony" outside the Chicago induction center. Standing on a table, clad in a World War I–style doughboy uniform, a five-piece band playing off to one side, he happily offered himself up to the army. "I gave a speech about how I was enjoying going into the army, getting paid by the government for two years to do antiwar organizing among the troops, and that I hoped to be back soon and bring my whole unit with me," he recalled. Kissinger was not asked to report for duty.[22]

Many draft boards eventually became reluctant to draft such agitators. Columbia SDSer Mark Rudd was found physically unfit for service after informing his board he planned to pursue his occupation of "professional revolutionary" inside the army. After Steve Hamilton passed out leaflets at his induction physical announcing, "I would love to be inducted—because then I could organize mutinies," he was granted a 1-Y deferral, which was "sort of a dumping ground," one draft counselor explained, "for guys the Army just doesn't want."[23]

As peace activists debated the political merits of noncooperation, another controversy was flaring over how to best channel public support for it. It reflected growing doubts among young radicals that nonviolent protest could end the war.

The four Resistance co-founders had initially agreed to ask their supporters to participate in a demonstration outside the Oakland induction center. They differed on how to build the action. Steve Hamilton thought all interested parties should collectively organize it. David Harris felt this was "the whole wrong approach." He worried that many of the Bay Area's youthful "revolutionaries" would want to battle the cops. "I knew what would happen if we brought people together and then said, 'Let's find a plan,'" Harris remembered. "Especially in . . . *Berkeley*, where there were four thousand political groups and more bullshit than you could shake a stick at." He and Dennis Sweeney believed Resistance organizers should design the demonstration.[24]

But Hamilton doubted Harris and Sweeney would support an action militant enough to appeal to working-class youth. And he was feeling pressure from other Bay Area radicals to begin building a series of antidraft actions at the Oakland induction center October 16–20. The National Mobilization Committee (the Spring Mobe renamed) was planning a large national antiwar protest on October 21, and the close proximity between that date and the date of the turn-in seemed to offer the perfect opportunity for a solid week of resistance activities.[25]

When Harris and Sweeney were out of town, Hamilton called a meeting to plan "Stop the Draft Week" (STDW) in Oakland. When Harris and Sweeney returned, they were "furious."[26]

The summer planning meetings for STDW were stormy, further dividing a Bay Area left already fragmented into a multitude of slivers. Many traditional pacifists wanted to sit in the doorways to the induction center. Harris advocated *decentralized* nonviolent civil disobedience. Groups of protesters should head to outlying towns where inductees were picked up and wheeled into Oakland, he exhorted. When government buses pulled up to these stops, the protesters should "whap—chain them down." After the buses were on the road toward Oakland again, other obstacles should greet them. "We were going to buy old used cars, under phony names, and get ahead of the bus on the freeway when it was going to make the turnoff," Harris reminisced. "And we were going to stop in the middle of the off-ramp. You know, park the son of a bitch, take the keys and run. And literally go for the practical effect of making it impossible for them to run the induction center that day—period."[27]

Many radicals desired something with more bite to it. They were frustrated by the inability of nonviolent action to end the war; some had even "started playing with guns as a way to forget their own hopelessness," one recalled. These radicals also shared Hamilton's conviction that a "new kind" of militant demonstration was necessary to reach working-class youth, particularly blacks. By "defending themselves" against police attacks, they maintained, protesters would demonstrate the "strength" and "seriousness" of the middle-class antidraft movement, thereby encouraging "young workers" to resist. "Vicariously intoxicated by the summer riots" that erupted in cities across the United States, these radicals modeled their plan for STDW "after a black street rebellion." They talked of "mobility," "spontaneity," "outflanking the police," and "kicking ass." Exactly how this white riot would shut down the induction center—or end the war—was "left unanswered." Hamilton conceded, "It was all vague."[28]

For Harris, STDW planning came to a painful head at a turbulent session in August. "All these weird SDS-types from Berkeley turned the meeting into what I felt was a farce, a shambles," he remembered. They were

> hostile to the Resistance . . . calling us a bunch of "middle-class mor-
> alists," denouncing us and all this shit. And talking about how we
> "have to follow the path blazed by the Black Panthers and make our-
> selves credible to black people in Oakland." . . . [There] was just all
> this *rhetoric*: "Ya, one of these fucking honk cops gets on my ass I'm
> going to blow this sucker away." And this guy's a math major at
> Berkeley, you know. "What? C'mon, *man*. Where are you from?
> Mission Hills?"

Hamilton remembered the dominant reaction to Harris's claim that nonviolence was used successfully by Gandhi in India: "Are you shitting me?"[29]

Harris stormed out of the meeting. "I wasn't trying to blaze the trail of the Black Panthers," he loathingly recalled. "And while I certainly wanted to be credible to whoever we could be credible to, I did not adopt the theory that you had to act like a young Huey Newton in order to be credible to black people in Oakland, or anybody else. If you had to behave that way, then I'd just as soon sacrifice our credibility in that community and keep it in others." And Harris found the militants' plan for "milling around" in the street outside the induction center and then "free-lancing" in the face of police sweeps "absurd, mostly. You'd get a lot of people needlessly beat up. You know, you're going to terrorize the police, because they ain't going to know what you're going to do, and they're double-scared because of that. . . . I thought these guys were off-the-wall. I didn't want to be associated with them." Harris ceased formal participation in STDW.[30]

Staggering toward the Pentagon

Meanwhile, the National Mobilization Committee was planning the most au-dacious national demonstration yet. Despite bitter clashes over antiwar strategy at an organizing conference in May, Mobe activists agreed to hold a multi-tactical protest in Washington, D.C., on October 21. They would combine a legal demonstration with a "non-violent confrontation" designed to "create a social drama that could become the object of national focus." Given the huge turnout in April, they perceived, one million marchers was not unrealistic.[31]

But the Mobe had trouble just getting the project off the ground. The in-spirational A. J. Muste had died of a heart attack in February, Mobe director James Bevel fell ill, the indefatigable Dave Dellinger was out of the country for much of the summer, and the Mobe was up to its eyeballs in debt. Many activists were at each other's throats over the significance of the June Arab-Israeli war and the ghetto riots in the United States. Some doubted another national demonstration would achieve anything. SDS expressed its "regret" over the Mobe's decision to hold the protest, stating, "We feel that these large demonstrations . . . can have no significant effect on American policy in Vietnam." Come August, the precise location and character of the action remained undecided.[32]

A desperate Fred Halstead suggested that the former Vietnam Day Committee leader Jerry Rubin be brought in from Berkeley to coordinate the project. The Mobe called Rubin, and he agreed to take on the task.[33] Halstead quickly came to regret his advice.

Rubin, it appeared, had changed since his days with the VDC. His thick, curly hair now jutted out six inches in all directions, and he had developed an affinity for hallucinogens and the religious practices of Native American Indian tribes. To Halstead, he "seemed less relaxed than before." Rubin felt the action should take place at the Pentagon. Not only was the Pentagon the nerve center of the American war machine, but, as a five-sided figure, it was, he said, a symbol of evil. By "exorcising" the building, protesters would drive the evil spirits away.[34]

Halstead was unamused. His confidence in Rubin was further shaken when, on a reconnaissance mission to the Pentagon, Rubin displayed ignorance of the fact that the building wasn't located in Washington but across the Potomac River in Virginia.[35]

On August 26, the Mobe agreed to hold the protest at the Pentagon. Two days later, it held a press conference in New York to announce its plan. On October 21–22, Americans would "shut down the Pentagon," one Mobe leader declared. "We will fill the hallways and block the entrances. . . . This confrontation will be massive, continuing, flexible, surprising." Surprising, indeed. Abbie Hoffman, a countercultural former civil rights activist brought into the Mobe by Rubin, informed the nation, "We're going to raise the Pentagon three hundred feet in the air." Dellinger warned that protesters would disrupt other federal offices as well: "There will be no government building left unattacked."[36]

The conference played poorly with the Mobe's moderate members. Their apprehension over the protest persisted in the weeks ahead. Most of it concerned the civil disobedience scheduled. Despite their agreement to hold a multi-tactical operation, many Mobe activists were jumpy about including illegalities in the demonstration. As Dellinger, who was the main driving force behind the Mobe's transition "from protest to resistance," would recall, "We ran into *tremendous* opposition . . . from most of the organized movement."[37]

But before exploring this opposition, let us examine the thinking of the Mobe's bolder members. Just what was so appealing about civil disobedience anyway?

When I interviewed him years later, Dave Dellinger was living in Vermont. A burly man with ruddy cheeks and a neatly trimmed white beard, he was amiable and modest, occasionally even self-effacing. His voice was gentle and several notches higher than might be expected of a man of his frame. Not surprisingly, this veteran organizer continued to devote much of his time to political activism, including environmental and antimilitarist activities. He was also at work on his memoirs.

Dellinger's enthusiasm for civil disobedience at the Pentagon reflected a longstanding tactical preference. He felt legal demonstrations wielded limited political clout. They were important for "displaying" a movement's strength, but to actually "exercise" this strength, direct action, or "the next stage of inconvenience," was necessary. "We were trying to show that we were stepping up the militance," he recalled of the Pentagon protest. "That . . . we were going to actually make it impossible for them to continue business as usual." Dellinger expected that U.S. officials would then realize "that they had something bigger on their hands than they'd thought. . . . They'd know there wouldn't be any peace at home if there wasn't peace abroad."[38]

Dellinger also favored civil disobedience because of its effect on protesters. Over the summer he had observed that some people "who had marched over and over again" in legal protests "were beginning to become dispirited." He felt civil disobedience would help rejuvenate them. "Something happens when people put their bodies on the line, or when they get arrested," Dellinger explained. "There's a certain invisible barrier, psychologically, which is crossed, and things happen differently." Dellinger thought any police brutality that resulted from the illegalities would strengthen protesters' resolve as well. "I knew what it did to people when they had their first . . . cattle prod or their first club," he said.[39]

The Mobe's Doug Dowd favored civil disobedience mainly as a way to "educate" the American public. He knew it would attract greater public notice than a mere legal demonstration. Just as a tough old farmer Dowd had met in the South got the attention of his mule by whacking it over the head with a stick, direct action at the Pentagon would get the attention of the American people. Many would then become more cognizant of the war and turn against it. Dowd recognized that many Americans wouldn't react kindly to the protest at first, however:

> I was very conscious of the fact . . . that it would alienate large segments of the public. But . . . I had come to the conclusion that every time that people did something that was in some sense breaking the

law . . . if they were doing it for a cause that could be rationalized and explained, that even though people were alienated at first, finally they began to say, "Well, I guess it's okay for them to do that." And the reason . . . is they began to pay attention.[40]

Brad Lyttle, the coordinator of logistics for the Pentagon protest, felt civil disobedience would influence Americans by conveying the deep political commitment and courage of antiwar demonstrators. "People tend to take folks who commit civil disobedience more seriously than folks who don't," he argued. What's more, Lyttle said,

> every time you can get somebody to act in a nontimid manner, it stimulates other people to do the same. You can take a guy like Dan Ellsberg. Well, Dan Ellsberg's sitting up there with all of these [government] documents at his disposal. He's got to make a courageous decision. Well, if he sees somebody else making a courageous decision sitting down in the street somewhere, he may say, "Well, what the hell? If that guy's got the balls to do that, I'll have the balls to do this." That's what we were trying to do, to a certain extent, all the time.[41]

Many activists' interest in civil disobedience at the Pentagon was shaped by their perception of the domestic political climate in 1967. They felt that the peace movement's continuing growth would allow for a much larger civil disobedience protest than ever before. And larger meant more credible with the public and government. Activists also noticed there was now much broader public support for civil disobedience than before. Those who broke the law were therefore less likely to be politically isolated and repressed by the government. In addition, there would be a large political "buffer zone" of supporters at the protest itself.[42]

Moving beyond mass demonstrations to mass civil disobedience thus seemed completely logical to some activists. "It was a natural evolution," Lyttle reflected. "It developed just as it was supposed to."[43]

Now, the objections. SWPers were particularly antagonistic to direct action at the Pentagon. Committing civil disobedience would hinder the turnout for the legal demonstration, they maintained. Illegalities also tarnished protesters' public image. And SWPers were themselves unexcited about going to jail. "We didn't think that that was the best way to spend our money or our time," Fred Halstead recalled. "So it just wasn't . . . our dish of tea—it's too expensive."[44]

The SWP believed that perceptions of political impotence were stoking interest in direct action at the Pentagon. SWP leader Don Gurewitz:

> From the very first demonstrations, a layer of student participants became frustrated. Once they became convinced that there was a horror show going on in Vietnam, they wanted it over. And we had

all been raised in this polite milieu: "You write to your congressman, you rationally debate things." And nothing changed—it just got worse. And I think under that pressure a layer of the student move-ment . . . just was continually groping for some dramatic thing to do to end this fucking thing. . . . And I think the Pentagon demonstra-tion was the first real expression of that on the national level. . . . It caught . . . a desperate, confrontational mood of a large number of people.

There was "just a sense of, 'We've had these successful demonstrations and the war goes on,'" Dowd echoed. "'We've got to do something more. . . . ' Out of this, of course, comes Weatherman."[45]

WSP activists argued that civil disobedience would restrict the participation of women and children in the protest. Dellinger remembered receiving a tele-gram signed by prominent WSP leaders, Dr. Benjamin Spock, and others "say-ing in effect we'd be betraying . . . the women and children who came to the demonstration if we had civil disobedience because they might get hurt."[46] Also, as mothers they could hardly take a chance on getting arrested. Who would then care for their husbands and kids?

The anxiety of many activists over the Pentagon protest was accentuated by the particular *style* of direct action planned. Dellinger and others were openly gearing up for "something with far more teeth in it" than "passive," "pre-choreographed" civil disobedience. They projected "flexible" and decentralized "probes and thrusts." Dellinger remembered his strategic reasoning:

> I did not feel that we should be an isolated minority of pure people who were holding absolutely pure nonviolent demonstrations, but that there was the youth movement, there was the . . . traditional political left, there were all of these people who were upset by the war . . . and that we should have a place for them and they should have a place for us. They should feed into the movement and be part of it. It should be a mighty waters of many streams. . . . What [that] meant was that it would be tumultuous. You had to recognize that if you didn't say to the Yippies, for instance, at a slightly later date, though it first began to happen at the Pentagon action . . . "I'm sorry, you can't work with us because you're too impure, because you want to piss on the Pentagon and all this crap" . . . then obviously you had a lot of tumult and diverse forces—and you couldn't always guarantee exactly how it would work out.

Dellinger believed a mighty waters of many streams spelled a broader move-ment, since many young people would stay away from the protest were it not for the militance on the agenda. It also spelled a more reasoned one. Without the "steadying influence" of "being part of a larger whole," adventuristic youth "would get worse instead of better," he thought. And it would provide the peace movement with a badly needed cutting edge of militancy. "My conscious thing always was to hold everybody together and move it to the left," Dellinger avowed.[47]

David McReynolds was among the skeptics:

> Mass civil disobedience? Absolutely! I was for that from the beginning. Tumultuous? What does that mean? That means if you're eighty, you can't go to the demonstration. It means if you're a coward you can't go to the demonstration. It limits. It also means you end up with things like burning the American flag and turning off Archie Bunkers, and instead of reaching out to the labor movement . . . you're seen as rejecting American values . . . and, I thought, playing into Johnson's hands. . . . Insulting values that you hold important when I want to change your mind is not, in my view, sound. It may make me feel better, but it may not get what I want done. . . . And my argument was to downgrade those things that I thought were making us feel happy but didn't achieve things.[48]

Doug Dowd worried that unwary protesters might get caught up in rougher waters at the Pentagon than they'd expected. "I was very much opposed to having any kind of c.d. unless people knew exactly what they were getting involved in," he recalled. "If there was anything I didn't want to see it was people getting trapped into becoming heroes that didn't want to be heroes."[49]

It was a common concern. Many activists feared the protest would turn violent. Fred Halstead knew that many of the young people who opposed the war were "very frustrated" and scheming, "'Well, I'm just going to do something terribly nasty, and you're going to pay attention to me.'" Halstead "had no such illusions: 'If you do something terribly nasty, they'll pay attention—by hitting you over the head, that's all they're going to pay attention to.'" Brad Lyttle had no confidence in Rubin and Hoffman's plans. "They're brilliant people, but I just could see very little other than disaster at the end of their strategies and their organizing," he remembered.[50]

McReynolds felt personally threatened by the specter of violence. "I'm a coward," he said frankly. "And the idea of 'upping the ante' means getting your head cracked open, and I'm not in the least eager to do that." McReynolds also worried that the violence would alienate Americans and even promote public sentiment for government repression of protesters. "One of the things which people in the radical movement underestimate is the degree to which everybody is conservative and is unsettled by disorder," he asserted. "And if they see disorder, one of the things they want, no matter what class they belong to, is more police."[51]

Many activists also objected to the provocative rhetoric and countercultural air of spokespeople for the protest. They were irritated to hear of Abbie Hoff-man—odd garb, unkempt hair, impish grin, and all—announcing that protes-ters would make the Pentagon rise into the air, turn orange, and vibrate until all evil emissions had fled. That act would hardly foster public support. The black Student Mobe leader Gwen Patton said evenly, "Black people are not going to go anywhere to *levitate* the Pentagon, okay. We don't find that cute." "In a society where millions of Americans really had felt cut out and were very en-vious of this group of kids—envious of their sexual freedom, envious of their beards, envious of their lifestyle, and envious of the fact that 'those kids have something that my kids do not have,'" McReynolds perceived, such silliness would inevitably burn rather than build political bridges between working Americans and antiwar youth.[52]

Nine months before he killed himself with a massive drug overdose, a loqua-cious and defiant Abbie Hoffman responded to the charge that he and other countercultural activists had alienated the public and thus hurt the peace move-ment. "We deliberately chose to go for the children of the Bunkers, because we could not get the Bunkers," Hoffman told me. "It was kind of hard to appeal to . . . that class of Americans because many of them were beating us up and sending us to jail." And "of course" countercultural protesters turned Ameri-cans off. "First of all, fighting against your government at a time of foreign war is *not* a very popular sport," Hoffman chuckled. Second, "most Americans don't give a shit, period"; they have "always" supported the status quo and distrusted protesters, he contended. "Inevitably you *do* alienate people. I am convinced, from all the readings that I've done, that the dumping of tea in the Boston harbor alienated the majority of Americans at the time." While talk of levitating the Pentagon turned people off, Hoffman conceded, it was "how we got every-body there." Hoffman found it curious that someone would question his politi-cal savvy, "having been cheered by more than half the delegates" to the 1988 Democratic Party convention, "knowing that one of the biggest publishing houses in America is now reissuing my first three books as classics," and having been called "the best grass-roots organizer in America" by one newspaper ("I don't argue with them," he said of the last accolade). "So I don't feel particularly apologetic."[53]

Dave Dellinger reconstructed and analyzed his own reaction to the charge that involving countercultural youth in the Pentagon action would narrow its public appeal:

> What I remember is just being thrilled and excited that this whole
> new element of humor and creativity and youthful zest was coming
> into things. . . . [I felt the levitation] showed the breadth and diver-
> sity and vitality of the opposition. But especially it was a lively,
> imaginative thing that just appealed to me. . . .

You must remember that this struggle had started long before, in somewhat different terms, when SANE had asked everybody to come [to protests] in suits and ties, and women in dresses, and had even been worried about people with beards. . . . Well, it just had too conservative and staid and conventional an emphasis. . . . For that reason, SANE got completely bypassed for that period. So this was merely an extension of that. You know, "How long do we wear masks to look like we're no different than anybody else?"

See, I was trying to walk a narrow line. Because I believed that we should appeal to such traditional, conservative people. So on the one hand I was trying to oppose any kind of hostility, or anything that would just seem too outrageous, I guess. On the other hand, it was clear that the traditional antiwar organizations were much too staid and conventional to grasp the seriousness of the occasion, and also to reach out to [countercultural] people. . . . So the whole idea was to broaden the scope and yet at the same time . . . not to do it in a way which narrowed it on another end.[54]

Activists' anxieties about the Pentagon protest jeopardized its success. As late as two weeks before the demonstration, the SWP, WSP, Dr. Spock, and SDS were all considering withdrawing.[55] The goal of a million marchers now appeared to be a pipe dream.

Protecting the Pentagon

As peace activists fought each other, the Johnson administration continued to apply a "slow squeeze" to North Vietnam. On August 9, the president approved sixteen additional Rolling Thunder targets and an expansion of armed reconnaissance. Two weeks later, he suspended the bombing in the ten-mile radius around Hanoi. The suspension remained in force through September as the administration pursued a backdoor peace feeler to Hanoi. The North Vietnamese accurately pointed out that Rolling Thunder had actually been intensified, as the United States had redirected to other cities the strikes deflected from Hanoi.[56]

Fueling the government's escalation was hawkish congressional sentiment. A vocal minority of legislators continued to urge the administration to pour it on in Vietnam. Congressman George Andrews (D-Ala.) declared in the House chamber that "if this great and powerful nation . . . cannot whip a little country like North Vietnam . . . then we have no business in the war business, and we ought to beat our swords into plowshares and declare to the world that we are a nation of Quakers." Hawkish congressional opinion was strikingly apparent in hearings on Rolling Thunder undertaken by the Preparedness Subcommittee of the Senate Armed Services Committee on August 9–25. Appalled at the curbs the "unskilled civilian amateurs" in the government were placing on the bombing campaign, the "hard-line" committee was "on the warpath." Its members adamantly disputed Robert McNamara's testimony that Rolling Thunder would never significantly affect the progress of the war. U.S. military leaders summoned to testify on Rolling Thunder's merits were also on the warpath. Chief of U.S. Naval Operations Admiral Thomas Moorer argued vehemently that only heavier bombing would end the war. Moorer later groused that U.S. officials

> screwed around so long. . . . They'd say, "A hundred sorties up to latitude twenty degrees." Then they'd say, "Fifty sorties to twenty-two degrees." They'd try to fine-tune the bombing. And I'd say, "What's that for?" People in McNamara's office, they'd say, "We're trying to get the message to Ho Chi Minh." I never did know what message they were trying to get to him, but I know one thing—he never did get it.

As the Pentagon Papers historian asserts, it was "no coincidence" that Johnson authorized additional air strikes on the day the Senate hearings began.[57]

Yet it would be a mistake to conclude from this that the administration was more concerned about the bombing zealots than about its liberal and left-wing critics. In May, McGeorge Bundy had told Johnson that "those against extension of the bombing are more passionate on balance than those who favor it." The president himself proclaimed at a meeting with his advisers on September 5, "The major threat we have is from the doves."[58]

On September 29, Johnson announced that the United States would stop bombing North Vietnam "when this will lead promptly to productive negotiations." The president's proposal merely restated U.S. communications during the backchannel peace feeler and was quickly rejected by Hanoi as a "faked desire for peace." With the administration's peace initiative now dead, ongoing escalatory pressures from the military "could no longer be resisted." On October 4, Secretary of Defense McNamara approved a request from General Westmoreland for expanded B-52 raids. McNamara also agreed to accelerate the deployment of ground troops already ticketed for Vietnam. Two days later, Johnson approved six new Rolling Thunder targets.[59]

Meanwhile, the war's defectors were mounting. Between July and September, some fifteen million Americans switched from support for the conflict to a belief that the United States should "try to end the war and get out as quickly as possible." According to one journalist, "travelers through American cities and countryside noted a strong and widespread falling off of war support." Dominoes were falling in Congress as legislators scampered "in search of a stance that took account of the growing distaste." Among the noteworthy defectors that summer and early fall were Congressmen Tip O'Neill (D-Mass.), Claude Pepper

(D-Fla.), Al Ullman (D-Oreg.), and Morris Udall (D-Ariz.) and Senators Thruston Morton (R-Ky.) and Joseph Tydings (D-Md.). A survey in late September showed forty-three representatives had recently shifted from strong support for the war to "more emphasis on finding a way out."[60]

There was accelerating criticism of U.S. policy in the press. Seven major newspapers expressed second thoughts on the war. *Time* and *Life* magazines also voiced new doubts. Even the business community was getting edgy. When Marriner S. Eccles, a senior corporate officer, attacked the war before the Commonwealth Club of San Francisco in August, the businessmen in attendance reacted surprisingly sympathetically.[61]

A group of young Americans in South Vietnam began making waves. In mid September, the director and three key staff members of International Voluntary Services (IVS), a major relief organization in Vietnam partly financed by the U.S. government, resigned over the war. Fifty IVS workers signed a letter to Johnson calling for negotiations with the NLF and an end to U.S. bombing, defoliation, and other refugee-producing policies. Many of the IVSers had gone to Vietnam supportive of U.S. policies only to be repelled by the war's brutality and angered by USIA propaganda characterizing them as "responsible" American youth in contrast to the "hippy protesters." Their work had become intolerable when the Pentagon placed them under the control of the U.S. military the previous spring. "Our purpose is to help people, not to kill them," they complained to U.S. Ambassador Ellsworth Bunker in Saigon. Bunker did not take the IVSers' dissent well. Don Luce, the resigning IVS director, remembered that when he and a co-worker formally presented the ambassador with their letter to Johnson and mentioned that they were thinking of giving it to the press, Bunker "got very upset." He "said that it would be impolite to send the letter from Vietnam, and particularly to give it to the *New York Times*. That we were blackmailing the U.S. government." The IVSers responded, "Okay, we won't send the letter if you promise to stop the bombing, stop the defoliation, stop making refugees and negotiate with the NLF. Or any one of the three, and we'll give you your choice." The red-faced Bunker only "got more angry."[62]

As its domestic rear guard continued to deteriorate, the Johnson administration stepped up its surveillance of peace activists. It knew they were partially responsible for this deterioration and would remain a major political problem. By the late summer, the administration had in place a vast domestic intelligence collection network. The FBI and local police Red Squads had, of course, been dealing in antiwar surveillance since the movement's inception. Under pressure from Johnson, the CIA had illegally begun its own domestic spying operation in early 1967. In August, it significantly expanded this enterprise by setting up a Special Operations Group to investigate protesters' suspected links to foreign powers.

Later known as Operation CHAOS, the program included wiretaps, mail openings, burglaries, and other black bag jobs. On orders from Johnson, the U.S. Army established its own domestic intelligence-gathering operation in July. Conus Intel relied heavily on the yields of Army intelligence agents placed discreetly inside antiwar groups. Their findings attracted the attention of the Justice Department, FBI, police departments, and other official bodies. "We created addicts for this stuff all over the government," a source close to Conus Intel recalled.[63]

The government's intelligence exchange paid particular heed to the upcoming Pentagon protest. It promised to be the largest of the fall's antiwar activities, and the administration could hardly afford to be caught with its political and logistical pants down as subversives moved on its military headquarters. Government operatives inside the National Mobe kept abreast of the coalition's plans and the organizations and individuals involved. To estimate attendance at the protest, agents tracked the Mobe's transportation arrangements and contacted bus and train companies in the United States. They even examined listings of "rides to Washington" on college bulletin boards. The government formed a secretive intelligence unit in the Pentagon to coordinate information on the protest and secure additional data.[64]

President Johnson was kept intimately apprised of the harvest. A full month before the demonstration, a meeting between the president, McNamara, Attorney General Ramsey Clark, and three other officials was devoted virtually exclusively to it. On October 3, Johnson told Clark that he wanted "some kind of report every night" on what Clark and Deputy Attorney General Warren Christopher were "doing on the demonstration," its "progress," and "any new FBI information." "Have in my office before 8:00 P.M.," the president tersely directed. Johnson began receiving daily memoranda from the Justice Department on the protest from that point on. The White House aide Joseph Califano, who also possessed a healthy thirst for antiwar intelligence, relayed to Johnson a steady stream of reports on the demonstration as well. The president's literature consisted of detailed descriptions of the antiwar activities scheduled for October 21–22 (even down to rally speakers), the Mobe's leaders and their organizational affiliations, and the administration's preparations. Johnson was passed at least one movement leaflet on the protest.[65]

What did the administration see coming down the pipe? For one thing, a turnout considerably smaller than that for the April Spring Mobe demonstrations. On September 20, the FBI told McNamara to expect a crowd of 40–50,000. By the morning of October 21, with the Mobe—much to the administration's pleasure—having canceled many bus and train orders owing to inadequate finances and interest—and government sabotage—attendance for that day was projected at slightly over 28,000. Clark told Johnson on October 18 to expect "'under 30,000' for total weekend attendance."[66]

For another, violence. Not more than could be contained, mind you, but violence nonetheless. Clark wrote Johnson on October 4 that there was "considerable evidence" for this. Officials observed Mobe leaders acting publicly "evasive" about what might transpire at the Pentagon and stressing that "'nobody can predict what forms of resistance will take place.'" The administration knew there would be "a large number of people without central control" on the scene—and hadn't Dave Dellinger stated flatly, "We are not all pacifists?" A small Revolutionary Contingent was "conducting a 'course' in basic karate, street fighting, and how to break through police lines." Phone calls to White House staff from friends around the country "with knowledge of March plans" warned of "a bloody weekend."[67]

Deputy Secretary of Defense for ISA Paul Nitze, the self-described "mastermind" of the Pentagon's defense, was counseling officials that some young radicals were bent on inciting state violence. They were "past the point of no return," Nitze perceived, and wanted to "tear down the entire institutions." According to Nitze, they felt that by provoking the application of "excessive force" against the demonstration, they would increase protesters' "alienation" from American society.[68]

The administration was aware that the fifty to one hundred American Nazis of various oddball stripes who would be counterdemonstrating at the Pentagon would be unlikely to calm the protesters. The Nazis' "potential for violence and causing violence is considerably greater than their numbers," Johnson was informed on October 5.[69]

Officials believed some violence might be self-directed. Norman Morrison was not forgotten. Bryant Wedge, a Princeton University professor, confided to one White House aide: "They want to impale themselves on bayonets . . . and they will because sometimes you just can't pull a bayonet back fast enough."[70]

Violence also loomed in the nation's capital. Intelligence sources reported that Columbia SDSers planned to lead "a snake dance . . . through the streets of Washington with the intention of diverting police, break[ing] through police lines, and grabbing their clubs." Some anarchists were even threatening to assassinate the president. Most ominous was the specter of black violence. The White House aide Tom Johnson told George Christian the morning of October 21, "A large group of the protesters are expected to go into the Negro neighborhoods to try to incite civil disorders tonight." Disturbingly, some blacks would head toward the White House. Nitze later remembered that the summer's ghetto riots were "something you very well had to take deep cognizance of" when preparing for the protest. Officials perceived that if black militants Stokely Carmichael ("Brother Stokely" to one derisive White House aide) or H. Rap Brown attended the protest, it would increase the chance of black violence.[71]

Finally, the administration expected many arrests, particularly at the Pentagon. Secretary of the Army Stanley Resor, who helped organize the defense of the building, remembered, "You had to assume the worst, that people were going to try to break in and stop your business." The government "frantically" cleared a Virginia workhouse of its regular inmates to create space for two thousand prisoners.[72]

Yet the Johnson administration was not simply a defensive player in the Pentagon battle. It moved to shape events according to its liking. Officials considered it crucial to dampen the protest's political import in the eyes of the public. One way was to inhibit its size. On top of obstructing transportation to the event, the administration briefed journalists that it was being organized "under irresponsible auspices."[73] The government was thus being forced to mobilize a large military and police force to protect people and property. Those traveling to Washington allegedly risked getting caught up in a violent clash.

The protest also had a reddish color. At a cabinet meeting on October 4, Clark noted that "extreme Left-wing groups with long lines of Communist affiliations" were heavily represented among the demonstration's sponsors. "They are doing all they can to encourage the March," the attorney general reported. Johnson's ears apparently perked up. "Is that a secret?" he asked. After Clark said no, Secretary of State Dean Rusk opined, "Wouldn't it help to leak that?" Secretary of Health, Education and Welfare John Gardner then declared, "The people have got to know that. . . . They must know that!" Following "strong vocal agreement" from the rest of the cabinet, Clark indicated that "the fact of Communist involvement and encouragement has been given to some columnists." The president was unsatisfied. "Let's see it some more," he commanded. Clark evidently had little zeal for the task, however. On October 16, Califano wrote Johnson, "So far the demonstrators have been getting very little news, but what they are getting tends to be sympathetic. The Justice Department has not done much in this area." Califano informed the president that he and other White House aides were pressuring Pentagon officials to pick up the slack. "I asked them today to release to certain reporters some FBI material showing the very heavy Communist involvement in the demonstration. This should discourage many less extreme antiwar sympathizers from attending."[74]

Clark advised Johnson that his absence from Washington during the protest would also help discourage attendance. It would dissuade demonstrators from targeting the White House too. Clark counseled the president that if he were to attend a governors' conference in the Virgin Islands during the protest, "I do not believe this would be viewed as your leaving the city to avoid unpleasantness and would tend to deflate the demonstration." Johnson elected to stay put. One reason may have been his deep-seated view that, as Christian put it, "if anybody ever got the notion that they could stampede him, by demonstrations or whatever, that that was all she wrote." Another may have been Clark's additional offering that remaining in Washington would "heighten the offensiveness of the demonstration to the nation because it is being done in your presence."[75]

The Justice Department hoped to shunt people away from the protest by "working with interest groups" in the capital to "create other diversionary events" on October 21. It apparently thought that refusing to furnish the demonstrators "facilities and amenities" would impede the Mobe's organizing efforts and further cramp attendance. The prospect of a restroom shortage unsettled Dean Rusk, though. "That means they'll all be in on top of us at State," he noted at a cabinet meeting. "We're the closest to them."[76]

Officials acted to hamper participation in foreign antiwar demonstrations scheduled for October 21–22 as well. Califano informed Johnson that White House staffers had asked Under Secretary of State Nicholas Katzenbach to prod the USIA's director, Leonard Marks, and Richard Helms of the CIA to "work up some activity" overseas to "deflect" the organization of these demonstrations "as much as possible."[77]

The White House aide Charles Maguire believed the administration could reduce the domestic political import of the Pentagon protest if it coaxed prominent Democratic congressmen to endorse prowar parades slated for the same weekend. Maguire urged John Roche to "quietly" encourage such legislators to "wire an expression of support" to the sponsor of the parades, the "National Committee for Responsible Patriotism" (NCRP).[78] The NCRP's director, Charles Wiley, it may be recalled, had "dealt so frequently" with the White House during preparations for a prowar parade in May.

Clark suggested that antiwar protests scheduled for October 20 at the White House, Justice Department, and other federal buildings would look unimpressive if the government's work seemed to proceed full steam ahead. "Above all, we want to maintain the appearance of business as usual," he advised other cabinet officials.[79]

The administration considered it important to minimize outbreaks of violence during the Pentagon protest. Coming hot on the heels of the summer's ghetto uprisings, substantial dissident violence might alarm the public and allied governments, officials worried. The administration would seem in precarious command, and more Americans would wonder if the war was worth all the turbulence it was causing at home. As James Reston wrote, officials dreaded "the impression of a nation in actual revolt."[80] Violence against government officials and property was unwelcome for simple health and financial reasons as well. And if significant violence was wielded by the state, or more protesters immolated themselves, criticism of America's "moral bankruptcy" would become shriller still.[81]

Richard Helms well remembered the government's fear of unruliness at the

Pentagon. Helms was the director of the CIA at the time. He was also an occasional participant in the administration's famous power lunch sessions on Tuesdays. Years later, Helms was the president of an international business consulting firm in Washington. When I interviewed him, he initially exhibited marked disdain and suspicion of his visitor from Berkeley, California. Helms said that the Pentagon demonstration

> was viewed seriously by the administration for the simple reason that getting a circle of Americans around your Defense Department could mean that you could strangle the place. You know, you would have to drive them away if you wanted to do business there. And this is nothing that anybody wants to face. In *any* country. I want to tell you that mobs in the streets for a government are almost unmanageable. . . . I recall that in places like Indonesia, a mob in the street, a mob of students, literally threw Sukarno out at the end. It's a devastating thing. What are you going to do to control it? Are you going to shoot your own people? Are cousins going to shoot cousins? . . . Mobs are nasty things. And the fact that the antiwar demonstrators thought this was one of the greatest inventions since sliced bread is a mark of their intellectual incapacity to understand what they were turning loose in this country.

Mobs, Helms added, warming to the subject, are "antidemocratic . . . against our system of government . . . and the vision we have of ourselves. And the people who took place [*sic*] in this thinking they had a holy cause and so forth should very well think back over exactly what they were doing." Especially since mob tactics "will be used again when there's anything unpopular in this country, I'm sure. And those who decide to go this route are going a very dangerous route indeed."[82]

Administration officials felt that barring civil disobedience at the Pentagon would diminish unruliness. A traditional demonstration was fine, General Services Administration Counsel Harry Van Cleve told Mobe leaders on October 6. But the government could hardly be expected to permit anything illegal. Furthermore, if the Mobe did not renounce civil disobedience, even the legal demonstration would be disallowed. (Two days earlier, Ramsey Clark had informed Johnson that the administration was trying to "maneuver" the Mobe into relinquishing civil disobedience.) Van Cleve warned Mobe leaders, forebodingly, "Don't put too high a measure on the Government's unwillingness to fight citizens in its capital." The previous month, officials had considered trying to secure an injunction or legislation outlawing the protest.[83]

The administration's ultimatum to the Mobe went up in smoke. Activists immediately hit the phone lines to solicit the reactions of antiwar groups around the country. The response was overwhelmingly combative. Many people previously hesitant about joining the protest took the government's threat as an omen of serious political repression and felt the action had to go on for civil liberties reasons alone. SDSers now saw something sufficiently revolutionary in store. The government's political clumsiness, in fact, served to rally virtually the entire antiwar movement behind the protest.[84]

The administration's intelligence apparatus surely noted this change in sentiment, as Van Cleve subsequently changed his tack with Mobe leaders. He turned untypically polite (although Fred Halstead still gathered the impression that the official "felt he was dealing with people from another planet").[85] Henceforth, the government's effort to reduce the likelihood of violence during the protest revolved mainly around confining the march to the Pentagon, the legal demonstration and civil disobedience to favorable locations and time frames.

Van Cleve denied the Mobe's request to use one of two main arteries for the trek from the Arlington Memorial Bridge to the Pentagon. The protesters could be more easily contained on a narrow side road, the administration calculated, and one, moreover, that did not offer the same arousing view of the Pentagon. The demonstration would be held in the Pentagon's north parking lot, over 1,000 feet away, and separated from the building by a wire fence, highway, and embankment—quite a contrast with the Mobe's choice of the Pentagon mall, located perilously close to the building. Van Cleve also insisted that protesters wishing to commit civil disobedience gather on the mall rather than the Pentagon's upper plaza and parking area. A high wall would separate them from the building, and tight approaches would hinder a mass onslaught. Van Cleve promised that anyone proceeding beyond the first row of steps at the Pentagon's mall entrance or trying to slither around to other faces would be promptly busted.[86]

The administration also restricted access to the Pentagon mall until 4 P.M. on October 21. This would limit the time during which the majority of demonstrators would be practicing civil disobedience, decreasing the possibility that a riotous crowd spirit would develop. Van Cleve undoubtedly knew that the many buses protesters had chartered from New York were scheduled to leave Washington at 5 P.M. In fact, the administration may have influenced this departure time. Officials were aware that preventing civil disobedience until "as late Saturday as possible" would restrict coverage of it in the Sunday papers as well.[87]

The administration prepared to circumscribe the demonstrators' access to other government buildings too. It arranged to erect a wire barrier on both sides of Pennsylvania Avenue in front of the White House. East Executive Avenue—"the only street," Califano informed Johnson, "from which someone can throw something and hit the White House"—would be closed in response to a demonstration for the first time. The government denied permits for protests in Lafayette Park across Pennsylvania Avenue from the building. It would allow only "limited VIP tours" in the White House on the morning of October 21.[88]

Anxious congressional officials made sure their workplaces would also be safe from the malcontents. Speaker John McCormack (D-Mass.) ordered the House of Representatives locked up. On October 10, McCormack expressed his view of antiwar dissidents plainly enough. "If I were one of those," he roared, waving his arms and banging a table, "my conscience would be such that it would disturb me the rest of my life." Congress passed a bill to safeguard the Capitol from armed intruders. Senator John Stennis (D-Miss.), one of the bill's supporters, said that the protest was "clearly a part of a move by the Communists."[89]

The Justice Department attempted to pinpoint potential "troublemakers" and help "responsible" demonstrators develop "self-policing activities." Justice also schemed to "keep those arrested from returning to the central area" and thus unable to foment more trouble.[90]

The government readied a massive armed force to contain any violence. More than six thousand Army troops would be close at hand. Twenty thousand additional soldiers would be placed on alert status across the country, poised to be airlifted in pending major (i.e., black) disorder. Some two thousand National Guardsmen would be mobilized; most would work with two thousand Washington police. Eight hundred cops would protect the Capitol. Despite concern that it might appear overly provocative, a Secret Service helicopter would hover over the White House. The Executive Office Building would be "confidentially" stuffed with "special policemen." Hundreds of other lawmen would be on the scene as well. To alert the leaders of these contingents to what was going down and help coordinate their responses, the administration set up a central command post in the Pentagon.[91]

Human torches would be nipped in the bud. "We had the orders, neatly mimeographed: anyone setting himself on fire was to be extinguished," one of the Pentagon's defenders revealed afterward. "At convenient locations barely out of sight, blankets were ready."[92]

The administration took precautions to minimize use of its might. "We must act in a way which holds to the absolute minimum the possibility of bloodshed and injury," Under Secretary of the Army David McGiffert directed Army Chief of Staff General Harold Johnson. "We played it very carefully so that there was no excess use of force," Paul Nitze recalled. Said Ramsey Clark, "The *effort* at restraint was substantial."[93]

The administration took steps to make it later appear that whatever level of muscle *was* applied was quite reasonable, even miniscule. By telling the press the approximate size of the force lying in wait, it would convince people that things could have been far rougher. Officials also prepared to recall one or another famous American's words on the delicate relation between freedom of expression and the need to maintain public order.[94]

Arrests were to be kept to a modicum. A large bust would draw greater domestic and international attention to the protest and consequently worsen the administration's opinion problems. Furthermore, arrests were expensive, and there were limitations on confinement space. McGiffert directed General Johnson to instruct his troops to behave in a way that minimized the need for arrest and distinguished "to the extent feasible between those who are and are not breaking the law."[95]

On October 20, demonstrators streamed into Washington. The government's hollow threat to block the protest was a major reason for its now widespread appeal. Also influential was the Mobe's decision to hold a legal rally at the march's Lincoln Memorial assembly point in addition to the one scheduled for the Pentagon. Apprehensive of the disorder that might unfold down in Virginia, WSP leaders and Dr. Spock had been pressing for this tactical separation since early September. Some black militants had also advocated it on the grounds that they were "prepared to defend themselves in their own community but not at the Pentagon or the bridges where they might be stranded by the white participants."[96]

Shortly after dark, Army troops began cramming into the Pentagon. They lugged field kits, rifles, tear gas machines, helmets, C rations. Trucks and jeeps of the First Army were parked in four underground tunnels. By morning they would sit "bumper to bumper, the front rank draped in beige cloth to conceal their identity." There was an "exciting and dramatic atmosphere in the usually drab corridors," one person present wrote. "Everything was there to give us that defender-of-the-castle feeling."[97]

A combat mentality was also setting in over at the White House. At dinner that evening, amidst the tinkle of fine china and the shuffling of servants' feet, there was "much talk of tomorrow," Lady Bird Johnson jotted in her diary. "There is a ripple of grim excitement in the air, almost a feeling of being under siege."[98]

As Washington nervously braced for the coming assault, fresh returns were pouring in on sharpening resistance to the war in other locations. They could not have been welcomed by officials increasingly concerned that the war's awful mess was now coming home in earnest.

Oakland Stop the Draft Week

On Monday, October 16, at 5 A.M., more than two hundred pacifists blocked the doors to the Oakland induction center. Opposed to the violent inclinations of Oakland STDW's militant organizers, the pacifists had pulled out of that committee and organized their own protest. They were methodically arrested.

Eight hours later, David Harris addressed the two thousand people congregated in front of San Francisco's federal building. A basket was being passed back through the crowd, Harris announced. The time had come: draft-age males could either be accomplices to murder or "outlaws." After three trips through the crowd, the basket returned to the front stuffed to the brim.[99]

As the receptacle was circulating for the last time, Cecil Poole emerged from his office in the building to observe the ceremony. Dickie Harris, a black draft resister, approached the black federal attorney and asked, "Brother Poole, you head nigger here?" Harris then dumped the container of draft cards on Poole's head. Poole turned the approximately four hundred documents over to the FBI.[100]

The same afternoon, Rev. George Williams, a Harvard divinity professor, issued a call for draft cards in the still, anxious air of Boston's Arlington Street Church.

> No one knew what would happen. Maybe fifty, or seventy-five? A
> trickle of men started down the aisle. . . . The aisle soon filled, the
> line grew longer, the doors were opened to let in those from outside
> who wanted to join. The organ played, flash bulbs popped, and TV
> cameras hummed away. It must have been twenty minutes before it
> was over. More than sixty burned their cards at the candle, and over
> two hundred handed them in.

Observing the ceremony was NBC News commentator Sander Vanocur. Tears welled up in his eyes. "What a country this would be," Vanocur told Rev. William Sloane Coffin, who had spoken at the ceremony, "if something like this were now to take place in every church." On television that night, following an excerpt from Coffin's speech, NBC's John Chancellor quietly told the nation, "If men like this are beginning to say things like this, I guess we had all better start paying attention." From twelve to fifteen hundred youths returned draft cards in eighteen cities that day.[101]

What explains the unexpectedly large number of rejected cards? Many youths gathered the fortitude to return their certificates while watching others do so. The birth of Resist, an adult draft resistance support group, was also impelling. In late September, Resist's "A Call to Resist Illegitimate Authority" was published under 158 (mostly prominent) signatures in the *New York Review of Books* and the *New Republic*. "It may have been the single most important statement during the Vietnam War," CALCAV's Richard Fernandez reflected. It "gave a lot of resisters a lot of courage" and was "a *huge* influence. . . . Not only for what it said, but for the [political] cover and the sense of energy, synergism it created within the resistance movement." Most stimulative of all was youth's swelling frustration over the continuing escalation of the war. Michael Ferber remembered that his September decision to participate in the turn-in was mainly a result of "feeling that we had to do something beyond the big demonstrations that we'd been having. . . . I just felt, 'We've got to do more.'"[102]

Early the next morning, three thousand demonstrators converged on the Oakland induction center. It was time for the STDW militants to do their number. Some of the protesters were equipped with primitive shields and motorcycle helmets to ward off police blows. Soon a dense phalanx of cops, heads rattling with "off the pig" threats relayed to them by their undercover brethren in the STDW committee, hands clasping clubs, business faces on, their wives watching breathlessly from a nearby parking garage, advanced ominously toward the demonstrators. They "went to work on them." More than twenty people were injured (including innocent bystanders and journalists); twenty-five were arrested. By 9 A.M. the streets bordering the building had been cleared.[103]

Forty minutes later, Joseph Califano penned a progress report on the situation to President Johnson. Although the mess in front of the induction center had been mopped up (with the aid of Mace, "which makes an individual lethargic"), Califano reported, circumstances remained "tense." Two to four thousand people were still "milling around" the area. Johnson was undoubtedly pleased when later informed that the rabble had retreated. The previous week, at his request, the president had obtained a report from the Attorney General's Office on preparations for STDW.[104]

That night protesters held a mass meeting on the University of California campus in Berkeley to decide how to respond to the day's bloodletting. Shaken and wounded STDW leaders were "unable to run a coherent rally." Charges of police brutality and empty promises of smashing the state punctuated the session. Some speakers advocated moving on the university chancellor's office. David Harris considered this "crazy." "The Berkeley chancellor's office?" he thought to himself. "For Christ sake, these guys, they were going to 'off the pig,' I thought." The militants had turned "chickenshit," Harris perceived. "They'd gotten scared." He urged the crowd to return to the induction center for a nonviolent protest in the morning. That motion carried, and on Wednesday some four hundred people picketed the center. Ninety-one sat in its doorways and suffered arrest. There was no violence.[105]

The scene was less placid two thousand miles away. On the University of Wisconsin campus in Madison, a throng of students strode into the Commerce Building and proclaimed an end to the job interviews being conducted there by recruiters from the Dow Chemical Company. They would leave when Dow's bagmen left. A university official initially agreed to shoo the recruiters away, but, when asked to put his commitment on paper, "lost his cool." In came the local police riot squad. Students were swiftly streaming out of the building, battered and dazed, only to be beaten again by a gauntlet of cops. The two thousand onlookers who had gathered outside, "smelling trouble as sure as any turkey buzzard," were furious at the wanton police violence. "Sieg heil," they chanted, arms upward. Many were gassed. They pelted police with rocks and bricks. When Mace failed to make the protesters lethargic, the county sheriff's office dispatched a riot team with snarling dogs. The tired and bloodied crowd gradually disbanded.[106]

The next day several hundred protesters peacefully picketed the Oakland induction center. In neighboring Berkeley, STDW's militants made plans to hold another "new kind" of demonstration the following morning. Wednesday's action had not sat well with them. Watching frightened young draftees file into the induction center while ineffectually shouting "Don't Go" at them had been demoralizing. Their "impotence" had been "exposed." They would try to shut down the building again. But this time they would exhibit greater mobility and aggressiveness in the face of police assaults. No one would get trapped and beaten by the pigs again. The cops might even take a pounding. Steve Hamilton fixed to set up a "command central" for the assault in a hotel adjacent to the induction center. From there, STDW generals, in touch with walkie-talkie-wielding lieutenants in the field, would direct the troops to the most exploitable ground. Hamilton asked the hotel's manager for a room overlooking the center. The manager "rented us the room and immediately called the police," Hamilton recalled.[107]

By 6 A.M. on Friday, nearly ten thousand demonstrators were gathered in the streets around the building. Many wore headgear and carried placards conveniently attached to hard wooden poles. Some had Vaseline on their faces to reduce Mace's sting. At 7 A.M. the cops launched their opening thrusts. The protesters retreated as planned, expanding the perimeter of the battle. They barricaded intersections using potted trees, garbage cans, unlocked cars. Some surrounded policemen, coercing them into harried retreats. A county bus lost its ignition wires. As they gained confidence in their ability to feint, jab, and withdraw at will, many young demonstrators began to feel like urban guerrillas. One seized a cop's baton and whacked him crisply over the head with it. "I was a little amazed at how far it went," Hamilton recalled of the protest. Hamilton was particularly stunned when an aged CPer asked him to help flip a car over. When the dust had settled, arrests and injuries were surprisingly few.[108]

That afternoon in the nation's capital, members of Resist collected unwanted draft cards on the steps of the Justice Department. After amassing 992 cards, William Sloane Coffin, Benjamin Spock, Arthur Waskow, and seven others disappeared into the Justice Department building to present the certificates to Ramsey Clark. The Resisters were "led down a long hall, secretaries peeking out their doors at us as if we were wild animals," Coffin remembered. Clark refused to see them. He felt that receiving "evidence of potentially criminal conduct" was "not the role of the attorney general," he later told me. It would "distort" and "politicize" the law enforcement process, Clark believed. He and his colleagues had decided earlier that Assistant Deputy Attorney General John McDonough would meet with the protesters instead. As a former professor and a "balanced, mature guy," McDonough would be less likely to "insult" or "provoke" them than an FBI official, the most appropriate witness to their deed, the officials reasoned. As a jittery secretary clattered cups of coffee, the Resisters each read McDonough a short statement expressing their support for draft resistance, an act that carried the same criminal penalties as noncooperation itself. When they had finished, McDonough stiffly read them the draft law. Coffin then tried to hand the official a briefcase containing the rejected cards. "Dr. Coffin, am I being tendered something?" McDonough asked. "*Tendered* something?" Coffin responded. "Yes, *tendered* something," came the return. McDonough refused to accept the briefcase. "*What!?*" Waskow screamed. "Ever since I was a *kid* I was brought up to respect the law in the United States. Here you have just read this statement alleging that we are guilty of crimes for which we offer you proof! And you [slamming his hand down on the briefcase], the number three man in the Justice Department, refuse to accept the evidence! Where, man, is your oath of office? I demand a response!" The Resisters left the briefcase on a table before departing.[109]

At his request, President Johnson was kept closely advised of the protest. Later that afternoon or evening he ordered Clark to "promptly" inform him of "the progress of investigations by the Federal Bureau of Investigation of any violations of law involved" and "steps you are taking to prosecute lawbreakers in accordance with established procedures. It is important that violations of law be dealt with firmly, promptly and fairly."[110]

It was a portentous order.

The Siege: "It Was Terrifying"

On October 21, more than one hundred thousand Americans gathered at the Lincoln Memorial. As in past protests, youth predominated. Also present, however, were lawyers, accountants, teachers, housewives, and veteran political organizers. Placards spanned from the mild ("Negotiate") to the wild ("Where Is Oswald When We Need Him?").[111] After listening to a round of speeches, the marchers inched haltingly toward the Arlington Memorial Bridge. Government helicopters buzzed overhead.

Brad Lyttle was in front of the procession. As the Mobe's logistics coordinator and a familiar face from previous demonstrations at the Pentagon, the sandy-haired, bearded, Amish-looking activist had been allowed by the police and FBI agents on duty to move freely ahead of the mass. Some greeted him by his first name as he passed. Under Secretary of the Army David McGiffert, director of the troops defending the Pentagon, might have said much more if encountered. He was a boyhood friend of Lyttle's in Chicago. "We played base-ball and football together," Lyttle remembered.[112]

Near the Pentagon, Lyttle's stomach started churning. Scores of protesters were frenetically pummeling a dozen Nazi counterdemonstrators. "Bloody faces and missing teeth were everywhere." The Nazis sprinted off with their tails between their legs. "They would have gotten worse if they'd stuck around," Lyttle said. His concern that the protest might overheat grew. "It didn't seem to me that this was nonviolence," Lyttle dryly recalled.[113]

Back at the southern end of the bridge, several hundred young militants abruptly severed themselves from the other marchers and tore off through the Virginia woods toward the Pentagon. At the front of the woolly pack, several youths carried fifteen-foot staffs bearing the red-blue-and-gold flag of the NLF. After the militants' first probe at a coordinate far to the left of the Pentagon was repelled, they regrouped, toppled a section of wire fence, and raced across the Pentagon's mall onto the left side of its plaza. They were immediately sur-rounded by MPs and U.S. marshals.

On the heels of these shock troops were much larger forces, also unwilling to proceed tamely from one rally to another, regardless of whether the scenery and even state had changed. They, too, skipped the speechmaking in the Pen-tagon's north parking lot, felled barricades, and streamed toward their target before the appointed time. Greg Calvert and Tom Bell, a fellow SDSer, "tore the fence down so people could get to their Pentagon, the People's Pentagon," Calvert recalled. "This was not the People's Fence. . . . And we made a hole big enough so that lots of people could get through. Tom was very effective, and so was I; I was an old farm boy and he was an ex-football fullback, so we were pretty good at taking down fences."[114] Several thousand protesters garrisoned the center of the plaza and stairs.

Suddenly, another, more daring, thrust. Two dozen members of the libera-tion army on the plaza, flushed from their penetration of enemy territory but far from satiated, sprinted toward a poorly guarded side door of the Pentagon. At least ten pierced the security shield and began running down the corridor, exhilarated.

They were routed. Army troops inside, overwrought by "the tension of endless hours waiting for unseen anarchists, bomb-throwers, Communists, poi-son gassers . . . nymphomaniacs, drug addicts, insane Negroes," and the like, slammed into them. Afterward, crusty trails of blood decorated the Pentagon's floor.[115]

By late afternoon, Calvert and Bell didn't like the smell of things. Some demonstrators were urging further combat, the rally in the north parking lot had ended, over thirty thousand people were gathered in the mall below, and many were trying to reach the forbidden plaza. "If there had been bloodshed at that point, the potential for hundreds of people being just killed, trampled to death on these staircases in the panic, was enormous," Calvert remembered. "It was a very tense moment." From the top of a wall, Calvert and Bell pleaded for people to sit down. Most did.[116]

As the action near the building stilled, that in the perimeter heated up. Protesters were testing the Pentagon's defenses at every conceivable point. The results, often enough, were bloodshed and arrests. On the fortress's west flank, Dave Dellinger was talking to a wall of troops through a megaphone. Dellinger, Calvert, and the Mobe lawyer Arthur Kinoy had agreed over dinner the previous evening to turn the protest partly into a teach-in with the many soldiers present. In "a real knockdown, drag-out session" lasting until 4:30 A.M., they convinced the Mobe's steering committee of this approach. "We beat Jerry Rubin on that," Calvert pridefully recalled. Rubin felt the soldiers should be treated as "fascists." "You are our brothers!" Dellinger's gentle voice sailed out into the warm afternoon air. "Join us!" Instead, the soldiers kicked and rifle-butted Dellinger and his comrades and deposited them in a paddy wagon.[117]

The battlefield also bred kindly encounters. A protester from Berkeley walked along a line of MPs placing flowers in rifle barrels. Abbie Hoffman and his wife, outfitted in tall Uncle Sam hats and high on acid, made love in front of U.S. marshals and troops. After finishing, the couple offered to shake hands with the marshals. The marshals declined. Hoffman later seemed embarrassed about his "genitalia-oriented" form of protest. Three other sexually engaged demonstrators shouted to marchers, "We'd rather fuck than fight."[118]

Up on the Pentagon's roof, military brass surveyed the disturbance below. Army sharpshooters "crouched uneasily, weapons at hand." Inside the building, "a siege mood prevailed." Officials peered anxiously out their office windows to get a taste of the angry horde. They didn't like what they saw. Richard Helms: "I don't think there was any doubt that they took a look at that mob around the Pentagon and nobody liked the look of that at all. And I certainly least of all. I'd had experiences with mobs all over the world and I didn't like the look or sound of this one one bit." Stanley Resor recalled, "It was a very impressive thing, thirty-five thousand people right there under your nose." More than one official realized uncomfortably that the mob had a personal element. Close friends and relatives of theirs were out there.[119] His later denials notwithstanding, Paul Nitze could not have been pleased to know that three of his children were staring his way.

Robert McNamara was alternately up on the roof of the building and at his office window. He also inspected the crowd from just behind a wall of troops at the Pentagon's mall entrance. McNamara was beside himself. "It was terrifying," he admitted later. "Christ, yes, I was scared. You had to be scared. A mob is an uncontrollable force. It's terrifying. Once it becomes a mob, all the leaders are useless. It was a mess." But he wouldn't run. "There was no question I would be up there," he averred. "You don't delegate something like that."[120]

McNamara was a profoundly tormented man by this time. To one of his associates, he seemed "increasingly tired and depressed" and persistently "thin." The president wondered aloud whether he was "on the verge of cracking up," possibly even doing himself in. "An emotional basket case," Johnson called him. McNamara would sometimes cry while at work; to hide his increasingly frequent tears from office visitors, one of his secretaries divulged, he would turn away and pretend to be looking out the window. "He does it all the time now," she said. "He cries into the curtain." Vietnam was McNamara's main scourge. He continued to be rattled by the resilience of the Vietnamese revolutionaries. They were tough little SOBs, he brooded, maybe tougher, even, than he. "The goddamned Air Force, they're dropping more on North Vietnam than we dropped on Germany in the last year of World War II, and it's not doing anything!" he would exclaim to startled colleagues several months later, then falter amid suppressed sobs. McNamara found the political situation in South Vietnam appalling—there didn't seem to be a viable government in sight! He also worried that the war was undermining U.S. preparedness vis-à-vis the Soviet Union. And innocent Vietnamese peasants were still getting killed and mutilated in high numbers. He might even be considered a murderer.[121]

McNamara had hoped that researching the war's history would suggest fruitful new policies. "In his office in the Pentagon he had a bookshelf right in back of him, and you could see the books on Vietnam begin and increase a little more and more as the two or three years went by," Eric Sevareid recalled. In June, McNamara had ordered the gargantuan Pentagon Papers study. When the study was completed, he was more shocked than enlightened. It revealed an enduring pattern of official duplicity and awareness that U.S. policies were inflicting monstrous civilian casualties in Vietnam. "You know," McNamara remarked to a friend, "they could hang people for what's in there."[122]

Accelerating public distaste for the war was particularly agonizing to McNamara. A continuation of present U.S. policies promised to be "unsatisfactory to our people," he would write Johnson ten days after the protest. But flattening North Vietnam "would stimulate severe criticism . . . the most unfortunate public reaction in the United States and world-wide." Invading the North also guaranteed "alarm" at home and overseas. McNamara's advice to Johnson to halt Rolling Thunder and put a lid on U.S. troop deployments was "based, *almost entirely*, upon an assessment of U.S. public opinion," Supreme Court Justice Abe Fortas wrote the president. McNamara recognized that both he and Dean Rusk had "pretty much lost their credibility" on Vietnam among the public. That his son Craig was among those doubting his credibility drastically compounded McNamara's agony.[123]

But that wasn't all. The war had recently spawned serious health problems within McNamara's family. In July, his wife Margaret had been hospitalized for treatment of her ulcer. Her condition "more equitably should have been his own," he told his colleagues. Craig had also gotten a serious ulcer. Again, it didn't take a genius to figure out that Vietnam was to blame.[124]

As McNamara gazed out at the mob surrounding the Pentagon, he may have taken solace in the knowledge that his days in office were numbered. In April he had tentatively been offered the presidency of the World Bank. He wanted the job; it would be a welcome change. But loyalty to the president came first. Then, in August, there had been that little matter of telling members of the Senate Armed Services Committee—and the rest of the nation—without prior White House clearance—that Rolling Thunder was not all that the hawks were making it out to be. McNamara had known such testimony would set the president off, and it sure as hell had. "Johnson hated it," Paul Warnke remembered. McNamara "was summoned to the White House to receive a full blast of presidential anger." "That's when Bob became a prime candidate for the World Bank," Warnke wryly remarked. Days before the protest, Johnson had informed McNamara that the bank position was "in the cards."[125]

As McNamara was eyeing the surly crowd outside the Pentagon, alone in his office save for a secretary or two, in walked another troubled man. The lean, dark-haired young visitor was not unknown to McNamara. In 1964–65 he had served as special assistant to the assistant secretary of defense for ISA. He had even written some of McNamara's most important speeches. In 1965–67, the visitor had worked with the State Department in Vietnam; he had sent McNamara at least one letter on conditions there. Upon returning to the United States, he had had "a very frank discussion" with McNamara about the war. Now the visitor had office space, the TFX (Tactical Fighter Experimental) room, to be precise, right next to McNamara's. Dismayed by the "stalemate" he had observed in Vietnam, the visitor had suggested to another senior Pentagon official in May that the government conduct a high-level study of U.S. policy to sort out what had gone wrong. He would even be willing to head the project. Lo and behold, McNamara had commissioned the study several weeks later. The visitor had been urged to participate and had agreed.

So there he was in the TFX room researching the war. To get a better view of the commotion outside, the visitor had left his workspace and wandered into McNamara's office. He would never have thought of doing so unannounced on a normal working day, but "there was nobody else around, and I just happened to walk in thinking that it was empty," he recalled. He took up a position at a window near McNamara.

The visitor had mixed emotions about the scene below. He was "totally sympathetic" to the protesters' goal of ending the war, but was feeling "quite resistant to a lot of the arguments being made" by peace activists on the whys and hows. "I didn't feel I had a lot to learn from them, particularly," he would say later. "I believed that people who didn't have access to the classified information I was getting were not in any position to judge the broad-scale considerations we were bringing to bear. . . . I didn't listen too closely, in other words, to what they were saying." And although "their instincts had led them in the right direction," the protesters clearly had at least a few things to learn yet on sticky issues of morality.

But some arguments advanced by peace activists had already "raised questions" in the visitor's mind; they "worried me a little bit," he remembered, "given that there were no clear answers in the classified literature." U.S. violations of the 1954 Geneva Accords, for instance. "'Could this be true?'" he had even asked his boss at the Pentagon, John McNaughton, a full two years earlier. "'No, I never heard anything like this,'" McNaughton replied.

As the visitor peered out at the demonstrators, McNamara looming large to one side, he thought to himself, "I hope this is making a strong impression on him. But I'm afraid that it looks too jolly. It's such a bright sunny Saturday afternoon. . . . I wish it were snowing, I wish it were a weekday, I wish it all looked a bit more serious. . . . There [is] a lot of a picnic flavor to it . . . and I'm not sure it will impress him with the commitment." Not that the visitor felt the protesters lacked political commitment. No, he knew better than that—he'd just been among them. For he had marched from the Lincoln Memorial to the Pentagon's north parking lot that day, where he'd hung around for a while to watch before moseying on up to his office. His reasons for marching hadn't been entirely political; he'd just wanted to "be part of" the big gathering, and, indeed, had ended up running into numerous familiar people during the afternoon, including his brother from New York. But he was now so fed up with the war that limiting his opposition to writing "policy options" papers just wouldn't do. Since walking in a sea of humanity allowed for a certain amount of anonymity, it was a feasible way for someone inside the government to take a stand. The visitor's motivations for marching were certainly more noble than those that had guided his only previous act of public protest against the war, in 1965. Then, as we have seen, his presence had been a consequence of his romantic interest in a female demonstrator.

Still, Daniel Ellsberg worried as he looked out through the glass, the protesters' political seriousness might not be getting through to McNamara. It clearly hadn't gotten through to some other Pentagon officials he had encountered already that day. "'Yeah, sure, it's nice for them to take the day off and have a nice picnic out on the mall'" was how they had dismissed the protest. For his part, Ellsberg wished the demonstrators

> had chosen a Friday and had really totally blocked, closed down, the
> Pentagon. In those days it was easy to get into the Pentagon. You
> didn't have to show passes usually: you just walked in. They could
> easily have flooded the place with people. . . . If they had chosen to

infiltrate a few at a time, and ultimately hundreds, there was no reason they couldn't have gotten a very large number inside the Pentagon and really made a fuss. . . . Even if they weren't allowed in, they could have had a blockade of the actual employees and made it hard for them to get in and out. There were enough people to make it hard.

McNamara may have been thinking along similar lines. "They did it all wrong," he exclaimed years afterward, slapping his fist. "The way to have done it would to have been Gandhilike. Had they retained their discipline, they could have achieved their ends. My God, if 50,000 people had been disciplined and I had been the leader, I absolutely guarantee you I could have shut down the whole goddamn place."[126]

Although standing only feet apart, Ellsberg and McNamara spoke nary a word to each other, not even saying hello. "I didn't bother him," Ellsberg remembered. "And he wasn't paying any attention to me." Finally, Ellsberg left and sauntered back to the TFX room.

It was over twenty-five years before he saw Robert McNamara again.[127]

Across the Potomac River at the heavily guarded White House, President Johnson was receiving frequent progress reports on the protest from Joseph Califano. He was surely relieved to read that angry black ghetto residents were not heading his way as earlier predicted. Johnson was also apprised of the hundreds of thousands of "emotional anti-Americans" (as *Time* magazine described them) then demonstrating overseas. Some of these emotional people were chanting "Death to Johnson!" Reporters occasionally dropped in to visit with the president. They did not arrive uninvited, for Johnson had solicited their company in order to document his "busier-than-usual" Saturday schedule and merely passing interest in the protest. The president pointedly spent much of the day out in the sunny Rose Garden, undisturbed by the clamor. One of his companions, Walt Rostow, remembered thinking that that was "a most unlikely thing to be doing . . . at the time."[128]

As darkness fell, the force assailing the Pentagon shrank. Buses were leaving, stomachs were growling, it was getting cold. Soon there were only four hundred hardy souls left on the plaza and a few thousand on the stairs and mall. But the confrontation was far from over. Draft cards began igniting one after another. More than two hundred would burn before the evening was through. At around 8:45, a soldier reportedly dropped his rifle, removed his helmet, and walked toward the protesters. He'd had enough, he was switching sides. Officers grabbed him and hauled him away. Word of the attempted defection swirled through the crowd. Protesters were ecstatic. Rumors of another switch in allegiance followed. Some female protesters pawed at soldiers' zippers and offered to accompany them to the bushes if they changed loyalties.[129]

As the night wore on, the minds of many demonstrators turned increasingly toward the satisfaction of unmet physical needs. Food and blankets were secured, fires started. One girl breezed through the crowd with a bottle of aspirin, inquiring, "Any headaches? Any headaches?" After another protester announced a "Piss Call," a large group "faced the Pentagon and urinated en masse." As Califano reported to an interested president afterward, "Small groups of males and females were observed in close contact, going through sexual motions."[130]

Shortly before midnight, the government decided it was time to get the intruders off the plaza. In a dense V-shaped pattern, its forces pushed slowly, deliberately into the demonstrators. Those still standing were powered backward; those sitting felt the hard thud of Army boots hitting their behinds. Riot-seasoned U.S. marshals collared and clubbed many protesters. Some "really had their faces bashed in" by rifle butts. Women got the worst of it. Several demonstrators directed a spotlight on one marshal as he was pummeling a female SDSer. "The look on his face could only have been that of someone having an orgasm." A few soldiers even "turned away in disgust and pain" at the state's brutality. One official who helped coordinate the government's security arrangements wrote Ramsey Clark hours afterward, "I would be less than candid if I did not pass along reports that the marshals . . . in a few cases used more force than was warranted." Clark called this early morning period "a bad time."[131]

Some demonstrators lusted to fight back. The Mobe's Doug Dowd noticed Jerry Rubin and others in the back of the crowd "goading people on, yelling and screaming, and throwing live, fiery pieces of wood up front . . . at the marshals." Dowd was furious. Such antics would only incite more state violence, he seethed. "That was one of the occasions on which I would have killed Jerry Rubin if I could have," Dowd said many years later, his anger still evident. "I mean, honest to God, if it had physically been possible to get up and go after the son of a bitch, I would have done it."[132]

At 2 A.M., Greg Calvert was on the bullhorn. He too had little patience for those who wanted to battle the troops. "You are our brothers, we want you to come home to us," Calvert appealed to the soldiers. "You don't belong to them, the generals, who are going crazy up there in the top part of the Pentagon because we're talking to you." Calvert also spoke against a proposal by another orator that the demonstrators walk toward the soldiers and offer themselves up for arrest. "Nonsense!" Calvert shouted. "We've won. We've made our point, we've talked to the troops. We should go home." Many agreed and left. The thousand or so who remained suffered sporadic beatings and arrests throughout the night.[133]

The next day the protesters' ranks climbed to two thousand. As Califano reported to Johnson, "'Motherfucker' was a common expression used over the bull horn by the leaders."[134] The several hundred demonstrators still present at midnight were busted. The siege was over.

The line score: 683 arrests (including two UPI reporters), 51 jail terms ranging up to 35 days, $8,000 in fines, untold injuries, no deaths.[135]

International Communist Conspiracy

Media commentary on the Pentagon protest was nearly unanimous. It was fine for opponents of the war to exercise their constitutional right of peaceful expression, although, tragically, they might be prolonging the conflict by strengthening Hanoi's resolve. But antiwar violence was inexcusable. The *Washington Post* praised the "honest" dissenters while rebuking the "lawlessness" of the "extremists." According to the *New York Times*, these extremists were not "genuinely troubled" by the war but merely hungry for media attention. They had purposes "alien" to America, warned James Reston. Jimmy Breslin of the *Post* condemned the "small core of dropout[s] and drifters and rabble" on the Pentagon plaza. They were "troublemakers" with no "taste," "decency," or even "humor," he charged. *Time* magazine intimated that more such "outbursts" would threaten the very "quality of life in America."[136]

The media considered the government's violence appropriate. "The rights of free speech and assembly . . . do not mean that everyone with opinions or beliefs may address a group at any public place and at any time. The constitutional guarantee of liberty implies that existence of an organized society maintaining public order," *Time* quoted approvingly from a 1965 majority Supreme Court opinion written by Arthur Goldberg (then ambassador to the United Nations) and probably furnished by the White House. The protest was also ineffectual. "They came and they confronted and by the end of the day everyone was fulfilled and nothing changed," wrote a *Post* reporter. "The war goes on." Many congressmen joined the hostile chorus. The Republican legislative leadership demanded that "the malcontent, the misguided and, yes, the malicious" who comprised "the greatest part" of the demonstration be "brought to justice." "These wretched few can no longer be tolerated."[137]

The Johnson administration was also unhappy with the protest. Although relieved that the violence on both sides had not been greater and pleased by the media's unkind words for the demonstrators, officials worried that the tumult painted a picture of a badly divided nation held together at the point of a bayonet. In addition, the protest was much larger and lengthier than intelligence sources had predicted. For their miscalculations, senior Army officers involved in Conus Intel caught "undiluted hell" from high-level officials, Johnson apparently included.[138]

The administration moved to allay the political damage. There were not simply "good" protesters and "bad" ones, said officials. The whole unsavory lot that marched to the Pentagon was responsible for the ugly spectacle. The White House political adviser Fred Panzer counseled Johnson on October 26 that the "official report" on the demonstration should "give the lie to" attempts to "blame an unruly minority for the mess." "The speeches at the Memorial, I am sure, set the stage for the violence at the Pentagon," Panzer wrote. "Friendly columnists should be backgrounded on the facts, so that the myth of restrained and responsible peaceniks can be exposed."[139]

And the communists were indeed behind the rumpus. On the evening of October 24, Johnson read excerpts from a "secret report" allegedly documenting communist masterminding of the protest to a select group of congressional leaders. Passed to Johnson by Walt Rostow, a key White House liaison to the intelligence community, the previous afternoon, the report apparently dealt mainly with protesters' contacts with North Vietnamese and NLF officials at a conference in Bratislava, Czechoslovakia, in September. The president gave a convincing presentation. House Minority Leader Gerald Ford (R-Mich.) said he had been persuaded by his commander in chief that the "disgraceful display" at the Pentagon had been "cranked up in Hanoi." House Majority Leader Carl Albert (D-Okla.) claimed it was "basically organized by international communism" and that "the marchers included every communist and communist sympathizer in the United States who was able to make the trip." When Ford pressed the White House to make the report public, however, it refused. Dean Rusk contended that doing so would unleash a new wave of McCarthyism. Ramsey Clark even paid Ford a personal visit asking him to cease his requests.[140]

The administration was bluffing. Meetings with Vietnamese revolutionaries were hardly evidence of communist subversion to those not already peeking for Reds under their beds. Moreover, the Pentagon protest had been in the works long before the Bratislava conference. As Clark would say later, Johnson and other officials probably "didn't find that the report was persuasive. If they had a persuasive report, I think they would not have given it to Jerry Ford—they would have released it themselves." The administration had no other evidence to offer for foreign communist influence in the peace movement either. Pressured fiercely by Johnson to secure such documentation, the FBI had previously come up with nothing. So had the CIA.[141]

Still, the communists were out there, they were behind his problems, the president maintained. Richard Helms:

> There's no doubt that President Johnson, if he wasn't convinced at
> least he was very much concerned, that the antiwar opposition *was*
> promoted by the communists, by foreign elements. And he wanted
> this thoroughly investigated. And he put a lot of pressure on the CIA

and the FBI to try and find out about this, to try and nail it down. There's no doubt about it. And when we would come back with reports that we couldn't find any evidence of this, that hardly changed his mind. He still felt that there was a strong foreign influence in all of this. Otherwise, Americans wouldn't be behaving the way they were.

Johnson was "after us all the time" to document foreign communist influence in the peace movement, Helms recalled. The topic "came up almost daily."[142]

The first symptoms of the president's paranoia had surfaced much earlier. In June 1965, Johnson confided to his cabinet, "I will see a line from Peking, Hanoi, and Moscow . . . about a month ahead of the time I see it here." Four days later he ranted to Bill Moyers and Richard Goodwin, "I am not going to have anything more to do with the liberals. . . . They all just follow the communist line—liberals, intellectuals, communists. They're all the same." On July 5 he told the increasingly frightened Goodwin that "the communists are taking over the country." Johnson blustered to Moyers the same month that "he was going to fire everybody that didn't agree with him, that Hubert [Humphrey] could not be trusted and we weren't to tell him anything; then he began to explain that the communist way of thinking had infected everyone around him, that his enemies were deceiving the people and, if they succeeded, there was no way he could stop World War Three." Later that summer, the president gloomily announced to members of his staff, "I'm going to be the one who lost this form of government. The communists already control the three major networks and the forty major outlets of communication. Walter Lippmann is a communist and so is Teddy White. And they're not the only ones."[143]

Johnson's paranoia extended to media coverage critical of the war. He revealed to aides that summer, "Hell, you can always find [Soviet Ambassador Anatoly] Dobrynin's car in front of a columnist's house the night before he blasts me on Vietnam." The president wondered whether the *New York Times's* Tom Wicker was "caught up in some sort of conspiracy against him." In August, the day after the Canadian-born CBS correspondent Morley Safer did a news piece showing U.S. Marines torching Vietnamese huts, CBS President Frank Stanton received an early morning wake-up call from Johnson. "Frank, are you trying to fuck me?" asked the president of the United States. Safer, "a Communist" if ever there was one, had "shat on the American flag." Johnson dispatched investigators to probe the correspondent's past. Safer checked out clean as a whistle, but Johnson was incredulous and continued to insist to anyone who would listen that he was subversive. When White House aides argued that Safer was merely a Canadian, the president got in the last word: "Well, I knew he wasn't an American."[144]

By the next year, Johnson was keeping tabs on which dovish senators were attending social receptions at the Soviet Embassy. Some of their children were dating the children of Soviet officials, he knew. And some of their speeches were being written at the embassy—he'd seen copies of them before they were given.[145]

Johnson's conviction that "good-thinking Americans" (as Helms put it) would support the war short of communist trickery was only one reason for his belief in foreign subversion of the peace movement. He was also reading a steady stream of FBI reports that grossly exaggerated the roles played by American communists—all of whom were obviously working at Moscow's behest—in the movement. The FBI persistently referred to SDS as a "militant youth group" that CP General Secretary Gus Hall claimed his organization "has going for us." Of the twenty Mobe activists one FBI report chose to describe, ten were CP or SWP members and the rest were portrayed as having communist links (e.g., proto-Yippie Stew Albert was noted to have once "introduced himself to [California] Governor [Edmund G. "Pat"] Brown and said, 'I'm a Communist, PLP'"). Johnson told his aides, "You'd all be shocked at the kind of things revealed by the FBI reports." That FBI information on protesters in front of the White House was generally relayed to Johnson through his aide Marvin Watson, "a man of limited intelligence" (as former official Richard Goodwin observes), did nothing to alleviate Johnson's suspicions.[146]

What's more, Walt Rostow was close at hand, and Walt knew communist treachery when he saw it. Raised by Socialist Party parents (his brother Eugene had been named after the famous American socialist Eugene Debs), Rostow had been a student of Marxism as a youth. At Yale in the 1930s, he had tried to push some of his classmates, including one Dave Dellinger, toward Marxism. "Rostow was a communist at that time, and he kept trying to convert me," Dellinger remembered. "I think he helped radicalize me, though he also helped prevent me from turning into an orthodox Marxist communist, because it [Rostow's brand of Marxism] was so abstract and mechanical and lacking human-relatedness." Dellinger thought it "ironic the way things turned out." Rostow, who when I met him was a professor of economics and history at the University of Texas, denied flirting with Marxism. He was merely an "anticommunist" "democratic socialist," he maintained.[147]

No, the wellspring of the American peace movement wasn't communist, according to Rostow. But foreign Reds were helping coordinate the whole thing. "Certainly there were those throwing kerosene on the fire," Rostow said. And Dellinger himself was a bona fide "working communist," a real "professional." Hadn't he been cavorting with the enemy in Czechoslovakia?[148]

Rostow tried to convince Johnson that the hand of international communism was behind some of the racial violence in the United States as well. He spent hours gathering "such evidence as there is" on this subversion from intelligence reports. But the data was unsupportive. Two studies Rostow forwarded to the president in late July 1967 categorically denied any Cuban or Chinese influence in the black power movement or ghetto riots. Not even J. Edgar Hoover was eager to side with Rostow on this one. Stanley Resor recalled having dinner with President Johnson, Hoover, and General Harold Johnson shortly after the summer riots in Newark. The president asked Hoover if the riots were "incited by outsiders." The FBI director responded, "No, Newark was indigenous, although after it got started people came from New York City to try to make it a bigger thing." Resor was surprised at Hoover's response, since if anybody could be expected to attribute the riots to external forces "it would be J. Edgar Hoover."[149]

Rostow did have a prominent ally outside the administration, though. Maryland Governor Spiro Agnew declared at a press conference that the ghetto disorders were the product of an external conspiracy. His voice oozing contempt, Ramsey Clark remembered:

> I came out one morning and picked up the *Washington Post* and saw the headline, and went back in and got the White House operator and said, "Get me Governor Agnew." He said, "You're catching me on my way out. I'm in a big hurry. Can I call you back in a little while?" So I go on down to the office, and he doesn't call. And in the afternoon I call him, and they say he's not available. I catch him the next morning. I say, "I need to know what your evidence is. I've got responsibilities." He said, "I'll get back to you. I'll get it together for you." A couple of days later he had an assistant call and say he had [received] an anonymous telephone call . . . [150]

The Pentagon protest strengthened Johnson's suspicion of foreign involvement in the antiwar movement. During an October 31 discussion with Democratic congressional leaders, "the President noted that he did not want to be like a McCarthyite, but this country is in a little more danger than we think and someone has to uncover this information," a memo on the meeting records. Consulting with Rusk, McNamara, Rostow, Helms, and George Christian four days later, "the President turned his attention to the troubles at home and said 'I'm not going to let the Communists take this government and they're doing it right now.' The President pointed out that he has been protecting civil liberties since he was nine years old, but 'I told the Attorney General that I am not going to let 200,000 of these people ruin everything for the 200 million Americans. I've got my belly full of seeing these people put on a Communist plane and shipped all over this country. I want someone to carefully look at who leaves this country, where they go, why they are going, and if they're going to Hanoi, how are we going to keep them from getting back into this country.'"[151]

On October 31, the CIA began preparing a lengthy analysis entitled "International Connections of the U.S. Peace Movement." Submitted to the White

House two weeks later, the results were not what Johnson had hoped for. The only "extensive" government contacts maintained by peace activists were with Hanoi, reported the CIA. The movement was simply "too big and too amorphous to be controlled by any one political faction," communist or otherwise: "the most striking single characteristic of the peace front is its diversity." Furthermore, "most of the Vietnam protest activity would be there with or without the Communist element." The CIA's researchers perceptively noted that American communists "seem more concerned about countering each other than about countering the non-Communists." In sum, said the CIA, "We see no significant evidence that would prove Communist control or direction of the U.S. peace movement or its leaders."[152]

Johnson wouldn't budge. The evidence was there, he fumed. Those people at the CIA just didn't know where to look. Better keep them looking. On December 21, the CIA submitted another report on the movement's international connections. A third came two months later. But no "new information" had "come to light," reported the agency, "that would lead us to alter the conclusions reached in our original study."[153]

Johnson was fit to be tied. This protest thing was happening all around the globe, he knew. He wasn't the only world leader with a pack of hippies at his front gate. De Gaulle over in France was having the same problem. Those kids over there in Scandinavia were going off the deep end, too. Yet European troops weren't fighting in Vietnam. Johnson realized something besides the war had to be responsible for his plight.

On September 18, 1968, the president's cabinet gathered around a table to discuss yet another CIA report on student activism. "Restless Youth" examined the possible causes of student protest worldwide, including, in particular, communist subversion. Helms told the assembled that the study found "no convincing evidence of Communist control, manipulation, or support of student dissidents." "No support?" Dean Rusk asked, incredulously. "That's right," Helms responded. "But there is support," the president piped in, suspiciously. "There is, isn't there?" "Aren't they giving the same kind of support that the Communists gave to the labor movement in this country?" inquired Secretary of the Treasury Henry Fowler. "Well, it is the difference between rape and seduction," Rusk analyzed. Secretary of Agriculture Orville Freeman said he found Helms's conclusion "very hard to believe. I'm travelling around this country and all kinds of people tell me about Communist involvement in this thing." Rusk wasn't through. "Let me say one thing. I was told by a trustee of an Ivy League University that he has 30 Communists on his faculty. He said that to me." Declared Johnson, "I just don't believe this business that there is no support. I've seen it in my own school. I've seen them provoke and aggravate trouble. I know that Students for a Democratic Society and the DuBois Clubs are Communist infiltrated, Communist supported and aggravated."[154]

Helms later claimed that he took these objections to the CIA's research in stride. Something as "complicated" as the war was bound to provoke "disagreements," he said. The most important thing was "to try and keep the whole affair organized and moving." His reaction, he recalled, "was simply that, 'Oh, I don't seem to have made my case convincingly enough. I guess I've got to go back and see if I can get some more evidence.'" It's unlikely that Helms was so unruffled. Ramsey Clark recalled that the dispute during the September discussion was quite sharp. "I vividly remember Johnson and Rusk, in particular, giving poor old Helms hell at that [meeting]: 'What kind of idiots do you have working over there?' . . . They were contemptuous. And they were, I thought, pretty insulting." Helms had probably expected a rough session. In a memo to Johnson on September 4, he expressed regret at his failure to produce "a more positive report" and suggested that the president might "wish to consider having the Bureau [FBI] authorized to use more advanced investigative techniques in dealing with this problem."[155]

How common were foreign conspiracy theories of the peace movement inside the Johnson administration? Very. Many officials believed overseas communists were nourishing antiwar activity in the United States. For one thing, the Soviet Union could hardly be expected to pass up such a golden opportunity to harm its superpower rival. Irritated at an insinuation that he might have perceived an international communist combine lurking in the antiwar movement, McGeorge Bundy snapped, "Now, *look*, there is a reality to the notion that the communists, the Soviets, do what they can to louse up American policy whenever they get a chance." George Christian said "we saw a connection" between overseas communists and domestic protest partly "strictly based on the fact that it would have been remarkable if our enemies hadn't tried to take advantage of it, and fanned it. . . . As far as demonstrations go, particularly some of the more violent ones, yeah, there had to be some linkage."[156]

And what else could explain the undeniable efficiency with which the peace activists organized protests? Christian remembered:

> I think there was always a question of what was spontaneous and what wasn't. I know in Johnson's travels around the country he became convinced, based on what the Secret Service told him, and the FBI, that he could not even announce such a thing [his travel schedule] off-the-record to the press, or let me announce it off-the-record to the press, because there were reports made straight from the White House to somebody to get something started. And I think that was very true. We had an open White House, we had a lot of people accredited. We also had [representatives of] Eastern bloc countries. We had foreign reporters of one kind or another. We had some domestic reporters who may not have been security risks but at least could have been targeted by somebody. And I think we learned a bad

lesson. We really did learn that you couldn't really say much about what Johnson was going to do in traveling, or you were guaranteed a demonstration. . . .

You know, there's no way some of these things were spontaneous. I don't care what anybody says, some of the demonstrations were *not* spontaneous! . . . They had an efficient network of some kind. And I think one of the things that really bothered us at that time about some of the campus activities in particular were the people that were on the campuses stirring things up—they *weren't* students. They were *not* students. And yet when you go around complaining about professional agitators and that sort of thing, a lot of people tend to pooh-pooh that, particularly academics. Although a heck of a lot of college presidents at that time learned that a lot of this was not as spontaneous as it might appear.[157]

The antiwar movement's funding was certainly suspect. "I know one thing," Christian said. "Some of the campus demonstrations where a lot of money was involved—there was more than just a suspicion that some of the money came from other sources." Admiral Thomas Moorer asserted, "You know damn well that if you charter fifty or sixty buses, and you're spending all your time rioting, you're not going to be able to [fund] it yourself."[158]

Moreover, CIA studies or no CIA studies, there *were* telltale signs of outside manipulation of antiwar organizations, officials believed. Dean Rusk remembered receiving a copy of an antiwar telegram from intelligence sources two weeks before he received the exact same telegram from a "perfectly innocent" peace group. "So I think it would be foolish to suppose that such communists as there were were not doing what they could in opposition to the war," Rusk argued. They obviously had "under-the-rug activities" going. Many officials also shared Johnson's disbelief that, as Califano remarked, "a cause that is so clearly right for the country . . . would be so widely attacked if there were not some [foreign] force behind it."[159]

So why was this communist infiltration so difficult to spot? Because the Reds were wily. Paul Nitze, who Paul Warnke said "can see a communist plot almost anyplace," explained that while the communists tried to "stimulate" the peace movement "by every means they could think up . . . the thing that limited their involvement in it was the very danger of it becoming obvious that they were involved. So they went up to the limit of being so obvious as to be counterproductive. Because if they had been identified with it, of course, it would have killed the peace movement."[160]

Visions of communist treachery were even more prevalent among U.S. military leaders than civilian officials. Admiral Moorer griped, "These people always accused me of seeing a communist under every bush. Well, that's because there *is* a communist under every bush." Communist conspiracy theories also had powerful proponents in the media. James Reston considered it "just standard operating procedure by the communists" to involve themselves in the peace movement. They were "always around the edges of it," he perceived. [161]

Some of those I spoke to would have nothing to do with communist bogeymen theses, however. Paul Warnke said of the notion of foreign communist intervention in the peace movement, "You've got to be a real dummy to believe that! How many American communists have you met? I think the last one I saw was when I was at Columbia law school back in 1948. . . . It's like this business about the [nuclear] freeze movement being inspired by communists. It's nonsense." Ramsey Clark chafed that "anybody who knows anything about the real world" recognizes that communist conspiracy theories are "bunkum." Clark found the accusations of communist infiltration "constantly" lodged by officials "really nauseating." [162]

No evidence has ever been produced for foreign communist involvement in the anti–Vietnam War movement. Nevertheless, many Johnson administration officials would remain adamant for years that such chicanery was substantial. Walt Rostow was particularly defiant on the subject. "There was!" the combative and erratic ex-official blurted when I mentioned the administration's attempts to document a link between protesters and foreign communists. "I mean, Dave Dellinger was a classmate of mine." [163]

Administration officials had noteworthy explanations for antiwar protest besides communist infiltration. Paul Nitze's theory that militant students were trying to prove their "manhood" in the face of questions about their refusal to fight has already been noted. At an October 31 meeting, Johnson pointed to FBI reports alleging that large numbers of draft-card burners "were crazy people who had previous history in mental institutions." The president also believed that university professors opposed the war because "for so long, their salaries, their economic status, their prestige had been so low," Lady Bird Johnson writes. "They were now feeling power for the first time." Moorer felt these professors "had a guilty complex" over avoiding military service, "so they tried to teach their students to do the same thing they did to show that it was alright." Moorer complained that "some of the things they used to tell my son [at Duke University] were *unbelievable*." The admiral felt such guilt-inspired pedagogy explained "the very excess of extreme liberals in the academic community today." [164]

Rostow was the White House expert on student protesters. As he recalled, "I knew more about them than almost anyone. Because I'd been a teacher, and I'd sit down with them on every opportunity I was permitted to. . . . I knew their minds, and I knew the nature of their anxieties." A "very significant" factor in student dissent, Rostow told other cabinet officials, was "the high number of dissident leaders and followers who come out of sociology and the soft subjects. They are accustomed to dealing in generalities and abstractions. The hard-subject people, economists and engineers, do not seem to have the same trouble fitting in. They can find their place." Rostow also offered that many young people were "impatient" and thus having problems deciphering "how to get from here to there" in this "period of great and complex transition in the world."[165]

Johnson's own meditations on youthful demonstrators extended to their life-styles. On October 22, the president, Lady Bird and daughter Lynda drove around the Lincoln Memorial because he was "interested in what a hippie looked like." Four days later, Johnson obtained—for his "NIGHT READING"—a report on "obscene" sexual activity and references during the Pentagon protest.[166]

Mounting Rage

After the Pentagon siege, the administration continued to slowly escalate the war. On October 24, the president authorized air strikes against a key North Vietnamese airfield and renewed strikes on Hanoi's power transformer. He also briefly lifted the moratorium on bombing in the Hanoi "donut." Johnson approved additional Rolling Thunder targets on November 9, but rejected military proposals to reduce the restricted zones around Haiphong and Hanoi. Five days earlier, he wondered aloud to his top advisers whether bombing certain factories and airfields was "worth all the hell we are catching here." The president rebuffed ongoing military requests to mine North Vietnam's harbors. The same month McNamara accelerated the deployment of U.S. troops already earmarked for Vietnam. On December 16, the administration placed ten new bombing targets on CINCPAC's hit list; most were in the Haiphong-Hanoi regions. In early December, the Pentagon announced that the United States had dropped more tons of bombs in Vietnam than it had in the entire European theater during World War II.[167]

As the war escalated, so did anger and despair among protesters. They had assaulted America's military command post, shaken officialdom to its roots, yet the bloodshed only mounted. Few recognized they were helping to prevent even greater horrors in Vietnam, or fully appreciated the tremendous political power that was building. Doug Dowd remembered that the very "next day" after the Pentagon demonstration there was "a real letdown among an awful lot of the young people I knew because the war was . . . still going on. It was as though Johnson was going to look out of the White House and say, 'Okay, we'll stop the war.'" It was "just an *insane* position," Dowd felt. Dave Dellinger recalled that acute political frustration "became a much more visible phenomenon" among peace activists following the Pentagon protest. "I began to notice after that [that] old friends with whom I had worked, let's say for two, three years in the anti–Vietnam War movement, some even on other things earlier, they began to drop out. It was literally true." The movement "had come to a climax for them," Dellinger theorized. Despite "two magnificent actions in a row" (the April and Pentagon demonstrations), "the war just kept right on mounting, and there was no indication of effectiveness." The frustration was greatest "amongst younger people, the kind that later became Weatherpeople," Dellinger said. "In fact, that was in a sense the beginning of that tendency."[168]

Father Philip Berrigan, a longtime crusader for peace, was feeling the pain. It was "clear" to him even before the Pentagon protest that the many antiwar demonstrations in which he'd participated "hadn't had any effect at all." Nor had other traditional dissent tactics. "From I guess about 1963 on we had tried all the legitimate and legal forms of protest," Berrigan recalled over the phone from Virginia's Yorktown County Jail, his residence after hammering and spattering blood on two of the U.S. battleship *Iowa*'s missile launchers in 1988. "And I had been running back and forth to Washington talking with dove congresspeople, both in the Senate and in the House." He had even sat eyeball-to-eyeball with Dean Rusk and other administration officials, trying to educate them. "After you try all of these things you know that it's not sufficient," Berrigan said. Influenced by talk of raiding draft boards among SDSers, Berrigan and three other pacifists in Baltimore decided to pour blood on Selective Service files stored in that city's customshouse. Using blood, "a very alive symbol" and "the stuff of the covenant," to deface the files would, they hoped, stimulate other Americans "to assume responsibility for this awful war."[169]

At high noon on October 27, Berrigan and his three friends strode purposefully into the customshouse. The clerical-collared priest asked a receptionist if he could speak to someone in charge of the draft-card records. The receptionist got on the phone, and the four men sat down. Then one of them "gave a signal." They walked through a small gate into the draft hall, opened drawers that they knew from previous detective work contained the 1-A draft files, and began drenching them with blood. One handed out copies of the New Testament to the office clerks, only to be pelted with the books in return. The protesters stopped the defacing without resistance when grabbed from behind by clerks. The press burst into the building minutes later. "There was blood all over the place," Berrigan remembered. "It had been beautifully coordinated so that the press arrived at exactly the right time, and got these key photographs, which went all over in the newspapers and on TV." The four pacifists were subsequently sentenced to six years in prison. "That was practically predictable," Berrigan said.[170]

On November 14, fury over the war's upward spiral turned the streets of midtown Manhattan into a combat zone. After learning that Dean Rusk would be speaking at New York's Hilton Hotel on that day, the Fifth Avenue Peace Parade Committee had called for a legal picket. The New York regional office of SDS (under the coordination of one Jeff Jones) and other militant youth would have nothing of it, however. Inspired by Oakland STDW, they decided to fight the cops and torment the arriving dignitaries. "Dine with the Warmakers!" SDS invited other protesters. "Embroil the New York Hilton. . . . Revolution Begins: Nov. 14, 5–5:30 P.M." By 6 o'clock that evening nearly ten thousand people were congregated in the chilly streets and sidewalks around the hotel. Over a thousand cops were on hand to prevent them from choking the building. Demonstrators were crammed "like sardines" into designated areas. "It was a very uptight situation," the Parade Committee leader Norma Becker recalled. Suddenly, a group of militants charged the police lines. They were clubbed or forced backward by horses, their strike triggering police assaults on others nearby. Some protesters heaved bags of red paint and eggs. Many blocked nearby streets, hammered on luxury automobiles, overturned trash cans, and set off fire alarms. Seventeen gallons of animal blood were sloshed on assorted symbols of injustice. Bands of young demonstrators launched forays into Times Square, trapping frightened theatergoers inside restaurants and stores. "It was an angry demonstration," Becker said. "Very angry. An expression of the despair and outrage that people were feeling over the mounting escalation." Predictably, the combat begot casualties. Kids could be seen "lying in the street bleeding all over"; one was "out colder than a mackerel." Forty-six were arrested, more than twenty hospitalized.[171]

The same spirit of militant resistance to the war was spreading like wildfire across college campuses. The main targets of students' ire were recruiters from the military, the CIA, and Dow Chemical. Activists also took university officials to task for their schools' research contracts with the CIA and Pentagon. The justifications officials offered for the contracts only fanned the flames of campus indignation. One college president told protesters war research was "valuable." "Valuable for what?" he was asked. "Valuable," the official unguardedly exclaimed, "for killing people." Obstructionist sit-ins mushroomed. "No one goes limp anymore, or meekly to jail," the SDS leader Carl Davidson exulted in mid November. "Police violence does not go unanswered." Students were out to stop the war "BY WHATEVER MEANS NECESSARY."[172]

The fall militance and surging black radicalism in the United States stoked SDS's revolutionary hopes. In December, Davidson and Greg Calvert announced that the American empire was teetering. A massive explosion of student resistance in the spring—under the slogan "Ten Days to Shake the Empire"—would advance imperialism's fall, they argued. The SDS leaders advocated direct action at factories and other corporate institutions on top of shutting down the universities. Their proposal was shot down at an SDS National Council meeting, however. Many SDSers considered it too radical to facilitate effective organizing. "It *was* too left," Davidson conceded afterward. "If I had to do it over again, I would have toned it down a bit."[173]

Throughout the fall, antiwar activists passionately debated the trend toward militant resistance. Some were unenthusiastic. "I thought 'mobile tactics' were self-indulgent and bullshit," David Harris recalled. "Running through town turning over a garbage can? *C'mon.* Rupturing the tires of local buses? It may make you feel powerful—what the hell does it do?" The passengers on the county bus that lost its ignition wires to Oakland STDW protesters "didn't want their bus disabled," Harris pointed out. "That bus wasn't taking them to the army—that bus was taking them to work." Harris considered STDW "just a wasted amount of energy." Norma Becker felt "it was a tactical error to take to the streets and stop the motorists" during the Rusk demonstration. "The motorists were not the enemy," she noted. "To evoke their annoyance and irritation was not a way to win friends and influence people." The Resistance activist Marty Jezer lamented that the drift toward "disruptive confrontation" sprang more from "frustration (even boredom!)" than "any clear sense of why one goes into the streets."[174]

Sidney Peck was also apprehensive of the trends. "One of the great political fallacies of the movement," the Mobe leader wrote in December, "is to make a direct association between the choice of tactics and the degree of radical commitment to end the war and change the system." Judging confrontational actions inherently "revolutionary" "just didn't make any sense at all to me," Peck recalled. He considered it "absurd" for some protesters to conclude that urinating on the Pentagon lawn "signified *real* radicalism, particularly if the participants were women!" Peck believed many young protesters were ignoring the symbiotic relationship between militance and mass dissent. Although resistance tactics required broad public support to be successful, he wrote, "'super-radical'" actions not only failed to communicate "any meaningful political message" to many Americans but "actually alienate[d]" them. Peck thought the countercultural lifestyles popular among young radicals were contributing to their strategic errors. He remembered:

> During this time I was still teaching and engaged in the normal activities you do for making a living. When you do that, you're constantly in touch with people who don't agree with what you're doing. And so you're getting constant feedback on exactly those people who have to be brought into the movement. . . . If you're into, now, an altogether new lifestyle . . . in many ways you're shut off. And while you may now have a support community to do activities that take courage and engage in some kind of risk, you're not that sensitive to what the [public] reaction's going to be.[175]

Even some prominent militants harbored doubts about youth's growing fascination with disruption. "After the Pentagon it was quite clear to me that the most dangerous thing that could happen is that we take the road to revolutionary adventurism," Greg Calvert recalled. On the eve of the demonstration, Calvert had observed wild-eyed veterans of STDW pulling into Washington hot to battle the police and troops. "People were just turned on to what we used to describe . . . as the 'wild in the streets' mentality," he said. "People wanted action, they wanted movement." Many "were very impressed with gimmicks. You know, you get some walkie-talkies and set up command posts, and it all starts to sound very much like, not guerrilla theater, but guerrilla warfare." The "infantile leftism" Calvert observed at the Pentagon exacerbated his concern. He consequently "developed a deep conviction that we had to hold the line on violence." The "next step" down the path of revolutionary adventurism, violence would both further divide activists, he worried, and cost them public support. As a result of this stance

> I was defamed and discredited by my opponents "by any means necessary," as they said, including a vicious and disgusting gay-baiting campaign. . . . It was real ugly. It was important to get Greg Calvert if you wanted to lead SDS in a revolutionary direction. . . . It was a very homophobic movement. People talk about sexism—they should talk about homophobia in the movement. And one of the things that some people need to do, some of the early "feminists" need to do, is a little fessing up about how they used gay-baiting against Greg Calvert. . . . It's a very, very ugly story. It did a lot of damage to me. . . . I lost a lot of friends. [176]

Although he was the leading national proponent of the trend "from protest to resistance," Dave Dellinger believed that verbally or physically attacking police and damaging property provoked unwelcome police violence and turned off potential adherents. Dellinger was "ambivalent" about the new mobile civil disobedience. "It did coincide with something that I believed in, namely this stepping up of tactics and the avoidance of just being so quickly disposed of," however, and so he felt activists should "experiment" with it. "But I was nervous about what might happen; it might get out of hand. I thought it had to be very carefully disciplined at the same time," he said with a laugh. [177]

Other protesters had no such qualms. Steve Hamilton felt Oakland STDW protesters had not only expressed their "seriousness" but shown that "the system was not invulnerable." Another protester called Friday of STDW "the greatest day of my life." According to an inspired Marvin Garson, it was time for even bolder actions, ones that might "require us to take a few casualties." [178]

Linda Morse, the Student Mobilization Committee's executive secretary, quickly proclaimed STDW "very successful." Morse considered mobile civil disobedience a tactical breakthrough of major proportions. She felt "blown away by it." Morse's passion for mobile tactics is reflected in her predominate recollection of the fall of 1967. "That was a wild period," Morse, later a physician, recalled. "I was exhausted the entire time. The main thing I remember is total exhaustion, physical and mental." Morse admitted that her analysis of mobile tactics' *strategic* value was not deep. "It was definitely vague," she said. The "core" of her political beliefs was then "getting muddled." Although unready to abandon her pacifism, Morse was "questioning it." The ability of nonviolent protest to end the war appeared increasingly doubtful. And mobile tactics seemed a more fitting existential expression of her soaring moral outrage over U.S. policy than "passive" civil disobedience. [179]

On November 4, Morse proposed that the Student Mobe organize another Stop the Draft Week. It would kick off in conjunction with the Resistance's second national draft-card turn-in, scheduled for December 4. Protesters would shut down induction centers and draft boards across the country "a la Oakland style," Morse submitted. In New York, they would close the Whitehall induction center. The plan included a nonviolent sit-in at Whitehall on December 5 organized by David McReynolds of the War Resisters League. "They said the first day we could have 'old-fashioned' c.d.," McReynolds amusedly recalled. "I thought, 'How far we had come that the first day was "old-fashioned" c.d. . . .'" Morse's proposal passed. [180]

On Monday, December 4, young Americans returned 375 draft cards to their government. Before sunrise the next morning, five thousand demonstrators were gathered around the red-brick, nine-story Whitehall building. More than twenty-five hundred police were there to greet them; some were grumbling over canceled leaves. Dr. Benjamin Spock led the first wave of blockaders. His move thrilled McReynolds. "I didn't know what Ben was going to do," the WRL leader remembered. Although Spock had agreed earlier to co-sponsor the protest, McReynolds had been "afraid to call him to ask whether he was going to be arrested or not, because Ben was a moderate at that time, a major figure, never been arrested before, and we didn't want to push him." Spock's task was not an easy one. Under the glare of television lights, the tall, smartly dressed pediatrician got down on his hands and knees and tried to slip under a wooden barricade, only to run into the resistant legs of solemn-faced cops on the other side. He was finally allowed to penetrate forbidden turf, incur arrest, and get hauled away. McReynolds and author Grace Paley led probes of other faces of the building. "My group got physically thrown into the air by the police, but not hurt," McReynolds recounted. He advised his followers, "Let's just stay where we are." McReynolds was "just happy to sit" after his excursion into the atmosphere. Mounted police charged into Paley's contingent, whacking heads. Paley's piqued reaction to the violence prevented worse. The diminutive woman screamed directly into a police captain's face, "I demand that you stop this! This is an absolute outrage! Pull your men back!" The captain "was so *stunned* at seeing this housewife yelling at him that he pulled his men back," McReynolds recalled. By the time the sun was up, 264 people had been arrested.[181]

The next morning, twenty-five hundred protesters congregated in Battery Park near Whitehall. It was obvious both from Tuesday's heavy police presence and the multitudinous cops then close at hand that shutting down the center would be impossible. The demonstrators thus had two options, one wrote later: either engaging in "ritual sit-ins" and legal picketing or "running through the streets of the city with our flies open, raising hell." They decided to open their flies. The protesters' weaving incursion on Whitehall proved no match for the thousands of police in the area, however. Everywhere they turned, lines of cops quickly appeared. "We were trapped like fleas," Morse remembered, also likening the experience to bouncing around "in a big plastic bag." "It was almost like they were laughing at us," she said of the police. "They had it quite together." Few protesters actually made it to Whitehall. That evening, an upset Morse "publicly criticized herself for timidity in failing to storm one lightly defended police barricade."[182]

On Thursday, some eight hundred demonstrators gathered to try their luck again. For Steve Cagan, the day got off to an embarrassing start. The second person the STDW leader approached to whisper the identity of four heretofore secret targets for the morning's assault was a plainclothes policeman. The officer promptly clamped handcuffs on Cagan's wrists and led him away. Hundreds were arrested in all.[183]

Friday's action saw the fiercest police attack of the week. Club-swinging cops teed off on a crowd of protesters pinned against an iron fence. One hundred and forty were arrested.

All in all, New York STDW invoked mixed reviews. Some young demonstrators again found street-fighting invigorating and thought it valuable training for U.S. Che Guevaras. Linda Morse and many other protesters were deeply frustrated. Their test drive with the highly vaunted mobile tactics "had failed," Morse remembered, "which was a disappointment to all of us." Some tactical tinkering was obviously in order if mobile civil disobedience was to be wheeled out for another run. David McReynolds, for one, was appalled at this new political fad:

> I thought that was stupid as hell. *Incredibly* stupid. *Militarily* stupid. They hadn't even looked at a fucking map! Where did they think they were going to have "mobile tactics" down in that area? What did they think the cops were going to do? You don't play games. You see, I am a pacifist, but I'm also a Marxist. If your enemy is the cops, all right, get organized and go shoot them or something. But if your enemy is not the cops, *don't bait the police*. Don't do that. They have guns and they have clubs and they're tired and they're overworked

and they don't get paid that much for overtime. *Don't bait the cops.* If you want a revolution, if that's your objective—and that's my objective—*don't bait the cops.* Do what Lenin did. I have other disagreements with Lenin, but I thought his appeal—steadily, relentlessly—to the troops was absolutely sound. . . .

What did mobile tactics accomplish? You didn't close the draft board down. If you were young and you wanted some fun, okay, you had it. If your objective was changing people, you didn't do it. If you wanted to see how many heads you could get cracked, you got some cracked.[184]

Fingers in the Dike

Meanwhile, Americans were losing heart for the war in rapidly growing numbers. The conflict seemed endless, the chances of victory slimmer by the day. The peace movement continued to provoke doubts about the war's merits. As *Time* magazine noted, people were also troubled by the domestic strife Vietnam was breeding. Amid the fall militancy, more wondered whether the war was worth a split society. Opinion polls indicated that, for the first time, more people thought U.S. intervention in Vietnam had been a mistake than did not. Only 35 percent looked favorably on the president's handling of the war. In Cambridge and San Francisco, some 40 percent of voters advocated prompt U.S. withdrawal from Vietnam. Five hundred union leaders mounted the first national challenge to the AFL-CIO's support for the war. As McGeorge Bundy wrote President Johnson on November 10, "public discontent with the war is now wide and deep."[185]

Johnson was obsessed with his faltering domestic rear guard. At a meeting on November 4, "he pointed out that it's very possible that we could get a no confidence vote any day now." The president also griped that antiwar senators were "going to all the colleges and stirring up problems." Johnson lashed out at his critics, proclaiming them "simpletons" and cowards with "no guts." He had a special dislike of dwindling enthusiasm for the war within his official family. "That military genius, McNamara, has gone dovish on me," the president gibed. There were too many "disloyal" officials around. "It's gotten so that you can't screw your wife without it being spread around by traitors," Johnson growled.[186]

Antiwar sentiment was also becoming more distressing to Lady Bird. At a January luncheon on juvenile delinquency in America, the entertainer Eartha Kitt sternly lectured Mrs. Johnson on the war's contribution to the problem. "We send the best of this country off to be shot and maimed," Kitt said, advancing a step toward Lady Bird. "They rebel in the streets." The first lady—her face pale, her voice quivering—could only meekly respond that the war's burden should not deter efforts to "make this a happier, better-educated land." (President Johnson was furious at Kitt's insolence and reportedly sicked the FBI and CIA on her. Soon stories appeared in the press claiming Kitt was a sadistic nymphomaniac; many of her performance contracts were canceled. Kitt says Johnson's vendetta against her derailed her career for years.)[187]

By late 1967 most administration officials probably agreed with McGeorge Bundy that the war's "principal battleground" was "in domestic opinion." They bombarded Johnson with prescriptions for rallying the public. The group of influential private advisers known as the Wise Men proposed developing "friendly" television programs to "explain" the war to confused Americans. They also suggested organizing "committees of speech-makers," bringing "responsible" university administrators to Washington to voice support, fetching Ambassador Bunker or South Vietnamese President Nguyen Van Thieu for speaking appearances in the United States, and publicizing favorable intelligence on the conflict. McGeorge Bundy advised the president to "keep calm." The administration had already "tried too hard to convert public opinion by statistics and by spectacular visits of all sorts," said Bundy. Since most Americans' qualms about the war centered on its duration and cost in lives and money, "changes in what actually happens in Vietnam are the only effective way of changing public attitudes at home," he argued. Bundy urged "some visible *de*-escalation," excluding a bombing pause and without negotiating.[188]

Harry McPherson and Walt Rostow agreed that changes in U.S. policy were needed to rally the public. McPherson told Johnson that "indefinitely postponing further bombing around Hanoi and Haiphong" would "recapture" considerable lost support from "middle-road Democrats." That a "big mechanized white nation" was "obliterating a small agricultural brown nation" was not agreeable to them, the White House counsel argued. Rostow, evincing what McPherson later called his "rugby player's view" of international affairs, continued to recommend invading Laos and southern North Vietnam. The majority of Americans were hawks and would back this bold move, he contended.[189]

Dean Rusk apparently felt that testifying before Congress was *not* a feasible tactic for winning over Americans. In response to a request from Senator J. William Fulbright to appear in open session before the Senate Foreign Relations Committee, Rusk hedged, citing "questions of military operations and planning," "the most delicate relations with other governments" and other dubious constraints.[190]

The administration ultimately pursued a variety of actions to help recover lost domestic support for the war. Officials apprised the nation that the United States was hanging tough in Vietnam to prevent nothing less than World War III. "Within the next decade or two, there will be a billion Chinese on the mainland, armed with nuclear weapons, with no certainty about what their attitude toward the rest of Asia will be," Rusk warned at a carefully prepared

October press conference. The United States was being "tested," he said, and it was time to "find out what kind of people we are." Three days later, Vice President Hubert Humphrey thundered that "the threat to world peace is militant, aggressive Asian communism, with its headquarters in Peking, China." Yet vilifying China hurt the prospects of international peace. Paul Warnke revealed that in 1967 and 1968 Rusk vetoed a State Department proposal to normalize relations with China because it would have undercut the we-are-containing-Red-China rationale for the war.[191]

The administration also helped prominent prowar Americans issue public expressions of support. On October 25, the reader will recall, the government-inspired Citizens Committee for Peace with Freedom in Vietnam announced its existence. On December 19 came the statement of the fourteen prowar intellectuals coaxed by John Roche.

And officials assured the public that the fighting was going well. Chaired by Rostow, the administration's "Psychology Strategy Committee" leaked favorable intelligence on the war to the media. It also rebutted congressmen's criticisms with prompt personal visits, telephone calls, letters, and counterspeeches by supporters. One legislator "found a man from the State Department on his doorstep within hours of press stories on his disaffection from official policy." Johnson ordered production of a pamphlet answering the "ten most asked questions" about the war. On Veteran's Day weekend, the president went on a frenzied journey to eight military installations to spread the word of U.S. progress in Vietnam (and to salute the men "who keep me free," he told his aides). In Saigon, U.S. military officers called in reporters for an upbeat three-hour briefing. Fresh from a trip to the war front, Humphrey told the public, "We are on the offensive. Territory is being gained." The government also flew other politicians and, starting in early 1968, "selected private citizens," to Vietnam to proclaim the outlook bright.[192]

The administration's "Success Offensive" reached its peak in mid-November when Johnson summoned General William Westmoreland, Ambassador Bunker, and Robert "Blowtorch" Komer, an expert on counterrevolution, to the United States for a slate of public appearances. The general was the government's "big gun."[193]

Years later, when I interviewed him, Westmoreland was retired and living in his native South Carolina. Ruggedly handsome, with erect carriage, square jaw, firm stare, and a handshake of nearly bone-crushing force, he continued to look and act the part of the quintessential military leader. During a walk through the streets of Charleston's old town district, he marched briskly like a soldier on a mission. Westmoreland's past was evident in his home decorations as well: U.S. and Army flags hung conspicuously just inside the front door of his modest home, Southeast Asian artifacts dotted his living room. Yet the general had also mellowed with age. Gone was much of his earlier hostility toward America's internal enemies. Immediately upon sitting down to lunch with me, fellow restaurant patrons hanging on his every word, Westmoreland remarked, good-naturedly, "So, I heard Berkeley's got a communist government. How's it working out?"[194]

Westmoreland had previously been summoned back to the United States to rouse Americans in April 1967. Before one speech during that stay, he witnessed antiwar protesters torching his effigy. It was "sobering to see a representation of oneself go up in flames," he writes. Upon landing at Andrews Air Force Base on November 15, the general told reporters, "I have never been more encouraged in the four years that I have been in Vietnam. We are making real progress." Six days later, he announced to the National Press Club, "We have reached an important point when the end begins to come into view." Westmoreland projected that the United States could "phase down" its involvement in Vietnam "within two years or less," which he would continue to believe was "a legitimate feeling at the time."[195]

Westmoreland visited with Johnson until nearly midnight on the evening of November 20 in the White House living quarters. The president was profoundly troubled. Westmoreland remembered:

> Mr. Johnson had a lot on his mind at that time. A lot of it was political—he was a very politically sensitive man, as you well know—but a lot of it was personal. He told me . . . that he didn't think that he would run for reelection, and he attributed that to his health. He was in a very poor state of health. And then as he talked he said that Lady Bird and Lynda and Luci [Johnson] didn't want him to run, and that very few people knew about it. And he said, "Very frankly, I'm telling you because I trust you, and I don't want you to tell anybody, not even your wife."
>
> . . . He was not a healthy man. He was carrying a tremendous burden. He realized that he was losing public support for the war.[196]

FIVE   1968

Peace by Ballot?

Ten days after Johnson told Westmoreland that he was leaning against running for reelection, Senator Eugene McCarthy issued a major public pronouncement that assumed quite the opposite. He was challenging the president in the upcoming Democratic presidential primaries. His main campaign issue: Vietnam.

McCarthy had been pondering a presidential bid for many months. The war seemed to him increasingly impractical and immoral, and he was irked by administration propaganda smearing its opponents as communists or cowards. Clergy and Laymen Concerned About Vietnam's winter 1967 mobilization in Washington had suggested to him that there might be enough domestic antiwar sentiment to wage a respectable campaign. The young protesters in the streets didn't appear to be making any headway on their own. "I thought that they had a right to some directed action against the war," McCarthy would recall. Belligerent utterances by administration officials also fed the senator's interest in running.[1]

But it was the Reform Democrat mover-and-shaker Allard Lowenstein who ultimately nudged McCarthy into the race. The former college wrestler had concluded that ending the war required defeating Johnson, and had begun building a "Dump Johnson" movement. Lowenstein boldly ignored the many political pundits who claimed the president had a lock on his party's nomination. "He never believed, indeed, the conventional wisdom about being unable to unseat a sitting president," David Hawk, a Lowenstein follower, remembered. "He'd had enough experience in electoral politics to have this sense that if you did well in some of the early primaries, everything thereafter could change." Over the summer, the stocky, tireless, perennially untidy Lowenstein had "goosed up" hundreds of liberal political organizations to impel the Dump Johnson movement off center. By building a national body of antiwar Democrats, he argued, activists could demonstrate the "enormous" unpopularity of Johnson's policies inside his own party. Encouraging protest votes in the first few primaries would also help surface this discontent. Lowenstein contended that a major political figure would then step forward to take on the president. "He argued that if one created a political bandwagon, the politician would emerge to ride the bandwagon," Hawk recalled. Lowenstein dismantled walls of skepticism during his recruiting trips. "This guy can't be serious," Hawk remembered thinking upon first hearing Lowenstein outline his strategy. The former Cornell diving star and Union Theological Seminary student "had to hear it explained five or six times" before joining the crusade.[2]

The man Lowenstein felt had the best chance of toppling Johnson was unenthusiastic. Calculating and ambitious, Robert Kennedy was pessimistic about his chances, and worried that he wouldn't get the Democratic nomination in 1972 if he threatened party unity. Other potential candidates also reacted coolly to Lowenstein's scheme. Only McCarthy seemed open to running. Then, on October 20, McCarthy met with Lowenstein and three associates over breakfast to discuss his plans. The uncharacteristically merry senator became merrier by the minute. At 10:15, he let the cat out of the bag. "You fellows have been talking about three or four names," McCarthy said with a smile. "I guess you can cut it down to one."[3]

McCarthy's candidacy got off to a rocky start. On December 2 at Chicago's Conrad Hilton Hotel, he delivered his first campaign speech to a meeting of the Conference of Concerned Democrats (CCD), the organizational leadership of Dump Johnson. McCarthy was not completely comfortable with these people. Lowenstein and other CCD spokespeople were taking their attacks on the administration a bit too far, he felt, neglecting important political realities. "I didn't really look upon them as a solid base upon which you could build a campaign," McCarthy recalled. "There were some good people there, but they were pretty much in a protesting mood." He remembered being "surprised" to see so many in the noisy crowd of ten thousand "wearing straw hats and waving banners . . . like in an ordinary campaign or convention." Lowenstein was at the podium. "It was Allard at his most demagogic," a friend recounted. "He was supposed to be leading up to the candidate, but after a while it seemed like he had forgotten about Eugene McCarthy and thought he was the candidate himself." Those officials over in Washington were a pack of liars and public relations hucksters, shouted Lowenstein. The American people would have no more, they were going to exercise their democratic rights. Lowenstein "introduced" McCarthy for more than half an hour. Offstage, McCarthy was heating to a boil. He began "stomping around . . . kicking a crushed dixie cup, and muttering to himself." Somebody tell that son of a bitch to sit down! A dull speaker, McCarthy feared Lowenstein's theatrics would eclipse his own talk.

Finally, someone gave Lowenstein the hook. McCarthy walked onto the stage and turned to address his supporters. His tone was calm, professorial. "After he had spoken for twenty minutes, some listeners were dozing." Lowenstein later tried to convince McCarthy to say a few words to the two thousand people gathered outside the hotel, unable to enter. Angrily, the senator refused and withdrew to his hotel room.[4]

McCarthy remained frosty toward Lowenstein throughout the campaign. He suspected the Dump Johnson leader was using it to advance his own political ambitions and, worse, that he continued to wish Kennedy was running instead. Many years later, McCarthy seemed visibly annoyed when Lowenstein's name was brought up and claimed to have no recollection of the organizer's overtures to him to enter the race.[5]

The friction cut both ways. Lowenstein was appalled at McCarthy's lackadaisical campaign habits. The senator seemed gutless—defeatist—to Lowenstein. McCarthy was not running to win, but passively posing as a high-minded receptacle of antiwar votes.[6]

McCarthy was indeed doubtful of his chances. Sure, he expected to receive far more votes than the 12 percent public opinion polls were forecasting. "Anybody can get 12 percent against Johnson," McCarthy figured. He knew that "opposition to the war was growing," and that he "wouldn't just be in all alone." He might even "be able to build up enough pressure to force a change of policy." But actually seizing the nomination was unrealistic.[7] A big time loser in big time politics, his political career would then lie in ruins. That was hardly worth busting his butt over.

McCarthy's pessimism about his electoral fortunes was shared by many of the young activists who flocked to his campaign. For them, McCarthy's challenge was primarily a way to broaden and mobilize domestic opposition to the war. Frustrated by the continuing escalation of the conflict and uncomfortable with the rising militancy in the peace movement, some were desperate for a new way of registering antiwar sentiment. David Hawk, for example, felt that peace protests weren't "getting anywhere" and that a fresh political tack was needed. Its precise strategic logic wasn't important. "Basically what was true then, and later became even truer, was that if it had a reasonable chance of showing opposition to the war policies, people would try it," Hawk, a human rights activist, recalled. "They would try anything that had the *remotest* chance of influencing policy [laughs]. . . . So you didn't have to know that McCarthy would win" to want to work for him. Youth for McCarthy director Sam Brown remembered entertaining hopes of a McCarthy victory "sometimes for up to thirty minutes at a stretch." The campaign appealed to him mainly because "it gave an opportunity and gave an excuse to walk up to people's doors and say, 'Hi. I'm Sam Brown. I'm here because I'd like to talk to you about the war in

Vietnam—and about Gene McCarthy.'" Brown hoped it would also show that protesters were "not some crazy minority" and encourage elite figures to speak out against the war.[8]

Other peace activists were less than enamored with McCarthy's campaign. Upon announcing it, McCarthy had expressed hope that it would alleviate the "frustration" and "helplessness" then leading protesters to pursue "extra-legal" and lawless activities as well as "make threats for third parties and other irregular movements." He wished, he said, to "restore . . . a belief in the processes of American politics and of American government." Those were repellent words to many radicals. With the slaughter in Vietnam rising still, this was no time to abandon the streets for the polling booth, said they, less so for a politician curiously late to the cause of peace. If the American political system really worked, they wouldn't have been in the streets in the first place. "McCarthy had made it all too clear that one of the reasons he was out there was to get us back into the system," SDS's Carl Oglesby remembered. "And that made a mockery out of everything we were doing. I mean, get us back into the system by ending the war in Vietnam and getting rid of racism!" McCarthy readily conceded to me that many of his young supporters "would have been in the streets if we hadn't had the campaign."[9]

The Socialist Workers Party was particularly antagonistic to McCarthy's candidacy. It attacked the senator as merely a hired prizefighter of the bourgeoisie who would accomplish nothing more than preserving the capitalist system. The SWP offered voters its own candidate for president, Fred Halstead, instead. The SWP considered Halstead's campaign a tool for purifying the ideological air. Its primary purpose was even more sectarian. "The *main* reason you run it is to build the SWP—you recruit," Peter Camejo admitted. SDS also sniffed at McCarthy's candidacy. "'Be Clean for Gene' for us was ridiculous," Carl Davidson recalled. "Of course, for another whole section of American youth who had yet to become politically active, that was their first step. . . . But we had been around for five years, and we saw it as an imperialist plot . . . "[10]

Activists eager for Robert Kennedy to enter the race were also unenamored by McCarthy's candidacy. They felt Kennedy was more electable than McCarthy. The New York senator could reach workers and blacks along with students, and he had the political savvy and muscle to handle Johnson at the convention. "The difference is very clear," Oglesby said emphatically. "McCarthy wouldn't have had anything to do with real power. That was pure symbolism. It was empty. McCarthy was *not* going to be the president of this country. *Period. No way, no how.* But Bobby Kennedy? *Ah, ha,* a very real chance to be the president of the United States. *Very real, very practical.*" Oglesby scolded McCarthy organizers, "Get out of this! This is sandlot politics!"[11]

Kennedy supporters were also more sanguine about their man's performance in office. Pressured from below, working in an "implicit social coalition" with Rev. Martin Luther King, Jr., Oglesby believed, Kennedy would "complete . . . the bureaucratic civil rights revolution that had begun in the last days of Jack's presidency." Granted, he would suck antiwar protesters out of the streets just like McCarthy. "But he does it by stopping the war." And "nobody wants to be in the streets—that's abnormal." Oglesby considered a Kennedy campaign to be "a logical expression of what we'd been doing. . . . I mean, all that stuff about having to organize the 'interracial community of the poor' in order to get power in the Democratic Party and work your way up was *baloney*."[12]

In early 1968, a New York businessman contacted Oglesby to ascertain the attitudes of student antiwar activists if Kennedy entered the fray. Members of his organization, "Business International," felt the war was economically costly, muddying U.S. relations with Europe and "unsettling our domestic politics in a very, very ominous way," Oglesby recalled. "I said I would do my damnedest, personally, to bring them in behind [Kennedy]." Soon five or six SDSers were sitting around a table talking politics with "a bunch of vice presidents from various big companies."[13]

Peculiar bedfellows? Mike Klonsky, soon-to-be SDS national secretary, thought so. Serious revolutionaries should be smashing liberals, he sneered, not collaborating with them. Klonsky put out the word: Oglesby was "the most dangerous man in the Movement." Exasperatedly, Oglesby remembered: "Num-nuts types like Klonsky would raise the bugaboo of cooptation. To me, there was no cooptation about it. If anyone was getting coopted, it was the Democratic Party. The movement was coopting the Democratic Party. . . . The thing is, you can't be against making compromises and moving in new directions and joining up with people to your right—above all if you're on the left."[14]

Some radicals assailed both McCarthy and Kennedy supporters "with such vitriol that a visitor from Venus would have concluded that McCarthy and Kennedy advocated escalation and genocide rather than restraint and concessions," Dave Dellinger writes. They "showed more interest in maintaining their doctrinal purity . . . than in finding ways of working with [others] outside electoral politics to end the war." As Dellinger observes, the acridity of the dispute among activists over the two senators' respective political value "disrupted [antiwar] planning sessions," "made enemies," and "drastically weakened" the National Mobe, "both materially and spiritually."[15]

As the McCarthy campaign was getting under way, many peace activists were gearing up to leave their mark on the 1968 congressional elections as well. CALCAV Director Richard Fernandez and Lou Frank, a Communist Party member and adviser to Henry Wallace's 1948 presidential campaign, were meeting with rich liberal businessmen to cajole financing of an antiwar mailer to voters. Enticing dollars proved remarkably easy. "In four months I went to more dinners and lunches with [Frank] with wealthy businessmen," Fernandez would recall. "And it taught me that these wealthy businessmen are more concerned with scale-matching problems [i.e., how far their money would go] than they are with whether they give you $5,000 or $50,000. I mean, you can literally stick zeroes on the end of numbers, I found out. It was a whole new world. We'd have dinners with three or four people and walk off with thirty-eight grand." CALCAV used the money to put together a 14-page tabloid entitled, "Who's Right? Who's Wrong on Vietnam?" The tabloid quoted scores of distinguished Americans opposed to U.S. policy. CALCAV flooded several primary states with it. "Then we sent it to every barber shop and beauty shop in America," Fernandez said. Not everyone was pleased. "We got back more hate mail," Fernandez remembered. "We got shit in the mail, literally dung."[16]

On February 5–6, twenty-five hundred CALCAV activists invaded Washington to visit with their congressional representatives and demonstrate. They gave every U.S. legislator a copy of *In the Name of America*, CALCAV's freshly released book documenting wholesale U.S. violations of international rules of warfare in Vietnam. Distribution of the book had been "blocked for about five months" by CALCAV's Rabbi Abraham Heschel, however, Fernandez recalled. A German refugee, Heschel "had all these feelings about Nazi Germany and feared that the book would so outrage the right wing that there'd be a lot of repression."[17]

Women Strike for Peace was pursuing a "woman power" voters campaign then. WSPers informed congressional and other political candidates they would have to pledge to help end the war to receive women's "peace vote." Other women were encouraged to exercise their political power. The campaign involved "saturation leafleting," vigils at officials' homes and offices, demonstrations, and car caravans. WSPers also conducted "interviews" with candidates "to separate the phonies from those genuinely committed to peace."[18]

On January 15, WSP co-sponsored a 5,000-strong march on Capitol Hill by the "Jeannette Rankin Brigade." The elderly Rankin was the first woman to serve in Congress and a longtime member of the Women's International League for Peace and Freedom. Preparations for the march had received an inadvertent assist from the government during the Pentagon demonstration the previous fall when it corralled several hundred female arrestees in the same room for the night. "That was when we really discussed the Jeannette Rankin Brigade," WSP's Dagmar Wilson recalled. "I said, 'See, this is what happens: they put us all in jail together and for the first time . . . we really have a chance to talk about these things!' So that drummed up a lot of interest." Police prevented the mainly black-clad women from entering the Capitol en masse. Many hungered for civil disobedience. WSP leaders had solicited the participation of moderate groups leery of illegalities, however; they checked that step. The women held a rally and their own "Congress" instead. "A lot of today has been bosh," one complained. Such frustration was widespread.[19]

In California, WSPers were persevering with a year-old campaign to get their state assembly to petition Congress to determine whether the war was in "the national interest." Similar resolutions had already been passed by the Colorado and Arkansas legislatures. The WSPers asked California's governor, Ronald Reagan, to back such a motion. Few were surprised by his persistent refusals, but Reagan's manipulative manner toward the women infuriated them and hardened their resolve. Particularly enraging was a meeting two hundred WSPers had held with him in Sacramento the previous spring. Under the glare of television news cameras, the women had flooded into Reagan's outer office to drop off a letter to the allegedly unavailable governor. Minutes later there had been "a great stir of excitement." In the event of a break in his busy schedule, an aide had officiously announced, Reagan would be happy to see them. But they would have to wait. Just when the women were "ready to give up," Reagan smilingly strolled out. Madeline Duckles and Mary Clarke, the spokeswomen for the group, were short feet from him. "He had put his makeup on," Duckles remembered. "You could see it. Pancake makeup; dark skin, a sun-tan effect. His eyebrows were brushed. His hair was brushed (it was grayer than it is now). And here were Mary and I with our bare faces hanging out." Reagan went into a canned rap. He was a man of peace, had always been one. But the North Vietnamese were not: they were the culprits. "He tried to smooth-talk us," WSP's Alice Hamburg recalled. Duckles and Clarke "exchanged glances and knew immediately that if we wanted to be heard we were going to have to interrupt him." No, they had come to tell *him* a few things, the women cut in. But Reagan was a poor listener. Gosh, wasn't it nice that people who disagreed could still "talk to each other and not about each other?" he remarked. The women left the meeting feeling "very much abused," Hamburg remembered. "It just told us a lot about him," Duckles said disgustedly.[20]

The Spock Indictments: Going after "the Biggies"

Following the Pentagon demonstration, the Johnson administration intensified its actions against the peace movement. It recognized that the protesters in Washington and those clamoring in other cities that fall had advanced still further public opposition to the war, in large part because of their unnerving fracture of domestic order. The FBI beefed up its surveillance operations, interrogating campus subversives and recruiting university officials to report on them. The CIA launched Project Resistance to combat student protests against government recruiters. The Pentagon's intelligence net grew too. ROTC instructors enlisted their pupils to scout campus radicals. The intelligence output of the U.S. Army's Conus Intel swelled to the point where Ramsey Clark pleaded with army officials to forward the Justice Department only the most pertinent reports. The administration moved to punish draft resisters. SSS Director Lewis Hershey fired off a letter to all local draft boards recommending they deny deferments to youth involved in resistance activities. The White House prepared a draft Executive Order to the same end. Both punitive measures were undertaken over Clark's strong objections. "We went round and round," he recalled. "I felt that you could not accelerate [induction] on the grounds of an exercise of free speech or protest, or unrelated conduct, even criminal conduct." (Clark assured Joseph Califano that he was "working on the matter with a positive attitude," though.) Other administration officials also saw potential legal snags to cutting off protesters' deferments. Califano cautioned Johnson that Hershey's recommendation raised "serious constitutional problems." Not so serious as to merit its retraction, mind you, but serious enough to embarrass the president if he were identified with it. "I believe it is important that you stay out of this controversy," Califano counseled his boss. Thousands of protesters were routed into the military before appeals courts repudiated the practice.[21]

Johnson directed White House aides to prepare a rundown on all federal statutes that could potentially be used to snuff out the "'resistance' now being spoken of by extremists." Califano's aide Matthew Nimetz reported that felony charges might be lodged against those who assisted deserters, advocated insurrection through the U.S. mail, impeded the Secret Service's protection of the president, urged insubordination by U.S. soldiers, willfully damaged government property, or sabotaged U.S. military facilities, among other acts. White House and Pentagon officials also began "discreetly" investigating federal, state, and local "relief" available to prevent demonstrators from "inhibiting the speeches or travel of the President." In January, Johnson ordered that all "civil disturbance matters" receive the government's "full attention."[22]

The combined menace that growing black unrest and militant resistance to the war posed to the status quo led to some rather dramatic White House discussions. Clark warned officials that urban guerrilla warfare might break out in the United States. He told Paul Nitze that he might have to request assistance from the Pentagon if power generation and electrical transmission lines were blown up.[23]

On January 5, the administration raised the ante in its battle with the peace movement a mega-notch. It indicted five prominent advocates of draft resistance—Benjamin Spock, William Sloane Coffin, Mitchell Goodman, Marcus Raskin, and Michael Ferber—for conspiracy to "counsel, aid and abet young men to violate the draft laws." Their potential fate: five years in the slammer. Word of the indictment swiftly shot through the antiwar movement. The

Draconian state repression long expected by many activists had apparently arrived.[24]

Michael Ferber is the author of three books, two on William Blake, the other on Percy Bysshe Shelley. In the early 1990s, he was professor of English at the University of New Hampshire. He also chaired the state chapter of the anti-militarist group SANE/Freeze and ran the peace studies program on his campus. Before teaching at New Hampshire, and following a six-year stint at Yale, he worked for the Coalition for a New Foreign and Military Policy, an anti-intervention organization that grew out of efforts to cut off congressional funding of the Vietnam War in the 1970s. Ferber was a friendly, unaffectedly self-confident man with a patient, attentive ear. Lunching with me in a Chinese restaurant, his face perspiring over a steamy and rapidly disappearing vegetarian entrée, the former Resistance organizer remembered his indictment with amusement.

On January 5, Ferber, a graduate student in English at Harvard, had just returned to his Boston home after spending Christmas vacation with his parents in Buffalo, New York. He envisioned a quiet semester ahead. The Resistance was in a lull following its December draft-card turn-in, and its next big action was several months away. Ferber's own clash with the SSS would probably not come until the end of the semester. If diligent, he might be able to catch up on neglected schoolwork in the meantime.

Ferber's telephone rang, and he picked up the receiver. "Mr. Ferber?" "Yes." "This is United Press International. Do you have any comments?" "About what?" Ferber queried. "Oh, haven't you heard?" chortled the newsman. "You've been indicted for conspiracy with Dr. Spock." "No shit!" Ferber exclaimed. "Can I quote you?" replied the reporter. "Wait a minute," Ferber sputtered. "Let me think of something else." The startled resister then "pulled myself together and . . . said some sort of militant remark that he could quote." Ferber's phone didn't stop ringing for two days, forcing him to leave the house.[25]

On January 8, when Ferber received his indictment notice in the mail, the only other letter in his mailbox was his draft order. Upon discovering an army regulation prohibiting conscription of anyone facing a felony charge, he drolly wrote his draft board, "Sorry, but you're a day late . . ."[26]

Ferber said that his initial reaction to the indictments was

> *delight.* . . . Not only because I was indicted—I wasn't so sure I was delighted at that—but I was delighted that there was an indictment of such famous people. I remember thinking, "Oh, boy, *Dr. Spock.* The government's actually going after Dr. Spock." On the one hand it was scary because it meant the government . . . might really crack down, but I was already feeling that the student movement . . . was

growing so fast that this would only help it. That having a baby doctor of the world on trial for supporting young men who don't want
to fight would only help enormously. And then Coffin was another
important figure. So aside from my own sense of excitement and
privilege of being with these guys (because I was not famous at all)
was this feeling that the government had made a wrong move. I just
sensed right away that they had screwed it up and that we were going to reap the benefits of this.[27]

Ferber's mood plummeted several days later. The five conspirators gathered
together—for the first time—at the New York home of the radical lawyer Leonard Boudin, Spock's attorney. Marcus Raskin "set the tone" for the meeting,
Ferber recalled:

Raskin was depressed. Because he thought Johnson was riding
high . . . was unassailable. That this resistance was going to be
cleaned up. That Johnson owed favors to the right and that he was
going to mop it up. Raskin used the phrase "decimation of the intelligentsia": "We're in for a decimation of the intelligentsia." And I'd
never met Raskin—very impressive. I thought, "Oh, my God!" I
was so flattered to be part of the intelligentsia—I was only a second-
year graduate student—but to be decimated was not what I felt was
going to help . . .

An attorney, Raskin had firm prescriptions for the defendants' legal strategy.
"We've got to be very careful and run a very good defense," he argued. "We're
just the opening shot. They're probably going to indict Chomsky and Mailer
and Paul Goodman and everybody else on this list [the "Call to Resist"], Martin
Luther King and who knows who. So we have to run a real strict legal defense
and try and get out of this." By challenging the conspiracy law before the
Supreme Court, contended Raskin and several other lawyers present, the defendants could forestall its use against other activists.[28]

Ferber was troubled. "But, but," he stammered, "we did this to get *into* this.
You guys knew what you were doing. You knew it was illegal. The whole point
was to take a stand with us [draft resisters]." "Yeah, well, okay, well, we've done
that now," the attorneys responded. "We're in it."[29]

Ferber thought William Sloane Coffin had a better idea. The trial should
raise the larger legal issues posed by the war, Coffin admonished, including U.S.
violations of the 1954 Geneva Accords, the draft's unconstitutionality, and U.S.
war crimes. If the judge ruled these points irrelevant, as seemed likely, the
defendants would stand mute: "Well, your honor, we have nothing further to
say. Put us in jail." Now, this was the way to go, Ferber believed: "The jury
would be instructed to convict, the judge would sentence us, and we would
march off to prison as heroes, with a huge antiwar movement making us into

martyrs. Dr. Spock with his head held high marching to Danbury Prison. I thought it was great. And I was willing to do it, too, because I thought I would go to jail anyway for my own draft case in another year. I had nothing to lose."[30]

The lawyers ultimately won out. In their late spring trial, the "Boston Five" fought the government's conspiracy charge on its own terms. Prevented from arguing the broader legal issues by the judge, they spent most courtroom time wrangling over narrow questions like who was sitting with whom when the Justice Department protest and "Call to Resist" were planned, and was that *really* them in that NBC videotape urging draft resistance? In June, all but Raskin were found guilty. An appeals court later acquitted Ferber and Spock and decreed a new trial for Coffin and Goodman. Justice then quietly dropped the charges.

Ferber's intuition that the peace movement would benefit from the indictments proved accurate. The media covered the Boston Five's trial extensively, giving wide and often sympathetic play to the defendants' views. Thousands of Americans came forward to sign complicity statements. The Boston Five were constantly sought after for speaking engagements, allowing them to spread their message further. "Thanks to the United States government," Coffin writes, "the five of us had become celebrities." Ferber relished the renown and sense of civic engagement the trial afforded:

> I loved it. I was a hero in Boston. . . . Every weekday morning during the trial I would just put on my coat and tie, walk out my door (it was nice spring weather), wind my way through Beacon Hill, come down through the Boston Common, go by my lawyer's house, and the two of us would march over to the Federal Court a few blocks away. He knew everybody, because he was an old Boston Brahmin, and I ended up knowing everybody else because my picture was in the paper and I had all these people coming up and saying, "Congratulations." So I felt more like a citizen of Boston, like someone who really belongs in the city. I felt like this was like Athens: this was a real city-state, a public, and I was . . . exercising my political rights. I loved that feeling, even though I was under indictment by the feds. I felt that at least half the population was on my side.[31]

That the Boston Five were all bright, articulate people with impressive credentials led Ferber, Coffin, and others to conclude that Ramsey Clark had the antiwar movement's best interests in mind when he drew up the indictment. He could just as easily have indicted thousands of young, hairy draft resisters of widely suspect character, they pointed out. An opponent of the war himself, he went after people who commanded considerable respect and would make a strong public impression at the trial.[32]

Right?

In 1988 Clark was a civil rights and criminal lawyer in Manhattan. His small, modest office provided scant hint of his privileged political past. On the wall directly facing his desk hung a picture of one of his guiding lights, Thomas Jefferson. On other walls hung three portraits of another of his heroes: his late father, Tom Clark, the former attorney general and Supreme Court justice. The tall, lanky, slow-paced Clark was also a dedicated antiwar activist. He included among his good friends many prominent protesters of the Vietnam War, including both Coffin and Spock.

Clark said that domestic pressure to clamp down on protesters was one reason for his decision. "The demand for more aggressive action was growing in the Congress and the press and the public," he recalled in a slight Texas drawl. "I felt *enormous* pressures for repression." Many of his colleagues in the administration were also hot for action. The president was among those leaning on Clark—but only lightly. "He was not aggressive on it at all," Clark said. Johnson didn't appear to have "much stomach" for prosecuting demonstrators "as an individual. But I think as a president he felt the responsibility to seem firm." (Informing Johnson's sense of responsibility were partisan political concerns. Clark remembered the president telling him over lunch that spring that his "softness" toward demonstrators might be "ruining the Democratic Party's chances" in the November elections.)[33]

Clark also felt compelled to uphold the law. "Law has an obligation to protect governmental institutions, even when they're engaged in erroneous policy," he explained. "And you have to hope or assume that democratic or other processes will get you on the right course in time, but you can't merely twist or evade or ignore the law to achieve an end if you believe in a rule of law as a means for achieving social justice. So I felt something had to be done. The question was what and how."[34]

Clark was loath to lower the boom on the thousands of vulnerable young draft resisters. During World War II, some of his "most sensitive" friends had refused military service. "I found out as the years went on that, overwhelmingly, they paid a terrible price for that," Clark recalled. Jobs were denied, families were torn apart, self-concepts were damaged. "There are very few people who know themselves well enough to live a fulfilling life of their own aspiration when they have defied powerful social norms," Clark said. "You keep getting hit, both from within and without, as the years go by. . . . I felt that we had needlessly damaged many of our best young people and that that ought to be avoided. . . . You just don't go out and tear up 150,000 youngsters because they think they are opposed to something." Clark perceived that American society as a whole had also paid "a terrible price" during World War II. The draft resisters of the time "were talented, their capacity to contribute was great—and it was wasted." Clark mused on the Vietnam War resisters: "These are the gentlest that we have. And these are the ones that we should want to protect the most, perhaps. They tend to have more initiative—it's a hell of a lot easier to go than not to go."[35]

Prosecuting only a small minority of the young draft resisters was unappealing, too. "You could grind them up," Clark said. Most would fail to secure adequate legal representation, and "except where you had a student body president or somebody like that, the ability for people to rally around or even know about [a resister's case] would be fairly insignificant."[36] Clark "strongly" believed that whatever action the government took should result not only in a "fair" and "thorough" "legal test" of the draft laws but in "a public appreciation of the legal test." The government was engaged in "a profound conflict with its own people" over the war, he reasoned. As a democratic institution, it should proceed in a manner that would maximize public scrutiny of this conflict and its actions.[37]

Clark and his aides elected to follow an "elaborate" and "fairly mechanical" procedure for choosing their victims. After examining a "whole series" of anti-draft protests, Clark remembered, "we tried to cull it down to people who were what you could call 'ringleaders,' in speaking for, creating, organizing and moving toward dissolution of the Selective Service System." Concerned about governmental imposition on civil liberties, Clark and his co-workers "spent a lot of time trying to analyze the free speech aspect of it." They consulted outside legal experts "to see if we could find a pure conduct basis" for prosecutions, he recalled. Finally, "we thought we had." They then selected ringleaders of "greater maturity" and "greater responsibility" so as to "enable us to test laws against people who . . . could defend themselves and protect themselves and who could focus attention on the problem." These activists would be "capable of rallying . . . support and legal assistance and all the rest," the attorney general and his aides believed. "That doesn't mean it wasn't traumatic for them," Clark hastened to add. "I think it was extremely traumatic for them. They were amazed that it happened. . . . But that's OK. . . . Think how it would be to a youngster."[38]

Clark's account of his decision smacks of antiwar sympathies. A proponent of U.S. policy wouldn't care to "protect" draft resisters or to maximize public debate over their actions, would he? Clark admitted to being opposed to the war by this time. Significantly, the very people he was feeling pressure to repress had shaped his opinion. The mounting demands on the Justice Department to "do something about" demonstrations and draft violations in 1966 and 1967, he remembered, caused him to pay considerably more attention to the war than he had previously done. Clark recalled 1966 congressional proposals to enact a federal law against obstructing shipment of military equipment—prompted

mainly by the Vietnam Day Committee's 1965 troop-train demonstrations—
and official pressure to cart draft resisters off to Vietnam as two noteworthy
spurs to his shift in focus. Also impelling was the evident "erosion" of civil
rights activity (a cause close to Clark's heart) into the peace movement. "Finally," Clark recalled, echoing Doug Dowd's thoughts on civil disobedience
strategy, "it was just like hitting a mule with a two-by-four." The war "got my
attention." It didn't take Clark long to turn against it. By the fall of 1967, he
was virtually a closet booster of the peace movement. While observing firsthand
the assault on the Pentagon, Clark received word of the militants' penetration
of the building "with some pleasure."[39]

Clark's opposition to the war was widely known—and detested—within the
administration. Johnson kept him off the National Security Council because of
it, he came to believe. Clark's relations with the president and other officials
eventually became "very strained." The Foreign Intelligence Advisory Board,
infuriated at his persistent refusal to grant wiretaps of protesters, "claimed I was
undermining not only the war effort then but generally the national security
of the country," Clark recalled disdainfully. During the second half of 1968
"the president and many others were *extremely* unhappy" with him. Johnson
"really didn't contact me significantly in the last six months. At the end of the
administration, when there were going-away parties and all that kind of stuff, I
was not invited, or present."[40]

Clark was so repulsed by the war that he considered resigning. His ultimate
decision to remain in office had two main impulses, he said. Since he was "quite
young" and "not a real public figure of any magnitude," the effect of his resignation on the war "would be minimal." In addition, "I could feel the passion of
the country overrunning constitutional rights. . . . I really felt a powerful need
to hold on and resist those emotions. One thing I remember thinking very
clearly is, 'If I walked away and they put [a hard-line attorney general] in
here . . . I would feel like I had done an awful thing.'" Clark calculated that he
"raised as much hell" about the war and curbs on demonstrators within the
administration "as was consistent with remaining in office."[41]

Still, Clark seemed uncomfortable with the notion that his opposition to the
war colored his choice of defendants. "I don't *think* it did," he responded tentatively. "If it did, it was in a subjective way. . . . I would personally feel that that
sort of strategic use of the law would be wrong. That's a government of will
rather than principle." Clark reflected on the young Vietnam draft resisters, "I
think I would have been very protective of them—I hope so—even if I had been
passionately committed to the war." He saw his decision to indict people who
could muster public support and attention as really just "legal statesman-
ship . . . the appropriate way for government to function through democratic
institutions" during a divided time. "It's funny, you get accused from both

sides," Clark said pensively. "The Johnson people thought I did it to throw a bone the other way. To show I was doing something. . . . Because symbolically it looked like you were aggressive: you're not afraid to go after the biggies."[42]

Dangerous Designs: Planning for Chicago

As the government was raising the stakes of the political battle at home, peace activists were preparing to do likewise. Dave Dellinger and the ex-SDSers Tom Hayden and Rennie Davis, who was "on fire" from an October trip to Vietnam, were pushing for a concentrated week of protests at the Democratic Party convention in Chicago in late August. The three radical organizers envisioned several hundred thousand people marching legally in Chicago's streets. They also saw sharpening militance. The antiwar movement, Dellinger would recall arguing, should continue moving beyond the "passive" style of civil disobedience "where it was all prechoreographed: they knew what you were going to do, you knew what they were going to do, you were arrested and it was over. We wanted to keep the pressure on." By launching a multitude of flexible yet nonviolent assaults on symbols of the war and racism in Chicago, Dellinger maintained, protesters would prevent "business as usual" and raise official fears of uncontrollable social disorder. Some might even disrupt the convention to "expose" its "hypocritical and undemocratic nature."[43]

But the three activists "immediately ran into problems," Dellinger remembered. At a National Mobe meeting in December, they were "surprised" by the "lack of enthusiasm" for protests in Chicago. Many worried that demonstrations at the convention would hurt the political fortunes of Eugene McCarthy and Robert Kennedy. Doug Dowd detected adventurism. He later recalled that Davis and Hayden, involved in the Mobe for the first time and "carrying the ball" on the project, handed out copies of "a very thick memo" that winter outlining a "scenario" for Chicago. "I didn't like it," Dowd said. "It sounded bad to me. . . . It seemed to me clear that there was going to be a contrived confrontation." Dowd also considered it unwise to write a detailed script for a drama still many months—and untold intervening events—away. "Hayden was making plans for . . . eight months ahead as though there was a kind of straight line going from January to August," he marveled. The Mobe postponed making a decision on Chicago.[44]

Hayden and Davis plowed ahead undeterred. In February, they opened an office in Chicago to prepare for the demonstrations. Their designs continued to arouse concern. Although publicly committed to nonviolence, Hayden and Davis seemed to many to harbor a less gentle private agenda. They sure were acting shifty. Staughton Lynd recalled that "on Monday, Wednesday, and Friday [Hayden] was a National Liberation Front guerrilla, and on Tuesday, Thursday, and Saturday, he was . . . on the left wing of the Democratic Party, and it just wasn't together." Brad Lyttle remembered that Davis "knew exactly how to say things in different ways to get different people interested." When talking to Quakers one day, "he'd be nonviolent." Speaking to militant students the next, "it would be 'anything was going to happen.' . . . You didn't know *what* was going to happen if you listened to Rennie Davis." Lyttle added, "I'll tell you, when Rennie Davis got his fingers on anything, I just saw nothing but disaster. I couldn't *stand* Rennie Davis. I didn't think he understood the notion of honesty for one second. I didn't think he had any idea of what it was to . . . level with people." During his recruiting trips for Chicago, Dellinger was invariably asked whether Hayden and Davis wanted a "bloodbath" there.[45]

Dellinger himself was edgy about Hayden and Davis's intentions. He knew both were rapidly losing enthusiasm for nonviolent protest and felt "armed struggle" was inevitable. Hayden's eyes would "light up" at the prospect of armed struggle, Dellinger writes, while Davis would "look sad but determined." In private, Dellinger clashed "repeatedly" and "heatedly" with the two activists about their waffling on nonviolence. He was particularly distrustful of Hayden. "What worried me coming up to Chicago was that I was getting word of things he was saying to SDS people," he would recall. But Dellinger was also uncertain where Davis would "come down in the end." Although he had "more common sense" than Hayden, Davis was "capable of being a little slippery." Plus Davis was feeling Hayden's potent political spell. "Tom was a very powerful person," Dellinger explained. "And Tom had a way of scapegoating people who disagreed with him, of badmouthing them. . . . Tom had this kind of single-minded determination and drive of his own and . . . could make life difficult for those who disagreed with him. I felt that I was lucky that I was that much older and more trusted amongst a wide range of people, and that therefore he had to handle me with kid gloves. So that he rarely challenged me openly in meetings." But Davis "had to deal very cautiously" with Hayden, Dellinger said, particularly because "Tom was a factor to be figured with" in the crowd of ex-SDSers they both ran with. "Rennie wasn't prepared, maybe, to feel the full extent of Tom's attacks." Dowd painted Hayden's influence on Davis with a rougher brush. "Rennie was always sort of a tail on the dog of Tom Hayden. . . . He always went along with anything Tom wanted."[46]

In March, Dowd was the target of a Hayden political assault. Some two hundred and fifty people met at a YMCA camp north of Chicago to discuss the convention protests. In anticipation of the conference, Hayden and Davis had prepared another controversial position paper. Although explicitly rejecting violence in Chicago, the paper left room for interpretive license. It spoke of a "massive confrontation with our government," an "attack on the Democratic convention," "pinning the delegates in the International Amphitheatre," and "final days of militancy." Dowd remembered:

It sounded to me as though they were preparing for exactly what happened. . . . It sounded to me as though they were going to kind of pull off a fucking disaster and get the American people to learn that way. . . . So I argued very, very heavily against this thing. . . . And Tom got up after I got through and he just went into a kind of character assassination of me that was really interesting. He just got into a big emotional kick about the whole thing. . . . It was as though the apocalypse was around the corner and the apocalypse was going to be a good thing and I was trying to stop it. Well, I thought the apocalypse was around the corner, too, but I didn't think it was a good thing . . .

At one point the conferees voted to forgo a national action in Chicago for a strategy of local organizing. Hayden would have nothing of it, however. He "kept the meeting going on for another two hours, waited for attendance to thin out, and got the original vote rescinded." The conference failed to formulate a plan for Chicago.[47]

Meanwhile, some strange new hats had entered the ring. Led by Abbie Hoffman and Jerry Rubin, the Yippies announced plans for a "Festival of Life" in Chicago. Their declarations worsened fears that the scene would turn ugly. Pot-smoking youth would "roar like wild bands" through the city, Rubin forecast. Although many would get their heads split open, their blood would nourish the movement. "Repression . . . forces everyone to pick a side," Rubin lectured. "A movement cannot grow without repression." SDS's Greg Calvert remembered hearing Rubin proclaim, matter-of-factly, "Radicalization involves smoking dope in the park and fighting the pigs in the street." Calvert could only mutter in response, "You're crazy. You're absolutely insane."[48]

But what a compliment. "We've got to get crazy," exhorted one Yippie. "So fucking crazy that they can't understand it at ALL. . . . They can deal with a demand. We put a finger up their ass and tell them, 'I ain't telling you what I want,' then they got a problem."[49]

Specters of bloody street battles and contaminated Democratic presidential hopefuls were the outstanding obstacles to organizing for Chicago. Other misgivings nagged as well. SDS national officers worried that the demonstrations would bolster the liberal wing of the Democratic Party. Some felt "there would be no way to distinguish ourselves from the Clean-for-Gene people," Carl Davidson recalled. Also, the Chicago police might use the protest as a pretext for repressing SDS. The SWP wanted no part of another civil disobedience spectacle, particularly one that might strengthen the hated Democrats. Some activists were simply tired of protesting. Many doubted another antiwar march would accomplish anything. Not least inhibiting were the movement's political schisms. "Because of the incredible division of opinions within the peace movement, there was no way to agree: 'What are we going to do? When are we going to do it? Who's going to be in charge of it?' or anything like that until about a month before [the convention]," one Mobe organizer lamented. According to Dellinger, some peace groups now seemed to feel that domestic antiwar sentiment "was sufficiently great for them to be able to organize relatively successful actions on their own."[50]

Turnaround

As the Mobe groped for a follow-up act to the Pentagon drama, events in Vietnam took a stunning turn. In early morning darkness on January 31, a platoon of NLF sappers emerged from a dingy automobile repair shop in Saigon and climbed into a Peugeot truck and taxicab. They wheeled slowly toward the U.S. Embassy, five blocks away. A South Vietnamese policeman noticed the vehicles' lights were off and "ducked into the shadows to avoid trouble." An explosion jolted the compound. The sappers had blown a three-foot hole in its high protective wall and were scurrying through. "They're coming in! They're coming in! Help me! Help me!" a frantic military policeman called out over his radio. Within minutes anti-tank rockets were piercing the building's front door and bullets were ricocheting across its lobby. As four Americans lay dead, others prepared to die.[51]

Outside the embassy grounds, the fighting was hotter. In shocking concert, NVA and NLF forces were storming every major city, town, and military outpost throughout South Vietnam. Usually hidden under lush jungle canopy, "Charlie" was now everywhere. Among his specific targets were, astonishingly, the U.S. military headquarters in Saigon, South Vietnam's presidential palace, and the headquarters of all four military regions.

For weeks the enemy's Tet offensive rocked the scorched, bloody land. U.S. and ARVN forces counterattacked mercilessly. Death and destruction seemed to know no limit. Half of Mytho, a city of seventy thousand, was obliterated by artillery and air strikes designed to dislodge NLF troops. After U.S. troops finally expelled an enemy contingent from the cultural and religious capital of Hue, 80 percent of the city's buildings lay in ruins, two thousand of its residents lay dead. "The mind reels at the carnage, cost, and ruthlessness of it all," mourned one veteran combat photographer.[52]

At 9:20 A.M. on January 31, five hours after the onset of the attack on the U.S. Embassy, General William Westmoreland walked resolutely through the building's shattered front gate. The compound was now secure. Ravaged bodies, some still in their death throes, littered the area. According to one observer, the place resembled "a butcher shop in Eden." Westmoreland addressed a half circle of journalists. "The enemy's well-laid plans went afoul," he announced. Although the embassy was slightly damaged, the communist invaders had all been killed. And elsewhere, Westmoreland declared, "the enemy exposed himself by virtue of his strategy and he suffered great casualties." U.S. troops were now tracking a wobbly opponent. Standing in the wreckage, the journalists "could hardly believe their ears."[53]

Washington also erected a buoyant public facade. Militarily, the Tet offensive was "a complete failure," the president informed the nation. The South Vietnamese had "pulled up their socks," gushed Walt Rostow, repeatedly, to the entertainment of those aware that most Vietnamese did not wear socks. Rostow had seen this kind of thing before, he confided to some: the international communist combine was at work. "Walt was very much of the belief," recalled Paul Warnke, that the Tet offensive, a routed North Korean commando raid on the South Korean presidential palace on January 21, and the seizure of a U.S. intelligence ship by North Korean forces two days later "were part of a coordinated communist effort to sap American morale . . . a global putsch."[54]

Privately, officials were agitated, frightened. Although they had expected an enemy offensive ("something was coming that was going to be pretty goddamn bad," figured one senior U.S. military commander), the exact timing, scope, coordination, and intensity of the offensive staggered them. A U.S. Military Academy textbook later called Tet "an allied intelligence failure ranking with Pearl Harbor." According to Under Secretary of the Air Force Townsend Hoopes, "One thing was clear to us all: the Tet offensive was the eloquent counterpoint to the effusive optimism of November. It showed conclusively that the U.S. did not in fact control the situation, that it was not in fact winning, that the enemy retained enormous strength and vitality." Tet may have been particularly jarring for the staff of the eternally sanguine Ambassador Ellsworth Bunker in Saigon. Only one month earlier, the invitations for the New Year's Eve party at the American embassy had read, "Come see the light at the end of the tunnel."[55]

By early March, intelligence reports from the front showed the enemy had suffered monstrous casualties. Moreover, the sweeping popular uprisings hoped for by North Vietnamese and NLF strategists had not materialized. But it mattered little. For the U.S. domestic rear guard was now crumbling by the minute.

The Tet offensive was dubbed a disaster by the American media. Although echoing the official bravado about a U.S. military victory, they emphasized the surprise and power of the enemy's attacks. On television the bloodletting in Vietnam assumed a stark and concentrated form unprecedented for the war. Shocked viewers watched the chief of South Vietnam's National Police calmly gun down a bound enemy prisoner at point-blank range; some were allowed to take in a fountain of blood spurting from the victim's head. Many were unsettled by the sight of U.S. bombers pounding South Vietnamese cities into rubble.

Influentials were shaken. "What is the end that justifies this slaughter?" asked James Reston of the *New York Times*. NBC's Frank McGee avowed that the enemy "now has the initiative" and that the war "is being lost"; further escalation would only "waste more human beings and more buildings." Senator George Aiken (R-Vt.) dryly remarked that if Tet was "a failure, I hope the Viet Cong never have a major success."[56]

And then there was Cronkite. The fatherly, trusted dean of television news was unnerved by Tet and the challenge it posed to the administration's cheery accounts of the war; he zoomed off to South Vietnam to see what was up. While there, Cronkite broadcast a report wearing a steel helmet and flak jacket. His act did not go over well inside the White House. "It's cheap as dirt," one senior official snorted years later. "That phony Walter Cronkite . . . wasn't in any danger." On February 27, Cronkite solemnly told nine million Americans that the United States should negotiate an end to the stalemated war, "not as victors but as an honorable people who lived up to their pledge to defend democracy, and did the best they could." Cronkite's words marked "the first time in American history a war had been declared over by an anchorman." Washington was horrified. William Bundy thought Cronkite's defection "an absolute landmark" in declining domestic support for the war. "Palpably, you were in a different ball game."[57]

The media's snowballing criticism of U.S. policy was too much for Dean Rusk. "There gets to be a point when the question is whose side are you on?" the usually unflappable official snapped to reporters on February 9. "Now, I'm Secretary of State of the United States, and I'm on our side!" Rusk went on to mutter, "I don't know why . . . people have to go probing for the things that one can bitch about."[58]

Some members of the administration seemed to be losing their grip on reality. Under Secretary of State for Political Affairs Eugene Rostow wrote in late March that the "vast inarticulate majority" of Americans still supported U.S. policy; an "excellent" way of "dramatizing" one's feelings, he proposed, was to "wear a safety pin in your lapel, to demonstrate that we favor preserving the safety of the nation and the world." Johnson's approval rating on Vietnam then registered 26 percent.[59]

For the other team, Tet was a shot in the arm. "Following Tet, it was clear to us that Vietnam would eventually win," the SDS leader Jeff Jones recalled. "Now we're going to get somewhere, because the mask is off," Michael Ferber thought.[60]

In early January, two NVA divisions had moved ominously toward the U.S. Marine base at Khe Sanh near the North Vietnamese border. Westmoreland ordered the base held. Striking an eery resemblance to France's fatal battle at

Dien Bien Phu in 1954, the fighting that ensued quickly garnered the scrutiny of the press. Johnson became obsessed with it. He spent hours hovering over a detailed terrain map of the combat zone set up at his request in the White House War Room, playing general. "I don't want no damn Din Bin Phoos!" the exhausted president roared to one visitor after spending most of the previous night with the map.[61]

On February 3, worried about losing Khe Sanh and another round of enemy attacks, Johnson directed JCS Chairman General Earl Wheeler to ask Westmoreland whether he needed reinforcements. Wheeler sent Westmoreland several cables, ostensibly to solicit his assessment, but in reality to coax a request for more troops. "Washington panicked at that time," Westmoreland irritatedly remembered. "They almost shoved the reinforcements down my throat." Troubled by inadequate U.S. military readiness worldwide, Wheeler viewed the crisis in Vietnam as an opportunity to secure a large U.S. reserve call-up. After "a little sparring back and forth," Westmoreland solicited and received a modest increase in manpower.[62]

Meeting with Westmoreland in South Vietnam on February 23, Wheeler told him that both President Johnson and L. Mendel Rivers, the powerful chairman of the House Armed Services Committee, seemed "in the mood" to pursue "a more aggressive strategy." Westmoreland liked what he heard. Given the enemy's heavy Tet losses, lifting the shackles on U.S. firepower might deal Charlie a death blow, the general calculated. Among the operations on Westmoreland's impatient mind were accelerated air strikes against the North, mining Haiphong harbor, and invading Laos, Cambodia, and southern North Vietnam. "If there was anything to the business of 'sending a message' to Hanoi," he writes wryly, "surely that was a way."[63] Westmoreland and Wheeler floated up another troop request. This one was contingent upon Washington's approval of a new war strategy. Consisting of three deployments, it totaled 206,000 men. Wheeler formally presented the request to Johnson on February 28.

Disturbed by recent events in South Vietnam and mindful that they were Johnson's immediate concern, Wheeler made no reference to depleted reserves or the two generals' appetite for an expanded battlefield. Cunningly, he stressed the precariousness of the U.S. position in Vietnam. The enemy's resolve "appears to be unshaken," Wheeler warned, forebodingly, and he was "recruiting heavily." Tet had been "a very near thing." Westmoreland needed more troops, the JCS chairman implied, to prevent even worse reverses and, eventually, U.S. defeat.[64]

Johnson was "visibly shaken." Only a month earlier, Westmoreland had told him the enemy was faltering badly and "resorting to desperation tactics."[65] Now Westy wanted 206,000 more troops? What was going on out there? The president decided it was time to take a step back and sort out what had gone wrong.

He ordered a high-level study of U.S. policy. The incoming defense secretary, Clark Clifford, a wealthy Washington lawyer and political insider of legendary personal charm ("Mr. Smooth," some called him), would direct it.[66]

Clifford, an old friend and adviser of Johnson's, was also, it seemed, a hard-liner on Vietnam. True, he had cautioned against a major U.S. troop commitment in 1965; the war "could be a quagmire" with "catastrophic" effects in the United States, he had told the president. But he was no cut-and-run man. In December 1965, Clifford had adamantly opposed the bombing pause over North Vietnam. And he *despised* Robert McNamara's November 1967 recommendation for another halt to Rolling Thunder and a lid on further troop deployments. It was "common gossip" within the administration that Johnson's own distaste for bombing pauses was fueled by evening nightcaps with Clifford and Abe Fortas.[67]

Yet seeds of doubt about the war were sprouting in Clifford's mind. In the late summer of 1967, at Johnson's request, he had joined General Maxwell Taylor on a tour of Southeast Asian countries to squeeze additional troops from them. It was "strikingly apparent" to Clifford that the leaders of these potential dominoes were not believers in domino thought. He wondered whether the U.S. government wasn't being a bit paranoid about creeping communism. Especially after Tet, Clifford also wondered whether the United States was really making meaningful military and political gains in Vietnam. The whole thing might turn out to be a loser after all, he ruminated. Moreover, Clifford was bothered by the domestic turmoil over the war. "I didn't like what I was seeing going on at the time," he would recall. "It was a period of the deepest concern because of the very sharp divisions among our people. It was very distressing."[68]

On the afternoon of February 28, at the opening meeting of his task force, Clifford spelled out his reading of its chore: to devise a way to come up with the 206,000 men Westmoreland apparently needed. Within minutes the new secretary of defense was overwhelmed. It was unlikely enough soldiers could be dispatched to Vietnam in the coming weeks to make a dent in the fighting, he learned. What if the communists really did launch a second burst of attacks the following month? The economic repercussions of a major mobilization staggered him. More alarming, even with upwards of 700,000 American troops in Vietnam, some of the men in the room seemed to suggest, U.S. objectives might still remain unachieved. And just what *were* those objectives anyway? The lack of clarity distressed Clifford. The next day, he told the group it was a whole new ball game: the entire course of U.S. policy was now up for debate. Westy might not get his troops after all.[69]

In the days ahead the task force met in long afternoon and evening sessions. Clifford also holed up virtually every morning with task force members Paul Warnke and Paul Nitze and three others from the Defense Department. The two senior Pentagon officials were to advance Clifford's education in the profoundest of ways.

Years later Paul Warnke was a Washington attorney. Until recently he was Clifford's law partner. The renowned Clifford and Warnke law firm closed in 1992 after most of the attorneys left in the wake of federal and state investigations of the Bank of Credit and Commerce International scandal, for which Clifford was ultimately indicted. Warnke was a political liberal and noted arms control advocate; as Richard Helms derisively said, "Hell, he's *antiwar.*" Warnke smiled at this. He'd heard worse: Admiral Ulysses S. Grant Sharp, the Johnson administration's head bomber in Vietnam, once remarked that Warnke was "as close to being a Communist as one could be without actually becoming one."[70]

Unlike Clifford, Warnke was already opposed to the war when he joined the Pentagon in 1966. "I think that superpower intervention is a poor idea," he told me. "There are very, very few instances in which it is in the security interest of the United States to intervene in an internal dispute." Sure, if the commies went after Canada he'd be as gung ho for action as the next man. "But Vietnam, Nicaragua—it's absurd," Warnke scoffed. "All you're going to do in those circumstances, probably, is weigh in on the wrong side. And even if the side you weigh in on when you start off is not the wrong side, you'll make it the wrong side."[71]

Warnke's opposition to the war hardened in 1967. He flew to Vietnam, buzzed about in a CIA helicopter, and was appalled. "It became clear to me that the only thing that was happening was that we were waging an increasingly successful occupation of South Vietnam," he remembered. "And that the other side could not win as long as we continued to occupy South Vietnam, but also we could not win, that there was no way that we'd be able to build up any sort of indigenous [political] structure." The turbulence over the war in the United States enhanced Warnke's desire to end it. But, he stressed, "I would have been trying to deescalate the war even if it had uproarious public support."[72]

When Clifford was appointed secretary of defense, Warnke saw his own job as conversion. His prospects of success were hard to gauge. "As far as I was concerned, Clark was an unknown quantity," Warnke recalled. Sure, he was aware of Clifford's hawkish reputation. But he also knew the man had real reservations about the war.[73]

Clifford directed Warnke's office to prepare a memorandum for Johnson on U.S. options in Vietnam. Morton Halperin joined with fellow Deputy Assistant Defense Secretary Dick Steadman and Warnke in reviewing it. Halperin was also opposed to U.S. policy; he felt the administration was "not supporting a serious government that had serious support." The memo offered a discouraging appraisal of the war. No troop strength or ground strategy would end the fighting soon, it emphasized; only effective South Vietnamese leadership could do that. A large force increase would also have major domestic costs. America's international balance of payments would worsen dramatically, the government would have to enact a large tax increase or wage and price controls, and there would be spreading draft resistance and urban unrest. Still more body bags coming home would heighten citizens' dismay. By granting Westmoreland's request, the Pentagon analysts warned, the administration ran "great risks of provoking a domestic crisis of unprecedented proportions." The memo had a "tremendous" impact on Clifford.[74]

The crash course continued. Clifford was astounded to discover that U.S. military leaders had no clear plan to win the war. He became convinced U.S. military victory was impossible. The prospect of endless fighting magnified his domestic political concerns. He recognized that public support for the war was diminishing dangerously as it was, and that "the divisions would only get worse, they would only grow." As Clifford wrote afterward, "I was more conscious each day of domestic unrest in our own country. Draft-card burnings, marches in the streets, problems on school campuses, bitterness and divisiveness were rampant." Clifford was impressed by the argument of Phil Goulding, another Pentagon official, that deescalating the ground war would evoke broader public support than any other policy.[75]

William Bundy, Dean Rusk, and Morton Halperin all later contended that domestic opposition to the war played a crucial role in turning Clifford against it. "Clark was intensely public opinion conscious," Bundy stressed. "That had always been his responsibility in the Truman White House, and he was an adviser to Johnson on, in effect, public opinion." Rusk said that Clifford was "much more of a political animal than some of the rest of us" and that domestic antiwar sentiment "weighed very heavily on his mind." Clifford himself remarked, "What influenced me was the attitude of the public. I didn't think the public was willing to support the policy we had been following."[76]

The task force report Clifford presented to Johnson represented a compromise between the Pentagon's dovish civilian officials and U.S. military leaders. It advocated sending twenty-two thousand more troops to Vietnam and mobilizing over two hundred thousand reserves, while fundamentally reassessing U.S. strategy and shoring up South Vietnam's political and military performance.

In early March, J. William Fulbright tried to line Clifford up to testify before the Senate Foreign Relations Committee. Clifford begged off, with the assent of Johnson, who didn't appreciate his old friend's changing political perspective. The officials agreed Deputy Defense Secretary Paul Nitze was a better man for the job. Aware that he would have to defend the war, Nitze felt otherwise.

In the 1980s Nitze was President Ronald Reagan's senior arms control adviser. Sitting amidst the elegant decor of his State Department office during an interview, secretaries attending to his every need, the white-haired, aristocratic offi-cial seemed much at home: an accomplished world statesman enjoying his repu-tation as a savvy arms negotiator.

Nitze's aversion to testifying before the Senate reflected long-standing doubts about the war. He had been queasy about the conflict way back in early 1965. With a fragile government and surging NLF guerrillas, South Vietnam was, he worried, a political lemon. By 1967 Nitze had grown extremely restive about the harm Vietnam was causing to U.S. preparedness vis-à-vis the Soviet Union. "This diversion of effort from the main show, certainly I deeply regretted," he remembered. Even more disturbing to him was the conclusion of a Navy study that it would take five to seven years to wrap up the war. Nitze thought it "unlikely" the American people would put up with the fighting that long. "A lot of problems were going to arise," he believed.[77]

When Nitze scanned the sea of rising domestic opposition to the war, one group of dissenters leaped out at him, distressed him the most: the young street demonstrators. "My reaction was that the most damaging consideration was the disaffection of the youth," he recalled of the war's critics. Sure, those antiwar journalists, whose reporting was often "totally irresponsible" ("90 percent" of Jonathan Schell's much-acclaimed 1967 *New Yorker* piece on the wasting of the village of Ben Suc was "pure imagination," Nitze thought) and who evinced a "wholly destructive" defeatism, were extremely influential in the United States as well. But "this corruption, really, of the patriotism of the youth seemed to me to be the *fundamental* source of all the other differences" on the war in the country, Nitze remembered:

> They were against the entire business, not just arguing about ways and means. They were radically opposed. They were against the whole goddamn show. They wanted to tear it down. That's the kind of thing that one was worried about.
>
> One saw it particularly with the busts in the universities. I spent a lot of time working with some of those students during that period. My daughter had taught at a school in New York, a professionals' children's school. And one of her fellow teachers taught French there. They'd come to the conclusion that these kids had never known the countryside and so it would be a good idea to put them on a bus and take them down for a weekend on the farm we had . . . outside of Washington. And they came down. This French teacher had a very attractive boyfriend who was one of the leaders of the SDS at Co-lumbia University. So I spent a lot of time that weekend talking to him about what he was about and why. And then he came down again a second time, because he said that it would be a good thing if some of the other leaders of the opposition at Columbia, including the Maoist group, including the black group, and including the Soviet [group] . . . came down. The Maoists refused to come, and so did the

black group, but the Communist group did come [laughs]. So I had a long discussion with them on that succeeding weekend. They were telling me about how they were going to destroy the Democratic convention in Chicago . . . how they were going to force the convention of Mayor Daley to take offensive action against them, causing casualties to them and to other people who were there, and [how] this would cause all the mobs that they would recruit to become thoroughly alienated. This was their tactic.

Nitze perceived that the young militants were "building widespread disaffection from the government's efforts" by triggering state violence against protesters. Such "entrapment" of officialdom was among the "important mechanisms by which this thing was growing," he believed.[78]

In early 1968, Nitze was "very much concerned" that the unpatriotic views of the young demonstrators would eventually pollute the ranks of the U.S. military too. "Not that we'd had any evidence that it had yet taken place, but I thought it would take place," he recalled. Already, the previous year, while still secretary of the navy, Nitze had felt "deeply troubled by the [low] morale of the young people coming into the navy."[79]

After President Johnson personally ordered Nitze to testify before Fulbright's committee, the deputy defense secretary spent a torturous weekend mulling over his options. "I decided, 'Goddamn it, I didn't approve of the policy and that I was not the person to do it,'" he remembered. "And so I reported that to Clark. And Clark was shocked that I felt that strongly about it. Because I was prepared to resign over the issue."[80]

Clifford's mind was spinning. The secretary of defense respected Nitze, needed his expertise (he had been virtually running the Pentagon since McNamara's fall from Johnson's grace), and now he was ready to leave office over the war that was churning Clifford's own stomach. Aggravating Clifford's trauma, Fulbright was tossing the ball back into his court, stipulating that the Senate would accept testimony from only him or Nitze. Clifford's predicament apparently had a profound effect on him. According to several observers, his booming doubts about the war now crystallized into a firm conviction that it was necessary to end it. Clifford realized that he couldn't simply stand up and regurgitate his old views on the conflict, "that he really had to think it through as to how he was going to defend the policy, before klieg lights and before the full attention of not only the Senate but also the world," Nitze recalled. "And when he began to think about it that way he changed his mind about 180 degrees. He was way to the left of me before I could say 'Jack Robinson.'"[81]

Lyndon Baines Johnson saw the world slipping out of his control. His enemies were everywhere, and they were multiplying. The faint-hearted McNamara had jumped ship, and now his new secretary of defense, Mr. Smooth, was getting the heebie-jeebies too. Clifford was pestering him constantly, arguing, in that suave, high-priced lawyer voice, "Mr. President, it's just not going to do." Johnson refused to invite the secretary to some meetings. "The bloom was off our relationship," Clifford recalled.[82]

The White House staff was also infested with doubters, weaklings. Even Harry McPherson, his loyal counsel, speechwriter, and close confidant, had developed serious qualms about the war. McPherson still believed in its goals; "whining" about America's "responsibilities" in a world plagued by "sordid socialist powers" was not for him. But the more hours McPherson logged surveying the evening news on his office television set, the more the war's blood and gore—"all of that terrific messiness"—got to him. Those tons of bombs exploding on the villages and people of North Vietnam weren't having any effect at all: "It just broke your heart," McPherson recalled. That "so many of the sensitive and intelligent people in the United States seemed to be totally disposed against the war" gnawed deeply into his resolve. He wished he could share Rusk and Rostow's view that the campus protesters were merely misguided children, but he just couldn't; he knew they were much more than that. "If you were, as I was (and I think this would be true of a number of people around the president), . . . a liberal arts graduate, somebody who just instinctively paid a lot of attention to the views of liberal intellectuals," McPherson remembered, "then you saw that the vast majority of liberal intellectuals were violently opposed to the war. And that had a very large effect on people like me." It disturbed him to see Dr. Spock, Norman Mailer, and Robert Lowell marching on the Pentagon. The views of such *"clercs "* were "terribly important" to McPherson. The fresh "insights" on Vietnam he got directly from antiwar students were also discomforting. These students were "the really important young" in America, McPherson believed, not those conservative types. He recognized that their activity was influencing other Americans as well. "I thought it was a massive problem for us," McPherson recalled. Now they had "left the roads for the fields, and there was no avoiding them." McPherson wanted to "cut our losses, get the demonstrators off the streets and reelect Lyndon Johnson."[83]

On March 10, the president's troubles mushroomed. The *New York Times* printed a page-one scoop on the Westmoreland/Wheeler troop request and the policy debate raging within the administration. The report was swiftly snatched up by other newspapers from coast to coast. If Tet was such a crushing defeat for the enemy, the public wondered, why did Westmoreland need 206,000 more troops? Johnson was "furious." News leaks by the administration's traitors always enraged him, but this one seemed particularly damaging. Which of those goddamn doves in the Pentagon was trying to destroy him now?[84]

On March 12 came another blow. In the New Hampshire Democratic presidential primary, Eugene McCarthy captured 42.2 percent of the vote. Counting Republican crossovers, he fell a mere 230 votes shy of Johnson. Although the president's name was not on the ballot, his forces had run a serious write-in campaign and expected impressive returns. The press judged the vote a major defeat for Johnson and a repudiation of his war policies. The president himself interpreted it "the same way everybody else did—that that meant he was in trouble," George Christian remembered. Later surveys showed many of McCarthy's voters actually favored stronger military action in Vietnam.[85]

On March 16, smelling blood, Robert Kennedy entered the ring. Why, Kennedy reasoned, should McCarthy be grabbing all of these anti-Johnson votes when he himself could be doing so even more efficiently? For months past the president had been telling others that Kennedy would enter the race. Now Johnson's fears had been realized, and his torment was excruciating.[86]

Exacerbating Johnson's pain were ghastly economic trends. As inflation boomed, word of the Westmoreland/Wheeler troop request, and the predictable steep rise in U.S. government expenditures, sparked a major outburst of speculative fever. The gold pool suffered a heavy drain. Morton Halperin remembered being shocked when the powerful budget Controller of the Defense Department, "a very hierarchical institution," wandered into his lowly office one day and declared that the war had to be cooled down or terminated because the dollar was on thin ice.[87]

In late March the president received more bad news. A dismayed Clifford, fearful that Johnson was bent on riding out the storm and escalating the war despite his efforts, had decided some "stiff medicine" was required to "bring home to the president what was happening in the country." He lined up another meeting of the Wise Men. Clifford had gotten wind that many of these influential private advisers were also losing heart for the war.[88]

The Wise Men gathered for a joyless candlelight supper in the State Department's opulent eighth-floor dining room on March 25. They quietly questioned Rusk, Rostow, Clifford, Nitze, Helms, and others about the war. Afterward, the State Department's Philip Habib, Major General William DePuy, and George Carver of the CIA presented briefings on the war: corruption was rampant in the Saigon government, pacification was a shambles, and the enemy were all over the place, they reported. The Wise Men were agitated.

They chewed on these tidings far into the evening and again the next morning. Most were now firmly convinced the war would be, at best, a long-drawn-out affair. And the bottom line was quite simple: the American people wouldn't stand for it. The jig was up. "We were weighing not only what was happening in Vietnam, but the social and political effects in the United States, the impact on the U.S. economy, the attitude of other nations," one of the Wise Men remarked afterward. "The divisiveness in the country was growing with such acuteness that it was threatening to tear the United States apart." In the eyes of Dean Acheson, the dominant force among the Wise Men, the militant antiwar protests of the previous fall had been "the worst yet." The Wise Men were "shaken by the opposition in this country," Richard Helms recalled. Johnson later observed that certain former officials "seemed to feel that the bitter debate and noisy dissension at home about Vietnam were too high a price to pay" for the war. His allusion to Wise Men is obvious.[89]

Acheson was particularly outspoken about the war's domestic constraints. Meeting alone with the president the week before, he had bluntly averred that the time required to secure America's military objectives in Vietnam was no longer available; the public had turned against them. Resting in Acheson's pocket when the Wise Men met was an editorial written by his good friend Walter Carroll, publisher of the *Winston-Salem Journal*. The essay contended that the war had caused Americans to "lose sight of our national priorities," with the "most crucial priority of all" being "of course, the home front." The "racial revolution" and "ominous chasm . . . between our youth and their elders" was poisoning the country, wrote Carroll. So was foreign communist infiltration of the peace and student movements. Acheson told Harry McPherson that evening that the editorial represented his views "precisely. I could have written it myself." Acheson's turnaround seemed to have "considerable impact" on the other Wise Men. It also strongly impressed the president, as well as Acheson's son-in-law, William Bundy.[90]

At lunch on March 26, the Wise Men gave Johnson their verdict. "It was like a chorus of old farts in a Greek play," McPherson remembered. "'Ooohhh! Wooohhh! Wooohhh! Cecilia is doomed!'" All of the Wise Men "expressed deep concern about the divisions in our country," the president wrote in his memoirs. "Some of them felt that those divisions were growing rapidly and might soon force our withdrawal from Vietnam." Johnson was visibly rattled by the Wise Men's gloomy mood. During a meeting only months earlier, he recalled, they had communicated general support for the war. "Who the hell brainwashed those friends of yours?" the president grilled the notoriously dovish George Ball. Smelling a rat, Johnson ordered Carver and DePuy into the cabinet room for an encore performance. "Did you tell them something different than what you told me?" he barked. "No." "Well, how could they come to one conclusion while I came to another?" "I don't know." The president was "nonplussed." Turning to Rostow, he groaned, "What the hell do they want me to do? What *can* we do that we're not doing?"[91]

Rostow sure as hell knew what to do. "Well, Mr. President, you know, as we've talked about before," and he started making his standard case for invading North Vietnam and Laos. "Johnson just *flinched*, just *jumped*," McPherson remembered. "No, no, no, I don't want to talk about that," the president quickly cut in. Explained McPherson, "He just simply didn't want me and the others [in the room] to know that he had given much consideration to [Rostow's advice] at all, because one of us might have gone out and said, 'Oh, my God, we're going to invade North Vietnam!'"[92]

As Johnson trudged back to the Oval Office, he pondered the Wise Men's views and their reflection in "broader opinion." The president and other administration principals were now keenly aware that public support for the war was rapidly going south and that something had to be done to stop the exodus. "You just couldn't see the country supporting a major force increase," William Bundy recalled. "That simply wasn't on. . . . You were standing with the water going up to your shoulders. . . . The country was fair fed up." Johnson's most trusted political adviser perceived that "any kind of escalation . . . is going to hurt us badly."[93]

Momentum for another partial halt to Rolling Thunder rapidly picked up throughout March. Few words were minced over its purpose. "In all of the discussions in which I participated," Bundy revealed, "the general consensus was that the utility of the partial bombing pause lay in persuading the American people that we were seriously concerned about peace. The proposal, it was thought, would help to bring dissent down to a manageable level." None of the policymakers expected the curb to accomplish its public objective: to bring the enemy to the conference table.[94]

Johnson was in utter agony. He wanted to *win* the war and was rankled by the softies around him. And he absolutely abhorred bombing halts. "I'll tell you what happens when there's a bombing halt," the president was known to say. "I halt and then Ho Chi Minh shoves his trucks right up my ass. That's your bombing halt." Johnson found pessimistic evaluations of the war maddening. If the American people could only read those juicy intelligence reports from Vietnam, he brooded, they'd see this was no time to get skittish. Lady Bird noticed that sties were "popping out on her husband's eyes, red and swollen." Others detected "erratic" behavior. Sleep did not come easy to the president.[95]

But Johnson knew the score. "Deeply conscious" of the burgeoning domestic opposition to his policies, he realized he "didn't have the votes" for war-as-usual. As the president told General Wheeler, he "had no choice . . . but to try to calm the protesters." In the closing hours of March, following more arm-twisting by Clifford, Johnson agreed to cut back Rolling Thunder. Facilitating his decision was hope of a brighter future. When the North Vietnamese failed to respond, the president schemed, he would *really put the screws to them.*[96]

On Sunday, March 31, at 9:01 P.M., a haggard Lyndon Johnson addressed the nation. "Peace" was the sole reason for U.S. intervention in Vietnam, the president proclaimed in the Orwellian style long since typical of the administration. The United States was halting its bombing north of the demilitarized zone to get negotiations started and save lives. Johnson failed to mention his disbelief that the move would spur talks. He casually announced that 13,500 more U.S. troops would soon be on their way to Vietnam. After more talk of peace and jabs at communist treachery, the president turned to his Big Problem: opposition to the war at home. "There is division in the American house tonight," Johnson solemnly observed. "I would ask all Americans . . . to guard against divisiveness and all its ugly consequences." He ended with the electrifying kicker: "I shall not seek, and I will not accept, the nomination of my Party for another term as President."[97]

Johnson's personal case of the willies stunned the nation. Yet it was relieved. The president's popularity rating darted upward, as did support for a bombing halt. For the first time, the number of Americans describing themselves as doves nearly equaled the number describing themselves as hawks.[98]

Hints immediately surfaced of Johnson's bellicose clandestine designs, however. The next day, U.S. jets delivered their bombs up to the 20th parallel, 250 miles north of the demilitarized zone and the administration's *real* boundary for the pause. Rolling Thunder was actually intensified after the president's speech. Was this the work of a man intent on enticing negotiations, asked the critics?

Clark Clifford was nobody's fool. He knew Johnson, Rusk, and Rostow were plotting to unleash the war after demonstrating Hanoi's "intransigence" to the American people. The secretary of defense put on some moves of his own. He repeatedly declared that a lid had been placed on U.S. troop deployments to Vietnam. Whenever the White House seemed particularly antsy about lifting the bombing pause, Clifford publicly praised the March 31 decisions and pointed out that reopening up the air war conflicted with Johnson's position. "In the press conferences following the March 31 speech, I was constantly trying to push toward deescalation," Clifford recalled. Paul Warnke was in cahoots with him. William Bundy annoyedly remembered, "Every morning, for that whole period of months, they met in conclave. You could never get them on the phone and get on with the day's business until about 10:30 in the morning, because they were chinning on, 'How do we better get our case put forward to Johnson . . . to get this war wound down and get the hell out of it?'" A grinning Warnke said, "We had a good group of conspirators."[99]

In the meantime, quite unexpectedly, Hanoi had agreed to peace talks. The administration feigned enthusiasm while dragging its feet. Finally, in May, it consented to meet in Paris.

When the American people applauded the apparent turn toward peace, Johnson knew he'd been had. To declare Hanoi implacable and then substantially intensify the war "would have produced such an outcry domestically that it became politically impossible," as Morton Halperin argued. "And then Johnson decided that he should ride the crest of this and allow it to be seen that he withdrew from the race to be a man of peace. Because that was the only option at that point."[100]

Johnson's continuing aversity to good faith negotiations, refusal to trot out a full bombing halt until five days before the November elections, and inability to even *contemplate* U.S. withdrawal from Vietnam do not belie Halperin's point. The die was now cast. With a collapsed political base, the administration's war was dead in the water. The troop deployments announced on March 31 were the last undertaken. A slow, uneven, and extremely bloody unraveling of the U.S. occupation of Vietnam had begun.

"That Kind of Mass Protest Activity . . . Is Quite Effective"

Let us now weigh more precisely the antiwar movement's role in forcing this monumental turn of events. How did it color official perceptions of inadequate domestic support for the war? What contribution did it make to broader opposition? And did it, as many claim, give Johnson the boot?

Paul Nitze is not the only Johnson administration official to regard the peace movement as the most important locus of domestic antagonism to the war. Richard Helms remembered "student activism" as "rather central to" antiwar sentiment in the U.S. "They were the ones throwing the eggs," he said, "and they were the ones that didn't want to be drafted, and they were the ones that didn't want to go to war, and they were the ones who didn't want to stand up for their country, and they were the super-intellectuals and all the rest of it." There was no question in Helms's mind that the antiwar movement played a crucial role in forcing Johnson's hand in Vietnam. In his opinion, such "mob activity" "inevitably" sways government policies. "I don't think there's much doubt about anything of that sort. Because this is a threatening action when you put mobs in the streets." The large mobs in Washington during the war were "particularly" effective, offered Helms.[101]

George Christian said the "divisiveness" Johnson "felt the most" when he gave his March 31 speech "was the campus unrest and the demonstrations, and whatever contributing factor all of this might have been on the racial troubles. . . . The demonstrations were certainly something that he noticed. They wanted to be noticed and he darn sure noticed them." Katzenbach's aide Lawrence Eagleburger recalled that campus protesters were "to a large degree the cutting edge of the opposition" to the war in the United States. "If I think back to that time, the thing that I remember is the students," Eagleburger commented. "And I suspect if you talk to anybody who went through that period, that's basically what they remember." William Bundy said he was keenly cognizant of campus demonstrators, a perception heightened by the enrollment of his son, nephews, and nieces in college. "That sixties generation was very much a part of one's sentiment," he recalled. Harry McPherson, a key proponent of the March bombing pause, devotes six pages to student activists in his memoirs; as we have seen, the peace movement as a whole had much to do with his growing disenchantment with the war. Paul Warnke stated flatly that the antiwar movement "strongly affected general governmental sentiment" on Vietnam and made "a major contribution" to U.S. deescalation. "That kind of mass protest activity, I think, is quite effective," he said.[102]

Wherein lay the peace movement's strength? It was vocal, articulate, disruptive, and persistent. Protests were blatant signs of diminishing domestic tolerance of the war. They were "good evidence that we were losing public support for what we were doing," Christian thought. Officials considered them influential in the United States. "I think that the feeling on the part of President Johnson and Walt Rostow and some of the other war enthusiasts was that . . . even a very vocal minority might make other people wonder, 'Are they right? Is my position wrong?'" Warnke remarked. As many protesters had hoped, the peace movement also caused officials to fear for the very fabric of American society. "The country was in turmoil from the war," McPherson sighed. And, as Clark Clifford perceived, that turmoil "would only grow." In addition, the protests seemed fortifying to the enemy. "If the opposition had remained only a state of mind, a condition of the public not unlike atmospheric pressure . . . detectable only by the barometers of opinion pollsters," Thomas Powers aptly writes, "then Johnson's policy of escalation would not have ended as and when it did." Helms considered it patent that mobs exert greater influence on government policies than opinion polls.[103]

Officials paid only minimal attention to the particular forms of protest. True, large demonstrations suggested broader public opposition than small ones and apparently had superior political legitimacy among the American people. Media coverage added political import to the events. And street-fighting apparently hurt the peace movement's public image; as McGeorge Bundy wrote Johnson in November 1967, "One of the few things that helps us right now is public distaste for the violent doves." In the end, however, these were lean distinctions to officials. Never particularly attentive to political differences on the left and suffocating under the weight of domestic criticism of the war, most viewed the protesters as part of a single hostile force. Richard Helms told me:

> I realize as a sociologist that you are interested in being more precise about who had influence in the dissident movement and who didn't, but from the vantage point of Washington I think it was the *totality* of the turn-off that was the pressure on [officials]. I mean, certainly the sight of the demonstrations, the letters, the telephone calls—all of the things putting pressure on the administration. There's no doubt about that. But I don't think that President Johnson or Nixon

tried to sort out which groups this was coming from. Just the fact
that there was a lot of it.

Rostow recalled, "We didn't enter into what tactics they were using."[104] Thus,
insofar as protesters considered Washington their immediate target, their endless tactical disputes were a waste of time.

But the antiwar movement did not pull it off alone. Not by a long shot. And
that it didn't helps explain official indifference to the movement's tactics. On top
of the incredible resilience of the Vietnamese revolutionaries, Saigon's feeble-
ness, and the bleak economic picture—a potent triad indeed—a whole arsenal
of domestic political needles was jabbing the Johnson administration simultaneously. As Nitze said, the war's critics in the media were damaging. Christian
was certain that dissenting television and newspaper commentaries had a "tremendous influence" on Johnson. "There was a great tendency in the Johnson
government to judge the national sentiment by what one read in the New York
and Washington press," he writes.[105]

Congressional criticism also badly wounded the administration. Johnson's
political skin was notably tender when it came to barbs from legislators; the
Congressional Record was "ever on his mind." By 1968 even many of the
bombing zealots in Congress were ready to dump the war. Officials considered
Congress an especially clear reflector of grass-roots opinion.[106]

Other expressions of domestic antagonism to the war also stung the administration. The results of national public opinion polls plainly conveyed the souring domestic mood. So did conversations with relatives, friends, and acquaintances, and communications to the White House from troubled everyday citizens. The explosive ghetto riots were another sign of the war's unpopularity
and its threat to social stability; to McPherson, they were even "more disturbing . . . than the opposition that came on college campuses." The criticism
of prominent business, church, and university leaders hurt the administration
as well.[107]

The peace movement's effectiveness was thus wedded to broader forces. It
sounded the dominant note in a powerful cacophony of antiwar voices. Protesters were, in fact, ultimately so dependent upon allies for political influence that
their particular leverage on the war is impossible to pin down. Asked which
segments of domestic opinion most swayed the policymakers, Helms responded,
"I don't think that really can be ascertained. It was the totality of it." McGeorge
Bundy recalled that the war's foes were "all part of the same ball of wax." "You
name it," McPherson quickly answered when asked which social groups Johnson worried an invasion of North Vietnam would incite. "That was the big
problem," McPherson said intently. "That was the terrible problem. That he
was concerned about the whole can of worms. And he was trying to manage
the war in such a way that he created the least amount of grief for himself

among all [social] groups." Morton Halperin went so far as to argue that government officials don't distinguish between segments of mass oppositional opinion. They merely have "a sense that the 'public mood' will not sustain," he said. "I mean, the level of analysis in the government on any issue would surprise you, and domestic politics is something that's even less well analyzed—if that's possible—than what's happening in Vietnam, for example. . . . It's all very instinctive. That may be too good a word for it. And it's certainly not differentiated." William Bundy similarly pointed out, "You have a sort of instinctive sense of what public opinion is doing."[108]

Officials' sweeping perceptions of domestic attitudes toward the war are reflected in the State Department's "American Opinion Summaries" of the time. They included excerpts from the *Congressional Record*; media commentaries; national poll results; protests; resolutions of civic groups, labor unions, and religious bodies; statements by governors and mayors; and incoming mail. Queried about what officials based their perceptions of public opinion on, McGeorge Bundy breezily responded, "It may be any one of 66 things."[109]

Still another aspect of domestic grumbling was on Dean Rusk's mind. The secretary of state shared Paul Nitze's concern about declining morale among U.S. soldiers; those shipped off to Vietnam were bringing with them "reflections of the discontent on the home front," he perceived. Rusk later said this might have been "part of the mix" of public disillusionment with the war that provoked his own call for a bombing pause in March. His doubt that a sense of declining GI morale contributed much to U.S. deescalation rings sound, however; of the officials I interviewed, only Rusk and Nitze recalled harboring concerns about it in early 1968.[110]

The acrimonious split between hawks and doves in the United States also pained the administration. The country seemed to be devouring itself. But officials' frequent allusions, then and later, to "divisions" and "polarization" can be misleading. Helms said bluntly, "These are just words to describe the fact that the country is not with you." And, as McGeorge Bundy observed, "Opposition *is* division." We have seen that George Christian regarded protesters as the chief originators of the cleavages tormenting Lyndon Johnson; the president's memoirs lend some support to this claim. Other administration officials accorded demonstrators the same honor. Asked what the concept "divisions" denotes, Nitze brought up the militant radicals. Antiwar protests admittedly fueled Clifford's distress over schisms in the United States too. An October 1968 speech by Bundy is also revealing. Immediately after expressing dismay over "the bitterness and polarization of our people," Bundy spoke of "a special pain in the growing alienation of a generation which is the best we have had."[111]

The peace movement also advanced antagonism to the war among the general public. Although the citizenry's defection probably sprang mainly from the war's length and cost, protesters helped focus scrutiny on the government's bankrupt policies. They challenged official lies, putting the administration on the defensive and widening the credibility gap. The light they shed on atrocities in Vietnam touched some, although most Americans were less concerned with Vietnamese casualties than with American ones. Activists heightened public awareness of the war's domestic economic price, and their willingness to suffer arrest or injury to stop the war provoked questioning, as did the movement's sheer size. The participation of their own children, friends, and acquaintances in the peace movement influenced some citizens. The movement then helped amplify the cries of the converted.

Activists also dished out a disturbing dose of social disorder. Many people got sick of the interminable controversy over the war. More than a few were shaken by the utter pandemonium it was generating. "You talk about turmoil—they still haven't forgotten that out there," CALCAV's Richard Fernandez chuckled. Revolution seemed more than idle talk. Of course, many citizens *hated* the protesters. A December 1967 Harris poll found that 40 percent opposed the right to hold peaceful demonstrations.[112] Some Americans may have backed the war longer and more strongly as a result of such sentiment. But others grew so tired of the disorder that they were willing to accept defeat in Vietnam if it would "get the country back to normal." And their hatred of demonstrators did not prevent bits and pieces of the antiwar message from slipping through.

The peace movement advanced opposition to the war in Congress too. Activists from the FCNL, AFSC, CALCAV, and other organizations provided legislators and their staff with information that countered the government's handouts, vexing already restless congressional minds. Acutely opinion-conscious legislators also saw the peace movement as a clear sign of public discontent with the war: "No way they could isolate themselves from the flak that they were getting from home and getting in their districts when they went home," as George Christian argued. Senator John Sherman Cooper later reluctantly conceded that "of course" the "constant stream" of people flooding his Washington office "affected me," although they failed to budge his belief in a president's prerogative to set foreign policy. (Cooper's main influence on the war would come later, when President Nixon's invasion of Cambodia violated his definition of constitutionally sanctioned presidential action.) Eugene McCarthy's decisions to speak out against the war and take on Johnson, and his stunning success in New Hampshire, clearly owed much to peace activists. Draft protesters grabbed Senator Mike Mansfield's attention: he warned the president on March 13 that a large troop increase might incite "serious resistance to military service at home." Finally, legislators had their own disgruntled children to reckon with.

At dinnertime, Congressman Tip O'Neill was "bombarded" with questions from his son Tom and daughter Susan, both college students. O'Neill would head off to government briefers for answers, but his kids "shot those official answers full of holes each time."[113]

Antiwar activists also nourished doubts about the war in the media. As Tom Wicker writes, a "powerful impulse" toward press skepticism of official pronouncements

> was provided by the peace movement—particularly by its student component. In the late sixties no one writing in the press or speaking on campus about the war escaped challenge, argument, confrontation—not only about the war itself but about American institutions and assumptions generally. Reluctantly, often painfully, members of the press were as profoundly affected as were many other Americans by the disillusionments and unwelcome revelations of the sixties.

Gingerly, James Reston and Eric Sevareid both told me they thought the antiwar movement caused them to question the war more. "There were a lot of eloquent people involved," Sevareid recalled. The peace movement also nagged at John Oakes, editor of the influential editorial page of the *New York Times* from 1965 to 1973. "It would be crazy to argue that that kind of thing didn't have any impact on my mind and on the minds of my associates," Oakes said. "I would have had to have been deaf, dumb and blind not to have felt . . . an impact. . . . *Of course* an impact—just like the air you breathe has an impact."[114]

The peace movement infiltrated some newsrooms. "As dissent built up in the nation, it crept slowly up the hierarchy of Time Inc. in New York, beginning with copy boys who might be drafted and spreading to researchers out of Vassar and Smith, and to the staff writers and editors," Don Oberdorfer writes. Sevareid said that "an awful lot of young journalists were very vulnerable or sensitive to [the movement], and receptive to a lot that went on in the colleges. And then they came into the papers, as a matter of fact. A whole lot of reporters suddenly show up in the *Washington Post* and the *Times* and other papers who are essentially part of that college generation and who carried those views in with them."[115]

Activists' valor stirred a few journalists. The attempt by California's four "napalm ladies" to block bomb shipments in 1966, the reader will recall, had a "profound" effect on Tom Wicker. The open support of William Sloane Coffin and other notables for draft resistance impressed John Chancellor.

The peace movement also roused the media indirectly. By fostering skepticism and opposition toward the war among the public, members of Congress, and other influential people (including administration officials), the movement helped catapult Vietnam into the "sphere of legitimate controversy." Media disparagement of the war became more acceptable. Sevareid thought Walter Cronkite's reversal, to take one example, was made under the goad of public opinion. "In effect he was just echoing back what most people had come to feel," Sevareid said somewhat disdainfully. "Whether he would have [changed his position on the war] if public opinion still favored it, I don't know. . . . Walter's a very popular man, and if you become a really popular celebrity you don't like to waste any of that popularity."[116] Since elite figures are routinely used as sources for news stories, their shifts in sentiment meant more publicity for antiwar views.

Granted, most journalists shared the citizenry's distaste for "Vietniks" (as they called protesters). Even from 1968 on, despite a marked increase in critical war coverage, media comments on the peace movement were twice as often unfavorable as favorable. Sevareid, for one, was never fond of noise in the streets. Speaking in plodding, soft tones amidst the lively chirping of the birds clustered one spring day around the flowery patio of his Georgetown home, sipping an iced refreshment served by his servant, the elderly newsman recalled:

> I didn't like the demonstrations and all the student stuff. A lot of it was arrogant and only connected with the draft, really. And I certainly couldn't approve of things like trying to stop a munitions train. . . . You can't interfere. . . .
>
> A lot of the things the youngsters did—the obscenities, the violence, preventing others from going to their classes, preventing the administration from running a school—it *offended* me. I was in college in the thirties when the first real student movement, ever, went on in this country. I was in Minnesota. I lost out as editor of the college daily for that reason. The president of the college intervened to stop me, because we got compulsory military training kicked out. . . . But it never occurred to us to use any kind of force, to try to tie up the campus physically, deny other students the right to speak or go about their business. We thought of the university as an oasis, somewhat, of reason. And we used the usual methods a lot: propaganda, meetings, writing and talking, and yelling our heads off. But not what a lot of these kids were doing. I didn't like it much.[117]

Yet many journalists of this sentiment were unnerved by the threat the malcontents posed to domestic stability. The war was "causing too much disaffection in the country," fretted the Hearst newspaper chain in explaining its slip from the fold. Walter Carroll complained it was "giving our home-grown Muscovites, Maoists and Castroites a chance to pursue once again the divisive tactics of the 1930s." The war "really *was* tearing apart American society," John Oakes remembered; antiwar violence and illegalities "certainly" fueled the *Times's* pleas for an end to the conflict. Sevareid admitted to sharing this response. "It was fragmenting the country," he said. The *Times* reporter David Halberstam was also concerned about the war's cost in domestic peace. James Reston said his growing antipathy to the conflict was shaped by a perception that the bitter public debate over it was "diverting the attention of the people from much more important things."[118]

Prominent Americans of other social stripes felt the antiwar movement's push as well. The domestic turbulence protesters fomented had a "considerable" impact on Arthur Schlesinger. Richard Goodwin's aversion to the war accelerated after he left the White House in the fall of 1965 partly because he came to realize that it was "wreaking perhaps irrecoverable damage on the fabric of American society." Goodwin also began listening more to "the voices of informed and reasoned dissent."[119] Demonstrators shook those weighty pillars of the Establishment known as the Wise Men.

The peace movement must thus receive a large chunk of the credit for turning back the tide in Vietnam. But what of Johnson's decision not to seek reelection? His senior aides later fell all over themselves denying that protesters kicked their man out. The president's judgment, they maintained, was made months—even years—before the country's defection on Vietnam. His primary motivation, Rostow and Rusk asserted, was fear of a stroke. Johnson also felt he'd used up his political capital with Congress. Furthermore, he genuinely believed, his aides insisted, that stepping down would bring Americans closer together. And, in Clark Clifford's measured words, the *"constant, unrelenting, unending* pressure" from Lady Bird to opt out was irresistible. Mrs. Johnson, too, feared the president would suffer serious health problems.[120]

Each of these explanations holds water, particularly the first. But they hardly tell the whole story. During much of March, Johnson did not act like a man set on relinquishing his powers. He continued to hold political strategy sessions and line up support. Then came his poor showing in New Hampshire, Kennedy's entry into the race, and word of a sure defeat in Wisconsin, maybe in Oregon, Indiana, and California as well. Vietnam had carved huge slices from Johnson's political base and torn the Democratic Party apart. The president knew he faced a grueling battle to secure the party's nomination. Even if he did pull it off, the Democratic coalition would lie in a shambles.[121] Johnson's "bitch of a war" had become his assassin. As mighty troops in the public barrage against that war, peace activists had exerted critical force indeed.

The antiwar movement may have assisted Johnson's tumble in other ways. To grant the president's concern with mending the country's internal divisions is to grant his concern with hushing the protesters. No protesters, no humanitarian gesture. Also, Johnson *was* tired, he *was* in poor health, he and Lady Bird *were* scared he'd end up an invalid (or worse), and these considerations *did* bear on his decision. It is difficult to conceive that domestic opposition to the war failed to leave a physical mark on Johnson, to grind him down a bit, and stoke fears of more stress ahead. Clifford believed the likelihood of continuing domestic "divisions" over the war counted heavily with Lady Bird.[122]

Johnson would not go down easily, though. He had notions of standing and fighting until the very end. On March 30 or 31, he told Vice President Hubert Humphrey he was unsure of his intentions. The day of his withdrawal statement, Richard Helms recalled, the president cautioned his wife and several others "that he would make a certain signal if he was going to end his speech with his retirement." William Bundy observed, "I think Johnson never decided the thing until he'd actually said it. Whenever he says he decided a thing, you knew damn well when you worked for him that he hadn't decided it until he'd actually signed his name to the piece of paper." "When did I make the decisions that I announced the evening of March 31, 1968?" Johnson writes. "The answer is: 9:01 P.M. on March 31, 1968."[123]

Restless Victors

Antiwar activists were ecstatic. Following Johnson's speech, they sailed out into the streets, whooping, laughing, getting down. The "wicked old witch" was dead, and they had fired some puissant rounds. "We felt it was a crowning achievement on our parts that we were going to be shed of that character," WSP's Alice Hamburg remembered. "Because we felt that he was the original war criminal par excellence." Hamburg and her friends "hated him very thoroughly." SDS's Bill Ayers: "You can't quite imagine the feeling, but to spend several years and several arrests and a lot of human energy opposing the war, and then to realize that you have had some small part in toppling this warmaking president, was a tremendous feeling of power and relief. . . . We were high as a kite. It was a *wonderful, wonderful* feeling." To another SDSer, "just the thought that we wouldn't have to see that awful face any more and hear those continual lies in that syrupy backwoods drawl, and thinking we all had something to do with that" was cause for exaltation.[124]

Others were restrained. "It is of the utmost importance," exhorted Fifth Avenue Peace Parade Committee leaders, that activists "not overestimate" the triumph. U.S. bombers were still dropping their grisly loads; more U.S. soldiers were on their way. The orgy of violence persisted. Protesters did not have the luxury of resting on their laurels.[125]

Some were disoriented. "There was a combination—I remember very well—of tremendous celebration and *tremendous* unhappiness," recalled Sam Brown, who had watched Johnson's "April Fools speech" from a Milwaukee hotel, spent from 90-hour workweeks in the McCarthy campaign:

> We didn't have Lyndon Johnson to kick around anymore. . . . I was devastated by it. . . . Rationally, it was a tremendous victory. Emo-

tionally, it was like, "Oh, my God . . . tomorrow morning we have to get up and see what all this means, and this afternoon it was so simple. . . . We had this guy that we could point a finger at, and now it's more diffuse, it's impossible to get a handle on it, you can't see it anymore." It was a crazy emotional reaction. It was like the loss of a valued enemy. I was crushed. [126]

Most were profoundly uncertain. Just how tasty *were* the fruits of their victory? If Johnson's peace initiative was only a scam to pave the way for more bloodletting, had they been prime time political players or simply a sideshow to the main action, capable of wresting passing acclaim but ultimately obscure? If the war's flames were now subsiding, who had really played fireman? *What did all this mean for future strategy and tactics?* The questions burned, the answers were elusive.

There were many road maps for the taking, and they pointed every which way. Rennie Davis and Tom Hayden continued to prepare for the Democratic Party convention protests, scrambling after city permits and commitments from the movement. On April 3, the Resistance collected a thousand draft cards for return to their maker. Some three weeks later, the Student Mobilization Committee held the largest student strike in U.S. history; hundreds of thousands of college and high school students boycotted their classes. The next day, a hundred and fifty thousand people demonstrated in New York, twenty-five thousand in San Francisco. On May 8, CALCAV activists picketed the annual stockholders meeting of the Dow Chemical Company in Michigan. Several managed to enter the 1,500-person assembly and hold the first "teach-in" before a big American corporation. "We were booed. You really felt like you were in the lion's den," Richard Fernandez recalled. The perturbed Dow chairman called Fernandez a "fascist." The protest received national news coverage. [127]

On May 17, the ultra-resistance struck again. At high noon, Fathers Philip and Daniel Berrigan and seven other Catholic mavericks strode into the draft board office in Catonsville, Maryland, with containers of homemade napalm concocted from a recipe in a Green Beret handbook. Since the Baltimore customshouse raid of October 1967, Philip Berrigan had concluded, "after talking it over with considerable numbers of people, the best people in the movement," that using blood to destroy draft files had been "counterproductive, because it put people off." "On the one hand, we're members of a very, very bloodthirsty society," Berrigan lamented. "We shed an awful lot of blood, almost habitually. On the other hand, we don't understand the symbol of blood." At Catonsville four female clerks confronted the intruders. "They put up quite a struggle, especially the head clerk. She kept saying, 'Don't you take my files!' She was clinging to them." During the scuffle, one of the resister's pants were ripped down. "That's why I say, when you do CD [civil disobedience] always wear belts," he later commented. The resisters managed to grab more than 300 1-A classification folders and dump them in wire mesh baskets. They then headed outside and napalmed their booty in the parking lot. In October they received prison sentences ranging from two to three years.[128]

After regrouping, Sam Brown and company plowed forward with McCarthy, bringing home the bacon in Wisconsin, Pennsylvania, and Oregon; meanwhile, Robert Kennedy was winning Indiana and Nebraska. Communist Party organizers touted CP General Secretary Gus Hall as the movement's presidential candidate of choice. Peace and Freedom Party activists scoured New York and California for signatures to secure that party's place on the two states' ballots. The Black Panther Party leader Eldridge Cleaver ran for president under the Peace and Freedom banner in both states. The Mobe's Doug Dowd reluctantly ran for vice president alongside Cleaver in New York. Dowd, who came to view the campaign as something of a joke, recounted the bizarre circumstances surrounding his selection to the ticket:

> I just happened to be in New York the weekend on which they were having their convention, on the east side of New York. . . . And I thought, "Well, as long as I'm here I might as well drop in on the goddamn convention before I go to Ithaca." So I go to the convention, which is a tawdry kind of a thing in some creepy old hotel. . . . I walked in there: "Jesus Christ, Doug. Thank God you've come! You've got to be vice president!" "What are you *talking* about? . . . I not only don't *got* to run for vice president, as I've told you I don't believe in this thing at all." "If you don't do it, Rubin's going to get it. Do you want *Rubin* to be running for vice president?" And they knew damn well I hated Jerry Rubin. . . . So I said, "Jesus, you've got to find someone else." "No, we *can't* find anybody else. It's too late. You've got to do it, Doug." So in order to keep Jerry Rubin from getting on this goddamn [ticket], I said "OK."

The gathering reminded Dowd of "a bunch of little kids, high school kids, playing mayor for a day or convention for a day." People were giving rousing nominating speeches and cheering like it was an earthshaking political event. Dowd would "never forget" when the Yippie Stew Albert, who "barely knew me and probably didn't care for me because I was way over thirty," rose to nominate Rubin. Rather than emphasizing Rubin's virtues, Albert wittily tore into Dowd. "Are we going to have the Peace and Freedom Party led by a man in a pinstriped suit with a martini in his hand?" the long-locked, hulking Albert asked the delegates. "He was characterizing me as a stuffy old goddamn professor who's wandering around with his gray flannel suit . . . and his cravat," laughed Dowd, who was dressed in his typical casual style.[129]

Yet despite the numerous road maps available to peace activists in the spring and summer of 1968, many paused to consider new political paths. The prominent road maps did not seem to them to account for major features of the American political landscape. Chicago looked even less inviting than before. Johnson's abdication had deprived the convention protests of a clear target. The surges of McCarthy and Kennedy exacerbated apprehension that demonstrators in Chicago would fortify the Democratic Party; the SWP urged people to stay away. Chicago's mayor, Richard Daley, was acting like "a small town southern bully." He refused to grant demonstration permits. Following urban riots in early April, he told Chicago police they should "shoot to kill arsonists and shoot to maim looters" (inciting "a big run-in" with Ramsey Clark, who snarled at Daley, with uncharacteristic anger, "That's murder, and if you're not indicted in Cook County, we'll indict you for civil rights violations"). On April 27, in Chicago's Loop, Daley's police hunted down peaceful demonstrators and onlookers alike, cracking skulls and ribs. The Yippies were still talking like the inmates of an asylum. By late summer their alleged plans included spiking Chicago's water supply with LSD, releasing greased pigs in downtown streets, and dispatching "super-potent" Yippie males to seduce the wives and daughters of convention delegates. [130]

The campaigns of McCarthy and Kennedy continued to evoke hostile reviews in many antiwar circles. While the two senators had helped dethrone Johnson, argued their detractors, they were still cozy with the system ("Pied Pipers of American capitalism," one SMC leader dubbed the pair) and reeking of opportunism. In late March, Marvin Garson called one of Kennedy's talks on Vietnam "the vaguest, emptiest speech I have ever heard, and I have heard Lyndon Johnson speak on numerous occasions." [131] Peace and Freedom was either too radical or too liberal. The April student strike and mass demonstrations were all fine and dandy, but they were hardly enough.

As for the Berrigans, they had apparently gone too far. Americans frowned on their actions at Catonsville. David McReynolds, for one, was bothered by "the Catholic intervention of the priests between the masses and the state: 'You don't have to confront the state, we'll take it on ourselves. *We* will burn your draft card.'" Dowd felt the Berrigans had "established a model of action which is too heroic to suggest *effective* steps to ordinary people." [132]

The incertitudes many activists felt over their political direction—over what worked and what didn't—imperiled the health of numerous antiwar organizations. Among the most seriously afflicted was the Resistance.

Following the April draft-card turn-in, the Cornell Resistance leader Bruce Dancis and other resisters went into a funk. Resistance strategy had predicted a dramatic, exponential expansion in noncooperation with the Selective Service System over time. But it wasn't happening. "After the April 1968 turn-in, it was really evident to me and to the people I was close to at Cornell that this movement was not going to grow on the scale that we thought it would," Dancis recalled. "We didn't achieve the things we hoped to in terms of clogging the courts, filling the jails, affecting the government's ability to raise an army." High draft calls of the country's young eggheads had not ensued; the government was going after nonstudents less likely to raise Cain. The McCarthy campaign had cut into the Resistance's ranks. So had prison. And many would-be resisters had parachuted out at the last minute. "We lost a lot of people who just thought better of it," Michael Ferber remembered. "They would take their draft card back or they would go to Canada or do this or that. That was somewhat demoralizing."[133]

What's more, the Resistance's effect on the war was hazy. Although encouraged by Johnson's downfall, many noncooperators despaired over the continued killing. With media interest in draft resistance waning, some were skeptical they were reaching the public. Others hadn't a clue: "It was impossible to gauge the impact of the Resistance on mass audiences," one antidraft activist wrote later. Many feared that, having in fact aroused lots of middle-class consciences, they'd "reached the point of 'diminishing returns'—increasing the number of draft resisters would do little or nothing to move people."[134]

Even sanguine resisters were often unsure of their next step. "I think the Resistance was at something of a loss over what to do after awhile," Ferber reflected. "We had these guys who turned in their draft cards, but that was an act you did once: it took five minutes. Other than organizing more of that, there wasn't a lot for a resister—as a resister—to do." And many resisters had never been keen on organizing in the first place. "So many of the guys were essentially moralists," Ferber recalled. "They were pure about their own stance . . . but they weren't good at organizations, they weren't good at coming to meetings, they didn't *like* meetings. And we couldn't build much of a program around them. . . . That was a problem."[135]

Dancis faced a different sort of problem. He had been indicted the previous April for mutilating his draft card: prison was now straight ahead. When Dancis reported to a Kentucky prison the following year, "it was sort of bittersweet," he said. For over two years he'd been expecting to go "at any time, so I was ready for it, I was psychologically prepared to face whatever was going to come." But, convinced draft resistance had "failed," Dancis regretted traveling that route. "I felt that, in some sense, 'It's a waste. I'd be more effective outside—I'm a good organizer, I'm a good speaker—and here I am in jail for the next how many years?'" Dancis's nineteen-month stay behind bars went better than he had expected, though:

> It was a youth prison. It was mostly people . . . in their early twenties, generally doing five- to ten-year sentences: car thieves, bank

robbers, drugs. . . . We formed an alliance in prison which we called "The Family" that included the draft resisters, some of the more political black and white inmates, and some of the drug users. . . . It was both a defense organization for us, so we wouldn't get hassled by other inmates—and we had real muscle in our group—but also we had study groups, which I put together. We didn't do organizing per se in terms of leading strikes of prisoners or stuff like that, but we did political education, we shared books. I led a study group on the history of the Russian revolution at one point [laughs], and on Marxism and the history of the New Left. . . . We were a support group for each other. . . . I'm not a very big person, so I was somewhat concerned for my physical safety, but that never really was an issue.[136]

Other draft resisters were in no mood to shift course in mid-stream. "I was just disappointed in a lot of other people in the Resistance because they were prepared by April 1968 to say it hadn't worked," David Harris remembered, his frustration still evident. Harris and his comrades in Palo Alto had never fully shared Dancis's expectation that the number of noncooperators would increase exponentially. "We weren't cutting it quite that mechanistically," he said. "We assumed nobody wanted to go to jail. We assumed that the option could be made palatable." They also believed that the government's decision to refrain from mass prosecutions was undercutting its credibility and thus a sign of the Resistance's power, not weakness. Furthermore, there was no question they were moving people. Many middle-class Americans "like my parents," Harris recalled, "were tremendously affected by the simple and human morality of the position that we took. And we found an enormous support base." Harris and his friends were reading more Sartre and Kierkegaard than resisters back east too. "We went at it primarily from the principle of 'How do you, as an individual, speak the truth, make yourself free of the machine and work to stop it?'" Harris said. "'How do you do all those things at once?'" Harris thought that many Resistance organizers were incredibly impatient. "Back east a lot of them said, 'OK, if enough of us do this, we'll grind the war to a halt.' So they wait a year and it hasn't ground to a halt—and you're up shit creek." The antiwar movement's "real problem" was not political weakness, Harris stressed. It was that it

> kept looking for a new tactic every week. It was, "Oh, well, this is not effective, let's try something new." The capacity to sustain an action as long as the government could sustain its policy was part of the test we had to go through, I thought. . . . People wanted to be able to stop the war right away and I thought that was tremendously naïve: "Jesus Christ, this is the goddamn American government waging a war, for Christ's sake! You don't just pry them off that like

that. . . ." And I thought the cycle of escalating rhetoric that those illusions generated was in itself a great mistake. It ends up with the Weathermen, for Christ's sake—a bunch of looney tunes.[137]

When Harris reported to prison in 1969, he had no regrets. "From the time I decided I was going to do it, I never looked back," he recalled. "I felt comfortable with it, always." With a three-year sentence hanging over his head, he told national student leaders the previous August, "I find no more honorable position in modern America than that of criminal." And Harris was eager to leave the movement. Nonviolence was being increasingly ridiculed; antiwar groups were splintering. "I thought the place was crazy," he said. "Jail was a better place to be than the streets." But Harris's time behind bars wasn't soft:

My attitude was to make it as big an adventure as possible, to learn as much and grow as much as possible. And to push it, that prison was not the place to back off. So I spent four of my twenty months in prison in isolation cells . . . because of various incidents . . . mostly going on strike. I was in four different strikes. I lived twelve months in maximum security. My attitude was, just because they lock you up, you don't stop what you're doing, and that it was important for Resistance people to be organizers in prison. And there were a bunch of us. . . . You know, nobody ever had to ask us twice to go on strike. And we built a good reputation amongst prisoners because of that. The place I did most of my time, La Tuna, Texas, there were only six draft resisters in the whole place, but I didn't have any problem with other prisoners—I had problems with guards. I was getting hassled all the time. And I was paroled with more disciplinary reports on my record than anybody else in the institution.

Harris considered it "unfortunate" that more antiwar activists didn't go to prison. "It gives you clearance," he argued. "I know a lot of people who are still living in the sixties because they never got clearance, they never did anything that made them feel that they had done something. . . . [Prison] made you feel like 'you'd done it, you'd paid your dues.'"[138]

Who was the more politically astute? Resistance organizers who concluded by 1968 that noncooperation had flopped, or those who detected meaningful yields? The second group. Dancis and his friends were right to infer that noncooperation had failed to make much of a dent in the supply of cannon fodder available for shipment to Vietnam. "It didn't substantially attrit the base of manpower," Paul Warnke recalled; echoed Secretary of the Army Stanley Resor, "The draft delivered enough people without any problem." And, save for scattered locations, the courts, indeed, remained unclogged. But the work of the criminal justice system was hampered nonetheless. As the authors of a highly acclaimed study of the draft argue, the Resistance contributed to a grass-roots movement of more than half a million young men who violated various Selective Service laws. Many who could not get themselves to return their draft cards to the government found the courage to refuse induction when called. Monstrous draft-case backlogs soon confronted U.S. attorneys. They could not keep up with the avalanche—and increasingly tired of trying to.[139]

Actual courtroom outcomes of draft battles also made the government gun-shy. By 1968 skillful antidraft attorneys had piled up an "astonishing" record of checking convictions. Federal judges were dismissing draft cases for Selective Service procedural irregularities hand over fist. Many magistrates were taking their cue from the early, exceptional leniency of their brethren in the San Francisco Bay Area. The Resistance's high visibility there was not unrelated to this practice. "One San Francisco judge privately acknowledged that the turmoil and bitter feelings about the Vietnam war affected the way he and his colleagues handled Selective Service cases. Had the war been more popular, he might have been less receptive to technical defenses." Behind many judges were young law clerks fresh out of universities teeming with antidraft activity.[140]

U.S. attorneys and their assistants also noticed the war's unpopularity—and proceeded accordingly. San Francisco's federal prosecutor, Cecil Poole, felt he couldn't pursue draft cases "'in the abstract,'" but only by "giving due consideration to community standards. In light of the attitude of young people in the Bay Area, Poole did not believe that draft offenders should be vigorously prosecuted." In 1967 and 1968 Poole's office dropped more than 90 percent of its draft cases. One U.S. attorney said he sometimes had to remind his assistant "that he was not a defense counsel."[141]

Selective Service officials complained to the Justice Department about the low indictment rate. The response, often enough, was unsympathetic. The department's chief draft prosecutor, William Sessions, was not about to satisfy what he called "a continuing, open, obvious expressed intent by many groups to absolutely swamp the system." Attorney General Ramsey Clark developed a finely tuned disappearing act: "Whenever I tried to call Ramsey for help," SSS Director Lewis Hershey recalled, "he just wasn't around."[142]

The upshot of all this was that of the many young Americans who committed draft violations during the war, fewer than 2 percent were convicted. The draft had not collapsed, as some Resistance leaders had envisioned, but its enforcement was in a shambles. Many lives were saved in the process. "We had in fact done exactly what we said," David Harris contended. "We'd ground the judicial system to a goddamn halt. It was 'Olly Olly, All Home Free' on the issue of the Selective Service Act." Less convincingly, Harris also claimed the Resistance successfully bogged down the penal system. "We *did* fill up the prisons," he spat. "Christ, I was in the prisons—let me tell you they were full."[143]

Yet the Resistance's main yields lay elsewhere. In fact, the bureaucratic knots it tied may not actually have burdened the war makers at the top. The *political* knots it tied obviously did, however. The Resistance was a conspicuous component of that cutting edge of active opposition to the war that played such a crucial role in turning U.S. policy around. It promoted official and public perceptions that war-as-usual had unacceptable domestic costs. Resisters' personal courage increased the peace movement's credibility with some Americans. Their sheer numbers nourished public questioning of the war as well. Perhaps most important, *the Resistance inspired greater dedication and resolve among other antiwar activists.* As Harris said, "We were the shock troops." Many people "marched in parades they wouldn't have marched in if we hadn't been doing what we were doing, passed out leaflets they wouldn't have passed out. We energized a great number of people." Dancis eventually came to concur: "When I look back on it, I think our major impact was on the antiwar movement. . . . We had a profound impact on other students. It's funny, to this day I get letters from people whom I never met . . . saying, 'I remember you at Cornell and you had a big impact on me.'"[144]

During the summer and fall of 1968, however, Harris and other Resistance stalwarts were feeling increasingly alone. Enthusiasm for draft resistance was fading. That November, the organization held its last national draft-card turn-in. A year later, the Resistance was, for all intents and purposes, dead.

Where did all the resisters go? Besides entering prisons, some helped provide sanctuary for AWOL American soldiers. A few gave up political activism. The largest group expanded their political pursuits to target issues "beyond" the draft and war. Many latched onto the most militant of the various multi-issue agendas making the rounds—revolution.

Resisters' shifting priorities reflected profound political rumblings in the antiwar movement as a whole. Not all of their consequences were beneficial.

Multi-Issuism versus Vietnam Protest: A "Savage" Dispute

Since the first batch of U.S. troops hit the beach at Danang in 1965, peace activists had, of course, organized protests against a host of political ills. To many radicals in the movement, a wide world of injustice demanded rectification. Some otherwise intelligent radicals felt the war could never be stopped until capitalism was overthrown. Many believed mobilizing Americans around domestic issues would facilitate political action in the postwar age.

As the conflict mounted, radicals multiplied. Maybe the entire system really did have to go before the nightmare would end, activists increasingly concluded. Political eyes were opening wide. "When I started out I didn't think of certain people as evil and certain institutions as evil, but I came to really feel that way because I learned a lot about them," the Student Mobe leader Linda Morse remembered.[145] Her education was hardly unique.

Of the many domestic injustices antiwar activists took aim at, racism was preeminent. Numerous demonstrators had worked in the civil rights movement in the South; their sympathies had not changed. When Rev. Martin Luther King, Jr., tied the war to racial oppression in 1967, the issue's salience skyrocketed. "What do you do when Martin Luther King has made the link between civil rights and peace?" David McReynolds asked. "Do you *reject* it?"[146] Three summers of urban riots enriched activists' understanding of the suffering endured by blacks. With their brothers in the ghettoes on the verge of insurrection, many white radicals deduced, they'd better come to their aid. State repression of radical black groups was enlightening as well. And as the black liberation struggle gained momentum, some activists believed, the repression was bound to get worse.

Carl Oglesby certainly thought so. In late March 1968, three weeks after a government-sponsored commission had blamed the 1967 ghetto riots on horrendous ghetto conditions and recommended corrective social programs, Oglesby went before the SDS National Council. The commission, he later recalled,

> had said all the right things, all the Yankee liberal kinds of things, about why there were these terrible disturbances in the cities. I was saying, "This might make us think that the powers-that-be, having at last understood the problem in realistic terms, are now prepared to take steps to rectify the situation that gives rise to the disturbances. . . . *Ah ha, this would be wrong.* The real truth is that there is nothing for them to do. So their accurate perception of the real causes of the riots is not going to lead to increased social welfare. It will lead, on the contrary, to increased repression. Because the more . . . the fascists come to understand the true sources and wellsprings of the rebellion against them, the more they will sharpen their weapons accordingly.

The overwhelmingly white, middle-class SDSers voted to give support for the black struggle their highest priority.[147]

The Tet offensive, plummeting public support for the war, Johnson's March 31 speech, and the start of peace talks accelerated multi-issue propensities among peace activists. With the Vietnamese revolutionaries dealing a decisive blow to the war makers, some reasoned, it was safe to confront other problems. Carl Oglesby told the SDS delegates that "the point had been made, the debate, having been properly staged, had been won. . . . On some 'each one, teach one' model, we have taught the ones next to us, and the ones next to us have taught the ones next to them, and now at the highest levels in Washington, in the White House itself, the anti-Vietnam War movement continues." Thus, argued

Oglesby, "antiwar organizing as such no longer needed to be done as a program at the local or capillary level." Paul Booth remembered that after March 1968, "we held back from participating in antiwar stuff on the theory that [the war] couldn't last more than six more months, this thing was so obviously harmful to the country that at that point it had to collapse of its own weight." Booth added ruefully, "There were four more years of *that*."[148]

For some radicals, the Establishment's defection on Vietnam was disquieting. The war had become a "liberal issue," they perceived. No radical worth his or her salt could now deny that a revolution could only grow out of agitation around domestic issues, they maintained. And working in a movement full of liberals was existentially unappealing in any event.

Martin Luther King's assassination on April 4, the firestorms of black rage that swept America in its wake, and state repression of the rebels fed multi-issue sentiment in the peace movement. According to many radicals, the revolution was being forced on blacks and whites alike by an unyielding, tyrannical system upheld by tanks and rifle fire. If The Man wouldn't even tolerate liberal church leaders like King, who was safe? Organizing more peaceful protests against the war seemed at best irrelevant, at worst immoral.

That white students could play a significant revolutionary role was promptly underscored by startling events on America's campuses and overseas. Columbia University students occupied five buildings for the heady span of eight days (inspiring the university's president, Grayson Kirk, to issue his first public statement against the war). The police violence used to dislodge the invaders only whetted appetites for wholesale social change. Following Columbia, obstructionist student protests snowballed. Shaken educational leaders deemed the unrest their "number one problem." Congress was also unsettled by it: assisted by the Johnson administration, it passed legislation denying financial aid to campus militants. In Paris, students squared off against police in fierce street clashes, instigating a general strike that nearly toppled the government. Other foreign students were also on the move, and they weren't messing around either. "It felt to many of us . . . that things were coming very quickly to a head world-wide," Bill Ayers remembered. And if Vietnamese peasants could defeat the most advanced military technology in the world, why couldn't Americans?[149]

When Robert Kennedy was murdered on June 5, hours after winning the California Democratic presidential primary, the politics of reform died for many with him. "So now it was time to take your turn in the line of people who would probably be repressed, brutalized or killed," Tom Hayden thought. Remembered Oglesby:

> I felt terrible. It confirmed all my fears and made me feel like, "That's it for my politics, because now the other side is going to say, 'Look, you played by the rules, and you won the debate, and just as you're about to pluck the fruit of it all the criminals come along and wipe

it out again. And they'll keep doing this, no matter how close you come. You will always be thrust away at the last moment by the underlying power structure that doesn't want to see democracy work.'" . . . The next years were terrible years. . . . People were very agitated and up and out and doing things, but to me it was all energy from before. . . . There was no life at the center that was pulsing new stuff out. That had died.[150]

When SDS met for its annual convention in June, "the revolution" dominated conversation. It was a time for determining who had the mettle for battle and who didn't. When Bernardine Dohrn, a candidate for national office, was asked whether she was "a socialist," she sniffed at the reformist implications. "I consider myself a revolutionary communist," Dohrn retorted.[151]

As multi-issue sentiment rose in the peace movement, so did controversy over it. The degree to which activists should target domestic injustices relative to Vietnam had always been a touchy matter in the movement, but now it was positively explosive. "The arguments over the multi-issue question were really savage," Brad Lyttle remembered. Many activists claimed a moral obligation to assist blacks' struggle. "It is incumbent on all concerned citizens and groups to respond to the racial crisis," Norma Becker exhorted other Parade Committee members in June. "The two questions . . . are equally grave." Recalled Becker, "It just didn't make any sense as Americans to be fighting against the injustice and oppression being experienced by people 6,000 miles away while not responding to the sufferings and injustice being experienced by people next door."[152] Many activists argued that organizing against racism would bring more blacks into both the peace movement and the struggle for radical social change.

With the war far from over, others maintained, it would be a serious strategic error for peace organizations to shift their central focus from Vietnam. The Parade Committee's "primary job" should continue to be "anti-war action," one activist submitted; otherwise, Vietnam might be "swept under the table" and "Johnson will succeed."[153]

The SWP was adamant that peace organizations concentrate solely on Vietnam. It feared targeting domestic issues would invite Democratic Party "cooptation" of the movement. SWPers considered civil rights organizing especially vulnerable to Democratic subversion. "They saw the black struggle as dominated by the Democratic Party," the SWP refugee Lew Jones remembered.[154]

Even some blacks felt the antiwar movement should stay focused principally on Vietnam. The SMC leader Gwen Patton counseled fellow blacks that while their own oppression was "serious indeed . . . *my God*, do not exalt this struggle to what's going on in . . . Vietnam. They have yet to drop napalm on us in this country." Could anybody in the United States tell Patton what *that* felt like? Unlike American blacks, she stressed, the Vietnamese "have got the whole U.S.

state apparatus kicking their behinds." Patton helped form the National Black Antiwar Antidraft Union in January 1968.[155]

Advocates of single-issue Vietnam protest suffered considerable abuse for their view. They were accused of "racism." Already feeling guilty about the advantages their skin color provided, many whites acquiesced in the charge. "Now, you couldn't be anything worse than a racist," Lyttle remembered. "So nobody spoke against the multi-issue position." The "honky-baiting" of its proponents constituted, said Lyttle, "the most powerful single political attack I've ever heard in the radical movements in this country."[156]

The acrid bickering among peace activists over political targets further fragmented the movement and hindered coordinated antiwar activity. It also dampened many an antiwar spirit. It was discouraging to work with people constantly at each other's throats. The arguments were *absolutely exhausting,"* the Mobe activist Madeline Duckles said. "Meetings would go on for hours and hours and hours." Some people dropped out of antiwar activity as a result. Tragically, the fighting probably hurt black participation in the peace movement. Patton thought many blacks stayed away from antiwar groups because of "all the doggone *talk*. . . . Working-class people don't have that kind of luxury to sit at meetings for six and seven hours," she pointed out. Later, at demonstrations, after countless speakers had outlined countless connections between countless issues, "you've lost your audience entirely," Duckles noted. Yet Norma Becker wryly commented that while disputes over racial protest wore peace activists down, "I'm inclined to think that if we weren't debating that issue and spending long hours over that crisis, we would have been doing it over something else . . . "[157]

In May, strife over acceptable political targets was combining with Old Left sectarianism to cripple the only national student antiwar coalition in the United States. The Student Mobe would survive the discord in name only.

The Devastation of the Student Mobilization Committee

Linda Morse, the SMC's executive secretary, was tormented. Since the SMC's inception she had been the glue that held the factionalized group together. But now Morse's mediatory role felt stifling. Her own political views were evolving; "socialism" held heightened appeal. Morse's pacifism, though still kicking, was on the ropes. As chief political arbitrator, however, Morse felt uncomfortable expressing her new beliefs. "When you have hundreds of people expecting certain things from you in terms of how you function, how you act, how you think, etc., it was extremely difficult to say, 'I am a person and I'm changing my political views,'" Morse remembered. "If I had announced I was in favor of armed revolution, half the group would have fainted!"[158]

Morse had correspondingly grown dissatisfied with the SMC's agenda. The group could no longer merely organize large antiwar protests, she contended. It had to move forthrightly on the question of black liberation. Although "without a clear understanding of how that would work out politically or structurally," Morse felt the SMC simply had to "figure out some way to make things more multi-issue." Many other students shared her impulse, she knew.[159]

Morse perceived that the SMC's decision-making structure was inhibiting its political development. On the national staff, power was concentrated in a "troika" between the YSA/SWP, CP, and herself. The arrangement was breeding "perverted" political relationships involving the exercise of "veto power" by occupiers of political "slots" on the staff, Morse observed. Most annoying, the YSA was always dashing about to block political initiatives incompatible with YSA Group Thought—including multi-issuism. On May 8, the SMC's working committee agreed that "the staff shall be composed entirely of independents in order to relieve some major tensions in the office." The two YSA staffers thus had to step down.[160]

Incensed, the YSA honed its political weaponry and prepared for war. It was not about to stand by twiddling its thumbs while the Democrats stole the movement. That was obviously what the new policy was all about. After the SMC agreed to debate the policy at a meeting in June, the YSA issued a call to its troops: EVERYBODY COME![161]

Morse reminisced:

> The Trots overreacted. . . . They saw everything going down the tubes and they just went bonkers at that [Student] Mobe conference. . . . They brought every single one of their folks in for it. They signed up Harry Ring, who was sixty-six years old and on the Central Committee of the SWP, as a Student Mobe representative [laughs]. It was ridiculous. . . . They packed the meeting. And the entire discussion that day was based on who could be allowed to vote. Period. I mean, we never got past that, we never even got into any substantive discussions. Period. There were all of these large Trots [laughs] who were pretending to be students . . .

After some caustic exchanges, a livid Morse took the microphone and called for a walkout of the SMC's independent activists. "We'd reached the end," Morse remembered. "I'd had it up to here and so had other people. When you spend a whole day debating whether Harry Ring can vote as a student—I mean, give me a break. I think we thought it was lost at that point."[162]

The next morning, Morse and her troops formed the Radical Organizing Committee. By the end of the summer, the group was no more. "It was a blip on the face of the earth," Morse admitted. "The only time it existed was at the Chicago demonstrations, and it existed more in the minds of Daley and the Chicago police and the FBI than anybody else."[163]

As a national antiwar coalition, the SMC also went kaput. Now merely a "Trot front" for organizing legal peace demonstrations, it was snubbed by most activists unaffiliated with the YSA. Anonymous FBI propaganda against the YSA fed their distrust.[164] The result was a weaker peace movement. Indeed, there would never again be a national student organization capable of uniting all youth who opposed the war.

Who was responsible for this loss? "We made a major error in just saying 'fuck it' and walking out," Morse conceded. But the SWP was ultimately to blame for the SMC's rupture; its gladiatorial approach to politics made dialogue virtually impossible. As Lew Jones admitted, the SWP's packing of the SMC conference and other antiwar gatherings was not only "greatly insensitive" but politically foolish. "You're dealing with forces coming into political motion for the first time, and you want to broaden [the movement], you don't want to scare them away," Jones pointed out. "And the SWP's heavy-handedness some-times had that effect." Other activists had even harsher words about the SWP's strong-arm methods. "The SWP was the biggest group of troublemakers that we had to deal with," cracked WSP's Cora Weiss, who worked with SWPers in the National Mobe. "We had to not only deal with government interference, but we had to deal with the SWP. And it's amazing that we all came out of it."[165]

The U.S. government undoubtedly watched the SMC's disintegration with sat-isfaction. The more the peace movement splintered, the better. To further "dis-rupt" and "neutralize" New Left and antiwar groups, the FBI launched an ex-tensive COINTELPRO program that spring. COINTELPRO's arsenal of dirty tricks included infiltration, poison-pen letters, forged literature, and leaked dis-information to the media. COINTELPRO operatives also set protesters up on drug charges and acted to "bad-jacket" movement leaders as government infor-mants. The program's main objectives were to discredit protesters, hinder their recruitment, and worsen their internal divisions. "Ridicule is one of the most potent weapons that we can use," J. Edgar Hoover instructed FBI agents in July. The FBI director ordered the bureau's field offices to distribute articles showing the "depravity" of New Left activists. Hoover also relayed that the "definite hostility" of the New Left toward the SWP, YSA, and PL "should be exploited wherever possible." He added that COINTELPRO "must be approached with imagination and enthusiasm if it is to be successful."[166]

Blood in the Windy Streets

Come August, most antiwar eyes were on Chicago—from a distance. No more than five thousand adventuresome souls trekked to the Windy City for the convention protests. Why participate in a bloodbath? Mayor Daley continued to withhold demonstration permits, while carrying out intimidating and well-publicized plans for "protecting" the convention from "extremists." "I felt in my bones that Chicago was going to be bad, that it was just going to turn sour," one peace activist remembered. Even Tom Hayden was edgy; he confided afterward that he ventured to the city "expecting death, expecting the worst."[167]

The action began pacifically enough. On Friday, August 23, at the Chicago Civic Center, the Yippies unveiled their presidential candidate—a pig—while singing "God Bless America." They demanded the government fly "Pigasus" to the Texas White House for foreign policy briefings like the other presidential challengers. Police put him in the pokey instead. The next day, WSP led a "very, very serious" women-only picket at the Hilton Hotel, home of the convention delegates. The women were serving as "guinea pigs," Cora Weiss recalled. "We did it to literally see what the police reaction was going to be."[168] There was no violence.

Late that evening, six hundred young people gathered around a bonfire in Lincoln Park. Allen Ginsberg, poet and high priest of beatnik mysticism, sitting in his customary lotus position, led the youths in a chant of "Om." "A thousand bodies vibrating om can immobilize an entire downtown Chicago street full of scared humans, uniformed or naked," he once claimed. Shortly before the 11 P.M. park curfew, most youths began ambling out of the park. Those who didn't were shoved out by police. "Red Rover, Red Rover, send Daley right over," they gibed. Suddenly, several hundred began sprinting through Chicago's Old Town. The streets were theirs and they were exhilarated. Just as abruptly, they ended their foray and melted into the surrounding citizenry. "A guerrilla army had found its jungle."[169]

The next day's Festival of Life was a bust. After police aborted a rock music performance, many of those present became abusive. One offered an officer a sandwich filled with excrement. Shortly after 11, a thousand protesters charged out of Lincoln Park into the streets. They turned over garbage cans and pounded on cars. Back in the park, police spewed tear gas. Its victims hurled rocks and thrashed blindly about. Some were clubbed to the ground by cops conveniently lacking badges and nameplates. Then another wave of protesters pulsed out into the streets. "Your wife sucks cock!" was a popular cry. Some spent the evening in emergency medical centers.[170]

The next afternoon, Tom Hayden was arrested. "I oughta kill you right now," one cop grumbled to him in the back of a paddy wagon. During a rally downtown to protest Hayden's arrest, several demonstrators scampered up onto a statue of a Civil War hero and decorated it with NLF flags. Police ripped them down, breaking one youth's arm. With nightfall came greater violence. In Lincoln Park, protesters heaved bottles and rocks at an approaching police car, shattering its windows. Cops then invaded the park and clubbed people indiscriminately. Near the Hilton, Hayden was slammed to the pavement and carted off to jail for a second time. Late the following afternoon, he resurfaced on Chicago's streets wearing a fake beard, sunglasses, beads, and yellow-brimmed hat. It was time, he said, "to get the pig off my back." That evening Hayden moved virtually undetected through the city. To some, he was now merely a "random weirdo." "He was doing all kinds of crazy things," Doug Dowd recalled. "He was just having the time of his goddamn life." Hayden delivered one network TV interview in his new persona.[171]

Tuesday night was a repeat of nights past, with one difference: the violence was worse.

On Wednesday afternoon, ten thousand gathered at the Grant Park bandshell. Daley had seen fit to allow a rally, but rejected petitions for a march to the Amphitheatre. An hour into the speeches, a shirtless longhair shinnied up a flagpole to turn Old Glory upside down. Several cops yanked the youth down and delivered their nightsticks to all parts of his body. Enraged demonstrators heaved bricks, eggs, chunks of concrete, balloons filled with urine. From the stage, Dave Dellinger, the master of ceremonies, pleaded for restraint. When a half dozen youths (possibly agents provocateurs) hoisted a red piece of cloth on the flagpole, cops plowed into the crowd, clubbing. Many protesters were battered senseless. Rennie Davis ended up on the ground with his head split open; blood drenched his face and shirt. A Naval intelligence officer hovered over Davis's body with a microphone and tape recorder. There was no response.[172]

On the platform, chaos. Dellinger announced that there would be an attempt to march nonviolently to the Amphitheatre. Hayden was furious. He and his crony Tom Neumann—along with "their strong-arm people"—strode menacingly toward Dellinger. It was not Hayden's finest hour. "Hayden tried to remove me, physically, from the platform," Dellinger remembered:

> I had to stand them down. Tom said that I had been immoral, that
> the police had charged and Rennie Davis was knocked out, and that I
> had told people to sit down and not to fight back. . . . That I had
> betrayed the Mobe. And that they were taking the microphone away
> from me. I looked around for some support, but nobody was there.
> And I just shouted them down. I said, "Fuck you, Tom Hayden! . . .
> That's not the way we operate. If you think that I'm doing it wrong,
> we're a coalition, and there's a little bit of a difference in views. I'll
> give you the microphone and you can say what we ought to do, and
> then I'll say what we ought to do. Or I'll say it first if you want and
> then you do it." And Tom, the bastard (forgive me), Tom says, "No,
> I won't do it." He says, "Tom Neumann will do it."

Dellinger handed Neumann the microphone after reiterating the plan for a nonviolent march. "That was my civil libertarianism at its best," Dellinger said. "Because I was scared shitless about what he was going to ask people to do."

Neumann directed the protesters to reclaim "their" streets. "That's no good, he didn't say anything," Hayden jabbered. "I'm going to tell them." "Rennie has been taken to the hospital, and we have to avenge him," Hayden shouted to the crowd. "We must move out of this park in groups throughout the city and turn this overheated military machine against itself. Let us make sure that if blood flows, it flows all over the city." Near Hayden stood the burly Sidney Peck. "I was ready to physically remove him," Peck recalled. Peck was "absolutely astounded" at Hayden's adventuristic political inclinations at the time.[173]

Few followed Hayden's cue. The five thousand demonstrators who tried to make their way peacefully out of the park were repulsed by police, guardsmen, and fortified jeeps. After deliberations, they decided to attempt to maneuver to the Hilton Hotel in small bands. Soldiers greeted them at major thoroughfares with tear gas "freely dispensed" from converted flamethrowers. The gas wafted over onto Michigan Avenue in front of the Hilton, where it upset the coat-and-tie and Chablis-and-Brie sets and, eventually, Hubert Humphrey in his shower. Vomit stains—compliments of those "who could not hold their gas"—soiled the plush carpet in the hotel lobby. Feinting, circling, slicing, most of the protesters finally made their way to Michigan Avenue; the vanquished were seen licking their wounds along the attack routes. By early evening the congestion around the Hilton was total. Flushed youths quoted Lenin for tactical guidance. "This was so surreal I couldn't believe it," Peck said later. Some threw missiles and swore at police. Then, Doug Dowd remembered, "all hell broke loose." Waves of helmeted cops, "big guts" sticking out, meaty red faces contorted with rage, filed out of buses. They lined up, platoon-style, and began jogging in place. Arms raised upward, chanting, "Kill, Kill, Kill," the police wheeled to face the demonstrators. They went to work. It was a sight Dowd would "never forget. . . . What a *traumatic* experience!" Heads cracked, knees buckled, arms were jerked "until they had almost left their sockets." The plateglass window of the Hilton's Haymarket Lounge shattered with a "sickening" crash; shrieking protesters and onlookers spilled through, some sliced horribly by the glass. The cops pursued them inside, clubbing wildly, "like mad dogs"; when they departed, seven writhing bodies adorned the floor. For twenty packed minutes, the bloodletting ran its course. "It was one of the most awful experiences of my life—which has had a lot of bad experiences—like wars and so on," Dowd said. At home, America watched it all on live TV.[174]

Inside the Amphitheatre, Hubert Humphrey was being nominated as the Democratic Party's presidential candidate. Humphrey had entered the race in late April proclaiming it time for "a politics of joy." Although McCarthy and Kennedy had received the overwhelming majority of the primary votes, the joy was now his. Humphrey knew thanks were due Johnson's and Daley's backroom magic and a stacked delegate selection process.

Thursday brought more street combat. At the front lines now stood many young McCarthy workers, outraged by the week's police violence and their man's blistering by Democratic Party powerbrokers. "The McCarthy kids wound up . . . throwing rocks at the cops," Linda Morse recalled. "I got hit by one of them because they had bad aim! They were so pissed. Even the ones who were putting down the demonstration [earlier] because it was going to harm McCarthy's chances were out there in the streets throwing rocks." When the senator's young organizers were roughly rousted from their hotel suites by police early Friday morning, their anger deepened. "Well, from now on it's the Battle of Algiers," one declared.[175]

On Friday afternoon, Doug Dowd parked his tender, exhausted carcass on a train back to New York. "I had flown out there," he remembered. "I went back on a goddamn train deliberately. I just couldn't bear getting on a fucking airplane. . . . I needed some time." It was quite a journey. "It looked like an ambulance train," Dowd laughed. "There were people with things around their heads." He still can't recall how long it took to get home: "I was sitting there in a *fucking daze.*"[176]

Convention week was almost as upsetting to officials in the Johnson administration. As Under Secretary of the Army David McGiffert wrote Clark Clifford on August 20, they knew there was a "potential for serious disorder" in Chicago. And no one doubted a few heads would roll—least of all Paul Nitze. "Are you somebody to complain?" Nitze retorted to his Columbia SDS friend when queried after the convention what he thought of Daley's act. "You laid out the entire strategy for me before you went there. You organized all of this. And now you blame all the fracas and . . . casualties . . . on Mayor Daley? You *plotted* to have these things done." Ramsey Clark had expected "problems" in Chicago given Daley's "extremely headstrong" character.[177]

But nobody foresaw the sheer ugliness of events. "It surprised the devil out of me what happened in Chicago," George Christian remembered. "I don't think anybody could have anticipated that mess. . . . I think it was just plain shocking to most everybody that I knew that something like that could have happened." "What the heck's going on here?" Christian said officials were asking themselves. "What's the game?" They couldn't understand why anyone would want to "disrupt the process." The convention turbulence, King's and Kennedy's murders, and black unrest suggested to Walt Rostow that the nation was "about to become unhinged."[178]

The tumult disturbed the administration on two main counts. First, Democrats' chances at the polls in November might suffer. Officials despaired that a party seemingly so riddled with conflict would appear incapable of effective leadership. Humphrey's presidential bid might be injured. "I was sick about it,"

Rostow recalled. Second, Chicago bode poorly for the war. Johnson, Rusk, Rostow, and other officials intent on hanging on in Vietnam feared that the violence in the streets—stark evidence that the war was breeding domestic chaos—would hasten public demands for U.S. withdrawal. It would thereby weaken the U.S. negotiating posture as well. In fact, Johnson seemed more concerned with winning the war than with his vice president's fortunes. Prescribed by one of his staffers, the pro-administration Vietnam plank accepted at the convention rejected calls for a full halt to the bombing of North Vietnam, although Johnson surely knew this would take votes out of Humphrey's pockets.[179]

Officials lashed out at the media. Television coverage of the protests had not only wooed demonstrators' violence, they groused, but exaggerated the police's dirty work. "A lot of us," said Christian, felt "the way that at least two of the networks handled the situation exacerbated the public's perception of what was going on." Rostow sputtered, "I knew that this was a put-up job between the TV people and the demonstrators. It was all mounted. . . . Just the way the Buddhist thing was mounted in Hue. . . . They made sure the cameras were there when these guys set fire to themselves." The media had made Humphrey out to be some sort of *bad guy*, for Christ's sake. "I think the thing that really annoyed me and I think a lot of other people at the time was the impression that Humphrey and everybody around Humphrey were the villains of peace," Christian remembered. "The impression was that the McCarthy people were the heroes and the Humphrey people were the villains." Reporters had portrayed the vice president and the rest of "the whole Establishment bunch" at the convention as "trying to beat everybody in the head," Christian perceived. But "Hubert Humphrey had no more to do with that than I did." Humphrey's media battering "was not something any of us enjoyed at the time," Christian recalled.[180]

As the Democratic convention was getting under way, Johnson was pondering another threat. Peace activists were stepping up their organizing within the U.S. military. Vietnam veterans close to VVAW in Chicago were churning out an antiwar newspaper called *Vietnam GI*; soldiers in the United States were its main recipients, but some copies were being sent over to Vietnam. Other subversive GI sheets were also popping up at military installations. Disloyal soldiers were organizing the American Servicemen's Union; one of its demands was the right of GIs to refuse illegal orders. Peace activists were setting up antiwar coffeehouses near military training bases; there, GIs were free to exchange ideas about the war and the military unmuzzled by their superiors. The Mobe was organizing a stimulative "Summer of Support" project to spread and fortify the coffeehouse movement. Many activists were promoting soldier desertions.[181]

Thus nourished, GI protest was growing. In February, thirty-five soldiers at

Fort Jackson, South Carolina (site of the first coffeehouse), held a silent vigil against the war. Forty servicemen marched at the head of a San Francisco peace demonstration in April. In July, two hundred GIs from Fort Hood, Texas (home of another coffeehouse), attended a "Love-in."[182]

Over lunch on August 20, Johnson discussed the peace movement's creeping infection of the military with new U.S. Army Chief of Staff William Westmoreland (who had been replaced as commander of U.S. troops in Vietnam and kicked upstairs). Five days later, Westmoreland sent the president a SECRET memo providing additional information on the coffeehouse virus and his assessment of its strength. The general was not happy. "I was pretty much shocked by some of the things that I saw and I was very sensitive to the trends," he recalled. Westmoreland told Johnson that he was "deeply concerned" about the spread of coffeehouses and

> related matters potentially affecting discipline such as outside-
> encouraged desertion to foreign countries, the concept of a soldier
> union, increased drug abuse, and other possible disciplinary vulner-
> abilities that may be exploited by those dedicated to doing so. All
> agencies responsible for action, however, have independently con-
> cluded that suppressive action is not yet warranted. The consensus
> is that coffeehouses are not yet effectively interfering with signifi-
> cant military interests and, consequently, suppressive action may be
> counter-productive.

Westmoreland also informed Johnson that he had assembled an Army task force to "analyze continuously all available information" on the coffeehouse movement and to "maintain close and coordinated surveillance of all aspects of antiwar-motivated actions adverse to Army morale and discipline. We intend by this means to detect any outside-induced problems sufficiently in advance to prevent any real damage to military effectiveness."[183]

Official tolerance quickly flagged. As Westmoreland reported to Johnson on September 9, authorities arrested numerous frequenters of the coffeehouse at Fort Hood on drug charges. Its manager, who, as Westmoreland had earlier conveyed, had agitated among soldiers mobilized for the Democratic convention, was jailed with a $50,000 bond on his head. Another leading GI organizer was arrested for possession of such a puny amount of marijuana that it vanished during laboratory analysis. He was found guilty and sentenced to . . . eight years at hard labor.[184]

Westmoreland was also concerned about the black liberation movement's infection of the military at this time. Black GIs were asking why they should fight "a white man's war"; some had occupied the Fort Bragg stockade; others had announced they would disobey orders to quash the Chicago protests. In Vietnam, racial disturbances were becoming "a serious and explosive problem" (as

U.S. military commanders apprised the Pentagon). In the late summer or fall, Westmoreland directed one of his most trusted officers to conduct a covert A-to-Z investigation of "the status and attitudes of the blacks." The officer "was black as the ace of spades, but his name was White," the general recalled. White "came back with a very hard-hitting report. . . . The racial problems were very real."[185]

Licking Wounds

After the Democratic convention, the National Mobe went into a protracted slump. The liberal and moderate antiwar forces that were its primary political base had been turned off by the street-fighting there and were wary of joining future demonstrations. Chicago "scared the shit out of an awful lot of people," Doug Dowd remembered. "And an awful lot of people withdrew from active participation" in the movement.[186]

But the expanding corps of radical militants judged the convention protests a resounding success. They'd shown the government and public that continuing fighting in Vietnam carried a very high domestic price indeed. Chicago "went right across the country and across the world and said, 'There's a civil war going on in America—right now!'" Abbie Hoffman recalled. They'd exposed the true nature of the beast. "Our presence in Chicago caused the guilt-ridden Johnson-Humphrey-Daley administration to bring out into the open the forces of intimidation and political suppression which are used far more brutally and regularly in the ghetto and in Vietnam," wrote Dave Dellinger in September. They'd held a mirror up to the beast for additional clarity. "When you see Mayor Daley with triple chins and all his cohort looking that way and actually talking with a kind of grunt," Hoffman commented, and you notice the cops are "all beefy as hell, too," then you *know* that running a pig for president is "right on track, symbolically." A shocked public had felt their pain and applauded their guts. "It was a clear-cut victory because the police acted abominably and our people showed courage, aggressiveness and a proper sense of values," argued Dellinger. Doing battle in the streets had been invigorating as always, and their casualties were limited, when you stopped and thought about it. "It's amazing that so *little* blood was shed," Hoffman contended. They certainly couldn't be held responsible for the cops' nastiness. "Being accused of inciting a police riot makes no sense at all to me," Hoffman snapped. "A good police force cannot be incited to riot. It's just that simple." And they'd done that miserable Humphrey in, taught him a lesson or two about the politics of mass murder in Vietnam.[187]

But the public was unimpressed. Opinion polls showed most Americans supported the police's storm-trooper tactics in Chicago; nearly 40 percent of whites who advocated U.S. withdrawal from Vietnam felt Daley's cops had used insufficient force (blacks showed less taste for blood). Americans hated antiwar protesters more than ever before. They were the most despised political group in the country. The independent presidential candidate George Wallace, who had bragged that "if any demonstrator lies down in front of my car . . . that'll be the last car he lays down in front of," was running a strong third in the race.[188]

On the campuses and in the streets, battle lines were being drawn. A few hard feelings were inevitable and a sign of their strength, sniffed the actionists. For many, Chicago's radical lessons were so overwhelming that the bad tidings scarcely registered. Linda Morse found the convention a forceful educational experience. She had hoped that dual pressure of street demonstrations and liberal challenges inside the Amphitheatre would compel meaningful changes in the Democrats' war policies. She had been sorely deceived. Like most other convention protesters, Morse had also been sobered by "the really naked, brutal police power that was put out against us. . . . It was at that point the worst that I had been trapped in before. . . . I think at that point I gave up on pacifism," she recalled. After the convention, Morse began organizing M-1 target practice for movement rifle squads and took up karate.[189]

Bruce Dancis was also a close student of Chicago. "By late 1968 I felt I could no longer call myself a pacifist," Dancis remembered. "It no longer worked for me." That winter Dancis helped organize an action against corporate recruiters at Cornell. Rather than employing "the old way" of protesting unwanted recruiters (i.e., peaceful picketing), he and five hundred others "just busted past the campus guards and threw them off campus," Dancis recalled. "We had moved to the point where we were going to take active actions and we didn't care whether they were nonviolent or not." Among the expellers was Huey Lewis, later a rock star.[190]

For SDS leaders, Chicago demonstrated conclusively that revolution was the only option for those serious about changing America. It showed that substantial numbers of young people were ready to kick some ass and brook a few shots for the revolutionary cause. And with SDS flourishing, it proved that bold action was a nifty organizing tool. Over the fall, actionists in SDS chapters hawked militant programs with growing obstinacy. At the University of Michigan, when older SDSers argued for patient educational work and announced they had formed the "Radical Caucus," sparks flew. "It was a group we couldn't relate to at all," Bill Ayers remembered. They were "very, very staid and very, very intellectual in their approach to politics" and promoting "polite, university give-and-take" forms of protest. During the chapter's first autumn meeting, one actionist denounced a critic's appeal for broad outreach as "one long stream of bullshit." The chapter should be pushing "aggressive confrontation politics," he and his comrades harangued, not catering to "backward" students. "What we wanted to do was to shake it up," Ayers said. Finding it "ludicrous" that measly "democratic socialists" would call themselves the Radical Caucus, the actionists made a hasty stab at one-upmanship. "Fine," they blustered. "We're the Jesse James Gang."[191]

Militant SDSers put forward two dominant reasons why bold action was a potent organizing tool. The first was standard movement fare: it incurred personal risk and thus woke observers up. But the other was a new contribution to political theory. According to the actionists, militance would make the revolution by *breeding confidence*. Audacious political deeds would alleviate widespread, crippling feelings of powerlessness in the United States. "In 1968 and 1969, when we were considered real crazy about all this stuff," Ayers recalled, "we said, 'Look, you see that map of the U.S.? That's not . . . etched in stone forever. That's a map that's socially constructed and it can be socially deconstructed.' . . . We wanted to kind of expand people's sense of what was possible."[192] It was with this strategy that Weatherman would be off and running inside a year.

How confident were the confidence-builders? "When I was involved in Chicago in 1968, when Johnson resigned, when we played the role we played in the defeat of Humphrey . . . I saw the potential for tremendous power growing," Ayers remembered. "And that was heady stuff. It was exciting. It was scary. I thought that a revolution was possible . . . [and] that we were going to participate in it in a very active and full way. . . . So I think we had a sense of its immediacy." Ayers felt the U.S. government could fall "right now." The New York actionist Jeff Jones said he fully expected revolution "within a decade."[193]

Many years later, Ayers and Jones were both cautiously critical of their revolutionary zeal. A doctoral student in education at Columbia University's Teacher College and husband of Bernardine Dohrn, the still militant Ayers offered: "We talked a lot about revolution—we knew very little about it. . . . We made lots of mistakes. We were not particularly erudite. We were not particularly educated in political philosophy or ideology, and yet it seemed to all of us that we'd better catch up. . . . So we all read wildly and discussed things that were sometimes certainly beyond our experience and sometimes over our head." He and his largely youthful comrades were "very ill-equipped for political leadership and very ill-equipped for politics at all," he acknowledged. "So a lot of what was said was stupid, I'm sure." The name Jesse James Gang, he conceded, sounds "silly and childish, or kind of like madness, kind of crazy." Jones, a reporter for a radical newsweekly in New York, granted: "The estimation that we made, as teenagers and young people in our early twenties, about how soon the revolution would come proved to be quite fantastic. . . . Now I think I have a much more realistic assessment of what it will take."[194]

In October, armed with the knowledge that the collapse of America's political "'center'" was "irreversible" and that its duty was to "build the left 'pole,'" SDS called for militant protests against November's "fraudulent" presidential election. Its demands included "the right of black people to defend and liberate themselves by any means necessary" and disarmament of the police. Trumpeting the slogan "No class today, no ruling class tomorrow!" SDS directed high school students to march out of their academic "jails" and college students to strangle the campuses.[195]

The protests were an utter flop. The revolution would have to wait.

Over the autumn, Humphrey choked slowly on Johnson's leash. Whenever he summoned the courage to put some distance between himself and the administration's war policies, his master snapped his neck rudely back. Humphrey had intended to announce in a September speech in Philadelphia "that there would be some troop withdrawals," remembered Melvin Laird, then a U.S. congressman. "Paul Warnke had the plan worked out. . . . And it just drove Johnson right up the wall. He called Humphrey and said he had to decide whether he wanted his support or not." When Humphrey merely suggested to questioners in Philadelphia that the United States *might* be able to bring some troops home in early 1969 (or even late 1968), the president, who was increasingly moody and irritable, immediately proclaimed that "no man can predict" when troops would be withdrawn. And when Laird revealed the plan for troop reductions to reporters, Johnson ordered Clark Clifford to go on the next *Meet the Press* and deny that the Pentagon intended "to withdraw one person from Vietnam." The public discerned little difference between Humphrey's vague burblings on the war and those of the Republican candidate, Richard Nixon.[196]

Antiwar protesters showed the vice president no mercy. He was stalked everywhere. Despite the repellent alternatives of Nixon and Wallace, most deemed voting for him far beyond the pale. Some would later come to consider their rejection of Humphrey rash. "I think that the Cambodians paid a very high price for our taking that position," AFSCer John McAuliff argued. Humphrey, he believed, would not have invaded Cambodia as Nixon did. Warnke agreed— and more. Since Humphrey had planned to appoint Clifford secretary of state and Cyrus Vance secretary of defense, and Clifford had asked him if he would serve as deputy secretary of state, Warnke asserted, a Humphrey administration would have ended the war in short order. How short? "I think during 1969."[197]

Humphrey lost to Nixon by a narrow margin. His failure to break clearly with Johnson on Vietnam was one reason. Nixon's superior manipulation of the ubiquitous "law-and-order" issue in a country hungry for domestic peace was another. So was Nixon's claim that he had a "secret plan" to end the war. Melvin Laird, Nixon's secretary of defense, later huffed and puffed at Nixon's assertion. "I don't care what anybody else told you," Laird growled, wagging a fat finger in the air. "He had no plan. *I* developed the plan."[198]

The national antiwar demonstration in Washington sponsored by SDS, April 17, 1965. (SHSW)

Donna Allen, a WSP activist. (Courtesy Donna Allen)

Norma Becker (left), leader of the New York Fifth Avenue Peace Parade Committee, before the first International Days of Protest march in New York, October 16, 1965. Her daughter, Diane, is in the middle. (Courtesy Norma Becker)

Richard Fernandez, leader of CALCAV. (Records of CALC, Swarthmore College Peace Collection)

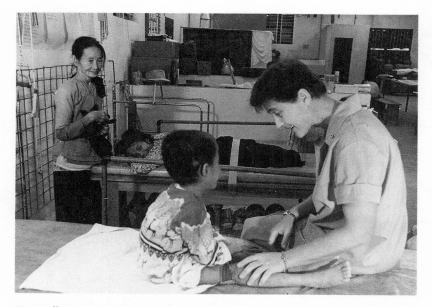

Dot Weller trying to cheer up an injured eight-year-old Vietnamese boy in the AFSC's rehabilitation center in Quang Ngai, South Vietnam. The boy is paralyzed below the waist. Behind them are the boy's grandmother (left) and mother, a twenty-five-year-old widow of four years who recently lost both legs to shrapnel. (Courtesy Dot Weller)

Craig McNamara, son of the secretary of defense, beekeeping in the early 1970s. (Courtesy Craig McNamara)

The CP student leader Bettina Aptheker, pregnant with her first child, speaking at a rally in 1967. (Courtesy Bettina Aptheker)

Spring Mobilization demonstrators in Sheep Meadow, Central Park, New York City, April 15, 1967. (Records of *WIN* magazine, Swarthmore College Peace Collection, Diana Davies)

Another draft record stoking the flaming coffee can in Sheep Meadow, Central Park, New York City, April 15, 1967. (Diana Davies Collection, Swarthmore College Peace Collection, Diana Davies)

General William Westmoreland (left) in the cabinet room briefing officials on the progress of the war, April 27, 1967. Across from Westmoreland are (from left) Nicholas Katzenbach, Dean Rusk, Lyndon Johnson, Cyrus Vance, and General Earl Wheeler. (LBJL, Frank Wolfe)

The draft resister David Harris.
(Courtesy David Harris)

A weekly luncheon meeting of the Johnson administration, October 11, 1967. With Johnson are (clockwise) Robert McNamara, George Christian, Walt Rostow, Tom Johnson, Richard Helms, and Dean Rusk. (LBJL, Yoichi R. Okamato)

A deeply troubled
Robert McNamara,
late 1967. (LBJL,
Frank Wolfe)

Oakland Stop the Draft Week protesters blockading a street, October 1967. (Jeffrey
Blankfort)

The antiwar leader Dave Dellinger speaking at a rally in Hawaii. (Courtesy Dave Dellinger)

Military police confronting demonstrators at the Pentagon, October 21, 1967. (Records of *WIN* magazine, Swarthmore College Peace Collection, Diana Davies)

Robert McNamara watching demonstrators from his Pentagon window, October 21, 1967. (UPI/Bettmann)

Attorney General Ramsey Clark conferring with Johnson. (LBJL, Yoichi R. Okamoto)

The draft resister Michael Ferber. (Courtesy Michael Ferber)

Deputy Defense Secretary Paul Nitze. (LBJL, Yoichi R. Okamoto)

Secretary of Defense Clark Clifford getting some points across to Johnson. (LBJL, Yoichi R. Okamoto)

The Wise Men meeting with Johnson, March 26, 1968. The Wise Men were "shaken by the opposition in this country," Richard Helms later recalled. (LBJL, Yoichi R. Okamoto)

A worried Lyndon Johnson the day after the Wise Men meeting. With him is Vice President Hubert Humphrey (left). (LBJL, Yoichi R. Okamoto)

Soldiers wearing gas masks sealing off a bridge in Chicago during protests at the Democratic convention, August 1968. (Brad Lyttle)

Chicago, August 1968. (Records of *WIN* magazine, Swarthmore College Peace Collection)

A medic treating a bloodied protester in Grant Park, Chicago, August 1968. (Brad Lyttle)

The Johnson cabinet debating the causes of student protest, September 18, 1968. "I just don't believe this business that there is no [communist] support," Johnson declared. (LBJL, Yoichi R. Okamoto)

Richard Milhous Nixon. (NP)

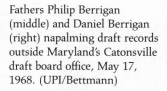

Fathers Philip Berrigan (middle) and Daniel Berrigan (right) napalming draft records outside Maryland's Catonsville draft board office, May 17, 1968. (UPI/Bettmann)

Henry Kissinger, John Ehrlichman, Richard Nixon, and H. R. Haldeman in the Oval Office. (NP)

Assistant Secretary of State Marshall Green, 1979. (Courtesy Marshall Green)

Weathermen readying themselves for battle with the cops during the Days of Rage, Lincoln Park, Chicago, October 1969. (Henry Wilhelm)

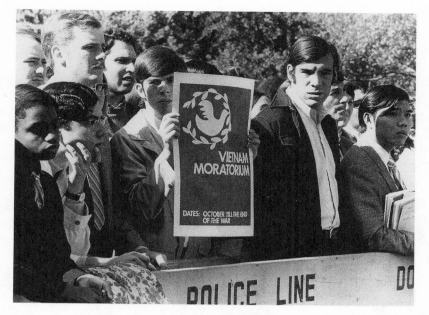

Vietnam Moratorium protesters in Washington Square, New York City, October 15, 1969. (Records of *WIN* magazine, Swarthmore College Peace Collection, Diana Davies)

Nixon and Haldeman consulting behind stacks of congratulatory telegrams after the president's "silent majority" speech, November 1969. (NP)

Mark Rudd (left, wearing a fake moustache) and other Weatherleaders getting dragged off by police during the Days of Rage, October 1969. The man in right front clenching a female Weatherleader is a Chicago city official who minutes later dove to tackle a demonstrator and smashed into a wall instead, leaving him paralyzed from the neck down. (Henry Wilhelm)

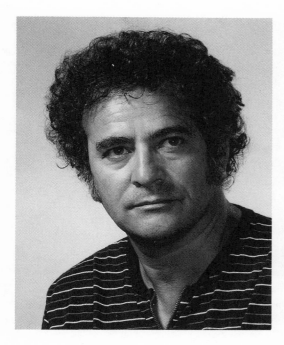

The antiwar leader Sidney
Peck. (Courtesy Sidney Peck)

Nixon announcing the invasion of Cambodia, April 30, 1970. (NP)

Nixon and Melvin Laird facing reporters and Pentagon employees in a Pentagon hallway the morning after announcing the invasion. "You see these bums, you know, blowing up the campuses . . . burning up the books," Nixon remarked. Behind Nixon is Henry Kissinger. (NP)

Kent State University, May 4, 1970. In foreground are remains of the burned-down ROTC building. During a campus demonstration, National Guardsmen shot and killed four people on the other side of the building at upper left. (AP/Wide World Photos)

Nixon meeting with Kent State students in the Oval Office, May 6, 1970. At far right are Ronald Ziegler and John Ehrlichman. (NP)

Nixon trying to engage demonstrators in conversation at the Lincoln Memorial around 5 A.M., May 9, 1970. "I hope it was because he was tired, but most of what he was saying was absurd," one protester commented. (UPI/Bettmann)

Demonstrators gathering on the Ellipse, May 9, 1970. At center are Bella Abzug (wearing a hat, as always) and Dr. Benjamin Spock. Behind the crowd are buses safeguarding the White House. (NP)

May 9, 1970, on the Ellipse: "A picnic in the park." In foreground are Senators Jacob Javits (R-N.Y., in white shirt and tie) and Edward Brooke (R-Mass., in suit). (NP)

Weatherleader Jeff Jones's FBI wanted poster. There was "a lot of frustration" in the Nixon administration over the Weathermen's ability to elude the FBI and the police, John Ehrlichman recalled. (Courtesy Jeff Jones)

Nixon administration officials (from left) Alexander Haig, Henry Kissinger, and Admiral Thomas Moorer. Flanking Nixon at right are William Rogers and Melvin Laird. (NP)

Daniel Ellsberg (center) surfacing from underground for his arraignment for leaking the Pentagon Papers, Boston, June 30, 1971. His wife Patricia is beside him. (Courtesy Daniel Ellsberg, Cary Wolinsky)

White House Counsel John Dean. (NP)

SIX

1969: Part I

The Madman and the Taps

When I interviewed him, Melvin "Bom" Laird held a comfortable *Reader's Digest* sinecure. His plush Washington office functioned more as the headquarters of "Melvin Laird, sage statesman" than of "Melvin Laird, Senior Counsellor, Reader's Digest Association" (his official title). Between puffs on a cigar, he casually let it be known that his next caller was a high-level Defense Department official in the Reagan administration interested in receiving words of wisdom from an old Pentagon pro. Laird was a cunning man with a massive bald dome, plump face, small piercing brown eyes, and a roguish smile; his eyebrows slanted upward. He frequently finished his sentences with the words "as you know." Although Laird was "not as dumb as he appeared . . . certainly it was not Laird's style to engage in serious, substantive exchange," one senior Nixon administration official recalled. Henry Kissinger, Nixon's national security adviser, "used to joke about Laird's horrible syntax." Nixon "certainly didn't have a high regard for his intellect" either.[1]

The "plan" Secretary of Defense Laird devised for ending the Vietnam War was twofold: to steadily and unilaterally draw U.S. troop strength in Vietnam down to a residual contingent of around two hundred and sixty thousand men and to beef up ARVN. He dubbed his plan "Vietnamization." Laird's overriding motivation was political. He was "acutely" conscious of the American people's distaste for the war. "They were fed up with Vietnam," he recalled. A 16-year veteran of Congress who maintained close contact with his many friends and acquaintances on Capitol Hill, Laird was keenly aware, too, of congressional discontent with the war, which he considered a clear sign of broader dissatisfaction. "The Congress is a *reflection* of our country," Laird practically shouted. "Public opinion is reflected in the Congress faster than any other place." Secretary Laird feared Congress would abruptly terminate funding of the war and force an unconditional U.S. withdrawal if American ground combat troops were not sent home. He also had his eye on antiwar protesters. He hoped Vietnamization would shut them up and buy time to marshal public support for a protracted U.S. air and naval presence in Vietnam. Laird worried that the protesters would really get out of hand if U.S. troops were not withdrawn. During an interview in August 1969, "he repeatedly expressed concern over 'what we're going to have on the campuses this fall.'" That Vietnamization would help Laird realize his ambition of election to the U.S. Senate after leaving the administration had no small impact on his thinking. "He is a consummate politician," Lawrence Eagleburger said, not disapprovingly.[2]

Laird had other reasons for reducing U.S. involvement in Vietnam. As guardian of the nation's military, he was bothered that the war was usurping resources needed to maintain and improve U.S. military capabilities elsewhere, particularly in Europe. "We were draining our assets. It was like a rathole," he said. Laird was also troubled about Vietnam's impact on the economy and on the reputation of the U.S. military both at home and overseas.[3]

Laird's views were not shared by many other senior Nixon administration officials. Nixon himself entered office favoring the withdrawal of *some* U.S. troops. He hoped a force reduction would stimulate serious negotiations with Hanoi. More important, it might "calm domestic public opinion." But Nixon was averse to unilateral U.S. withdrawals. Both in public and in private, he asserted that American troops would only leave South Vietnam if North Vietnamese troops did too. And he opposed steady troop reductions. Nixon realized Laird was pushing Vietnamization partly for personal political gain, and was infuriated by the secretary of defense's incessant use of press leaks to push the program forward. Roger Morris, then a senior National Security Council (NSC) staffer, recalled reading a series of White House memos recording Nixon's reactions to articles in the morning papers: "'I see this goddamn, cock-sucking story about troop levels. This is Laird again. The son-of-a-bitch up to his old games. What's he trying to do?' Next page. 'Henry, what is this goddamn, cock-sucking story by [*New York Times* reporter William] Beecher? Is this Laird? It must be Laird. It's Laird, isn't it?'" Yet despite his rejection of unconditional U.S. deescalation, Nixon believed that if the United States could significantly weaken the enemy in South Vietnam and modernize ARVN, unilaterally pulling out some troops would be "a public relations coup."[4]

Henry Kissinger strongly opposed Vietnamization, feeling it would seriously weaken the administration's bargaining position vis-à-vis Hanoi. He, too, seethed about Laird's machinations. "For a long time I thought Laird's last name was crook," one Kissinger aide remembered. "'Mel Laird's a crook,' Henry would always say."[5]

Secretary of State William Rogers argued in January for withdrawing fifty thousand U.S. troops from Vietnam. He felt that would "buy an indefinite amount of time at home" for developing a viable Vietnam strategy. His counsel reflected one of his basic roles in the administration: advising on public opinion. "He was very interested in public opinion, and he knew what influenced public opinion," Assistant Secretary of State for East Asian and Pacific Affairs Marshall Green said. Rogers ultimately had little impact on actual policies in Vietnam, however. For Kissinger and Nixon had concentrated the power to make foreign policy in the White House. "They didn't trust us," Green bitterly recalled. "Kissinger and the president wanted to do their high-wire act unimpeded by us earthlings. . . . We were continually, by one device or another, cut out of involvement in decision making. . . . Often times I felt like getting out. And sometimes my thoughts were on the suicidal side. And they were with a lot of us." Undermining Rogers was, in fact, one of Kissinger's primary preoccupations. He slanderously told his aides that Rogers was a "fag" who kept a Georgetown house with a young male lover in it. He also suggested that the secretary of state and Nixon had "indulged" in the past. Kissinger repeatedly threatened to resign if the "incompetent" Rogers did not go. (Laurence Lynn, then a senior NSC staffer, remembered that Rogers was "really not substantively up to the role of secretary of state" and incapable of "carrying on sustained substantive discussion of complicated policy.")[6]

Although unenthusiastic about Vietnamization, Nixon and Kissinger did believe that the war had to be ended—one way or another. The public's patience with the conflict was obviously wearing thin. "We knew that it was not a popular war," White House Chief of Staff H. R. Haldeman recalled. "I mean, Johnson [had] made that very clear." Officials also recognized that the war inhibited progress on the administration's domestic agenda. And Nixon and Kissinger considered Vietnam a vexatious impediment to superpower diplomacy. "The war was an Achilles' heel," Morris said. The USSR and China were "much bigger fish to fry."[7]

The president and Kissinger decided early on against going for a quick kill. Attempting "knockout blows" by bombing North Vietnam's dikes or using tactical nuclear weapons would have triggered a "domestic and international uproar that . . . would have got my administration off to the worst possible start," Nixon writes. Resuming Rolling Thunder, mining Haiphong harbor, and invading North Vietnam, Laos, or Cambodia would also have incited angry protests. "I doubted whether I could have held the country together for the period of time needed to win," Nixon records. The president knew that "if he made a warlike move . . . antiwar protesters would explode in riots," Haldeman recalled. Officials were also concerned that going for broke would damage U.S. relations with China and the Soviet Union. It might prove ineffectual as well.[8]

The strategy Nixon opted for involved *threatening* the North Vietnamese with major escalation, offering them substantial financial aid, and warning the

USSR that relations depended upon progress toward a peace settlement. The threat was central to Nixon's thinking. Walking along a foggy beach during the 1968 campaign, he had told Haldeman that he would end the war within a year. "I'm the one man in this country who can do it, Bob," he said. His long record of fierce anticommunism was the reason. "They'll believe any threat of force that Nixon makes because it's Nixon," Nixon asserted.

> I call it the Madman Theory, Bob. I want the North Vietnamese to believe I've reached the point where I might do *anything* to stop the war. We'll just slip the word to them that, "for God's sake, you know Nixon is obsessed about Communism. We can't restrain him when he's angry—and he has his hand on the nuclear button"—and Ho Chi Minh himself will be in Paris in two days begging for peace.[9]

Nixon understood he had to relay his threat to Hanoi secretly. Otherwise, he would rouse the peace movement. To convey its willingness to strike hard, the administration began clandestinely bombing the neutral country of Cambodia with B-52 aircraft in March. Both Laird and Rogers were restive about the policy. They argued that it would be impossible to keep the strikes secret and warned of domestic tumult. "I was an advocate of the Cambodia bombing," Laird remembered. "I wanted to make it public. I didn't want it secret. And I refused to sign the secret order. . . . I had a big fight over there in the National Security Council with the president [over it]." Few senior officials were told of the strikes. Kissinger was nervous about being found out. One day Senator John Stennis was briefed on the bombing in the White House Situation Room. After the briefing was over, Kissinger and his aide William Watts discovered to their horror that a highly sensitive memo used during the session was nowhere to be found. "Henry was absolutely bonkers as to what happened," Watts remembered. "We went back and found it in the room, but we were afraid Stennis had taken it off with him."[10]

The first raid on Cambodia bore the macabre code name "Operation Breakfast." It was less than successful. When a Special Forces "Daniel Boone" team helicoptered into the target area immediately afterward to gather any enemy survivors, there was "instant carnage." Rather than annihilating the Vietnamese as expected, the bombing had the same effect as "taking a beehive the size of a basketball and poking it with a stick," one Green Beret recalled. "They were mad." Few of the mop-up men survived. When another Daniel Boone team was ordered to go in and pick up "dazed" enemy troops the same morning, its response was simple: "Fuck you."[11]

Over the next fourteen months, 3,630 B-52 raids were carried out along the Cambodian border. "We were dropping a hell of a lot of bombs," Chief of U.S. Naval Operations Thomas Moorer airily recalled. "Breakfast" was followed by

"Lunch," "Snack," "Dinner," "Dessert," and "Supper." The entire operation was dubbed "Menu."[12] It was concealed from the public and Congress for more than four years. In its impeachment inquiry in 1974, the House Judiciary Committee weighed the bombing as an article in the mooted impeachment of President Nixon.

On May 9, the *Times's* William Beecher reported that the United States had undertaken several bombing raids in Cambodia. The story attracted almost no public attention, but "it got a lot of attention over in the White House," as Laird wryly remembered. In the words of the NSC staffer Morton Halperin, Kissinger and Nixon "went berserk." That morning Kissinger asked J. Edgar Hoover to make "a major effort" to ascertain the source of Beecher's report. He vowed they would "destroy whoever did this." Hoover said Halperin was the most likely culprit, but Kissinger had his own suspect. Kissinger and Nixon had Laird paged off a golf course that afternoon "to bitterly accuse him—'you son-of-a-bitch'—of leaking the story." "It was a hell of a go-round," Laird said. "They were furious."[13]

And not only over Beecher's story. For it was only the latest in a series of troubling leaks in the press on the administration's foreign policies. Indeed, Kissinger and Nixon had been stewing over leaks since assuming office. "There was an enormous amount of distrust," Marshall Green remembered. "The way Henry would run his meetings with the NSC [is] they would always start out with Henry saying that the president was furious with the latest leak. He left a clear impression that somebody at that table had created the leak, or a member of his staff. And in that atmosphere of mutual suspicion we would then proceed . . ." (Many years later, while lunching at Washington's Metropolitan Club, a favorite gathering spot of officialdom, Green suddenly raised his right hand and exclaimed, "I never leaked . . . *once* all the time I was assistant secretary of state. God, Witness of God, I *never* leaked.")[14]

Beecher's story prompted the White House to begin wiretapping suspected leakers. The home telephones of Halperin, two other NSC staffers, and Laird's military aide, Col. Robert Pursley, were bugged within seventy-two hours. Over the next eighteen months, the White House ordered taps placed on four more Kissinger aides, three other White House staffers, two senior State Department officials, and five journalists.

Although Nixon and Kissinger subsequently claimed the wiretaps were necessary for "national security" reasons, their motivations were hardly so noble. The White House was paranoid about internal enemies and rife with personal intrigue. By bugging Pursley, Kissinger and Nixon could monitor Laird's plotting. Tapping the State Department officials allowed Kissinger to gain information on his arch-rival William Rogers. By bugging his aides, Kissinger could learn what they thought of him and prove his loyalty and "toughness" to

Nixon, Hoover, and Haldeman, all of whom suspected his NSC staff was in-fested with (as Laurence Lynn put it) "pinko-weenies." That four of the first six NSC staffers tapped were Jewish led the writer Seymour Hersh to another conclusion: Kissinger was playing to Nixon's rabid anti-Semitism and demon-strating that his Jewish background was not tainting his policies. "Nixon would talk about Jewish traitors, and the Eastern Jewish Establishment—Jews at Har-vard," White House Counsel John Ehrlichman recalled.[15]

The wiretaps on reporters had no more noble motivations. The White House hoped mainly to check on officials' allegiances. Kissinger was aware that his loyalty was doubted and concluded that his own phone was bugged. "Time and again," Haldeman writes, "he would pass me in the hall and say, 'What do your taps tell you about me today, Haldeman?'"[16]

To the White House's disappointment, the wiretaps produced little useful information: "just gobs and gobs of . . . gossip and bullshitting," Nixon later said.[17] They constituted the first of the series of abuses of governmental power now known as Watergate.

Down but Not Out

As Nixon was assuming his madman persona, the antiwar movement was mired in a slump. The Democratic Convention protests had cost the National Mobe considerable support. The SWP-controlled Student Mobe was widely scorned and "only a shadow of its former self"; attendance at a national "GI–Civilian" antiwar conference it sponsored in December was dismal. Many protesters continued to believe the war was on its way out and considered peace activity less than pressing. Others were disheartened by the continuing fighting in Vietnam; they, too, questioned the point of more protest. Nixon's election discouraged many. "We felt that that was really bad, that obviously Nixon did not have a secret plan to end the war," Bruce Dancis remembered. "The hope-lessness of having to acknowledge to ourselves that Nixon is really the same old tricky Dick was enervating," wrote the WSP leader Barbara Bick, who called the 1968–69 winter "one of the most depressed periods of our work."[18]

At a Mobe meeting in December, Dave Dellinger and Rennie Davis proposed a series of "counterinaugural" protests around Nixon's January 20 inauguration. The session was "stormy." Many participants opposed the countercultural tone of Dellinger and Davis's plans and feared a low turnout. More than a few saw another Chicago in the works. Sidney Peck felt "there was no way that we were going to get people out to it, and to just go there to disrupt the inaugural didn't make any political sense." The Mobe decided to organize a "political confron-tation." Planning proceeded slowly and in "an atmosphere of distrust." "Many people feel stalled by doubts," Dellinger observed on December 23.[19]

The counterinaugural increased the Mobe's political isolation. Only ten thou-sand demonstrated on January 19. Activists clashed over access to the microphone. While a disfigured Vietnam veteran was addressing the crowd, a group of protesters ranted, "Stop the bullshit and take to the streets. Stop the bullshit and *let's go!*" Their leader was a plainclothes policeman.[20]

The next day several thousand protesters gathered along the inaugural route. Government agents jammed the airwaves of their walkie-talkies. The protesters chanted antiwar slogans and waved signs; a few threw sticks, stones, and smoke bombs at the sealed presidential limousine as it edged slowly up Pennsylvania Avenue. Nixon was furious that the demonstrators had turned him and the first lady into "captives inside the car," unable to stand up and wave to spectators. He tersely ordered the Secret Service to have police arrest anyone seen violating the law. Eighty-seven were busted, although the SS concluded afterward that Nixon's order had not precipitated the arrests. Four days later, the president questioned giving permits to demonstrators in the future. "They seem to aggravate the situation by making it lawful and easier to congregate," he jotted in the margin of one memo. Nixon's anger at the counterinaugural protesters would linger for months, nurturing a growing siege mentality.[21]

When the Mobe's steering committee met at Norma Becker's apartment in early February, the coalition was critically ill. Once again it had failed to mobilize large numbers for a protest, and its authority in the peace movement had declined further. The "highly developed factional cross-fire" in which the counterinaugural had taken place had demoralized many Mobe activists. An anonymous FBI letter ridiculing the protest exacerbated tensions inside the group. Few Mobe members were eager to organize another demonstration. Peck and others argued that a new coalition was needed to mobilize Americans on a massive scale. The group decided to suspend activity. "For all practical purposes the National Mobe had become inoperative," Peck wrote afterward. "It could not move."[22]

Yet other segments of the antiwar movement could and did move, providing the Nixon administration with ample evidence that the movement was by no means dead. Local organizers around the country continued to speak out door-to-door, on the street, in the press. SWPers and others organized for GI–Civilian actions in the spring. On February 3–5, a thousand members of Clergy and Laymen Concerned About Vietnam gathered in Washington to demonstrate and see their legislators. CALCAV leaders also met with Henry Kissinger in the White House. Richard Fernandez, a participant, recounted that Kissinger "couldn't deal with Rabbi [Abraham] Heschel in the room." The bearded Heschel, who "looks like Moses" and, "in a place like this, always talked as if he was reading off a tablet," asked Kissinger, a fellow refugee from Hitlerism, "Don't you think if we keep doing this, America will look more and more like Nazi Germany?" Kissinger was visibly flustered. "The air was just electric," Fernandez recalled. "And I don't know what Kissinger said to this day. I mean, he just didn't . . ." At another point in the discussion, after Kissinger complained that protest was impairing the health of the body politic, Rev. William Sloane Coffin remarked, "Well, our job is to call down justice like rolling waters, and yours is to figure out the irrigation ditches." "I gave him a big elbow," Fernandez remembered: "'Jesus Christ, that's the problem—we don't want them figuring out the irrigation ditches.'" But Coffin "thought that was quite clever. He still repeats it . . ." Two weeks after the meeting, CALCAV announced it was ending its moratorium on criticism of the new president.[23]

In March, Catholic protesters tossed files of the Dow Chemical Company out a fourth-floor window in Washington. They also poured human blood on Dow office furniture and equipment. CALCAV mailed a poster listing the number of American and Vietnamese soldiers killed in the war to sixty thousand people. More than a thousand WSPers, many dressed in black and wearing dark veils over their faces, picketed the White House. The picketing agitated Richard Nixon. The next day, he requested a report from White House Director of Communications Herb Klein or John Ehrlichman on WSP's apparently sinister nature. "Herb—Let's dig out the background on this outfit," Nixon wrote. "As you probably know, it's a front."[24]

On Easter weekend, roughly a hundred thousand people marched in a GI–Civilian demonstration in New York, despite another FBI poison-pen letter, which hindered the organizing of the march. Forty thousand paraded in San Francisco; thirty thousand in Chicago. Quakers held sit-ins at draft boards and committed other acts of civil disobedience in more than thirty cities. Some publicly read the names of American war dead. On Easter Sunday, four protesters were symbolically crucified on giant crosses in front of the White House. "As long as this war continues," they declared, "it is always Good Friday."[25]

On April 29, seven student leaders met with Kissinger and Ehrlichman in the White House Situation Room. The students were representing 253 campus editors and student body officers who had signed a public declaration refusing to enter the armed services as long as the war continued. Accompanying the students was David Hawk, a draft resister, National Student Association staff member, and the architect of the declaration. Sitting in his sweltering Manhattan apartment one hot spring day in 1986, his infant son squirming in his arms, Hawk remembered the meeting:

> It was clear from the way Kissinger was talking that Nixon was going
> to continue the war. . . . He wouldn't talk about the origins of the
> conflict, and whether or not we should have been involved—the fact
> is we *were* involved, our honor was at stake, our credibility was at
> stake. . . . And he was really saying, "Don't protest now, don't
> undercut . . . don't create the impression that the public is not behind
> the president in his search for an honorable end to the war." . . . It

went on for a long time, about two hours, and he was very professorial. I mean, he was acting like he was a honcho professor with a
group of graduate students. . . .

Ehrlichman was so unbelievably hard-line that he threw everybody for a loop. He didn't say anything while Kissinger was in the
room. . . . And then Kissinger left and . . . Ehrlichman turned on
the students and said, "If you guys think that you can break laws just
because you don't like them, you're going to force us to up the ante
to the point where we have to give out death sentences for traffic
violations." "Uuuuhhhh!!!???" . . . I mean, whoooaaa, that's pretty
hard line. . . .

The consensus was, easily, among the students—as everybody
was shaking their heads—"These guys are going to be worse than
the last bunch." Everybody after that just looked at each other, and
everybody knew, it was clear, that they weren't going to stop the
war—and they were going to be hard-line nasties.

"Pretty frightening," sighed one student of his hosts.[26]

Six days later, five Quakers met with Kissinger. They were among the hundreds conducting a vigil outside the White House that afternoon. As adherents
of the same religious faith Nixon once claimed to embrace, the Quakers had
tried to meet with the president, to no avail. "People finally got to see Kissinger," David Hartsough remembered. "And people felt it got nothing. They just
said, 'They're completely committed to continuing this war. . . . The "secret
plan" is to escalate the war.'"[27]

The next evening, religious protesters held another meeting with an adversary six hundred miles away. CALCAV activists were in Michigan to demonstrate at the annual Dow Chemical stockholders meeting. While preparing to
hold a press conference, they received a phone call from Dow's president, Gil
Doan, a "very good Episcopal lay person," who invited several of them over to
his luxurious home to discuss their concerns. Doan told his guests "that for the
last three months he'd been discussing this book in church called *Situational
Ethics,*" Richard Fernandez recalled. "And the problem with this stupid book is
it's all personal ethics: you know, should you sleep with fifty people at once,
and if so, what kind of contraceptives? But there's no corporate sense of responsibility." Doan said that "if we could prove to him that napalm was being used,
intentionally or not, primarily on a civilian population, he would do all he could
do to get the company out of the contract." Fernandez thought to himself,
"What's he want—to be on the ground when it's dropped?" At the stockholders'
meeting the next day, Dow's officials were "very, very subdued," Fernandez
said. "They weren't mad at us, they let us speak, etc. And the next year, they
had no contract." Reportedly, Dow purposely overbid on the napalm contract
because it had cost it quality student job applicants.[28]

In May protesters in Chicago and Pasadena, California, burned over twenty thousand Selective Service records. Quakers read the names of American war dead on the steps of the Capitol and were arrested, only to reappear on the steps again the next week. After getting busted and hauled away a second time, one of the Quakers, David Hartsough, asked Congressman George Brown (D-Calif.) for help in sustaining the readings. Brown then coaxed two other congressmen to join him on the Capitol steps to recite the names of war dead themselves. The legislators were not arrested, and the readings received national publicity. "Then people started reading the names of the war dead at post offices and federal buildings all over the country," Hartsough recalled.[29] The ceremonies heightened the public's awareness of the war's immense human toll.

Over that winter and spring, activists continued their efforts to reach GIs. Antiwar coffeehouses and GI newspapers were cropping up in growing numbers. Many protesters were leafleting bus stops, airports, and other places frequented by servicemen. Some launched forays onto army bases. Don Gurewitz remembered that after one fellow YSA leader was drafted and sent to Fort Knox, Kentucky, for basic training, twenty protesters invaded the base:

> We got a plan of the base . . . and we figured out where people would be. And that morning we divided up in cars, in couples, men and women, so we would look like routine visitors—we were all really clean. . . . Then we just zipped onto the base, leafleted all the barracks, went to the bus station, went to the PX—just busted in everywhere. It took them about an hour and a half to track us all down and arrest us. They organized this car caravan off the base . . . and of course they had a police car in front of us and one in back, with their lights flashing. So the whole fucking base turned out to see what the hell was going on. . . . GIs were cheering and going like this [raising clenched fists]. It was great.[30]

The GI–Civilian demonstrations in April involved many soldiers in peace activity for the first time. Among them was David Cortright, who later served as the national head of the antimilitarist group SANE/Freeze. Cortright recalled his experience:

> [In] early 1969 I had been in the army a few months. My mind was really spinning around. I was reading a lot, and I was thinking, "Boy, something's really screwed up here. And I'm not the type that can desert—it's not part of my family or culture—but I've got to do something." I was basically wandering around New York really kind of like in a daze . . . wondering what the hell I was going to do with my life—"How did I ever get stuck in this kind of war, in this army?" . . . And I saw a poster: "GI–Civilian Mobilization. Come to a meeting." . . . So I went. . . . You know, I just wanted to do

something against the war, and here was a group inviting GIs. So I remember I . . . was sort of sneaking around the edges, not knowing (a) if these people were going to laugh at me because I had short hair and I was a GI, or (b) if it was a setup or something. And somebody came up to me and was nice to me and talked to me and sat me down and we actually had a meeting. I felt good and I kept on it.[31]

Antiwar soldiers were banding together. In February, GIs United Against the War in Vietnam was formed at Fort Jackson, South Carolina. The group attracted considerable media attention; even NBC's Huntley-Brinkley news program did a piece on it. Eight leaders of GIs United were arrested following a mass on-base meeting in March, but the charges were dropped when peace activists rallied behind the GIs and challenged the military's violation of their civil rights.[32]

Opposition to the war was also growing among GIs in Vietnam. Drug use was widespread. Soldiers were murdering abusive or overzealous officers with fragmentation grenades. A bounty of $10,000 was placed on the head of one officer.[33]

And on America's campuses, student militants were more active than ever. At Stanford, protesters commandeered the Applied Electronics Laboratory, a site of war research, for nine days. Students at Harvard yanked deans out of their offices and occupied the administration building, only to suffer mass arrests and injuries, sparking a ten-day student strike. Major protests erupted at nearly three hundred campuses over the spring, striking at the rate of almost two a day; a quarter involved building occupations or strikes, another quarter disruption of classes and administration.[34]

Political violence was escalating. There were at least eighty-four bombings, attempted bombings, and acts of arson on campuses in the first half of 1969, twice as many as the previous fall. America's high schools were the scenes of twenty-seven bombings and attempted bombings. Off school grounds, activists bombed ten targets; the destruction of four electrical transmission lines in Colorado earned one SDSer a spot on the FBI's Ten Most Wanted list. Street battles raged. Trashing and petty vandalism rose to new heights. Talk of armed revolution was as common as hot dogs at a baseball game. The peace movement's inability to end the war was "leading to outbursts of frustrated anger," as Barbara Bick observed. "A gigantic tantrum," Bettina Aptheker later called the movement's violence; it "reflected this tremendous frustration—'We can't change it, so we'll blow it up.'" Norma Becker sadly recalled the many "good, decent people who were pissed and felt compelled to resort to violent means out of real frustration and cluelessness." More than a few protesters had come to believe that the only way to stop the war was to make America ungovernable. Others simply craved existential satisfaction. "Terrorism, in its modified form of breaking windows and so on, became very popular because that was like the moral expression, 'I'm good, I took real action,'" Peter Camejo argued. "It was emotional release."[35]

Many activists continued to shake their heads at their adventuristic comrades. The McCarthy organizer Sam Brown felt the militants had to ask themselves, "'If you make [society] ungovernable, what happens next?' And my answer to that was always, 'They come down on you—and it's the end.'" David McReynolds was "horrified" at the torching of ROTC buildings on campuses. "We should have been asking for them to be turned into day-care centers," he said intently. "We were just burning up the public, we were just closing out masses of people." Yet even many tactical moderates were sympathetic to the violence. McReynolds pensively offered:

> I think most of us working in the movement at that time were so
> heartbroken by the war, and so progressively shocked at what the
> government was doing, that we didn't care too much what happened,
> if you want an honest [recollection]. The alienation that we felt, pro-
> gressively, starting with people like myself who came out of a Re-
> publican background with a father who was a lieutenant colonel and a
> grandfather who was a lieutenant colonel. . . . I am among many
> people who did not believe that America could do what it did do as
> long as it did it. . . . How radicalized I was by that war. And how
> great the distance is now [between] me and others who didn't go
> through that process. So I don't think in some ways we gave a damn,
> as long as something was happening. That's an existential agony that
> we all felt. . . . We lost our own way many times because of the
> psychic anxieties produced by that war. . . . And a lot of the things
> that I think were *stupid*, against which I fought then, I was sympa-
> thetic to their being done anyway.

And some tactical moderates believed a genuine revolution wasn't totally out of the realm of possibilities, either. "You have to remember the time," the SWP leader Fred Halstead commented years afterward. "It was a time in which things were coming apart a little bit. And one could walk around campuses in those days and get the idea that, 'Jesus Christ, this is about to go.'" A blue-collar worker in the workaday world, Halstead himself had no such illusions, however. "I was too close to that goddamned garment factory—I knew fucking well it wasn't about to go," he laughingly recalled. "The real world out there was pretty solid."[36]

Troubled Ted

Hardly a day passed when the media failed to warn the public that a pernicious radical menace was loose in the country, tearing up campuses, terrorizing law-abiding citizens, turning America into a war zone. The result was an increasingly restive public already unnerved by years of unprecedented domestic dissent. As *Time* magazine observed, many Americans were crying, "Enough!" A spring Harris poll found that 52 percent now opposed peaceful demonstrations by students. A Gallup poll indicated that 82 percent thought student demonstrators should be expelled from school. [37]

But "Enough!" was also directed at the war. The faraway conflict that was apparently wreaking so much havoc at home seemed more costly to the public with each passing, battle-scarred day. The press was not immune from this sentiment. John Oakes, the editor of the *New York Times*'s editorial page (which called the student militants "left fascists" in May), said that the mounting threat they posed to American social stability "surely would have been another factor in that later [Nixon administration] period in making us even more antiwar than we had been earlier. . . . We certainly were concerned about what this was doing to American society." Oakes was "absolutely certain" that it fueled the *Times*'s pleas to wind the war down. "I would think that this would have been quite natural," he said. [38]

Acutely attuned to public sentiment, congressmen queued up on the floors of both houses to denounce the militants' conduct. Senator Gordon Allott (R-Colo.) warned that "there is an active, aggressive national conspiracy to destroy by force and violence, including the use of dangerous weapons, the peace and dignity of the academic communities." Senator Karl Mundt (R-S. Dak.) called for "drastic remedial action" to cure the sickness on campuses. "They're about the most contemptible people I know of," Senator Russell Long said of SDS during a floor debate. "Is the Senator familiar with the fact that the parents of these people have put up the money to pay all their expenses and buy soap for them? But they refuse to take baths. . . . That they put up the money to buy food for those children? And they spend it on marijuana." More than twenty bills were introduced to cut off federal funds to student and faculty rebels and their universities. Congressional committees launched investigations of the malcontents. Goaded by the Nixon administration, which hungered for a televised exposé of "student rioters so that the country might see just what they are up to" (as one White House memo records), two congressional subcommittees commenced fist-pounding public hearings on them. The administration fed the Senate Internal Security subcommittee FBI reports on the fiendish nature of the militant leaders and their organizations. It also provided individual senators "evidence" of their communist links. [39]

The dons of American higher education took keen note of all this. Fearful that the government would quash campus protest unless they subdued the militants themselves, university officials moved to clamp down. Admissions offices were told to screen out potential troublemakers, financial aid offices threatened to cut protesters' funds, psychiatric counselors were encouraged to seek out and "treat" them, and records offices turned over their names to the congressional witch-hunting teams. Police and National Guard units were called in as never before. Arrests and expulsions swelled. Prison sentences were meted out to the most offensive recalcitrants, and they weren't slaps on the wrist either: one SDSer was given a one-year term for grabbing a dean's elbow.[40]

By now, after several years of crescendoing student protests, many university officials were shaken to their bureaucratic boots. The "campus crisis" seemed to be "out of control," as one wrote later. Where was it all going? What fate awaited American higher education—indeed, American society as a whole—if the tumult persisted? No one was more distraught, more restive of the country's future, than the man the *Nation* would call "the most influential cleric in America, and the only possible rival to Dr. Billy Graham as preacher to the nation": Father Theodore Martin Hesburgh of the University of Notre Dame.[41]

"Ted the Head" Hesburgh was then fifty-two and in his seventeenth year as Notre Dame's president. A handsome, well-built priest with a square jaw, swarthy complexion, otherworldly stare, and grueling, peripatetic lifestyle, he had watched the campus troubles since the early 1960s with growing concern. His "very conservative" attitudes toward student behavior had increasingly been challenged by disgruntled youths at his own school. Although less and less enamored of the war ("the more tragic it became, and the more futile . . . it became, and the more the projections proved false at every turn of the road," he remembered, the "more turned off on it" he became), Hesburgh could hardly accept the notion promoted by many of the protesters that Vietnam was some sort of moral abomination. He felt many of them simply didn't have their heads screwed on straight. Hesburgh theorized that the editor of Notre Dame's student newspaper was "working out personal hostilities" by attacking the war and restrictive campus regulations. Each year between 1965 and 1968, Hesburgh presided over a full-dress military review of Notre Dame's ROTC program while pretending to ignore antiwar demonstrators nearby.[42]

The Columbia student rebellion in 1968 turned Hesburgh's concern over campus protests into outright alarm. "For a long time I thought [the 1964 Free Speech Movement at] Berkeley was just an isolated incident," he recalled. "We all did. It wasn't until the Columbia disturbances in 1968 that we really started to worry." Hesburgh said he and other university presidents then began running scared. "Everybody who was in charge of his place got up in the morning with a knot in their stomach, wondering, 'What are they going to do today?' and 'What am I going to do to react to it?'"[43]

By early 1969, Hesburgh had become convinced that student militants posed a major threat to the survival of American higher education. They were manu-

facturing issues, he perceived—any issues—in order to provoke police intervention, radicalize other students, and spark campus shutdowns. Hesburgh listened
closely to fellow university educators who told him that the militants had an
"almost nihilistic lust for confrontation." Hesburgh believed many antiwar protesters were simply manipulative opportunists. "There were, of course, a lot of
people who had their own agendas that had nothing to do with Vietnam—and
they were never going to go there—but it gave them a convenient target," he
recalled. Hesburgh uneasily watched his fellow university presidents bite the
dust one by one. He began keeping a list of those forced out by protesters:

> I filled two sides of a yellow sheet with names. And I decided that
> there wasn't anybody left, really, except [Yale President] King[man]
> Brewster and myself. . . . There was just no question that at each
> firing of a president there was this terrible feeling that we were just
> wiping out a whole generation of very good guys. I don't think we've
> necessarily had presidents since then as good as these guys. But they
> all went down the drain, just about 100 percent of them. . . . I recall
> one period [in which] one guy got fired, for all practical purposes, for
> calling the cops, and another guy within a short period of time got
> fired for *not* calling the cops. Everything was improvisation, and
> that's not a very good thing to live on.[44]

In early February, Hesburgh met with his "good friend Dick Nixon" in the
Oval Office. The president had just appointed him chairman of the U.S. Civil
Rights Commission. Hesburgh advised Nixon to end the war "as soon as possible." It was, he said, "a major irritant, a red flag to most students." Hesburgh
advocated ending the draft to placate students too.[45]

But Notre Dame's celebrated president did not think appeasement alone
would calm the turbulent campus waters. It was time for university officials to
lay down the law. On February 17, Hesburgh issued a famous letter to Notre
Dame students and faculty. Declaring that he had "studied at some length the
new politics of confrontation" sweeping America's campuses, Hesburgh decreed
that "anyone or any group that substitutes force for rational persuasion, be it
violent or non-violent, will be given fifteen minutes of meditation to cease and
desist." Those who refused would be suspended from school or arrested. Hesburgh claimed that applying "the forces of law" was "a last and dismal alternative to anarchy and mob tyranny."[46]

The letter touched a nerve across America. More than three hundred newspapers rushed to congratulate Hesburgh for having had the guts to stand up to
the militants. Fan mail streamed into his office. Nixon sent Hesburgh a congratulatory letter. Ray Price, a Nixon aide, recalled that the president "felt very
strongly that it was up to the college administrators to bring peace to the college

campuses, that this was not a federal role, and that it wouldn't happen unless they kind of pulled up their own socks themselves and took the responsibility." Nixon, Price said, "had a large measure of contempt for college administrators . . . who were craven and knuckling under and letting their institutions be transformed into nothing but hotbeds of rebellion." The president took advantage of Hesburgh's letter to denounce protesters in even stronger terms.[47]

At Notre Dame, Hesburgh was "a villain." Students were irate. Not only was he acting like a petty tyrant, they fumed, but their campus had never been threatened by anything approaching "mob tyranny." And now it was more unsettled than ever. Many sensed Hesburgh had buckled under pressure from trustees and powerful alumni.[48]

It was strong medicine for a man who desperately craved the admiration and affection of his students. Hesburgh felt personally hurt. In the spring of 1969, visitors to his high-ceilinged office, decorated with photographs of Hesburgh hobnobbing with popes and presidents, encountered a defensive, moody, seemingly out-of-touch administrator. Hesburgh would often begin conversations by reading from his collection of fan mail, his mind lost in a strange reverie, his hand dipping deeper and deeper into the pile. "I will not be forced out by pressure from any group," he exclaimed to more than one caller. Of legendary physical stamina (Hesburgh's well-known "18-hour days" really *were* 18-hour days), he "looked terrible," Notre Dame's vice president recalled. Hesburgh was pale, his forehead was creased with worry lines, large pouches hung below his eyes, and his expression was frequently testy during public engagements. He reportedly had incipient heart disease.[49]

Hesburgh decided to leave the country to get out of the firing line and pull himself together. "Nineteen sixty-nine was so bad that I took off for three weeks," he remembered. "I took off and went around the world just to get out of here, and to cleanse my mind, even. Then when I got back, I said, 'If I hadn't done that, I wouldn't have made it.'" During his summer travels to distant lands, Hesburgh pondered his unpopularity at Notre Dame, the campus crisis, Vietnam, civil rights. The embattled administrator encountered angry American youth overseas, too. "Those kids were all soured and bitter and frightened," he said of the Peace Corps workers he spoke with in Malaysia and Ethiopia. "I had a terrible time just dealing with them, until they found out I was more liberal than they were; then they kind of opened up a little bit. But they were *very, very nasty* about anybody coming and talking to them."[50]

When Hesburgh returned to the United States, he acted like a new man. Speaking at an antiwar event in the early fall, Hesburgh called for accelerated U.S. troop withdrawals from Vietnam. "Were I in a position to do so," he declared to a stunned Notre Dame audience, "I would end this war tonight before midnight." The "Ted Offensive" intensified the next year. Following the

U.S. invasion of Cambodia and Kent State killings, he called for the immediate termination of U.S. involvement in Vietnam; "mental midgets," Hesburgh dubbed U.S. policymakers. "There has been an almost existential change in the man," one close observer commented in 1971.[51]

Years later, Hesburgh made no bones about the fact that it was antiwar youth—the same antiwar youth who had made his life miserable, who nearly destroyed him—that turned him around on Vietnam. "There's no question about it," he avowed. "I have said very often that this is the only case I know of in the history of the country where the younger people pulled their elders around to a position they didn't really go with in the beginning. I think that's true. I think the young people really turned the tide on this one. . . . Most of us underwent a complete transformation from A to Z." Asked to describe his views on the war in early 1965, Hesburgh responded, "Well, it wasn't that big of a problem at that point in the universities."[52]

"The Sectarianism Is Staggering"

Ironically, the primary target of the domestic outcry against student militants in the winter and spring of 1969 was in no condition to foment much of anything. During the previous fall, SDS had been debilitated by its ultraleftist national leadership and factional warfare. Most of the nation's college students were not enamored of its talk of armed revolution and thought SDSers were either naïve or nuts. SDS actionists around the country had forced splits in a long list of SDS chapters; the schisms were exacerbated by the FBI's COINTELPRO machinations, but they were preponderately internally generated. And the recruit-hungry Progressive Labor Party had launched an all-out push into the organization, splintering SDS chapters with remarkable efficiency and poisoning the atmosphere in the national office. Countless youths dropped out of SDS rather than dodge the crossfire.[53]

PL also damaged SDS in another way. Its neatly packaged orthodox Marxism was attractive to many newly radical SDSers looking for a tidy world view. "They seemed to know their Marx and Engels," Bill Ayers smiled. Partly to blunt PL's appeal, SDS leaders turned increasingly to Marxism themselves. "PL said that they were the communists," Carl Davidson remembered. "We said, 'Wait a minute. . . . This is bullshit, this is not communism.' . . . We wanted to show that PL[ers] were phony communists and that they were giving communism a bad name."[54] SDS leaders advanced a variant of Marxism that emphasized organizing the *youthful* working class. By thereby turning away from student politics toward proletarian politics, SDS was effectively abandoning its natural constituency.

SDS's death knell sounded at its national convention in June. By all accounts, it was a truly bizarre gathering. The opening morning found more than a thousand SDSers milling restlessly around in front of the Chicago Coliseum, held up by an intensive security check at the door. The targets: knives, guns, tape recorders, "the capitalist press," police agents. The check was too intensive for many female SDSers: a spokeswoman for the Women's Liberation Caucus later took to the floor of the arena to angrily report, "The men doing the frisking are reaching inside the women's blouses and feeling their breasts, and running their hands up the women's legs." Mingling with the SDSers were hundreds of government agents of every conceivable institutional stripe. Inside the grimy, cavernous, cement-block-walled coliseum, normally the home of roller derby, delegates were handed a jumbled, rhetoric-laden essay entitled "You Don't Need a Weatherman to Know Which Way the Wind Blows." Its purpose was to wage political war. "That was very much a response to PL," Ayers, one of the essay's authors, recalled. "And it was very much an attempt to be more ideological than they were." According to the "Weatherman" statement, the world was embroiled in a war between national liberation movements and U.S. imperialism. Revolutionaries who ignored this "principal contradiction"—that is, PLers—were propagating "a very dangerous ideology." The main national liberation movement inside the United States—the black struggle—was the "vanguard" of the American revolution. The tract was designed to refute PL's curious view that "all nationalism is reactionary" and "a bourgeois idea."[55]

The first afternoon witnessed escalating political clashes between PLers and SDS regulars. The next evening, pandemonium. Rufus Walls, a leader of the Black Panther Party, which Weatherman had deemed the vanguard of the black liberation movement, decided to enlighten the delegates on the issue of women's liberation. The Panthers supported "pussy power," cracked Walls, who wore sunglasses and was flanked by bodyguards. After shouts of "Fight male chauvinism!" erupted from the floor of the smoke-filled arena, Walls issued a shocking off-the-cuff: "Superman was a punk because he never even tried to fuck Lois Lane." Now "Fight Male Chauvinism!" was deafening. After another Panther heavy, Jewel Cook, declared that the "strategic position" for "you sisters" in the revolution was "prone," there was bedlam.[56]

The next night came the denouement. Cook told the delegates that, "after long study and investigation," the Black Panther Party had concluded that PL had "deviated from Marxist-Leninist ideology on the National Question." Consequently, PL either had to change its politics or get its privileged white butts out of SDS. If it didn't, the Panthers would not look kindly on SDS. After a PL leader, in an "eerie calm voice," declared that PL would not be bullied out of SDS and went on to set the record straight about PL's politics, a coiled Bernardine Dohrn, "hair flying, jaw set," rushed onto the stage. SDSers had to decide whether the racist PL was fit political company, she cried. Anyone interested in doing the deciding should follow her to the next room.[57]

The delegates were stunned. Even Dohrn's fellow Weathermen were dumb-founded. "She did that unilaterally," Jeff Jones recalled. "Several of her most loyal supporters felt [it] was a disaster," remembered her husband, Ayers. "Jim Mellen was just livid. He thought it was an absolute disaster." The six hundred revolutionaries who followed Dohrn's cue decided to expel PL from SDS out-right. Protected by two rows of bodyguards, Dohrn delivered their verdict to the PLers (including *their* bodyguards, ominously lined up on the perimeter of the room) the following evening. When she finished, there was "dead silence." One PL leader recounted:

> At that point I . . . ran around the room from person to person, shaking them . . . and saying, "Don't you hear what she's saying? She's saying that you are bad, that you are an enemy of the working class." The people started shouting, "Shame!" . . . Everybody, in-cluding the leaders, was frozen. . . . They were in tears. That's what the reaction was . . . stunned horror, because we saw them destroy-ing the organization. We looked around and we saw potheads and crazies and maniacal Panthers—we're talking about sickies.

Fists thrust upward, screaming "Power to the People!" and "Ho! Ho! Ho Chi Minh!" Dohrn and her contingent marched out of the coliseum and into the night.[58]

SDS was for all intents and purposes dead, yet another casualty of the po-litical sectarianism riddling the antiwar movement. "Nothing could have served the interests of the ruling class more," one prominent radical lamented.[59] In-credibly, both of the nation's two largest antiwar student organizations—the Student Mobe and SDS—had now self-destructed.

SDS's fracture was given front-page coverage in the next day's *New York Times.* That morning, apparently seeking even more publicity for their lunacy, the SDS heavy Mike Klonsky called a press conference. "The first thing Klonsky does is to read a telegram that he, Klonsky, has *personally* sent to Mao Tse-tung, announcing the 'great victory,'" SDSer Clark Kissinger remembered with a roll of his eyes. "I was always trying to get somebody to draw a cartoon of Mao sitting at his desk throwing these papers around, saying, 'Who is Michael Klonsky, and why does he send me a telegram every day?'"[60]

The White House was both pleased and amused by SDS's decomposition. "The image created by SDS . . . at its June 18 Chicago convention did more than anything else to educate the American people as to its goals and interna-tional political affections," one official gloated. The conference suggested that SDS might well "destroy itself both on and off campus," he perceived. Stephen Hess, a presidential aide, forwarded John Ehrlichman a "confidential" AFL-CIO report on the convention, with the following attached comments:

Perhaps it is my perverse sense of humor, but I found it hysterical
(and a little raunchy in places!).

The sectarianism is staggering, even by leftist standards, as the
SDS divides, amoeba-like, into less and less significant cells. The process, as the report says, is surely "self-isolating."

. . . The moral for us: Don't over-react.[61]

"The Youth Problem"

Hess's advice was not the watchword of the Nixon administration during the
winter and spring of 1969. As Ray Price writes, senior White House officials
were "spending long hours agonizing over" the dilemna of youthful protest,
pondering its roots, analyzing its potential, concocting schemes for blunting
it. "The youth problem" was the topic of many a White House memo. For
the Nixon administration, like that of Lyndon Johnson, considered protesters
the most nettlesome manifestation of domestic distaste for the war. "It was the
noisy public opinion . . . that would have created concern," Haldeman recalled.
"You know, 'end the war now,' 'peace at any price' . . . the heavy attempt, as
the president put it, to make policy in the streets." "They were noisy and they
squeaked a lot, and when the wheel squeaks that's the one you pay attention
to," echoed Kissinger's aide Lawrence Eagleburger. Officials worried that the
protesters would convince Hanoi that Nixon did not have sufficient domestic
support to carry out his madman war strategy. "The hope, obviously, of the
negotiators on the other side," Haldeman said, "was that as this din kept up, as
the violence developed, as the moratoriums and marches and more covert displays took place, that those pressures would force the president to make greater
concessions at the bargaining table than he was originally prepared to make."
Officials also worried that the dissent was feeding public sentiment for a pre-
cipitate U.S. withdrawal from Vietnam. "A lot of people took the students seriously—a lot more seriously than they should have been taken," Price told me.
"This itself was a kind of snowballing political problem for us." Nixon underlined a warning in a memo from his aide Daniel Patrick Moynihan about youth's
"incredible powers of derision."[62]

Not that officials felt the demonstrators reflected public sentiment as a whole.
"The Nixon people didn't feel that this was their constituency, didn't feel that
this in any way represented the heart of America—the great 'silent majority'
was out there," Roger Morris remembered. But, Morris added:

> We saw the seriousness of the early antiwar movement not so much
> in an analysis of whether it was a minority or a majority—it was
> always a minority. We saw that as affecting overall public opinion, we
> saw that as affecting the Congress, and as furthering the defection of
> the press. . . . This might be a bunch of wild-eyed kids or little old

ladies in tennis shoes walking down Pennsylvania Avenue . . . but it had an insidious effect in public opinion and in the Congress. . . .

I think Nixon's sense . . . of American politics is based in the activity of vocal minorities anyway. . . . Nixon had been the beneficiary of a very vocal minority: raising anticommunist issues in the late 1940s. [Senator Joseph] McCarthy may have had wide sort of national approval, and the [Alger] Hiss case may have eventually won national approval, but those things were initially prosecuted and pushed and got to the point of sort of national consensus on the backs of a very vocal and active minority of people. . . . [So] I don't think he ever underestimated the power of people who were organized and hard-working, regardless of how kooky they might seem or how small their numbers.

Said John Ehrlichman, "Nixon viewed all minority political opposition as bearing watching. It was in the nature of the man. He was pugnacious."[63]

And not that officials believed the protesters had anything worthy to say, either. Morris:

It's one thing to say that this thing presents a political problem and it may translate into votes down the line. It's another thing to say that, "Look, these people in the streets are thoughtful, they may have *a point* about the war, it may behoove us to rethink some of our assumptions." They never did that. They thought they were insubstantial and capricious, they thought it was basically a draft protest, they thought they were cowardly, they thought they were there for frivolous reasons, they thought the antiwar movement was manipulated in part by subversive elements—I mean, you could see the far left out there. . . . They just never took the protest seriously in an intellectual sense. . . . And their disdain and their contempt for the antiwar movement was part of the defense mechanism for keeping them out. . . . If you could dismiss them as a bunch of flukes and phonies and kids, you didn't really have to think seriously about what they were saying. . . .

Now, that didn't mean that they weren't a serious threat. That didn't mean that other people couldn't be conned or beguiled or misled, and that you still didn't have problems on Capitol Hill.[64]

Officials understood that the ultramilitant youth were hurting the peace movement's public image. "What we learned in the general sense of evaluating public opinion was that . . . the violent efforts were alienating people," Haldeman remembered. "There were people who honestly believed in the peace movement—'let's get this war done' . . .—who were totally turned off by the bomb-throwers and the window-busters." "Everybody knew it," White House Press Secretary Ronald Ziegler impatiently snorted—"anybody knowledgeable in public opinion or knowledgeable about what's happening in their society." But officials were far from happy with the violence. For one thing, it raised the frightening specter of truly uncontrollable social disorder; there was always "the potential for substantially greater damage as those things escalated," Haldeman recalled. "That you do worry about." For another, it suggested the government was in questionable command, and for a government that had swept into office on a wave of law-and-orderism, that was a major political liability. The violence also appeared to fuel Hanoi's intransigence. Most of all, it was nourishing public demands for U.S. withdrawal from Vietnam. Haldeman recalled observing that "there were people who were opposed to the antiwar people but who were afraid enough of the violence to be willing to give way to their views just to stop the violence." Thus, "I don't think it was a plus for us," he said firmly. "I think it was an overall negative. . . . In the overall perspective, I wouldn't say that *any* facet of that [movement] was good for us." Correspondingly, "you wanted to try to calm the waters as much as you could," Price revealed. The costs of antiwar violence, he said, "would lead [Nixon] more towards trying to conduct our policy in Vietnam in a way which would contribute as little as possible to further inflaming the violence." Still, if opponents of the war "were going to do something *anyway*," Haldeman added, "the less attractive they were in the process of doing it, the more harm they did themselves, was the feeling."[65]

Official concern over antiwar violence mounted during the Nixon administration's early months. Special Assistant to the President Robert Brown warned in March that "violence in colleges and high schools threatens to increase rapidly over the next four to six weeks and lead to a very heated summer." Moynihan agreed, counseling Nixon that campus unrest was "one of the most serious situations you face." The president solicited the opinions of his aides on "whether or not we should openly predict what lies ahead." Wary of further unsettling the public, Nixon decided against it. By the late spring, he was apparently girding up for the worst. His aide Alexander Butterfield reported to Ehrlichman, Attorney General John Mitchell, and Secretary of Health, Education and Welfare Robert Finch on June 2 that Nixon shared the perspective of a recent *Wall Street Journal* article that argued that "Lincoln should be kept constantly in mind. He took extreme liberties with the Nation's laws 'but he saved the Union. President Nixon faces an even harder task, for he must save the Union not from a civil but a guerrilla war.'" Butterfield transmitted that "the President wants each of you to know that . . . in his opinion we may soon have to face up to more than dialogue.'"[66]

Officials were probing the youth problem from all sides, hoping to get a better grasp of their adversaries. The president was among the most ardent students. Deputy Counsel to the President Egil Krogh wrote the FBI's Deke DeLoach (Lyndon Johnson's main man in the bureau) on February 25: "We are in the midst of putting together a complete analysis of the current student disorder problem in the country. As you know, President Nixon has taken a very strong stand opposing such disorders, and we would like as much information as we can get on this subject for his further study." Krogh asked De-Loach for data on the "numbers of non-students involved" in the disorders, "effect of professional organization" (particularly communist and socialist), "number of students involved who are on federal scholarship," "who is responsible for violence," "categories for student grievances," "value of property damages," and "number of lost teaching hours," among other subjects. Six weeks later, Nixon directed Henry Kissinger to prepare a memorandum "setting forth your views on the reasons for student unrest," adding, "This is only for my background purposes." In early June, the president ordered Ehrlichman to assemble an annotated bibliography on student protest. Ehrlichman, in turn, told two co-workers to "assemble all the good, recent literature in the field of campus unrest for [Nixon's] review." White House aides fed the information-hungry president a steady diet of articles on the campus ferment.[67]

Nixon asked Presidential Counsellor Arthur Burns to solicit the opinions of university professors around the country on the nature of the youth problem. After contacting "thoughtful members" of the academic community, Burns reported to Nixon on May 26 that they generally agreed that "a small, nationally organized, group of protesters, usually associated with SDS," was "behind the demonstrations" on campuses. This group enjoyed "the widespread support of other students and faculty members." Burns also wrote: "A few professors noted that of the students admitted to colleges and universities, many are unequipped for the work or have no purpose in going to college."[68]

Ehrlichman was meeting secretly with student leaders, "trying to understand better what it was we were up against." He recalled that he "learned a lot about what was going on on the campuses. . . . About the depth of their passion, about their attitudes toward the draft and the all-volunteer army, and things of that kind." He also tried to measure support for Nixon among students. Ehrlichman advised that "every member of the White House staff, particularly the younger members," make such contacts with students. "I am sure that it will pay dividends," he wrote in late March.[69]

The White House was obsessed with maximizing its intelligence on protesters. For Nixon, they were yet another political enemy in a long line of people out to get him. The president craved information that might help him fend off his attackers. John Dean, who was then in the Justice Department, commented:

> I think that a lot of the stuff that later resulted in Watergate was that
> mentality. After I got to working with Nixon a little bit more and
> more directly, I realized that he was in many regards a very insecure
> man. And I sensed that [the purpose of] intelligence was twofold.
> First of all, what was your opponent up to? And secondly, did you

have any [way to] control it? I think that the knowledge and then
some factor that gave him some control over the situation gave the
man comfort. And I think that was in evidence during the antiwar
movement and all of his political things. He liked information.

Nixon harbored "distrust of anybody unless he really knew what they were up
to and [discerned] some way to deal with them," Dean believed.[70]

Ehrlichman's thirst for antiwar intelligence rivaled the president's. Haldeman
once compared his attraction to demonstrations to that of "a firehouse Dalma-
tian at a blaze." "Ehrlichman loves intelligence," Haldeman smiled. "What he
really wanted to be was director of the CIA. And John got quite absorbed in
that [antiwar intelligence] on a personal basis—much more so, really, than the
president did." Dean remembered "Field Marshal Ehrlichman's" taste for monitoring large demonstrations in Washington:

> He seemed to like all of that. A lot of those guys did. Ehrlichman
> would go down to the bomb shelter [in the White House] and set up
> all sorts of elaborate information equipment. We never did that in
> my office—we used the telephone. . . . I was often struck with the
> attraction of men in high places to the toys of government, if you
> will. And the demonstrations became a time to be sort of a command
> general and set up a command post and all this sort of thing, and
> play a whole different game. . . . It was a weird atmosphere [in the
> White House during demonstrations].[71]

In the 1980s Ehrlichman was a novelist in New Mexico: a bald, bearded man
with a conspicuous paunch, high waist, and sloping shoulders. Slouched across
from me at the Pink Adobe restaurant in Santa Fe in jeans and a wool sweater,
his down vest at his side, this friendly, relaxed L. L. Bean Buddha bore little
resemblance to the pompous, haughty Ehrlichman of the Nixon years. He
seemed to genuinely enjoy giving interviews; mulling over intellectual issues,
he spoke in a carefully measured manner. ("John should have been a professor,"
Haldeman said.) Ehrlichman admitted to being attracted to antiwar demonstrations. "I thought they were an interesting phenomenon," he recalled, "and one
that certainly had not been seen in my lifetime in this country. So I was interested in them from that standpoint. And I went and looked at a lot of them. I
was also concerned that the administration might seriously overplay its hand"—
that is, use excessive force against the demonstrators. Ehrlichman worried that
would "hurt the president's cause." In addition, his boss had designated him the
chief White House watchdog on protests. "Nixon wanted to have one person
he could talk to about every thing," Ehrlichman said. "For demonstrations, I
was that person."[72]

Through Ehrlichman, Nixon solicited the views of other officials on whether the administration's intelligence on protesters was up to snuff. He himself had little doubt that it was not. Moynihan shared the president's sentiment. He told Nixon on April 14 that "in general the intelligence system of the U.S. Government in these matters is deplorable." Arthur Burns, however, disagreed. "It is not clear to me whether we should try to follow more closely than we now do the activities of students on college campuses," he wrote Ehrlichman.[73]

Burns was overruled. During the first half of 1969, the Nixon administration stepped up governmental surveillance of protesters. The FBI and other branches of the Justice Department expanded their intelligence operations. Attorney General Mitchell significantly relaxed restrictions on federal wiretapping of "subversive" organizations. The CIA's Operation CHAOS grew. Regular liaison was established between the CIA and Justice on domestic intelligence matters. Military agents were swarming about campuses in record numbers; friendly university administrators regularly granted them access to confidential student files. "Once the military [liaison] is established with the university, you have pretty much free run of the place," one agent disclosed. Encouraged by federal action, state intelligence agencies escalated their efforts too. "I've never seen anything like the intensity of current investigations in all my years in law enforcement," remarked the superintendent of the Illinois State Police. Among protesters, the expansion of intelligence operations was palpable. "The Nixon administration was different in that sense," Fred Halstead remembered. "I mean, suddenly you were covered like a blanket. You could feel it." One federal agent commented that spring on the effect of governmental surveillance on SDS:

> Our inside information has caused S.D.S. to get more conspiratorial in a lot of places. They make their plans at the last minute now to fool us. But that doesn't leave them much time for getting the word around, and it . . . makes it harder for them to draw the kinds of crowds they used to get at their rallies.
>
> We also find that the more conspiratorial S.D.S. becomes, the less they appeal to the hippies and people like that who think everything should be wide open and who are afraid of . . . secret political planning. I think the conspiratorial mood is hurting S.D.S. a lot.[74]

Yet the White House was unsatisfied. Asked by Ehrlichman for advice on improving the administration's intelligence, the White House political sleuth Jack Caulfield recommended on June 20 that it place new "Federal Intelligence undercover units" on "major campuses." They would "supplement the existing intelligence gathering methods (paid informants, cooperative citizens, etc.) and provide an effective tool to aid in accurately predicting the potential for violence and unrest on a campus by campus basis," the ex-cop submitted. He proposed that the agents be recruited from the ranks of the military, where "ideal talents for undercover work" like "unquestioned loyalty" and willingness to submit to discipline were bred. Caulfield's prescription was too strong for Egil Krogh. Although the operation had potential benefits, Krogh cautioned, it also entailed "great risks," including exposure, which would politically damage the administration. After further discussion of Caulfield's plan, officials apparently shelved it.[75]

Communist Dupes and Spoiled Children

Richard Nixon's deep-seated paranoia about political enemies was the dominant force behind the administration's lust for antiwar intelligence, but delusions of another sort were impelling the administration as well. Like their predecessors, Nixon administration officials believed foreign communists were aiding and abetting the antiwar movement. "They had the same feeling," CIA Director Richard Helms recalled. "Some were pretty paranoid over there about that," chuckled Melvin Laird. Nixon yearned for hard evidence of communist penetration of the movement. He had read the earlier CIA studies that found no basis for foreign conspiracy theories, but he distrusted the CIA's intelligence generally and had little confidence in Helms personally, often treating the CIA director with unveiled disdain at meetings, to the point of snidely correcting his frequent butchered pronunciations. (These lessons apparently left Helms eager to turn the tables: he sternly corrected my pronunciation of *harassed*, then added, man-to-man, "If you think of it as 'her ass,' that's the wrong way to pronounce it.")[76]

The president turned to other investigators to document foreign communist trickery. On June 2, he directed Ehrlichman to "gather all the information you can on this matter" and assemble a report. Three days later, Ehrlichman reported that "the conclusion of the intelligence community is that our Government does not have specific information or 'ironclad proof' that Red China or Cuba is funding campus disorders. But, this is not to say that it could not be concluded from the evidence that such funding is taking place," especially since radical activists traveled often to communist countries. Responded Nixon:

John—(1) Please keep after this.
(2) Give [White House aide Tom] Huston the job of developing hard evidence of this probable support activity (. . . or if not Huston, someone with his toughness and brains).
(3) Please get with [White House aide] Bryce Harlow on this. I want to pass the information to Senators Mundt and McClellan.[77]

The Subcommittee on Investigations chaired by Senator John McClellan (D-Ark.), it should be noted, was then gearing up to hold public hearings on campus violence.

Ten days later, Nixon directed the FBI to prepare a report on communist subversion in the United States. The FBI's research also failed to uncover any foreign intervention. Again, Nixon concluded that it was U.S. intelligence—not his thinking—that was faulty.[78]

Haldeman was equally skeptical of the intelligence reports. Years later, Haldeman was a businessman living in Santa Barbara, California. He was involved in numerous commercial ventures, including Sizzler restaurant franchises in Florida, a small manufacturing company in Seattle, and enterprises in the former Soviet Union. I found him a cordial yet guarded man, with a weathered face, high rectangular forehead, and thin frame. His smiles often seemed forced. Like Nixon, Haldeman had been an observer of international communist subversion for many years. His grandfather had founded a precursor to the John Birch Society. As a student leader at UCLA in the 1940s, he had tried to purge the campus newspaper of communist influence. Haldeman directly witnessed Red orchestration of student protest on the University of California at Berkeley campus in the early 1960s. Stroking a cup of coffee in a Santa Monica hotel restaurant, he remembered his early education about communist subversion:

> I had seen a lot of that going back to my days on the [University of California] Board of Regents before I went into the White House, when we were getting the Sproul steps activities at Berkeley. . . .
> There was a Regents' meeting [one day], and there was a demonstration going on down below. And one of the people—I can't remember who it was—at a break in the meeting said, "Come on down, let me show you something down in the square." And we went down, and he said, "See the guy at the microphone?" I said, "Yeah." He said, "He's a student. He's doing all the shouting. But watch his eyes. Watch where he's looking." I watched, and he was looking over here [to his left]. All the time he was looking over here. I said, "Okay." Then he said, "Now, look at who he's looking at." There's three or four people over here. And they're older. I said, "Are they students?" And he said, "No, that's my point." I said, "Do you know who they are?" He said, "Yes, that's my other point." I said, "Who are they?" And he said, "They are longtime communist organizers in this country. They work the cause. And they're over there directing this guy's activities." Now, you knew that kind of thing was just a surface thing, but I remembered that, and so it wasn't hard for me to accept the notion that there was some validity to getting some intelligence [on antiwar protesters]. . . .
> Because a lot of the kids were being manipulated, there's no question about that. And it's easy to manipulate kids, because they love to get excited. You can foment them up for a panty raid, or, in the old days, gold-fish swallowing. You know, this was just another version, for some of them, of that. It's the need, at that age, for stimulation and excitement. . . .
> There was no question, I don't think in any of our minds, but that [the peace movement] was a cause that had its own natural roots, but those were being manipulated, or played upon, and utilized, by

what you might call more sinister causes. And I think often unknowingly.[79]

Many officials believed the Soviet Union simply *had* to be aiding the movement. Ray Price remembered "the sense that if you were sitting in Moscow, you would be a fool not to be trying to do this." Kissinger's aide William Watts said:

Certainly, that somehow or other the Soviet Union, KGB or whatever operatives were able to infiltrate the antiwar movement, to foster it, was something that I think people did very much feel. . . . It seems inconceivable to me—I served in the Soviet Union for two years, and my original background is Soviet studies, I speak Russian, I think I know something about the Soviet Union—it really seems inconceivable to me that somehow or other in their black operations that there would not have been some attempt to influence that movement. . . . If they hadn't tried to influence it, it seems to me they were derelict in their own duty. When you've got something like that going in the heart of the enemy camp, it seems to me only natural that you would try to promote it. Now, that can mean, at least among other things, to try and make sure you get as much attention paid to it as possible. So that you use assets that you've got, say, in other countries, particularly . . . where you can control newspapers . . . to make sure that they get *every bit* of information. And you're supplying them pictures and maybe forged documents and all kinds of stuff to fan the flames.

Ronald Ziegler recalled: "There was certainly the point of view that funds were flowing to certain segments of the radical community from communist sources. . . . I think certainly the communist world in the East saw the benefits of social unrest in a free democracy, and would do anything that they could to support those types of events. I think most of the radicals were more duped in that regard than they were conspirators."[80]

Officials believed other foreign communists were promoting the peace movement too. Haldeman was convinced the North Vietnamese were working behind the scenes. "We know they were involved in that," he confidently said of the October 1969 Vietnam Moratorium protest. Hanoi, he thought, had to have said, "'We'll get this cranked up and see if that doesn't grind them down, and then we'll keep up an unremitting program off of that type of thing.' . . . It was clearly in their interest to have it keep going." Haldeman commented on the violent antiwar protests, "I think Hanoi was instigating them to begin with." In his memoirs, Haldeman claims that "North Vietnamese agents advised the Students for a Democratic Society how to mount the so-called Days of Rage in Chicago in 1969. The North Vietnamese advised the SDS to choose youngsters who would battle with the police. They suggested that the antiwar movement needed not just intellectual protesters but also physically rugged recruits."

Haldeman also alleges that the Weathermen were aided by Cuban operatives after going underground in 1970. "Some were sent to Europe, given new identities, and sent back into this country by way of Czechoslovakia—all paid for by Cuban intelligence."[81] All of this would have been news to the Weathermen.

J. Edgar Hoover was still churning out memos on communist infiltration of the movement, of course. "Hoover would flag things like that," John Dean recalled. "There'd be little special reports." The FBI's lack of evidence didn't faze most officials. "I read the reports and took them at face value," Ehrlichman admitted. Echoed Dean, "It [the FBI] was taken at face value. And this was the only FBI we had." Dean still maintained that "there *was* evidence that, indeed, communist money and what have you was part of the whole picture," although he said he often wondered if Hoover wasn't "taking little threads and running them into grander schemes to justify something. Was it before the fact or after the fact? And I never could tell."[82]

Some officials later downplayed talk by their colleagues of an international communist conspiracy, however. "I never took them seriously when I heard things like that and I don't think they took it very seriously either," Roger Morris scoffed. "They weren't *that* dumb." Laurence Lynn said, "There were some strange ones . . . but I don't know that they were crazies." And Lawrence Eagleburger offered, "By and large, the sophisticated people—of whom there weren't a great number within the administration, but some—I don't think believed it."[83]

Yet Nixon and Haldeman certainly *did* believe that foreign communists were fueling the antiwar movement, and that "basic problem" (as the White House aide Jeb Stuart Magruder later called it) would, in the end, play a significant role in the administration's demise.[84]

During 1969 Nixon administration officials were entertaining other theories of antiwar protest besides communist subversion. Henry Kissinger felt permissive child-rearing practices were partially responsible for the dissension. Explaining the "special feeling" he had for antiwar students, Kissinger writes in his memoirs: "They had been brought up by skeptics, relativists, and psychiatrists; now they were rudderless in a world from which they demanded certainty without sacrifice. My generation had failed them by encouraging self-indulgence and neglecting to provide roots." Morris recalled "a collection of acid Kissinger observations to his staff on the neurotic character of the demonstrators" that fall. "'They don't know who they are,'" Kissinger said. "'They need fathers, not brothers.' 'They are going through an identity crisis.' 'This is like dealing with thumb-sucking.'" Kissinger's aide Anthony Lake remembered, "He saw them as spoiled children." Nixon shared Kissinger's view of rudderless youth. "They don't know what to do with their lives," he mused in his diary.[85]

Kissinger believed most protesters were also "casualties of our affluence," as he told Nixon in November. "They have the leisure for self-pity, and the education enabling them to focus it in a fashionable critique of the 'system.'" Bashing the establishment was "a major thrust of contemporary academic literature," he pointed out. Furthermore, the protesters' upbringings had conditioned them to scorn their affluence. "Stimulated by a sense of guilt encouraged by modern psychiatry and the radical chic rhetoric of upper middle-class suburbia," Kissinger wrote, youths were rebelling against the society that had delivered them the goods yet proved "a spiritual desert." They were suffering from "metaphysical despair," he deduced. "Vietnam is only symptomatic," Kissinger informed Nixon. "When that issue is gone, another will take its place."[86]

Haldeman agreed. He felt many of the protesters were simply out for fun and thrills. "There are people who want to get excited about something, and they don't really give much of a darn what it is they're excited about," he recalled perceiving. "And they move from one cause to the next. They get fired up on civil rights, then on antiwar, then on ecology, and it moves from one thing to another. Antinuke and so forth." Haldeman thus believed that "a lot of them are not really motivated by *the* cause that they are espousing at the moment. They are motivated by the desire to be in *a* cause." And, what's more, "there were a *lot* of people in that movement, especially the younger segments of it, that were simply motivated by the desire to get out and raise hell, without the slightest concern of what they were raising hell about. You know, they had some concern about it, but their motivation really was to get out and do something—it wasn't to stop the war." Haldeman didn't think that all of the protesters were merely issue-hoppers, though. "That's not all of them by any means," he said. "There are some of them—the highly ideologically oriented—that believe deeply in the peace movement and couldn't care less about civil rights or the environment."[87]

Ray Price, who called the 1960s "the second most disastrous decade in the nation's history—the only worse one being the 1860s when it was literally tearing itself apart in civil war," felt much protest was simply an attempt to be cool. "It was in fashion at the time," the mild-mannered former Nixon speechwriter matter-of-factly remarked. "It became the latest hula hoop." Price considered it a mindless fad. "Each time I talked with a group of students, I was dismayed anew at how abysmally ignorant most of them were," he writes in his memoirs. They were "unaware of even the most elementary facts about whatever issue they were currently inflamed about. They rushed to embrace any rumor, as long as its effect was to discredit the war or the 'Establishment.' And, sadly, they had no idea of how little they knew." The protesters were "strangers to linear logic," Price discerned. They saw "'truth' not in terms of observable, hard facts . . . but rather in terms of emotional 'truth'—what seemed right because it felt right, what felt right because it made them feel good, what pleased the senses, what excited the libido or gratified their hungers." They were engaging in "an orgy of right-brain indulgence," Price perceived.[88]

As Price was considering the problem of youthful protest in 1969, it occurred to him that one of its "key elements" might be a "pervasive fear" that the dissenters "neither articulated nor even explicitly recognized." He advanced this hypothesis in a memo to Kissinger and other senior White House staffers on October 2:

> The most overwhelming characteristic of our society today is its complexity. To those just entering on the mysteries of adulthood, this complexity is not merely a phenomenon to be observed; it is a direct, personal threat to their capacity to manage their own futures, to their achievement of "manhood," to their sense of identity, to their place in a world they yearn to call their own.
>
> . . . I suggest that a lot of today's young see the complexity of modern life not as a challenge, but as a barrier, precisely because they see no way . . . by which they can master it; and thus, instead of expending the energy needed to meet the "challenge," they rebel against the system.
>
> . . . Rebellion can be many things—and one of those things is a crutch for those who fear they can't make it, just as Black Studies is often a crutch for the black student fearful that he can't compete in a white milieu. . . . By rebelling against the "system," the youth sets up an excuse for failure; by rejecting its values, he rejects in advance the anticipated negative judgment of the society that embraces those values.
>
> It's no coincidence that so much of the youthful rebellion . . . is focused on the search for *simple* answers, *simple* relationships, *simple* truths. Or that in its inarticulateness, this same set . . . reduces communication to little more than simple grunts and code phrases. . . . It's as though, by instinct, the herd is running from the thunder, seeking shelter: and its shelter is the simple, even the primitive.
>
> This same set of circumstances might also explain much of the passionate arrogance so characteristic of much of today's youth. . . . Arrogance can be rooted in fear—and it may well be that the fear of insufficiency in the face of overwhelming and oppressive complexity would produce precisely the sort of arrogance we have witnessed.

Nixon felt perceptions of *actual* failure were motivating young antiwar professors. "They wanted to blame somebody else for their own failures to inspire the students," he pondered in his diary in 1972.[89]

Robert Brown told Nixon in March that nice weather tended to stir students up. "Most large campus disruptions, whether political or otherwise, have tended historically to develop in the first warm days of Spring," Brown noted. "Such disruptions are generally spontaneous and usually reflect a widespread *restlessness* caused by a combination of factors including the warm weather and the tedium of the daily class routine. . . . Such disruptions are generally not issue-oriented."[90]

Officials recognized that the draft was stoking the peace movement. "Drawn into the moral vacuum of the 1960s," Nixon wrote later, most "draft dodgers" themselves "were not acting out of moral convictions." Rather, they were scared of dying. Other protesters also wished "to keep from getting their asses shot off." Moynihan told the president in August that the draft was giving rise to "a generation of college youth afflicted by intense and persistent emotional crises." Middle-class kids witnessed the poor going to Vietnam in their place, greatly disturbing them, he observed. "At the very least they can prove their manhood by roughing up the administration. But the true demand on them is to transform (i.e. overthrow) the system that put them in this pickle in the first place." Moynihan also informed Nixon that campus protest was partly just plain youthful alienation; kids typically find circumstances "intolerable" until they reach the age of twenty-five, he asserted. Then they learn to adjust.[91]

Anthony Lake aptly characterized the Nixon administration's grasp of the roots of antiwar protest when he commented, "They were so clueless as to what was going on that Kissinger was their resident expert, and would write memos on what students think—which is silly." David Broder of the *Washington Post* was no less perceptive when he wrote in August 1969, "The government under Richard M. Nixon is as ill-equipped to understand and deal with the student movements as it was under Lyndon B. Johnson."[92]

Tackling the Youth Problem

But deal with them it did. Officials were meanwhile weighing and implementing a variety of strategies for combating the youth problem. "We passed many . . . ideas back and forth among ourselves . . . as we groped for answers," Price writes. Many shared Ehrlichman's view that the administration should undertake greater communication with the youth. Robert Brown wrote Nixon on March 17:

A. Problem

1. A *relatively small* group of students (and non-students) across the country are trying to disrupt our Nation's high school and college campuses. The success of the efforts of such students depends on their ability to bring with them the *large majority* of students who, though not basically oriented toward disruption, share with the disruptive elements many of the same attitudes and uncertainties.

2. . . . Although [big campus] disruptions are generally not . . . instigated by individuals or groups, they are *highly susceptible* to outside leadership.

3. If widespread student disruption and violence is to be avoided or at least minimized, efforts must be made to attract the large uncommitted majority away from the instigators and troublemakers. . . .

B. Recommendations

1. Efforts should be undertaken immediately to establish *lines of communication* between this office and student groups of *all* types, including the most radical. These efforts should be made by the younger members of this office and should be strictly informal and off-the-record. Such efforts would help to establish the following objectives.

   a. *An early-warning system* which would enable us to learn of potential trouble areas before they explode so that *preventative action* might be taken.

   b. *Working lines of communication* which could be relied upon in time of crisis. Such lines would be extremely difficult to establish once a crisis has developed.

   c. *Working knowledge of individuals, groups and issues.* In the shifting sands of student politics it is quite important to know who can be relied upon and who should be dealt with in any given situation. It is also important to know which groups should be encouraged to help calm or control a situation rather than be forced by default to rely upon often clumsy means of control offered by government-related institutions. [93]

Both Ehrlichman and Moynihan agreed with Brown's analysis of student disruptions and supported his recommendations. They suggested that a White House program for establishing and maintaining contacts with students be coordinated by Bud Wilkinson, a former University of Oklahoma football coach who was the president's "special consultant" on youth policy. On April 22, Haldeman directed Wilkinson to formulate such a program and to apprise the head of each government department of it. Haldeman pointedly added, "It should be emphasized that this program would not relieve any staff member of any of his normal duties, nor should it require so much time that it would interfere with the performance of his regularly assigned tasks."[94]

Some officials saw limitations to this approach to the youth problem, however. Special Assistant to the President Pat Buchanan disagreed "entirely" with Brown's memo. He felt that the White House was "too busy and understaffed to be serving as an early warning system on disturbances on the 1,000-odd university and college campuses." And "the universities have to solve their own problems," Buchanan believed. White House aide Tom Huston, a 28-year-old ultrarightist and recent national chairman of the Young Americans for Freedom, advised Haldeman on May 20:

> More is involved in the "student problem" than merely listening to the grievances of the small, but vocal minority. I suspect that the basic problem is not one of communication, but of organization and politics. I have known the SDS leadership personally for years; in fact, I knew Tom Haydan [sic] and the others long before the Huron Conference at which SDS was organized. These fellows are careful students and skilled practitioners of the art of revolution. Dialogue is a tactic, not a solution. You don't win their confidence by talking with them, and you certainly don't accomplish much since you must first establish common premises before a discussion can profitably take place—and we don't share common premises about the nature of our society with these people.

Nixon also doubted that talking to the militants would achieve anything. In a memo to Price in February, he sneered at a recent column by Tom Wicker that argued that the administration should "listen to them and treat them as adults." Nixon commented: "The extremists do not want to be listened to and do not want to discuss their problems rationally. Some simply want to disrupt and others want nothing less than complete capitulation to demands that would destroy the higher education system." The president was all for sitting down with the less emotional youth, though. "John—We should make some real efforts towards setting up some positive contacts with the decent kids throughout the country . . . and towards putting a stop to the media's giving so much attention to the bomb throwers," he told Ehrlichman.[95]

Huston agreed that the administration should link up with the decent kids. He advised Haldeman in March that it should "pour money into" the Association of Student Governments (ASG), a centrist-to-conservative organization, "so it can mobilize the resources necessary to effectively cope with the militants where it counts: within student governments on individual campuses." Huston also urged that Nixon meet with a hundred and fifty student body presidents whom the ASG was planning to bring to Washington for a conference in May. He told Haldeman that the ASG was "the best possible vehicle for coping with the militants and I hope we will not fail to take advantage of it." In May, after Nixon had rejected his advice to attend the conference (inducing the ASG to postpone it), Huston again took his case to Haldeman. "The press is anxious to publicize and support the activities of campus moderates, and I believe that we could take advantage of this opportunity with a minimum of effort, but to a great deal of advantage," he wrote. Huston counseled that Nixon speak at the ASG's rescheduled conference in September.[96]

The president was not opposed to aiding pro-administration youth groups.

Agitated over spreading student militance, he wrote Haldeman on March 17, "The only way to stop this dangerous drift is for the decent young students to take up the fight. Why don't Huston, Buchanan, et al get the Young Republicans and other young groups to lay off RN [Richard Nixon] and take on these clowns. *Give me a report.*" Spurred by Haldeman, Buchanan quickly got moving. He reported to Nixon four days later:

> In response to the President's [i.e., your] request, I have contacted the national chairman of the College Young Republicans. He is coming in this week; and we will discuss at that time a program whereby he can inform every *Young Republican leader on campus of the political dividends—and the political rightness—of getting their organizations into the media on the right side of the campus violence issue. The American people are hungry for some neatly dressed young Americans to applaud.*

Buchanan cautioned his boss not to expect earthshaking results, though. "We can do this at the top level. But the President, I am sure, is aware that most Young Republicans have had little or no experience in political combat—other than civil wars. Their speciality is scrimmaging with each other over 'titles' like 'Regional Coordinator' and 'State Chairman.'" Huston was even more pessimistic. The Young Republicans "are not presently capable of positive action at the grassroots, particularly on the campus," he advised. [97]

The administration's program for communicating with antiwar youth was apparently slow in getting off the ground. As the spring school term was drawing to a close, the administration was still debating whether to send "listening teams" to campuses or to make "quiet, unpublicized contacts" with student leaders, as one Ehrlichman memo attests. And Egil Krogh was still writing about "*potential* forays into the campus" by "young White House staffers." But some officials were nonetheless meeting with protesters, ushering them into their lofty White House offices to discuss their concerns. Kissinger was among the most active hosts. As a Harvard professor, he had more at stake than U.S. policy in Vietnam. He had his reputation inside academia to consider. "He was very sensitive to where he stood with his colleagues in the academic profession," the State Department's Marshall Green recalled. "Eventually he was going to go back to those circles, and he did not want to create permanent enemies." Said Price, "He was very deeply troubled by what [antiwar protest] did to his own personal relationships with the campus." Asked which opponents of the war most unsettled Kissinger, one official with whom he worked closely answered, immediately, "Intellectuals. . . . I don't think he'd admit that, but I think it was where he was most sensitive." [98]

Kissinger was a smooth talker. "He would desperately want to . . . portray himself as the sympathetic person within the administration," his aide Anthony Lake remembered. "And he was very good at leaving the impression at meetings that he was—not a secret dove, because they wouldn't have believed that—but at least sensitive to their concerns: 'Nobody has a monopoly on anguish,' deeply moved by the human suffering—all those things that would ring their chimes." Price complained: "He might say one thing to them and another to us."[99]

Neither Lake nor Price believed Kissinger's sensitivity to academic dissent influenced his policies, however. "I don't think he would ever say to himself, 'I am going to pursue a policy that is softer than I would otherwise pursue for the sake of my standing with my academic colleagues,'" Lake argued. "If anything—because he had contempt for them at the same time, and he dripped with contempt when they weren't there—it would be more of, 'Precisely because they're such jerks I'm going to pursue the right policy.'" Green had a different view. Kissinger's concern for his reputation in the universities, he contended, fed a recurring inclination to give up on the war. "I think quite often the president had to buck him up and tell Henry, 'For God sakes, get in there and fight,'" Green said. "I think Henry was much more prepared to back away."[100]

Nixon attempted to communicate with the young protesters through public statements. Preceding each statement were extensive White House deliberations on the appropriate line. The president's first major pronouncement took officials more than a week to compose. Price warned against a hard stance. "Insensitive intervention can make the situation far worse instead of better," he wrote in mid March. "Reagan loves to blast the campus rioters—and every time he does, he gets another couple of riots." Robert Brown concurred with Price. "Great care must be exercised not to force the uncommitted majority into the hands of the disruptive few," Brown counseled Nixon. "The mood of the campuses is such that overreaction in speech or in action by the Government could easily antagonize a great many presently uncommitted students and facilitate their alienation."[101]

The president found merit in his aides' advice. "Students today point to many wrongs which must be made right," Nixon told the nation on March 22. He criticized "a depersonalization of the educational experience" and inadequate "student involvement in . . . decision-making." But the president was not simply Mr. Understanding. "It is not too strong a statement to declare that this is the way civilizations begin to die," he darkly warned of campus violence. "The process is altogether too familiar to those who would survey the wreckage of history."[102]

Nixon soon concluded that he had been too soft with the dissenters. "The President wants to seriously consider another statement on the student crisis," Haldeman wrote the White House speechwriter Jim Keogh on April 28. "This time he does not want to sympathize with the students; he feels that they need a stiff jolt. He feels the first statement may have been too much of a compromise and this time we should express less concern—although we should mention it—regarding understanding them and listening to them." The next day, speaking to a national meeting of the Chamber of Commerce, Nixon declared that there must be "no compromise with lawlessness and no surrender to force if free education is to survive." He specifically condemned students who "terrorize other students and faculty members," including ones who "carry guns and knives in the classrooms." The president applauded peaceful dissent. He also expressed faith in the future. "This is an exciting time to be alive," Nixon said.[103]

On June 3, at minute General Beadle State College in South Dakota—one of the few campuses he could set foot on safely—Nixon lashed out at protesters again. "We live in a deeply troubled and profoundly unsettled time," he gravely observed. "Drugs, crime, campus revolts, racial discord, draft resistance—on every hand we find old standards violated, old values discarded, old precepts ignored." Nixon lambasted "the student who invades an administration building, roughs up the dean, rifles the files and issues 'non-negotiable demands.'" He ominously declared, "We have the power to strike back if need be, and to prevail. The Nation has survived other attempts at insurrection. We can survive this." And the next day, at the U.S. Air Force Academy, Nixon decried the "open season on the armed forces" in America.[104]

Based on his conversations with university professors, Arthur Burns urged the administration to denounce one rampageous youth group in particular. He wrote Nixon on May 26:

> The government should inform the nation about the nature of SDS and its goals, so that students, faculty, and others can distinguish between legitimate issues and the demands of a group whose ultimate goal is destruction rather than reform. If the government's information concerning the SDS and related groups is not sufficient, it should be quickly augmented. It is essential to know the exact nature of this new, rather frightening, movement.

The president agreed. He queried Ehrlichman: "(1) Will the Senate or House investigation [of protesters] meet this need? (2) Could Justice or H.E.W. do anything on it? (3) Possibly a University indigenous group should investigate and report (4) Or a respected newspaper team?" After inquiring into the first issue, Ehrlichman concluded that the summer hearings planned by Senators James Eastland (D-Miss.) and John McClellan would "meet the need of public exposure called for by Dr. Burns." Because of the "great respect enjoyed by Senator McClellan's investigations, it would seem unnecessary and imprudent to attempt to augment his efforts by executive branch disclosures." Ehrlichman smugly added, "If these congressional hearings do not adequately expose the illegitimate, nihilist goals of some of these groups, then I think it necessary for the executive departments involved to focus their attention on some of these groups and to educate the public accordingly."[105]

Officials debated what role congressional legislation should play in quelling the campus turmoil. Some felt a bill passed the previous year denying federal aid to students convicted of criminal conduct was sufficient. Others backed pending legislation that would require universities to adopt codes of appropriate student and faculty conduct in order to receive funds. Virtually all, however, opposed proposed legislation that would cut off aid to universities where major disturbances occurred. Such legislation would greatly increase anti-administration sentiment on campuses, they knew. As John Mitchell told a congressional subcommittee, it "would certainly play right into the hands of the militants."[106]

Brown advocated using federal resources to entice the militants to abandon the barricades for more wholesome political pursuits. "Efforts should be made to harness the energies of the students in constructive activities which both serve the public interest and fulfill the growing need of many students to contribute meaningfully to society," he advised Nixon. "An example might be a large student-manned and managed nationwide program to gather and organize data relating to nutrition upon which a broad-scale anti-hunger campaign might be launched."[107]

Another prescription of Brown's had been on the minds of officials since the administration's inception: draft reform. "It was obvious that the draft was a major factor in all the unrest that was limiting our options and so forth in terms of [Vietnam] policy," Price recalled, "and that to the extent that we could get rid of that we would reduce a lot of the frictions." Many officials preferred a lottery system limiting draft liability to one year. Secretary of Defense Laird was a particularly strong proponent of the system. "That was Mel Laird's baby," General William Westmoreland remembered. "He was trying to defuse the younger generation." Acknowledged Laird, "That was a very important thing in order to relieve some of the dissatisfaction" with the war. He considered conscription "the most combustible element in the campus tinderbox" and hoped to eventually abolish it. In May, Nixon proposed a lottery to Congress. To no one's surprise, the proposal languished on Capitol Hill into the summer.[108]

The administration showed its stick. In early March, John Mitchell announced that the Justice Department would prosecute "hard-line militants" who crossed state lines to foment trouble on campuses. "If there are subversive influences disrupting the academies," the dour, jowly attorney general told an interviewer, "then the Department has to step in." Mitchell drew a distinction between "demonstrators" and "activists," contending that the latter should be denied permits to protest. "If you can sort out the wheat from the chaff," he explained, "the good cowboys are less likely to be induced into [disruptive] activities by the militants." To curb criminal conduct in general, Mitchell proposed preventive detention of "dangerous hard-core recidivists." Richard Kleindienst, the mercurial deputy attorney general, declared, "This Administration is prepared and willing and ready to act immediately. As soon as we're notified of danger, we'll have the National Guard in the armory and the Army on two-, four-, or six-hour alert." Student militants, he said, "should be rounded up and put in a detention camp." Will Wilson, the Justice Department's chief prosecutor, concurred, asserting that "if you could get all of them in the penitentiary, you'd stop it. The ringleaders, I'm talking about." Of protest in general, Wilson was no more accepting. "In the area of balancing the right of dissent against public order, my heavy leaning would be on the side of public order," he avowed. "On the question of where does free speech move towards public disturbance, my answer would be 'pretty soon.'" The administration formulated contingency plans to quash an insurrection in the United States.[109]

Government bodies intensified their harassment of protesters. Nixon's General Beadle tirade aside, intelligence and police agents were responsible for most of the rifled files in the country. Many an antiwar group had its records ransacked or stolen. David McReynolds remembered that "someone came in and took the membership lists and wrecked the office" of the War Resisters League's national headquarters in 1969. "It was a fast, efficient operation," he said. "It was a government agency, I don't have any doubt about that." Agents spread false information about protesters, promoted violent acts, and even disrupted lawful peace activity. (Suppressing legal protest was not new to Nixon administration officials then. During the 1968 presidential campaign, Nixon had ordered Ehrlichman to put together a "flying goon squad" to "rough up" demonstrators at his speeches. "Occasionally, we would even pay cash money for that kind of help," Ehrlichman disclosed.)[110]

At Nixon's request, Tom Huston and Arthur Burns pressured the IRS to go after tax-exempt radical organizations. Huston sent the IRS "background material on some of the more conspicuously offensive groups." He and Burns also leaned directly on IRS Commissioner Randolph Thrower. "*Good,*" Nixon commended Burns when apprised of their work. "But I want *action.* Have Huston follow up *hard* on this." Although Thrower failed to audit or otherwise harass the conspicuously offensive groups, the IRS established a staff in the early summer to investigate "Ideological Organizations," including their funding sources. Discretion was the watchword: "We do not want news media to be alerted to what we are attempting to do or how we are operating because the disclosure of such information might embarrass the Administration," Huston cautioned. An FBI agent recalled visiting a locked, soundproof basement room in the IRS's Washington headquarters that summer where hundreds of files on antiwar protesters and black militants were assembled.[111]

The Nixon administration's stick came down with a loud thud on March 29, when, at Mitchell's direction, a federal grand jury indicted eight protesters for conspiracy to incite a riot during the 1968 Democratic Convention. Those charged included Dave Dellinger, Rennie Davis, Tom Hayden, Abbie Hoffman, Jerry Rubin, Bobby Seale, John Froines, and Lee Weiner. Most of the career lawyers in the Justice Department considered the indictments groundless or iffy and had advised against them. The previous year, Attorney General Ramsey Clark had found their counsel persuasive and rejected pleas from the White House and members of Congress to take the same action. "I wasn't about to indict any of the protesters," Clark recalled, disgustedly. "I knew, for instance, that the idea that Bobby Seale had participated in any conspiracy was *utterly* false, and was *known* to law enforcement to be utterly false. He hadn't even planned to come to Chicago. . . . Bobby came at the last minute. He doesn't know who these other seven people are and what the hell is going on." Far from prosecuting demonstrators, Clark had ordered the indictment of eight Chicago policemen for civil rights violations. "I've always believed that the reason there were eight [protesters charged] was because there were eight police," he said. The "Chicago Eight" (later Seven when Seale's case was separated) became a cause célèbre and rallying point for antiwar activists. Nixon subsequently seemed fixated on the Jewish protesters indicted. "Aren't the Chicago Seven all Jews?" he asked Haldeman during an Oval Office conversation in 1971. "Davis's a Jew, you know." "I don't think Davis is," Haldeman responded. "Hoffman, Hoffman's a Jew," the president returned. "Abbie Hoffman is and that's so," Haldeman said. Nixon said of protesters then in Washington, "About half of these are Jews." "I think more now," Haldeman corrected him.[112]

A month after the Chicago indictments, Mitchell let it be known that more prosecutions would be forthcoming. "The time has come for an end to patience," he declared. Mitchell denounced the "members of a small core of professional militants" behind major university disruptions. "Campus militants . . . are nothing but tyrants," he spat. The same day, Kleindienst condemned "ideological criminal[s]" on campuses.[113]

On June 8, with South Vietnamese President Nguyen Van Thieu standing obediently by his side, Nixon announced the withdrawal of twenty-five thousand U.S. troops from Vietnam. The announcement was made on uninhabited Midway Island in the middle of the Pacific Ocean "because of the fear that a visit by Thieu to the United States would provoke riots," Kissinger recalled. It was designed to calm not only youthful protesters but dissenting congressmen and the general public. "I don't think there can be any question but that the Nixon administration was obliged to make some gestures to indicate that they were trying to get the war over," Richard Helms said. "And one of the more visible ways to convince the public that they were working in that direction was to withdraw troops." Nixon and Kissinger recognized "that they were sitting on a very volatile political situation, that people thought that Johnson was moving toward withdrawing us, and that if they had any sense that Nixon was not, the whole thing would blow up," Morton Halperin argued.[114]

Placating the public had grown increasingly important to Nixon and Kissinger over the spring, lessening their aversion to unilateral troop withdrawals. Despite the secret Cambodia bombing and private threats to Hanoi, the North Vietnamese had failed to agree to U.S. peace terms; much to the administration's chagrin, they denounced a U.S. proposal on May 14 for mutual withdrawal from South Vietnam. Nixon decided that the madman inside him would have to be made clearer to them. But the president and Kissinger recognized they needed to convince Hanoi that they had sufficient domestic support to actually carry out their threat of savage escalation. They also needed more time for the threat to work. "Buying time at home was one of the most crucial factors in dealing with the war," as Price said. Although withdrawing troops was also designed to force the South Vietnamese to pull up their boots, Price recalled, "we absolutely had to from a domestic standpoint."[115]

And even as antiwar voices were pressuring Nixon and Kissinger from outside the government, Mel Laird was leaning on them within it. "Laird was very intense in the implementation of this program [Vietnamization]," Westmoreland remembered. Laird persuaded General Creighton Abrams, commander of U.S. forces in Vietnam, that troop withdrawals made political sense, creating a valuable ally in his crusade. Laird also helped convince Nixon that the South Vietnamese could ultimately be trained to stand on their own feet. Not until later did it become apparent how faulty the data informing that assessment were. Roger Morris recalled

> how bad the intelligence was from Saigon and how phony the numbers were. It was just one great ongoing sort of crap game of fraud that was being perpetrated on Washington. To find an honest man in the American government dealing with that war in . . . 1969 would have been *a miracle. Everyone* was compromised. . . . It's really true that the truth wasn't in us. We had been lying to ourselves and others for so long about that problem that you just couldn't get decent, open analysis. . . . The American government was saying to itself the same kind of horseshit that it was peddling on the outside. . . . It was a form of structural insanity taking place in the organism of the government at large. . . . It was a very scary experience.

Yet move Nixon Laird did. "His influence on the president was *considerable,"* Laurence Lynn said. "Laird knew how to deal with the president. He knew how to get his way with the president. He knew how to get his way even *without* the president."[116]

But Laird could only push Nixon so far. The secretary of defense had urged him to withdraw fifty thousand troops at Midway, twice the actual figure.

"I wanted the announcement to be fifty to start with," Laird remembered. "I thought there would be more impact with fifty. And I got Abrams to agree on fifty. But Kissinger, Nixon and the State Department felt that that was *very bad*."[117]

Following Midway, "Nixon was jubilant," Kissinger writes. "He considered the announcement a political triumph. He thought it would buy him the time necessary for developing our strategy. His advisers, including me, shared his view. We were wrong on both counts."[118]

Planning an Autumn Attack: The Vietnam Moratorium and New Mobe

As officials were scheming to blunt domestic antagonism to the war, their opponents were gearing up for a major fall offensive. In April, the Boston envelope manufacturer and peace activist Jerome Grossman proposed organizing a nationwide general strike against the war. The strike would last one day in October, he submitted. If U.S. troops were not withdrawn from Vietnam by November 1, citizens would strike two days in November. Another day would be added to the strike each month until the war was over. Grossman's proposal was greeted skeptically in many antiwar circles. "What are the new conditions that make it more plausible now than it was last year?" asked Richard Fernandez. "Any peace action is good, but we do not think the strike will have much support."[119] Nevertheless, Grossman was able to entice the interest of a number of seasoned antiwar organizers. Their leader was Sam Brown, the former head of Youth for McCarthy.

When I interviewed him, Brown was a real estate developer. His interest in the business was all-consuming: he worked long hours, and during a stroll through downtown Denver his attention focused on the anatomies of buildings under construction. Before trying his hand at real estate, Brown was director of VISTA under President Jimmy Carter and Colorado's state treasurer. After Vietnam, his politics moved somewhat rightward. The former antiwar leader agonizingly supported the 1991 Gulf War with Iraq.

In the winter of 1969, Brown was teaching a seminar on American politics at Harvard. He was lying low on the antiwar front. "There was a political sense that you couldn't attack [Nixon] until he'd been in office long enough that he owned the war," Brown recalled. "I mean, to sort of go after him in January or February would have been silly. People would have looked at you and said, 'Wait a minute. The guy says he's got a plan. Give him a chance.'" Brown himself had little faith in Nixon. "It seemed that he was going to get out of Vietnam as slowly as possible, while selling the idea that he was getting out as fast as possible," he wrote afterward. And the former Young Republican leader thought the country was ripe for a massive display of antiwar sentiment. The 1968 McCarthy campaign had not only surfaced widespread public disenchantment with the war, he noticed, but vitalized the peace movement. "By the time the McCarthy campaign was over, the antiwar movement didn't any longer have to be such a fringy operation," Brown said. "We did, after all, have both more developed talent, more money, more sources of knowledge on how to raise money. . . . I mean, I saw that year [1968] as a major breakpoint in what we could do."[120]

Brown found the localist slant of Grossman's proposal compelling. Despite substantial public opposition to the war, he was not interested in organizing another big demonstration in Washington. Brown explained:

> It all goes back to the theoretical question, "How do we end the war?" If it's to make things unworkable, if it's to create a revolution, then you've got to get a large mass of people together where the center of government is. . . . If you think what that's likely to do is to drive the rest of the country away from you and in the long run create the opposite of what you hope for, then you shouldn't do it. And what you needed to do was to figure out, not how to convince the people in Boston and New York and Washington—who were already pretty much against the war—that the war had to be ended, but how do you demonstrate that there is a much broader base? . . . I mean, there was some legitimate concern that if the country withdrew and it was seen as an act of cowardice . . . that we'd be right back to Joe McCarthy in 1951. That somebody would have to be blamed. . . . And nobody wanted to hand the right wing that kind of club. . . . So what you had to do was to have a broad enough consensus that it couldn't be blamed on a sellout, it couldn't be "that secret closet commie FDR running off giving it away." . . . And I thought that marches and demonstrations in Washington by that time tended to be seen in a large part of the rest of the country not as representing the will of the American people but as representing a threat from a small minority of the American people. Also . . . some people were so pissed, so incapable of controlling themselves, and just so angry and bitter and generally upset, that no matter how hard you tried, it seemed to me if you had a half a million people together in the same spot, you were going to get a certain number of crazies, and . . . a certain number of agents provocateurs, who understood that if they could attack the Justice Department or carry Viet Cong flags or burn the American flag . . . that it was going to undercut the intent of what you were doing. And therefore it seemed to me at that time that it was the wrong time to do marches. You don't bring a half a million or a million angry people together in the same place and expect it to be a nice afternoon in the sun.[121]

Brown had his Harvard seminar—which he'd creatively turned into a roundtable discussion on antiwar strategy—weigh Grossman's proposal. "In the course of that discussion we sort of came around to the conclusion that 'strike' had a kind of stridency to it," he remembered. "You could do the same thing with other kinds of language that kind of softened the edges of it without changing the substance. . . . You could say, 'For one day, we're going to put aside our normal business and think about the war.'" Brown and his students also concluded that *strike* wrongly suggested action against the institutions struck rather than against the war. He and Grossman agreed to use the word *moratorium* instead.[122]

Brown approached David Hawk, who had been a fellow Youth for McCarthy leader, about the protest. Hawk was intrigued by its potential. "That seemed to me to be a very interesting idea—'That's kind of wild.' But it had teeth in it," he recalled. Hawk knew there was already a "terrific network" of student activists in place that could get the ball rolling on the project: the 253 signatories of the April antidraft statement. "Essentially that spring we had created a network . . . of mainstream student-body-leader types who had access either to the editorial pages of their college newspapers and the resources thereof, or else to their student governments," he said. "That's a good network to have, because your people can get stuff done. . . . We were really well on our way to a nationwide network for a fall activity." Excited, Hawk "got a little bit of money together and brought a bunch of [the students] in, and laid out the idea of the Moratorium."[123]

Activists would spend the summer and early fall organizing the campuses, Hawk and Brown explained. On October 15, they would strike out into the communities, canvassing, holding vigils, leafleting. Their primary goal would be to build a base for November's two-day protest. The Moratorium would escalate in breadth, visibility, and strength over time. "People would come at their own pace, so that people who were already committed before the first month would be doing one set of things, and people who started in the first month would be doing another set of things," Brown recalled thinking. "As the mood of the community changed, we expected the [antiwar] events would change." Who knew what the spring might bring? A truly enormous citizens' revolt against the war was possible. The student leaders were interested.[124]

Brown and Hawk set up shop in a dingy, barren office in Washington. Joining them at the helm of the "Vietnam Moratorium Committee" (VMC) was David Mixner, another former McCarthy organizer. On June 30, the three young activists held a press conference to announce the Moratorium. "We want to make it clear that the 2 percent that people talk about on the campuses are really 70 percent—that they're not just 'crazy radicals' but 'your sons and daughters,'" Brown stated. "People want desperately to talk with kids," Hawk said. "A big part of our success in New Hampshire was that people were just so happy to have a kid knock on the door and talk to them." The youths criticized Nixon's "token displacement" of twenty-five thousand troops.[125]

Over the summer, the VMC secured endorsements from student leaders and got campus groups started. "In several years of antiwar work we have never seen such enthusiasm or unanimity over strategy," exclaimed a VMC letter. The group attracted other veteran organizers to its steering committee—including Richard Fernandez (who would come to speak of "the genius of the Moratorium"). Congressional support was much slower in coming, however. Mixner, the VMC's point man on Capitol Hill, "got nothing but smiles and encouragement from everyone but the handful of consistent doves" in Congress. "There was a perceptible lack of raw courage on the part of most elected officials," Brown writes. Media interest in the Moratorium was also low, although a few journalists—aroused by the spring campus militance and sniffing around for stories on "Just what do those students have planned for the fall?"—reported the VMC's activity. [126]

Antiwar activists were also planning a traditional mass demonstration in the fall. In April the Socialist Workers Party asked the Cleveland Area Peace Action Council (CAPAC) to sponsor a national antiwar conference for the purpose of organizing another big mobilization. The moribund National Mobe had lost too much authority in the peace movement to sponsor such a conference, the SWP knew, but the CAPAC—situated in the Mobe's birthplace and with a certain political standing—might be able to pull it off. Enhancing the CAPAC's attractiveness was its growing SWP flavor; in fact, its chairperson, Jerry Gordon, was such a "close friend of the party" (as SWPer Lew Jones recalled) that he attended SWP steering committee meetings, and his wife was the daughter of a party heavy. On May 10, the CAPAC agreed to host the conference. There was a snag, however. Sidney Peck, who had headed the CAPAC until recently and was a widely respected figure in the movement, refused to go along. [127]

Peck was all for organizing an autumn demonstration. The April pacifist and GI–Civilian actions had convinced him that large numbers of people could again be brought out into the streets. And Peck was all for convening another national antiwar conference. But he was leery of the SWP's intentions. He remembered:

> There were two things that I was concerned about. One, that they
> would pack the conference. And two, that they would try to exclude
> some of the forces around Dellinger and to the left of Dellinger, par-
> ticularly some of the youth forces, some of the SDS people, including
> those that had moved into a Weather[man] direction. Because they
> just did not trust Dellinger; they didn't really want to work with him
> and those other people. Their attitude toward what they considered
> to be ultraleftism was to keep them away. So that while the Trotsky-
> ists were into nonexclusionism, politically, they would have loved to
> have had a conference that did not include Dellinger and those other
> forces. [128]

Sharp conflict erupted over the SWP's proposal. Peck warily decided to help build the conference, "but only if Dellinger and others went along with it. So I tried to convince David and others to be part of it. And of course they along with myself were concerned about the effort on the part of the SWP to pack the conference." "That was the fear," Norma Becker recalled. Dellinger was also unready to junk the National Mobe. The conflict was finally resolved at an emotionally charged meeting in the kitchen of Peck's Cleveland home in June. The session ran into the wee hours of the morning. According to the SWP leader Don Gurewitz, a participant, Peck phoned Dellinger in New York and bluntly asserted: "Dave, the movement's going to go forward with or without you. You can keep the National Mobe as long as you want, but somehow the movement is going to move forward. So if you want to be part of it, you'd better come up with a compromise." And compromise Dellinger did. The discussants agreed to an invitation-only conference, scheduled for July 4–5. Although observers would be permitted to attend, only invited delegates could vote. That way the SWP would be unable to ram its positions through the assembly. Also, observers could petition for voting status. The SWP was far from happy with the arrangement. "We agreed to that *extremely reluctantly*," Gurewitz remembered. "As far as we were concerned, that wasn't real good."[129]

Short days later, the SWP-controlled Student Mobilization Committee put out a call for its own conference in Cleveland on July 6. It didn't take a genius to figure out what the SWP was plotting: it would flood the earlier meeting with party members and sympathizers who, claiming to represent "independent" antiwar groups, would demand delegate status. "They had a whole approach to that," Peck said wearily.[130]

The CAPAC-hosted conference was tense. At a steering committee meeting on convention eve, tempers flared over recommendations for fall antiwar activity. Dellinger and others advocated helping build a militant "National Action" Weatherman was cooking up in Chicago to mark the opening of the conspiracy trial of the Chicago Eight. According to Fred Halstead, Dellinger and Rennie Davis argued that the trial should be the focal point of fall activity. "For them, in truth, the movement became this case," he scornfully recalled. "The *football game* was more important than that trial as far as I was concerned." (Dellinger said that he would be "shocked" and "ashamed" if he had urged that the conspiracy trial be the main focus of fall protest.) Jerry Gordon proposed organizing a peaceful demonstration in Washington. Good SWP front man that he was, Gordon was adamant that civil disobedience be prohibited. Doug Dowd later remembered getting so steamed over Gordon's self-righteous tone and obvious adherence to the SWP line "that I just wouldn't put up with it. And so at some point . . . I said, 'Gordon, if you don't shut your fucking mouth, I'm going to come over the table, and although I'm not a violent man, I'm going to beat the shit out of you. Just cut out the shit. . . . ' And Halstead said, very quietly . . . 'Jerry, cut it out.'" Sidney Lens eventually persuaded the steering committee to recommend to the conference that it promote both the Chicago and Washington protests.[131]

The next day SWPers were running around the convention site in droves. As expected, many demanded delegate status. Other conventioneers were livid. Norma Becker recalled:

> The SWP stacked that conference. . . . And they did it with consummate skill. And I was very enraged over that. Because a lot of us had great trepidation in going along with that conference and lending our names to it. I only did that . . . through Sid Peck's pressure. He said that Jerry Gordon swore that it wouldn't be stacked, that it would be a representative conference with legitimate representatives from legitimate groups that were functioning and not just paper groups. But they stacked it.

In its zeal to ward off the SWP's onslaught, the conference's credentials committee mistakenly rejected petitions for voting status of representatives of popular antiwar groups, infuriating them. "Are you conducting an inquisition?" some bitterly asked.[132]

The Weatherman Mark Rudd appealed for support for the Chicago protest. His raving speech about kicking ass and fighting pigs was "so poor," so "really bad," Peck remembered, that it received scant support from the delegates. "The SDS proposal lost because it was presented very honestly," Halstead chortled years later. "He presented it just the way it turned out." "Did you pay him to say that?" an appalled Lens jested to Halstead when Rudd had finished. Gordon spoke again for a mass demonstration in Washington. Halstead thundered about the need for nonviolence. "You faced these guys and you had to spell it out!" he boisterously recalled—"'No, no, no. This has got to be a legal, peaceful demonstration. No nonsense!'" Coaxed by Lens, the conferees decided to support both Washington and Chicago, but with the proviso that further negotiation "on tactics" in Chicago was necessary.[133]

The conference made several other important decisions. It endorsed the Vietnam Moratorium. To help build the demonstration in Washington, the delegates scheduled it for November 15, the time of the second Moratorium. The conference also endorsed a single-file "Death March" in Washington proposed by the AFSC leader Stewart Meacham. The venerable, silver-haired former pastor was planning a massive reading of the names of American war dead that fall running for thirty-six straight hours and involving forty thousand people. The conference supported Meacham's proposal despite doubts about its viability. "Stewart, that won't work," one antiwar leader lectured him around this time.

"Why not?" Meacham patiently responded. "Well, no one's going to [march] at three o'clock in the morning." The skeptic's name was Richard Fernandez. "And those buses pulled in at two o'clock, three o'clock—all night long," Fernandez amusedly recalled of the wildly successful march.[134]

The conference's steering committee selected a name for the rebuilt antiwar coalition: the New Mobilization Committee to End the War in Vietnam. Even that seemingly innocuous task prompted hours of heated debate, lasting until 2 A.M.[135]

Few of the exhausted, emotionally racked discussants would have been surprised to learn that their new coalition had less than a year to live.

New Mobe and VMC organizers banded together over the summer to build the Washington protests and the Moratorium. Small teams composed of representatives of each project traveled from city to city trying to pump up interest in them. "We went all over the country giving speeches together, pushing the Moratorium and the Mobe," Doug Dowd, one member of this "flying circus," remembered. "The audiences that we had tended to be audiences that either had to be convinced that the Mobe was okay, knowing the Moratorium was okay, or vice versa. So the two of us would sort of throw the ball back and forth." The New Mobe leaders Sidney Peck and Ron Young organized Moratorium committees in cities where none existed.[136]

Relations between the Mobe and the Moratorium were not all harmonious, however. "There was a tremendous amount of suspicion of the Moratorium" within the Mobe, one activist recalled. Many Mobe organizers considered the Moratorium "liberal," overly diffuse, undisciplined, and thus ineffectual. VMC activists, on the other hand, worried about violence on November 15. Many thus wished to avoid association with the Mobe. And some felt national demonstrations hampered grass-roots antiwar organizing. "It seemed a centralized thing was a diversion from the building of local stuff," David Hawk said. "And people go back [from national demonstrations] and think they've done it for awhile." November 15 might let steam out of the Moratorium, VMC activists feared. Dowd and Meacham smoothed over the rough edges in relations between the two groups, but as late as October 16, Sam Brown announced that the VMC's support of November 15 was still "an open question."[137]

Weathermania

Meanwhile, the Weathermen were madly organizing for their National Action in Chicago. They would "Bring the War Home," they blustered, tearing "pig city" apart and thereby "striking blows" at U.S. imperialism. Militant action was the only thing "the Man understands," declared three Weatherleaders. "As long as militancy isn't a threat, pig and ruling-class approval is forthcoming."

The "Days of Rage" (as they increasingly billed the protest) would also attract more working-class youth to the barricades and thus build a "white fighting force" that could "attack the beast from within as the peoples of the world attack it from without." The action would recruit youth by showing the movement's confidence and strength. "Being on the side of victory . . . that's the essential thing that we have to show people," Bill Ayers told fellow Weathermen. "Our theory was that, by fighting, we were proving that it was possible to fight, and therefore, theoretically, ultimately possible to win," the Weather-leader Jeff Jones reminisced. "It was a leap. It's not completely logical. I mean, we only did it once . . ." Some recruits, it was hoped, would pick up the gun. "We're . . . going to make it clear that when a pig gets iced that's a good thing, and that everyone who considers himself a revolutionary should be armed," Ayers stated.[138]

The Weathermen rejected the Mobe's demand for input on tactics. "We said, 'Well, write them off,'" Ayers recalled. "That was the mentality that we [had]." For a change, they, the actionists—not wimpy liberals or phony communists—would be calling the shots on a national demonstration. Ayers remembered:

> Our initial idea for proposing that . . . action was that all these dem-
> onstrations that had happened through the years, from 1965 on,
> were sponsored by large umbrella organizations, but it was the mili-
> tants who both took the licks and were the shock troops of the dem-
> onstrations, who made the demonstrations effective. So those of us
> who'd been arrested in demonstrations [in 1965–68], in 1969 we said,
> "Let's have our own demonstration where we're the ones who set the
> slogans, and let them join *our* demonstration. . . . Instead of saying,
> 'These are the slogans and everybody has to unite around them,'
> we'll say, '*These* are the slogans and everybody should unite around
> *them*.' And instead of saying, 'We'll be nice, and we won't do any-
> thing [provocative], and negotiate it all out,' say, 'No, it's going to be
> a militant demonstration—we're militant.'" And we felt that we ap-
> pealed to the militants who made up the . . . foot soldiers of the
> other demonstrations, and that we would have thousands and thou-
> sands of people in Chicago.[139]

Weatherman organized "action projects" in a handful of cities over the summer to recruit working-class youth. They were among the most bizarre enterprises ever undertaken by an American left group. The predominately affluent, student Weathermen hung out on inner-city street corners "rapping" with local teenage toughs about imperialism, kicking ass ("one of the Weatherpeople's favorite phrases that year," Dave Dellinger writes), "getting us a few pigs." To demonstrate their toughness, they scrapped with police and potential recruits alike. In Detroit, nine Weatherwomen organized a "jail break" at a community college; after invading a classroom, chanting, the women barricaded the door with the teacher's desk and "rapped" to the dumbfounded students about "the revolution" and the Days of Rage. When two male students "got uptight" and charged the door, the women assaulted these "pig agents" using "karate" (in their version of the story) or their teeth and fingernails (in the males' version). In Pittsburgh, scores of Weatherwomen tore through a high school yelling "jail break!" at the top of their lungs, some with their breasts exposed, to the delight of male observers. Weathermen bound and gagged two teachers at a Brooklyn high school before haranguing their students. Although Ayers boasted that kids across America "loved the fuckin' action," most, in fact, sensed that the Weathermen were lunatics. Some booted them out of their neighborhoods. Ayers later lamented:

> In some ways we got, I think, caught up in a romantic vision . . . that we were going to show that we were courageous. . . . And a lot of things that happened were quite nutty. . . . Some of the stuff was ridiculous. And some of it was ineffective and meaningless. And some of it was the stuff of Zap comics. . . . And I think that we made . . . tremendous, tremendous errors. And as I look back on it, that was a hard time to live through. We were both kind of driving ourselves in a way that wasn't completely healthy and we weren't seeing things particularly clearly. . . . I think that our political sense of sparking something had really lost touch with both the moral vision and any kind of [political] base that might have been moved by that. So I think it became kind of a frustrating, self-denying kind of activity.

Ayers tried to explain how he and his comrades had arrived at this state:

> I think probably what it was was a sense of tremendous frustration coupled with the need to remake ourselves to kind of overcome our own middle-classness. . . . [The frustration involved] a feeling of isolation, and a feeling of not being able to somehow do enough, that somehow the war was inexorable and you couldn't stop it. . . . My God, it was just awful. You would just watch the war building, and then even with the withdrawal of American troops you'd just watch it expand, [with] more people being killed. And no matter what you did, there was a sense that we couldn't do enough. So there was this kind of driven quality to that whole time. We were driven to do more.[140]

The Weathermen's drive to transform themselves was as maniacal as their drive to transform society. "We have one task, and that's to make ourselves into tools of the revolution," Ayers lectured. "And that means a lot of heavy stuff." Living in collectives around the country, the Weathermen moved to "smash" the myriad everyday habits and notions that seemed to prop up capitalism. To smash attachment to personal property, many limited themselves to one set of clothes. To smash individualism, everything—including a person's wish to go to their bedroom to read—had to be decided by group discussion. To smash sexism, remarks that hinted of it had to be immediately confronted by the entire collective (leading to "a few fistfights" between the sexes). To smash racism, more up-against-the-wallist meetings. To smash monogamy, Weathermen swapped sexual partners virtually at random. Grueling "criticism–self-criticism" sessions—"Weatherfries," some dubbed them—left no liberal stone in a Weatherman house unturned. The objective was "to live . . . revolution twenty-four hours a day," Jones recalled. Many Weathermen couldn't handle the strain and left the collectives, some as emotional basket cases. Jones would come to regret this frenzied attempt to create new men and women:

> I look back on that as a political low point in my life. . . . I feel that there were tremendous interpersonal abuses in that [process], that it was a very unhealthy political phenomenon. I don't see that many people trying to repeat that particular political experiment. A lot of burnout occurred, a lot of good people were damaged, a lot of bad things happened in the way that that was done. . . . [To] confront other people's racism in a way that you actually are projecting yourself as exceptional on this issue, better than them, is really a total fraud. None of us were qualitatively superior to any of the people we were confronting. In other words, it was not effective organizing. It was somewhat dishonest, and it certainly wasn't effective.[141]

In August the Weathermen's organizing for the Days of Rage suffered two major blows. Piqued by a political disagreement, the Black Panthers broke with them in a less than amicable way. Panther Chairman Bobby Seale denounced them as "jive bourgeois national socialists and national chauvinists," and Panther Chief of Staff David Hilliard warned, "SDS had better get their politics straight because the Black Panther Party is drawing some very clear lines between friends and enemies. . . . We'll beat those little sissies, those little schoolboys' ass if they don't try to straighten up their politics." This from the group the Weathermen had deemed the vanguard of the revolution. Panther leader Fred Hampton later called Mark Rudd a "motherfucking masochist" and floored him with a single punch. A previously allied SDS faction called Revolutionary Youth Movement (RYM) II split with the Weathermen in August as well, accusing them of "fighting the people" rather than organizing them. The RYM II leader Mike Klonsky predicted the Days of Rage would be a "flop." Ayers responded by calling RYM II "running dogs" and asserting, "There's a lot in white Americans that we do have to fight, and beat out of them." Stung by widespread movement criticism of the Days of Rage, Ayers also criticized "this kind of right-wing force, this weirdness that's moving around." He remembered:

> We were quickly developing a bunker mentality. . . . And the more isolated we got, the more it confirmed our sense that it was just us, it was just us who were capable of doing anything, because nobody else wanted to do anything. . . . Instead of us righting that [growing isolation] or correcting that or understanding that or getting on top of it, it kept confirming to us that everybody else was wrong, and that we had to continue down this road.[142]

But not without trepidation. "As the summer wore on, it became clearer and clearer to us that we weren't going to have a lot of people" in Chicago, Ayers recalled. "And then the question was, 'Should we go through with it?'" The verdict was reached after scant debate: "We've *got* to do it. We're doing it for ourselves, we're transforming ourselves. We're doing it to show people not to be afraid."[143]

The White House was keeping an eye on the Weathermen's plans. "Through his daily news summary, the President has been made aware of the forthcoming SDS and Panther protests scheduled for Chicago," the White House aide Ken Cole informed John Mitchell on September 23:

> As you know, the October 11 demonstrations in Chicago come only four days before the nation-wide Vietnam Moratorium activities. From all reports, leftist leaders are counting on serious disorders in Chicago with resulting "police brutality" to polarize student opinion and increase participation in the Moratorium activities.
>
> The President asked that you be advised of his feeling that it would be a good idea for the Justice Department to work closely with Chicago officials in an effort to keep the October 11 activities from getting out of control. It is the President's feeling that while the "scene" in Chicago may help Mayor Daley, it would make problems on a national basis much more difficult.

Mitchell conveyed to Cole two days later that Justice had been "monitoring" the protesters' plans in coordination with state and local officials who also desired "to keep the situation as cool as possible."[144]

Other Summer Voices

The summer of 1969 witnessed an abundance of antiwar activity besides that organized by the Mobe, Moratorium, or Weathermen. For most protesters, Nixon's grace period was now decidedly over. A coalition of peace groups held a two-day "Speak-Out" against the war in Washington. Some demonstrators poured blood on the Pentagon steps. Twenty thousand marched in New York.

CALCAV, WSP, AFSC, and other groups continued their grass-roots organizing in hundreds of cities and towns across America. CALCAV took the war issue to the floor of the conventions of major religious denominations. Activists counseled troubled GIs and provided sanctuary for AWOL soldiers. Resisters continued to raid draft boards; in New York, five Women Against Daddy Warbucks mutilated several thousand Selective Service records and seized the *1* and *A* (as in 1A) from a board's typewriter. More than two hundred psychologists denounced the war as "the insanity of our times" outside the White House. WSPers met with women from Hanoi and the NLF on the U.S.–Canadian border, expressing their sisterhood over ice cream cones. The Vietnamese invited the WSPers to come to Vietnam in the fall, at which time they made arrangements to forward mail from U.S. prisoners of war to their families through a Committee of Liaison. Cora Weiss, a woman of tremendous political dedication and almost as tremendous self-importance, assumed the reins of the project. "She said that the Vietnamese wanted to meet with *her* about the issue of political prisoners and that the rest of us . . . could go to nursery schools or something," Madeline Duckles, who accompanied Weiss to Vietnam, remembered. Weiss even ordered Duckles to leave one meeting with the Vietnamese after she joined it near its end. "I was embarrassed for her!" Duckles exclaimed. The WSPers had the misfortune to arrive back in the United States amid the rampant commercialism of the Christmas season—a stark contrast with the grim material realities they observed in Vietnam. "Everything was so garish and so bright and so *phony*," Duckles said loathingly.[145]

Protesters launched a sea invasion of Fort Lewis outside Tacoma, Washington. "If it becomes necessary to destroy Fort Lewis in order to save it, *we will not shrink from that task*," they declared before landing in rowboats, rubber rafts, and a canoe. The invaders were captured and released.[146]

Several thousand protesters descended on Nixon's estate in San Clemente, California. Nixon administration officials were beginning to suffer the same harassment at the hands of demonstrators that Johnson administration officials had. The problem would intensify in the months ahead. "Sometimes it was so loud you couldn't even go to sleep at night," Nixon would recall of protest in front of the White House. Melvin Laird remembered that "they did things to my house. . . . People came up and urinated on my front door and threw bricks through the windows."[147]

As campuses opened in September, protesters organized teach-ins. University of Michigan President Dr. Robben Fleming denounced the war in a jam-packed Ann Arbor auditorium. Nixon got wind of Fleming's performance, and was not pleased. "The President wants you to know that in the future Robin [*sic*] Fleming is not to be included in any White House conferences," Ken Cole informed John Ehrlichman.[148]

Antiwar sentiment continued to grow among U.S. soldiers in Vietnam. On August 24, an entire Army company refused its captain's order to move out down a perilous mountain slope. It was the first reported mass mutiny in Vietnam. Literate in Vietnamese, rebellious psy-war soldiers were secretly rewriting propaganda so that it condemned the GVN instead of extolling it; some dumped whole bundles of pro-U.S. leaflets into the ocean. One GI expressed a common attitude among American troops when he remarked, "I just work hard at surviving so I can go home and protest all the killing."[149]

SEVEN

1969: Part II

"The Campuses Are Gonna Blow"

Over the summer and early fall of 1969, Nixon administration officials continued to ponder the youth problem. Many remained advocates of greater communication with youth. "That young people must have a feeling they are being 'listened to' . . . has thread[ed] through all discussions as the most important factor in the beginning stages of any youth policy," Deputy Counsel to the President Egil Krogh recorded in August. "What we are aiming for is *communication*, with the possible objective of closing the gap—the chasm—which apparently exists between younger people and middle-age[d] and older people today." President Nixon hoped to reach the same youth the Weathermen were targeting. As John Ehrlichman informed Special Consultant to the President Leonard Garment on October 1, Nixon was after "that group of young people which goes directly from high school to the factories."[1]

Officials believed one way to persuade youth they were being "listened to" was to involve them in government affairs. Krogh suggested engineering "a youth Congress. It may well be that some of the younger Congressmen would respond favorably to the idea of allowing the responsible members of the younger generation to participate in moot Congressional hearings, floor debates, etc.," he wrote another White House official. Director of Communications Herb Klein advised the president that the administration could demonstrate its "interest in the ideas of young people" through "the formation of a council of young people on the White House staff who could give their opinions on public policy." Krogh hoped such governmental participation would instill patience into restless youth. "By an on-going arrangement whereby young people's views are being listened to, they will appreciate the time involved in developing a new policy and putting a program into effect," he argued. "Hopefully they would understand that patient pressure is the best device for accomplishing something.

Merely because they have spoken, will not necessarily mean that developments will follow immediately."[2]

Another way to convince young people they were being listened to, Krogh suggested, was to hold a "Youth Weekend" in San Clemente. He proposed to Ehrlichman that Nixon and other officials meet with a small group of youths "with the aim of nurturing a kind of 'spirit of San Clemente.' . . . We want to leave the impression with the press that the President and his staff can develop meaningful dialogue with young people . . . and that the young people were impressed with our openness, sincerity and interest." The conference's "Hidden Agenda" would include: "(a) Recruit youth for Nixon, (b) Attempt to defuse student unrest in the autumn of 1969, (c) Begin process of developing a 'national youth policy' for the United States."[3]

Tom Huston remained a strong proponent of working with the decent kids. He complained to Haldeman on August 8, "We have made no gestures to indicate support for those young people who supported us, to encourage the vast majority of young people who reject violence, but who seek reform." Krogh joined Huston in urging that Nixon make an appearance at the Association of Student Governments conference in September. He pleaded with Ehrlichman:

> The struggle on the campuses is a struggle of *ideas* as well as of actions. The radicals have articulated—and acted upon—their concepts of revolutionary, dictatorial change. The defense of the traditional methods of cooperation, discussion, and majority rule must be the foundation of the administration's approach to youth problems in general and campus problems in particular. Without a clear, precise—and perhaps most important, early—statement by the President on this point, the battle of ideas will be won by the radicals. . . . [The President should] make this point by praising this group for its adherence to the traditional methods of change.
>
> . . . This is one way of reaching the vast, silent student majority through the media at a time when it will make maximum impression, at the beginning of this administration's first academic year.
>
> The young hate two things above all others: indifference and hypocrisy. The proposed appearance in itself will do much to offset charges of indifference to youth problems; the praise of a group which has chosen to "seek answers together" will show all segments of youth where we stand and the kind of change we will support.[4]

Nixon apparently found Krogh's and Huston's counsel persuasive. On September 20, he proclaimed to the more than five hundred ASG conventioneers then in Washington that his administration was "concerned about the same problems you're concerned about, and we want to find answers with you." The president also said that among the "lessons" he had learned over the years as a political leader was that "a great deal more is learned by listening" than by talking and that "usually the man who talked the loudest had the least to say." Selective Service Director General Lewis Hershey also addressed the convention delegates. Asked about the uncertainty students faced under the current draft system, the elderly, nearly blind Hershey waxed philosophical: "Life is pretty much made of uncertainty. You don't want everything beer and skittles because nothing will destroy life faster than that."[5]

The administration continued to toy with the idea of debating youth on the campuses. Warning that "college America is tense," one White House student intern proposed that a "mobile team of high-level government officials" reason with students. Ehrlichman's aide Todd Hullin felt the team would have to be particularly mobile. Trips onto campuses "could be very dangerous," he cautioned; in fact, they might "risk the lives of members of the administration." Bill Gavin, another White House staffer, was also leery of taking the debate to enemy ground. "If we were to go on the campuses, we would run the risk of playing an SDS game of confrontation," he advised. Gavin and other officials urged that Nixon appeal to youth over the safe medium of TV instead. "Over television we are in control," Gavin argued. "Why not use our power?" Other officials felt Nixon would accomplish little through a televised appeal, however. "The students will measure us several years from now by what we've done, and not what we said," one scoffed. Contended another, "Such a speech would be recognized on campus and in the press as a transparent device to cool the campuses. This would seriously impair its effectiveness." Huston worried that a televised pitch to youth would make Nixon appear to be on the defensive and thereby benefit the Moratorium and Mobe protests that fall. The president "should not act precipitously, or as if he believes himself under pressure," Huston counseled. "I would be reluctant for him to do such a thing between now and the showdown on November 15."[6]

Daniel Patrick Moynihan was unexcited about any form of communication with youth, televised or otherwise. He wrote Nixon on August 19:

> I would expect there will be considerable anti-war protest in the coming academic year. . . . I am not sure what you can do about all this, except of course to end the war. . . . I would imagine there can not be much successful dialogue between the students and the Administration on this issue *per se*. Until the war is over, or its gradual subsidence becomes manifest to even the most skeptical, any American president will face more or less bitter opposition from the now radical children of the Republican middle class.

Such opposition, Moynihan observed, "constitutes an immediate and direct threat to the day-to-day effectiveness of the national government." Moynihan further offered that the "struggle" between America's "centrist political forces" and "the intense radical views of the coming generation of educated youth will almost certainly go on, and will almost certainly become more disruptive." What's more, the "effects" of the "profound movement of opinion" leftward among youthful and other Americans "will be with us for generations. It will, for example, drastically limit the role which the United States can play in foreign affairs."[7]

Seven weeks later, Moynihan reiterated his basic prescription for tackling the youth problem. "The fundamental thrust of your administration," he bluntly told Nixon, should be "to bring an end to an ill advised, badly conducted, and shockingly misrepresented war." Jonathan Rose, another White House aide, was thinking along the same lines, and was no less frank. Young people were "looking for action rather than rhetoric, particularly from Richard Nixon," he wrote Krogh. "I regard the problem of youthful discontent and student unrest as one of the greatest we will face until a dramatic reduction occurs in the level of hostilities in Vietnam."[8]

Moynihan did not feel communicating with the young was a complete waste of time, however. He urged Nixon to sympathize with their painful search for firm existential ground. "I believe as President you *can* do something about this ethical yearning," he wrote. "You can acknowledge it. You can make clear that you know what's going on out there."[9]

Ray Price also advocated expressing understanding of youth's frustrations with life. Officials should try to convince young people that the "challenge" of "the complexity of modern life . . . *can* be mastered," he argued. This would not only "defuse a threat to our institutions" but "rescue a generation from a despair more deeply felt than its own members would admit."[10]

Officials considered organizing conferences of university heads, law enforcement professionals, and federal authorities on ways to cramp campus unrest. The conferences would have to be private, they understood, as visible sessions "could have unpredictable and undesirable political overtones," as one official pointed out, and "be a target for demonstrations which might exacerbate the situation." The administration also pondered arranging a meeting of university dons in Washington. Nixon had a definite idea of what political tone the meeting should take. When informed that eight college presidents in the New York area had publicly taken a hard line against protesters, he remarked to his aide Alexander Butterfield, "These are the types I should have in for a conference."[11]

The administration discussed submitting legislation to Congress that would prohibit protesters from gathering near the White House. Nixon was keen about the legislation, as he hated the near-constant sight of demonstrators in front of his home. Even a lone picketer was enough to set him off. Nixon later spied a man holding a ten-foot banner in Lafayette Park. Within minutes Presidential Assistant Dwight Chapin was scurrying around looking for "thugs" to remove the picketer, John Dean recalled. Nixon "didn't like his sign," Dean said dryly. The administration decided against submitting the legislation for fear of harmful political fallout. Sources on Capitol Hill indicated that it would spawn "numerous political attacks on the President" and promote "the alleged image the President has of 'cloistering' himself in the White House," one official apprised Egil Krogh. Thus, "the general recommendation was that any White House Picketing legislation not be proposed until well after the demonstrations take place this fall." Nixon later authorized infiltration of groups of Quakers picketing the White House. Officials tried to set the Quakers up on drug charges, to no avail. [12]

Officials urged stepped up efforts at draft reform. Moynihan advised Nixon that making such reform "a national political issue" would build momentum behind the initiative and thus help end a system of military service "which has driven a generation of American youth half mad." Even if the administration's efforts failed to spur Congress to act on the draft, officials believed, they would be worth political points with youth. To "take the edge off campus antiwar protests during the coming school year" (as the *Washington Star* theorized), Nixon suspended draft calls for two months in September. In mid October his proposal for a lottery system emerged out of the House Armed Services Committee. [13]

Nixon knew that further U.S. troop reductions in Vietnam would also help take the edge off antiwar protests and soothe broad public opinion. On September 16, over the objection of Henry Kissinger, he announced the withdrawal of another thirty-five thousand U.S. soldiers. "We are going to reduce the fight to a level the American public will tolerate for a long time," one senior Pentagon official remarked. "We were under immense domestic pressure to give an appearance of a kind of steady diminution of the American role," Ray Price recalled. "And we had to keep bringing troops out at a pace which would sustain that appearance. The appearance became as important as the fact in the U.S." [14]

The administration continued to move against protesters. Judging from released FBI documents, there was "a *lot* of government presence" at the July antiwar conference in Cleveland, Sidney Peck noted. "They had folks all the way around. They had people in every one of the factions." Liaison between Justice and military intelligence was moving forward. Relations between the CIA and local police were expanding. The CIA's Operation CHAOS infiltrated the peace movement for the first time. IRS spying continued. Ehrlichman began investigating the possibility of revoking the license of the leftist Berkeley radio station KPFA after a car bearing its sign was seen being "used very actively" in an anti-Nixon demonstration on August 21. The car was "hardly engaged in 'public service' at the time," Ehrlichman observed. [15]

The administration undertook other measures to counteract the youth problem that summer and early fall. It coaxed the American Bar Association to hold a conference on legal standards on campus unrest and helped fund the session. To enrich the government's understanding of restless youth and suggest remedial policies, it set up a "Youth Advisory Group," composed of young officials and chaired by Krogh on Ehrlichman's behalf. The White House directed its student interns to prepare periodic memoranda on the campus mood. And Nixon appointed a blue-ribbon committee on student protest.[16]

For all its handwringing over the youth problem, however, the Nixon administration's overall response was essentially a meager one. Official advice to undertake greater communication with youth continued to go largely unheeded. No "Youth Weekend" in San Clemente was held, no officials toured the campuses, few met with protesters in Washington, Nixon never appealed to youth over TV. Proposals for youthful participation in government affairs remained "just words on paper," the columnist David Broder lamented.[17] And no conferences of university heads on campus unrest took place. For a variety of reasons—skepticism that protesters could be placated, fear of compounding the problem, concern about alienating supporters, just plain bureaucratic inertia—the administration did little to blunt youthful rebellion.

Many officials bemoaned the administration's sluggishness. Tom Huston wrote Haldeman on August 8:

> At the present time the Administration does not have a youth program; it has manifested no particular interest in youth problems; it has made no effort to convince young people that their problems are of interest or concern. . . .
>
> The President recognizes inflation as a serious domestic problem, and he would not for a minute think of assigning it a priority somewhere between arranging church services and planning for the Bicentennial Celebration. Campus disorders and student unrest is perhaps the second most pressing domestic issue in the country today, yet it is receiving little serious attention. Young people constitute a significant and volatile portion of our population, a group which we can ill afford to ignore. I urge you to consider this problem and evaluate whether, in your opinion, we are doing as much as we should.[18]

The specter of major fall disruptions fueled official concern over the administration's inertia. Huston dramatically warned Haldeman:

> I recognize the dangers of shouting "wolf," but I am willing to state unequivocally that we will witness student disorders in the fall which will surpass anything we have seen before. Student militancy will sweep major campuses and flow into the streets of our major cities as the competing factions of SDS strive to prove that each is more "revolutionary" than the other and as antiwar protest organiza-

tions seek to escalate the fervor of opposition to the Vietnam war. You will see it most likely by October 15, certainly by November 15. . . . We are confronted with more than a youth problem. On no other domestic issue is the President's credibility more at stake than on the issue of law and order. Widespread student disorder will further polarize the country, the people will insist on prompt action to quell it, and we will be faced with the sole alternative of repression once the crisis is at hand. It is possible to contain if not prevent future student disorder. But this will not happen by wishing for it. Action is required, and time is running out.[19]

Huston was equally urgent with the president. Escalating racial disorder was "cause for great concern," he wrote Nixon on August 18. "Add to this the volatile situation which exists on the campuses and in the cities as a result of New Left and anti-war activism, and I think we find a situation which could reach crisis proportions [in the fall]. . . . The best evidence indicates that the youthful militants are determined to create as many disturbances as they possibly can. And they won't be peaceful."[20]

Huston's prediction was widely shared within the administration. Todd Hullin told Krogh in July that a recent trip his father-in-law took to seven campuses suggested it was a "foregone conclusion that the violence will increase this coming fall. . . . The hard core militant groups are preparing and organizing themselves for large-scale violent demonstrations. Specifically, arson is the one problem which repeatedly crops up in discussions." The fall outlook was "becoming increasingly worrisome," Hullin fretted. Krogh and two other younger officials personally advised Nixon and members of his Cabinet on September 29 that campus disruption was "quickly reaching the proportions of a national epidemic." In early October, the White House aide Dick Blumenthal reported to Krogh that a meeting he had just had with National Student Association leaders revealed that "the threat of disruption hangs over all the campuses. . . . 'The campuses are gonna blow' was one of the most common ways to buttress or close an argument."[21]

The administration publicly expressed little concern over what the fall might bring, however. In fact, it was positively upbeat. "High U.S. officials" believed prospects were "very promising" for a quiet year on the campuses, one prominent member of the administration anonymously told reporters in August. Nixon questioned the political wisdom of such sanguinity, though. "Perhaps we shouldn't be so optimistic in our public predictions on this," he mused to Ehrlichman. "We might look like McNamara on Vietnam."[22]

Blunting the Moratorium and Mobe

Official nervousness over the administration's lack of a youth policy was fed in no small part by the upcoming Moratorium and Mobe protests. The administration "felt threatened, put on the defensive" by these protests, Special Assistant to the President Jeb Stuart Magruder recalled. They promised to be the largest public expressions of antiwar sentiment since Nixon took office. "It seems clear to me that the results will be fairly impressive," one White House aide warned of the Moratorium. Estimates of attendance at the Mobe demonstration ranged from a hundred thousand to "well over several hundred thousand." Such imposing turnouts would attract considerable media attention, officials worried. And press coverage sat especially poorly with the public relations addicts who held sway in the Nixon White House. "Whether television covered the demonstrations was a major factor in how we viewed them," Ehrlichman remembered. [23]

Officials feared the Moratorium and Mobe protests would have injurious political effects both at home and abroad. "I think the President, Henry Kissinger and the people in the foreign policy process were concerned about what effect these demonstrations might have on the climate in Washington, on the Congress," Ehrlichman said. White House officials "knew that [they] would have an impact on public feelings," the State Department's Marshall Green recalled. Equally disturbing, the protests would further Hanoi's resolve, undercutting Nixon's threat strategy. "They were viewed as a problem because of their effect on the negotiating process, primarily," Haldeman remembered. "It was clear it was creating a problem . . . in terms of the president's credibility to the opposition." And the demonstrations might get out of hand, officials worried, fueling public disquiet over the war's cost in domestic social peace. "We were concerned about potential damage to persons and property. We had reports of possible violence," Ehrlichman noted. Huston warned Nixon that intelligence indicated that even leaders of the Moratorium—hardly a riotous group—"refused to make . . . a disavowal of violence." [24]

The fall protests also troubled officials because of their timing. Some feared the dissent would set the wrong tone for the entire school year. Special consultant on youth policy Bud Wilkinson warned Kissinger in July that if nothing were done to counter the Moratorium

> the organizers of the strike may accomplish much more than closing down some well-known schools for a day. The TV cameras will show students walking out of famous colleges and universities in protest. The strikers will flaunt the Administration's position that the way to work for change is to work responsibly within the system. With such a beginning, there is no telling how the academic year will go from then on out. [25]

And the administration was concerned about the fall protests for the simple reason that they reflected a broader political trend in the United States. Public impatience with Nixon's war policies was rising. Something "was boiling up around the country," Price observed. "There was a kind of an anger in the White House over these demonstrations, and a desire to crack down on them, and play to them only really in the sense that they represented a rising tide that they found very difficult somehow to repress," Green commented. Of course, the tide might shape Nixon's personal political fate. "He was always concerned that [the antiwar opposition] might increase and affect his political viability in terms of getting reelected," Ehrlichman remembered. "We always had one ear cocked toward the 1972 election."26

Most officials saw virtually no difference between the Moratorium and Mobe protests. They were identical political threats. "Basically it was all part of the same cloth," Haldeman said. Officials did not differentiate between them "on any perceptible or definable basis." In fact, like its predecessor, the administration tended to put all protesters "in the same bag." Still, Tom Huston felt the real "showdown" would come in November. "The important date will be November 15, when the Moratorium Committee plans a second strike in conjunction with the antiwar activities of the larger National Mobilization Committee," he counseled Nixon. "This November demonstration could have not only domestic, but foreign policy implications as well," since it might impair the U.S. negotiating position in Paris.27

Always attuned to what his enemies were up to, Nixon himself expressed concern over the two protests during their early planning stages. On June 24— one week before Sam Brown and other Vietnam Moratorium Committee leaders publicly announced the Moratorium—the president asked Ehrlichman to come up with a "game plan" to counter the protest by July 1. Nixon apparently leaned only lightly on his aides, however, for come August 19, no game plan had yet arrived, as one document attests, although the matter was "under consideration" by key Haldeman aides. And as late as September 25 Krogh could still inform another official of the president's request for a plan for blunting both the Moratorium and Mobe, and admonish, "Generally, we need to think through what *specifically* can be done to offset the fervor which is building up advocating a precipitous withdrawal. As you know, we need time [in Vietnam], and we have to do everything possible to get it."28

Yet officials had plenty of advice to offer on the matter, some of which was quietly put into practice. Bud Wilkinson wrote Kissinger on July 7:

> This office believes that the organizers of the proposed student strike in opposition to Vietnam [i.e., the Moratorium] care less about the immediate issue of the war than they do about using the war issue to keep their political organization intact and strengthen it for the future. Last year this group organized the young people's part of the McCarthy campaign. Their proposed strike again gives them a rallying point.
> We believe opposition to the maneuver can be achieved if respon-

sible students recognize the effort for what it actually is—an attempt
to exploit students for the organizers' own purposes. Since no one
likes to be "used," we believe this idea can be effectively communicated.

The White House should *not* be directly involved with this effort.
It must appear to be a spontaneous reaction by students.

Wilkinson reiterated the same advice six weeks later, but seemed less hopeful.
"The problem of dealing with the Vietnam Moratorium Committee is difficult,"
he admitted.[29]

Other officials advocated mobilizing administration sympathizers. Nixon
asked aides to set up a prowar group of notables, including the "real goer," Leo
Cherne of Freedom House. William Safire, a White House speechwriter, proposed organizing a "citizen's committee" called "The Middle Americans" to
speak for "forgotten" people. Both Nixon and Ehrlichman liked Safire's concept
(although the president preferred the "more positive action word" *working* to
middle). Nixon also suggested to Haldeman that they "game plan the possibility
of having some pro-Administration rallies, etc. on Vietnam on October 15, the
date set by the other side. Inevitably, whenever we plan something, they are
there to meet us; perhaps we can turn the trick on them." The White House
might have friendly political leaders and groups urge Americans to fly their
flags and keep their lights on that day, officials submitted. Leonard Garment
argued that since "sentiment is beginning to crystallize in support of the President's position on Viet Nam, *despite all the surface noise to the contrary . . .*
there is a real chance that the Mobilization[30] will be a flat event . . . if we take
steps to help the silent millions articulate their opposition *both* to the war and
to some mindless process of withdrawal."[31]

Not coincidentally, a group calling itself the "Citizens Committee for Peace
with Security" surfaced shortly before Moratorium day. The group placed full-
page "Tell It to Hanoi" ads in newspapers. Also on cue, members of veterans'
groups, police, and firemen denounced the Moratorium and announced plans to
drive with their headlights on and fly flags on the day of the protest. To further
rally political support, the White House asked friendly congressmen to condemn the Moratorium.[32]

The administration engineered political attacks on legislators supportive of
the protest. It had conservative congressmen assail colleagues who would "bug-
out" and thereby allegedly cause "the slaughter of untold millions of Vietnamese."[33] It also generated pro-administration letters to the doves, supposedly from
private citizens. For this it utilized a "discreet" "Nixon Network" (as Nixon
himself called it) set up by Lyn Nofziger and Pat Buchanan for manufacturing
such letters and phone calls to the media. Haldeman directed Magruder to "get
with Nofziger" to generate telegrams and letters to Senators Charles Goodell

(R-N.Y.), Charles Mathias (R-Md.), and Charles Percy (R-Ill.) "blasting them" for their opposition to Nixon's policies. "This program needs to be subtle and worked out well so that they receive these items from their home districts as well as other points around the country," Haldeman instructed. Soon an "avalanche" of telegrams arrived in the senators' offices. The president also ordered aides to "have the Chicago *Tribune* hit Senator Percy hard on his ties with the Moratorium."[34]

Nixon was particularly eager to have Senator Edward Kennedy (D-Mass.) get hit hard. Spiteful with respect to Kennedy generally, he was also enraged by criticism the senator made of his September troop withdrawal and draft announcements; he felt Kennedy was "trying to divert attention from" the summer Chappaquiddick incident by "enlist[ing] the McCarthyites and all the far left on Vietnam, leading up to the October 15 mobilization date for the college campuses," as he told Haldeman. Nixon suggested that they prod a senator "with plenty of guts" to "hammer" Kennedy and that they direct the Nixon Network to "get a major mailing out" smearing Kennedy as cozy with Hanoi. "I think Teddy's is the first round of Federal syllables [i.e., congressional statements] we are going to get on Vietnam leading up to October 15," he wrote Haldeman. "It is absolutely essential that we react insurmountably and powerfully to blunt this attack." Nixon cautioned Haldeman that White House plans for "the Teddy Kennedy fight" "should be discussed only orally."[35]

Some officials proposed holding a "National Day of Prayer" on October 15 to divert attention from the Moratorium and express the administration's interest in peace. Others felt that would be counterproductive, however. As one White House aide, Tom Whitehead, reasoned:

> It is more likely to dramatize rather than ameliorate the growing cleavage between the students and the institutionalized "establishment." . . . We simply have to face the fact that we have large numbers of extremely well informed young people who are well educated and who think for themselves; that they tend to be overly idealistic and unrealistic does not alter the fact. To attempt to draw attention away from the activist element casts us in the light, however strongly and rationally we may argue to the contrary, of being unresponsive, uncaring, and, perhaps worst, unhearing.

Plans for a prayerful day were aborted.[36]

Charlie McWhorter, another White House aide, warned strongly against saying anything that might provoke the protesters. He suggested to Herb Klein on September 25 that "word be passed out to appropriate officials . . . to make sure that any comments they offer about the Vietnam Moratorium . . . reflect . . . a responsible and enlightened view. . . . It is important that the

Administration avoid any confrontation." In reiterating his advice the following day, McWhorter reported that the VMC leader Sam Brown had just told him that a critical or provocative official comment would be "the best thing that could happen to" Moratorium organizers. McWhorter urged that Nixon express "concern for the thinking which is reflected by those who do participate in the Moratorium."[37]

Other officials shared McWhorter's concern. Lyn Nofziger cautioned that "trying to ridicule the October 15 demonstrations . . . could really backfire. Nobody takes the war lightly today. To attempt to laugh off or sneer at any effort—however misguided—to stop it would be disastrous." The president should instead acknowledge "the sincerity of many of those involved." Whitehead proposed a presidential pronouncement and a paper conveying that "we feel it is healthy for students and people generally to reflect on the problems of public policy posed by the war" and that "we will do our share to see that the facts are available." "Such a statement and paper would be a healthy and responsible offset to the overly emotional demands of the students," he submitted.[38]

On September 26—the date of McWhorter's second warning not to incite the protesters—Nixon did precisely that. In reply to a question at a press conference about the Moratorium and other antiwar activity, he declared that "under no circumstances will I be affected whatever by it." Although the president's "stiff-arming" was deliberate, he misjudged its political consequences. "Nixon goofed," as the VMC leader David Hawk later said. "It sounded like he didn't care what the American people thought." To make matters worse, the media turned Nixon's remark into a lead news story. Reporters turned to Hawk and Brown for a response. "It gave us the most extraordinary opportunity," Hawk marveled. "By saying what he did, [Nixon] put us in the position of actually calling a press conference and responding to the president of the United States. It was very heavy stuff." The Moratorium's press conference, held the following day (a Saturday and hence "a light news day—it would give us this good shot at the Sunday papers," Hawk recalled VMC leaders strategizing), was packed with reporters. "It was like a presidential campaign," Hawk laughingly recounted. "I mean, [usually] if you try to . . . have a press conference, you get five or six reporters—that was great. And here was a room with all the networks, the TV cameras and all the wires and the Washington press corps. There were thirty or forty people!" Brown and Hawk reeled off the names of supporters of the Moratorium on Capitol Hill, where endorsement of the protest was growing. "It's not just kids," they pointed out. The press conference made the evening news and the front page of the *Washington Post*. As Hawk told it:

> Then the media realized that there was a major story happening and they didn't know anything about it. So . . . reporters who were as-

signed to cover us at that point switched from being your people who did "education" or the "student protest" beat to your national political reporters. And there it is there on CBS—you know, Walter Cronkite—they've got the story and they're using our logo. You know, our little dove was on the set! So then we just got huge amounts of press.

Said Brown, "It's a pain in the neck to have all these reporters running around your building, but you know it's sort of valuable."[39]

White House officials realized Nixon had blundered. "There were people in the staff who were very concerned that he be more outgoing and . . . try to mollify or placate" the protesters, Ray Price recalled. McWhorter complained to Egil Krogh that "much of the positive reaction we had begun to generate" over Nixon's recent appearance at the Association of Student Governments conference had been "wiped out" by the president's remark. Supporters on Capitol Hill lamented that it would reinforce Nixon's image as a cloistered president. To mitigate the political damage, the White House marshaled reasons why the administration should not heed the Moratorium. Chief among them was its irrelevance to Nixon's own "complex strategy to secure peace in Vietnam." "We are rather like an arrow in mid-flight, on course," John Ehrlichman coached Nixon to say in "expanding on" his remark.

> Whether school keeps [open] on October 15 or not, whether people march for peace or not, does not put in question any of the basic factual assumptions underlying our choice of means [for attaining peace]. . . . I was asked whether the moratorium would make any difference in how we went about the achievement of our common national goal. . . . I'm sure you see that it cannot, under the circumstances. That is the full meaning of my earlier answer.[40]

To express this and other points to Americans and show that he was not totally deaf to youthful dissent, Nixon had his staff prepare a response to one of the many letters it had received from students criticizing his remark. The letter was written by Randy J. Dicks, a sophomore at Georgetown University and—the White House assumed—a typical student. Kissinger's aide Anthony Lake composed the initial drafts of Nixon's response. It was not a pleasant experience for him. "I really lost my on-surface cool," Lake remembered with amusement.

> I must have written three drafts, and Kissinger kept rejecting them on the grounds that they were too soft. . . . I was trying to make it so that a student might actually find it appealing. And on about the third try Kissinger had thrown it back to me, saying, "Make it more manly." And since I considered myself at least as manly as Kissinger,

I took umbrage and stormed out of the office, slammed the door and punched out the Coke machine. . . . I hated that letter.

On October 13, a White House courier summoned Dicks from his French class to hand him Nixon's statement. At about the same time, the administration released the letter and Dicks's own communication to the press. The president's statement argued, among other things, that "to be swayed by public demonstrations . . . would invite anarchy," that "there is nothing new we can learn from the demonstrations" and that the administration was already "on the road to peace." A half hour later, the balding, bespectacled, suit-and-tie-clad Dicks was plucked from his French class again by a pack of reporters eager to get his reaction to Nixon's letter. Facing three network television cameras and a handful of microphones, Dicks seemed a bit dazed. After he repeated his criticism of Nixon's earlier comment, Dicks offered another political opinion of even greater interest to his questioners. Monarchy, said the 19-year-old, was "the superior form of government." What's more, he was the head of the Student Monarchist Society. White House officials were less than amused. This "little mix-up" (as Price called the Dicks episode) elicited more chuckles than support for Nixon's remark. Lake, though, was "just thrilled when it all turned into such a mess."[41]

The administration was then undertaking other measures to counteract the Moratorium and Mobe protests. Its intelligence operatives targeted protest organizers. The two groups' Washington phones were tapped. FBI and CIA agents slithered in and out of their offices. "We got two FBI agents up there now," a Moratorium activist told a reporter outside the group's national headquarters. "They're pretending to be students. But we spotted them right away. Everybody knows who they are." Plainclothesmen attended Moratorium and Mobe meetings. The FBI sent the Mobe a bogus letter allegedly from a militant black group in Washington demanding one dollar for each person who demonstrated in November "because of the expressed strong opposition to any white-led convention in our Black City." Tom Huston, a former U.S. Army intelligence agent and self-styled supersleuth, reported to Nixon in August on sources of financial support for the Moratorium while taking the opportunity to bemoan the lack of "a mail cover on the operation." Ehrlichman tried to pin down the funding source for a full-page Moratorium ad in the *New York Times*. The Justice Department produced "Daily Intelligence Summaries" on Moratorium and Mobe activities starting at least in early October. Utilizing the findings of undercover agents, Huston prepared detailed reports on Mobe planning and political divisions inside the group. The White House examined Moratorium and Mobe leaflets.[42]

The administration moved to shape press reports on the Moratorium. "There should be a meeting with the network leadership regarding their plans for coverage of this," Nixon instructed on September 30. The White House apprised the media of communist involvement in the protest. Nixon suggested to Haldeman that they "triple-estimate the results" to the press "so that it will look like a failure."[43]

Senior officials emphasized that the administration was deescalating the war. Henry Kissinger said a new peace initiative was anticipated. In the same vein, the White House announced two days before the Moratorium that Nixon would be making a major address to the nation "on the entire situation in Vietnam" on November 3. Meanwhile, the administration made plans to deny the day after the Moratorium that the protest had changed anything. Nixon's September troop withdrawal announcement, temporary suspension of draft calls, and the firing of SSS Director Lewis Hershey were also intended, in part, to blunt the Moratorium.[44]

Officials were simultaneously taking steps to keep Moratorium activity in Washington from getting out of hand. They "agreed that it would be unwise to have thousands of people congregate in front of the White House, but a procession would be more appropriate," as one memo records. The administration refused to allow a rally in Lafayette Park or the Ellipse behind the White House. Protesters would have to gather at the Washington Monument a safe distance away, the government decreed, and then march past the White House. "At no time shall the participants stop along the agreed upon route and participants shall not remain stationary except on the Washington Monument grounds," the permit for the protest read. The Pentagon made plans to place at least a thousand National Guardsmen on drill status at the Washington armory. Armed troops would be hidden in the Executive Office Building and the White House. Others would be placed on alert status at nearby bases. The Secret Service planned to set up remote cameras on the White House grounds. In the elaborately stocked presidential bomb shelter in the White House basement, officials established a command post to monitor the protest. There, Field Marshal Ehrlichman and other officials would have access to a closed-circuit television system and direct telephone lines to Washington's police chief and mayor, the National Guard, FBI, and Pentagon.[45]

"I Can't Believe That a Fourth-Rate Power Like North Vietnam Doesn't Have a Breaking Point"

Meanwhile, Richard Milhous Nixon was pulling out all the stops with Hanoi. Faced with an impending escalation of antiwar dissent and a probable enemy offensive over the winter, he decided in early July to try to end the war by either negotiations or a roundhouse knockout punch. That month he directed a courier to warn Ho Chi Minh that, unless significant progress was made in the Paris peace talks by November 1, he would be forced to turn to "measures of great consequence and force." Henry Kissinger passed the same message to North Vietnamese leaders in Paris. The president and his national security adviser also leaned on Moscow. On September 27, by prearrangement, Nixon telephoned Kissinger while he was meeting with the Soviet ambassador, Anatoly Dobrynin. After the two men had talked for a few minutes, Kissinger hung up, turned to Dobrynin, and solemnly declared, "The President just told me in that call that as far as Vietnam is concerned, the train has just left the station and is now headed down the track."[46]

In October, Nixon and Kissinger sent an even more ominous warning to the USSR and its allies that their "November 1 ultimatum" was for real. They ordered the Strategic Air Command to place its nuclear-armed B-52 bombers on full alert. The planes were wheeled into take-off positions on runways across the United States. No announcement was made of this extraordinary development—but Moscow was bound to notice. The alert lasted nearly a month without public detection.[47] For at least one participant in the exercise, however, it was far too real.

Joe Urgo was an Air Force Security Police sergeant in a small detachment assigned to help guard four nuclear-armed aircraft at the Atlantic City airport. Although "most of our time on duty was spent sleeping and fucking off," Urgo remembered, he was responsible for monitoring the alarms for the nuclear weapons. One day "the normal day-to-day routine was totally disrupted," Urgo recounted. Members of the detachment were placed on 24-hour alert—"a complete lockdown." Two of the aircraft were positioned outside their hangars at the end of the runway. A team of soldiers was ordered to stand guard around the planes, day and night, guns loaded. Whenever Urgo walked into the detachment's day room, "there was always two pilots in there," toting weapons. The pilots were carrying the guns for two reasons, Urgo said: "both to protect themselves and also if the other guy starts to fuck things up they've got to shoot the other guy." Urgo had been "constantly around nukes and security procedures for nukes" since joining the Air Force in 1966, but this was an unprecedented situation for him. "I'd never seen them do anything like that," he said intently. "I knew that this was just fucking heavy." He scanned the newspapers and television news to try to figure out what international development might have prompted the alert. "I'm saying, 'Jesus, we're at the edge, and I don't know what's going on!' . . . I'm getting real agitated. It's like, 'Why are we going to die?'" One night, Urgo surreptitiously entered the detachment's guard shack and phoned a U.S. military installation in Iceland over the military WATS line. "I got a guy from Keflavík, Iceland, to dial the Associated Press in New York," he recalled. "And I got this guy on the midnight shift, a sleepy guy. I said, 'Look, man, I'm on a military alert. We are, like, ready for war. Could you tell me what's going on in the world?'" The tired AP employee could shed no light

on the situation. "I was scared shitless doing it [too], because I figure I'm violating some kind of national security rule." Only years later, through an encounter with Daniel Ellsberg, did Urgo learn what the alert was all about.[48]

In the White House, planning for Nixon's roundhouse punch was moving
forward. Working through a backdoor liaison with U.S. naval officers, Kissinger
commissioned top-secret studies of the operation, code-named, curiously, "Duck
Hook." The studies were completed without Secretary of Defense Melvin Laird's
knowledge. They called for intensive bombing of North Vietnamese population centers and military targets; mining North Vietnam's harbors and rivers;
bombing the North's dike system and main rail lines to China; invading the
North; and destroying—possibly with low-yield nuclear devices—the major
passes along the Ho Chi Minh Trail. A separate study considered exploding
tactical nuclear weapons on the rail lines. The operation was planned to last all
of four days, and be repeated, if necessary.[49]

Talk was tough. "Savage was a word that was used again and again," Roger
Morris recalled. Kissinger directed a "Top-Secret-Sensitive" working group he
had convened to analyze the military's studies to devise a detailed plan for a
"savage, punishing" blow. "I can't believe that a fourth-rate power like North
Vietnam doesn't have a breaking point," Kissinger told the group.[50]

The scheme sparked doubts among members of the body. William Watts
had just entered the White House when asked to join the group. He was raring
to carry out his duties as a public servant. "I arrived with huge idealism," Watts
remembered. "You know, the day I went to work I was on the phone to Nelson
Rockefeller about something. I mean, I came in at full speed. . . . And [two
days later] I'm flying off to California on a special flight to meet with Kissinger—that's where I first heard about this Duck Hook thing. It was extraordinary. You really thought that you were saving the world." Watts was shown
the military's Duck Hook plans while working at the Florida White House in
the late summer. "I didn't know what the hell they were," he reminisced. "I
had just very newly arrived on the scene and we were down in Key Biscayne
and Henry asked me to look at these things. I went through them and I was
boggled by what I saw, I'll tell you." The plans included estimates of the number
of civilian casualties for particular bombing strikes. "There was one, something
like a 'railroad yard at noon,'" Watts recalled. "Projected civilian casualties was
'one.'" Watts turned to Kissinger and remarked, "Henry, it is very hard to
figure out how this is going to work this way." "My reaction was that it was a
lot of crap," he remembered. "It seemed to me that it was *fairyland* in terms of
the projections." Watts also worried about the domestic reaction to Duck Hook.
"The nation could be thrown into internal physical turmoil," he warned Kissinger in a highly sensitive memorandum. Blacks would erupt in riots. So would
students and other youth. "Widespread mobilization of the National Guard

could become inevitable," Watts forecast. "The Administration would probably be faced with handling domestic dissension as brutally as it administered the November plan."[51]

Roger Morris coordinated the research of the Duck Hook working group. He, too, worried about the domestic reaction to the operation. Morris's concern was compounded by a perception that the assault would fail to subdue North Vietnam quickly. He felt the military's plans were less than brilliant. Morris remembered:

> I don't want to be unkind so many years later to gentlemen and officers here, but it was a shoddy job. And these things had been lying around with cobwebs on them. The [Joint] Chiefs had been trotting this crap out for years. It was one more quick fix in a war which had no quick fixes. . . . It all had what I would call the "Gallipoli syndrome" about it. It was a military and political fiasco which had taken on reality in these little neatly typed papers somewhere in the Pentagon, where, to put it kindly, some not-very-gifted minds were applying military solutions to these problems.

And Morris had "little confidence" in the U.S. military in the first place. "The people I dealt with in the military were uniformly intellectually inferior people," he said. "And that always gives you a start. I mean, if the best guys are supposedly assigned to the policymaking roles . . . and these guys are . . . sort of C- or D+ students, then you really had cause for worry."[52]

Another member of the Duck Hook working group, the senior NSC systems analyst Laurence Lynn, wrote a "scathing" critique of the operation's military potential. He argued that intensive bombing of North Vietnam would not significantly impair Hanoi's war-making capabilities, while fueling enemy resolve and costing numerous B-52 planes and pilots. "The fact is that at that particular time the Chiefs' proposals would have been insane," Lynn said fervently. "[It] would have been *insane* for Nixon to endorse those proposals. It was just quite obvious from examining what they proposed to do and from applying any kind of critical analysis to their plans that the President would have been very badly advised to engage in something like that. In effect, they were revealing by their plans that a 'short, vicious, punishing blow' was impossible. They did not know how to do it."[53]

Kissinger was impressed by Lynn's paper. His skepticism about the operation grew during a series of meetings on it attended by U.S. military officers. Under questioning, the officers progressively toned down their claims for Duck Hook. "Things got more and more equivocal," Morris recalled. "So that the ass-covering and the general inferiority attending the whole process became more and more apparent." Kissinger, who felt the Joint Chiefs "were a bunch of fools and clowns," became "very frustrated."[54]

Kissinger presented Lynn's paper to Nixon, who was also having doubts about the operation's military potential. The president had a more immediate worry, though. He realized that "the only chance for my ultimatum to succeed was to convince the Communists that I could depend on solid support at home if they decided to call my bluff," as he records in his memoirs. "However, the chances I would actually have that support were becoming increasingly slim." There were "signs of a new level of intensity in the antiwar movement," he writes. Most troubling, the Moratorium was scheduled to take place "right in the period most crucial to the success of my . . . ultimatum." "Nixon was very worried that the October 15 moratorium, just two weeks before this deadline that he had privately given Hanoi, would be seen by them as evidence that he could not deliver," Ray Price recalled.[55]

Desperate Dan

Antiwar protesters were unaware that the Nixon administration was actively considering a major escalation of the war. Most had little doubt that Nixon wanted to win the conflict and wished to use stronger military measures. But the Duck Hook planning and November 1 ultimatum were not public knowledge. Had they been, the "new level of intensity" in the peace movement that Nixon observed would have been many times greater.

The president's threat strategy was not a total secret, however, and that it was not would ultimately exert a critical influence on the war. For among those who learned of Nixon's machinations, one person judged the situation sufficiently urgent to take extraordinary action to head Nixon off at the pass—action that would play a pivotal role in the downfall of his administration.

Daniel Ellsberg was then a research analyst for the RAND Corporation in Santa Monica, California. He was, in many ways, a peculiar staffer of that paragovernmental think tank on "national security" issues. Although more than a few of his colleagues at RAND opposed the war, Ellsberg's opposition to the conflict seemed, to many, overzealous. And his freewheeling lifestyle was hardly typical of defense researchers. "I'd heard of Ellsberg," one NSC staffer remembered. "He was a wild man."[56]

Ellsberg had gone through some serious changes since the Pentagon demonstration in October 1967. In March 1968 he had attended a conference on revolutionary change at Princeton University co-sponsored by the American Friends Service Committee. Ellsberg was conducting a study for the Defense Department at RAND at the time on "lessons of Vietnam, and in particular, a study of pacification process, which is basically a counterrevolutionary study." Hence, his primary reason for attending the conference was to gain "insight" into the revolutionary process "from the point of view of *countering* it." Although supportive of the antiwar movement, Ellsberg still felt that the United

States "had a right, in principle, to oppose communists where feasible." Early in the conference, Ellsberg met a number of Quaker peace activists, some of whom had sailed on the *Phoenix* to deliver medical supplies to North Vietnam in 1967. A few of these Quakers had also sailed to Bikini in the South Pacific in 1958 to try to halt nuclear testing there. Ellsberg was "very sympathetic" to the Bikini protest and impressed by much of what the Quakers had to say. "And that was very unusual for me to hear and meet people like that," he later noted. But most thought-provoking to Ellsberg was a woman sitting across a table from him. "I was both attracted by her *and* very interested in what she was saying, which had to do with Gandhian thinking," he reminisced. "And I began talking to her about it. And we ended up, really, spending all of our time together for the next several days. And she got me very interested in Gandhian thought, which I knew nothing about . . . and also in Martin Luther King." The woman, a Ph.D. student at Harvard from India, had a "very strong impact" on Ellsberg. Before leaving the conference, she gave him a reading list to further his education. "Through her I read a lot of pacifist and Gandhian literature for the first time," Ellsberg remembered. "And *that* then had a steady influence on me from about then on." Ellsberg stayed in contact with his new friend after returning to RAND, and she continued to shape his views. "She's the one who had the strongest influence on my life," he said.[57]

Other events in Ellsberg's personal life were also stoking his distaste for the war. That spring he began undergoing psychoanalysis, leading him to reassess many aspects of his life. His growing indulgence in hallucinogenic drugs also provoked questioning. And Ellsberg's zestful participation in Los Angeles's swinging singles scene over the summer (apparently under the alias "Don Hunter") increased his exposure to anti-establishment views. Feeling shell-shocked by the assassinations of Martin Luther King and Robert Kennedy, "fighting an extreme case of powerlessness" over the war, he decided "it was better to be screwing than getting screwed."[58]

In December, Henry Kissinger asked Ellsberg to prepare a paper on policy options in Vietnam for the incoming Nixon administration. Kissinger had known Ellsberg for years, had met with him in Vietnam, and respected his knowledge of the war. Ellsberg's feeling of powerlessness over the war now began to wane. Here was an opportunity to persuade the Nixon administration to end the conflict, he thought to himself. Ellsberg also felt inspirited simply by his close proximity to power again (which, some friends believed, he enjoyed). The RAND analyst prepared a comprehensive list of policy options in Vietnam ranging from pulverizing North Vietnam to unilateral withdrawal. He spent two days going over them with Kissinger at the Pierre Hotel in New York, where the incoming Nixon team was gathered. Ellsberg left New York "with considerable expectation that they would act on this and get us out."[59]

But it was not to be. Over the winter and spring of 1969 Ellsberg stewed as Nixon talked peace while continuing the war. Meanwhile, he continued his foray into pacifist literature, not feeling "that open to the actual pacifist part" of the literature, but finding the Gandhian emphasis on truth-telling compelling. Then, in the late summer, Morton Halperin informed Ellsberg of the secret bombing of Cambodia and the Nixon administration's direct threats of savage escalation. "The president will not go into the 1972 elections without having mined Haiphong," Halperin predicted. He also told Ellsberg that Nixon intended to withdraw U.S. troops as slowly as politically feasible and keep a large residual force in Vietnam indefinitely. Other friends in the government substantiated Halperin's claims. Ellsberg was outraged: Nixon was trying to *win* the war, he now realized, not disengage from it. "So this was what the 'options exercise' . . . had come to," he caustically wrote later. Ellsberg began ruminating about publicly speaking out against the president's policies. "It seemed to me the situation was quite desperate and it was important to head him off, to create a political climate unfavorable to the war before he committed himself to an escalation," he remembered.[60]

But it took several additional circumstances to spur Ellsberg—an adviser to four administrations who had never publicly criticized U.S. policies in Vietnam—to act. In August he began reading the only volumes of the Johnson administration's secret study of the war (to which he had contributed) that he had not previously examined, those considering the war's origins during the period 1945–54. Ellsberg was troubled by what he read. The United States was the aggressor nation in Vietnam, these early volumes of the Pentagon Papers study attested, not North Vietnam. What's more, American presidents had been receiving pessimistic counsel about the war from day one; hence, it would hardly be worth his while to try to influence U.S. policy from the inside.[61]

Shortly after beginning his reading about the war's origins and learning of Nixon's plans, Ellsberg attended a conference of the War Resisters League in Pennsylvania. His pacifist friend from India had invited him to attend "on the grounds that I should speak there as somebody from RAND who was now increasingly interested in this [Gandhian] approach," Ellsberg recalled. "And I said, 'Well, that would be ridiculous'—I had just gotten into it, and here I was at RAND, and I didn't have that much to say—but that I would go as a participant." Ellsberg talked with scores of pacifists at the convention, including famous ones like the Reverend Martin Niemoeller, who had spent seven years in Nazi concentration camps for opposing Hitler. Niemoeller deeply impressed Ellsberg. So did many of the young draft resisters he spoke with. "I found them to be sober, intelligent, principled," he writes. But most impressive of all was one particular draft resister, Randy Kehler, a member of the WRL's international board, who was then bound for prison. "I had met him a few days earlier and had been very taken with him," Ellsberg said. "I thought he was a very likable, attractive person, and that he represented the best of American youth. . . . And to discover that he found that he had to go to prison as the best thing he could do to end the war just really tore my life in two." Ellsberg remembered listening to Kehler address the convention:

> He was speaking to a plenary session of several hundred people from all over the world. And I was thinking as I listened to him that I was glad the foreigners were there . . . because I thought, "He's the best we have, he's the best kind of American for them to meet." And suddenly I heard him say that he was the last male left in the San Francisco office of the War Resisters League, because the others had all gone to prison. And he said, "And I'm happy to say that I will soon be joining them." Actually, his voice broke at that point. . . . And it was so stunning to hear, suddenly, that he was on his way to prison, that I started to cry. And I went to the men's room—he was still speaking, there was nobody there, just a little men's room—and I sat on the floor and just sobbed hysterically for about an hour, close to an hour. I couldn't stop crying. And just almost screaming . . . just shaking with sobbing. I've only done that a couple times in my life. And my thoughts were that America was eating its young. That we were relying on the young people to end the war, and so just as we relied on them for cannon fodder we were relying on them for peace fodder, to go to prison for it. That we somehow had to share those risks and that burden. And then I felt so bad for my country, that this is what we had come to, that the best thing that a young man like this could do would be to go to prison. And the third thought that came into my mind around then—either in that hour or within hours—was, "Well, what can *I* do, if I'm willing to go to prison?"[62]

Among the actions that occurred to Ellsberg was making the Pentagon Papers public. In fact, "the Pentagon Papers suggested themselves very quickly," he recalled. Ellsberg felt distributing the study—a copy of which was sitting in his top-secret safe at RAND—would "greatly discredit the war" by documenting its "illegitimate origins" and by "showing that people had been lied to consistently, that what they had been told were our objectives were not the real objectives, that the costs always loomed much larger" than U.S. officials claimed. Releasing the papers might also "unlock Nixon from the war," Ellsberg thought, by allowing him to "identify it as a Democrats' war and say 'it's just not worth continuing it' and cut it off." Both effects would prevent a major escalation. Ellsberg realized as well that "the Moratorium was coming along as a vehicle for expression of mass sentiment against the war," and that it "was going to be quite large. So [it] seemed an opportune time to put out the Papers, to get fuel for the Moratorium." But most impelling of all, Randy Kehler had put the ball in his court. Ellsberg had previously considered trying to persuade Robert McNamara or other senior Johnson administration officials to release the Pentagon Papers, but that would no longer do. It was time to put his own body on the line—time to do his own truth-telling. Encountering Kehler "was crucial," Ellsberg said:

> It didn't really occur to me to put [the Pentagon Papers] out myself until this Kehler incident. Because I did assume I would go to jail for the rest of my life. Flatly—"For this, I will never get out." And so you just didn't think of doing such a thing . . . it wasn't something you weighed, until you were confronted by somebody who was actually ready to go to jail. And then the very fact that Kehler was sufficiently like me in my background—he had gone to Harvard (he was a graduate student), he was a young, articulate, white male, and intelligent—[meant] that I could identify with him enough to say, "Well, if he can do this, *I* can do it." And I immediately thought, "If I were willing to get killed in Vietnam, get captured or whatever, then I should be willing to go to prison—why not?"[63]

Still, Ellsberg hesitated. He was by no means *eager* to go to jail (certainly not for the rest of his waking days), and he thought that if he could convince a group of influentials to come out against the war with him, they would have greater political impact than himself alone. In September Ellsberg approached five other RAND analysts who had opposed the war for some time. The researchers decided to compose a letter to the *New York Times* calling for unconditional U.S. withdrawal within a year. "Written by men of considerable expertise who normally shun publicity," as the *Times* commented, the letter "provided new impetus to the growing public demand for swift disengagement from Vietnam." The same month, Ellsberg tried to coax a blue-ribbon group of Establishment Democrats who had criticized the war two years earlier to issue another antiwar statement. "Mr. President, this is not your war," Ellsberg proposed that the group declare. "This is our war. You should get out of it. We were wrong to get in it, we were wrong to continue it. You should not make that same mistake." The group refused. "The general reaction was . . . 'Good idea, but not yet, not now,'" Ellsberg remembered. "The thing was, it wasn't yet Nixon's war, and they did not want it to be just the Democrats' war." Shortly thereafter, Ellsberg called the former Johnson administration officials Harry McPherson and Paul Warnke, both members of the Democratic Party's policy advisory committee, and proposed that they spearhead a similar Democratic call to end the war. Again he was rebuffed. "If the Democrats urged Nixon to get out this year," McPherson warned Ellsberg, "there would be a political bloodbath such as you have never seen. And that means you and me, Dan."

Ellsberg was nearly speechless. "Harry, you may well be right," he responded. "In fact, I think you probably are right. But I am not willing to be protected from that by seeing Vietnamese bombed. I'm not willing to see a war prolonged to save you and me from a political bloodbath in this country, because there's a bloodbath going on over there right now."[64]

Ellsberg decided to move while lying in bed reading the *Los Angeles Times* on the morning of September 30. The paper's lead story was on the U.S. government's decision to drop charges against six Green Berets accused of murdering an alleged South Vietnamese double agent. Although Ellsberg had no doubt the White House had ordered the dismissal of the charges, Secretary of the Army Stanley Resor insisted to reporters that it was his decision. Ellsberg was outraged. "This is a system that I have served for fifteen years," he seethed. "It is a system that lies automatically from top to bottom to protect a cover-up murder. I've got a safe full of documents that are full of lies." Ellsberg got out of bed, put on some clothes and went over to the home of his friend Anthony Russo, a RAND colleague, who lived down the road in Santa Monica. "Tony, can you get ahold of a Xerox machine?" Ellsberg asked. That night or the next, they started copying the 7,000-page Pentagon Papers study. Ellsberg recruited his two children, Robert and Mary, aged ten and thirteen, to help with the operation. "My son was Xeroxing and my daughter was cutting TOP SECRET off the top and bottom of the pages," he recalled. The group "went into a very heavy night-and-day operation," until, Ellsberg said, "I thought I would go blind from the green light of the Xerox machine."[65]

"It was something that came to a suicide mission that I thought had to be done," Ellsberg reflected. "It was . . . a desperate situation that justified desperate means. And justified self-sacrifice. . . . I thought it was virtually obligatory to do what I did. To do less would be wrong."[66]

More Defections

Over the summer and early autumn public discontent with the war was mounting. Despite the Nixon administration's troop withdrawals and claims of progress, most Americans could see no end to the fighting. New York's Mayor John Lindsay observed that if Nixon's pullout continued at the same rate, it would take nine years to quit Vietnam. Body bags were still arriving home in high numbers. The war's toll in American lives was vividly imprinted on the public's psyche in late June when *Life* magazine ran pictures of young American men killed in one week in Vietnam. There were over two hundred photos in all. "We must pause to look into the faces," *Life* said. Most of the victims looked like wholesome, all-American boys. "It was almost unbearable," David Halberstam writes. "It was an issue to make men and women cry." The story "probably had more impact on antiwar feeling than any other piece of print journalism" during the entire war; "almost nothing else . . . brought the pain home quite so fully."[67]

The peace movement continued to fuel antiwar sentiment. By September, Charles Goodell was the Senate's leading dove; only a year earlier, he had been a dutiful supporter of Richard Nixon. According to a top aide, the turning point in Goodell's transformation came in the spring when he spoke to a group of radical students at Cornell University:

> It was an inquisition. I don't know how many other politicians would have stood for it. His answers were a lot of the old cliches. It wasn't enough to say he was opposed to the war. The students wanted to know when and how he proposed to end it. He said that if substantial progress has not been made within six months, he'd make a proposal. They booed and hissed. It was very painful, but it was a very good lesson. It caused him to think through his position.

Goodell's rethinking continued during the summer, when he held daily sessions with the student interns in his office. The sole issue in these sessions was, almost always, Vietnam. "Like any open-minded individual, he could not help but be influenced by it," the aide recalled. Goodell met through the summer with Sam Brown and other VMC leaders as well.[68]

Public disquiet over the war's cost in domestic peace continued to grow. Protests and youthful alienation were impairing the health of American society, many Americans worried. In August, the president of the Los Angeles Chamber of Commerce declared that America's No. 1 problem was "a generation of youth that is discontented, restless and rebellious." Youthful recalcitrance was "infecting a whole generation—the generation which will succeed us," he warned other businessmen.[69]

Though in June the public backed Nixon's Vietnam policies by a slim margin, 47 to 45 percent, by September 57 percent opposed them and only 35 percent expressed support. Eleven antiwar resolutions were introduced in Congress during one three-week period in the early fall, including one by Goodell that would bar the appropriation of funds for the U.S. military in Vietnam after December 1, 1970. "You could sense the change in the country," remembered the traveling peace organizer Sidney Peck.[70]

Support for the Moratorium was mushrooming. On hundreds of campuses, students were organizing protests; some meetings drew over a thousand participants. Housewives, teachers, lawyers, and others were planning events in their communities. "We're seeing one of the benefits of the McCarthy campaign," the VMC's David Mixner said. "You call four people in Iowa and you don't have to tell them what to do. They know how to organize, get up literature, deal with the press, rent halls. They know how to handle it." Establishment endorsements of the Moratorium were plentiful—more plentiful than for any previous peace protest. No fewer than sixty-four members of Congress expressed their support; twenty-three announced plans to keep the House in all-night debate on the war on Moratorium eve. Other heavyweight supporters included Averell Harriman, Arthur Goldberg, Bill Moyers, Theodore Sorensen, Walter Reuther, and the United Automobile Workers of America. John Laird, a student at Eau Clare State University in Wisconsin, also expressed support for the protest and indicated his intention to participate in it. The 21-year-old's announcement sent reporters scurrying off to the Pentagon for a reaction. "I never raised hell with him for his position," his father, Melvin Laird, recalled. "I understood his position. . . . We'd have a good go on things, but he was always very supportive of me. . . . There was always great love." (Immediately after making these comments, Laird walked to one wall of his *Reader's Digest* office, grabbed a picture of his son's 1969 wedding—at which he was the best man—and proudly handed it to me.)[71]

Aware of the swelling support for the Moratorium, the Nixon administration made a last-ditch effort to discredit the protest. On October 14, at the president's direction, Spiro Agnew denounced a letter North Vietnamese Premier Pham Van Dong had sent to antiwar groups expressing support for the fall protests and demanded that VMC leaders "repudiate the support of a totalitarian Government which has on its hands the blood of 40,000 Americans." Agnew claimed that VMC organizers and congressional backers of the protest were now "chargeable with the knowledge of this letter" and had to distinguish their views from those expressed in it. "Now have to take offensive," H. R. Haldeman's notes of a meeting with Nixon that day tellingly read. "Tag those involved with left wing—and take the heat." Officials judged Dong's communication a "kiss of death" to protesters.[72]

"They Are All with SDS. They Are All Fucking Crazy!"

On Monday, October 6, shortly before midnight, antiwar protesters blew up the nation's only monument to policemen. The statue in Chicago's Haymarket Square was blown clear off its twelve-foot pedestal, throwing chunks of the legs onto a nearby expressway. A hundred windows in the surrounding area shattered from the force of the explosion. The blast was the opening salvo of the Weathermen's Days of Rage. "We now feel that it is kill or be killed," a Chicago police official ominously declared.[73]

Over the next forty-eight hours, youths steeled themselves for the first mass action of the Days, a rally in Lincoln Park on Wednesday night followed by a probe into Chicago's streets "to feel out the city and the pig situation." They "struggled" over their fears of violence and anxiety about "offing the pig." Most practiced the "basic moves" of "stick fighting," "some awkwardly, others with obvious experience," as one wrote. Many honed their karate and judo skills. "If you have anything short of a mortal wound, you are expected to fight on," one Weatherleader commanded his troops. Mused a wide-eyed teenager, "It's amazing that in a couple of hours I might be dead."[74]

Come Wednesday evening, only three hundred had gathered in Lincoln Park. Most found the paltry turnout unsettling. "This is an awful small group to start a revolution," one student remarked. The young revolutionaries were outfitted in full battle gear: helmets, "shit-kicker boots," goggles, gas masks, heavy clothes, first-aid kits. Less visible were clubs, lead pipes, chains, brass knuckles. The youths tried to screw their courage up by screaming high-pitched "Battle of Algiers" war whoops. Observing them were hundreds of cops.[75]

At around ten o'clock, Tom Hayden of the Chicago Eight addressed the crowd. A proponent of armed revolution who had begun organizing target practice for movement rifle squads, Hayden conveyed the Chicago Eight's support for the protest. A few minutes later, the Weatherleader Jeff Jones, his blond hair dyed black to conceal his identity, stepped into the flickering light of the bonfire in the center of the group and announced, "I am Marion Delgado."[76] The nearby Gold Coast district was "where the rich people live," Jones told the crowd, including the rich judge in the Conspiracy trial, Julius Hoffman. "Marion Delgado don't like him and the Weatherman don't like him, so let's go get him," Jones exhorted the demonstrators. His tough talk notwithstanding, Jones was shaking in his combat boots. "More than once I have said that that particular night required the strongest act of will to overcome personal fear," he commented years later. "I mean, to say 'we're going to march out of this park and we're going to march to Judge Hoffman's house, and we're going to fight anyone who gets in our way,' and then *do* it, is not my natural personality . . ."[77]

The ragtag army charged out into the streets, whooping and unveiling their weapons. After one youth heaved a rock through a bank window, glass began shattering in every direction. Bystanders caught in the onslaught were knocked to the pavement. Police watched with their jaws open as store and car windows splintered one after the other. "I just don't believe it," one officer gasped. Said a pedestrian, "I don't know what your cause is, but you have just set it back a hundred years." Dave Dellinger, who had secured a safe house for the Weathermen outside of Chicago, was also appalled by the destruction. On the scene as "a disgusted observer," he noticed "that a disproportionately high percentage of the cars wrecked were Volkswagens and other old and lower-priced cars," and that youths were trashing "small shops, proletarian beer halls, and lower-middle-class housing." With each broken window, each trashed automobile— each blow against the pig state—the youths' courage rose another notch. Some cops separated from their brethren were "vamped on severely."[78]

Soon police lines began forming ahead. Jones and other youths in the front of the mob charged directly into one line, screaming and swinging. At last they were going to get to test their mettle, at last they were going to get themselves a few pigs. Jones pierced the line and was immediately pounced on by six cops:

> They grabbed me and knocked me down. I got kicked a few times. The worst thing that happened . . . was that someone Maced me right in my eyes from about two inches away. It blinded me for a couple of minutes. And that scared me. While that was happening . . . they said, "Who are you?" And I identified myself. And they said, "No, you're not," and kicked me a couple more times, because my hair was dyed. So I said, "I have my wallet." So they took out my wallet, and they said, "Sure enough, it is Jones." And then I was thrown into a wagon.

For another hour, the chill Chicago night air was filled with the sound of breaking glass, war whoops, police sirens, burglar alarms. By the end of this "Gandhian violence," as Abbie Hoffman called it (his definition: you announce the time and place and then show up and commit an act of violence), six Weathermen had been shot, a great many had been injured, and nearly seventy were in police custody.[79]

The next morning, Weatherman's "women's militia" took to the streets for more hand-to-hand combat. "Showing considerable bravery if not much military sense," the leaders of the militia (helmets, goggles, and all) also stormed into a police line, flailing away. They were swiftly subdued.[80]

After a day of calm, the two hundred Weathermen not out of action returned to the streets for "the second battle of the white fighting force" on Saturday. They swooped through Chicago's Loop, bullying more pedestrians, smashing more windows, and swinging at more cops. Within thirty minutes, more than half were sitting in paddy wagons or police cars, bloodied and bruised. The day's worst injury occurred when a city official fond of joining in police roundups of protesters dove to tackle one and smashed into a wall instead. He was paralyzed from the neck down.[81]

That night and the previous two, Weathermen held interminable "criticism–self-criticism" sessions on what had gone down. Many bemoaned the small turnout for the protest. "Some people in the leadership did feel it was a defeat. Some people thought, 'Where were the trainloads from Michigan?'" Bill Ayers recalled. More than a few wondered whether fighting armed cops wasn't a loser. Some "warned against the 'death trip.'" A blue-collar teenager who had participated in one action said from jail, "The guys in here are war-monguls. They all want a revolution and they are all with SDS. They are all fucking crazy!"[82]

But other Weathermen felt they'd shown that white kids could "do it in the road" and win. "We'd . . . proven that it was possible—we didn't all die, we were still there," Ayers said. Carrying out the protest despite forbidding circum-

stances was itself a victory. Perhaps most important, they'd strengthened themselves. "People felt, 'We'd proved ourselves, we'd toughened ourselves, this is a
necessary step, we're finding out who's really committed,'" Ayers remembered.
That most observers thought they were nuts was hardly cause for concern.
"Most people will be turned off, you have to expect that," lectured one Weatherleader. "They are going to be fighting on the side of pigs if they ever fight
at all." "As you might expect, those of us who had really pushed this thing
through had a lot invested in calling it a success," Jones frankly stated. [83]

Some Weathermen felt the military battle was the right battle but that it
could ultimately only be waged successfully from underground. The Man
would continue to come down hard on militant public demonstrations, they
argued. Also, "we had gone to this level of militancy and still the war was going
on," Jones recalled thinking. "Even that wasn't enough." Said Ayers: "We felt
that there was a need to escalate the opposition to the war and to make it [more]
painful to the warmakers. We felt that we were ineffective . . . and if we can't
stop the war by convincing the majority of people, we can certainly make the
price greater. . . . We can build an underground force that's not going to be
constantly persecuted and prosecuted by the state." This force would carry out
bombings and other terrorist acts while its members continued to participate in
public political activities. [84]

The Days of Rage had attracted few working-class youths to the struggle and
had not even begun to tap the rising reservoir of antiwar sentiment in American
society as a whole. Jones conceded the failure, even while exaggerating the
turnout: "We were mobilizing for the National Action at a time when literally
tens of thousands of people would come to an antiwar demonstration—and we
got eight hundred people. And the reason we got eight hundred people was
because we demanded that people come to a level of struggle where they were
willing to fight the police in the streets of Chicago as their antiwar statement.
It didn't make sense—although we did it. . ." "I don't want to equivocate on
just how big a failure it was," Jones reflected. "Violent, aggressive fighting with
the police and property destruction just wasn't something that was going to
mobilize masses of people." The Days of Rage also promoted public perceptions
that antiwar protest and violence were one and the same, hurting the peace
movement's image; as Bill Gavin gloated to Haldeman, "the *vital force* of radicalism has . . . been . . . driven into outright physical violence for all to see."
The protest hurt the Weathermen as well; most were injured or arrested (many
of the leaders faced stiff charges), their bail bonds were gargantuan, and, according to Dave Dellinger, at least half defected from the group afterward, having
seen the light on kamikaze-ism. [85] Yet it must also be acknowledged that the
Days of Rage contributed to the growing sense of domestic crisis in America
and fed both public and official perceptions that the war was risking social co-

hesion at home. Gavin's exultation aside, the White House was certainly not pleased that it occurred. As Haldeman said earlier, *no* antiwar protest "was good for us." And, as we have seen, Nixon felt violence in Chicago would harm him politically. On balance, then, damaging to the peace movement, but not a *complete* disaster.

Reaction to the Days among other protesters ran from admiration to disgust, but tended heavily toward the latter. The most common response was summed up in the remark of a Wisconsin SDSer: "You don't need a rectal thermometer to know who the assholes are." Years later SDS's Greg Calvert maintained that the Weathermen's actions as a whole "did more to set back the development of a meaningful American left than anybody else in the country. And I think in that sense that they played right into the hands of the state."[86]

Following the Days of Rage, Weatherman became increasingly taken with the notion of building an underground. "From about the National Action on, that's what we . . . spent our time doing," Ayers remembered. "I think we all felt it was something we had to do," Jones said. "And I think we all each in our own way felt pretty scared. . . . That period . . . had a lot of sort of ominous feelings to it. And the feeling that you'd never come back from it, you know. That doing this was . . . sort of like victory or death. If not death, then long years in jail."[87]

Weathermen began cutting themselves off from family and old friends. Facing March 1970 court dates for charges stemming from the Days of Rage and having no intention of showing up, some started living under assumed names. "We wanted to get a head start on the official date at which we would become fugitives," Jones recalled. With each step underground, their bunker mentality grew.[88]

Moratorium

Three days after the Days of Rage, a protest of an entirely different nature commenced. At 7:30 P.M. on October 14, antiwar congressmen set in motion their plan for keeping the House in all-night debate on the war in solidarity with the Moratorium. The protest had been organized by peace activists on Capitol Hill, particularly the Quaker David Hartsough and Cliff Hackett, an aide to Congressman Benjamin Rosenthal (D-N.Y.). "While everybody around the country was stopping business as usual, Congress was going to stop business as usual and really focus on the war," Hartsough envisioned. "To me it was just psychologically important that Congress was kind of 'out in the streets' at the same time that people around the country were." The debate was halted after only four hours by Republican congressional leaders, who claimed it would undercut their commander in chief. "There can be only one quarterback," the Republican Minority Leader Gerald Ford, a former football player, had lectured earlier in the day. "We have a good quarterback and I believe he will do the job." The protest "turned out to be a flop—a dud," Nixon perceived. Nevertheless, it was the most extensive discussion the House had ever held on Vietnam. "That was certainly a massive step ahead from where we had been," Hartsough recalled. [89]

The next day witnessed an outpouring of public dissent unprecedented in American history. More than two million citizens participated in the Moratorium. Many of the predominantly white, middle-class protesters were speaking out for the first time. In cities and towns across the nation, Americans rallied, leafleted, canvassed their neighbors, held candlelight vigils, attended church services, showed films, and engaged in discussions. Church and school bells tolled for the war dead. In community after community, citizens publicly read the names of Americans killed in Vietnam; one reader in Houston burst into tears upon discovering the name of a friend on his list. Flags were displayed at half staff. Black armbands, symbols of participation in the Moratorium, were everywhere. [90]

Businessmen and professionals turned out in large numbers, even holding their own demonstrations. Some of the nation's biggest capitalists participated in a rally of twenty thousand on Wall Street, where they listened to Bill Moyers; afterward, several read the names of American war dead in nearby Trinity Church. That many of the businessmen were more concerned about the war's economic cost than its morality did not bother Moratorium organizers in the least. "I'll take people who were against the war for whatever reason they're against the war," Sam Brown said ardently. "I wanted the killing to stop. . . . We're not dealing here with the entryway to heaven—we're dealing with how do you end the war. And that frequently got confused. . . . There was a good deal of 'holier-than-thou' going on: 'I'm more against the war than you are. And the reason why I can know I'm more against the war is because . . . I've been busted seven times. You've been busted six? Well, *Christ*.'" Brown considered such thinking "nonsense." [91]

More than a thousand high schools participated in the Moratorium. While many youths merely used it as an excuse to cut classes, others pondered the gravity of the occasion. Among them were two seventeen-year-old classmates in New Jersey. Craig Badiali was president of his school's dramatic society, Joan Fox a cheerleader. Both were profoundly disturbed by the war. The two teenagers joined in an afternoon rally. The next morning, they were found parked on a deserted road in Badiali's parents' car—dead. A vacuum-cleaner hose was attached to the exhaust pipe and fed through a hole in the floor of the vehicle. Said Badiali's brother, "My brother died for his convictions. He was against the war." [92]

In the nation's capitol, thousands of federal employees partook in Morato-

rium activities. HEW workers had their choice of at least twelve different discussion sessions on Vietnam to attend during their lunch period. Participation
in the Moratorium by government workers led the U.S. Civil Service Commission to issue a directive the following month declaring that "any day set aside
by a private group for an event of interest to that group does not change that
day to an other-than-normal Government business day. On such a day, the regular leave and personnel policies of the Government apply and are unchanged."[93]

Antiwar leaders were moving at top speed, hopping planes, trains, and automobiles to fulfill multiple speaking engagements. Rallies, teach-ins, and panel
discussions were held all over the major cities, often simultaneously. Some two
hundred thousand people turned out for myriad events in New York. Mass
demonstrations took place in many locations. Coretta Scott King addressed a
crowd of fifty thousand at the Washington Monument. At least as many gathered at Manhattan's Bryant Park, clogging rush-hour traffic and listening to
speeches by Shirley MacLaine, Woody Allen, Stacy Keach, and Senators
Charles Goodell and Eugene McCarthy. Thirty thousand congregated on the
New Haven Green, where they heard no less than the previous year's state
chairman of Citizens for Nixon-Agnew assail the war. Crowds of twenty thousand turned out for rallies in Ann Arbor and Madison, fifteen thousand in
Minneapolis, Detroit, and Philadelphia. On Long Island, Averell Harriman addressed another assemblage of fifteen thousand—the largest antiwar protest
ever there.[94]

In the biggest demonstration of the day, about a hundred thousand people
converged on Boston Common. The highlight of the afternoon was provided
by the SWP leader Peter Camejo, the last speaker. By the time it was Camejo's
turn to talk, many in the audience were tired of speeches and some were starting
to head home. Intent on halting the exodus, the fiery Camejo began his speech
while still a step or two from the microphone. He spoke "in a high pitched,
stacatto cadence, and his whole body vibrated to the rhythm." The war was not
a mistake but an inevitable product of the system, he shouted. "And to those
politicians who are joining the bandwagon, this antiwar movement is not for
sale. This movement is not for sale now, not in 1970 and not in 1972." The
exodus of bodies quickly ceased. Disdainful of the VMC's call to *think* about the
war for a day, Camejo told the gigantic throng, "We are not here to reflect on
the war! We have already decided that it is wrong! We are here to *stop* it!"
Waving his arms about, bouncing and gyrating, tearing into the war with a
vengeance, Camejo stirred the crowd's passions. "He made us hate the war
perhaps more than we ever thought possible," one listener writes. Wild bursts
of applause punctuated his oration. This was the first time that Camejo had
spoken to a hundred thousand people, and he was having a ball. "I could actually
see the front of the crowd react to what I was saying before the back did, in a
wave," he recalled. Camejo ended his speech at its peak.[95]

Two hours later, the rally at the Washington Monument concluded, and the demonstrators, led by Coretta Scott King, began marching toward the White House. They proceeded ten and twelve abreast, holding candles. The tone of the procession was solemn, almost funereal. Signs and placards were considered inappropriate for the march and were prohibited. In less than an hour, the demonstrators virtually encircled the White House. A drumroll sounded for the war dead. Candles could be seen stretching back to the Monument. Nothing but a sea of candles in the darkness. The Justice Department's John Dean was at the front of the procession. The government's chief negotiator with Moratorium leaders over the protest, he was on the scene to keep tabs on the action. Over his walkie-talkie, Dean was reporting to Ehrlichman in the White House bomb shelter and other officials. Dean was impressed by the march. "The Moratorium was not an unpleasant demonstration," he recalled. "It wasn't ugly, it didn't have that feel. The anger wasn't manifest. . . . I thought if people behaved like this more people would be attracted to the movement and it would make a bigger impact." When "you've got the candles burning and the nice atmosphere," Dean perceived, people "will listen more."[96]

NSC staffer William Watts was inside the White House during the march. He was working on a presidential speech announcing a major escalation in Vietnam—the Duck Hook option. At one point, Watts "came up for a breath of air" and strolled out onto the White House lawn. He, too, was impressed by the protest. "I think that had to have a lot of effect," he said later. "It was a very moving night, that's for sure." It was also a painful one for Watts. To get a better look at the marchers, he walked over to the White House gate. Lo and behold, there were his wife and children walking by, each holding a candle. "I felt like throwing up," Watts recalled. "There they are demonstrating against me, and here I am inside writing a speech." "You talk about a sense of siege mentality inside," he said. "It was pretty strong. . . . It was very painful to be on the other side of the fence. . . . It was astounding."[97]

Watts was not the only administration official with loved ones on the other side of the fence. Also among the marchers was Antonia Lake, wife of the NSC staffer Anthony Lake, who was working with Watts on the Duck Hook speech. Antonia had been opposed to the war for several years and had protested it since 1967. Her differences with Tony on Vietnam were a source of considerable strain in their relationship. Sometimes they led her to wonder whether the marriage could survive. But Antonia had caused her husband to question the war more.[98]

Numerous children of administration officials were involved in the antiwar movement, many of whom undoubtedly participated in Moratorium events. "*All* of us . . . had sons or daughters who were involved in this," Marshall Green fervently recalled. "I mean, everybody did. I had a son who was poised to go to Canada. I had to keep arguing, 'For God sakes, *don't*,' you know, and trying to pull him back. All of us were torn in our own family lives." Ray Price said that opposition to the war inside officials' families "was a problem for most members of the administration." Susan Haldeman was a peace activist at Stanford, the scene of considerable Moratorium activity; her boyfriend was an antiwar leader there. "She didn't throw any bricks through windows, but she went to rallies and things like that," her father, H. R. Haldeman, said. Two of John Ehrlichman's children participated in antiwar protests. Peter Ehrlichman was active at Stanford as well. "During the height of the demonstrations there, he and I talked quite frequently," his father remembered. "He was very concerned about [the war]. . . . We had a need for a lot of communication." Peter traveled to Washington for some demonstrations. For John Ehrlichman and his kids, the war period was a "rough time" replete with "anguish." Ronald Ziegler said both Secretary of the Treasury George Schultz and Director of the Office of Management and Budget Caspar Weinberger had children who opposed the war. Ziegler remembered observing "compassionate feeling" within the administration over officials' antiwar kids. As promised, John Laird participated in Moratorium activity in Wisconsin. Kim Agnew, aged fourteen, had wanted to join in the Moratorium, but was prevented by her father. "I wouldn't let her," Spiro Agnew said. "She was unhappy for a day, but she got over it." As in the Johnson administration, antiwar sentiment inside officials' families heightened their awareness of the conflict's unpopularity and caused great personal pain. "I do think that [antiwar] friends and relatives had a great deal to do with people's emotions," Green said. "They're bound to." Did his own son's views affect him? "Of course!" he exclaimed.[99]

Many officials also had friends who participated in the Moratorium. One of these officials, the NSC staffer Winston Lord, recalled that the protest pushed him in a dovish direction.[100]

Some of the young men responsible for fighting the war took part in the Moratorium too. In Vietnam, about fifteen U.S. soldiers went out on patrol wearing black armbands that day. Another half dozen donned armbands at the gigantic Tan Son Nhut air base. The draft resister Michael Ferber remembered visiting with some American psy-war troops in their Saigon apartment shortly after the protest. Between drags of "unbelievable" Cambodian grass, the GIs "wanted to know all about the Moratorium," Ferber recalled. "They were all against the war. . . . I was amazed that morale had degenerated to that extent."[101]

As some Americans protested the war, others protested them. They taunted Moratorium activists, ripped their armbands off, flew flags at full staff, and demonstrated. At least one parachuted down on the Washington Mall. Although most of the counterdemonstrators were acting on their own volition, the White House aided and abetted their activity. "We were asked to demonstrate the way we feel the best way we know how," the parachutist revealed to a reporter.[102]

For the first time since the war began, the press sympathized with a protest. Media commentators praised the Moratorium. Walter Cronkite called it "historic in its scope. Never before had so many demonstrated their hope for peace." The *Washington Post* and other newspapers did VMC organizers the service of printing schedules of protest events in their cities. Both CBS and NBC broadcast 90-minute prime-time news specials on the Moratorium on the evening of October 15; Sam Brown appeared on one, David Hawk the other. The media stressed the wide range of Moratorium activities and participants, the large crowds, and the many Establishment supporters. On television, Americans saw that what was happening in their own community was happening all over the country.[103]

VMC organizers were euphoric over the turnout. "It caught on way beyond our expectations, and it just took off," Hawk recalled. "We knew that we were building an enormous momentum of opposition to the war. We thought the administration is going to have to respond." Nixon himself had to be listening, Brown believed—"he couldn't miss it." But there was also concern, overshadowed by the ecstasy of the moment, that the momentum had built up too much, too quickly. "It was very clear by October 15 that we had shot our wad, that we had accomplished in October what we thought we might have built up to by December, January, February, or March," Hawk said. "I mean, when you get your chance to go on prime-time television and give your five-minute antiwar rap . . . that's why you organize a couple hundred thousand people—so you'll have [an] event that'll allow you to create media interest, that'll allow you to talk to millions. You know, we'd talked to millions." What could the country do for an encore, VMC organizers wondered.[104]

Nixon Blinks

The White House emphasized that it was business-as-usual for officialdom on Moratorium day. Ron Ziegler told reporters that President Nixon had met with the National Security Council to discuss Latin American issues in the morning and with his economic advisers to consider inflation in the afternoon. Chirped Mrs. Nixon, "I haven't seen a single demonstrator—and I've been out." Ziegler disclosed, however, that the president was receiving reports on Moratorium activity from his advisers.[105]

The chief dispenser of these reports was John Ehrlichman, who was intently tracking Moratorium activity around the country from the presidential bomb shelter and other locations. Ehrlichman took time out from his sleuthing to direct Egil Krogh to obtain FBI information on Sam Brown and David Mixner (who Krogh believed was "the brain behind this problem"). By the end of the day, Ehrlichman and other officials were apparently impressed with the organizational skills of Moratorium leaders. Haldeman recalled that Sam Brown "seemed to be a genius for organization. He seemed to be awfully good at setting up a structure to run a vast operation from a central command post." Haldeman was impressed with the organizational talents of other antiwar leaders as well. "We knew that these people were good at coordinating and planning," he said. "John did in his intelligence. . . . They used walkie-talkies, and we had their frequencies.[106] You could listen to their command post and all their stuff going through. I mean, they were well-staffed and skillfully operated. . . . They did it well, and that was recognized." "They *were* good," Ehrlichman confirmed. "They were very efficient." Ehrlichman was loathe to admit any special admiration for the organizational skills of Sam Brown, however, saying, "I didn't think he was any particular genius organizer. . . . Brown was much more kind of an ideologue, I think. And I finally came to the conclusion that Sam Brown was in it for himself."[107]

Officials met with Moratorium protesters in their offices. Some, including Ziegler, walked down to the Washington Monument during the rally to check out the scene—"just kind of mingling around and seeing what it's like," Ziegler remembered.[108]

Despite claims of business-as-usual, officials were agitated by the Moratorium. Leonard Garment recalled being somewhat "shaken up" by it. The "awesome crowds," evidence of widespread domestic opposition to the war, suggested to Garment that the situation was "out of control." Moynihan bluntly apprised Nixon the day after the protest:

> The Moratorium was a success. It was not perhaps as big as some
> may have anticipated . . . but in style and content it was everything
> the organizers could have hoped for. The young white middle class
> crowds were sweet tempered and considerate: at times even radi-
> ant. . . . The movement lost no friends. It gained, I should think, a
> fair number of recruits and a great deal of prestige. . . . I believe the
> administration has been damaged.

With equal frankness, Moynihan told Nixon that "we have only ourselves to blame for some of this damage." Agnew's "clumsy and transparent attempt to link [the protesters] up with Pham Van Dong," he said, "was a blunder of the first order." Moratorium organizers "know that it was just about the best thing that happened to them. The middle class, academic, intellectual world will now be solidly with them. More importantly, as they move into alliances with much more questionable groups . . . [for the November protests] they will be immune to charges of fellow travelling. Howsoever well founded. . . . They can now more readily associate with organizations that are nominally concerned with peace, but in fact have far more complex agendas." Moynihan argued that "what the Vice President should have done, of course, was to go before the television cameras and punch Premier Pham Van Dong in the nose." Moynihan urged Nixon to *"stop the red baiting."* "If we are to get through this period," he admonished, "we are going to have to act a lot smarter than we have done lately."[109]

Pat Buchanan was also disturbed by the Moratorium. "The war in Vietnam will now be won or lost on the American front," he wrote Nixon two days later. "The morale of the American people is roughly equivalent to the military posture of the South Vietnamese in 1965. . . . [They] are confused and uncertain and beginning to believe that they may be wrong and beginning to feel themselves the moral inferiors of the candle carrying peaceniks who want to get out now."[110]

Officials chafed over the sympathetic press coverage of the Moratorium. "The theme in the media . . . is that the protesters have us on the run," Tom Huston wrote Haldeman. The White House felt D.C. Police Chief Jerry Wilson had aided the Moratorium's image in the press by giving out an artificially high crowd estimate for the Washington march. "What is he trying to tell us?" Ehrlichman queried Krogh later.[111]

Nixon himself was deeply distressed by the Moratorium. His fear that it would undercut his November 1 ultimatum to Hanoi had intensified in the days leading up to the protest, as momentum for it had swelled. "Although publicly I continued to ignore the raging antiwar controversy," he writes in his memoirs, "I had to face the fact that it had probably destroyed the credibility of my ultimatum." When Pham Van Dong sent his letter of encouragement to antiwar groups on October 14, "I knew for sure that my ultimatum had failed," Nixon records. "I knew . . . that after all the protests and the Moratorium, American public opinion would be seriously divided by any military escalation of the war." By the night of October 15, Nixon's mood was dark indeed. "I thought about the irony of this protest for peace. It had, I believed, destroyed whatever small possibility may still have existed of ending the war in 1969."[112]

The Moratorium had undermined the November 1 ultimatum partly by encouraging the North Vietnamese to hang on during the initial phase of Duck Hook in the knowledge that strong American opposition to it was guaranteed. The likelihood of a quick little victory—one of those swift military operations the American people always went for—had thus gone way down. And a longer attack was sure to engender enormous opposition. "It's all in place: the telephone networks are there, people will come out, everybody knows where to go," as Daniel Ellsberg observed. "[Nixon] knew he was going to face an unprecedented opposition. So the odds now looked just terrible." The president's perception that Duck Hook would incite serious domestic turmoil was reinforced by his advisers. "Laird was *very* strong about that," Roger Morris recalled. Laird was reluctant to discuss Duck Hook with me, but verified that he was mainly concerned about its political consequences at home. "*That* was really the [issue]," Laird said. "And I really felt that you could accomplish the same thing without using the assets that they wanted to use. . . . I thought that at that time we should test the South Vietnamese . . . and throw responsibility to them in a very tough way."[113]

Inextricably linked to Nixon's disquiet over the Moratorium was his uncertainty about U.S. military capabilities. If Duck Hook was sure to bring Hanoi to its knees in short order, regardless of enemy resolve, then the antiwar movement was of little concern. The job would be accomplished before a domestic crisis could develop. But there was no such guarantee. In fact, the more Nixon learned about the military's capabilities, the more it seemed a decisive blow was impossible. And the longer the Duck Hook attacks had to go on, he understood, the worse the domestic furor would be. Of course, there was also a potential "face-saving problem," as Morris pointed out. "If the U.S. announced this 'savage, punishing blow' to bring North Vietnam to its knees, and nothing happened, it was a little like Rocky throwing his knockout punch and the other guy's still standing there saying, 'Hit me again.' It was a real moment of truth . . . for . . . the application of American military power." Laurence Lynn's critique of Duck Hook's military potential probably had a substantial influence on the president's decision to back off. Lynn himself came to believe it was "a major factor." "I think it may well have been the case that Nixon would have decided against it anyway," he said. "But the fact that he had a rather powerful critique would have made it extremely difficult for him to go ahead with it."[114]

Roger Morris contended that it was ultimately this uncertainty about military efficiency that led Nixon to forgo Duck Hook, not domestic political concerns. Nixon's assertion in his memoirs that the Moratorium thwarted his ultimatum, Morris said, was simply "a fig leaf. That's what I call 'memoir history.' . . . I think Richard Nixon would like to think that he was somehow undercut or stabbed in the back by the protesters, but . . . I think [he was] much more pragmatic and cold-eyed than that." Other officials, however, disagreed. Laird said he believed Nixon's account; the Moratorium "had a tremendous influence on him," he thought. Like Laird, Haldeman was reluctant to discuss Duck Hook with me (claiming, curiously, to have no knowledge of it), but he unwittingly confirmed Nixon's account. The antiwar movement prevented a peace settlement in the fall of 1969, Haldeman maintained. He singled out the Moratorium for special blame. At a second interview, a year later, Haldeman's memory of Duck Hook had improved. Asked this time whether he agreed with Nixon's account, he said yes. The Moratorium, Haldeman recalled, meant that Nixon's ultimatum was "so substantially reduced in credibility that it'll no longer be effective." Ray Price also "would credit the memoir on this."[115]

Of course, Nixon's complex personality and rapid swings in temperament also have to be factored into the equation. "A lot of it probably has to do with Richard Nixon's own mood and psyche at the time," Anthony Lake argued. Although he believed the Moratorium and military considerations shaped Nixon's decision, it was Lake's "impression at the time, from remarks of others around the White House, that he simply couldn't bring himself to do it. . . . Just for personal reasons or something."[116]

The Duck Hook plans were shelved. They would be trotted out again later, though, with deadly results.

Isolating the Black Sheep

Following the Moratorium, officials debated how to respond to the protest and counter the upcoming November demonstrations, including the "March Against Death" planned by the AFSC leader Stewart Meacham and the Mobe's mass demonstration in Washington. Both Secretary of State William Rogers and Moynihan recommended trying to convert young opponents of the war and cautioned against further alienating them. Moynihan warned Nixon of their substantial influence on their parents. He urged that officials meet with Moratorium leaders. "Part at least of the difficulties involved here is that the players don't know one another, and not unnaturally suspect the worst," Moynihan reasoned. The presidential assistant did not think the administration could exert any great influence on the November protests, however—it was too late for that. Mobe organizers "hope to have a million people in Washington, and one would have to bet they might just," he told Nixon on October 16. "There is not much you can do about this. Or at least not much I can think of. The course of events in the near term is pretty much set. . . . For the moment the most we can hope to do is to keep matters from getting worse than would otherwise be the case." Moynihan pointedly added, "Having watched our responses as yesterday's events approached, let me say in all candor that this will be no small achievement."[117]

Other officials advocated playing political hardball. Bill Gavin pressed for a "full-scale" "campaign of counter-revolution" against the November demonstrations "that can blow the other guys out of the water in twenty-five days." The campaign should be "directed from people close to us," he proposed to Haldeman on October 16, and involve pro-administration "front groups," rallies, buttons, newspaper ads, leaflets, and an "unrelenting propaganda drive against those politicians who have chosen to become bedfellows of Sam Brown." Gavin felt domestic political conditions were ripe for such an offensive. "I think the nation just may be a bit weary of hearing the same old junk, and, what is *infinitely more important,* the *media* might be getting wise to the fact that they've been *had* by the radicals for the past few years," he wrote Haldeman. "This might be just a time to seize the day and break the back of the sell-out movement in this country."[118]

Tom Huston was thinking along similar lines. The same day he "strongly" urged that the administration "immediately" launch a campaign to rally public support for Nixon's policies and isolate the protesters. The campaign "must be directed from the White House (secretly, of course, but nevertheless decisively)," he stressed to Haldeman, "through the use of a series of front groups around the country." Its main objectives: "discrediting the leadership of the New Mobilization Committee (a heavily Communist-infiltrated group . . .)," arranging public appearances by administration spokesmen and supporters, mobilizing prowar veterans "through easily attainable projects like flying the flag and turning on headlights," organizing rallies "in carefully selected sites where it is possible to turn substantial numbers of people out," and running newspaper ads "by local groups." In addition, proposed Huston, the front groups should circulate bumper stickers, posters, and pins reading SUPPORT THE PRESIDENT AND END THE WAR IN VIETNAM (to which the advertising-trained Haldeman responded, in the margins of Huston's memo, "No. Need to work on wording—there's no sex in *Support the P.*"). Huston emphasized that White House command of the campaign "must be unified—no committee effort, but centralized direction with sufficient stroke to get the job done" ("Agree!" scrawled Haldeman). The president's speech on November 3 should serve as the occasion for surfacing pro-administration sentiment, Huston argued. "We should know well in advance the thrust of what he is going to say and, on the basis of that knowledge, program support for it beginning one minute after he finishes speaking." Huston informed Haldeman that he had already instructed an underling to scour newspapers from around the country to identify people who had publicly supported Nixon during "yesterday's show" but were not yet linked up with the White House's propaganda network. "I am confident that through this effort we will turn up the names of perhaps a hundred contacts around the country who can be mobilized quickly for action in November," he wrote. Huston argued that the administration could "regain the initiative" in the political battle over the war at home "if we utilize all the resources potentially at our command."[119]

In still another memo to Haldeman on October 16, the White House aide Dwight Chapin also made the case for splitting the protesters from the public. "Following our discussion in the car tonight, the objective is to isolate the radical leaders of the 'Moratorium' event and the leaders of the 'Mobilization' committee," he wrote. "They are one and the same and their true purpose should be exposed." Contradictorily, Chapin advocated warning congressional supporters

of the Moratorium "not to rush off on the November 15 thing—it is differ-
ent." The administration should orchestrate "a full-fledged drive . . . against
the media." To network officials in New York, "cold turkey should be talked."
Chapin recommended mobilizing support from the business community
("*FAST,*" commanded Haldeman). Justice Department officials should warn the
public of communist involvement in the protest. At a meeting with the press,
Nixon should act the part of "a dedicated President—not detoured by the
Moratorium . . . a man who has been working for peace and has stepped up
the activity. . . . He is strong, confident, undeterred." Like Huston, Chapin
advised that support for Nixon's policies be surfaced "immediately after the
November 3 speech. . . . It should be shown by all—each in their own
way—but what they do must be visible." Citizens might "ask the networks to
tell it to Hanoi. . . . Thousand of wires, letters, and petitions to the networks."
All of this—"if done right—will pre-empt much of the publicity which the
November 15 group will be trying to generate at that time," Chapin envisioned.
"If properly handled, many of those who might be considering becoming involved in the November 15 activity can be won over. It will also tend to make
the November 15 group more vocal—less rational and appear properly as the
fringe groups they are." Chapin further prescribed that the White House engineer pro-Nixon festivities at halftimes of football games on November 15.
Nixon himself might even attend a game. [120]

The president and Haldeman were eager to isolate the protesters. Both felt
that strategy had more political mileage than trying to win them over. In the
margin of a memo from Moynihan alleging that there were potential Nixon
supporters among youthful protesters, the president wrote, "No, RN $ and
votes came from West and South." Following a discussion with Nixon on October 16, Haldeman stressed to William Rogers in an EYES ONLY memo that
while it was important to try to capture young people who had not gone too far
off the deep end, it was more important not to "alienate our friends" in the
process. "We don't want to say to the 199,000,000 people who didn't demonstrate yesterday that they were wrong, while we are trying to show our cooperation with some of the thousands who did demonstrate," Haldeman wrote.
Moreover, "we must make it clear that we do not, in any way, embrace the
extreme elements that [were] in the demonstrations," including "those who
lowered the American flag to half mast"—which would include New York's
Mayor John Lindsay. However, the administration should also make the point,
Haldeman told Rogers, "that the majority of the people yesterday were demonstrating for peace, and that in this goal we have absolutely no quarrel with
them . . . that we are on a peace course . . . but that our ability to achieve peace
will be greatly enhanced by cooperation rather than opposition within the country." Haldeman added:

The trick here is to try to find a way to divide the black sheep from
the white sheep within the group that participated in the Moratorium
yesterday. We need to separate, in any statement we make, those
who are honestly for peace from those who are for their own purposes trying to rally support against the Administration and/or
against the U.S. The problem is to find a way to divide the good
guys from the bad guys in the demonstration movement without
discouraging the people who have backed us all along.

There was an additional problem, Haldeman perceived. In response to Huston's
assertion that the White House's campaign against the November demonstrations had to be conducted secretly, he wrote—after nine months of infuriating
leaks—"there is no such thing."[121]

The administration decided to rally the honest Americans and discredit the
bad ones. White House public relations operatives shifted into high gear. According to John Ehrlichman, countering the November 15 demonstration was
the "first major project" of the administration's "propaganda mill" for shaping
public opinion. Haldeman, the head of the project, admitted, "It was a serious
effort." Haldeman agreed with Huston and Chapin that Nixon's November 3
speech should serve as the focal point for displays of pro-administration sentiment. He directed White House propagandists to "focus on Nov. 11 Armistice
Day / Veterans Day" too. To prepare the ground for pro-Nixon activity then,
officials drove home the point that the administration needed unity at home to
achieve peace; the White House distributed a "fact sheet" detailing steps it had
taken to facilitate a settlement of the war. Congressmen were pressured to support their commander in chief. Officials planted stories in the press on favorable
public reaction to Nixon's stiff-arming of the Moratorium and to the Tell It to
Hanoi newspaper ads. The administration manufactured more prowar letters to
the media.[122]

The president turned Spiro Agnew loose on the black sheep. On October 19,
the vice president called antiwar leaders an "effete corps of impudent snobs who
characterized themselves as intellectuals." Mobe organizers were "hard-core dissidents and professional anarchists" intent on holding a "wilder" demonstration
than the one in October, he warned. Agnew offered Americans his own personal theory of youthful protest: "The young, at the zenith of physical power
and sensitivity, overwhelm themselves with drugs and artificial stimulants.
Thus, subtlety is lost and fine distinctions based on acute reasoning are care-
lessly ignored in a headlong jump to a predetermined conclusion." In another
diatribe against protesters, Agnew complained that "anarchists and Communists," aided by "ideological eunuchs" in American political circles, were, like
"vultures who sit in trees" and "prey upon the good intentions of gullible men,"
transforming "honest concern" into "something sick and rancid." Referring to

the impudent snobs, the vice president declared, "We can . . . afford to separate them from our society with no more regret than we should feel over discarding rotten apples from a barrel." Agnew clarified the administration's call for national unity: "When the President said 'bring us together' he meant the functioning, contributing portions of the American citizenry." To lend weight to his attacks, Nixon appeared in public with Agnew and assured Americans that he was "very proud to have the Vice-President, with his Greek background, in our Administration."[123]

Members of the media and Congress were passed intelligence reports claiming that communists were pulling the strings for the November demonstrations. Thus primed, prowar legislators made sure their less vigilant colleagues were aware of the full magnitude of the deception. Obviously up to his ears in FBI documents, Congressman Richard Ichord (D-Mo.) revealed on the House floor that the Mobe was "top-heavy with Communists and pro-Communists" with "invaluable expertise" in planning "blatant Communist manipulation, exploitation and subversion." The July antiwar conference that organized the fall protests "was characterized by an extra-ordinarily conspicuous Communist presence," Ichord asserted.[124]

The administration impressed upon the public that it anticipated violence on November 15—this was, indeed, an animal different in kind from the October Moratorium. At a Justice Department press conference on November 6, John Dean warned of "serious violence." Intelligence indicated that Weathermen would be on the scene, Dean reported, trying "to disrupt traffic, to cause vandalism, and to close the downtown business area." An unnamed "militant group" was "attempting to bring street gangs to Washington." Another "militant organization" planned to "'confront' federal officials." (Asked to name these militant bodies, Deputy Attorney General Richard Kleindienst refused, saying, "In most cases, it is impossible to label them by a name.") Dean also stated that "informal reports" from campuses revealed "there may be a general mood of violence and antagonism toward established authority." Much to the administration's delight, the press was soon awash with predictions of bloodshed. Charged the *New York Times*, "The Justice Department has been turned into a funnel for alarmist reports . . . of the type that exacerbate tensions and thus serve as self-fulfilling prophecies." To the irritation of Tom Huston and the FBI, an intelligence report later leaked to the press admitted that the administration engaged in "scare tactics."[125]

The administration was not just being theatrical, however. John Dean, its main liaison with Mobe leaders, solicited the advice of more than a dozen government agencies on a Mobe request for a permit to march from the Capitol up Pennsylvania Avenue and around the White House. Virtually all of the agencies warned of violence. "Could be potential dynamite," said the National Park Service. The marchers would include "about 5,000–6,000 of the hard core," including "leftists, extremists and even Communists." According to HEW, the possibility of "uncontrollable action" was "considerable" (although by permitting activities that prevented "boredom" among the demonstrators, HEW counseled, the government would minimize disruptive behavior). Moynihan told Nixon that Mobe leaders were "likely to want as much [violence] as they can provoke. (That, after all, is why the 1967 march on the Pentagon was such a success.)" The FBI warned that the likelihood of violence was considerably greater than at the Pentagon march or 1968 Chicago demonstrations. The administration's concern about rioting was fed by a growing awareness that half a million or more people would turn out for the protest. How could anyone control a mob that large?[126]

Yet the administration greatly exaggerated the potential for violence. It also used it as a convenient excuse to deny the Mobe's request to congregate near the White House. By spurning the request, officials surely understood, they could hamper organizing for the protest. It would be difficult to publicize an event still up in the air. And the administration was hardly eager to let half a million Americans surround the White House even if they were nonviolent. How would that look on the evening news and the front page of the Sunday papers? Plus, these did not promise to be the staid candle-carrying types who had paraded around Washington in October. Many were seasoned practitioners of civil disobedience. Some might get the idea of scaling the White House fence and leading a large-scale move on the Executive Mansion. It didn't matter whether the intruders were all limp-wristed pacifists crawling on all fours, that would be a monumental problem.

For several weeks the Justice Department threatened to deny a permit for a march at all. After a series of negotiations with Mobe leaders, however, it offered to allow a parade from the Capitol straight up the Mall to the Washington Monument, a safe distance from the White House. Mobe leaders insisted on Pennsylvania Avenue. A subsequent administration offer of Constitution Avenue was also spurned, and negotiations between the two sides dragged on into November. John Dean remembered the Mobe's "disruptive" effect on the government during this and other predemonstration periods:

> I was always struck that the antiwar movement was much more effective in making its voice heard than they even perceived they were. The fact that they were able to tie the government up, and all that talent in the government up, in dealing with the minutiae of their demonstrations and the politics of the demonstrations—they were making an impact, no denying. My sense was that the government really disliked the nuisance of having to deal with it. . . . I thought it was a pretty effective tool. . . . It was clearly making its point.

But, Dean thought, "it was more of a pain in the ass, if you will, than an influencer of policy. . . . I never sensed that it was changing any policy."[127] Nixon himself, as we have seen, knew better.

On November 11—only four days before the Mobe demonstration was scheduled to take place—the government abruptly reversed its position and offered Pennsylvania Avenue. The mayor of Washington, D.C., who feared the Mobe would go ahead without permits, resulting in considerable bloodshed, was widely credited with persuading Nixon to make the concession. Encircling the White House was still out of the question, though. From Pennsylvania Avenue, the parade route would drop down Fifteenth Street to the Washington Monument, where there would be a rally. Nonetheless, the administration moved to fortify the White House by placing a solid ring of buses around the grounds.[128]

Officials were meanwhile making it easier for Americans to voice their support for Nixon following his November 3 speech. As Haldeman's assistant Lawrence Higby told Jeb Magruder on October 21, the president wanted the "maximum game planning cranked up for November 3." The White House helped set up pro-Nixon "citizens committees" around the country and planned supportive activities, including phone calls to the media and the display of bumper stickers and buttons. It also had Republican Party officials urge Americans to wire Nixon immediately following his speech to express their enthusiasm for it.[129]

Nixon spent the week before his speech in seclusion, logging long hours crafting it on a yellow legal pad. As Roger Morris said, the address was "a counterattack of a major kind" against the antiwar movement. Against the advice of his cabinet, the president took a hard line against the protesters. He would be "untrue" to his "oath of office" if he allowed national policy to be "dictated" by a "vocal minority" that attempted to "impose" its views on others "by mounting demonstrations in the street," Nixon said. If this minority "prevails over reason and the will of the majority," he warned, "this nation has no future as a free society." The president informed Americans that his unceasing peace efforts had elicited nothing but wooden rebuffs from Hanoi. On the brighter side, he had put into effect a "plan" to "win the peace" regardless of what Hanoi did. This plan, Vietnamization, called for "the complete withdrawal of all U.S. ground combat forces" from Vietnam. Nixon claimed that he could not disclose the timetable of that withdrawal lest he aid the enemy. To help offset his blinking on November 1, the president declared that he "would not hestitate to take strong and effective measures" if Hanoi escalated the fighting. Nixon asked for the support of "the great silent majority of my fellow Americans" in his struggle to win the peace. "Let us understand: North Vietnam cannot defeat or humiliate the United States," he said. "Only Americans can do that."[130]

Sam Brown, whose own unceasing peace efforts had influenced Nixon to give the speech, was glued to his TV set. He was feeling triumphant. "I said, 'That guy is running scared,'" Brown recalled. "I mean, that was a speech of somebody trying to recapture [lost support]. That was a defensive action, was the way I read it . . . [evidence] of real weakness on his part. . . . I mean, this is not the mayor of Cleveland giving the speech—this is the president of the United States standing up and responding directly to what you just did." Other antiwar activists were less pleased. "Never before has [Nixon] disclosed how committed he is emotionally and ideologically to this war," I. F. Stone lamented.[131]

The public expressed overwhelming support for Nixon's stance. The White House was deluged with congratulatory telegrams, letters, and phone calls. Nixon had expected a positive response, but even he was surprised by its magnitude. Not all of this praise represented heartfelt sentiment, however. White House operatives had orchestrated many of the laudatory communications, as well as other pro-Nixon activity that swiftly followed. "Clobber commentators, especially NBC," Haldeman's notes of a November 3 meeting with the president read. "Load the switchboard—crack them." Haldeman later conceded:

> The silent majority thing, we really *did* crank up. . . . We aided and abetted that activity, we encouraged it, and we had people volunteering to develop it. Alex Butterfield was the project guy on that for a while. We had little "silent majority" buttons and bumper stickers made up—you know, the normal kind of, in effect, countercampaign to the peace march stuff—the Mobilization and all that—to give people who did believe in us a way of overtly rallying to the cause. Because they weren't basically activists, so you needed to help them along, let's say.

The next day, Nixon posed for the press behind stacks of congratulatory telegrams arranged on his desk in the Oval Office. He kept them there "in such numbers that the Oval Office could not be used for work, and for days he refused to relinquish them," Kissinger writes. The president was euphoric. "We've got those liberal bastards on the run now," he told White House staffers on the morning of November 5, his feet up on his desk, a satisfied smile on his face. "We've got them on the run and we're going to keep them on the run." He'd "floored those liberal sons of bitches" and would "never let them get back on their feet." Nixon's language was "rough"; he was talking like a football coach back-slapping his team. The president's players "shared his satisfaction and his relief. The tension had been building in the White House for weeks" over the protesters' fall offensive, notes Jeb Magruder, one of those present. Now they had apparently "cut them off at the ankles." Nixon's mood quickly darkened, however, when Pat Buchanan informed him of a critical television report the previous evening by the NBC correspondent Marvin Kalb.

"Well, Mr. President, that man is an agent of the Rumanian government," Kissinger allegedly interjected. "That's right," Nixon snapped. "That guy is a Communist."[132]

Despite overwhelming public support for his speech, Nixon still needed bucking up. He called Kissinger repeatedly on November 4 for pats on the back. Anthony Lake was in Kissinger's office when one of these calls came in. Although he disagreed with Nixon's stance, Lake was telling Kissinger, the speech had clearly helped the president's cause. Even his sister in Connecticut, an antiwar activist, had told him that it was a good speech, Lake said. Over the phone, "Kissinger was saying, 'Oh, Mr. President, what a wonderful speech,'" Lake recalled. "'Everybody—Nelson Rockefeller—says it was a great speech. . . . Even the sister of my aide Tony Lake, who is an antiwar activist, said [so].' And then there was this pause, and then a 'No, no, no, Mr. President. He's alright, he's alright.'"[133]

The administration's counteroffensive against the antiwar movement continued following Nixon's address. Working through a front group chaired by Bob Hope, it proclaimed November 10–16 "National Unity Week." The White House's "game plan" for the week, as an Alexander Butterfield memo records, included orchestrating "increased display of American Flag . . . porch lights and automobile headlights during daylight hours . . . patriotic rallies throughout the country . . . second barrage of wires and letters to the President . . . distribution of 1 million handbills to college campuses . . . circulation of 30 million 'Support the President' coupons . . . [pro-administration propaganda] at all NCAA and professional football games nationwide." The Dallas business tycoon (and later presidential candidate) H. Ross Perot aided the effort. As Haldeman had earlier instructed, White House operatives concentrated their efforts on Veterans Day, when a series of prowar rallies were held across the country. Most of the events were less than impressive. Only forty-five hundred turned out for a flag-drenched "Freedom Rally" at the Washington Monument, despite considerable advance publicity. Nixon himself paid a visit to the D.C. Veterans Hospital, where he clumsily joked to a one-eyed war casualty, "All you need is one. You see too much anyway."[134]

On November 13, Spiro Agnew blasted the television networks for biased reporting and called for an end to criticism of the war. Forewarned of his attack, cowed network officials granted it unprecedented complete live television coverage. Afterward the White House sent both itself and the media more laudatory letters. Meanwhile, FBI agents visited bus companies that had contracted charters with organizers for the November demonstrations and warned of communists, violence, and subpoenas. Some companies buckled under the pressure and canceled the arrangements.[135]

The administration's counteroffensive paid dividends. Many of the recent peace activists in Congress decided it was wise to lay low for awhile; only a handful backed the November 15 demonstration. Senator J. William Fulbright canceled hearings on Vietnam scheduled by his Senate Foreign Relations Committee. His decision thwarted an attempt by Daniel Ellsberg to release about a thousand pages of the Pentagon Papers, then hot off the xerox machine. Invited by Fulbright to testify at the hearings, Ellsberg had arrived in Washington the week of Nixon's speech with a suitcase stuffed with top-secret documents. Some opponents of the war elected to stay home on November 15 to avoid potential violence in Washington; others were grounded by government sabotage. In New York, remembered Norma Becker, one of the leaders of the Fifth Avenue Peace Parade Committee, "we mobilized tens of thousands of people, but then the government got to the bus drivers of the bus companies, and thousands were stranded here. They never made it there. Also, there was a bomb scare on one of the trains. So they did everything that they could to sabotage that demonstration."[136] As a result of Agnew's attack on the media, not one television network provided live coverage of the demonstration, and only short snippets were shown on the evening news, although the protest—the largest in American history, despite the government's machinations—was clearly a momentous story.

The administration was meanwhile taking measures to minimize violence on November 15. In view of a forewarned press, nine thousand troops were flown in for positioning around the Washington area. This was a larger force than employed during the October 1967 Pentagon siege. Men of the Eighty-second Airborne Division prepared for "a possible paratroop move." A Marine contingent set up a machine-gun emplacement on the Capitol steps. The White House provided Mobe organizers with walkie-talkies and other communications equipment to facilitate both control of their army and official eavesdropping. Again, Ehrlichman prepared to man the White House's central command post in the presidential bomb shelter; although worried about the adequacy of police and military arrangements for the protest, Ehrlichman himself was well prepared for it: since late October he had been receiving "significant intelligence items" on the demonstration from Tom Huston, who had arranged for a "daily flow" of FBI reports.[137]

Two days before the protest, the administration's public relations campaign against the antiwar movement suffered a serious setback. Seymour Hersh filed the first of a series of reports in more than thirty newspapers on the American massacre of between 350 and 500 unarmed Vietnamese civilians in the hamlet of My Lai in South Vietnam. The incident had been covered up by the military for more than a year, as the White House was "very much aware," Roger Morris remembered. Now the peace movement's fall offensive had helped turn it into a hot news item. Although many Americans distrusted the story, others were appalled. Charges that the United States was committing war crimes in Vietnam gained considerable credence. Newspapers published stories on other American atrocities that would not have been published before. Members of Vietnam Veterans Against the War were deluged with requests to shed light on My Lai and similar U.S. barbarities in Vietnam. "People all rushed to us to say, 'Tell us about the massacre,'" the VVAW leader Jan Barry recalled. "We were astounded, because you couldn't talk about [American war crimes] prior to that coming out. Nobody wanted to hear it." The growing interest in U.S. war crimes had its seamy side, though. "You could foresee very quickly what it was going to degenerate into—*True* magazine confessions of the latest atrocity," Barry said. "People from those kinds of magazines contacted me. They say, 'Tell us somebody we can talk to who has a real grisly story.'" Some VVAWers began organizing public hearings on American war crimes in Vietnam.[138]

The uncovering of the My Lai massacre agitated White House officials. "That had a *big* impact," William Watts later exclaimed. "When those photographs showed up in the office one day—God! And the realization that this was going to be public." Nixon, who expected the exposé would spark more antiwar protests, was furious. He ordered the military to spy on the ex-GI who had first reported the slaughter. The president also directed aides to find out "who is backing him." Nixon spent more than two hours one night bitching about publicity on the massacre. "It's those dirty rotten Jews from New York who are behind it," he kept saying to Alexander Butterfield.[139]

The "Showdown"

The period between October 15 and the November protests was an uneasy one for leaders of the Moratorium. They had surfaced opposition to the war on an enormous scale and rattled Nixon's cage, and that was reason for tremendous satisfaction. But the Mobe demonstration on November 15 remained cause for concern. It would hurt their chance (poor as it was) of duplicating or bettering their October performance on November 13–14, the next Moratorium days, since it would be the focus of peace activity then. And the possibility of counterproductive violence seemed to be growing stronger. Nixon's hard-line speech on November 3 and Agnew's diatribes against protesters meant that the demonstration was "going to turn very anti-Nixon," David Hawk perceived. "It was now a personal thing. People were going to hate Nixon like they hated Johnson. . . . It's not a policy disagreement: 'They're after us, and we're going to storm them.' . . . One didn't have to be an old movement hand to see what was going to happen." Compounding the anxiety of VMC leaders, Jerry Rubin and Abbie Hoffman unilaterally called for a separate action at the Justice Department at the end of the demonstration to protest the trial of the Chicago

Eight; the attention-hungry Rubin hyped the event by posing in front of the building wearing boxing gloves. Hawk recalled with irritation that Rubin then

> came over to our offices and said, "We're going to attack the Justice Department at the end of this rally. What do you think? You're not going to denounce us, are you?" I was just furious. Because you knew it was going to be personal with Mitchell, you knew it was going to be violent, and you knew that the Chicago Seven was going to maintain its solidarity, which meant that Dave Dellinger was going to support from the stage the march on the Justice Department, and that that was going to be the end [of the day]. . . . I mean, you could see that that was coming. . . . So you felt enormous frustration.[140]

Despite their concern about the Mobe demonstration, the VMC leaders formally endorsed it on October 21. The Mobe had stressed its nonviolent intent, and an open breach among the major peace forces would look bad, they reasoned. By working with the Mobe on the demonstration, they could also "bring order and control to it," Sam Brown thought. As it was, the Mobe's logistical preparations seemed sorely deficient. "We did a lot of training in nonviolence of our own marshal force so that we could control the circumstances better," Brown remembered. There were also many "little things" left up in the air, "like, 'How many latrines do we need?'" "There's nothing worse than somebody who needs to take a leak and can't find a latrine," Brown pointed out. "It just makes them mad, and they go piss on the side of somebody's building, and that makes the guy who's inside say, 'You're like a bunch of bums out there in the alley, pissing on the side of my building.'" (Eventually the D.C. Health Department provided toilets "out of desperation.") Brown came to suspect his insecurity about his masculinity also shaped his stance toward the demonstration. Refusing to endorse it would strengthen the perception of other protesters that he was scared of tumultuous actions. "If the feminist movement had come along ten years earlier, the history of the antiwar movement would have been different," Brown said intently, "because I would have felt more comfortable with my own sense of not needing to be a man, not needing to be macho. And there was a lot of that macho nonsense in the antiwar movement." Brown felt "very strongly" in retrospect that the VMC leaders "should have simply said, 'No, we're not going to have anything to do with a major march next month. It fundamentally separates you.'" The demonstration "distorted the intent of what we were about, which was not to get people on buses and bring them to Washington—it was to get them to go talk to their neighbors."[141]

In early evening darkness on November 13, the March Against Death began. The take-off point for the march was beside the Potomac River at the west end of the Arlington Memorial Bridge; the Justice Department had rejected a Mobe request to assemble in Arlington Memorial Cemetery, claiming that funerals would be unfairly disrupted. Every hour, twelve hundred marchers crossed the bridge, single-file, and headed silently toward the White House. Each carried a placard around his or her neck bearing the name of an American soldier killed in Vietnam or a destroyed Vietnamese village. During night hours, they held candles. At the head of the march, drummers beat a slow cadence. "It was like a massive funeral," one participant remembered. To sustain the procession, buses unloaded marchers at the take-off point every three minutes on the average. Many of the protesters had just completed long rides from distant parts of the country, only to step out into the cold, grubby and tired, and embark on a two-and-a-half-hour walk. For almost forty hours, through rain, hail, and bright sunlight, the death parade continued unabated. Forty-five thousand marched in all.[142]

As they passed the front of the White House, each demonstrator paused to say the name of a dead American soldier. Some shouted it, others spoke it softly. It was a powerful moment for most of the marchers. "You just opened your mouth and it wasn't your voice; it was a very haunting sound that came out," Sidney Peck recalled. "It was a terribly emotional experience," said Sam Brown. "To be there was—whooaaa—overwhelming. Overwhelming."[143]

Behind the locked and barred White House gates, police patroled warily around the grounds. Silhouettes of White House staffers could be seen in the windows. The building's floodlights were turned around to illuminate the marchers, and a ten-foot-long mercury vapor lamp was attached to the front of the mansion. "The lamp dazzled anyone looking at the building," Brad Lyttle recounted. "It was easy to imagine machine gunners stationed in the building's windows ready to mow down the first wave of high school students who breached the fence."[144]

As the marchers passed government buildings along their route toward the Capitol, policemen peered their way. They deposited their placards with the names of the dead in twelve open coffins at the foot of the Capitol. A drum sounded with each addition to the coffins.

Hours before the parade began, Bill Ayers and three other Weathermen, "flat and grim in their shades and work clothes and heavy boots," strode into the Moratorium's Washington office. They demanded $20,000 in exchange for abstaining from violence during a march they had planned for the next evening. VMC organizers told them to "get lost." "These guys were off their tree," David Hawk recalled. At one point, a VMC activist asked the Weathermen what they were really after. "To kill all rich people," Ayers replied. "Aren't your parents extremely rich?" the activist queried. "You know what Abbie Hoffman says, 'Bring the war home. Kill your parents,'" Ayers responded. His comrade Jeff Jones remembered, "We were all at our most extreme. . . . We were both mimicking the Panther style and also feeling a certain superiority to the rest of the movement based on what we had done [during the Days of Rage]." The next evening Weathermen and others ran through the streets of Washington, whooping, starting small fires, breaking windows, "downing jugs of wine." The action was broken up by police spewing tear gas. The gas drifted into nearby buildings, including the DuPont Theater, which had to close: "House Full of Gas" explained a sign in front.[145]

Earlier that day, protesters had held a peaceful rally at the Justice Department. "We want to see the Wizard!" three longhairs yelled while banging on the barricaded doors of the building. Passersby "found it hard to suppress a smile."[146]

Moratorium activity was then unfolding around the country. Again Americans rallied, canvassed, read the names of the war dead, tolled bells; in Los Angeles, Kenneth Chotiner, son of Nixon's longtime adviser Murray Chotiner, organized a protest of Ad Hoc Lawyers for Peace. Most of the events were tiny compared to October: now the action was in Washington.

November 15 was a crisp, clear day in the nation's capital, with temperatures in the low thirties. Shortly after 10 A.M., the throng of protesters gathered in the Mall began marching up Pennsylvania Avenue. Mobe leaders assumed the lead, followed by three drummers, again beating a funeral rhythm. Behind them walked a single line of people carrying the coffins holding the placards with the names of the dead. Behind them, several marchers lugged a huge wooden cross. The demonstrators were predominately young, white, and middle class. Their mood was determined, dignified; the procession had a "majestic tone," observed the *Washington Post*. A chorus of "Give Peace a Chance" arose spontaneously from the multitude as it edged slowly up the Avenue. Many of the marchers smiled at police stationed along the way; some officers flashed the peace sign. Signs in the crowd included "Hitler Had a Silent Majority Too." Among the marchers were scores of active-duty GIs; six days earlier, 1,365 servicemen, including 189 in Vietnam, had signed an ad in the *New York Times* urging participation in the demonstration. "Pentagon officials were frankly surprised that this many GIs would permit their names to be used in a protest ad," the *New York Post* reported.[147]

So large was the crowd that thousands of demonstrators tired of waiting to move up the Avenue and simply streamed across the Mall's grassy acres toward the Monument. By mid afternoon more than half a million people blanketed the Monument area. "I've never seen anything like it," Sidney Lens remarked. "It's the biggest thing I've been connected with in more than 30 years. Look at that crowd." Many likened the atmosphere at the rally to that at the Woodstock rock festival the previous summer. Musical performers included Arlo Guthrie, Peter,

Paul and Mary, and the cast of *Hair*. "It was a wonderful, wonderful day," David Hawk remembered. "It was . . . culture and politics coming together in a way that was very exciting." Speeches at the rally were largely dull and ignored, although the comedian Dick Gregory perked up the crowd when he said, "The President says nothing you kids do will have any effect on him. Well, I suggest he make one long distance call to the LBJ Ranch and ask that boy how much effect you can have on him."[148]

As the marchers were making their way to the Monument, President Nixon was meeting with his senior advisers in the White House. He was well protected from the mob. Besides the ring of buses around the mansion, police barricades prevented unauthorized foot or car traffic for several blocks in all directions. Cops patroled the restricted zone. Military and police helicopters buzzed overhead. All over town, troops were hidden in the bowels of government buildings, "ready to move." Military intelligence agents saturated the crowd; plainclothesmen who had traveled from New York on buses with protesters "encountered so many other operatives in Washington that they were unable to report back as instructed because the phones were tied up by their colleagues from other areas under similar instructions." And, of course, John Ehrlichman was monitoring the action from below.[149]

The sounds of speeches and songs from the rally at the Monument could be heard inside the nearly deserted White House grounds. The voices were angry. Although muted, they could even be heard inside the Executive Mansion. "It was," wrote a *Post* reporter, "an eerie sensation."[150]

"Normality" was the theme of the day for White House spokesmen. "Abnormal efforts were made to get that point across." Officials repeatedly announced that it was business-as-usual inside. Although Nixon usually spent at least a portion of his Saturdays at Camp David, this time he remained pointedly at the White House. At 12:30, reporters were invited into the Oval Office to photograph the president at work. So unconcerned was Nixon with the demonstration outside, he suggested to the press, that he planned to spend part of the afternoon watching college football on TV. In reality, the White House was "about as normal . . . as it would be any time that there is an all-day air raid alert limited to the area immediately surround[ing] the Executive Mansion," the *Post* noted.[151]

The demonstration did not sit well with officials. "Threatened is not too strong a word," Roger Morris recalled. There was "a lot of sense of isolation. No one likes to have Pennsylvania Avenue filled up with people protesting your policy. I stood inside the Treasury grounds with Bill Watts and Tony Lake surrounded by armed guards and buses barricading the White House. There was a very real sense of the country, or whoever was making politics at that point, turning against you." Watts said that the demonstration and the earlier

Moratorium made "a big impression" on him. "There was no question that they had an impact. . . . You had to notice the size of them, the people and the violence and everything else." Laurence Lynn remembered "walking around absolutely in awe of how buses could form such a barricade around the White House. At least I hadn't realized what a good idea that was, to back them up [against each other]—you just couldn't get between them." The size of the mob surprised many officials.[152]

Henry Kissinger was among the most unsettled. "He repeatedly referred to the fate of Weimar [Germany] as the streets around the White House filled with marchers," Morris writes. The protesters were practicing "fascism of the streets," Kissinger groused to his staff. "They will be sorry." Morris remembered:

> Kissinger was very concerned about the overall impact of domestic
> dissent on the body politic. He had an almost gruesome obsession
> with the Weimar example, which I think was more than just play. I
> must confess I thought at the time that it was part of the theatrics of
> the whole business . . . but when I look back on it, I think that I and
> others should have taken that more seriously. I think he had a very
> European sense of the fragility of the American body politic, which I
> think was inaccurate and wrong but which nonetheless influenced his
> policy, and thank God it did—it was a restraining factor.[153]

True, Nixon and Kissinger considered the demonstrators a small segment of the public. "I think there was to some degree a sense that these were beatniks and hippies and drug addicts and weirdos and so on," Watts said. "It wasn't mainstream America." Indeed, the public's response to Nixon's November 3 speech had demonstrated that the "silent majority" was with him, the president believed. But Nixon and Kissinger also worried that the protesters would make Hanoi even more obstinate. They would influence Americans as well. The day of the demonstration, Kissinger wrote Nixon, "They become formidable by adding to their own votes an enormous outburst of political activism, bound to have an influence on others as well as on their parents." Morris commented, "You cannot have that kind of event without some erosion inside and a sense of erosion." He aptly added, "It's a very electric atmosphere in which there are very mixed feelings about what's happening."[154]

According to Marshall Green, officials at State were less disturbed. "We saw these people milling around—it didn't bother us particularly," Green remembered. "It wasn't aimed directly at us, and we didn't fear for our physical safety." And "we thought maybe this would have some effect upon the administration, in making them more amenable to compromises and solutions." Green felt the protesters "could be [our] allies to a certain extent." He and Secretary of State William Rogers were "worried about the White House more than . . . the mobs," he said.[155]

Come late afternoon, following an appeal from the stage by Dave Dellinger, thousands of demonstrators began flooding toward the Justice Department. Leading the charge were militants carrying a huge papier-mâché mask of Attorney General John Mitchell. After some protesters broke Justice Department windows and fired firecrackers and bottles at police, the cops unleashed "wave after wave" of tear gas. They drove the crowd into the downtown area, where marauding bands of youth trashed businesses and cars. Several took over a hot dog stand abandoned by its owner and started selling his dogs. Tear gas wafted over the area for hours, inflaming the eyes and throats of passersby. "I've seen this on television, but I never realized what it was like," said a real estate developer from Massachusetts trapped in the gas. Mitchell and his deputy Richard Kleindienst watched the action at Justice from fifth-floor office windows. One official recalled encountering tear gas in Mitchell's office—"so much you could hardly speak."[156] The protest made quite an impression on the attorney general. Shortly afterward, at an NSC meeting on whether to ban chemical and biological weapons, including tear gas, Mitchell told other officials that it looked like the Russian Revolution. The rioters were swinging chains and just really "out to kill," Watts recalled Mitchell recounting. "It was rather dramatic," Watts said. "I mean, here's this meeting of all these top people, and he's describing the streets of Washington as St. Petersburg in 1917. I mean, sometimes when I would think about it I would pinch myself." Mitchell asserted, "The tear gas was what stopped them." "Well," responded Nixon, "that takes care of the tear gas issue."[157]

Also on November 15, in the largest protest in that city's history, a hundred and fifty thousand people turned out for a demonstration in San Francisco despite a steady drizzle.[158]

Following the November demonstrations, the White House quickly moved to smear them. The next day, Mitchell and Director of Communications Herb Klein declared that the protests had pushed Washington to the brink of major disorder. "Had it not been for the highly effective work of the Washington police, of the National Guard, had it not been for the reserve forces of the Defense Department and the complete cooperation of all elements of the government in this," Klein stated, "the damage to Washington . . . would have been far greater than it was at the time of the previous riots after the death of Martin Luther King." Mitchell charged that the demonstrations were "marred by such extensive physical injury, property damage and street confrontations that I do not believe that—over all—the gatherings can be characterized as peaceful." Klein called the demonstration in Washington "small." Richard Kleindienst warned of prosecutions of Mobe leaders under the anti-riot act. John Dean began preparing an official report on property damage and injuries to police inflicted by the protesters; Egil Krogh advised him to include "a lot of the background material" on the Mobe leadership and militants. Krogh delightedly noted that some congressmen were "already" deploring the demonstrations' monetary cost. Nixon ordered Jeb Magruder to have the Nixon Network generate congratulatory letters and phone calls to ABC's Howard K. Smith on remarks he made critical of the protesters.[159]

Tom Huston was uncomfortable with the administration's smear campaign. "I suspect that we have far extended ourselves in an effort to discredit the New Mobe—to the point, in fact, that our credibility is likely to be seriously questioned," he wrote Ehrlichman on November 20:

> While the New Mobe Steering Committee is not made up of moderate, peace-loving individuals, I have not seen any evidence that they were interested in anything more than a large, peaceful demonstration. If we attempt to link the New Mobe leaders with the Crazies and other anarchistic elements, we will fail, because the case simply cannot convincingly be made. . . . In many important ways, the New Mobe types are a greater internal security threat than the SDS people, but this point cannot be put across to the public effectively by following the present course of action.[160]

The *Washington Post* responded to the White House's smear campaign thus: "The effort by this administration to characterize the weekend demonstration as (a) small, (b) violent, and (c) treacherous will not succeed because it is demonstrably untrue." Klein's claim that military and police forces prevented major violence was "sheer balderdash" that "would be difficult to exceed," the *Post* commented. "The Nixon administration was less interested in trying to keep the march peaceful than in trying to make it seem less large and more violent than it really was, and in trying to scare the daylights out of that putative Silent Majority at the same time." Of Nixon's talk of watching football, the *Post* said, "for sheer piquancy, we have not heard the likes of that since Marie Antoinette."[161]

The administration kept up its campaign to surface public support for the president. Also, to help stave off another invasion of Washington and defuse protest on campuses, Nixon signed into law a bill permitting a draft lottery on November 26. "'This will take care of a lot of the draft dodgers,'" William Watts remembered Nixon scheming at an NSC meeting. "I think he was very aware of what that would mean in terms of student protest." And to advance the administration's intelligence on Mobe practices, John Dean requested a copy of a report Brad Lyttle was assembling on organization of the Washington protests. After Lyttle complied with Dean's request, Dean sent the report on to Krogh, with attached note, "After you have a chance to look at it I wish you would return it as it is my only file copy and when these people take over the Government, I want to know how to organize a mass march!"[162]

In late December, FBI Director J. Edgar Hoover tried to reason with discontented youth. "Through free enterprise and equality of opportunity," he wrote in "An Open Letter to the Youth of America," "American life has become rich and full." Yet "our Nation" was "increasingly beset by the devastating forces of lawlessness and destruction," Hoover observed. Crime and violence had reached "terrifying proportions" and were "indicative of a moral deterioration and a pervasive contempt for properly constituted authority." "Violent extremists from all directions" were "ruthlessly trampling on the rights of all," he charged. Still, Hoover assured youth he had faith they would turn things around and that "the FBI will do all in its power to assist you."[163]

Restless Victors Revisited

Peace activists had reason to feel gratified after their fall offensive. In consecutive months, they had mounted antiwar protests on unprecedented scales. The cause of peace was more popular with the public than ever. They had exerted a critical influence on Nixon's decision to forgo Operation Duck Hook, thereby helping prevent bloodshed and human misery in Vietnam on an unspeakable scale. It was an accomplishment of momentous proportions. On the campuses, they were gaining converts left and right. As one White House student intern apprised Egil Krogh, "The tolerant neutrality that prevailed through last semester and the summer months is shifting at an accelerating rate to a hardened anti-Nixon stance. . . . The moderates and the apathetically neutral . . . are now leaving us . . . in droves. The anti-war mood is sweeping the campuses and taking the middle ground with them." The student intern reported that "nearly 25% of the former Youth for Nixon crew at my campus alone" had defected to the peace movement.[164]

Many activists were indeed feeling good. They had no way of gauging their influence on Nixon's war policies and thus no way of knowing just how great their accomplishment was, but their political gains were clearly substantial. "November 15 is now a part of American history and will be recorded as the largest, most effective demonstration this country has known," New Mobe leaders wrote the day of the protest. "The Nixon administration is feeling the impact of the demonstration despite all its attempts to ignore it." Sidney Peck felt that the fall offensive provided "a very clear showing . . . that the great majority of the American people were opposed to this war." Thus, "we were in a position to follow up to the Congress." Peace activity "now had to be focused on the legislature . . . because they held the purse strings," Peck believed.[165]

But other activists were feeling demoralized. "The mood at the time was characterized by frustration," Fred Halstead writes. More than a few protesters felt the administration "chose to ignore the peace sentiment," as Moratorium leaders themselves concluded. "We are quite desperate with the war continuing in spite of all efforts to the contrary, a bad down-hill careening nightmare, entirely out of rational control," Daniel Berrigan mourned. Some protesters were convinced the conflict would never end if *that* outpouring couldn't budge officialdom. And although the public wanted the war over, activists fretted, most people supported Nixon's "Vietnamization" strategy for ending it; according to a November Gallup poll, nearly 65 percent backed his policies in Vietnam (influencing Pat Buchanan to tell Nixon that "we have clearly won the 'fall campaign'"). The president further demonstrated his peace credentials to the public on December 15 by announcing the withdrawal of another fifty thousand U.S. troops from Vietnam. "It looked like they would be able to . . . stage phased withdrawals of troops . . . every time you got something going again that would take the steam out of it," David Hawk recalled. "Because then the argument is . . . 'He's doing exactly what you want, he's ending the war, he's just not doing it as fast as you would like.' And then you say, 'Well, no, because he's doing the bombing, the dying isn't stopping, they're just not American boys, the Asian boys are continuing to die.' But it really made it different. . . . We couldn't really ever get around that. . . . And we thought that that dynamic would just go on." "I always thought [Vietnamization] was a very clever strategy on his part," the Mobe's Doug Dowd said. [166]

At a Mobe steering committee meeting in December, most participants were unexcited about organizing another national peace demonstration. Many derided the November protests as having little political effect. "I just couldn't figure that out, because to me they had been fantastic!" Brad Lyttle exclaimed. "I couldn't understand where these people were coming from at all. I just didn't know what these people were talking about. I mean, here they just had before them an enormous success, and they couldn't see anything good about it at all." Peck was equally astonished at the critics, the most vociferous of whom were organized into the "Radical Caucus." "I'm telling you, you'd have to see it to believe it," he sighed years later. "That's when Stewart Meacham basically left [the Mobe]. He had killed himself getting the March Against Death thing going. He left, and I think Doug Dowd and I just took the attitude, 'Hey, if folks can do it better, do it.'" Norma Becker recalled that the Radical Caucus was composed mainly of younger activists, including "a lot of new feminists":

> This element had become extremely radicalized. I'd watched several
> of them who came into the movement [as] plain, ordinary, middle-
> class young people, and within a year or two had become *extremely*
> radicalized, terribly frustrated, enraged, and put their hearts and souls
> into their political work and experienced the despair of watching the
> war escalate. And the more successful the demonstrations became
> in terms of numbers, in terms of [media] coverage—it was like
> banging their head against a stone wall. So that they condemned the

type of action that took place November 15, 1969, as "a gathering in the park."[167]

The Radical Caucus advocated organizing decentralized civil disobedience against domestic injustices and the war. Fred Halstead was exasperated by what he heard. The Mobe's purpose was to organize mass peace demonstrations, the SWP leader shouted, and that's what it should continue doing! "I made a talk there that was terrible," Halstead ruefully remembered. "I just ranted and screamed at people. Lost my temper. Had no effect at all." Most of the conferees sided with the Radical Caucus, partly out of animosity to the SWP's rigid insistence on single-issue, legal antiwar demonstrations; the SWP front man Jerry Gordon provoked "real sharp antagonism" when he declared that, as a lawyer, he could never support illegal acts. The Mobe agreed to call for a "Winter-Spring Offensive" focused on domestic repression, the political economy of the war, GIs, and war crimes. The offensive would peak on April 15, tax day. Peck and other veteran Mobe leaders effectively turned over the reins of the coalition—and $60,000 in surplus funds—to the Radical Caucus.[168]

The Mobe was now in the hands of a loose alliance of left-wing pacifists and revolutionaries with a narrow political base. Few Americans outside radical political circles could be counted on to heed its call. The Mobe, to use a popular phrase, was outrunning its constituency. "It was a disaster," Halstead recalled. "It was a disaster."[169]

Increasingly fed up with young militants—most of whom apparently didn't know political organizing from pot smoking—Halstead and his comrades in the SWP wanted no part of the Mobe's latest incarnation. They began making plans to organize antiwar activity on their own. "That was the time the Trotskyists basically decided to prepare to go their own way," Dave Dellinger remembered. An anonymous FBI letter demanding that antiwar activists "flush" the SWP from the Mobe widened the breach between the group and other protesters.[170]

In the wake of a stupendous political success, then, with the Nixon administration on the defensive, the Mobe was once again, incredibly, disintegrating. "That's when things did begin to fall apart," Dellinger said. "That was the beginning of the end." The White House apparently didn't think so, though. Five days after the Mobe steering committee meeting, Alexander Butterfield sent Nixon a memo outlining each phase of the forthcoming enemy offensive.[171]

The Moratorium was in no better condition: its three-day demonstration in December flopped badly. White House propaganda had cost the group considerable political support, both in the country and in Congress. VMC organizers were also exhausted. "We underestimated the emotional burnout factor," Sam Brown remembered. The November march "was the real emotional drain point." It "took so much energy and organizational skill, it was such a climax. . . . I mean, you just couldn't do any more." Further, VMC organizers "made an error in analysis." It was naïve to expect antiwar sentiment to mushroom monthly, Brown reflected. "A month is not very long. . . . We should have understood that most of us had spent by that time five years getting to where we were [politically]. People don't move in thirty days to where it took us five years to get. And they don't move in thirty days particularly when they don't have the freedom and the latitude that people at the age I then was had." Thirty days also wasn't very long for getting out publicity on a nationwide protest. After one Moratorium was over, Brown recalled, "you go home and sleep for a day, and then you get up and tell stories to each other for two days about what happened . . . and then it's already too late to get ads in the newspaper, because the deadlines are passed, practically, for the next month's demonstration. You were almost out of business. . . . You do a mailing, you get that all ready to go, and by the time you get it mailed and people get it, it's five days before the events are supposed to happen." In addition, the Moratorium "succumbed to the cyclical rhythm of campus protest." In December "kids were home from school, finals were coming up, Christmas was happening," Brown noted. "And at Christmastime, [people] don't take three days off to be bitter and angry." And it turned out that many Moratorium activists didn't have the stomach for sustained organizing. "I became convinced that there was a serious lack of long-term commitment among many students," Brown writes. "Time after time, students came to the national office arguing that the system had failed to respond to their efforts but it almost always turned out that the students' efforts had consisted of little more than canvassing for a weekend in a 1968 primary, attending an October rally, and participating in some marches. They had not yet accepted the fact that ending the war would take a long time and a great deal of dirty work." Bureaucratic infighting and despair over public support for Nixon's Vietnamization policy also took wind out of the Moratorium's sails.[172]

After the December demonstrations, the VMC leaders junked their original plan for increasing the number of days of protest each month. "We clearly couldn't do it," Brown said. They decided to concentrate on grass-roots organizing mainly around the war's economic cost, culminating in "taxpayers' rallies" to take place on April 15 simultaneously with the Mobe's protests. By focusing on Vietnam's contribution to high taxes and inflation, the VMC leaders hoped, they might reach new constituencies. "We probably had delusions about . . . a populist sort of tax revolt," Hawk smiled. More impelling, "We were desperate. . . . I'm sure we were all desperately pipe-dreaming as to what to do."[173]

Youthful militancy was showing no signs of slowing down that fall. Campus disruptions, including building takeovers and clashes with police, were more plentiful, even, than the previous spring. Bombings and burnings of ROTC buildings were increasing dramatically. Off school grounds, government and corporate offices were popular targets of youth's fury. Feeding the ire of many young people was the trial of the Chicago Eight, then taking place in Chicago. The trial was widely perceived to be a judicial farce and revealed widespread governmental surveillance and infiltration of protest groups.[174]

Administration principals who ventured out in public for speaking engagements were given raucous receptions. "The President can expect large local dissent in connection with any announced political trips" and even "leftist planning for non-political trips," the White House intelligence operative Jack Caulfield advised John Ehrlichman on November 19. Caulfield proposed the "virtual elimination of Presidential motorcades" and "exclusive reliance on helicopters" to "thwart" such "attempts to embarrass the President." To counter a protest against Nixon at the Waldorf-Astoria Hotel in New York, the White House directed its head advance man Ron Walker to stimulate "pro-RN demonstrations . . . in and around the Waldorf."[175]

Despite the protests, the autumn was "a time of significant depression for the radical and revolutionary studentry," as Kirkpatrick Sale writes. The fracturing of SDS into rival political factions meant there was no single youth group in the United States capable of organizing and sustaining radical action on a national scale, no group capable of infusing youth with the sense of a powerful revolutionary whole. "Splintered and in disarray, student leftists floundered."[176]

That the Weathermen were incapable of leading the way was starkly apparent at their "National War Council" in Flint, Michigan, over the Christmas holidays. From the ceiling of Flint's "Giant Ballroom" hung a huge cardboard machine gun. A 20-foot poster on one wall was covered with bullets bearing the names of assorted Weatherenemies, including Nixon, the radical *Guardian* newspaper, and the actress Sharon Tate (recently murdered by the Charles Manson "family"). Among the four hundred participants were kids as young as thirteen or fourteen. The action was frenetic, nonstop. "Most Weatherpeople slept an hour a day; the rest was heavy, heavy rapping, heavy listening, heavy exercising, heavy fucking, heavy laughing, a constant frenzy-strain that went through the whole four days, all the time no flab, no looseness, no ease in anything that was done." Evening "wargasm" sessions started with group karate and other exercises, followed by Weathersongs, whooping, and raps by Weatherheavies. "It's a wonderful feeling to hit a pig," Mark Rudd raved. "It must be a really wonderful feeling to kill a pig or blow up a building." After apologizing for Weatherman's "wimpy" behavior following the Days of Rage, Bernardine Dohrn, dressed in a mini-skirt and leather boots, rhapsodized over the Manson murders: "Dig it: first they killed those pigs, then they ate dinner in the same room with them, then they even shoved a fork into pig Tate's stomach! Wild!" Four outstretched fingers, symbolizing the fork, became a popular Weathergreeting. (The Weathermen were not the only young radicals taken with Manson: after visiting him in prison, Jerry Rubin wrote, "I fell in love with Charlie Manson the first time I saw his cherub face and sparkling eyes on national TV. . . . His words and courage inspired [me] . . . and I felt great the rest of the day.") Racked by guilt over their "white skin privilege," the Weathermen debated whether killing white babies was politically correct. "All white babies are pigs," one Weatherman ejaculated.[177]

Amid the "group psychosis" the Weathermen came to two decisions. They would up the ante on revolutionary violence. "Armed struggle starts when someone starts it," one Weatherdocument proclaimed. "To debate about the 'correct time and conditions' to begin the fight . . . is reactionary." Shaken by the recent murders of the Black Panther leaders Fred Hampton and Mark Clark by Chicago police, the Weathermen also resolved to divide into clandestine cells and make the final descent underground.[178]

EIGHT

1970

Before the Storm

The winter and early spring of 1970 was a low period for the antiwar movement. Many activists remained skeptical of the movement's clout and questioned the point of holding more demonstrations. Public support for Nixon's
Vietnamization policy was disheartening. American troop withdrawals sapped
strength from the movement—why protest if the war was ending, some activists reasoned? As Nixon had envisioned, the draft lottery was also enervating.
With the hot breath of conscription cooling, antiwar activity seemed less urgent.
"There's no doubt that the switch to the draft lottery did take some steam out
of the draft resistance movement," Bruce Dancis said. "I hate to admit it, but
it's true." Doug Dowd, who felt that opposition to the draft was the motor force
of the antiwar movement and had thus been "hoping like hell that the draft
would continue," thought, "'Shit, we're lost now.'"[1]

The New Mobe was critically ill, riddled by conflict and led by radicals with
a tiny constituency. Organizing for its "Winter-Spring Offensive" was unimpressive. "A lot of money was spent, and not a lot came out of it," Sidney Peck
remembered. The Moratorium was also on the ropes. Weakened by Nixonian
propaganda, politically divided, and emotionally spent, the Moratorium was "an
all-but-forgotten movement," as one VMC organizer writes. "The great coalition of last autumn had fallen apart." Many of its student troops had thrown in
the towel on legal protest. The Moratorium also generated little momentum
behind the spring antiwar actions.[2]

But the peace movement was far from dead. There were ample signs of life,
despite its slump. Clergy and Laymen Concerned About Vietnam organized a
"Lent-Passover Fast" involving both daily fasting in front of the White House
and local abstinence. "With no illusions of the possible political effect," CAL-
CAV declared, "we fast because we feel there is a moral imperative at this time

to do so. We fast because we must." In Washington, participants in the fast burned dollar bills, income tax forms, and other "documents of repression." To "build new antiwar constituencies," CALCAV also organized peace conferences in small and medium-sized cities across the United States. And it placed antiwar ads on billboards, including the stark

Dear Mom and Dad,
Your silence is killing me.[3]

CALCAV, the AFSC, and other religious peace groups played lead roles in building nationwide antidraft protests sponsored by the New Mobe in March. Activists picketed, sat in, and staged guerrilla theater at draft boards across the United States. In Manhattan, 182 people were arrested for blocking the entrance to the office of four boards. In Philadelphia, the "Spectre of Death"—a figure robed in black—appeared silently at draft boards, seating himself unsettlingly aside board members and clerks. "Death" also appeared in San Antonio, Texas, where he paid a visit to a local lottery victim. David Hawk and other VMC activists circulated a "We Won't Go" petition on campuses. "That was a tactical mistake," Sam Brown reflected. "The draft was the best organizing tool we had." Opposing it, he said, was "stupid."[4]

A coalition called the "Citizens Commission to Investigate War Crimes" held hearings on American atrocities in Vietnam. Members of Vietnam Veterans Against the War helped document specific atrocities by tracking down multiple witnesses to them. "We double-checked the stories—'Do you have a name?'" the VVAW leader Jan Barry recalled. "We were not going to take any of these stories simply at face value. . . . Guys had to come up with as much documentation as they could come up with. And then, '*Who else* do you have a name of that we may be able to find who can tell us about that?' It was amazing. We could find two and three people after a certain point to talk about the same thing that had happened in some unit." Many VVAWers initially took an "arm's length" stance to the hearings, however. "I mean, this is really heavy duty," Barry explained. "We're almost charging our fellow veterans with war crimes."[5]

Antiwar sentiment was growing among GIs in the United States. At the Oakland Army Base, applications for CO status were skyrocketing. Dissenting sailors in southern California formed the Movement for a Democratic Military, which "specialized in weapons theft from military bases." In Washington, D.C., junior naval officers opposed to the war formed the Concerned Officers Movement. Joe Urgo remembered that when he and other troublemakers at the Air Force's Atlantic City airport detachment were released early from the military in the late winter, the Air Force brought in a dozen new Vietnam veterans to take their place. "These guys came in and unpacked their bags and put their antiwar posters up on the walls," Urgo marveled. "I mean, we didn't *do* that. . . . I thought, 'Holy shit.'"[6]

Acts of insubordination were also increasing among soldiers in Vietnam. On Christmas Eve 1969, Don Luce, who had earlier resigned as director of International Voluntary Services to protest the war, organized a prayer service at the National Cathedral in Saigon. Although only twenty GIs participated, the demonstration received significant publicity when a red-faced provost marshal descended on the scene in a tank and—standing in the turret and roaring into a loudspeaker—threatened to put the GIs away for life for praying. Several months later, under the watchful eye of a CBS television crew, members of one company refused their commander's order to proceed down a dangerous jungle trail; American viewers were then treated to a live "working it out" session between the captain and his troops. Fraggings, or attempts by soldiers to murder their officers, were mounting. Consequently, some commanders began restricting access to grenades and rifles, particularly among blacks, the most rebellious of U.S. troops.[7]

In February the Student Mobilization Committee (still a front group for the SWP) held an antiwar conference in Cleveland. More than thirty-five hundred people attended, only a small minority of whom had participated in any previous SMC conference. It was among the largest antiwar meetings to date. Many of the conferees were independent young radicals bent on breaking the SWP's stranglehold on the SMC and turning it into a multi-issue anti-imperialist organization that could fill the void left by SDS's demise. Most opposed holding more legal demonstrations against the war. Members of the SDS splinter group that called itself Revolutionary Youth Movement II flooded the convention with red-blue-and-gold NLF flags bearing their group's name on the edge of them. "The YSA people were tearing the 'Revolutionary Youth Movement' off the end of them," Clark Kissinger amusedly recalled. Debate was sharp. "There was a wild free-for-all of proposals—every kind of proposal under the sun," the YSA leader Don Gurewitz remembered. Internally divided, the independent radicals were unable to formulate a persuasive counterproposal to an SWP motion to organize mass actions against the war in the spring. The conferees resolved to call for demonstrations and a nationwide student strike on April 15.[8]

The April antiwar protests, sponsored by all three national peace coalitions (the Mobe, Moratorium, and SMC), were widespread, though much smaller than those of the fall. To call attention to the war's economic cost, demonstrations were held at IRS offices across the United States. Protesters reenacted the Boston Tea Party in several cities. Thirty thousand rallied in New York; militants disrupted the proceedings by screaming about revolution and attempting to take over the stage. Rally speakers "dwelled on what they called the uselessness of words and the futility of demonstrations," the *New York Times* observed. In Boston, nearly a hundred thousand people gathered on the Common. "Few were smiling," one participant writes. Increasingly skeptical of the effectiveness of legal protest, "most looked as though they were [merely] . . . giving it 'one last go.'" After the demonstration, young radicals smashed windows, looted stores, and set fires in Harvard Square. "How are the nation's elite?" some chanted jocularly outside Harvard dormitories. Thousands marched on Berkeley's ROTC building, sparking a five-hour battle with police; the university was declared to be "in a state of emergency" and closed the following day. Students boycotted classes at hundreds of college campuses and high schools on April 15, but shut down few schools.[9]

Nixon administration officials continued to face protests when they ventured out for public appearances. In April, Henry Kissinger was invited to address a group of graduate students at Johns Hopkins University. After he was introduced, most of the students rose to their feet, and one read a statement they had signed assailing the war. Kissinger chucked his speech and opened the floor to questions. "Dr. Kissinger, do you consider yourself a war criminal?" was the first. Kissinger turned to the chair of the proceedings, commanded, "Mr. Chairman, get your audience in order," and walked out. To avoid "an ugly incident," Nixon made "a very painful personal decision" to forgo attendance at his daughter Julie's graduation from Smith College in the late spring. Julie shaped his decision. "I truly think the day will be a disaster if he comes," she warned John Ehrlichman on April 28. "The temper up here is ugly. At a rally at M.S. one of the Chicago Seven led the audience of 10,000 in a chant of 'fuck Julie and David Eisenhower.'" The president worried that his absence at his daughter's graduation would look bad, though. "For your long-range planning, it will be necessary for me to plan some sort of trip out of the country at the time of Julie's graduation," he earlier wrote Haldeman. "We could not justify not being there unless we were gone at that time on some sort of special trip." Nixon later told a White House visitor that he would "love to go" visit campuses but the Secret Service wouldn't permit it because of the "danger." There was also the problem of "radicals without anything to say" who "shout obscenities" and "deny right to speak," the president said.[10]

Throughout the winter and early spring, youthful militancy remained a prominent feature of the American political landscape. In January, members of the "Vanguard of the Revolution" commandeered an ROTC plane and dropped three homemade bombs on a U.S. Army ammunition plant outside Madison, Wisconsin. The bombs landed in a snowbank and failed to ignite. The University of Wisconsin's student newspaper endorsed the act, arguing that the powers that be had failed to heed legal protests: "End of the Road," the editorial was ominously entitled. In February, following guilty verdicts in the case of the Chicago Seven, trashing and street-fighting erupted in numerous cities; in Isla Vista, California, protesters burned down the local Bank of America building. A "rising wave" of bombings swept the country. On February 21, at 4:30 A.M., a Weatherman cell detonated three gasoline bombs outside the Manhattan home of a judge presiding at pretrial hearings of Black Panthers; the explosions shattered front window panes, scorched an overhang, and seared one of the judge's cars. Early on the morning of March 11, a bomb blew out the side of a Maryland courthouse. Twenty-four hours later, within a time span of twenty-nine minutes, bombs rocked three midtown Manhattan skyscrapers, mangling walls and plumbing and sending showers of glass down onto streets. The buildings housed offices of Socony Mobil, IBM, and General Telephone and Electronics. No one was injured in the blasts; "Revolutionary Force 9," the group claiming responsibility for them, had given the police thirty-four minutes to clear the buildings of janitors before the first bomb went off. During the rest of the "tense" day in Manhattan, three hundred bomb threats were phoned in, forcing thousands of people out into the streets. "Are they blowing up that building, too?" one man asked a companion as he surveyed a crowd gathered outside a building. Campus ROTC buildings, draft offices, police stations, and police cars were also popular bombing targets. Commented one academic observer, "The young people have had protests and riots and disorders—they've done everything one can do in the way of peaceful and unplanned protest, and not much has changed. To that degree there is an increasing sense of desperation, and a sense of vengefulness."[11]

The Weathermen continued to build their underground network. More severed connections with family and old friends and began living under assumed names. Some altered their physical appearances. New revolutionary cells were formed; old ones were strengthened. Most Weathermen continued to engage in open political organizing as well, however. They would combine terrorism with public agitation.[12]

Then came the townhouse. Just before noon on March 6, several explosions rocked a luxurious Greenwich Village home owned by James P. Wilkerson, a wealthy businessman then vacationing in the Caribbean. An entire city block shuddered from the blasts. Two "dazed and trembling" young women, faces besmirched with soot, staggered out of the townhouse as parts of it crashed to the sidewalk. One was wearing only blue jeans, the other was naked. Behind them was "a sort of red, incandescent glow, more scary than flames, then the flames came very shortly after that," recalled a neighbor. The women were Cathy Wilkerson, aged twenty-five, daughter of the building's owner, and Kathy Boudin, aged twenty-six. Both were Weathermen. Several of their comrades, "coughing and partially blinded," hobbled out of the rubble through the manicured back garden and disappeared. Inside the townhouse, three Weathermen lay dead. One was headless, handless, and riddled by roofing nails; another was so badly blown apart that he could not be identified by police. The Weathermen had been manufacturing pipe bombs and bombs peppered with nails—antipersonnel weapons. The weapons had allegedly been intended for use at Columbia University. While demonstrating the art of bomb making to a comrade, one Weatherman had connected a wire to the wrong place.[13]

A neighbor, Susan Wager, former wife of the actor Henry Fonda, led the shaking Wilkerson and Boudin into her house, showed them a bathroom where they could clean up, dropped a pile of clothing outside the door, and returned to the burning townhouse. When Wager returned minutes later, the women had vanished.[14]

To avoid arrests, other Weathermen also ducked for cover. "When the townhouse happened, pretty much on a moment's notice we all went underground," Bill Ayers remembered. "Because they were after us." Recalled Jeff Jones, "The townhouse was a real galvanizing thing that *necessitated* . . . people disappearing, and sort of put the whole [move underground] into dramatic form." This mass vanishing act was not what the Weathermen had envisioned when they decided to launch clandestine revolutionary warfare months earlier. "We . . . didn't think that we would have to be underground in the [total] way that we were," Ayers said.[15]

A month after the townhouse explosion, a group of *nonviolent* militants was also running for cover. Fathers Philip and Daniel Berrigan and three other Catholic protesters convicted of destroying draft files refused to surrender to authorities to begin serving their prison sentences and slipped out of sight. "We didn't want to convey the idea that we would come hat-in-hand for a surrender date [and thus] give credibility to the notion that just because we were convicted we were guilty," Philip Berrigan recalled. We "went underground simply because we didn't want to create the idea that we acknowledged our guilt—we didn't at all." Philip spent his two weeks on the run "hiding out in New Jersey." "We found that a limitless number of people were willing to hide us out and protect us," he remembered. During his four months on the lam, Daniel Berrigan moved in and out of homes "all through the Midwest and the East." He met secretly with small groups for "hard rap sessions"; the priest appeared at these meetings "Tupamaro-style," arriving last and departing first. Daniel "surfaced" frequently through articles and interviews in the press. He also made an audacious appearance before a crowd of several thousand (including FBI agents) at Cornell University. As the lights dimmed for rock music, he put on a costume belonging to the Bread and Puppet Theater and disappeared into the night.[16]

Philip Berrigan was captured by FBI agents in a Manhattan church rectory on April 21. He was preparing to speak at a big rally in the church. He remembered:

> The monsignor, who was a pastor of the parish, had negotiated with the FBI because the head FBI honcho in the area was a seminary classmate of his. And the FBI person had told him that they wouldn't interfere until we had finished addressing the rally, and then they

would arrest us. And, of course, then they broke their word and they broke into his apartment on the very day that the rally was to take place. . . . In that one block where we were captured, they said they had a hundred and fifty agents, if you can believe that. I know that there were a lot of them there, because twenty of them poured in the door. They broke the door down.

Daniel Berrigan, whom the FBI had hoped to find in the church rectory as well, was apprehended on Block Island off the coast of Rhode Island in August. His capturers were FBI agents dressed in orange parkas masquerading as bird-watchers. Hours later, as he was being pulled down the steps of a Providence courthouse by two beefy agents, a television reporter asked Berrigan how he was feeling. "Fine!" he exclaimed, his wrists shackled together. "Glad to be here!"[17]

On April 19, Moratorium leaders announced the disbanding of their group's national office. "Full of jurisdictional squabbles and petty fights," it had ceased functioning productively. And there was little public interest in another Moratorium day. Demonstrations were "a political fad that has worn off," one VMC leader declared. Since there was "little prospect for immediate change in the Administration's policy in Vietnam," the group said, a "new direction and focus are needed for anti-war activities." Many Moratorium activists planned to work in the electoral campaigns of antiwar congressional candidates. "Congress has to do it," David Hawk recalled some VMCers thinking. "What else is left? . . . Where else can you turn—out of desperation?" Closing shop would at least allow the Moratorium to arrest its galloping debt. As it turned out, Hawk and Sam Brown had to spend most of the next year working to pay it off. "We finally settled out some phone bills and stuff by just [saying], 'Look, we don't have any money,'" Brown remembered. "'We don't have any money—period. Sue me. . . . Here, I've got seven dollars. Take it. Fifty thousand dollars in bills? Fine, I've got seven dollars.'"[18]

"We're Dealing with the Criminal Mind"

Meanwhile, the Nixon administration was continuing its efforts to counteract the antiwar movement. Officials recognized the movement was in a lull and felt they had the most breathing room since assuming office, but it remained a serious political problem. The problem was magnified by plummeting public support for U.S. policies in Vietnam: although 64 percent supported Nixon's handling of the war in January, only 46 percent did in April. Observing an increase in antiwar letters to the White House, "the President noted that it seems that our silent majority group has lost its steam," an aide told Haldeman on February 20.[19] And, lull or no lull, the Nixon White House thought even one protester was too many.

At the president's direction, the administration stepped up its aid to supportive youth groups. Officials distributed prowar propaganda to the College Republicans, Young Republicans, Young Americans for Freedom, Freedom Leadership Foundation, Association of Student Governments, and United Student Alliance. The administration also developed closer relations with the College Press Service, "the UPI and AP of campus newspapers," Jeb Magruder wrote Haldeman; consequently, while "their releases are not yet pro-Administration . . . their attacks have been toned down." Instructed by Nixon to set up a front group on campuses, officials worked through the College Republicans to establish the Washington Campus News Service. "News Service mailings periodically send the Administration point of view to every campus newspaper and radio station," Magruder proudly reported to Haldeman. The White House worked "very closely" with the College Republicans on other "imaginative programs" as well. Further, it began investigating the possibility of building the United Student Alliance into a "campus counterpart to SDS" that could "harness the silent student majority." Among friendly student leaders whom officials had spoken with, Magruder wrote, the White House was "particularly impressed" with Charles Stephens, the head of the USA, and was thus "having him thoroughly checked out." Also at Nixon's direction, the administration assisted the work of the Young Americans for Freedom and other conservative youth groups organizing for a "no" vote in a nationwide campus referendum on whether the United States should leave Vietnam. Nixon was apparently skeptical of the YAF's ability to organize students ("they are about as nutty . . . as the militants," he wrote Haldeman), but the group ended up "doing such a good job for us," Magruder reported.[20]

The administration's work with conservative youth groups was not free of problems, however. The student right was as factionalized as the student left, and close relations with one group often created friction with another. "The YRs are presently trying to fire the College Republicans' executive director, and are more interested in fighting YAF than working with it toward common goals," Magruder fretted to Haldeman.[21]

Magruder felt the administration could bring some of the disgruntled back into the fold if it projected a more youthful image. Officials should publicize the many "bright, young, well-educated men" in the White House "working on bold new programs," he proposed to Haldeman. "What sophisticated young professional man (or his wife) would not be interested in, say, an *Esquire* picture-story on the life-style of a Dwight Chapin or a Ron Ziegler, men who daily meet with the President and are not yet middle-aged? . . . Why not balance the society pages with the Administration's young swingers as well as the Mitchells and the Agnews?" The Justice Department's John Dean, suggested Magruder, was "an example of a sophisticated, young guy" ripe for publicity. Haldeman wrote in the margin of Magruder's memo, "*Absolutely*. Really work on this."[22]

White House Counsel Charles Colson advocated reviving the Citizens Committee for Peace with Freedom in Vietnam (CCPFV). It would counter a new, insidious offensive by the war's opponents. He wrote Haldeman on February 5:

> As you so well pointed out this morning, a campaign is being organized to discredit the Vietnamization policy. It began with an announcement in Hanoi that the war would drag on for years. It was followed by the commencement of the Fulbright Hearings and by [Senator Charles] Goodell's testimony. The campaign will intensify; major publications are planning articles to demonstrate that there really is no new policy and that Vietnamization can never end the war. . . .
>
> In my opinion, the strategy this time is quite different than it was before. The New Mobilization demonstrations proved counter productive. I believe the technique will be low key, and within the political structure. It will be designed to force us to accelerate our withdrawal plan. To this extent it is considerably more sophisticated and, by the same token, harder to deal with.

"I can't emphasize too strongly the urgency of this need," Colson wrote of the CCPFV.[23]

Haldeman was all for reviving the CCPFV. He approved Colson's recommendation to pour money into it, apparently to the tune of $250,000. The White House also restaffed the group. And it helped the CCPFV generate favorable articles in the press, run a speakers' bureau, distribute propaganda (inter alia to "a very influential mailing list"), and hold a press conference. The White House understood it had to keep its ties to the group invisible for the project to work. "Obviously, the enclosed must be kept completely secret as should this letter," Colson directed a co-conspirator upon sending him a "proposed budget" for an "expanded" CCPFV.[24]

The administration worked with another "citizens committee," too. In January, when a leader of the American Friends of Vietnam described the group's recent attempt at resurgence to Colson, the White House counsel responded, "It sounds very good and I will add it to our inventory of assets." Colson also promised to invite AFV leaders to luncheon at the White House after "we have our outside people lined up." In March, the administration coaxed the AFV to issue a supportive public statement on the war.[25]

Colson and Haldeman perceived that Clark Clifford was a key soldier in "the current anti-war campaign." They were aware from intelligence sources that the former defense secretary was preparing articles for *Life* magazine attacking the administration's Vietnamization policy. Alexander Butterfield directed Magruder to "get ourselves springloaded to a position from which we can effectively counter whatever tack Clifford takes." When Magruder came back with several options, Ehrlichman wrote Haldeman, "This is the kind of early warning we need more of. Your game planners are now in an excellent position to map anticipatory action." "Let's get going," Haldeman commanded Magruder. Haldeman also urged Colson to "get moving quickly" on efforts to "discredit" Clifford.[26]

On March 2 Nixon directed Haldeman to undertake a new campaign to politically isolate the militant protesters, writing:

> I have decided to initiate a program for teachers, judges, policemen, and others who take a strong stand against demonstrators and other militants when they engage in illegal activities. I am not satisfied with our program on this to date. It is too low key. I want information to be fed in from all over the country, and then I want letters to go out which will be publicized. . . . Whenever possible, I want to bring individuals here to the White House to commend them. One place to start is in the Mafia. Whenever you find a teacher, policeman or principal publicized for standing up against these people, bring them in.
>
> I do not want you to tell [Leonard] Garment or any of our liberal group of this matter. . . .
>
> I know that Garment, et al. would strenuously object on the ground that we would be [throwing] down the gauntlet to the militants, and that they would suggest that the way to get at this is to invite them into the White House and try to "reason" which was their line, of course, before the October 15th Moratorium and after the Moratorium up until November 3. As you know, my reaction to this whole matter has been along these lines, and I have not adequately responded to it. From now on, we are going to take a very aggressive "militant" position against these people, not simply because the public is probably with us, but because we face a national crisis in terms of this disrespect for law, etc., at all levels.
>
> . . . I consider this new direction as being of the highest priority. I want absolutely no deviation from it. . . .

Nixon hoped to include some young people among his guests at the White House. "Somewhere in the heartland of student America and young America are some decent types," he wrote Haldeman. However, "as far as universities are concerned, just rule out the east even though there are some good ones here and go to the Midwest to try to find some decent people."[27]

In April, the White House let it be known that it was stepping up its surveillance of militants through the use of informers, undercover agents, and wiretaps. The president was disturbed by the wave of bombings, bomb scares, and general youthful rebellion, highly placed officials told reporters. Political appeals or changes in policy wouldn't mollify these "potential murderers." "It wouldn't make a bit of difference if the war and racism ended overnight," one senior Nixon aide said. "We're dealing with the criminal mind, with people who have snapped for some reason." The situation was critical, declared another. "We are facing the most severe internal security threat this country has seen since the Depression."[28]

The White House wasn't just talking for public consumption. Noting "the seriousness of the increasing use of bombings as a revolutionary technique of violence," Tom Huston wrote Haldeman on March 12:

> While you may think I am paranoid, I want to go out on a limb and warn with deadly seriousness that this threat is terribly great . . . that we are not taking this problem seriously enough nor doing enough to cope with it, that you should be aware that the most logical target at some point in time for these people is the President and the White House, that ultimately innocent people are going to be killed, and that—unless I am completely wrong (along with most of the best informed men in the intelligence community)—this Spring may be the most violent on and off the campus that we have yet witnessed. The number of people involved may not be as great, but the level of violence is likely to be far greater.
>
> I urge you to consider taking two immediate steps: First, a thorough review of White House security procedures. For example, ask yourself how difficult it would be for a 23 year old beauty to place her handbag with 5 sticks of dynamite in the ladies room of the Residence while going through on a White House tour.
>
> Second, [consider] whether the resources of the Federal Government are being adequately mustered to cope with the threat which we may face.
>
> I would rather have you think I am nuts than have us find ourselves in six months confronted with a critical situation in which people live in fear throughout this country as a result of a rash of insane bombings, etc. Those kids in Greenwich village had a bomb factory set up and they weren't manufacturing toys. Six months ago I warned that this was where we were headed and nothing was done. In the past two weeks, we have had five bombings, two attempted bombings, and a bank burned down. I think a *prima facie* case has been made that perhaps I haven't been whistling Dixie in the dark.[29]

Daniel Patrick Moynihan, who was also unsettled by the bombings, wrote Haldeman the same day:

> For about a year now I have been keeping a file and thinking to send you a memo on the subject of terrorism. The time has come.
>
> It seems to me that we have simply got to assume that in the near future there will be terrorist attacks on the national government, including members of the Cabinet, the Vice President, and the President himself.

... The war has already begun. The level of political violence has been escalating steadily for the past two to three months. In the last week bombs have been exploding up and down the Eastern seaboard. So far only the terrorists appear to have been killed. But that has to be regarded essentially as part of the learning process. We have to assume, for example, that the Mad Dog faction of the Weathermen will in time learn to make anti-personnel bombs, as they evidently were trying to do in Miss Wilkerson's house. . . . We have to assume those folks blowing up corporation headquarters in New York City will turn to blowing up corporation heads. . . .

Political violence is not new to the nation. . . . But I do believe the present situation is different. What we are facing is the onset of nihilism in the United States. . . .

There is also an element of psychopathology in all this. . . . Consider that at the last convention of the Weathermen Charles Manson's photograph was everywhere.

Moynihan complained that the Chicago conspiracy indictments had contributed to the terrorism. "The trial of the Chicago Seven was a terrible setback to the cause of social stability," he bluntly told Haldeman. "Authority was made to look foolish, incompetent, impotent, corrupt. (Of all the people who buy judge-ships in Chicago, how *could* we have chosen [Julius] Hoffman?) Every possible opportunity was given the defendants to undermine the legitimacy of . . . the courts, and they used every opportunity." Moynihan advocated responding to the terrorism

in some systematic way. It simply won't do to add the extra guard detail here or there, or to pay for a few more informers. . . .

First, we must take a thorough look at the question of the security of the President. Times simply have changed.

Second, someone really ought to look into the question of just who is in charge of our intelligence in these areas. Really, dealing with the old Stalinist Communist Party was child's play compared to dealing with the Weathermen. The Communist Party was a hierar-chical, rational organization. We are dealing with diffuse, decentral-ized, irrational, even psychotic groups.

Third, we ought to ask ourselves how the government can act in such a way as to minimize the spread of the present mood and tactics of the left.[30]

That night, Nixon had dinner in the White House with Irving Kristol, a professor at New York University, who told him that "it was not unrealistic to expect the Latin American resort to political kidnappings to spread soon to Washington."[31]

In the early spring, Nixon directed Tom Huston to study possible new intelligence-gathering methods. Not only were the government's intelligence agencies failing to contain the spread of terrorism, but they continued to prove utterly incapable of uncovering the foreign communist support of protesters that Nixon knew was there. Huston proposed holding a meeting of the chiefs of the main U.S. intelligence bodies, at which Nixon would "bang some heads together" and demand they develop better plans. Nixon was more than a little interested. "The President is placing top priority on this Inter-agency effort," Dwight Chapin wrote Haldeman on April 24. "He expects full cooperation from all and desires that the White House be kept informed on an operational basis."[32] The meeting would take place in early June.

The administration took other steps to counter the protesters. The Justice Department initiated an "extraordinary" series of grand jury inquiries into their activities; those who refused to testify were charged with contempt and jailed. A federal grand jury in Chicago indicted twelve Weatherleaders on fifteen criminal counts, including conspiracy. Officials moved to stiffen congressional legislation denying federal aid to student lawbreakers. The White House continued its in-house efforts to uncover communist assistance to demonstrators. "I have reviewed your memorandum concerning the financial support of the various revolutionary groups and would like you to do some additional digging for the following groups," Haldeman instructed Egil Krogh. He listed the Black Panthers, New Mobe, Student Mobe, SNCC, SDS, and YSA. "Many of the sources are not determined," Haldeman chided Krogh. "We should be able to get a much better rundown on who the sources are and the amounts given." Nixon kept up his own close tracking of protesters; after reading conflicting press reports on the Student Mobe's February conference in Cleveland, he directed Ehrlichman to "get the facts concerning this session."[33]

The president and Henry Kissinger knew that further U.S. troop withdrawals from Vietnam were necessary to keep the demonstrators in line. In April, they decided that "the time had come to drop a bombshell on the gathering spring storm of antiwar protest," Nixon writes. The president announced the withdrawal of another hundred and fifty thousand troops—the largest cutback yet. He neglected to tell the public that only a "token withdrawal, if any" would take place over the next several months. Secretary of Defense Melvin Laird was unhappy and continued to push for faster reductions. "His clever game!" Nixon had earlier commented to Kissinger upon reading an obviously leaked press report on Laird's displeasure with the rate of withdrawal.[34]

"I'll Show Them Who's Tough"

Even while sending troops home, the Nixon administration was expanding the war. In February, the president secretly authorized B-52 strikes in northern Laos. The strikes would not only counter the growing communist threat in

Laos, but, more important, demonstrate to Hanoi Nixon's willingness to strike hard despite his having blinked the previous November. Although reported in military records as taking place in South Vietnam and along the Ho Chi Minh trail in southern Laos (which the administration had been bombing heavily since it took office), the strikes were publicly revealed by the *New York Times*, setting off harsh congressional criticism. The previous year Nixon had stepped up the secret U.S. ground war in Laos.[35]

In March, Cambodia's Prince Norodom Sihanouk was overthrown by right-wing officials led by Premier Lon Nol. Sihanouk had irritated the United States by permitting the NVA and NLF to maintain sanctuaries in Cambodia. His ouster was probably encouraged, if not actually inspired, by Washington. Immediately afterward, ARVN forces, abetted by the United States, began launching deep and frequent attacks inside Cambodia.

The growing U.S. military involvement in Laos and Cambodia did not go unnoticed by Hanoi. The New Mobe leader Doug Dowd recalled that when CALCAV's Richard Fernandez, Noam Chomsky, and he visited North Vietnam in mid April, "what they wanted to talk to us about in Hanoi—every day—and we didn't know that this was going on—was, 'What would happen in the U.S. if people recognized that the U.S. was invading Cambodia and Laos? What would people do?' . . . They just kept asking this day after day after day." According to Chomsky, "some form of direct American intervention in Cambodia was clearly anticipated" by North Vietnamese leaders.[36]

March and April were "months of great tension" in the White House, Henry Kissinger reveals. The president himself was "getting testy." Renewed secret peace talks in Paris were getting nowhere, NVA troops apparently posed a threat to the new Cambodian government, and the military situation in South Vietnam was not improving. Further rankling Nixon, the Senate rejected his second straight nominee for a Supreme Court vacancy on April 8. "Those senators think they can push Nixon around," the "Mad Monk" (as Ehrlichman nicknamed the president) fumed. "Well, I'll show them who's tough." When the *Times*'s William Beecher reported on April 22 that Nixon had secretly authorized the provision of captured enemy rifles to the Cambodian government, the president "exploded." "I've never seen Nixon so mad," acting JCS Chairman Admiral Thomas Moorer recalled. The president ordered lie-detector tests for all officials who had access to the leaked information and the firing of several possible culprits, including Assistant Secretary of State Marshall Green. The orders were never carried out. It was not a unique occurence for Green. "I was fired at least two or three times during the course of my tenure" in the Nixon administration, he remembered. And Green had witnessed Nixon angrily call for the hides of other officials as well, only to back off after calming down. "Nixon was *really* sulfuric in his comments about people and . . . he flailed about and fired people continually," Green said. "But he didn't mean it." He "was letting off steam." Green was not used to Nixon's "violent language," though. It "was totally incomprehensible to those of us who stayed on [from the Johnson administration] and worked for the State Department," he recalled. "We never hear that kind of language. . . . Johnson . . . was scatological, but very funny at the same time." Moorer was used to it, though. "Nixon couldn't even pass the first grade when it comes to cussing compared to Lyndon Johnson," Moorer said. "Lyndon Johnson—he was a guy who really knew how to cuss!"[37]

In an "increasingly agitated frame of mind," Nixon began talking about a "bold move" in Cambodia. By launching a ground invasion of that country, the president calculated, he could once again demonstrate his toughness and instability to North Vietnam. In the face of U.S. troop withdrawals, his madness would help keep Hanoi in line. Nixon believed "that you couldn't be completely predictable, you couldn't let the other fellow take you for granted, you had to strike out savagely from time to time, and certainly as we left we were going to 'go out with our teeth going out last,'" Green recalled. "That was one of his favorite expressions." Invading Cambodia would also give Lon Nol more time. Nixon considered launching a massive attack against North Vietnam simultaneously with the invasion, but decided "it would be very hard to hold the country together" and feared injuring U.S. relations with China and the USSR.[38]

Both Melvin Laird and William Rogers opposed employing U.S. forces in an invasion of Cambodia. They feared high American casualties and a major domestic uproar. At a "tense" meeting on April 27, one of the two officials, probably Rogers, warned Nixon, "If you do it, in my opinion the campuses will go up in flames." Green also opposed invading Cambodia. Consequently, Nixon kept the Defense and State departments in the dark on much of the planning of the operation. Only four days before it was launched, Green "had a feeling that we were going to unleash the South to go into Cambodia, but I didn't dream of American ground forces being involved in that."[39]

So opposed were three of Kissinger's closest senior aides to invading Cambodia that they resigned their offices. Roger Morris, Anthony Lake, and William Watts were already dissatisfied with U.S. war policies. And they and other NSC staffers had become increasingly disillusioned by the bureaucratic intrigue and backbiting in the Nixon White House. "There was a dawning recognition that this was a frightening place," one staffer recalled. "It was like walking into a room with a bad odor." Morris was also troubled by the apparent low level of intellectual ability inside the government. He had known from his earlier work in the State Department during the Johnson administration "that the people who were running policy over there were not at all gifted," he remembered. "I mean . . . I worked closely with Dean Rusk, and I didn't have a great regard for his intellectual candle power." But Morris had "just automatically assumed that the idiots that I was working with there were not duplicated elsewhere in the government. But that was not true. . . . And I was utterly appalled." Sitting at the cabinet table listening to CIA Director Richard Helms's frequent mispronunciations and butchered syntax, "I was really frightened," Morris said. Also disturbing to Morris, Lake, and Watts was Nixon himself. The president's instability was apparently not just a bargaining ploy. Each had listened in on phone conversations between Kissinger and an obviously drunken commander in chief. "Nixon drank exceptionally at night," Morris recalled. "There were many times when a cable would come in late and Henry would say, 'There's no sense waking him up—he'd be incoherent.'" One Kissinger aide overheard an intoxicated Nixon babble to Kissinger, "Henry, we've got to nuke them." Laurence Lynn divulged: "All of us were worried about this man's stability. We'd have glimpses of him and didn't know what to do with it." (Kissinger also worried about Nixon's character. "We've got a madman on our hands," he often told other officials. In 1968 Kissinger had claimed that Nixon was "not fit to be President.")[40]

But it took the invasion of Cambodia to push Morris, Lake, and Watts over the edge. In a "painful session" on April 24, they warned Kissinger that "there would be blood in the streets" if the administration carried it out. Watts gave back to Kissinger his October 1969 memo forecasting domestic tumult in response to Operation Duck Hook, saying "it still applies in spades." Watts felt "very strongly" that "this country was not far from really major domestic violence. I mean, really major." On April 26, Watts refused to go to an NSC meeting on the Cambodian invasion and announced his resignation. Watts's disobedience incited a "hostile and tense" exchange with Kissinger, who accused him of "cowardice." After Kissinger's military aide Alexander Haig told him that he'd "just had an order from your Commander-in-Chief and you can't refuse," Watts retorted, "Fuck you, Al. I just have and I've resigned." Morris and Lake stepped down on April 29, also to Kissinger's aggravation. (Kissinger was not the only official upset by his rebellious aides. Admiral Moorer, who came to suspect one of them was responsible for the April 22 news leak, huffed that they "should have been locked up until they resigned.")[41]

Days later, the former NSC staffer Morton Halperin showed his displeasure over the invasion of Cambodia by resigning as a consultant to Kissinger. When Nixon got wind of Halperin's act, he was not pleased. "Now Halperin is going to make a big thing out of resigning," he wrote Haldeman. "I want . . . to find out who consultants are around this government and let's do a little housecleaning and sanitizing in this respect."[42]

Nixon formally ordered the invasion of Cambodia on April 28. Both he and Kissinger were themselves uneasy over the operation. Its effect on the war was uncertain, and the domestic political risks were substantial. "Our feeling was that as long as Cambodia was announced as a limited undertaking and for a limited period of time . . . that the opposition would be manageable and tolerable," John Ehrlichman remembered. But sharp protest was nonetheless assured, Nixon recognized. And there was even a chance that it would be widespread enough to spell "personal and political catastrophe for me and my administration." Nixon and Kissinger logged many hours in anxious consultation, trying to steel each other's nerves. Both Green and Morris recalled that this was typical of their relationship. "You had a feeling often times that these two were bucking each other up all the time," Green said. "It was terribly emotional. . . . It was very unhealthy." Morris:

> The one common denominator throughout all of these four years
> is that they're never sure of themselves. They're putting on a great
> front, and they're doing the best they can, but there are a lot of
> sweaty palms. And Kissinger in particular. Kissinger's not some Met-
> ternichian manipulator of grand global vision. Kissinger is a very
> nervous, slightly overweight little man sweating a lot between his of-
> fice and the Oval Office. And he is very worried about his place in
> history and he is talking seriously about ending up teaching at Ari-
> zona State, and he's not kidding. I mean, he thinks that maybe in the
> end he's going to be sacrificed by the Establishment. . . . It's a very
> uncertain time.[43]

To help fortify himself, Nixon drank liberally. During a boozy cruise down the Potomac on the presidential yacht *Sequoia* with Kissinger, John Mitchell, and Nixon's pal Bebe Rebozo on April 25, "the tensions of the grim military planning were transformed into exaltation by the liquid refreshments," Kissinger records. The previous evening, while holed up with Rebozo at Camp David, Morris writes, an intoxicated Nixon gibed at Kissinger about the invasion, "If this doesn't work, it'll be your ass, Henry." The president thickly added, "Ain't that right, Bebe?" To further steel himself, Nixon repeatedly watched the movie *Patton*, an account of the pugnacious World War II general. The president was "a walking ad" for *Patton*, William Rogers remarked. Nixon gathered strength through solitary contemplation as well. In the days leading up to the invasion, recalls Kissinger, "Richard Nixon was virtually alone, sitting in a darkened room in the Executive Office Building, the stereo softly playing neoclassical music—reflecting, resenting, collecting his thoughts and his anger."[44]

The Storm

On the evening of April 29, the coordinating committee of the New Mobe was gathered at Cora Weiss's elegant Bronx home. The meeting was not going well. The turnout for the Mobe's "Winter-Spring Offensive" had been disappointing, the coalition was broke, and many participants were unsure what to do next. SWPers argued fervidly that the Mobe should hold another national conference for the purpose of organizing yet another mass legal demonstration against the war. Others were sick of the SWP's political tunnel vision and, moreover, knew the SWP would pack the conference. SWPers went into the meeting suspecting their proposal would fall flat. "We went for one last time to try to convince these people to call a conference so the movement could get off dead center," Don Gurewitz remembered. "And we were basically just going through the motions because it seemed very unlikely." They would have to organize legal peace demonstrations on their own, SWPers increasingly believed. A split in the Mobe seemed imminent.[45]

Suddenly the phone rang, and Dave Dellinger picked up the receiver. Nixon had sent troops into Cambodia, Dellinger stunningly related. "Operation Rock Crusher," the first thrust of the two-pronged invasion, had begun. It was unclear to the discussants how extensive the escalation was, but something had to be done. Word of the invasion "just changed everything," Gurewitz said. The participants unanimously agreed to call for a demonstration at the White House on May 9, only ten days away. "We went right down to Washington from there—bang," Fred Halstead recalled.[46]

Other Mobe organizers also shifted into high gear. In New York, Norma Becker was on the telephone with the Washington conferees. After receiving word of the scheduled demonstration, Becker remembered, "we just put out a 10,000-piece mailing overnight. We assembled something like twenty or thirty people up in the loft, and we mobilized the New York constituency."[47]

The next evening, President Nixon went on national television to announce the invasion. He was visibly nervous, perspiring, and tired; the previous night, he had been unable to sleep. The president told the nation that he was sending troops into the sanctuaries in Cambodia to save American lives. In one of the sanctuaries, U.S. and ARVN forces would be attacking "the headquarters for the entire Communist military operation in South Vietnam." Nixon stressed that the assault was "not an invasion of Cambodia" but a limited and temporary operation. Nonetheless, it was a test of American will. "We live in an age of anarchy, both abroad and at home," he declared. "We see mindless attacks on all the great institutions which have been created by free civilizations in the last 500 years. . . . If, when the chips are down, the world's most powerful nation, the United States of America, acts like a pitiful, helpless giant, the forces of totalitarianism and anarchy will threaten free nations and free institutions throughout the world." Nixon failed to tell the public that he had also ordered heavy bombing raids on North Vietnam, in apparent violation of the United States's private understanding with Hanoi prohibiting strikes there.[48]

No sooner had Nixon signed off the air than protesters expressed opposition. That night, demonstrations were held at Princeton, Rutgers, and Oberlin. The next day witnessed hundreds of protests and public meetings across the country. A national student strike began to take hold; within four days, strikes were in progress at over a hundred schools. A strike information center was established at Brandeis to provide coordination to the wave of campus shutdowns. Everywhere, people were passionately denouncing—and defending—the invasion. "It was something I'd never ever seen before and never seen since," remembered Joe Urgo, who was living in New York at the time. "I could feel the polarization. You could cut that with a knife in society, it was so incredible. . . . On that day or two after the Cambodian invasion, this whole city was filled with thousands of people all over the streets debating. You could just go from group to group arguing." Protesters engaged in civil disobedience and political violence in many locations. Maryland students launched a "hit-and-run attack" on their school's ROTC headquarters and skirmished with state police. At Princeton, students firebombed an armory. Students battled police for more than three hours at Kent State, inciting a dusk-to-dawn curfew. Shortly afterward, "a fire of undetermined origin" roared through the school's wooden ROTC building; firemen were impeded by students slicing fire hoses and throwing rocks. Ohio's governor called in the National Guard. Students at Stanford went on a rampage, breaking into shops and smashing windows; among the rampagers was Robert McNamara's son Craig. The National Student Association and sixty-eight Cornell faculty, claiming the invasion was unconstitutional, called for President Nixon's impeachment. Peace activists deluged Congress with telegrams. The Senate Foreign Relations Committee voted to repeal the Gulf of Tonkin Resolution. If the antiwar movement had needed a rallying point to pull it out of its lull, the invasion of Cambodia had provided it.[49]

Nixon's announcement of the invasion agitated more than protesters. Melvin Laird was shown a copy of the president's speech several hours before it was given. When he came to Nixon's claim that the United States was going after "the headquarters for the entire Communist military operation in South Vietnam" (otherwise known as COSVN), Laird hit the roof. He knew that COSVN in that grand sense did not exist. "I never thought there was a COSVN," Laird scornfully recalled. "And I tried to get that out of the President's speech. I thought that was a phony [claim]. . . . Kissinger put that in. And I had a *bad* argument at five o'clock that afternoon with Kissinger" over it. Around the same time, Marshall Green was sitting with William Rogers in the secretary of state's hideaway office on the seventh floor of the State Department. A copy of Nixon's speech arrived there as well. "We'd known pretty well what was going to be in the speech," Green remembered. "But then at the end the President had suddenly added all of this highly emotional stuff" about the invasion being a test of American will. "And Rogers's reaction was, 'My God, the kids are going to *retch* when they hear this kind of thing! This is the kind of thing that is going to touch them off.' . . . He could see right away that this highly emotional speech, in this atmosphere, was going to have an incendiary effect amongst the youth."[50]

It was an excruciating time for Green personally. His "good friend" Richard Nixon had just threatened to fire him. Once again, he—the senior State Department man on Vietnam policy—had been shut out of decision making on a crucial aspect of that policy. And although opposed to the invasion, Green had to testify in support of it on Capitol Hill. The potential legal problems of testifying to "the whole truth"—under oath—were worrisome. Most agonizing of all to Green, his son disowned him over the invasion. After Nixon's "diatribe" on April 30, he recalled,

> I came back to my house, and my son came into the room where I was talking to my wife. He denounced the position that the President had taken, and he said, "I don't want to see you again." And he left. And we didn't see him again for weeks. I mean, it was that kind of thing. It's hard to realize. *You were driven to the brink of suicide,* you really were. The only thing that stabilized me was my good old dog. I'd talk to him, and he'd never talk back . . . [51]

John Ehrlichman had two angry sons. "Ehrlichman was shaken by the student protest following the Cambodian incursions," Kissinger writes. "He had . . . teenage children caught up in the campus upheaval and their travail touched him deeply." Ehrlichman later remembered that although domestic political developments were his main worry at the time, "the personal thing had to be worked out, because I was getting phone calls from these kids and was talking to them about the reasons for [the invasion]." Secretary of the Army Stanley Resor also had an upset son. John Resor helped organize a one-day strike at Williams College over the invasion; he unsuccessfully tried to persuade Victor Reuther to get the UAW to strike over the operation too. Many other children of administration officials undoubtedly protested the invasion as well.[52]

Early the morning after he announced it, following another rough night in bed, Nixon went over to the Pentagon for a briefing on the invasion. He was heartened by cheering Pentagon employees in the halls. In the briefing room, sitting aside Laird, the Joint Chiefs, and other senior military officials, Nixon seemed "a little bit out of control," Laird's aide Daniel Henkin recalled. "It scared the shit out of me." "I want to take out all of those sanctuaries," Nixon impassionedly told the Chiefs. "Make whatever plans are necessary, and then just do it." Nixon spoke repeatedly and emotionally about destroying the sanctuaries. He also stressed that "bold decisions make history." After abruptly terminating the session, the president once again encountered supportive Pentagon employees in the halls. Visibly cheered, Nixon remarked, "You see these bums, you know, blowing up the campuses. Listen, the boys that are on the college campuses today are the luckiest people in the world, going to the greatest universities, and here they are burning up the books, I mean storming around on this issue—I mean you name it—get rid of the war, there will be another one." After leaving the Pentagon, Nixon joined a meeting in the basement of the White House. "He was in a *tremendous* emotional mood," Green vividly remembered. "He was so tensed up and so gratified that he'd had this kind of reaction from the Pentagon. . . . It was amazing! And I remember he sat down at that meeting, and he was just purring like a kitten, he was so glad at the way things had worked. But *terribly* tensed up [Green rattled a coffee cup]."⁵³

That afternoon, to calm his nerves, Nixon went on another cruise down the Potomac. He was still buzzing. Although "I had never seen him appear so physically exhausted," the president's military aide Jack Brennan recalled, "he seemed to feel exuberant inside." Nixon stressed the importance of playing the National Anthem "with feeling" when passing Mount Vernon. "He told me he wanted the National Anthem 'blasted out,'" Brennan wrote. "He wanted it to be heard! He emphasized this point by punching the air with his closed fist." As the presidential yacht approached Mount Vernon from a distance, "the president was quite anxious. He was standing in position at the bow of the yacht well in advance of the prescribed time for the ceremony." During the anthem, Nixon "stood at rigid attention." Later that day, Haldeman's meeting notes record, Nixon asserted that the invasion "will work—bold decision." The "lines" to take, said Nixon, were "cold steel—no give . . . courage—laid it on the line."⁵⁴

The White House took steps to rally public support. The night of April 30, Charles Colson briefed leaders of numerous prowar groups on the invasion; after watching Nixon's address in the White House with Colson, the leaders "departed with the mission to organize support for the President's position," Colson's aide George Bell told Haldeman. At the administration's request, one of the leaders sent copies of Nixon's speech "to student body presidents at approximately 2,000 colleges and universities (nearly all that exist in the country)," Bell reported. "We duplicated the copies and delivered [them] to their office." Herb Klein sent the text of the speech and "background material on Cambodia" to newspaper editors. The White House's Tell It to Hanoi front group placed pro-Nixon ads in more than forty newspapers. Officials moved to "really trot" out friendly congressmen, as Haldeman's meeting notes attest, and arranged television appearances for other prominent backers (including Bob Hope). Nixon directed his staff to assume a hard-line public posture toward critics: "Don't worry about divisiveness," he said. "Having drawn the sword, don't take it out—stick it in hard." The White House announced that private polls and communications showed "heavy" public support for the invasion; "get poll to opinion maker types by phone calls," Haldeman's notes of May 2 read. (The Harris poll evidenced widespread public questioning of the invasion,[55] as did letters to members of Congress.) Officials acted to convey that Nixon's decision was made by a steady, well-informed commander in chief. "His mood has been excellent and there is a confidence which all those working with him on the problem have noticed," one talking paper states. "As is the President's style, he did it in a cool, calm, rational and very Nixon-like way." By May 4, Nixon was considering a speech on student protesters if they got "more out of line"; while he shouldn't "react too defensively on student thing," Haldeman's notes read, the White House had "better get some ideas written."[56]

Early that afternoon, from the top of a hill, National Guardsmen opened fire on student demonstrators at Kent State. In a matter of seconds, more than fifty bullets whistled through the air, striking cars, trees, dirt, and students. Four protesters were killed, nine wounded.

Less than an hour later, an "agitated" Haldeman informed Nixon of the shootings. The president was "stunned." So were other officials. "Grim-faced White House aides, haunted by memories of the domestic violence which erupted after Martin Luther King's shooting two years earlier, clustered around the chattering ticker-tape machines in Ron Ziegler's press office as the ugly story unfolded," Colson recounts. In the White House staff mess that evening, "I looked around the crowded room," writes Colson. "Like a scene from a stop-action camera nothing was moving" as officials stared intently at a TV screen replaying scenes from the tragedy, including the sobbing father of one of the victims angrily blaming Nixon for his daughter's death. "Dinner plates were untouched, red-jacketed stewards stood frozen in place, White House staffers sat in stunned silence." Most officials were less shaken by the deaths themselves than by the specter of mushrooming protest;[57] indeed, more than a few blamed the students for getting shot. "I happened myself to be one who sympathized with the National Guard at Kent State," Nixon's speechwriter Ray Price remembered. "The National Guard themselves are a bunch of scared kids with guns, and as a mob charged, hurling rocks, at a bunch of scared kids with guns, you shouldn't be surprised if some of the guns go off." (Price's account of the shootings is inaccurate: the students were not charging the Guardsmen, although some had thrown rocks at them.) J. Edgar Hoover informed other officials that one of the female victims had been "sleeping around" and was "nothing more than a whore" anyway. The White House expressed its callous attitude toward the shootings in a statement it released that afternoon: "This should remind us all once again that when dissent turns to violence, it invites tragedy." That evening Vice President Spiro Agnew called the killings "predictable" and refused to criticize the Guardsmen; he went on to condemn "elitists" who encouraged the "paranoids" demonstrating on campuses and who advanced the Bill of Rights as protection for "psychotic and criminal elements in our society." No wonder, said Agnew, that "we have traitors and thieves and perverts and irrational and illogical people in our midst."[58]

America's campuses exploded. Student protest swept like an out-of-control brush fire across the country. Within three days of the Kent State shootings, the student strike sparked by the invasion of Cambodia had spread to several hundred colleges and universities. "The overflow of emotion seemed barely containable," observed the *Washington Post* on May 6. "The nation was witnessing what amounted to a virtual general and uncoordinated strike by its college youth." Faculty and administrators joined students in active dissent, and 536 campuses were shut down completely, 51 for the rest of the academic year. Many schools were turned into centers for antiwar organizing. In California, Governor Ronald Reagan temporarily closed down the state's entire university system in response. Nervous university officials in other locations granted students the resources they requested to sustain their activity. Fred Halstead was on the University of Illinois Circle Campus in Chicago. "That campus was completely an antiwar engine," he recalled. "And I remember I wanted to make a phone call to someplace—Japan, I think—about something, and I was trying to figure out how I was going to pay for this thing. And some student says, '*Don't be ridiculous! Just pick up the phone and make it!*' And I did. You know, the administration didn't [complain] at all—'Oh, yes, yes *sir*.' [Laughs.] They weren't quibbling. They weren't going to lose the whole thing." Protests were held at nearly 1,350 colleges and universities during the month of May, with perhaps half the nation's students participating in them. Many were moderates or conservatives protesting for the first time. "The general effect of May was one of radicalizing as well as politicizing student opinion across the board," Vanderbilt's Chancellor Alexander Heard later told Nixon. "The meaning of May [was] a big shove Leftward." The shove involved "growing class consciousness among students," Heard reported. "The self-identification by college students as a separate class in society is assuming extraordinary proportions."[59]

Clark Kerr, the chairman of the Carnegie Commission on Higher Education, was equally impressed by the outpouring of campus dissent. "The variety of protest activities—both violent and nonviolent—seemed to exhaust the known repertoire of forms of dissent," he wrote. Besides strikes and shutdowns, there were teach-ins and workshops, rallies and marches, building blockades and sit-ins, flag-lowerings and symbolic funerals. Students organized antidraft activity on many campuses; more than ten thousand youths pledged to turn in their draft cards. Numerous students canvassed in the community. Thousands of students, professors, and administrators descended on Washington to meet with officials and members of Congress; Father Theodore Hesburgh and other university presidents confronted Nixon in the White House. A massive congressional lobbying campaign took off. In many cities, students blockaded streets, bridges, or highways. Some harassed draft boards. Although the May protests were overwhelmingly peaceful, violent demonstrations erupted on many campuses. During the month's first week, ROTC buildings were exploding or igniting at the rate of more than four a day. The police and National Guard—toting bayonets and live ammunition—were called out at more than a hundred schools. Students in Buffalo, New York, pelted police with rocks, shouting, "Shoot me, shoot me." Arrests skyrocketed. The month witnessed the greatest display of campus discontent in American history.[60]

Fueling the explosion was a sense of growing state repression. Ten days after Kent State, police in Mississippi opened fire on a crowd of unarmed black students at Jackson State College, killing two and wounding twelve. Many students felt Spiro Agnew's diatribes against protesters had encouraged both sets of killings. (Secretary of HEW Robert Finch apparently agreed: he told a group of demonstrators that the vice president's "rhetoric" had "contributed to heating up the climate in which the Kent State students were killed," but he then promptly denied making the remark.) On May 8—only ten days after Agnew invited Americans to view protesters as Nazi Storm Troopers or Ku Klux Klan members and to "act accordingly"—two hundred construction workers in lower Manhattan assaulted a group of peaceful student demonstrators with their fists, crowbars, and metal wrenches. Seventy youths were injured, some "very brutally." Two men in gray business suits were seen directing the "well-organized" attack, which came from four directions. One construction worker revealed that the workers were offered a monetary bonus by at least one contractor if they would take time off from their work to "break some heads." New York police were also in on the assault and cheered the workers on. President Nixon told New York union leaders that he found their expressions of support for the war "very meaningful." (Despite evidence that the White House had both the capacity and an inclination to organize such attacks,[61] John Ehrlichman later denied any knowledge of administration involvement in the incident, although he told a reporter that he always "assumed" some of the attacks by hard hats on demonstrators that occurred while he was in the government were "laid on" by the White House. H. R. Haldeman sidestepped a question about White House involvement in the assault but admitted to feeling "some secret satisfaction" over it. "It had a sobering effect on the demonstrators," he told me. "It wasn't too bad a result. . . . [It was] kind of nice to see our side dishing some of it back.") Many youths also worried that Agnew wasn't just flapping his jaw when he talked about discarding rotten apples. Moreover, there was a widespread rumor that the administration had contracted with the RAND Corporation to investigate the possibility of canceling the 1972 elections. A late May Harris poll found that 58 percent of students agreed with the statement that, compared to a year earlier, the United States had become a highly repressive society, intolerant of dissent.[62]

But it wasn't just students, professors, and administrators who were up in arms in May. Other Americans were demonstrating in city after city and town after town across the country. Mass rallies were held in many places. GIs protested at a dozen military bases, some of which had no previous history of dissent. Clergy, doctors, lawyers, editors, and other professionals flooded into Washington to express their opposition to the war and domestic government violence. Sam Brown and David Hawk, who were feeling somewhat embarrassed about having closed down the Moratorium office just two weeks before the invasion of Cambodia, joined with a group of clergy to "pray for peace" outside the White House fence. "Got busted," laughed Hawk, later amused by the protest. "We congratulated ourselves on the scene, but nothing good was going to come of that. Shit. . . . It was just outrage." Former Peace Corps volunteers occupied six offices of the Peace Corps building in Washington; they named them the "Ho Chi Minh Sanctuary" and flew the NLF flag out a window, readily visible from the White House.[63]

The invasion of Cambodia and the Kent State shootings also evoked mounting union criticism of the war. On May 7, the American Federation of State, County and Municipal Employees called for U.S. withdrawal from Indochina. The same day, Walter Reuther, speaking for 1,800,000 UAW members, told Nixon of the union's "deep concern and distress" over the invasion and governmental repression of dissent. The General Executive Board of the United Electrical, Radio and Machine Workers of America called the Kent State killings "a tragic product of an Administration in Washington which has made escalation of war abroad and repression at home its most distinguishing characteristics." Other union leaders also spoke out. Organized labor's support for the war was faltering. And rank-and-file workers participated in antiwar protests in unprecedented numbers.[64]

"Powerfully affected" by the domestic dissent (as Kissinger writes), members of a divided Congress proposed two amendments to reduce U.S. military activity in Southeast Asia. Senators John Sherman Cooper and Frank Church (D-Ida.) sponsored legislation prohibiting funding of U.S. ground forces and advisers in Cambodia after July 1. The Senate approved the Cooper-Church amendment on June 30; a subsequent version was passed by the full Congress eight months later. Rankled, the Nixon administration did everything it could to subvert the legislation. "I think the most successful State Department man at that time was the man who knew how to get around the spirit of the law without breaking the law," Marshall Green frankly offered. "We found all different kinds of ways to try and get aid into Cambodia. . . . We did a great deal of monkey business that way." Also, Senators George McGovern and Mark Hatfield proposed an amendment that would cut off all funding of the war by the end of the year, later extended to December 1971. Many peace activists organized for the McGovern-Hatfield amendment; indeed, some, including David Hartsough of the Friends Committee on National Legislation, had helped draft it and attract Senate co-sponsors before it even hit the Senate floor. After a summer of debate on the amendment, it was defeated on September 1, by a vote of 55 to 39.[65]

Open dissent surfaced inside the Nixon administration itself. More than two hundred and fifty State Department employees signed a statement criticizing U.S. policy.[66] Melvin Laird and William Rogers leaked to the press their opposition to the invasion. Secretary of the Interior Walter Hickel wrote Nixon a letter—also artfully leaked to the press—that condemned the administration's "lack [of] appropriate concern for the attitude of . . . our young people" and advocated restraining Agnew. "Youth in its protest must be heard," Hickel counseled. The interior secretary also advised Nixon to listen more to his own cabinet. "This raised an ominous question," as Jonathan Schell writes: "If the President was out of touch with young people, and out of touch with Congress (whose advice he had not asked before he ordered troops into Cambodia), and out of touch with his Cabinet, then whom was he in touch with?" Nixon was furious with Hickel and spent much time with Haldeman and Ehrlichman discussing how to respond. To limit Hickel's contact with the press, they barred him from a White House church service on May 10, three days after his letter hit the papers. Hickel was angry and told Ehrlichman "that he and his wife had been very upset since their son was in town from San Francisco and they invited two couples to be their guests," Ehrlichman informed Nixon. The president subsequently fired Hickel.[67]

To many Americans, the domestic uproar following Cambodia and Kent State suggested that the country was becoming unhinged. Newspapers observed that the United States was as divided as it had been since the Civil War. The country was on the verge of a "physical breakdown," commented New York's Mayor John Lindsay. "The nation disintegrates," lamented John Gardner, the Johnson administration's secretary of HEW. "I use the phrase soberly: the nation disintegrates." McGeorge Bundy, one of the war's main architects, who was now president of the Ford Foundation, declared: "Not only must there be no new incursion of Americans across the Cambodian border, but nothing that feels like that to the American public must happen again, on the President's say-so alone. . . . Any major action of this general sort . . . would tear the country and the administration to pieces. . . . The chances of general domestic upheaval would be real." Many prowar students felt the war's cost in domestic turmoil now outweighed any benefits of continuing it. "The consequences of a prolonged war might be violent revolution," some cautioned officials.[68]

It was an exhilarating time for most protesters. The antiwar movement was alive as never before. The political possibilities seemed stupendous. A truly general strike against the war was not inconceivable—just shut the whole country down. Even a revolution was not out of the realm of possibilities. But other activists were feeling frustrated. With the extension of the war into Cambodia, "political powerlessness and personal frustration increased a hundred times for many," two analysts of the period noted. Surging political sectarianism was also disheartening. Doug Dowd, who was then speaking all over the country, remembered that despite "all these years" of antiwar activity and "all this effort" at building a movement, arguments at planning meetings

> would go on and on and on and on for hours. And finally what would happen is you'd end up with sixteen people out of sixteen hundred, who were either the heartiest or the most professional of the people. And what would happen is nothing. . . . The political arguments that went on in those Cambodian days were so maddening to people that just wanted to do something. While the pros . . . were contending against each other in very, very bitter ways. And it just became a goddamn stalemate. . . . There was so much energy that was dissipated in arguments in auditoriums. . . . There was an innumerable number of groups [fighting each other], each of which thought, "This is our opportunity. If we can take charge of this thing, we're going to really make it." There was a kind of greed for organizational triumph.

The Socialist Workers Party was acting particularly abysmally. "At the time of Cambodia we were just busy running around trying to sell *Militants* [the SWP newspaper]," Lew Jones said. "I mean, when Cambodia hit, the SWP central office's big thing was 'Sell *Militants*—Get out there and sell those *Militants*.' I was the head [of the SWP] in San Francisco and I couldn't figure out how in the hell we were going to sell all these papers. . . . We had stacks of *Militants* at our San Francisco headquarters for months afterwards." The SWP called protests on its own, which were "a total flop," the SWP leader Peter Camejo recalled.[69]

James Shea was apparently feeling particularly frustrated. The thirty-one-year-old Massachusetts state representative had recently sponsored legislation challenging the war's constitutionality, which was signed into law by the state's governor. Yet the war had only expanded. So much more had to be done, Shea painfully realized. "I think he had the feeling that the harder he worked for peace the more never-ending the war seemed to become," said a pastor who had proposed the legislation to Shea. The representative had already been working himself to the bone. Plus, he had other political pressures to worry about. After spending the evening of May 8 at the home of friends, Shea and his wife returned to their house shortly after midnight. Shea went to an upstairs room he used as an office. Moments later, Mrs. Shea opened the door of the room, only to see her husband raise a gun to his head with both hands, pull the trigger and tumble backwards to the ground. Shea was dead.[70]

On May 7, in New York, a memorial service was held for Jeffrey Miller, one of the Kent State victims. Thousands of mourners gathered outside Riverside Chapel on Manhattan's Upper West Side. As a coffin containing Miller's body was being carried out of the chapel, the mourners stood in complete silence. The tension was palpable. "All of a sudden . . . all these fists are just going up real quietly," Joe Urgo remembered. "You could just feel the cops on edge." Hundreds of youths walked alongside the funeral cars as they crept slowly up Amsterdam Avenue. "In his silence," a rabbi said during the service, "all [Miller is] saying is 'Give peace a chance—for God's sake, in the name of humanity, give peace a chance.'"[71]

Damage Control

The White House was profoundly shaken by the May uprising. Although expecting protest following the invasion of Cambodia, it had not bargained for dissent on this scale. Certainly not deaths. "I think we badly need to focus on the campus situation," Colson advised Haldeman on May 6. Herb Klein informed Nixon the same day that "the feeling of opposition to the war and the Cambodian strike runs deeper on the campus than has anything in recent years. All reports confirm this." Moreover, "there is a great deal of fear among adults today." Recalled Nixon, "Those few days after Kent State were among the darkest of my presidency. I felt utterly dejected when I read that the father of one of the dead girls had told a reporter, 'My child was not a bum.' Kent State also took a heavy toll on Henry Kissinger's morale." It was "a time of extraordinary stress," Kissinger writes. "Washington took on the character of a besieged city. . . . The very fabric of government was falling apart. The Executive Branch was shell-shocked. After all, their children and their friends' children took part in the demonstrations. . . . Exhaustion was the hallmark of us all. I had to move from my apartment ringed by protesters into the basement of the White House to get some sleep." Nixon, who was "deeply wounded by the hatred of the protesters" and realized that both his "bums" remark and divisive April 30 speech had fanned the flames of campus dissent, "reached a point of exhaustion that caused his advisers deep concern," Kissinger reveals. In fact, the president appeared "on the edge of a nervous breakdown." The White House "feared more demonstrations, more Kent States, a nation immobilized," Jeb Magruder writes.[72]

Many officials felt the press and protesters were blowing the Kent State shootings out of proportion. "That picture of that girl kneeling [and crying next to a victim] was really blown up in the media to the point where you would have thought that Kent State was a matter of great import to the president," Richard Helms recalled. "I don't want to be misunderstood here," said Haldeman,

> but if there were an accident out here on the highway and seven people were killed . . . there'd be a little notice in the paper . . . and that'd be the end of it. . . . If a policeman shot a robber running out of that restaurant, that, again, would be a little blip of a thing. When a National Guardsman shoots a student on a college campus, that's a horrible thing . . . but also because of the nature of it it had a much greater propaganda impact than the actual physical event would have justified under other circumstances. . . . It's like that little girl who burned up in the Saigon street in that picture. Well, there were thousands of little kids in Saigon who burned up, but that one became symbolic. And Kent State became symbolic. . . . And it was good fodder for the mill that wants to gin up strong adverse reaction. And that was clearly recognized and understood and therefore a matter of great concern.

Cambodia and Kent State "created this massive, absolute hysteria," Ray Price complained. "And all reason just fled out the window." Students "were reacting largely to things that never happened, that they imagined did."[73]

The nation's highest ranking military official was also vexed by the domestic outcry over Kent State. JCS Chairman Thomas Moorer felt the media—and the Kent State victims themselves—had been duped by a protester plot. The Alabama-bred Moorer drawled:

> Now, the Kent shooting had nothing to do with Cambodia. . . . That was masterminded from Berkeley, California. They had a regular command post out there. And these people that caused all of this were not even students at Kent. They were older than you are. And they just backed away and let the students run in and get shot. And here you had 17-year-old boys at school and 17-year-old boys in the National Guard. So they started shooting. And of course there was a *great* hue and cry over that. Somehow the press related that to the Cambodia cross-border [invasion]. It was just this disruption that this group in Berkeley were doing. . . .
>
> And they had ordered this same group that was at Kent to come to Washington to have a student killed on the White House grounds, charging the White House from Lafayette Park [during the New Mobe demonstration on May 9]. So what we did was to take practically every bus in Washington and put them down on Pennsylvania Avenue . . . bumper to bumper. We had two rows of them . . . so that you couldn't run between the bumpers. So they gathered on Lafayette Park but they couldn't get across. So they never managed to

get anybody killed on the White House grounds. But they were so delighted over the reaction to the killing of students on the college campus that if they could just get somebody killed on the White House grounds they'd think they'd really accomplished something.
. . . Berkeley, that was a mess during that period. They used to give messages across the country to riot in different cities. We were too smart for them, though. We monitored their communications. That's why they weren't able to carry out their plan to have one of them shot on the White House lawn. We kept track of what they were doing.

Just which group in Berkeley was behind all this? "I'm not sure what [group] it was," Moorer said, "but you could look it up."[74]

Laurence Lynn didn't think anybody was overreacting to Kent State. He was horrified himself. And Lynn thought the White House's response to it was "hideous." Consequently, he decided to resign from the National Security Council, of which he was a senior staff member. "What did it for me was the National Guard assault," Lynn remembered. "The combination of Kent State and Agnew's reaction to it led me to realize the danger that I felt the country was in. I started *feeling danger* at that point. And knowing what I knew about Nixon and the element of instability in his nature, I got kind of scared at that point." Also, "my wife at the time was certainly uneasy about it all, and Kent State made her conclude that continuing to serve the administration didn't make a lot of sense. And it was influential with me, given the family situation." Lynn recalled "spending an entire week virtually unable to function effectively psychologically. I was a wreck. All I wanted to do was sit and talk about what was going on—I didn't want to do my work. It was just the most powerful emotional blow that I had felt as a public servant. You know, the invasion happened, Kent State, Agnew, and thinking about what would come *next*. In fact, knowing that Nixon had turned down Duck Hook once but he might not always do that. . . . I felt that I didn't want to be hostage to future 'bold moves' by that president." Lynn left the administration in the early fall.[75]

White House officials anxiously discussed how to contain the uproar. They agreed it was important to avoid steps that would further incite the protesters. "Remember—the goal of the Left is to panic us," Haldeman's notes of a May 6 meeting with the president read. "Don't fall into the trap." As deprecating youthful dissidents would be counterproductive, many officials believed, Agnew now had to be muzzled. "I strongly urge that the Vice President be urged by you, to use major restraint during this moment of tenseness," Klein wrote Nixon on May 6. Otherwise, "he could undo what major gains he has made and make himself ineffective for fall campaigning." Haldeman's notes of another meeting with the president on that day read, "Agnew say *nothing* at all re student unrest in Atlanta [on May 9]. Do speech of reconciliation. . . . *Don't say anything* about students. Non-political in *every* respect." Agnew's rhetoric did indeed soften, but both he and Nixon denied to a skeptical press that he had been reined in.[76]

Klein advised Nixon to meet with dissenting students and university administrators. "The major things most people remember about the Johnson reaction to students were that he appeared . . . to be a hand wringer, and that he turned inward, becoming more and more isolated, almost hermit-like," Klein wrote the president. Meeting with campus dissenters "would not change the minds of the radicals . . . but the fact that you are listening and communicating in a non-violent dialogue is important now with the more moderate students and with parents." Nixon hated even the thought of sitting down with protesters and spineless administrators, but agreed that the overheated political climate required conciliatory action. That night, he invited eight university presidents to come to the White House to discuss the campus ferment. Officials also looked for a group of reasonable, moderate students with whom the president could meet without fear of disruption.[77]

An opportunity arrived that very afternoon when Ehrlichman received a call from an Ohio congressmen. The legislator said he had six Kent State students in his office who wished to voice their concerns directly to the White House. Ehrlichman invited them to his office. "They were passionately upset," he remembered. "Very well-spoken, upstanding kids. Not nutty at all, you know, not crazies. They said how upset they were, what had happened, how unprovoked it was, and so on. And as I listened to them, I felt strongly that the president ought to be given an opportunity to gauge this thing himself. So I went down and asked him to see them. And he did. . . . They were by then a little nervous, uptight, and he didn't get the full impact at all." Nixon and the students mainly just "drank coffee and looked at each other."[78]

"From that moment on," Ehrlichman recalled, "for several months, we just had waves of people coming into the White House from all over the country. Mostly young people, but not all. And it was inescapable, the impact was inescapable." Henry Kissinger met with many of the White House's young visitors. Although advocating "a particularly hard line on the demonstrators" to other officials, Kissinger, with characteristic dishonesty, acted sympathetic to his guests. "Give me six months," was his standard line. Not all his young visitors were taken in, however. "It was only the illusion of dialogue," one commented after a meeting with Kissinger on May 6. "He seemed to be aware of what we were saying but not really concerned." Kissinger also met with unhappy professors. On May 8 he was painfully chastised by thirteen former Harvard colleagues. Already fearful of his future in academia, Kissinger perceived that the professors had insinuated he would not be allowed back at Harvard unless he altered U.S. policies or resigned. In private discussions and leaks to the press, Kissinger repeatedly complained "that he was the target of a vast academic conspiracy." Even Arizona State might not take him now.[79]

Nixon directed other officials to meet with the protesters as well. To foster the image of a youthful administration, younger White House staffers bore most of the burden, but even "the most aloof and uptight" officials got in on the act. On May 8, John Mitchell met with three National Student Association officers, who demanded his resignation. Mitchell did not respond. The ultra-conservative Haldeman, who had about as much in common with the protesters as Tahiti has with the North Pole, also met with many students. "Some of them were very genuine and open and understanding and rational," Haldeman remembered. "Some of them were totally irrational. . . . They said, 'You're killers,' and that's it. And, 'All you want to do is kill Vietnamese and kill American boys.'" Haldeman said he never developed a thick enough skin to bear such criticism without unease. "You never get totally used to it," he admitted. "It's not comfortable or fun by any means."[80]

Some officials advised that Nixon make a public statement on the domestic dissent and Cambodian invasion. Colson's "political instincts" told him that the White House's brief May 4 comment on Kent State did not "go far enough," he wrote Haldeman two days later. Although there were "undoubtedly a lot of negatives to" a presidential statement, argued Colson, "the idea should be thrashed out quickly." Klein urged Nixon to hold a televised press conference. While this risked projecting an air of "crisis," Klein counseled, it would sustain "the picture of the President as the one leader who is cool and strong but also thoughtful and concerned."[81]

Nixon was leery of holding a news conference. Most of the press would be antagonistic, and a bitter session might "only make things worse," he believed. Yet the potential gains were great, and Nixon knew he could shun reporters who were "out to get us" (a practice he had earlier decided to follow at press meetings). The president elected to "try to defuse the tension" by holding a news conference the evening of May 8.[82]

Nixon was "very tense" during the televised conference. Again he was conciliatory toward the protesters. "I agree with everything that they are trying to accomplish," the president said. He might even invite some more into the Oval Office to talk. Nixon also made a major concession to the demonstrators. Firming up a loose projection he had offered to members of Congress three days earlier on the length of the Cambodian invasion, Nixon told the nation that, since "the action" in that country was "going faster than we had anticipated," all American troops would be withdrawn from Cambodia by the end of June.[83] The White House's original plan for the invasion had envisioned a temporary operation, but the time frame had been flexible. Now that was no longer possible. "The enormous uproar at home was profoundly unnerving," Kissinger recalls. "The panicky decision to set a June 30 deadline for the removal of our forces from Cambodia was one concrete result of public pressures." U.S. troops were "arbitrarily" withdrawn in two months. Laird, Haldeman, Green, Ziegler, and other senior Nixon administration officials I interviewed confirmed Kissinger's account. "I think it's quite clear that [Nixon] felt that domestic political pressure obliged him to curtail that operation before it really was finished," Richard Helms said. Laurence Lynn commented, "I think that the domestic political reaction to the incursions had a *lot* to do with Nixon saying, 'I'm just not going to bleed to death Cambodia.'"[84]

But it wasn't protesters alone who forced Nixon into a premature withdrawal. Many other Americans were obviously skeptical of the invasion, and the administration feared declining public support. Congressional dissent weighed very heavily on White House minds. "I think they were told by their people on the Hill that they could not hold the line on Cooper-Church or any of the [other] restrictions that were then being debated if those troops stayed in there," Roger Morris said.[85]

The Nixon administration took other steps in early May to counter the domestic uproar over Cambodia and Kent State. It used "every possible means" to publicize the reasons for the invasion. Officials mobilized the Nixon Network of support. The White House nourished the propaganda of the Citizens Committee for Peace with Freedom in Vietnam and other prowar groups. Colson prodded the AFL-CIO to "launch a major campaign among its members" in support of U.S. policies; to stimulate the campaign, Nixon visited AFL-CIO headquarters and briefed the body on the invasion. Colson also made plans for Nixon to speak at an Association of Student Governments conference; the ASG leader James Dunn, a "first rate fellow" (in Colson's eyes), urged the White House that "in whatever way the President addresses the students . . . he flood them with kindness—really love them." The administration released more favorable poll data ("more ammo," Haldeman called it). Officials moved to convey that not all of the protesters were reacting to Cambodia or Kent State—many had more complex, even sinister, agendas. Nixon summoned the governors of all fifty states to the White House to explain the invasion and solicit help in quelling the campus uproar. He appointed Vanderbilt's Alexander Heard his "special advisor" on campus problems and ordered the FBI to investigate the Kent State shootings. Meanwhile, for his own perusal, Nixon asked the FBI for the "same-day copies of all field reports. . . . These reports should be unabridged—not boiled down or condensed," Ehrlichman informed the Justice Department.[86]

"Heightening the pressure" on the White House at this time, as Jeb Magruder notes, was the demonstration the New Mobe planned at the White

House on May 9. Despite the short notice, as many as a hundred thousand Americans would turn out for the protest, officials realized. Many of the demonstrators planned sit-downs in the streets or other acts of civil disobedience. Some were bent on violence. Intelligence indicated that Mobe marshals would not be as effective at controlling the crowd as during the group's demonstration the previous November. Perhaps most disconcerting, some militants might attempt to incite state violence. The specter of another demonstrator killed at the hands of a government agent was more than a little frightening. Admiral Moorer was not the only official wary of a charge on the White House. "I was awfully concerned that there might be some people get over the fence, and that there would be violence," Ehrlichman remembered. "There was a lot of conversation about that in advance. We just didn't want that. . . . I thought if there had been excessive reaction on the part of the White House police, for instance, or the Secret Service, that that would certainly have put it more or less in the same category as Kent State, where there would be a backlash." The nation would *really* blow then.[87]

Officials acted to minimize unruliness. They placed a ring of sixty buses around the White House. "I remember going to work having to weave my way between two buses—it was the only way you could get in and out of the White House," William Watts said. Riot-trained police were positioned behind the buses. Secret Service agents in sunglasses cordoned off streets surrounding the Executive Mansion for several blocks in all directions. "My car was met at a checkpoint at Nineteenth and E Streets and escorted in by helmeted police," Colson recounts. Parking was restricted in a 130-square-block area. TV cameras were placed on top of the White House "so that we could see what was going on in different places," recalled Ehrlichman, who was preparing to monitor the action from the building's bomb shelter; so concerned was he about the demonstration that he slept in the White House the night before. The administration rejected a Mobe request to rally in Lafayette Park across the street, offering the Washington Monument instead; at the last moment, it granted the Ellipse. The Secret Service placed "intelligence gathering teams" on the streets of Washington "to insure a flow of current information" about the demonstrators' plans; SS offices around the country gathered intelligence on violence-prone protesters who would be attending.[88]

On the night of May 8, under cover of darkness, troops in full combat dress began moving quietly into the bowels of government buildings. Five thousand soldiers in all were positioned in the Washington area. "They should be capable of rapid reaction," the Pentagon instructed; "however, minimum visibility should be the key." Use of force should be kept to "the absolute minimum" and "all efforts should be nonlethal." The troops would be "brought to a state of readiness" on the morning of the protest, while still maintaining "low visibility." More than a thousand National Guardsmen would be deputized as "special policemen." Two thousand others would be positioned nearby. Also "to maintain control of the situation," the Pentagon would provide water trailers, salt tablets, and medical aid to the demonstrators.[89]

When it came to communicating with protesters, the White House now planned to pull out all the stops. It would send younger officials out into the streets to round up anyone who wanted to "talk things out." "We really had an organized outreach program," Ray Price recalled. "We had these whole units organized to go out and talk to them and bring them back in to talk to us." A telephone line was also set up to take calls from students who wished to visit. Not every young Tom, Dick, and Harry would be allowed into the White House, however. "Obviously, any radicals or way-out students would not be brought in," Chapin assured Haldeman in outlining the program. At the end of the day, Ziegler would inform the press of the administration's effort to communicate with troubled youth, despite the obvious security risks.[90]

When not meeting with protesters, White House staffers would call influential figures around the country "to get a late reading on the situation in their various communities and to suggest that they adopt a 'quietening down' approach," Chapin wrote. "Ministers would be asked to pass the word in their communities that perhaps it would be a good idea to call for some special prayers over the weekend for the President, students, and the men in Vietnam."[91]

May 9: "A Picnic in the Park"

Meanwhile, the coordinating committee of the New Mobe was locked in a non-stop debate over the demonstration at the Washington home of the WSP activist Barbara Bick. For six days, in a supercharged political atmosphere, the group met virtually continuously. "I don't think those meetings ever adjourned," Fred Halstead recalled. They went on "all night long." Sleep was a scarce commodity. So, it seems, was political accord. For the same divisions that had threatened to split the coalition before the Cambodian invasion surfaced sharply. Some activists wanted to engage in traditional nonviolent civil disobedience as close to the White House as they could safely get: just cross the police line and sit down. Dave Dellinger, Rennie Davis, and others, worried that the demonstration would turn into some sort of tired, choreographed Quaker exercise or, worse, another feeble day of listening to speeches in the sun, argued strongly for militant nonviolent civil disobedience, "with not too much emphasis on nonviolence on Davis's part," as Halstead remembered. "We serve notice that days of ineffective mass dissent are over," Dellinger told the press. Davis felt the country was on the brink of a truly major explosion and that aggressive confrontationism at the door of the White House would electrify the shut-it-down movement. (Davis had some credentials as a political prognosticator by this time: shortly before

Kent State, he had predicted that there would be "blood in the streets," so when the shootings occurred "everybody was taking a second look at Davis," Halstead chuckled.) Halstead and other SWPers not only despised the whole notion of civil disobedience but feared a military trap north of the White House; they pushed for a legal rally at the Ellipse to the south. Brad Lyttle, the Mobe's logistics specialist, who along with Halstead was in charge of training three thousand marshals for the protest, shared their position. Since most of the advocates of direct action either opposed a demonstration at the Ellipse (it seemed too far from the front of the White House to move easily into civil disobedience where it counted) or felt the government would never grant the site anyway, little planning took place over how to combine the two tactics. Come the day before the demonstration, the debate was still inconclusive. "You were going crazy there," Sidney Peck remembered.[92]

When the White House suddenly offered the Mobe the Ellipse at 4 P.M. that afternoon, the coordinating committee was thrown into greater turmoil. Halstead and Lyttle were delighted with the government's decision and moved immediately with the Mobe lawyer Phil Hirschkop to accept the site. "We don't even wait for the committee—we say, 'Okay, we take it,'" Halstead recalled. Other Mobe organizers were not pleased. When Halstead walked into a hotel room where the coordinating committee was then meeting, "instead of everybody being overjoyed that we got the Ellipse . . . there's all kinds of long faces," he recounted. The faces were hurriedly debating how to work civil disobedience into the protest under the new circumstances. The passionate discussion continued into the following day. "I got up early the next morning and went back, and they were still at it!" Halstead exclaimed. Abbie Hoffman and Jerry Rubin proposed that all of the demonstrators march from the Ellipse to the White House to back up a small delegation that would demand to "rap" with Nixon on the White House lawn. The delegation would feature Hoffman and Rubin. Few were enthusiastic. Later a plan was worked out whereby two streams of marchers would proceed to the White House led by "a delegation of caskets." The caskets would be placed on the front steps of the White House. The dead would deliver the protesters' message to Nixon: "the dead could speak for themselves," as Peck put it. The two streams of marchers would then ring the White House. "It would be a total encirclement," Peck said. "This would then symbolically, in effect, put Nixon under house arrest. And we would post our bill of particulars and so forth." The demonstrators would then sit down and remain through May 11, when the governors were scheduled to meet with Nixon. "They would have to fly in by helicopter," Peck envisioned. "And people would see the White House would be under political—not military, but political—siege." The plan was agreed upon at one or two in the morning. Shortly after sunup, Peck and his fellow Mobe leader Ron Young prowled the streets around the White House to work out the final tactical details.[93]

Richard Milhous Nixon was also prowling outside his residence early that morning. Following his press conference the previous evening, the president had been "agitated and uneasy as the events of the last few weeks raced through my mind," he records. Once again unable to sleep, he made fifty phone calls between 10:30 P.M. and 4:30 A.M. Nixon was in "an odd mood," the White House speechwriter William Safire, one of those with whom he spoke, recalled. "Keyed up and relaxed at the same time," the president "obviously" just "felt like talking" and was "rambling in his remarks." He assured Safire at one point that "if the crazies try anything, we'll clobber them." Shortly after 3 A.M., Nixon took time out from his verbal meanderings to listen to Rachmaninoff's First Piano Concerto, a dramatic composition, in the Lincoln Sitting Room. Awakened, his valet Manolo Sanchez appeared at the doorway in a bathrobe. Looking out a window at small knots of protesters gathered on the Washington Monument grounds for the impending demonstration, frustrated at his inability to communicate with disgruntled youth, eager to show that he was not a prisoner in the White House, the "very troubled" president asked Sanchez if he'd ever been to the Lincoln Memorial at night. Sanchez said he had not. "Get your clothes on, we'll go," Nixon directed. At 4:30 A.M., the president and his valet strode out onto the south lawn of the White House.[94]

Egil Krogh was then in the Secret Service command post for the demonstration. "Searchlight is on the lawn," the stunned Krogh heard a SS agent declare over the loudspeaker. "Searchlight has asked for a car." Krogh immediately awakened his boss John Ehrlichman to tell him what was going down. (Apparently few people in Washington were getting any sleep that night.) Ehrlichman remembered with amusement, "I got a phone call from Bud Krogh in the middle of the night, saying, 'Heeeee's going out there.' So I said, 'Well, you'd better go with him.'" "Petrified" SS agents were also scrambling to stick with the restless president. So were White House military staffers. "Our office was notified immediately that the President was on the move," Bill Gulley, the director of the White House Military Office, writes. "The Football—the famous black briefcase with our retaliatory information—was our responsibility, and it was imperative that it go with the President wherever he went."[95]

After taking in the Lincoln Memorial with Sanchez, Nixon approached some of the protesters. In what he later described as an attempt to "lift them a bit out of the miserable intellectual wasteland in which they now wander aimlessly around," he talked mainly about sports and travel, very little about "the war thing." "It was a surreal atmosphere," Krogh recalled. To many of the dumbfounded young people, the president of the United States seemed out of his mind. "I hope it was because he was tired, but most of what he was saying was absurd," one Syracuse University student told a reporter. "Here we had come from a university that's completely uptight, on strike, and when we told him where we were from, he talked about the football team." Anthony Lake smiled,

"If you look at Nixon's behavior after Kent State, it was not a true Alan Alda-ish, sensitive male performance." The president also discoursed to the youth on the "spiritual hunger which all of us have." He told Haldeman four days later that it was such "qualities of spirit" and "the depth and mystery of life which this whole visit really was all about." As the sun was beginning to come up, with the increasingly nervous Secret Service fearful that Mobe leaders would show up, the president and Sanchez got back into the car and drove off.[96]

Nixon was not yet ready to return to the White House, however. Had Manolo ever been to the Capitol? Manolo had not. So off they were for a tour of the Capitol, Krogh and SS agents close by, two demonstrators in a white Volvo giving chase. During the tour they asked a cleaning woman for a key to the Senate Chamber. Told she did not have one, the party headed off toward the House Chamber instead, leaving the astounded cleaner "shaking her head." After obtaining a key to the chamber, Nixon decided it was time for a little speechmaking. According to some accounts, including the president's own, Nixon had Sanchez sit in the Speaker's chair, at which point the valet delivered some spontaneous remarks about how proud he was to be an American. Nixon allegedly sat in the front row clapping. According to Haldeman and Ziegler, who caught up with Nixon outside the Capitol, however, it was the president who delivered the oration. "Nixon was giving the talk to Manolo," Haldeman said. "He was telling Manolo how the House of Representatives works." In any event, after the speech—it was now 6:40 A.M.—Nixon and his entourage headed off to the Rib Room of the Mayflower Hotel for some breakfast. Haldeman remembered that Nixon's mood at the breakfast table was "kind of strange. . . . I don't think he had slept much. . . . He didn't seem to be upset. He *seemed* to be at that point very pleased with having talked with the people up at the Memorial." Although a bit taken aback by the president's jaunt himself, Haldeman had seen Nixon roam the streets in the middle of the night before. "It wasn't an unusual thing," he said. "Going back to the campaigns, after a heavy campaign day or a big speech on a campaign night or something, he'd go to bed and not sleep, and then at four in the morning he'd get up and start walking through the town of Billings, Montana, or wherever we happened to be, and end up in a coffee shop or someplace, just sitting there at the counter. In fact, when he was vice president sometimes he'd sneak out without the Secret Service knowing he'd gotten away." Ray Price had also seen this kind of behavior from Nixon before. "I remember once bumping into him at six o'clock in the morning out in Fargo, North Dakota, when we were out there," Price recalled. "He couldn't sleep and I couldn't sleep, and we'd both gone out for walks. Down by the train station there I saw him standing talking to an old farmer. Then we went off to a pancake house and had pancakes together."[97]

But to most observers the president's nocturnal journey was quite extraordinary. "It's a strange episode," Marshall Green remarked. "It's the kind of thing that doesn't happen very often in Washington. In fact, it's probably a unique experience with a president wandering around the town in sort of a strange psychological mood." The *New York Times* aptly commented that "it provided a revealing glimpse of a man who has been under exceptional strain for the last few weeks." According to Henry Kissinger, Nixon's trek was "only the tip of the psychological iceberg." Another senior administration official waggishly called it, "King Lear Act VI."⁹⁸

Nixon's jaunt was a public relations setback for the administration. Press accounts painted a picture of a disturbed president awkwardly attempting to talk about trivial subjects with students who had come to Washington on serious business. "It's one of those things like so many in that period that backfired," Price said ruefully. Ehrlichman remembered that though Nixon's mood was "very good" later that morning and that "he thought that he had made a good contact [and] had communicated with some of the people out there . . . I felt that, in fact, he had *not* communicated well." When Ehrlichman criticized his boss for talking about sports to the protesters, the "tired and tense" Nixon "snapped at him about the problems a President has when even his own staff believes the false stories that are spread about him."⁹⁹

Several hours after Nixon had returned to his residence, Fred Halstead and Brad Lyttle were busily working on the rally platform at the Ellipse. There were still many logistical matters to be taken care of, including helping with the sound system, arranging access to water, and preparing the defense of the stage against any ultraleft attacks. Some eighty thousand people were already gathered below. Although the noon starting time for the rally was only an hour away, the key Mobe leaders Sidney Peck, Ron Young, and Dave Dellinger were nowhere in sight. "It took a long time [to arrange] for the casket to get there," Peck would later explain. "We could only get to somebody early in the morning to build a casket—not such a simple thing to do. . . . The other thing that we had to do was to organize a group of, like, prominent people who would be willing to initiate this mass sit-down thing. And included in that were a group of people from the Congress. But there had to be an orientation for that group. . . . And it took us a while, again, to get that organized." Come noon, the Mobe officers still had not appeared. "We have to stall," Halstead recalled. "We get up and make announcements. . . . We introduce prominent people we find in the audience. . . . And finally they show up" at 1 P.M.¹⁰⁰

Over a hundred thousand people were now congregated on the Ellipse, an extraordinary turnout for a demonstration organized in only a week's time. Again the crowd was overwhelmingly young, white, and middle-class. And once again, many were protesting for the first time. "What has happened in the last week was kind of the last straw," one explained. According to the *New York*

Times, the crowd "showed an undertow of deep resentment, perhaps more so than in any of the many anti-Vietnam demonstrations staged in the Capital since 1965." Some adults present were also demonstrating for the first time. The *Times* columnist Tom Wicker defied journalistic norms to participate. Anthony Lake, his resignation from the NSC staff not yet operative, slipped through the ring of buses surrounding the White House to join his wife and friends on the Ellipse. Several hundred federal employees waved banners declaring "Federal Bums Against the War" and "We Have Found the Enemy and He Is Us!" Roaming among the protesters were dozens of government officials trying to reason with them. Their task was not an easy one. "I'm not getting through to them," an agitated AID official complained to Lake.[101]

After starting the rally, the tardy Mobe leaders resumed their debate over civil disobedience on the platform. Informed only hours or minutes earlier that the plan for the march was to head up Fifteenth and Seventeenth streets to the White House, many Mobe marshals—trained by Halstead and Lyttle and heavily self-selected from the ranks of those opposed to civil disobedience—contended vehemently that the marchers would run smack dab up against a police line and get crushed. Nervous, the Mobe leaders agreed not to announce the march, then almost immediately reversed their decision. "There was so much confusion," Dellinger remembered. "It was all uncertain." "We were split right up to the end." Already disturbed by "minor shortcomings" in the organization of the demonstration, Lyttle became "despondent" during the argument on the stage; he sat down, made "several uncomplimentary remarks to New Mobe officers," bowed his head, covered his face, and cried. "I was sitting there listening to these people arguing about what strategy they were going to follow, which they'd been arguing about for four or five or six days," Lyttle recalled. "And it just *disgusted* me. I can wax vehement about that. Because these people are all arrogant, you know. I mean, I suppose they would accuse me of that, too, but they are arrogant sons of guns, and they were just fouling it up terribly." Lyttle emerged from his "brief paralysis" to join Halstead in telling Dellinger "that if I urged people to join me in civil disobedience—which is what I wanted to do—that they were going to cut the microphone," Dellinger remembered. Another dispute had earlier erupted over whether members of Congress could use the mike at all. "It was ridiculous," Peck sniffed. "And here you had members of Congress who were prepared to commit civil disobedience!"[102]

Amid the bickering, the nationally televised rally was not going smoothly. Pressured by assorted wannabe orators unscheduled by the Mobe, the group's coordinating committee proved unable to control the microphone. One of the many unscheduled speakers was the Chicago Eight defendant John Froines, who tried to lead the crowd in a chant of "FUCK NIXON!" "It seemed to me that Noam

Chomsky [who was sitting aside the stage] might have had more to say than that to 150,000 people," Lyttle dryly commented. Many in the sun-baked crowd ignored the speeches and headed off to frolic in the Lincoln Reflecting Pool.[103]

Over at the heavily barricaded White House, there was an air of "anxious expectancy," Colson writes. What did the mob have up its sleeve? officials worried. "You literally were afraid for your life," Colson recalled. John Dean remembered that "it was very strange when they ringed all those blocks with buses. It was a very weird feeling inside there. It was almost like they'd dropped the White House inside of a movie set or something. Because normal traffic [had stopped]. I mean, there was nothing inside. . . . It was like a picnic ground. . . . People were running around in their shirt sleeves . . . and you could walk up and watch a policeman Mace kids trying to crawl under buses. It was a strange sport, a great spectator sport." Ehrlichman was in no mood for a picnic; apparently irritated at having to hear the rally speakers from inside the White House, Haldeman noted, Ehrlichman complained, "Why P.A. so loud? Crank it down or cut some cords." To politically blunt the demonstration, Ehrlichman advised, "Be sure to go low on crowd count—give official estimate." Also, "Say what the hell—didn't work before. Why waste time now." Ehrlichman took a hard line against the protesters then occupying the Peace Corps building. "Bust the Peace Corps—get it rough," he counseled. "No soldiers do anything—let the kids break windows. . . . Get Peace Corps out." (The invaders were allowed to leave untouched that evening. "Like the Viet Cong," they proclaimed, "we escaped back into the people.") Many White House officials were meeting with protesters in their offices; two nursing students from Virginia were invited in to chat while simply walking by the area. The White House worried that holding too many such meetings would "debase" them, though.[104]

Around 4 P.M., Dave Dellinger, in an arousing closing speech, directed the demonstrators to head up Fifteenth Street behind a line of coffins to the White House. To avoid "skirmishes on the platform and in the crowd," he refrained from calling explicitly for civil disobedience. "Since there was so much confusion and divisions—I mean, we'd spent [six] days getting nowhere, getting to no unity—I felt that if I tried to do it and they cut off the mike, it would just lead to chaos," Dellinger recalled. "It would just be total chaos." Meanwhile the several hundred marshals who had been trained specifically to facilitate civil disobedience had been called to the other side of the Ellipse to prepare for a march up Seventeenth Street. "They make the wrong announcement," Halstead remembered. "And everything is just total confusion." Thousands of protesters followed Dellinger's cue, but the marshals on Fifteenth Street strongly discouraged them from turning off onto H Street, the logical place for committing civil disobedience, claiming it was "the path to violence, to Weatherman, to a disaster." Some marshals linked arms to block entry. Instead, they herded the protesters to the north, away from the White House. According to some observers, government agents were also herding protesters away from the White House. Ultimately, Peck bitterly recalled, "whoever directed that line of march took them off to Arlington Cemetery." "Boiling mad at the Mobe," about a thousand marchers pierced the line of marshals and made it onto H Street, where they shattered bus windows with rocks and bottles, tried to overturn buses or simply sat down in the street. "A warning was flashed from the command post in the White House basement," Colson recounts. "I could hear the rustling of the troops in the basement—loosening rifle straps, fixing bayonets, laying out ammunition clips." Police wearing steel helmets and gas masks waded into the mob, swinging clubs and spraying tear gas. "There were shouts and screams, the shattering of glass and steel," writes Colson. "A gentle breeze from the west swept the mist of tear gas through the White House windows; I felt the acrid, burning sensation in my eyes and nose." The police put down the assault, arresting several hundred. In nearby areas, roaming bands of youths crashed barricades, broke windows, and skirmished with cops into the night; an explosive device blew out the glass facade of the National Guard building. At 3 A.M., with the number of protesters dwindling, the unused and largely unseen army troops wheeled into Washington for the demonstration began moving out.[105]

The demonstration had been, in the eyes of most of the protesters, a dud. "A major disaster," the Mobe leader Arthur Waskow called it. Norma Becker:

> People went down there prepared to make a forceful protest. Now, I'm not talking about being violent. They went down expecting to be Maced, expecting to be brutalized by the police. Pratt Institute bought half a train. They had students who came. I remember that they were wearing turtlenecks, and they brought Vaseline. For many of them this was their first demonstration. . . . And people came prepared for heavy-duty action. . . . They were out there to express . . . outrage at a government policy that was slaughtering people in Vietnam and was now killing students on American campuses. There was a groundswell of intense passion. These for the most part . . . were not your full-time movement organizers who were out to organize the revolution at 5:30. They were out to go down to make a statement, and they were prepared to be arrested, they were prepared to be hurt. I wasn't prepared to be hurt—I mean, I'm terrified of police violence—but I was a little more experienced in how to run away from it, how to avoid it. . . . But a *large* number of those people went down there ready to be arrested, to sit down, to engage in nonviolent civil disobedience. And they would have done that [if given the opportunity]. I can't give you numbers, but I would say that easily—*easily*—50 percent of that crowd [would have].

The protest "turned out to be a picnic in the park," Becker said. "People returned from that demonstration very depressed."[106]

They had a right to be depressed. Had only twenty thousand of the protesters sat down in the street (a conservative estimate of the number so inclined), the action would probably have sparked similar acts of mass civil disobedience in other cities, greatly intensifying the national sense of crisis after Cambodia and Kent State. Increasingly politically isolated, Nixon would have seen his authority wane further. More Americans would have demanded an end to the war to stem the domestic turmoil. Spurred by their colleagues sitting down in the street, some members of Congress might have moved faster to cut off funds for the war. Nixon might have been forced into swifter U.S. troop withdrawals. "It was a perfect time!" Peck exclaimed. "It just would have been a perfect action. . . . And we failed. . . . I mean, that was one of our biggest, biggest errors. . . . We allowed him breathing space. We didn't sustain [the pressure]."[107]

Who was responsible for the Mobe's failure? The primary blame must lie with the Mobe leaders themselves. Politically divided, they simply failed to come up with a coherent and enduring plan for civil disobedience. "I and some of the other organizers should have handled the complicated relationships better," Dellinger admits. "We should have found an honorable way—without factionalism, backbiting, or manipulation—of offering two alternatives to the assembled multitude": leave at the end of the legal rally or proceed with the following plan for civil disobedience. "But we failed to work out such a common-sense solution." The government contributed to the Mobe's failure. By granting the Ellipse, it moved the demonstration away from the front of the White House, where civil disobedience would have been easier. And by doing it at the last minute, it gave the Mobe scant time to devise a plan. "A master stroke of public relations," Dellinger calls the government's move. Physical exhaustion made the Mobe's task harder still. Fred Halstead and Brad Lyttle must also bear significant responsibility for the Mobe's failure. Halstead and other SWPers violence-baited the protest, and Lyttle, who was impressed with the SWP's acumen in logistical matters, supported their arguments. Both Halstead and Lyttle imbued the army of marshals (many of whom were SWPers as it was) with strong anti–civil disobedience sentiment. "To this day I believe that it got undercut by the SWP," Peck said of the protest. And Lyttle "was their key figure. If they got Brad to go with them, then that did it."[108]

That night, weary and short-tempered Mobe leaders met to discuss the demonstration. Dellinger, Peck, Waskow, and others lambasted Halstead for derailing it. "I was just absolutely furious about it!" Peck remembered, his ire still evident. "There was a lot of anger at the SWP on that one." "*They were pissed,*" recalled Halstead, who was "greatly relieved that we'd gotten through without another Kent State." "Oh, God, they were just pissed. And they just blamed it on me. . . . So I told them to 'Go fuck yourself' or something—I didn't use that language, but I said something ungentle—and stormed out." Lyttle was also resentful of the accusations against the SWP. "That was a bum rap, a really bum rap," he later complained.

> I was really sore. I said, "These guys, the Trots, they were just standing around waiting to take orders. You guys didn't know what the heck you were doing. You didn't give them any leadership, you didn't give them any strategy, you had nothing when you went out on that platform, and you were arguing about it throughout the whole program." . . . I thought it was absolutely disgusting. You know, Mao talks about criticism and self-criticism. I would say that was about *zero* in most of the antiwar movement. . . . There was plenty of criticism, but there wasn't much self-criticism. That was a pitiful, pitiful demonstration. [109]

The Mobe activist David McReynolds thought the whole dispute was unnecessary. "The movement tore itself apart even though it had won a victory," he lamented. "We got a hundred thousand people there within a week's time. . . . Nixon got on television and said he was going to pull all the troops out [of Cambodia] in thirty [sic] days. I thought we'd won." [110]

The mood at the White House that night was undoubtedly one of anxious relief. Another Kent State had been averted, and the demonstration, though politically damaging, had been kept under control. But "within the iron gates of the White House, quite unknowingly, a siege mentality was setting in," Colson writes. "It was now 'us' against 'them.' Gradually as we drew the circle closer around us, the ranks of 'them' began to swell." [111]

More White House Game-Planning

Through the rest of the spring, the Nixon administration kept up its efforts to counter the domestic uproar. To exhibit concern and a youthful image, it dispatched eight young White House staffers to twenty-seven "strategically selected" campuses to meet with students, faculty, and administrators. In press briefings, Magruder wrote Haldeman, "we will emphasize that the trip occurred, not what will follow from it." Upon returning to the White House, the staffers urged Nixon to "create a conciliatory mood" between youth and the administration. "We fear that the universities may have a frightful destiny if polarization continues," they warned. The staffers stressed the magnitude of the opposition on campuses. "The depth, breadth and intensity of student disaffection is greater than any of us anticipated," they reported. In his own investigation of the domestic political fallout of Cambodia and Kent State, John Ehrlichman came to a similar conclusion. "There was a whole new set of realities," he remembered. "The opposition changed. There was an escalation in their ability to do us serious political damage in the Congress and among the electorate. . . . It was very clearly a problem. . . . I saw both a quantitative and qualitative escalation of the antiwar opposition." It "was making real inroads." Haldeman shared this perception. Cambodia had "backfired," he later acknowledged.[112]

The White House fostered additional displays of public support. After the conservative Stanford scientist William Shockley, who had shared the Nobel Prize for Physics in 1956, decided to circulate a counterletter to an antiwar statement by other Nobel laureates, it fed him propaganda. The administration coaxed a Kent State official to appear on a Sunday TV talk show to give his "side of the story." It continued to assist prowar groups, including the Association of Student Governments, which was "back under our control" after an internal power struggle, Colson noted. The White House asked some of these groups to "mount a special effort" on the Hill. With support from the CIA and Jay Lovestone, an AFL-CIO intelligence operative, it helped Peter Brennan and other right-wing New York union leaders organize a supportive demonstration of nearly a hundred thousand people in Manhattan. The union leaders didn't need much help, though. "This group required very little encouragement," Colson informed Nixon afterward. Union officials told workers they would lose their pay for the day if they failed to attend the demonstration. Colson regarded the event as "an enormous success." Probably with White House assistance, Brennan got union leaders in other cities to stage additional pro-administration rallies. Nixon later appointed Brennan secretary of labor.[113]

The evening after the New York demonstration, Nixon called Brennan to thank him. Colson raised the possibility of phoning other union leaders "either to thank them for what they've done or motivate them to do more of the same kind of demonstrating," but Haldeman rejected the idea, saying it would be "diluting." Against the advice of most of his staff, who felt that the hard hat had become symbolic of repression of demonstrators, Nixon invited Brennan and his associates to the White House. Although he "very much" desired the meeting, White House documents attest, the president opposed being presented with his own personal hard hat. "Shrinks with horror at idea of hard hat," Haldeman told Colson. "Delegation O.K.—but *no hard hat.* . . . Would never live it down." Nixon made it clear that he would "not under any circumstances" wear a hard hat for photographers. The morning of the meeting, Colson advised the president not to discuss "the student protest issue" with his guests. "They are very anti-student. Almost anything you say along these lines will be quoted and probably with more emphasis than you intended." The union leaders presented Nixon with a hard hat labeled "Commander in Chief." He did not, however, pose for pictures with it on. The labor leaders left their own hard hats on the cabinet table for photographers before departing.[114]

Nixon went on television to tell Americans that the invasion of Cambodia had been an enormous success. White House propagandists launched "an all-out effort" to substantiate his claim. (Before the speech, Moynihan had pleaded with Nixon not to use Cold War rhetoric in it. Students, whose "opposition makes it increasingly difficult for you to govern," "believe the cold war is a conspiracy to kill them. Literally," he counseled. "Obviously their education has been a bit of a disaster.")[115]

Nixon appointed a Commission on Campus Unrest chaired by William Scranton, the former governor of Pennsylvania. "Don't let higher education off with a pat on the ass," Nixon directed Scranton. The president continued to feel that most university presidents were "without spine—frightened of faculties and radical students," he told Scranton. So were many faculty. "Students used to follow teachers," Nixon complained. "Now vice versa." Instead of kowtowing to the militants, "faculties should toss them out," he remarked to Scranton. And Nixon felt there was a "tendency among educators to blame it [protest] all on the war." But if the war ended, it "won't then be peaceful," Nixon observed, partly because of "professional agitators" and partly because "educators have failed to give students something to believe in." The president's appointment of the Scranton Commission got him in trouble with Ronald Reagan, however, when it was discovered that one of the commission members had charged that the governor of California was "bent on killing people for his own political gain." Reagan repeatedly phoned the White House to demand that Nixon kick the bum off the commission. When Dwight Chapin asked Ehrlichman to call Reagan back, however, Ehrlichman claimed he didn't have time.[116]

The same month, as Tom Huston had earlier suggested, the president met with the heads of the main U.S. intelligence agencies. Amid the domestic uproar, Nixon had concluded that the agencies simply couldn't help in his battle with protesters and other internal enemies. He "didn't pull any punches in expressing his dissatisfaction with their work," Haldeman writes, especially their failure to document foreign communist support of the demonstrators. Nixon directed the agencies to devise a more aggressive domestic intelligence program; Huston would oversee it. The White House aide apprised the intelligence chiefs of Nixon's judgment that, in dealing with the internal threat, "everything is valid, everything is possible." The new interagency committee submitted a report to the president that warned that "the 'New Left,' involving and influencing a substantial number of college students, is having a serious impact on contemporary society with a potential for serious domestic strife." It recommended a wide assortment of criminal acts to combat the threat, including mail openings, burglaries, and phone taps. This criminal activity would be directed from the White House. The "Huston Plan" was approved by Nixon. But J. Edgar Hoover adamantly opposed it (he called Huston a "hippy intellectual" and "snot-nosed kid"), and since the FBI director knew where more than a few bodies were buried, Nixon was forced to junk it. The plan later became an important consideration in the Watergate investigation and impeachment proceedings.[117]

In response to flak from the "jackals of the press" (as Hoover called unfriendly journalists), Nixon wielded a much smaller stick, but a stick nonetheless. "*No one* from the White House staff under any circumstances is to answer any call or see anybody from the *New York Times* except for [Robert] Semple," Nixon instructed Haldeman on May 11. "No one on the White House staff is to see anybody from the *Washington Post* or return any calls to them" either. "Just treat the *Post* absolutely coldly," the embattled president directed. Nixon also ordered Haldeman to pass to *Time's* Hugh Sidey that, although the media "violently" opposed him on Cambodia, "the President has taken all this with good grace."[118]

The Death of the Mobe

The period following the May 9 demonstration was a depressing one for many protesters. "That was the worst period in the Movement," Norma Becker recalled. Most recognized they had forced Nixon into an early withdrawal from Cambodia, and that was reason for satisfaction. But most also recognized "that we had faltered when history demanded decisive action," Dave Dellinger writes. "Instead of being exhilarated by the ability of the people to stand up to the government and win at least the partial victory that was in fact won, they were disheartened to think that the war continued, even though somewhat abated, and that protest action was petering out as divisiveness and the summer doldrums took over. An unwarranted and unnecessary sense of powerlessness gripped the movement, contributing to the growing crisis of self-confidence." According to Doug Dowd, the "naïveté about power" that had always led many protesters to expect quick victories "really became murderous" at this time. "I think that really did us in," he said. "Sort of, 'Well, God, and we brought all these people.' . . . I think the disillusionment finally caved in people." It was very difficult to accept "that all that happened in 1970 was without visible effect." Dowd himself worried that Nixon's premature withdrawal from Cambodia might only be "a goddamn temporary trick." Some protesters feared the president might be planning an even greater escalation, possibly using tactical nuclear weapons.[119]

After May 9, the Socialist Workers Party decided it had finally had enough of mindless adventurists and sloppy organizers and moved to organize antiwar activity on its own. It called for a national antiwar conference in Cleveland in June for the purpose of planning legal and peaceful demonstrations. Given the movement's size and their growing contacts to the right (particularly in SANE and organized labor), SWPers believed, "we don't need these folks. We don't need to get into this pissing argument with them about . . . civil disobedience." A sympathetic Brad Lyttle remembered:

> The Trotskyists by that time had developed I would say a very deep contempt for a lot of people in the . . . peace movement. I think they felt that many of us were bad organizers, and we weren't committed. . . . And I think the Trotskyists were right. I mean, I was fed up with a lot of what was going on in the movement [myself]. See, I was involved with all of these practical details. And the irresponsibility concerning money just nauseated me. I mean, it was general policy that if you borrowed money from a rich person, you'd never repay it. . . . Well, that's bad enough, but the trouble was that it got into everything. If you borrowed money from a poor person you'd never repay it. And here I get a telephone call from a school teacher in Maryland who loaned the Mobe a thousand dollars. . . . You know, a naïve woman who wants to end the war in Vietnam. And she wants her money [back]. The leaders of the Mobe didn't have the slightest interest in repaying her her thousand dollars! . . . That really burned me up. Because not only did it strike me as being dishonest, but it seemed to me that you couldn't build a responsible and effective humanitarian movement on that basis.[120]

But the SWP operated differently, Lyttle perceived. It knew how to build a movement:

> The SWP was organized from top to toe. That was one of the reasons that I got along with Halstead and a lot of these people. Because my approach to movement work had always been that of methodical organization. . . . They had a handful of people . . . in the Fifth Avenue Parade Committee, [but] they were doing over 50 percent of the work. And they began to do that in the Mobe, too. In the Mobe, they were obviously the most effective organizers. They delivered. They delivered on leaflets, they delivered on fund-raising, they delivered on banners, they delivered on sound equipment, they delivered on permits. They knew how to do it. They did the nuts-and-bolts organization. And to me that was the bottom line. If a person did that, he or she was dedicated. . . .
>
> You know, there was a big ego trip going on. A lot of the other people in the movement didn't do it. They weren't interested in it, they wouldn't get their hands dirty. They wouldn't raise money. Good grief, some of these people, they felt they were getting dirty if they asked anybody for money. They were willing to spend it, they wanted the time in front of the TV cameras, but they wouldn't go out and ask anybody for money. That to me was terrible. And I

couldn't take those people seriously. And the Trotskyists couldn't take them seriously. So I got along pretty well with the Trotskyists. . . . And I could understand the Trotskyists' position [on wanting to go it alone] completely. . . . I didn't particularly like their vanguard party approach and their tight discipline and their manipulation—which was gut-curdling—but, boy, I respected their efficiency. Because to me it really meant that they were serious revolutionaries. [121]

Some Mobe leaders were also thinking about a divorce. Without the SWP to contend with, they could organize not only massive civil disobedience against the war but the multi-issue radical movement that many had long desired—and that now seemed a very real possibility. "We thought we were ready in terms of numbers of people," David McReynolds recalled. "There was an excitement." Some black groups were simultaneously pressuring the Mobe to target the war's economic effects on the black community. Not least impelling, many Mobe activists were simply fed up with the SWP's gladiatorial approach to coalition work. "It just got to be impossible to function any more," Dowd recalled. "Every time that there would be a convention or steering committee meeting, they would have two or three hundred people thrown in as ringers, with all these phony organizations. . . . So we started trying to go it alone."[122]

To build bridges to blacks, the Mobe met in May at the Atlanta headquarters of the Southern Christian Leadership Conference, where its leaders agreed to call for an "Emergency Action Conference" in late June "for developing a unifying offensive in the face of the deepening interrelated crises of race, war, and the economy." A strategy for "stepped-up, massive, disciplined direct actions" was to have been a "major focus," but in June the conferees proved unable to agree on a definite plan. [123] They decided to hold regional meetings over the summer to further deliberate and organize support.

The June meeting in Cleveland called by the SWP gave birth to the National Peace Action Coalition (NPAC). This new SWP front group would concentrate on building—what else?—legal, peaceful, single-issue antiwar demonstrations. It called for protests on October 31.

For all practical purposes, the Mobe was now dead. Rather than allowing elements of the coalition to organize and control actions of their choosing, thereby maintaining the strength that comes from broad-based unity, it had split into hostile camps. Like many divorces, the split entailed hard feelings. "It was a bitter period," Dowd remembered. "A sign of the tensions that existed was that my mere presence at a workshop led by Sid Peck [at the Emergency Action Conference] was so disturbing to him that he asked me to leave the room, which I did," Halstead writes. The split also entailed some regret. "I was sorry," Dellinger recalled. "There were old people that I'd worked with, like Fred Halstead . . . and others, who, whatever our differences in politics, and with the exception of a few times like the Cambodian thing . . . for about five years . . . we'd worked together profitably. So that was kind of sad." Dellinger felt the split was for the better, though. "The movement had become so big and the sections so energetic that . . . even though we could possibly set up an atmosphere in those meetings of some fraternity/sorority, it was almost impossible . . . to . . . carry that into other things," he said. "So . . . it had a certain logic." The coalition "had outlived its usefulness." Halstead later voiced a different opinion on the breach, however. "It was unnecessary," he told the author. "Shouldn't have happened. We could have lived with one another. . . . It's true we couldn't have lived with the total crazies—they had to go. But we could have lived with the pacifists and massive civil disobedience."[124]

The Mobe's fracture fueled the growing sense of powerlessness in the movement. It also sent all the wrong signals to the warmakers. "When the coalition divided, that gave them more room," Sidney Peck said. "So by the fall of 1970 the administration was once again on the offensive. You know, clearly at that point thinking about tactics to escalate the war."[125]

After the Storm

The summer saw a decline in visible antiwar activity. The national student strike sputtered out as the school year drew to a close. Other campus protests also ebbed with the summer student exodus. But many peace activists continued to lobby Congress. Others leafleted workplaces in the waning hope of fostering a general strike against the war. Antidraft protests, including sit-ins at draft boards, the destruction of draft files, and a national draft-card turn-in, persisted. Demonstrators greeted President Nixon in Los Angeles; the day before the protest, Ron Walker, the head of the White House's advance team, advised Haldeman that if Nixon walked past the demonstrators "it would be embarrassing to the President and it would lend itself to wide television and press coverage." Two days later more than twenty thousand protesters turned out for a National Chicano Moratorium demonstration in Los Angeles. Other activists continued to engage in grass-roots organizing in hundreds of communities across the United States; many placed ads in newspapers. Mobe organizers pulled together regional planning conferences in more than a dozen cities. Eighteen-year-old Miss Montana returned her crown rather than assent to the demands of Miss America pageant officials that she stop criticizing the war.[126]

The Weathermen were hardly silent. On June 9—nineteen days after issuing an underground communiqué promising to attack "a symbol or institution of Amerikan injustice" within two weeks—they audaciously bombed the New York City Police Department's headquarters, inflicting heavy damage. It was their first publicly acknowledged bombing. Seven weeks later, they exploded a pipe bomb at the entrance to a Bank of America building in Manhattan. "Don't look for us, Dog; We'll find you first," they warned Attorney General Mitchell the day before the blast. [127] Among the targets of later Weatherman bombings were the Long Island Court House, Capitol building, Pentagon, and State Department. Pensively, the Weatherleader Bill Ayers explained the Weathermen's motivations:

> We felt that we were building one part of a revolutionary
> movement. . . . And we saw the bombings as . . . one type of ac-
> tivity that would both build up the underground capacity—build up
> our ability to do illegal work—and also build up our reputation, I
> guess, and our influence in the movement. And I guess we thought
> that the targets that we picked were targets that were . . . related to
> stopping the war . . . supporting the black liberation movement
> and . . . retaliating when we felt that the movement was attacked and
> couldn't retaliate. . . .
> We felt that the [bombings of] antiwar targets were very effective.
> We had a lot of kind of formal as well as informal feedback. . . .
> We felt they were effective because we felt that they were popular
> and . . . condemned roundly by the Establishment and by the gov-
> ernment and by the FBI. And we felt that they [demonstrated] . . .
> that things are possible, that you can get away with a lot. . . . [We
> also felt they] played a role in limiting the options that this govern-
> ment had in how much terror they could rain on Vietnam. [128]

Weathermen were adapting to their new underground habitat. After scurrying for cover following the townhouse explosion, Ayers recalled, they "very quickly" developed

> an understanding that the way to survive underground, the strength
> of being underground, is if you have a base of support. And the base
> of support that we had was the youth movement. . . . We were very
> much a part of it. We lived very open lives. We only changed a detail
> here and there. I mean, we always changed our name. If you had
> very short hair, you might grow your hair long. If you didn't have a
> beard, you might grow a beard. If you had long hair, you might cut
> it short. But, basically, we were recognized *often* underground. *Of-
> ten*. And we were not turned in. Now, occasionally, someone was
> turned in. . . . Judy Clark was recognized in a theater in New York.
> But there were eight of us with her when she was arrested, and we
> weren't arrested. I was with her. She did a very smart thing: she was
> asked to step into the lobby, and she ran down Second Avenue, or
> wherever we were, and the rest of us went out the fire door. But the
> point is that we had a base of support that we felt was reliable. We
> lived quietly in apartments. We worked jobs. But we had a political

structure and a political organization and we did political work. And some of the political work we did on the job. I mean, I worked in a lot of different jobs, and I always was very much who I am, but without the name and without the organization. I believed in certain things, I organized for certain things. And we found life underground therefore to be full, and not frightening, and not isolating. We found it to be full and engaging and enriching. . . . There was a lot of different close calls, but more [important] than the close calls was a sense that we were part of a youth culture—and it was very widespread—and within that culture people really didn't want to see us get arrested.

The Weathermen felt "if we could just survive, let alone do anything," Ayers said, then "that in itself was a strong statement about . . . what was possible." By the end of the summer, Weathermen had apparently adapted well to life underground. "All I ever want to do is smoke dope and make revolution," Jeff Jones dreamily told Abbie Hoffman during a secret rendezvous in the Nevada desert. [129]

The Nixon administration was apparently *not* adapting well to this new underground army. John Ehrlichman vividly remembered "the difficulty we were having in securing information about what they were doing, and in there being some kind of a law enforcement response to it. . . . The police departments and the FBI were not very good at enforcing the law, so to speak, in these kinds of [bombing] incidents. And there was a lot of frustration. I was frustrated—a lot of people were frustrated—that the law enforcement people were not getting better results" (despite regularly undertaking illegal break-ins at the homes of Weathermen's friends and relatives). And although Nixon suspected the Weatherman bombings were hurting the peace movement's public image, officials also recognized that they injured the administration by making it seem in doubtful command and feeding public concern over the war's cost in domestic peace. Plus, as Huston and Moynihan had earlier warned, the White House might be the next target. Asked whether he considered the Weatherman bombings "a negative thing," Ehrlichman immediately said yes. He believed Nixon judged them politically harmful as well. [130]

Over the summer, Vietnam Veterans Against the War was growing. Disillusioned with the war, many veterans were also feeling utterly deceived and horribly used. "There was an enormous number of vets out there that were just seething with anger," Joe Urgo, who joined VVAW that spring, recalled. Stoking their anger was their inability to talk to others about what they'd been through in Vietnam. "You couldn't explain to people how you just got through murdering people, that you were nothing more than a murderer, a rapist, a baby killer," Urgo spat. "You couldn't come back to the society—with its bread and circuses, with the 'Beverly Hillbillies'—and tell people, 'This is what we were doing over there.'"[131]

Some VVAWers protested conditions in rat-infested VA hospitals. "You talk about rage," Urgo said. Hospitalized veterans "hated the war, they hated the VA, with an unbelievable passion." VVAW's Jan Barry remembered visiting an army hospital late that summer: "I didn't know what to say. You walk into a ward full of guys in wheelchairs who have got no arms and legs—mad as hell! And you don't know if they're mad at you. But, oh no, they're mad at the government." But the big activity for VVAWers then was "Operation RAW" (Rapid American Withdrawal). By conducting a four-day, simulated search-and-destroy mission between Morristown, New Jersey, and Valley Forge, Pennsylvania, VVAWers thought, they would show Americans what the war was like. "The argument behind this was to bring the war home," remembered Urgo. "To show people the truth . . . in a graphic way."[132]

Some eighty veterans began the ninety-mile trek on September 4. By the time Operation RAW was over, there were a hundred and fifty of them (bearing a hundred and ten Purple Hearts among them). The veterans wore their old jungle combat gear and carried plastic M-16 rifles. A mobile "chow unit" accompanied them. Marching through rural areas and small towns, the veterans conducted "sweeps" and "ambushes," "cordoned" villages, "interrogated" and "shot" "civilians," and distributed leaflets. "A U.S. INFANTRY COMPANY JUST CAME THROUGH HERE!" one leaflet announced. "If you had been Vietnamese— we might have burned your house . . . shot you . . . raped your wife and daughter . . . turned you over to the government for torture. . . . If it doesn't bother you that American soldiers do these things every day to the Vietnamese simply because they are 'Gooks,' *then* picture YOURSELF as one of the silent VICTIMS." A few observers heckled the veterans, but more encouraged them. "All along the route there was significant support for us," Urgo recalled. "People were waving. . . . A lot of people met us by the sides of the roads and came out and gave us food and water and stuff like that. Cars would drive by and fists would come out." In some towns, Barry remembered, "the mayor would come out to greet us." Authorities shadowed the veterans; Barry later saw FBI documents evidencing frequent reports to the White House on the march. Jane Fonda spoke at a concluding rally, as did amputees from a nearby army hospital, at risk of a court martial.[133]

Dissent continued to build among soldiers in the United States. Six major revolts shook army prisons and bases in mid 1970. Aided by civilian supporters, GIs circulated more antiwar newspapers. A peace petition was signed by 1,740 servicemen in the United States and overseas. One of the signatories at Fort Hamilton, David Cortright, was transferred to Fort Bliss for his act and subsequent dissent. "At Fort Bliss they were always checking on me," Cortright remembered. "I was being called in to go speak to this colonel or that colonel for one reason or another. Not to be scolded or disciplined, but to be asked what I was doing." During a big ceremony at Fort Bliss, Cortright, who played in the base's band, was warily eyeballed by the commanding general. "The general almost never came to see the band, so it was like a big event. . . . He walks right by the . . . commander of the band, and comes right up to the front row and . . . says to me, 'So you're Cortright, huh? . . . I just wanted you to know I'm watching.'"[134]

In Vietnam, morale and discipline declined further. In a private letter, forty combat officers warned Nixon in July that U.S. leaders "are perceived by many soldiers to be almost as much our enemy as the VC and the NVA." If the war persisted, they warned, "young Americans in the military will simply refuse en masse to cooperate." Drug use was now rampant. There was "a grave heroin epidemic." "The issue of drugs . . . surfaced right after the Cambodian invasion," Secretary of the Army Stanley Resor recalled. After returning from a tour of Vietnam then, "I remember . . . recommending that we should continue to acccelerate withdrawals," Resor said, "and that was really to work with the [drug] problem over there." He thought he was "pushing on an open door," however, "because Mel Laird . . . was at all times pushing for accelerated withdrawals." Nevertheless, Laird announced on July 9 that U.S. troop cutbacks would be quickened. Egil Krogh, who was tracking drug use in the military, advised abolishing the draft to alleviate the problem.[135]

A civilian American dissident in Vietnam was also troubling the administration at this time. Don Luce, a World Council of Churches worker and teacher in Saigon's College of Agriculture, was acting on behalf of South Vietnamese political prisoners incarcerated in the state's largest civilian prison on Con Son island. "It started when one of my students got arrested and I went over to the prison," the bearded, friendly Luce recounted. "The students had told me to take a bottle of whiskey, and I had taken a bottle of Johnny Walker Red. And the head of the prison gate gave me back my student in exchange for the bottle of whiskey—but also told me that he really liked Marlboro cigarettes also. . . . Then every time a student would get arrested they started coming to me. And I . . . would use my PX card to buy cigarettes and whiskey . . . take them to the prison director and get the students out." In late May, on its own, the South Vietnamese government released five students from the prison. The students had been confined in a "tiger cage"—a steamy, dark, filthy stone compartment measuring only 5' by 9'—with their legs shackled and held high to a metal rod. They were sick, severely malnourished, and unable to walk. "The idea was to make them an example to other students—'This is what happens when you get involved in student demonstrations,'" Luce said. But the students chose to use their plight to rally opposition to the government. Luce remembered:

They decided that they wanted to put themselves on display at the
university. And I was the only teacher at the university who was
willing to request a room, because the Vietnamese teachers would
have just been sent to the tiger cages too. But here was this weird
American who would. So I asked for the anatomy lab for that
weekend. . . . They just put themselves on the long benches, and the
students came through, and talked to them. So it just became complete chaos; like maybe ten thousand students were gathered there.
So then the police came and threw tear gas. Then we carried these
students off to my apartment, because that was a fairly safe place.

Afterward, the students wrote a report on conditions at Con Son. Luce and a
Quaker friend translated it and sent copies to hundreds of newspapers in the
United States.[136]

While Luce was stapling pages of the report together in the middle of one
night in early July, Thomas Harkin, an aide to a congressional committee then
touring South Vietnam, paid him a visit. Harkin asked Luce if he could arrange
a meeting with South Vietnamese student leaders. Luce replied that he would
have to go to the tiger cages, as that's where they were. Harkin, Luce, and two
members of the committee then flew out to Con Son. Aided by maps student
leaders had drawn showing how to get in between walls of the prison to get to
the hidden cages—and against the will of a U.S. official present—the group
managed to reach the stone pits and snap photographs. One of the congressmen
called the conditions "the worst I've ever seen." The group's exposé of the tiger
cages received considerable publicity in the United States and overseas, embarrassing the Nixon administration. When asked about it, Press Secretary Ronald
Ziegler refused to discuss it. One week after the story broke, the South Vietnamese government announced it was releasing five hundred prisoners from
Con Son. After Luce later revealed that a Houston construction consortium (co-
owned by Lady Bird Johnson) was making 284 more tiger cages under contract
with the U.S. government, he was kicked out of Vietnam.[137]

Worried that the invasion of Cambodia meant Nixon was going to go for
broke, Daniel Ellsberg was consumed that summer with the thought that releasing the Pentagon Papers might help block the escalation. He continued to
approach prominent politicians and journalists, to no avail. In August, just before he was to go back east to marry Patricia Marx, Ellsberg bumped into Lloyd
Shearer, the editor of *Parade* magazine, in Los Angeles. Shearer was headed off
to San Clemente to see Henry Kissinger. Ellsberg asked if he could go along.
Maybe he could persuade Kissinger directly that escalation wouldn't work, Ellsberg mused. "At that point, I didn't have the sense of revulsion at the thought
of meeting him, which I did acquire later," he recalled. When Shearer phoned
San Clemente, however, Kissinger said he would "under no circumstances" see

Ellsberg. "He's a madman," Kissinger said. "He likes to argue." When Shearer persisted, however, Kissinger gave in: "All right, Lloyd, we'll stick him with Al [Haig]."[138]

As Ellsberg was waiting in an outer office at San Clemente, large photos of Nixon lining one wall, he glimpsed the president driving a pink golf cart, "scowling, and looking very grim. His shoulders were hunched over and he was piloting this thing like the engineer of a toy train. Right behind him was another pink golf cart driven by Bebe Rebozo." When Kissinger appeared, Shearer quickly brought up the war. "We are not here to talk about Vietnam," Kissinger responded, looking "quite nervously" at Ellsberg. He began drumming the table with his fingers. Suddenly, Kissinger said, "Tell you what, Dan, why don't you and General Haig have lunch together while we talk on other matters, then we will all get together." When Kissinger saw Ellsberg again after lunch, he got rid of him without a discussion.[139]

No More Appeasement

In the White House that summer, U.S. policymakers were "spent from the trauma of Cambodia" and suffering from "psychological exhaustion," Kissinger reveals. "Fear of another round of demonstrations permeated all the thinking about Vietnam in the Executive Branch that summer—even that of Nixon, who pretended to be impervious." The president's mood on Vietnam "oscillated wildly," Kissinger writes. One day he was talking about hanging tough, the next the war simply had to be ended: he would end it by combining massive bombing of North Vietnam and a blockade with total U.S withdrawal. Kissinger cautioned Nixon that "in view of the trouble we had" following Cambodia, that option was not politically feasible.[140]

Administration officials continued to feel "under siege" from antiwar critics. To weaken the attack, Jeb Magruder advocated appealing to "uncommitted, moderate and liberal youth" through "a low key presence on campus" and in the media. Students would thereby have "an opportunity to grasp an intelligent alternative to the nonsense of the New Left," Magruder wrote Haldeman on July 24. Aware of Haldeman's distaste for trying to reason with discontented youth, Magruder warned him that "even if we write them off politically because their numbers do not mean anything vote wise, we cannot write them off because of their impact on public opinion." And a policy of assuagement would have the "incidental benefit" of "isolating the Far Left." Magruder proposed setting up a "White House Youth Office" to coordinate the policy. This office would "service" youth partly by giving them "someone to 'talk to' which is what they're always wanting." Its head would be "young . . . articulate, presentable, informed, 'cool,' and well dressed."[141]

Magruder's advice fell on deaf ears. For as the domestic clamor over Cambodia and Kent State subsided, "the President reverted to his basic belief that there was more political advantage in isolating his campus critics than in trying to win them over," Magruder recalled. This sentiment was reinforced by a new book by Richard Scammon and Ben Wattenberg entitled *The Real Majority*, which argued that the prototypical American voter was a 45-year-old Dayton housewife who was married to a machinist and who most worried about rising crime, blacks, demonstrators, and permissiveness. Thus, it maintained, Democrats had to reduce their appeals to youth, blacks, and the poor to win the 1970 and 1972 elections. Nixon felt the book's analysis was right on the money and would be useful in the fall congressional campaigns. In an August 24 memo from his aide Pat Buchanan, the president underlined Buchanan's statement that Democrats "must be branded—and the brand must stick—as permissivists, as indulgent of students and black rioters, as soft on crime"—that is, as "ultraliberals." Nixon also underlined Buchanan's advice that the administration should charge that "the Democratic Leadership has altered its foreign policy position to kow-tow to student radicals who bully-ragged those same leaders in the streets of Chicago, etc." Three weeks later, Ehrlichman's notes of a meeting with the president read, "Soft on students is the issue. *Any* students. . . . Administration is being read by the country as 'too soft on students.'" Nixon by then felt "very strongly" that campus unrest was "an issue we can make a lot of gain on," Haldeman informed Ehrlichman; in fact, it was "the key issue of the campaign."[142]

To help isolate opponents of the war, the White House engineered an "Honor America Day" rally in Washington on July 4. It conducted a telephone and propaganda campaign "to make sure we got a maximum turnout," Magruder discloses. During the rally, attended by fifty thousand people, Magruder repeatedly phoned Haldeman and Dwight Chapin "to let them know how large the crowd was and how it was responding." The event was marred by disruptive acts by hundreds of longhairs, some of whom waded noisily in the reflecting pool toward the Lincoln Memorial, where Reverend Billy Graham was addressing the crowd. Under White House–induced pressure, CBS covered the rally's entertainment live.[143]

The administration was then moving to set up another prowar front group. The immediate goal of "Americans for Winning the Peace" (AWP) was defeating the McGovern-Hatfield amendment. AWP's long-term goal was more ambitious. By "forming an outside support group to carry the fight for us on Hatfield/McGovern," Charles Colson wrote Haldeman, "hopefully we are building a permanent support apparatus around the country so that we will not have to go to our same old backers everytime we need help." Nixon put Colson in charge of the project. "It is a matter of the absolutely highest priority and we've got to move quickly and effectively," Haldeman directed other White

House staffers on July 14. Haldeman wanted "weekly reports" on AWP. Over the summer, Colson hammered out a "battle plan" for the committee with Gene Bradley, a businessman who had agreed to serve as its director. Colson also came up with money to pay the salaries of AWP officers and tried unsuccessfully to coax ex-President Lyndon Johnson to serve as an honorary co-chairman of the committee. The Johnson administration's Walt Rostow, who knew a thing or two about prowar front groups, advised the White House on the operation. By mid August there were fledgling AWP committees in twenty-five cities. The White House had to hide its ties to the group to maximize growth; many people said they'd join "only with the understanding that this activity is separate and distinct from the U.S. government," Bradley reported. Nixon phoned regional AWP leaders to stimulate their work. The AWP developed newspaper ads, letter and telegram campaigns, newspaper commentaries, and TV programs.[144]

It was a two-pronged offensive. While AWP "is to be the high level group that takes a positive line," Colson informed Haldeman on August 12, the White House's Tell It to Hanoi front group would "go . . . on the attack." Tell It to Hanoi smeared McGovern-Hatfield as "the surrender amendment." This "hardball attack," Herb Klein later wrote, "was developed and secretly directed by Colson and his staff." Colson also organized an "attack group" of senators, with Robert Dole (R-Kans.) serving as their "team captain."[145]

Bradley deemed "phase 1" of AWP's work a "success" when McGovern-Hatfield was defeated. So did the White House. "Damn Good," Haldeman praised Colson on September 8. Five months later, when anonymous officials told reporters that AWP was sponsored by the White House, Colson claimed that the administration "has not in any sense been the sponsor or moving force behind this group." Bradley, he said, had approached him in November (four months after the operation had started, it will be noted), and he was "only too happy to accommodate them."[146]

On September 21, in his own special way, J. Edgar Hoover tried again to reason with discontented youth. "You do have ideas of your own—and that's good," Hoover wrote in "An Open Letter to College Students." "You are outspoken and frank and hate hypocrisy. That is good too." But, Hoover warned, there were "extremists" on campuses who "have no rational, intelligent plan of the future" and "will try to lure you into their activities." "Based on our experience in the FBI," Hoover alerted students, there were many ways these extremists would try to ensnare them. "They'll encourage you to lose respect for your parents . . . trying to cut you off from home," Hoover counseled. "They'll ask you to abandon your basic common sense. . . . They'll try to envelope you in a mood of negativism. . . . They'll encourage you to . . . hate the law enforcement officer. . . . He is your friend." Nixon was impressed by Hoover's letter and directed his aides to distribute it nationwide under his stamp of approval.[147]

One week earlier, FBI agents attending a bureau conference on the New Left in Philadelphia were urged to step up their interviews of dissenters "for plenty of reasons, chief of which are it will enhance the paranoia endemic in these circles and will further serve to get the point across that there is an FBI agent behind every mailbox."[148]

Decline

Also in September, representatives of the Mobe's summer regional meetings and national peace groups met in Milwaukee. They formed the National Coalition Against War, Racism and Repression (NCAWRR). Many activists soon belittlingly referred to NCAWRR as the "coalition against everything." Even some of its organizers were unexcited about it. "It took on such a wide range of stuff that there was no clear focus," Sidney Peck remembered. "I felt that had blurred our opposition to the war to some extent." NCAWRR's fall agenda included demonstrations in support of jailed Black Panthers and welfare rights, multi-issue community organizing, and antiwar protests. As Dave Dellinger writes, many groups in NCAWRR "put only limited energy into its programs, preferring to 'go it alone' organizationally." Doug Dowd recalled that there was "real notable" and "increasing difficulty in holding the coalition together. . . . Each of the groups in the coalition increasingly became insistent that its position, its path, its goals, had to be primary. It got to the point where it came to be kind of a bad joke, you know, where you couldn't have a demonstration without having thirty-five speakers, and the only kind of position you could get any kind of agreement on was watered down or stupid." And "once you finally gave in, so to speak, and got agreement from two hundred different groups . . . then nobody would go out and organize for the fucking demonstration. . . . So you've got more people at the fucking organizing meeting than at the demonstration." It "became very, very difficult to move an inch," Dowd said. The antiwar leader felt the mounting sectarianism in the movement "was like a bunch of fucking vultures over a carcass. . . . They were making a carcass out of something that had been alive."[149]

Rennie Davis was then trying to garner support for a massive civil disobedience action in Washington early the next May if the war persisted. NCAWRR agreed to help build the "May Day" protest. In New York, activists were pressuring the city council to adopt a resolution to "Take New York City Out of the War—Now!" The campaign gained little momentum. In several other cities, activists campaigned for antiwar referenda. The referenda passed. VVAWers were meanwhile planning national hearings on American war crimes in Vietnam. They wanted to show that My Lai and other atrocities were not isolated incidents, but logical results of U.S. policies. The veterans debated whether to work with the Citizens Commission to Investigate War Crimes, which wanted to hold the hearings before Congress. "Some people in VVAW from the Midwest argued, 'No, it really ought to be out there in middle America,'" Jan Barry recalled. "'Everything's been directed at Congress for years, and what have those fuddy-duddies ever done? If we take it out to middle America and we shake up middle America, *they'll* shake up Congress.'" VVAW decided to hold the hearings in Detroit early the next year. They dubbed them the "Winter Soldier Investigation," a reference to Tom Paine's 1776 statement about "summer soldiers" who shrink from duty during crises. Jane Fonda promoted the hearings.[150]

The antiwar demonstrations called by the SWP-controlled National Peace Action Coalition on October 31 were small. Aware now that they couldn't organize massive demonstrations on their own, SWPers urged NCAWRR to participate in an NPAC conference on December 4. Peck and the handful of other NCAWRR leaders who attended requested that NPAC refrain from setting a date for the next spring's antiwar demonstrations until a NCAWRR meeting in early January so the coalition could shape the decision. NPAC refused. It issued a call for peaceful, legal demonstrations on April 24. "They were constantly setting dates and then compelling the rest of the movement to [go along]," Peck disdainfully recalled. "That was their big thing." This date had special significance—it would limit participation in the May Day civil disobedience, the SWP schemed, since few people would stay in Washington two weekends in a row.[151]

The autumn witnessed another wave of bombings. On October 7, in a tape-recorded message, Bernardine Dohrn announced a "fall offensive." "We are everywhere and next week families and tribes will attack the enemy around the country," Dohrn warned. "Guard Your Children, Guard Your Doors." Early the following morning, bombs rocked three buildings on the West Coast, inflicting extensive damage; another bomb was dismantled by police before exploding. John Mitchell called those responsible "psychopaths"; the next day, John Ehrlichman discussed both the bombings and Mitchell's statement with Nixon: "Send [FBI] agents," Ehrlichman's notes read. "Start investigating." In late November, Dohrn's leadership of Weatherman earned her a spot on the FBI's Ten Most Wanted list.[152] Nine days later, she issued another underground communiqué. "We want to express ourselves to the mass movement not as military leaders, but as tribes at council," she proclaimed. Dohrn criticized Weatherman for concentrating exclusively on armed struggle while neglecting mass organizing. "This tendency to consider only bombings or picking up the gun as revolutionary, with the glorification of the heavier the better, we've called the military error," Dohrn avowed. One White House official felt the communiqué might "signal a shift in tactics by certain revolutionary groups on the left," although it was "too early to project any significant trends in this regard." John Dean, who had recently been appointed presidential counsel, sent a copy of it to Assistant Attorney General William Rehnquist, offering, "I think you will find it a most interesting document."[153]

America's campuses were relatively quiet that fall. The sharp contrast with the previous spring "astonished almost all observers." Behind the calm lay widespread political pessimism. As Dellinger wrote, the antiwar movement was still "struggling to overcome the feelings of frustration and despair that have gripped people after they discovered that neither a million people in the streets (November 1969) nor several hundred schools and colleges on strike (May 1970) altered Washington's determination" to win the war. Protesters' frustration mounted in mid November when Nixon ordered two days of intense bombing of North Vietnam, including population centers. Concomitant with the bombing, U.S. commandos undertook a bold but unfruitful raid on Son Tay prison, twenty-three miles west of Hanoi. Nixon authorized the raid despite concern it would provoke a repeat of the spring uproar. "Christ, they surrounded the White House, remember?" he reminded other officials. "This time they will probably knock down the gates and I'll have a thousand incoherent hippies urinating on the Oval Office rug." Many protesters feared the bombing and Son Tay raid meant Nixon was poised to go for broke. "I thought, 'Now we're getting hot here, we're on the way,'" Daniel Ellsberg recalled. "We were getting pretty close to invasion [of North Vietnam]—that's what I was mainly worrying about . . . along with a total renewal of bombing. . . . I thought, 'These are the final hours. We're going to be escalating any time now.'"[154]

Domestic opposition to the war was continuing to inhibit the administration, however. "The fact of the matter is that we were continually trying to calm down the opposition—in Congress, the press, and the demonstrations, the academic circles—by making unilateral concessions," Marshall Green remembered. "We were not going to invade the North. We were not going to bomb the dikes . . . or try to topple the government."[155]

Radical Liberals, Terrorists, and Thugs

Throughout the autumn the White House took a hard public line on youthful unrest. An unshackled Spiro Agnew toured the country blasting protesters and their Democratic supporters. "Will America be led by a President elected by a majority of the American people," the vice president asked, "or will we be intimidated and blackmailed into following the path dictated by a disruptive, radical, and militant minority—the pampered prodigies of the radical liberals in the United States Senate?" Agnew called demonstrators who greeted him at one stop "pathetic" and "intellectually stagnant." After being harassed by "misfits" at another, he declared that it was "time to sweep that kind of garbage out of our society" and "get them out of our hair." Agnew compared the protesters to the "anti-social elements" who used to clog the doorways of Manhattan's Bowery but now "lie any place they can find."[156]

In a speech at Kansas State University, Nixon condemned the "cancerous disease" of "violence and terror" that was "spreading over the world and here in the United States" through "bombings and burnings on our campuses" and "wanton shootings of policemen." The carriers of this disease "deserve the contempt of every American," Nixon asserted. The president denounced the "passive acquiescence" or "fawning approval" of the terrorism by those "in some fashionable circles." After the speech, the administration's Americans for Winning the Peace front group distributed copies of it to campuses.[157]

Nixon ordered White House propagandists to keep up the drumbeat against protesters. "The President has expressed a keen interest in our doing all we can to sustain our line on campus unrest which was laid so well in the Kansas speech," Egil Krogh wrote other officials a week later.[158] Nixon knew one way to sustain the drumbeat was to "go all out for" a piece of hard-line legislation. Thus, on September 22, the administration proposed amendments authorizing the immediate dispatch of FBI agents to campuses that had experienced bombings; no requests from university officials were necesssary. Nixon asked for a thousand additional agents to do the job. "The President wants some action on his frequently repeated instruction that there should be something coming out every day for public consumption on the issue of law and order, control of crime, tough actions against bombings, etc.," Haldeman simultaneously informed Krogh and Magruder, who set up a task force to feed the public. When Professor Sidney Hook of New York University wrote an article rebuking protesters, Nixon had copies of it sent to "some 1,000 VIPs" and wrote a laudatory letter, which he ordered "leaked and used as a major news item."[159]

Campaigning for Republican senatorial candidates, Nixon delivered a standard law-and-order speech lambasting foul-mouthed demonstrators and murderers of policemen and calling on the "silent majority" to "speak up for America." The demonstrators and the murderers were allied with the Democrats, Nixon said; the decent Americans were with him. Thus, "the campaign was not a contest between candidates looking for votes—it was a contest between criminals, on the one hand, and the voters, on the other," Jonathan Schell comments. At each of Nixon's stops, White House advance men allowed protesters, "in carefully measured strength" (as the *Washington Post* observed), into the areas where he was speaking. Their numbers were not great enough to disrupt the rallies, but sufficient to serve as a foil for Nixon's condemnations of those who "shout obscenities" and "will not listen." The White House military aide Bill Gulley, who participated in the planning of all of Nixon's trips, divulges that Dwight Chapin and Ron "Roadrunner" Walker "would often plan what means they'd use to 'sucker in' the crowd . . . and put the protesters in the worst possible light. It was standard for them to tell [the] Secret Service to let any particularly unsavory-looking characters get close enough to the President so the news media would pick them up." John Ehrlichman recalled that Nixon felt ugly personal encounters with demonstrators helped his cause, although, overall, antiwar disorder was harmful. "He wanted to have it appear that these violent people were pitted against him . . . that he was not afraid and that he was standing up to them and so on," Ehrlichman said. The White House knew its stage-managing of protests would inevitably produce a tumultuous encounter with the demonstrators. Chapin wrote Walker in a CONFIDENTIAL memorandum just as Nixon was embarking on the tour:

> As Haldeman points out, it is not going to be long until we have a confrontation with the demonstrators and we probably should be thinking of how it is going to happen, where it should happen, and what we are going to do when it does happen. All of our advance men should be told to be sure to play it cool and that we just ride our way through it. The President, under a crisis situation, has the best instincts and we must be very careful to let him handle the situation and not to have the advance men jump into it and create an incident. [160]

The confrontation came in San Jose, California, the evening of October 29.

Before Nixon's speech that night, reporters had been told "there might be some sort of trouble," Schell writes. "They noticed, too, that police barricades to hold back demonstrators outside the auditorium were unusually close to the motorcade route." According to the *Post*, the Secret Service had ordered buses and trucks placed so that the president's limousine had no choice but to "run the gauntlet of a hostile crowd." Inside the auditorium, after finishing his speech, Nixon was "almost certainly" advised by the Secret Service that "the situation was dangerous" outside. But after exiting the building and talking to Secret Service agents for a minute, Nixon suddenly mounted the hood of his limousine, faced the crowd, smiled and raised both hands in a V-sign. "That's what they hate to see!" he said to no one in particular. Predictably, thrown objects and epithets followed. According to the columnists Rowland Evans and Robert Novak, White House aides were "jubilant." But Ehrlichman and Haldeman had a different recollection. They said things got out of control. "Judging by the post [incident] reaction in the White House to that episode," Ehrlichman recalled, "that was certainly not anything that anybody wanted to have happen." Haldeman said: "If it were eggs [being thrown], that would be one thing. It was rocks, and he had no interest in seeing them throw rocks at people, at the press bus, or his limo or anybody else." Still, Gulley considers it "well within the realm of possibility" that the affair was "rigged," given "how the Nixon advance team worked." "It was the kind of thing that was often discussed at pre-trip meetings," he says. [161]

The White House immediately moved to exploit the incident for political advantage. "The next morning Haldeman called my office with orders that we stress [it] in every possible way over the weekend," Magruder writes. Haldeman directed Magruder to distribute a statement calling it "the most severe attack on a President since the assassination of John Kennedy." Ronald Ziegler, a former Disneyland tour guide, gave reporters "an inch-by-inch, scratch-by-scratch tour of the President's supposedly battered limousine." Nixon called the incident "an example of the viciousness of the lawless elements in our society." In preparation for other public statements, Ehrlichman advised the president to "impart, first-hand, the run-amok violence inflicted on 'innocent Americans. . . . ' You can tell those of us who really don't know how it feels to be there the sheer fury and mindlessness and disregard for life and decency that is the essence of such an event. You can make the point that . . . press photographers in the open pool cars were hit not by rocks but by small boulders (show them how big they were with your hands)." Nixon should also follow the example of his son-in-law, David Eisenhower, who "referred to this as 'fascism' the other day," Ehrlichman counseled. "He's a student of history and knows how the Weimar Republic fell."[162]

The next morning in Phoenix, Nixon decried the "mob of about a thousand haters" he had confronted in San Jose. "We could see the hate in their faces as we drove into the hall, and in the obscene signs they waved," he related. "We could hear the hate in their voices as they chanted their obscenities. . . . The haters surged past the barricades and began throwing rocks. Not small stones— large rocks." Nixon reported that the many "decent citizens" who "brought their children" to the rally "were terrified." He stressed that the haters were not simply "romantic revolutionaries, but the same thugs and hoodlums that have always plagued a good people." Tougher laws were required to put these "terrorists where they belong—not roaming around civil society, but behind bars." Nixon also assured the public that "no band of violent thugs is going to keep me from going out and speaking with the American people." Afterward, Herb Klein passed copies of the speech to Republican senatorial candidates, saying, "I am sure you will find [it] a vital reference work."[163]

Reporters accused the White House of both inciting and exaggerating the disturbance in San Jose for political effect. The White House's machinations were an "insult to the intelligence," said the *Post*, which noted that only one of three top police officials on the scene recalled seeing any rocks thrown. Several journalists said they had left San Jose "thinking they had witnessed a minor incident."[164]

As Nixon and Agnew were linking Democrats to antiwar terrorists through speeches, Charles Colson was doing so through newspaper ads. For this enterprise, the official utilized a record compiled by aides of speeches by Democrats that were "very sympathetic to student radicals and revolutionaries." "We've got to show that their rhetoric over recent years has encouraged the kind of attitude of permissiveness that has allowed the revolutionaries to hold sway among the moderate students," Colson wrote a White House speechwriter. Colson's ads questioned not only Democrats' patriotism and morality, but their manhood.[165]

Fueling the White House's hard public line against protesters that fall was awareness that the peace movement was faltering and thereby vulnerable to attack. According to William Rogers, Nixon had "defused" the Vietnam issue. Haldeman recalled perceiving that the movement "had been significantly weakened." Yet officials recognized that it could by no means be written off. As Magruder told Haldeman, "trouble" was likely on the campuses after the election period was over.[166] The White House thus continued to take a host of other measures to counteract the movement.

In September the president ordered Magruder to formulate a game plan for blunting the NPAC demonstrations on October 31. The White House political hit man Lyn Nofziger spearheaded the planning; his recommendations, however, are classified. Days later, Haldeman and Nixon directed Colson to "mobilize the Silent Majority." Colson continued to work with the United Student Alliance on prowar propaganda. His aide George Bell enthusiastically wrote of USA President Charles Stephens, "It looks to me like we have a very effective guy." So effective, felt Nixon, that he should come work directly for the White House. "Frankly, I think we'd be better off financing his activities on the outside," Colson advised. "He is worth a lot more to us as an independent orator." Stephens stayed on the outside.[167]

Colson planned a national conference of leaders of Americans for Winning the Peace. Although he implored that Nixon address this "blue ribbon group" and "hard core of our support apparatus around the country," the president worried his participation would make AWP seem "too much our creature" and declined.[168]

The administration took steps to prevent "anticipated" acts of political terrorism, including attempted assassinations, kidnappings, and assaults on officials by Weatherman, the Black Panthers, and other revolutionary groups. After being advised that the White House had "no overall strategy or firm grip on the subject," Ehrlichman approved the formation of a task force to map countermeasures. Also, J. Edgar Hoover circulated a memo warning officials that "the possibility of abduction or assault is a real and present danger" and prescribing a quite remarkable series of "precautionary measures," including:

> Be alert to the repeated presence of strangers, loiterers and vehicles at the office, residence or while in travel status. . . .
> Travel should be confined if at all possible to main thoroughfares and limited to daylight hours. Unsafe locations, unknown areas, and those of potential unrest should be avoided. Doors to vehicles should be locked at all times. Avoid traveling alone. . . .
> . . . Every effort should be made to vary the pattern of living.

Adopting a routine with respect to business and social activities should be avoided. . . .

Information concerning travel, appointment schedules, et cetera, should be restricted to those who have a need to know and the number of individuals in this category should be limited.

The family or office should be aware of the official's whereabouts at all times. . . . On-person transmitters and receivers should be considered under certain circumstances.

Avoid wherever possible appearances before unfriendly elements. . . .

. . . Consideration should be given to the utilization of bodyguards and escorts. . . . Particular attention should be afforded screening and training of such personnel.

Office space and residences should be thoroughly checked by experienced security personnel. Particular emphasis should be placed on the residence insuring that there be adequate outside lighting and that all means of ingress can be effectively locked. . . .

. . . A simple code should be devised so that any member of the family may be alerted if one of the family is being held under duress and forced to make contact by telephone or otherwise.

Background of all servants or household personnel should be thoroughly checked.

. . . Consideration should be given to securing finger and palm prints for identification purposes from top echelon officials and their families. Along these lines a current photograph should be readily available (both portrait and full length front and side views). Dental charts and accurate physical descriptive data should be on file. Hair sample should likewise be on file.[169]

On November 27, Hoover warned the nation of a particularly despicable plot by the terrorists. A group of Catholic militants led by Fathers Philip and Daniel Berrigan planned to "blow up underground electrical conduits and steam pipes" in Washington, Hoover announced. The plotters were also "concocting a scheme to kidnap a highly placed Government official." The official, the Justice Department later revealed, was Henry Kissinger. (Kissinger informed Nixon that if he *was* kidnapped the government should "meet no demands of the kidnappers," and that "if you should receive any communication from me to the contrary, you should assume that it was made under duress.") Although Hoover's accusation evoked laughter in many circles, Philip Berrigan didn't take it lightly. "I thought something was afoot," he recalled. In prison, Berrigan had recently come to suspect that a fellow inmate might be passing information on him to the government. "I got a feeling that something strange was going on," he said, "and I had nothing more to do with him." It turned out that the inmate, a paid FBI informant and agent provocateur, was setting him up "in order to save his own hide," Berrigan said. "They [had] threatened him with another five years for carrying contraband into the penitentiary." Two months later, Berrigan and the others were indicted on conspiracy charges. Berrigan feared the government might actually make the charges stick. "I had to get my mind ready for the possibility of being in jail the rest of my life," he remembered. The case was dropped in April 1971, but Justice later filed another indictment against Berrigan and six others focusing on their antidraft activities. That case ended in a mistrial (the government's cause was not helped when the father of its only witness, the FBI informant, remarked that his son had "told so many lies practically all his life that I can't believe anything he says").[170]

Despite Hoover's veto of the Huston Plan, the White House had not given up on the notion of establishing one body for coordinating its intelligence activities against protesters. In early December, it set up the "Intelligence Evaluation Committee." The IEC was chaired by the Justice Department's Robert ("Crazy Bob") Mardian, a high-strung and abrasive man of "dogmatic," "very far right" political views with an "Armenian sort of drug salesman mentality," John Dean recalled. It led a highly secretive existence. "They had all these locked doors over there, and sort of security systems, and I could never tell what the hell they were doing," said Dean, who was the White House's link to the IEC. Dean did know that the committee's main task was to summarize and evaluate intelligence on protesters. He thought the IEC never moved beyond this "study group" stage. "It was nothing," he said. "It was just a bunch of ex-FBI and intelligence types sitting around and summarizing information. . . . Bob Mardian was sort of a cowboy when it comes to that. I don't think he'd had any background, any experience. They were looking for something for Mardian to do—there was no other job for him—so they gave him this one." However, as J. Anthony Lukas points out, over the next few years the intelligence agencies that made up the IEC carried out numerous wiretaps, break-ins, mail-openings, and dirty tricks against protesters, "strongly suggesting that the Huston Plan was implemented piecemeal."[171]

The White House pondered even more drastic measures if the terrorists and demonstrators really got out of hand. Dean solicited William Rehnquist's counsel on the legality of declaring martial law if a state of "insurrection" developed. Rehnquist thought some civil rights could be suspended, but had doubts about blanket restrictions. The White House also analyzed opinion polls to determine just why it was that so many young people opposed their government and what could be done to turn them around. "We need to find out if our problem with youth is a weakness of the GOP, or of Nixon, or of the establishment, or life in general," Haldeman wrote Robert Finch.[172]

And Nixon continued to demonstrate his peace credentials. He proposed a ceasefire in place in Vietnam, although he knew Hanoi was unlikely to accept the offer. Nixon also announced the withdrawal of another forty thousand U.S. troops. This acceleration of the administration's withdrawal schedule was "one unilateral concession occasioned by domestic pressure," Kissinger writes. Marshall Green recalled, "The [political] effects of Cambodia put more and more pressure upon the administration to show that we were getting out of the whole mess down there." When Nixon got wind that AFSCers were criticizing his continuing substitution of Vietnamese troops for American troops as "immoral" and planned to picket the White House, "the President commented with some consternation that [his Special Counsel] Dick Moore had strongly recommended he *see* this group," Alexander Butterfield told Dwight Chapin.[173]

The November election returns were a disappointment to the White House. Republicans gained two seats in the Senate, but lost nine in the House. They also lost eleven governorships. The administration's attempts to smear Democrats with the brush of terrorism had not worked as planned. If it wanted to hang on to the White House in 1972, the administration would have to tone down its talk of murderers and haters. Curbing Agnew again would be a good place to start, Nixon and Haldeman recognized. "The Vice President should attempt to de-escalate the rhetoric without de-escalating the substance of his message," Haldeman wrote the president on December 1. "He should be shown fighting for something, and not just fighting *against* something or somebody. He should not be exposed as our only hatchet man. . . . To a degree he is now coming across as a result of the campaign as being as radical as those he's attacked. He needs to develop an image as a reasonable and credible man."[174]

"*Excellent. I agree,*" Nixon wrote in the margin of Haldeman's memo.[175]

NINE 1971

*"The Next Six Weeks Will Determine the Future of
Western Civilization"*

In January 1971 the National Coalition Against War, Racism and Repression gathered in Chicago. The coalition remained seriously divided. Backed by Dave Dellinger, Rennie Davis continued to push for massive civil disobedience in Washington in early May that would "stop the government." Dellinger and Davis felt this May Day protest would help revitalize a movement increasingly skeptical of its power. "It was clear that there was a fatigue, a quasi-disillusionment" with legal demonstrations, Dellinger recalled. To many activists, they had become "yesterday's mashed potatoes." But by undertaking massive direct action, Dellinger and Davis believed, activists would feel their power. The government would, too. "The aim of the Mayday action is to raise the social cost of the war to a level unacceptable to America's rulers," a May Day "tactical manual" stated. "To do this we seek to create the spectre of social chaos while maintaining the support or at least toleration of the broad masses of American people." The protest, however, "may divide us from certain constituencies," Davis told the conference delegates. May Day would be decentralized and unchoreographed. There would be "no 'movement generals' making tactical decisions you have to carry out," the manual promised activists.[1]

Other protesters were apprehensive. Indeed, many "were scared to death" of May Day, as Dellinger remembered. Some felt Davis and Dellinger "had gone crazy." Although giving lip service to nonviolence, Brad Lyttle perceived, Davis had no intention of keeping things pacific. "I looked at what they were putting together and said, 'This is a disaster,'" Lyttle recalled. So did the War Resisters League leader David McReynolds. "I'll tell you, the May Days in 1971 scared the shit out of me," he remembered. McReynolds "didn't trust Rennie" either and feared he "was leading us into a trap, that we would all get down to Washington and . . . find out there'd be provocations that would allow Nixon to unleash the National Guard on us. The May Days looked to me like a real setup." Plus, "it was based on an apocalyptic vision," McReynolds felt—"'If they don't close the war down, we're going to close them down.' And that [suggested] we had more power than we did." Moreover, "we had to be aware politically that if we *did* close the government down . . . we would be violating where most people wanted it to go." The former SDS leader Carl Davidson, who was then covering the antiwar movement for the radical *Guardian* newspaper, also distrusted Davis and his May Day plan. "I thought that Rennie Davis was spaced out, and I thought he was burning out," Davidson reminisced. "I thought there was all kinds of weirdness developing around it. . . . It wasn't, like, really together." So distrustful were McReynolds and other activists of Davis that they suspected him of being a CIA agent. McReynolds even raised the possibility with Dellinger.[2]

Dellinger himself had doubts about Davis's commitment to nonviolence and agreed that his vision of May Day was apocalyptic (Dellinger was not pleased when Davis told prospective recruits to the protest that "the next six weeks will determine the future of Western Civilization"). However, Dellinger thought he could keep Davis on a reasoned path. "I used to be able to sober him up," he recalled.[3]

The January conferees could agree on only a very general program for the spring. They would organize to "implement" a symbolic "People's Peace Treaty" previously negotiated by Davis and others with Vietnamese students. They would also hold "nonviolent and militant" protests that went "beyond rallies and demonstrations" but included them too. "It was a hard meeting, that's all I can say," NCAWRR's Sidney Peck pensively reflected. "It was a real difficult meeting."[4]

Further splitting the conferees were accusations that some NCAWRR leaders were losing touch with their troops. "I went through a tremendous personal trashing on elitism and jet-setting," Peck remembered. Two of the accusers later turned out to be government agents.[5]

The following weekend, representatives of the SWP-controlled National Peace Action Coalition and NCAWRR met to consider uniting on a mass legal demonstration that spring. NPAC urged NCAWRR to help build the demonstration it had already called for April 24. NCAWRR preferred rallying on May 2, the day before May Day would begin, instead. The two groups failed to reach an agreement. "We had all kinds of games being played back and forth," Fred Halstead ruefully recalled.[6]

Shortly thereafter, NCAWRR disbanded. NCAWRR leaders set up another group—the People's Coalition for Peace and Justice (PCPJ)—in its place. Given the mounting sectarianism in the movement, the coalition leader Doug Dowd didn't think PCPJ was going to fare any better than NCAWRR. "I remember lacking any kind of enthusiasm or hope about PCPJ," Dowd said. "I remember believing that this was nothing that was going to get any place. It was already riddled with internal opposition."[7]

PCPJ established its headquarters in Washington. In the same building, one floor below, resided NPAC. One floor above sat the office of the May Day Collective (later known as the May Day Tribe), a largely countercultural grouping "filled with strange personalities" prone to using "lots of various kinds of chemical stimulants," Lyttle recalled. The three organizations were most unlikely neighbors. Lyttle remembered visiting NPAC's headquarters shortly after PCPJ set up shop in the building: "When I came in there I went up to their office, and it was a fortress. They had a steel-plated door, and they had two-by-fours that you could put across it. And I said, 'What the heck do you have all this here for?' And they said, 'Well, we don't want to be attacked by the police.' Well, obviously it wasn't the police [they were worried about]; the police could get in if they wanted to. What they didn't want was to be attacked by the rest of the movement."[8] *This* was what the peace movement had come to.

On January 31–February 2, at a Howard Johnson's motor lodge in Detroit, Vietnam Veterans Against the War held their Winter Soldier Investigation into American war crimes in Vietnam. Veterans testified that they had been conditioned to commit war crimes during basic training. By the time he had finished boot camp, one recounted, "I wanted to kill my mother. . . . I knew I was an effective fighting machine." Another described the "rabbit lesson" an officer gave all Marines upon leaving Camp Pendleton. "He has this rabbit and then in a couple of seconds after just about everyone falls in love with it, he cracks it in the neck, skins it, disembowels it . . . and . . . throw[s] the guts out into the audience. . . . That's your last lesson you catch in the United States before you leave for Vietnam." The veterans' accounts of atrocities in Vietnam were chilling. One remembered seeing sixteen enemy prisoners put on two helicopters. When the helicopters completed their flights, he noticed, there were only four prisoners left. Flesh from the hands of the missing prisoners was stuck to one of the craft's door frames, and there was blood on its floor. "They tried to escape over the Mekong Delta," a pilot explained. Another veteran described the "common" practice of cutting off the ears of dead Vietnamese to exchange for army badges signifying "kills." "Anybody who sat there in the room and listened to the testimony was blown away by it," Joe Urgo recalled. "It changed my life. That was a turning point."[9]

The Winter Soldier hearings were read into the *Congressional Record* by Senator Mark Hatfield. George McGovern and other senators called for congressional proceedings on American war crimes. But VVAW's investigation received scant media coverage. And what it did receive was largely hostile. Reporters questioned whether the veterans were, in fact, veterans. "People were really mad, frustrated," Jan Barry recalled. VVAW decided it would have to up the ante. "They didn't want to cover this Winter Soldier Investigation, all right, let's do something that's going to make them stand up and take notice," Urgo remembered thinking. "Let's really wake them up." VVAWers knew they now had the troops for it, too: a free full-page ad in the February issue of *Playboy* magazine had increased their membership dramatically. The veterans decided to hold a march on Washington. They would gather on April 19, Patriots Day in New England. The winter soldiers of America would now take their grievances directly to the halls of power. [10]

"We've Got Our Officers Tightened Up!"

In Vietnam, the morale and discipline of American soldiers was then "deteriorating very seriously," as one columnist observed. In fact, the entire U.S. Army there was "in danger of going plumb to hell." Drug abuse, the most rapidly growing cause of noncombat deaths, was "out of control." Combat refusals were mounting. "They have set up separate companies for men who refuse to go out into the field," one soldier related. "It is no big thing to refuse to go. If a man is ordered to go to such and such a place he no longer goes through the hassle of refusing; he just packs his shirt and goes to visit some buddies at another base camp. Operations have become incredibly ragtag. Many guys don't even put on their uniforms any more." Commented an infantry officer, "You can't give them an order and expect them to obey immediately. They ask why, and you have to tell them." A member of one platoon that refused to advance against heavy enemy fire explained, simply, "the reason given wasn't a very good one." Many officers were losing strength for ordering their men into combat; some tried to avoid contact with the enemy. Racial strife was growing. The gigantic U.S. air base at Danang was the scene of "virtually open racial warfare" for a week in early 1971; Camp Baxter near the demilitarized zone was "in a state of siege." Fraggings were "a very significant problem," too, the commander of the Americal Division acknowledged. So significant that fragmentation grenades were no longer given to soldiers on bunker guard duty at one of the division's base camps. GIs were placing bounties on the heads of unpopular officers. The officers were typically given two warnings before being hit: first, a smoke grenade was rolled under their bed; next came a tear-gas grenade. "Then comes the more lethal stuff," *Time* reported. In the Americal Division, fraggings were running at the rate of one a week. So nervous were many officers of their own troops that fraggings were not necessary to keep them in line. Said one young soldier in the 198th Infantry Brigade, "We haven't had a fragging in maybe four or five months. We've got our officers tightened up!" [11]

Military officials at the Pentagon were disturbed by the deterioration in discipline and morale in Vietnam. "Only 18 months ago, every general worth his stars was complaining that troops were being withdrawn too fast," *Time* observed. "Now, officers from Chief of Staff William C. Westmoreland on down are known to be arguing that they are not being pulled out fast enough." Westmoreland recalled, "I was very, very unhappy about the racial and drug problems. This was going absolutely to the heart of discipline." Westmoreland darkly commented on the drug problem, "Who was responsible for this, who was behind it, Lord only knows." JCS Chairman Thomas Moorer thought the fraggings were "a very dangerous thing. It's indicative of a mind-set that's very dangerous because it breaks down all the discipline when you start shooting each other instead of the enemy. . . . It was bad."[12]

The White House was also worried about the trends in Vietnam. "Of course they were a topic of concern," Ronald Ziegler recalled. According to Roger Morris, the deterioration in discipline and morale "was something that Kissinger was very concerned about" even by the previous year. Some officials later doubted the deterioration had much impact on U.S. policy in Vietnam, however. "I don't think that it was regarded as a very significant factor in the prosecution of the war," CIA Director Richard Helms offered. "The impression in Washington was that it had not attained the degree of seriousness that there was any reason that you couldn't put military forces into action." But H. R. Haldeman said the decline in discipline and morale "was another factor" in policy formation. "If the troops are going to mutiny, you can't pursue an aggressive policy," he pointed out. And Secretary of the Army Stanley Resor remembered that it "was a reason to accelerate [troop withdrawals] somewhat." It "would lead you to go faster with the withdrawals," he said. Writing in December 1970, the Washington insider Stewart Alsop went further: the deterioration, he asserted, was substantially responsible for "a growing feeling among the Administration's policymakers that it might be a good idea to accelerate the rate of withdrawal from Vietnam very sharply."[13]

Secretary of Defense Melvin Laird was certainly influenced by the decline in discipline and morale. During a trip to Vietnam in January, Laird was "shocked" by the magnitude of drug and morale problems among American troops, the *San Francisco Examiner* reported. Laird found these problems "considerably more serious than he had been led to believe" and worried that they might "approach crisis proportions unless the end of the U.S. involvement is brought more rapidly in sight." He was thus "planning a speedup in the U.S. withdrawal from Vietnam," the *Examiner* stated. Laird subsequently agreed that the article was "true" and that he was "very concerned" about declining U.S. troop discipline and morale. "I had many visits with General [Creighton] Abrams [in Vietnam] about that," he remembered. The problem fueled his efforts to get U.S. forces out of Vietnam, Laird divulged. "That contributed to the whole

Vietnamization program." Laird, who apparently spoke to the author of the *Examiner* article on background, told me he publicly exaggerated the problem for political effect, however. "I really was having to use that a little bit, too, to try to put some heat on within the administration," he recalled. "I had to have a little leverage." And he stressed that the overwhelming reason for his efforts to withdraw U.S. troops from Vietnam was low morale on the *home* front. "Over there it was a problem, but not as difficult as it was at home," he said. "Because the morale . . . here was *very* bad."[14]

Laird's trip to Vietnam in January had an agenda hidden from public view. For Richard Milhous Nixon was then planning another demonstration of his madness to Hanoi. In early February, the president decided, ARVN forces would invade Laos and block the Ho Chi Minh trail, thereby hampering a North Vietnamese offensive in 1972—and strengthening Nixon's reelection chances that year. The role of the United States in the invasion would have to be limited to air power and artillery "because of the problem of American domestic opinion" and a need to test ARVN's capabilities, Nixon writes. "I think he would have liked to have used American forces . . . but he knew that it was politically out of the question," the State Department's Marshall Green said. By sending Laird to Vietnam for briefings by General Abrams and South Vietnamese President Nguyen Van Thieu, both strong proponents of the invasion, Nixon hoped, Laird would become a persuasive advocate as well. He would then bring other officials on board. "Nixon was determined not to stand naked in front of his critics as he had the year before over Cambodia," Henry Kissinger recalls.[15]

The president had learned another lesson from Cambodia. He would keep this operation hush-hush. There would be no presidential announcement of the invasion, and a news blackout would be imposed. "Just as there were loud, overt attacks on the political opposition and quiet, covert attacks on the political opposition, there were loud invasions and quiet invasions," Jonathan Schell writes. "The invasion of Laos was one of the quiet ones." During late January and early February, a column of U.S. forces and equipment rumbled toward the Laotian border, and American B-52s pounded enemy positions inside Laos around the clock. ARVN troops massed at the border. Reporters concluded an invasion was imminent, but, for ten straight days, the White House remained silent. On February 8, ARVN troops made their move.[16]

They were routed. Hanoi had learned the details of the invasion ("Hell, they had every goddamned order, every change of plans," one CIA analyst recalled), and, in "the bloodiest fighting of the war," mauled the South Vietnamese badly. American television viewers watched as retreating and panicking ARVN soldiers clung to the skids of American helicopters to escape the slaughter. Many of the ARVN troops faked injuries to get on the helicopters. Angered, wielding screwdrivers and other instruments, some U.S. helicopter crewmen "gave them real ones."[17]

Several weeks later, after thousands of ARVN and enemy troops had perished in the invasion and nearly fifty thousand tons of bombs had been dropped, Nixon told an interviewer, "I rate myself as a deeply committed pacifist, perhaps because of my Quaker heritage from my mother."[18]

During the invasion, Nixon had tape recording systems installed in the White House, his EOB office, and the presidential cabin at Camp David. Bugs were embedded in desks and light fixtures, taps in telephones. Nixon's "primary intent," according to Haldeman, was to "protect himself from the convenient lapses of memory of his associates"—that is, public statements contradicting their private talks with him. Kissinger's memory problem especially concerned Nixon. "He knew that Henry's view on a particular subject was sometimes subject to change without notice," Haldeman writes. The taping systems were installed "in utmost secrecy."[19]

A Tenuous Alliance

Stalled by feelings of futility, hindered by subfreezing temperatures, just plain tired, the antiwar movement responded to the invasion of Laos with protests of only slight and modest size. During the first week in February, as word of the invasion leaked out, demonstrations of several hundred were mounted in many cities. On February 8, groups of protesters invaded the South Vietnamese Embassy in Washington and Herb Klein's White House office. Students at Stanford locked trustees and administration officials in the business school. Two days later, fifty thousand turned out for synchronized demonstrations across the nation. The largest was in Boston, where five thousand gathered; it was the biggest winter antiwar demonstration ever held there. In Manhattan, several thousand held a "mill-in" in Times Square, forcing police to close the area to automobile traffic. Three thousand demonstrated in Ann Arbor, two thousand outside the White House. During a march in Berkeley, militants set fire to a car belonging to the Atomic Energy Commission. Stanford students—on the move for the third straight day—occupied a campus computer center used for war research. Students in Madison took over the social science building. A few universities went on strike.[20]

Although the February protests received little media attention, one that took place on March 1 captured headlines across the country. Early that morning, a man with "a hard, low voice" warned a Senate switchboard operator: "This building will blow up in 30 minutes. You will get many calls like this, but this one is real. Evacuate the building. This is in protest of the Nixon involvement in Laos." Thirty-three minutes later, a Weatherman cell detonated a powerful bomb in a marble-lined men's restroom in the Capitol building, inflicting "considerable structural damage." The bomb "smashed the lavatory fixtures to smithereens," the *Washington Post* noted, blew out a row of windows, and sent "a hail of shrapnel" out through the closed restroom door into the Senate barbershop, propelling its swinging doors through outside windows into a courtyard. The shock wave also swept through a Senate hearing room and senators' hideaway offices. "It was a hell of an explosion," a Capitol guard commented. The bomb had been so well concealed behind a false wall in the restroom that a janitor who regularly cleaned the room didn't know it was there. Within an hour of the blast—and before the news media had been notified—two callers, from Chicago and Washington State, asked Capitol police if the explosion had caused any damage. The FBI immediately began a major manhunt.[21]

That afternoon, during an appearance in Iowa, President Nixon declared that "violent people" would not keep him captive in the White House. He was greeted at the Iowa State Capitol by a thousand demonstrators—students, farmers, and hard hats among them—who threw snowballs at Nixon and chased after his motorcade. The president told reporters they were "a little amateurish." "Mostly I see experts," he said. The White House had earlier tried to organize a friendly demonstration by hard hats. "Our contacts within the building trades union are doing what they can," Deputy Counsel to the President Henry Cashen informed Dwight Chapin on February 26. White House operatives were watching "the situation closely," Cashen reported. The administration had also considered orchestrating a confrontation between prowar hard hats and demonstrators. "[Ron] Walker and company could arrange for such a confrontation," Cashen told Chapin. "You know what the hardhats would do." Afterward, Walker, the administration's head advance man, apprised Haldeman of the "composition" of the crowd. In preparation for another presidential appearance, Chapin chided Walker, "As you will recall in the past, we are supposed to have a plan as to how we are going to handle the demonstrators on any given trip. I would like to have the plan in tomorrow."[22]

The invasion of Laos aroused some members of Congress. During February and March, five resolutions were introduced to restrict Nixon's conduct of the war. Over the next three months, seventeen votes were taken toward that end. On June 22, the Senate adopted Mike Mansfield's nonbinding "Sense of the Senate" resolution to the effect that "it is the policy of the U.S. to terminate at the earliest practicable date all military operations in Indochina."[23]

Some South Vietnamese also spoke out against Nixon's policy. A well-known Catholic professor commented, "Although the United States may have become as strong and as big as an elephant, she is being directed by the brain of a shrimp. Head of an elephant and brain of a shrimp. That is the tragedy."[24]

The invasion of Laos and the specter it raised of even greater escalation—

including an invasion of North Vietnam—spurred organizing for the spring demonstrations. On February 19–21, over two thousand young people attended a national student antiwar conference sponsored by the SWP-controlled Student Mobilization Committee at Washington's Catholic University. The conferees endorsed the April 24 demonstration. Prior to the meeting, the FBI had orchestrated a political pressure campaign to force the university to cancel it, including anonymous mailings charging that the Catholic Church had been "duped again" by the Trotskyists. "Considering financial support CU receives from Roman Catholics throughout U.S., majority of whom are undoubtedly anti-communist and loyal Americans," J. Edgar Hoover wrote FBI field offices, "it appears unique counterintelligence situation presented with potential to have SMC conference cancelled." The FBI's dirty tricks forced the SMC to secure a million-dollar insurance policy from Lloyd's of London against potential damage from "riots" at the conference.[25]

Given the new crisis in Indochina, many antiwar activists beseeched NPAC and PCPJ to set aside their differences and unite on a national protest. "NPAC set a date. PCPJ set a date. Beautiful!" Norma Becker sarcastically remarked. "Two 'massive' national antiwar actions are now scheduled to take place in D.C. a week apart. Great!" Becker went on:

> Certain outcomes of this division and its inevitable competitive
> struggle for support are predictable: smaller, narrower, less effective
> actions this Spring; mutual recrimination and bitterness among
> movement activists; demoralization and disgust within the ranks of
> the movement. We perhaps, placing priority on our rather petty
> power politics and pathetic ego trips, deserve this . . . but the people
> of Indochina don't![26]

In late February, faced with NPAC's apparent determination to plow ahead with April 24 regardless of other activists' wishes, PCPJ decided to cancel the protest it had planned for May 2 and support the April demonstration. NPAC refused to allow PCPJ any control over the organization of it, however, despite PCPJ's efforts to build it. Brad Lyttle remembered:

> We went over all of the aspects of the demonstration to see how
> PCPJ would be involved, and PCPJ *wasn't* going to be involved.
> "How's the money going to be divided once it's collected?" "Well,"
> the SWP said, "we're not going to give you any money. What we'll
> have is competitive fund-raising." . . . They were just so contemptu-
> ous of PCPJ's organizing machinery that they thought that PCPJ
> couldn't collect anything and they'd collect everything. "The sound
> system—who's going to pay for the sound system?" Well, they'd pay
> for the sound system, even though it was originally decided that
> we'd split the cost, because if you control the sound system you con-

trol the demonstration. . . . Physically, I had nightmares working with the SWP on that demonstration because they lied to me directly so many times. And finally I went up to their office and I said, "Syd [Stapleton, an SWP leader], just tell me exactly why it is that you believe that the SWP is going to control this demonstration at the end rather than PCPJ?" And he looked me straight in the eye and said, "Brad, it's because we have the permit for the rally site." I said, "In other words, you'd call out the cops to keep PCPJ from being involved." He didn't say anything, but that's what they would have done!

"I was absolutely appalled by the manipulations of the SWP in actually trying to take over complete control when they were in a united effort with the People's Coalition," Sidney Peck recalled. "I was just totally appalled by that."[27]

PCPJ decided to organize a "People's Lobby" in Washington during the period between April 24 and May Day. The lobbyists would "talk directly and forcibly with all employees of the federal government." They would demand an end to the war, the release of all political prisoners in the United States and a guaranteed income of $6,500 per year for a family of four. PCPJ also resolved to participate in May Day, including through nonviolent civil disobedience at the Pentagon, Justice Department, and Capitol. PCPJ would not organize illegalities on April 24; in return, NPAC would not interfere with May Day. "We just agreed not to get in each other's way," Fred Halstead recalled. Nevertheless, SWPers violence-baited May Day and advertised that it had been canceled. "They were basically divisive and really manipulative," Peck said.[28] Many PCPJ activists continued to be nervous about May Day as well. "I was spending a *tremendous* amount of time then running interference for the mostly young May Day Tribe . . . with my old colleagues, including Sidney Peck, [who] was very skeptical," Dave Dellinger recalled.[29]

Members of VVAW were then firming up their plans for their march on Washington. "Operation Dewey Canyon III," as they wryly called it, in reference to the invasion of Laos (code-named Operation Dewey Canyon II) and an earlier U.S. incursion into Laos (Operation Dewey Canyon I),[30] would target Congress, the Supreme Court, and the press. Mocking Nixonian rhetoric on the invasions of Cambodia and Laos, Al Hubbard, the executive secretary of VVAW, wrote:

> The incursion designated "Dewey Canyon 3" will penetrate into the country of Congress for the limited purpose of severing the supply lines currently being utilized by the illegal mercenary forces of the Executive Branch. And, for the limited purpose of ascertaining if any pretense of Constitutional Democracy exists in this country.
> The success of the incursion is dependent in part on a limited

penetration into the country of the Supreme Court for the limited purpose of demanding they meet their responsibility as a neutral country to rule on the Constitutionality of the Indochina War.

A reluctant limited penetration into the sacred country of the Fourth Estate is essential to the overall success of the incursion as any pretense of Freedom of the Press will seriously jeopardize the safety of our limited force of Vietnam Veterans.

We would like to make it perfectly clear that our primary concern, and the only reason the incursion was ordered, is to insure the eventual safe withdrawal of our limited force of Winter Soldiers from the countries of the District of Columbia. To meet our responsibility in this area it is absolutely necessary that the supply lines that weave their way through the country of Congress be severed, the havens provided by the country of the Supreme Court be eliminated, and the voice of the communist controlled country of the Peoples Republic of the Fourth Estate be silenced.

. . . Vietnam Veterans Against the War, the winter soldiers of today, have identified the enemy. He is us. Armed with this knowledge, we will not in this crisis shrink from the service of our country. Instead, we will press on with the winter soldier offensive; we will continue to bring the war home.

Following five days of lobbying, guerrilla theater, civil disobedience, rap sessions, and other activities, the veterans would conclude their incursion by returning all their war medals to the government—in body bags or even "shitcans filled with blood."[31]

"It Doesn't Take That Many Terrorists to Block All the Traffic Arteries"

The White House was meanwhile mobilizing prowar sentiment and mapping countermeasures to the peace movement's spring offensive. In January, Charles Colson and friends organized the national conference of Americans for Winning the Peace in Washington. To blunt potentially embarrassing inquiries from the press about AWP, Colson prepared, FOR INTERNAL USE ONLY, a list of likely questions and appropriate answers, including:

Q. "Is this a front for the President . . . ?"

A. "Decidedly no."

Q. "Where is the money coming from for this organization?"

A. "Thus far, we have been strictly 'operation bootstrap'. . . ."

Q. "Are the activities and positions of this organization cleared with the White House?"

A. "No."

Q.   "Is this a brain-washing operation designed to convince the American people that the doves and peace movement are wrong?"

A.   "Again—no. But let's stay out of simplistic slogans and arguments such as 'hawks and doves.' The world is not black and white. . . ."

Q.   "What are the origins of this group: who dreamed it up?"

A.   "No one 'dreamed it up.' . . . 'Americans for Winning the Peace' has been an evolutionary development [of efforts by citizens to support U.S. foreign policy]."

A letter from AWP Executive Director Gene Bradley to Colson after the conference was more honest about the White House's role in the group. "I have worked in and out of government for a number of years . . . but I have never seen an event . . . which better exemplifies how the government and the private sector can work together for the national interest," Bradley gushed. "Last Monday's event simply would never have happened had it not been for the White House, on the one hand, and the power of the Executive Committee, on the other." Colson was equally pleased with AWP's progress. "I think we have something going," he wrote Alexander Butterfield.[32]

Following the conference, the White House continued to nourish AWP. Colson garnered funds and plotted strategy. Bradley recognized the group would have to remain cozy with the administration to accomplish its mission. AWP "will take continuing White House involvement if the program is to be responsive to the needs of the President," he wrote Colson on May 8. "It will take some close watching, especially during the next few months."[33]

The White House kept up its work with prowar youth groups. Jeb Magruder and other officials moved to "use" a speech Nixon gave at the University of Nebraska "in a major way" with these groups, including through "comprehensive and massive mailings." Nixon was dissatisfied with his men's activity in this area, though. "The President feels strongly that we need to do a much better job of developing young people—college and high school age—who are on our side, instead of spending so much time trying to pacify those who are against us," Haldeman informed the White House aide Robert Finch on February 2. "For example, he would much prefer to spend his time meeting with a group like he had in during the 'open door' hour today, who support us in Vietnam, rather than the college editors he had in last week, who are opposed to us. He wants to see an active effort to develop some opportunities for . . . *our kind* of young people to see White House staff people as well as . . . the President."[34]

Nixon was also dissatisfied with White House efforts to rally prowar veterans. "What's happened to the President's request that we take steps to mobilize Vietnam veterans?" Haldeman reproached Colson on February 20. "Specifically, have we acquired lists of these people? Do we have ways of reaching them directly? Are we utilizing this source of support?" Colson responded that although the White House obtained the lists of returning veterans that the Veterans Administration provided to the prowar Veterans of Foreign Wars (VFW) and the American Legion, "we don't do anything else with the lists. . . . We work through the VFW and Legion to see that they use the lists for recruiting purposes." Colson also informed Haldeman that he had explored "the feasibility of setting up a separate Vietnam Veterans organization" but concluded "it would cut into the recruiting of the VFW and the Legion." Colson further reported that, "pursuant to the President's comments" several days earlier, Don Johnson, the head of the VA, was "instructing the VFW and the Legion that there is nothing wrong with their setting up all Black posts in inner-city areas" to expand their membership.[35]

Dwight Chapin urged Colson to surface expressions of support from another social group. In March, when Catholic protesters picketed the Newport Naval Base in Rhode Island, Chapin recalled the activities of the Berrigans and other Catholic dissidents and complained, "Once again, we're getting clobbered by the way-out Catholics. . . . We should be doing whatever we can do to offset the idea that Catholics oppose the President."[36]

The White House's efforts to counter the spring peace offensive directly began by at least early January, when John Dean started collecting intelligence on the "May Day invasion." One month later, the White House aide Tom Pauken advocated establishing a "task force on contingency planning" for these "major demonstrations." Pauken pointed out that "extreme leftist groups" were already organizing them. "With demonstration organizers working so actively this far in advance of the proposed protest dates, the possibility of a serious confrontation between the demonstrators and the government is very real," he warned Dean. "Assuming further that a situation might arise in which the President deemed it in the national interest to take additional steps in Indochina this spring or perhaps another unpredictable event (such as Kent State) were to occur, it should be expected that demonstration organizers would seek to inflame national emotions and encourage mass actions that might lead to serious consequences in terms of our domestic order and credibility overseas as a world leader." It was thus "essential," argued Pauken, that the administration "game plan" the protesters' tactics "well in advance of the projected demonstration dates."[37]

The administration's new Intelligence Evaluation Committee and Dean's office handled most of the game planning. On March 8, Ehrlichman directed IEC head Robert Mardian to "begin to keep us informed on a regular basis of the progress of the planning of these [April 24 and May Day] demonstrations in order that we're in a position to answer the President's questions on this subject." The same month Dean instructed Mardian to have the IEC "conduct an analysis of the Spring Anti-War Offensive for White House review" focusing on, among other issues:

To what extent will the anti-war forces be able to retain a sizeable representation of April 24 demonstrators for planned civil disobedience during the first two weeks of May?

. . . Should an unforeseen or planned violent act take place on, before, or after April 24th, what might happen?

Analyzing the announced disruptive tactics to be employed, how effective does the committee feel they will be?

. . . At what point would the hazards suggest a White House decision to secure the White House complex with buses . . . ?[38]

The administration was particularly concerned about May Day. The legal demonstration on April 24 and VVAW's Operation Dewey Canyon III were unwelcome, but if the protesters managed to paralyze Washington, it would be an absolute disaster. "The government can't simply sit by idly and say, 'Go ahead and bring us to a halt,'" Haldeman commented. "It was important, first of all, from a practical viewpoint that the government keep going. There are some functions of the government that are important—there are a lot that aren't, too—but we didn't want to permit a total shutdown. And we didn't want to let it become apparent to the world that the government *could* be shut down by a group of insurgents." Dean observed: "If the President can't even keep the government functioning, it sure doesn't look very good to the American people, not to mention foreign governments. . . . Here's the top law-enforcement officer in the country: if he couldn't control that city [Washington], what *can* he control?" Officials knew the protesters were capable of paralyzing Washington too. "The plans they had laid out had the potential for success," Haldeman remembered. "Because they were going to stop all the traffic . . . pull cars across the bridges and block the access. You can do that, as you know. You get in a traffic jam in any major city; it's not too hard to jam it. And if you have a coordinated and well-planned [operation, it's even easier]. . . . The threat to stop the government was viewed as potentially a real threat." Ray Price noted: "It doesn't take that many terrorists to block all the traffic arteries." Even if they weren't able to pull it off, officials worried, the terrorists could still wreak serious havoc. "A lot of life and property was at stake too," Price pointed out. "It wasn't just shutting down the government—it was what they were going to do to whom in the process of shutting it down." The antiwar movement "was evolving in a very nasty way," Dean perceived.[39]

In White House meetings, the president repeatedly declared it imperative that the protesters be prevented from shutting down Washington. "His mood was that individuals, no matter what their cause, should not be permitted through the process of civil disobedience to close down the government of the United States," Ziegler remembered. "He felt strongly about that." "Nixon was determined not to let the protesters succeed," Ehrlichman said. "He stressed that we could not let them succeed." Ehrlichman added with a smile, "Then he left the country . . ." (Actually, Nixon spent the first three days of May at San Clemente.)[40]

The administration took steps to keep May Day under control. CIA agents penetrated May Day groups. Dean tracked incoming intelligence on the protesters and relayed digests of it to Haldeman and Ehrlichman. He also passed them May Day leaflets. To enrich his understanding of the protest, Dean viewed a film on it by Rennie Davis entitled *Time Is Running Out;* he invited other officials to join him at the screening. At "summit meetings" the weekend before May Day attended by Ehrlichman, Dean, Deputy Attorney General Richard Kleindienst, and other officials, "there were detailed briefings on the precise transmission frequencies of the demonstrators' walkie-talkies, which would be monitored, and general estimates of the percentage of drug users in their ranks," Dean writes. "And there were constant updates on the intentions of the demonstrators, which was no great feat since the plans were printed in antiwar newspapers, complete with maps and arrows. Shortly before the battle, Assistant Attorney General Robert C. Mardian reported that the government knew the exact target areas of every antiwar group except one faction of Gay Liberation."[41]

The White House readied its basement command post for monitoring demonstrations. Direct telephone lines were installed between Dean's office and posts at the FBI, Washington Police Department, Secret Service, and Justice Department. "We had a very elaborate command structure set up," Price recalled.[42]

The White House proclaimed its willingness to cooperate with and assist all demonstrators who intended to act lawfully. In a televised press conference, Nixon said he shared the protesters' goals. "I would not want to leave the impression that those who came to demonstrate were not listened to," he said. "It is rather hard not to hear them, as a matter of fact." The White House prepared Washington Mayor Walter Washington to serve as a voice for its conciliatory stance. "Mayor Washington has a good image and will cooperate with us—as he has in the past—in setting forth the government's . . . posture," Dean told Haldeman and Ehrlichman on April 15. (The mayor ultimately said little about the demonstrations, however.) Officials also tried to reason directly with May Day leaders, but they were unsuccessful. "The organizers were not cooperative," Ehrlichman recalled.[43]

It would be strictly business as usual for all government employees during the May Day assault. At the White House's behest, the chairman of the U.S. Civil Service Commission directed the heads of all departments and agencies to "convey to their employees the importance of making every effort to report to work so that the operations of government will be carried on efficiently." "Hard line at departments this week," Haldeman scrawled on one memo. The White House made sure its key staffers would be on duty. Dean distributed a list of those "who should make necessary arrangements to be within walking distance of the White House on Sunday evening [the day before May Day] or should plan to arrive at their offices by 6 A.M. on Monday morning. The former alternative is recommended whenever possible, due to the uncertainty of traffic conditions early Monday morning. These arrangments should continue throughout the period of the demonstrations." The staffers should also "keep the White House operator advised of their whereabouts throughout [the] weekend" preceding May Day, Dean instructed officials. Other White House staffers should "use their best efforts to arrive at work at the normal starting time." Dean added, "All staff members are further reminded that the contents of this memorandum are classified, and should not be discussed with others except where absolutely necessary." The administration made "special arrangements" for some officials to stay at nearby hotels during the protest. Haldeman considered it essential that those staffers responsible for meal preparation in the White House and Executive Office Building be on duty. "Mess and EOB Cafeteria must be *operative* and fully stocked," he ordered.[44]

The administration initially planned to rely on Washington police for law enforcement. Federal troops would be ready and used only if necessary; Assistant Attorney General William Rehnquist counseled that they could be deployed without a presidential declaration of martial law, however. Dean was wary of the administration's preparations. "Observation: There are not sufficient police or troops to prevent some disruption in normal traffic if demonstrators pursue their plans," he cautioned Haldeman and Ehrlichman on April 27. Several days later, when it "became apparent," as Ehrlichman recalled, that "we would be dealing with a substantial number of people—considerably more than had originally been estimated by police intelligence," and when officials "had reason to think that great amounts of explosives had been brought into the city," threatening "violence of a severe nature," the administration decided to commit ten thousand troops to the fray. Attorney General John Mitchell immediately informed Defense Secretary Laird of the new policy. "It is quite plain that the announced intentions of those who seek to disrupt the operations of the Government during the beginning of next week may well be successful unless . . . armed forces are . . . made available," Mitchell told Laird, giving him authority to deploy as many troops as were necessary to foil the protesters' plans. When Lieutenant General Hugh Exton, who had responsibility for the use of army troops during domestic disorders, advised a delay in the deployment of forces, Ehrlichman said he was "amazed at the general's attitude." Ehrlichman informed him that "the President wanted the city kept open if it took a hundred thousand" soldiers, that "no fine tuning was necessary," and that "if we were short on troops someone will be in big trouble." Ehrlichman also ominously conveyed that "the President was ready to go further than had been discussed up to now in this meeting." Nixon was indeed thinking about tough action. "Hard line on Monday," he instructed in a meeting with Haldeman on May 1. "Use term party's over—time to draw line." (Earlier the White House had considered seeking a court injunction to block the protest, asking Congress to make participation in it a felony, or declaring martial law—utilizing preventive detention—with Mayor Washington invoking a curfew in the nation's capital the first two mornings of the demonstration.)[45]

Officials took other steps to keep traffic flowing. Pedestrians would be barred from four downtown bridges targeted by the protesters. Trucks, forklifts, and cranes would be positioned downtown to remove old cars and other heavy objects used as barricades.[46]

Two days before May Day, the administration decided to revoke a permit the demonstrators had to camp in West Potomac Park. There were already some 17,500 protesters there, officials fretted, and "upwards of 75,000," including "2000 hard core," could be expected by that evening, when an all-night rock concert would be held. "There was some indication that there were troublemakers—police began noticing a great deal of narcotics, a great amount of apple wine was being consumed and lots of disorderly conduct," Ehrlichman recalled. It was an "unwholesome situation" growing more unwholesome by the hour. Particularly unwholesome was the threat the encampment posed of a truly monstrous protest on Monday. As Ehrlichman subsequently informed other officials, the "tactical aspects" of revoking the demonstrators' permit "were recognized. By breaking up the concentrated group, it would eliminate their plan to have training sessions on Sunday. If they could not train their demonstrators on Sunday, they would [not] be as organized for the stoppage effort Monday and Tuesday." Officials considered several ways to end the protesters' party, including: "pen them in or hold them some other way," "arrest them on the spot on a trumped-up charge," or disperse them. It initially decided to "funnel them out" of the park using a phalanx of troops, then thought better of it, and, on the advice of Jerry Wilson, the Washington police chief, elected to move in in a "low key" manner at 6:30 on Sunday morning and tell them to leave by noon. No arrests would be made then, as that might "give the kids the wrong impression," as Dean put it, thereby inflaming them. Although officials expected the clearing operation would incite trashing, most of the protesters were too tired or drugged out after the all-night concert to mount any resistance. Many went home. "There was almost no reaction," Ehrlichman marveled four days later. Remarked Dean, "Crowd not even hostile—caught by surprise; 'the party's over' attitude." Afterward the White House judged the move a brilliant tactical stroke, making Wilson "the hero of the episode." Protesters conceded the government's shrewdness. "The effect of the park bust was something short of disaster," one observed. "Certain targets were eliminated because a lot of people left, and the organization was busted; a lot of people didn't know where to go."[47]

Officials were simultaneously debating how the police should handle the mob on Monday. Some advocated swift and massive roundups. Participants at one meeting agreed "that some type of strong penalty needs to be established to prevent all but the 'hard core' from taking part in the demonstrations and to prevent those who did take part from getting out quickly to continue their disruption." The administration and Wilson decided simply to disperse as many of the protesters as possible; Wilson would be in close touch with Justice in case a change in tactics was needed, however. Officials also debated whether to pick off protest leaders. One argued that doing so on Sunday would "confuse" the demonstrators. Ziegler, on the other hand, warned that "action against leaders at that time or later could give demonstrators [a] rallying point, increase their determination, and provide them an excuse for disruptive tactics, thus giving them new targets such as Free Rennie Davis," one memo records. "Ziegler also feels that the seizure of this new target could tend to diffuse in the public mind reasons for the demonstrators' disorderliness." Ziegler's advice was rejected, as Davis was arrested on federal conspiracy charges developed by Mardian's office on Monday. The White House may have taken another step to undermine May Day. On April 29, the telephone company cut off all five of the phone lines in the group's Washington office, citing a large overdue bill.[48] It seems possible the administration coaxed the crackdown.

The White House was then moving to counter the April 24 demonstration, People's Lobby, and Operation Dewey Canyon III as well. On April 24, not for the first time, President Nixon would be "postured on a 'business as usual' schedule either at the White House or at Camp David," Dean wrote. Demonstrators would not be allowed to march past the White House as had been requested. Police would ring the White House area, but a bus cordon would be unnecessary, even though as many as two hundred thousand protesters were expected. ID cards would be required at parking checkpoints. The public White House tour that day would be canceled. Announcement of this cancellation would be made in a "low key" manner and delayed until April 23 "to preclude this action becoming a demonstrator issue," Dean wrote.[49]

It would be business as usual for all federal employees during the People's Lobby protests, too. Prodded by the White House, the Civil Service Commission reissued the directive it had distributed after the October 1969 Moratorium proclaiming that such protests had no impact on the "normal Government business day." Dean fervently told Haldeman and Ehrlichman that the action was "essential to preclude such agencies as HEW from instituting a liberal leave policy!" (Secretary of HEW Elliot Richardson was refusing to toe the White House line on the protests, leading Ehrlichman's assistant Ken Cole to write Dean, "I personally do not think there is anything that can be done unless someone with the stature of John Ehrlichman or Bob Haldeman is willing to lock horns with Secretary Richardson.") The White House instructed departments and agencies that "they should not have 'rap sessions' or permit demonstrators in buildings for conducting acts of civil disorder." Access to buildings would be significantly tightened. The acting deputy director of the IRS wrote IRS employees, "If despite our best efforts demonstrators do get into the halls or offices, please understand that their intention is simply to engage in 'dialogue,' so you should deal with the situation in good spirit." Arguing with the intruders would be ill-advised.[50]

To blunt Operation Dewey Canyon III, the administration acted to show that it had taken "strong measures" to secure employment for Vietnam veterans. It placed Don Johnson on a TV talk show to tout government assistance to veterans and denounce VVAW. The White House hoped to place "positive" Vietnam veterans alongside Johnson, but apparently decided against it for fear the producers would "then have some VVAW (against war) types also," as one memo says. "We'd rather have Johnson alone." The administration tried to get some Gold Star Mothers (women who had lost sons in Vietnam) on the Mike Douglas Show. It had friendly veterans groups assail VVAW as unrepresentative of veterans. At Colson's request, Herbert R. "Chief" Rainwater, head of the VFW, held a press conference in Washington, at which he charged that antiwar veterans groups were communist-inspired. The conference received considerable media attention, prompting Colson to tell Lawrence Higby, "I think our boys are getting a little better." To Haldeman, Colson reported, "The President should know that we are continuing the effort [to discredit VVAW]." After Rainwater later tried to organize an encampment by VFWers in Washington to counter a VVAW encampment, Colson giddily wrote Higby: "HAIL TO THE CHIEF! My mad man has struck again."[51]

Colson's office worked with Johnson to start vocal prowar "subgroups" of the American Legion and VFW. VVAW's Joe Urgo would remember seeing John O'Neill, leader of something called "Vietnam Veterans for a Just Peace," debating VVAWer Robert Muller on the Dick Cavett Show. "Who's this guy John O'Neill?" Urgo thought to himself. "Who the fuck are the 'Vietnam Veterans for a Just Peace?'" Urgo and other VVAWers "even handed out leaflets saying, 'Where are these veterans? We want to debate you.' We pleaded with these guys to come out of the closet. We couldn't figure out, 'How could this guy go around talking [for] "Vietnam Veterans for a Just Peace" when nobody can find any of these guys?' There was like two of them, three of them. We really wanted the debate. . . . We were getting tired of them—we wanted a little fireworks. . . . We'd make mincemeat out of them, you know." Only years later did VVAW learn that "Vietnam Veterans for a Just Peace" was largely a creation of the White House.[52]

Colson dug for dirt on VVAW and its leaders. "The men that participated in the pseudo-atrocity hearings in Detroit [the Winter Soldier Investigation] will be checked out to ascertain if they are genuine Viet Nam combat veterans," a CONFIDENTIAL "Plan to Counteract Viet Nam Veterans Against the War" in his White House files reads. A propaganda piece prepared by Colson's aide Dick Howard tarred VVAW as

> a group that are apparently veterans, many of which are not Vietnam veterans and most of which are not combat veterans, who are apparently trying to compensate for some guilt feeling or psychological defect by participation in this organization. . . .
>
> Their friends and affiliation are cloudy. For example they have had full page ads in the February Playboy and in the April 11 New York Times. The cost of these ads had to be considerable. . . . They are stating they will furnish transportation to the demonstration for people from all over the country. Where does this money come from? They haven't said. Several of their regional coordinators are former Kennedy supporters.

Colson's aide John Scali "plant[ed]" "appropriate questions" with reporters for an appearance by the VVAW leaders John Kerry and Al Hubbard on a Sunday TV talk show. The White House also engineered letters to newspapers demanding they "expose" Kerry as "a fraud." And Colson helped his "very loyal friend" Jerald F. ter Horst, a reporter with the *Detroit News* (who was "not the best journalist in the world," Colson told Ziegler), prepare an article trashing Kerry. Although the piece was syndicated to about a hundred and fifty newspapers, Colson wanted greater circulation: he had copies distributed to editors and Republican legislators, as well as to "all veterans organizations and military groups in plain envelopes with no cover letter."[53]

Officials debated how to respond to VVAWers' plan to return their medals to the government. Although the veterans were thinking about depositing the medals on the steps of the Capitol, the White House perceived they were coming its way. Moreover, as Dean apprised Haldeman and Ehrlichman, the veterans "intend to throw a bag of such medals over the White House fence if no one receives them." Officials considered having a military representative accept the medals, but Nixon's chief military aide, General Don Hughes, found that idea distasteful. Having the Congressional Medal of Honor Society receive them, on the other hand, "would be a little bit too 'put on,'" officials worried. The administration finally decided to have a "low level White House clerk or messenger"—that is, "no one of real stature"—accept the medals "in the routine fashion—just as any other package or piece of mail would be received," Colson wrote.[54]

Three days before Dewey Canyon, the Justice Department asked a federal court for an order barring the veterans from camping on the Washington Mall, where they planned to set up a "fire base." The judge ruled they could stay in the Mall, but couldn't pitch tents or sleep there. Some veterans responded that they would "stand up all night."[55]

In addition to all this, Ron Walker, a veteran facilitator of prowar actions (including attacks on demonstrators) and unseemly displays by protesters, would handle some "special projects."[56]

Heightening the Nixon administration's concern about the antiwar movement's spring offensive was accelerating discontent with the war among the general public. An April Harris poll found that, for the first time, most Americans felt the war was "morally wrong." By a margin of 60 to 26 percent, Americans favored continued U.S. troop withdrawals "even if the government of South Vietnam collapsed." "I don't think you could find a hawk around here if you combed the place and set traps," a small-town newspaper editor in Kansas remarked. "The tide of American public opinion has now turned decisively against the war in Indochina," Louis Harris reported. There was a "rapidly growing feeling that the United States should get out of Vietnam as quickly as possible."[57]

The same month, Special Assistant to the President Jon Huntsman wrote Colson, Haldeman, and other officials on the "changing mood" around the country. There was "building antiwar sentiment in once hawkish San Diego" and a "new mood of tourists" there, related Huntsman, citing press reports. "They are now sympathetic to protesters and don't cast aspersions on them as used to be the case." And "across the nation, non-college youth . . . seem far less conservative than is generally assumed." To Nixon, a particularly disturbing sign of the changing public mood was growing support for Senator Edmund Muskie (D-Maine), seemingly the leading contender for the Democratic presidential nomination. Muskie was pulling ahead of Nixon in the polls.[58]

On April 7, to help rally the public, the president announced the withdrawal of another 100,000 U.S. troops from Vietnam by December 1, leaving 184,000 there. Nixon pointedly refused to set a deadline for the removal of all U.S. troops, as the "madmen" in Congress and other critics were increasingly demanding. Meanwhile, bombs continued to rain down on Vietnam, Laos, and Cambodia, and press leaks indicated that Nixon was preparing for five to ten more years of war, with 50,000 U.S. troops remaining in Vietnam "indefinitely."[59]

The Spring Offensive

On Monday, April 19, a thousand Vietnam veterans marched across the Lincoln Memorial Bridge to Arlington National Cemetery in Virginia. Many wore jungle fatigues and long hair. Some were in wheelchairs, others were on crutches. Gold Star Mothers—*their* Gold Star Mothers—led the procession. A small delegation of mothers, widows, and veterans was prevented from entering the cemetery to conduct a memorial service. It laid two large wreaths at the entrance. As the marchers trekked to the Capitol for a rally, some extended their middle finger toward a helicopter that zoomed by overhead. In the helicopter, unbeknownst to the veterans, sat Richard Nixon. Although the president was undoubtedly on other business at the time, his interest in Operation Dewey Canyon III was "intense." He reportedly received hourly reports on it. The same day, represented by former Attorney General Ramsey Clark, who was now openly on the side of the peace movement, the veterans obtained a federal court order rescinding the injunction against camping on the Mall.[60]

The next day, two hundred veterans returned to Arlington Cemetery. After the earlier affront, "it became a priority that we were going to go back and those gates were going to open," Jan Barry recalled. The cemetery superintendent initially tried to halt the veterans at the gates, then yielded. "These guys risked their lives to go out and pick up those bodies and put them in body bags so they could be shipped home," John Kerry said. "You can't bar these men from paying honor to their friends." In the cemetery the veterans held a silent memorial to the dead in Indochina. That afternoon some performed guerrilla theater at the Capitol:

> Jumping a low fence, they began shouting at a group of tourists. "All
> right. Hold it. Hold it. Nobody move. Nobody move." Their voices
> were full of tension and anger. A man broke out of the crowd and
> started running. Several soldiers fired at once, and the man fell,
> clutching his stomach. Blood could be seen on the clean sidewalk.
> The tourists turned away in horror. "Get a body count," a soldier
> yelled.

Later the Justice Department successfully appealed the rescindment of the injunction against camping on the Mall. "Justice has taken this action to insure a possible strong position against the desires of the militants to use Rock Creek Park" for camping during May Day, John Dean reported to Haldeman and Ehrlichman that afternoon. The veterans were given until 4:30 P.M. the next day to break camp.[61]

The following afternoon a contingent of veterans marched to the Pentagon. Their mission: to turn themselves in for war crimes. (Before they departed, a voice over the public-address system in the Mall had breezily instructed, "Will all war criminals please assemble across the street.") The authorities would not receive the veterans. "I'm sorry, but we don't accept American prisoners of war here—why don't you try the Justice Department," a general suggested. Some veterans engaged in guerrilla theater in front of Justice. A woman told one, "Son, I don't think what you're doing is good for the troops." "Lady, we are the troops," the veteran replied. On the Mall, veterans were debating how to respond to the latest court order. Rumors swirled that troops would be coming in if they didn't break camp. Soldiers from Fort Bragg who had joined the protest reported otherwise, however. "Don't worry about it," they told the veterans. "Because the guys . . . are not going to move from Bragg." There were signs of support from members of the Washington police force as well. "Cops would come and just talk to us. They'd come and say, 'Hey, yeah, you guys, I support what you're doing,'" Barry remembered. "They would just come and talk to us like professional to professional, just like guard duty, meeting another guard. There was a great deal of that." Many other residents of Washington also expressed support for the veterans. Some "would just come and start crying, say, 'I don't understand it, but it's beautiful,'" Barry reminisced. "They would be drunk, you know; they had gotten themselves really wigged out to be able to come and say this. And inevitably they brought a car full of food or some money." With the protest attracting national news coverage, endorsements arrived from distant points, too. "This postman arrives with mail addressed to 'Vietnam Veterans on the Mall in Washington, D.C.,'" Barry laughed. "He says, 'Where do I deliver this to?' It was the most astounding thing to suddenly discover that we had gone from being rather anonymous to being center focus."[62]

Inside the White House, there was no intention to move against the veterans. That would not play well politically. "The policy—which the VVAW are totally unaware of—is that there will be *no arrests* made of VVAW who violate the [court] order and it has been clearly and unequivocally given to the appropriate authorities," Dean told Haldeman and Ehrlichman that day. Pat Buchanan underscored the political wisdom of this policy in a memo to Haldeman. The veterans, advised Buchanan,

> are getting tremendous publicity; they have an articulate spokesman [i.e., Kerry]; they are being received in a far more sympathetic fashion than other demonstrators.
>
> I know we have [the court's] go-ahead—but my understanding is that these guys are leaving Friday the 23rd, anyway—they are *not* the guys we want the confrontation with. Those guys are coming in Friday and staying until May. . . .
>
> Seriously, the "crazies" will be in town soon enough; the whole public is antipathetic toward their violence; and if we want a confron-

tation, let's have it with them—not with the new Bonus Army.[63] This is not a recommendation that we not be tough—but that we pick the most advantageous enemy from our point of view.

"Don't bust the Viet Nam veterans on the Mall—avoid confrontation," the president directed in a meeting with Ehrlichman that day. Nixon later told reporters he feared the confrontation might be "rather nasty."[64]

At 4:30 P.M., an alarm clock rang over the microphones on the speaker's platform in the Mall. The appointed eviction time had arrived. Veterans cheered and thrust their fists defiantly into the air. No police or troops were in sight. An hour later, Ramsey Clark informed the veterans the Supreme Court had just ruled they could stay on the Mall if they didn't sleep there. But sleep would bring arrests. An impassioned debate then ensued. "This was *heavy duty*," Barry remembered. "Most of us had never been arrested, we did not come there intending to be arrested, civil disobedience was not our lifestyle or what most of us conceived of as being within tactics we felt comfortable with. And yet we're being challenged—literally, this is nose to nose with the federal government. They're saying, 'Leave or else.'" During the two-hour debate, Barry, who was unsure what to do, was approached by comrades for advice. "I was holding the telephone to give us an outside link [and] they kept asking, 'Well, what are you going to do?' I said, 'I'm just going to sit here, I'm going to hold this telephone, and I'm going to tell whoever is at the other end what happens.'" Barry was on the phone to the mother of one of the veterans to mobilize external support in case the cops moved in. "It was a field telephone wire; somebody had rigged up a field telephone wire across the Mall to someplace where I had telephone access," Barry laughed. By the time the veterans' votes were tallied, nightfall had arrived. His face bathed in TV lights, Kerry relayed the verdict: they would sleep on the Mall.[65]

After a night of undisturbed slumber, a contingent of veterans sat in at the Supreme Court. They were busted and walked off with their hands clasped behind their heads, POW-style. Later that day, the Justice Department slipped quietly back into federal court to request that the original injunction against camping on the Mall be terminated. Dean informed Haldeman and Ehrlichman that "discussions" with the judge who had invoked the order had been

> to no avail, leaving this as the only option to avoid confrontation or the situation where the government failed to enforce the order it had requested. It will be argued that the order should now be terminated because the VVAW have had use of park lands under color of legal permission since Sunday; there have been no incidents or problems in their use of the land; they are leaving on the 23rd; therefore—all factors considered—the order is not necessary. While the argument is thin, I personally agree with the procedure as the only reasonable course given our present posture.

The judge peevishly dissolved his order and assailed Justice's legal maneuverings, charging that the court had been "dangerously and improperly used" by the Nixon administration.[66]

That afternoon John Kerry testified before the Senate Foreign Relations Committee. It was a compelling presentation. "The country doesn't realize it yet but it has created a monster in the form of thousands of men who have been taught to deal and to trade in violence and who are given the chance to die for the biggest nothing in history—men who have returned with a sense of anger and of betrayal that no one so far has been able to grasp," the future U.S. senator stated. "Each day to facilitate the process by which the United States washes her hands of Vietnam someone has to give up his life so that the United States doesn't have to admit something that the entire world already knows . . . that we have made a mistake. . . . How do you ask a man to be the last man to die for a mistake?" Some VVAWers resented the media attention Kerry received, however. In fact, their resentment of this Yale-educated, articulate "star" with obvious political ambitions (he had earlier made an aborted run for Congress) had been building for months. "They knew that he was a rich guy, they knew that he was a politician, that he was in it to use us," Joe Urgo said. "When Personality Posters came out with his picture on a poster, it went up on a wall and somebody wrote PIG across it. And my attitude toward this was, 'Let's keep some unity here . . .'" For his part, Barry thought, "Geez, anybody who wants to come and use us, to run for Congress, ought to have his head examined, unless he's really serious, and if he's really serious then I'll take him."[67]

Many VVAWers were buttonholing their congressional representatives on Capitol Hill. Their encounters were often frustrating. Barry recalled that Congressman John Rooney (D-N.Y.), a staunch hawk, was in no mood for dialogue. "He pokes me in the chest and says, 'I'm going to tell you where I'm coming from. You got it?'" Complained another veteran, "The politicians sent us to Vietnam . . . now they don't want to hear us." Urgo remembered the education he received from Congress: "I did think that if I went there and told these people the truth . . . maybe it will wake them up. . . . I went down there half believing that stuff, and came back convinced, 'Fuck them. Fuck Congress.'" When the veterans could not find a legislator willing to receive their medals, their anger grew.[68]

By Thursday, frustrated over their treatment by both Congress and the Nixon administration, including an insinuation by Nixon that only 30 percent of them were veterans (prompting one VVAWer to shoot back, "Only 30 percent of us believe Richard Nixon is President"), many of the veterans wanted to do something more dramatic with their medals than simply place them on the Capitol steps. Meanwhile, they had been watching a fence go up around the Capitol for the April 24 demonstration. "We felt, 'Those motherfuckers are putting this fence up between us and that Capitol, the Congress,'" Barry remembered. "'We're going to go there tomorrow with our medals—let's throw them over the fence!'"[69]

The next day the father of a boy killed in Vietnam inaugurated the medal-returning ceremony by blowing taps on a bugle. On his back rested his dead son's army fatigue jacket. Nearby stood two mothers of boys killed in Vietnam; their hands held their sons' medals and American flags. Their eyes were misty. One by one, the veterans stepped forward and threw their medals over the fence. "You saw the faces on these guys—you didn't want to talk to them," Barry recounted. "It was like paratroopers lined up ready to jump. This was a *big* event in their lives, this was no small matter . . . to throw away their medals. There was no bullshit, there was no joking. They were very short-tempered. They stood there in line waiting to move another inch forward until their time came to jump out the door." Many of the veterans made emotional statements about the war or dead comrades before tossing their medals over the fence. Afterward, the emotions of some burst. "It was like two hours before I could stop crying," one recalled. "It was very, very, very heavy."[70]

That decorated veterans were protesting the war enhanced the antiwar movement's legitimacy. It also inspired other peace activists. Sidney Peck said the protest "set the whole tone" for the movement's spring offensive. "We could feel the dynamic beginning to build with the Vietnam vets. I mean, that just created such a positive atmosphere."[71]

The veterans were not the only ones moved to tears by the return of their medals. Three thousand miles away, a draft resister recently released from prison was driving down the freeway when word of the veterans' action came over his radio. Tears of happiness began streaming down his face. "This was the kind of thing we'd wanted for a long time," he later remembered. The resister's name was David Harris.[72]

Throughout the morning of April 24, demonstrators flooded onto the Ellipse in Washington, the staging area for the day's march to the Capitol. Most were young. Rank-and-file unionists, GIs, and veterans were present in greater numbers than at past peace demonstrations. According to a survey by the *Washington Post*, more than a third of the protesters were attending such a demonstration for the first time. "I'm a member of the silent majority who isn't silent anymore," a 54-year-old furniture store owner from Michigan remarked. The survey found that fewer than a quarter of the protesters considered themselves radicals; most were liberals. At least thirty-nine members of Congress endorsed the demonstration. So large was the turnout for it that cars and buses carrying protesters were backed up for three miles at the Baltimore Harbor Tunnel by 11 A.M. Many of the occupants never made it to the demonstration.[73]

The White House was keeping a close watch on the action. "John Dean will be in his office all day today," Haldeman's aide Bruce Kehrli informed his boss at 9:30 A.M. "He has direct lines to all command posts and will be giving you a report every 30 minutes on the size, reaction, movement and mood of the crowd, and any incidents or arrests." Kehrli also reported that, aside from the seventy-five thousand people already gathered at the Ellipse, there were several thousand "Rennie Davis-types" in West Potomac Park. "We are watching them for any unusual action," he wrote. One hour later, Kehrli informed Haldeman that the crowd had grown by one-third and that its "mood" was "typical of demonstrations," with "small groups gathering around signs," some emitting "small chants." Also, there were "no major political figures on the scene." Simultaneously, President Nixon was discussing demonstrations with John Ehrlichman at Camp David.[74]

At 11 A.M., the bulging throng at the Ellipse forced a premature departure for the Capitol. Leading the procession were several hundred U.S. servicemen and wounded veterans. Before departing, the GIs and vets "let out whoops and whistles that reverberated from the buildings and gave the sendoff an eerie, almost frightening quality," one participant writes. The marchers filled most of the west lawn at the Capitol and overflowed onto the Mall. "Every statue, every tree seemed to hold a demonstrator," observed the *Post*. At noon, inside the White House, Kehrli apprised Haldeman that the media were claiming a quarter of a million demonstrators were on the scene, though Dean still put the number at a hundred thousand. "He has called the Chief of Police to make sure they get the correct figures," Kehrli related. Not coincidentally, when the crowd later swelled to half a million, astonishing both antiwar organizers and officials alike, Chief Wilson repeatedly told reporters it was less than half that size.[75]

At the Capitol the demonstrators listened to a steady stream of speakers denounce Congress's inaction on the war. Some of the speeches received live national television coverage. Rock music blasted from the west stairway, and an "occasional smell of marijuana" wafted through the air. Alongside the stage, PCPJ and NPAC organizers clashed over the list of orators; when Sidney Peck tried to enter a roped-off area to exert pressure on behalf of certain speakers, Fred Halstead refused to let him in until he had obtained the approval of the rally chairpeople. Peck was furious and "never forgave" Halstead for the indignity.[76]

Despite the bickering, the demonstration—rivaling the record-setting November 1969 mobilization in size—was a tremendous accomplishment for the peace movement. Although bitterly split into two national coalitions, one of which was itself seriously divided, the movement had once again shown its ability to mobilize massive numbers in the streets. Once again it had shown its staying power.

In San Francisco that day, some two hundred thousand participated in the largest antiwar protest ever on the West Coast. The rally ended prematurely, however, after militants took over the stage for more than an hour, forcing protest coordinators to cancel the last few speeches.[77]

After the April 24 demonstrations, apparently displeased with the favorable media attention they received, Charles Colson compared their print coverage to that for the pro-administration Honor America Day rally in 1970. "To my horror, the protest did not outdo us by all that much," he wrote Haldeman. "The tube, however, is a very different story."[78]

On April 25, the People's Lobby commenced. One hundred and fifty-one Quakers were arrested for conducting a mass pray-in on the sidewalk in front of the White House. Photos of David Hartsough, his wife, and their two toddlers were splashed on the front pages of newspapers around the country after police refused to arrest the children. "The police had no scruples whatsoever about arresting anybody else, whether they were ninety years old or twenty years old or anything else, but these two little babies—you know, it was a little embarrassing," Hartsough recalled. "So the chief of police came over and spent about forty-five minutes trying to convince us that it was very irresponsible to take your kids to jail, that they would be separated from us, and all of this kind of stuff. We said, 'The kids in Vietnam are getting bombed, and we've got to take some risks to try to stop this. . . . We're not going to move. It's up to you whether you arrest us, but we're going to stay here and continue this worship.'" "I won't arrest them," the police officer kept saying of the children. Finally, after all the other protesters had been taken away in a bus, the officer persuaded the Hartsough family to get into an unmarked police car. "We said, okay, we would walk to the police car like we were under arrest," Hartsough remembered. "They took us to the police station—and let us out behind the police station. . . . They didn't want that publicity of arresting kids."[79]

The next day, "roving" bands of protesters engaged in "hit-and-run" actions on Capitol Hill, including bizarre guerrilla theater. In the Old Senate Office Building, a group of women, "cloaked in burlap sacks and with red liquid trickling from the corners of their mouths," ranged through the halls, shrieking and weeping. "God have mercy, don't kill my baby!" some of the "wailing mothers" screamed. Senate secretaries and staff aides who emerged from their offices to see what was going on were wide-eyed; one became visibly upset and ran back into her office crying. Several demonstrators dressed like Vietnamese peasants barged into one senator's inner office pursued by Vietnam veterans in combat gear. "A group of veterans were here last week to see the senator and he wouldn't see them," one of the vets explained. "Since then, 70 GIs have died in Vietnam, so 70 people are going to die here." The wailing women then began shrieking in the senator's office. Later, after police temporarily closed the building, one protester proceeded to scale its wall. "I want to see my senator," he waggishly declared. "Let him see his senator," a crowd of demonstrators chanted, "let him see his senator."[80]

Inside the White House, Nixon and Ehrlichman discussed the protests during at least two meetings that afternoon and evening. "Hippies on the Hill today," Ehrlichman's notes of one of the meetings read. "Young, peaceful. Tore down flag—maybe childish pranks, these days." Meanwhile, demonstrators staged a mock battle on the front lawn of Melvin Laird's home in Bethesda, Maryland, and hung an NLF flag on his porch. One protester also returned his draft card—in person—to Selective Service System Director Curtis W. Tarr, who called him "a fine boy."[81]

On April 27, demonstrators blocked the entrance to the SSS headquarters. Many remained throughout a nippy night after police failed to arrest them. More than two hundred were busted early the next morning. "I tried very hard to get arrested so I wouldn't be there when the May Days came by," David McReynolds remembered. "I really was terrified about the May Days." Also that day, the leaders of twenty-seven religious organizations with a membership of more than eighty-six million (three-quarters of all Americans listed as members of religious faiths) issued an unprecedented call for "repentance and renewal" over the war. "We are all sick at heart," the call stated.[82]

On April 28, demonstrators lobbied IRS and CIA employees. On Capitol Hill, five representatives of the May Day Collective testified before the Senate Foreign Relations Committee; two were selected by their comrades to testify because they seemed particularly in touch with "the spirit of the land" in West Potomac Park, where they were camped. One, "Kathy Sister," told the astonished senators about "our" experience on "the land"; the existence of strychnine in the LSD there, she said, showed that they were not yet capable of relating to each other as genuine brothers and sisters. Another May Day representative explained to the senators why many people considered them war criminals.[83]

The next day, welfare and civil rights organizers led a raucous rally of six hundred in the HEW auditorium. After the rally, the protesters tore down "every inch of" a freshly painted, thin wooden wall hastily erected the night before to bar them from offices. Shouting "To the White House," carrying large pieces of the wall, the demonstrators then headed outside, only to be quickly surrounded by police. Two hundred and twenty-four were busted.[84]

On April 30, over two thousand protesters ringed the Justice Department, blocking every entrance. Those at the FBI entrance requested to see any files the bureau might have on them. Justice Department employees had to climb over rows of protesters to get inside the building. Some were not happy. "Who told all of you to do this?" one man irritatedly asked. "I got a wire from Mao

Tse-tung this morning," a demonstrator responded, "and he told me not to move." Three hundred and seventy were arrested.[85]

Then things really got wild. On May 3 in Washington, May Day protesters, fearful of being trapped by police before getting started, began striking out toward bridges and traffic circles before dawn. As they were moving out, a message from President Nixon was read over the police radio network asking that Washington be kept "open for business." The mainly youthful demonstrators, many wearing jeans and fatigue jackets, with handkerchiefs around their necks for "the gas," concentrated their assault on nine targets, fewer than half as many as originally planned, given the reduction in their forces and disorganization spawned by the government's clearing operation in West Potomac Park the day before. The protesters were greeted at their targets by lines of police and soldiers, some toting rifles with fixed bayonets, others wearing flak jackets, steel helmets, and ammunition pouches. They were ready for battle. "The cops were in a very nasty mood," David McReynolds recalled. "Very early, as we were just arriving, they were zipping back and forth, gunning their motor scooters. God, I never saw them in such a nasty mood." Many of the demonstrators sat down in the streets, Gandhi-style; others danced and chanted in glee over traffic stoppages. Some moved trash cans, furniture, concrete slabs, tree limbs, and cars onto streets, then let the air out of the cars' tires. A group overturned a tractor-trailer rig. One longhair was seen "riding the back bumper of a civil servant's sputtering Volkswagen like a broncobuster as he tried to get the hood open and the distributor cap pulled." Police waded into the crowds, spraying tear gas and clubbing. This tactic of dispersal fostered hit-and-run attacks, including trashing, with many protesters abandoning plans hatched in their affinity groups. "If these kids were coordinated, we'd be lost," one cop commented. "They just don't have any communications system like we do." Police and military helicopters buzzed overhead, snapping photographs and radioing the demonstrators' positions to the authorities on the street. Police on motorscooters threaded their way through snarled streets in hot pursuit. Others sprang from their cars with their nightsticks flailing. Sirens screamed, army trucks and jeeps rolled through Washington, tear gas drifted through normally peaceful, tree-lined Georgetown streets and downtown Washington, seeping into offices. One cop lobbed a tear-gas grenade into a medical van used to treat injured protesters, contaminating medical equipment and wounding the medics inside. On the Washington Monument grounds, six huge Chinook helicopters staged a dramatic landing, disgorging 198 "combat-ready" soldiers, who ran out "at double-time." Smaller helicopters guided the landing by dropping pink and white smoke bombs on the grounds.[86]

In the streets the air was electric. Some protesters' adrenaline got the best of them. Rev. Richard Fernandez, a pacifist theoretically opposed to wild-in-the-streets-ism, helped flip over cars. "I only turned over two," he would recall with an impish grin. "I was supposed to be in the office helping to raise bail money, but we were out for a couple of hours . . ."[87]

At 6:15 A.M., PCPJ protesters led by Dr. Benjamin Spock marched from the Washington Monument toward the Pentagon. Attempting to cross the Fourteenth Street Bridge, they encountered May Day Tribesmen trying to close it. "An extraordinary tactical blunder!" McReynolds exclaimed afterward. "We were moving into our allies." Police spewed tear gas and Mace and swung nightsticks. Howard Zinn, a Boston University history professor, was present with a "funny little affinity group" of intellectuals, including Noam Chomsky and Daniel Ellsberg. "I remember sitting in the middle of the street and looking at Noam Chomsky and thinking, he is a very smart person and I don't want the police to hit him on the head—his head is very precious," Zinn recalled. Chomsky's noggin was spared. Ellsberg himself hadn't initially planned to attend the protest, as he was so busy with other antiwar activity then, including trying to release the Pentagon Papers through various senators (who "didn't seem pleasant about it," he remembered); plus he figured the papers "would be coming out before long, one way or another," and he "didn't want to discredit myself" by being arrested—"I wanted to blossom." But Ellsberg had given a speech at a teach-in a day or two earlier in which he had gotten a bit carried away and ended with a rhetorical flourish. "I had just seen *Little Big Man* with Dustin Hoffman," he recounted. "I said, 'How many people have seen this movie?' It had just come out so a lot of people had just seen it. I said, 'Well, you may remember that the Sioux [Indians] in there say, "Come brothers, this is a good day to die," before a battle.' And I said, 'Well, probably it's never really a good day to die, but tomorrow is a good day to get arrested. . . . Tomorrow is a good day to go to jail.' So I came home and said to Pat [his wife], 'Well, it looks like I'm going to go. I can't make a speech like that—everybody was cheering, you know, a standing ovation— . . . and not go there myself.'" Sitting on the Washington pavement with a copy of the book *Revolution and Equilibrium* by Barbara Deming, who was "a hero of mine" and a fellow May Day participant, in his pocket in preparation for jail, Ellsberg was Maced and beaten by police. "Nobody was arresting anybody in our vicinity; they were just clearing us off the street," he reminisced. After a few skirmishes with police, and sensing that the day's battle was already winding down, Ellsberg "flew to New York, went to my wife's apartment, changed clothes because my clothing was saturated with tear gas, showered, got the tear gas out of my hair, put on a new suit and went to the Council on Foreign Relations to hear McGeorge Bundy give the first of his [three] scheduled lectures on 'lessons of Vietnam' . . . that afternoon." Ellsberg angrily listened to Bundy deliver "a long collection of lies."[88]

PCPJ's Brad Lyttle also attempted to march to the Pentagon. "Somehow the government got it into their head that I was much more influential in the anti-Vietnam War movement than I was, and they were frequently out to get me. And that time they did," Lyttle remembered. "A couple of policemen pounced on me and beat me up, bloodied me. As soon as blood was pouring out of my mouth, they stopped beating me." After the cops arrested Lyttle, he tossed a bullhorn he had been using to other demonstrators. He was promptly charged with assaulting a police officer with it. Lyttle escaped a possible ten-year sentence when his lawyer, Phil Hirschkop, requested that the government make available to the defense all tape recordings it had of the phone conversations of PCPJ organizers, although Hirschkop did not know if any even existed. The judge ruled in favor of the request, and the government dropped its case.[89]

Ray Price, who "made it a practice to mingle anonymously with the demonstrators" during national protests in Washington "to pick up some sense of the mood and temper of the crowd," decided to get a firsthand look at the action in the streets that morning. Walking from his Georgetown home to the White House, he saw "ugly mobs of thugs" darting about, "ripping shrubbery out and throwing it into the intersections," "smashing windows," and "threatening lives." "It was murderous," he recalled. "It really was murderous. . . . They were throwing the bedsprings over the overpasses and so forth, and they didn't care who they killed or maimed in doing it. . . . It just was a very brutal, ugly scene. . . . The police [were] . . . having a very desperate time, really, trying to control it. . . . What stands out is just the ugliness of [the protesters]. I don't mean just physical ugliness; I mean just the venomous kind of ugliness of the people who were organizing it. Real beasts. . . . It was a hate-filled kind of exercise." Price arrived at the White House "with my eyes swollen shut and my lungs on fire from tear gas," although he "considered that my own fault for having pressed too close to the action." It was a memorable experience for him: Price volunteered that, of all the protests during his time in the government, May Day stood out. He was not alone: other Nixon administration officials I interviewed also had a particularly strong recollection of May Day. "If you'd been there, you'd remember it, too," Ziegler said when asked why. "It was a very dangerous point."[90]

John Ehrlichman and John Dean also decided to get a closer look at the battle. At 7 A.M., accompanied by aides, they climbed into a military helicopter for a flight over the theater of combat. "We saw burning cars in Georgetown, a confused maze of little figures running through the streets, and conclaves of demonstrators on university campuses," Dean writes. "Flashing police lights and pitched rock battles blended into a general scene of chaos." As was his proclivity during demonstrations, Ehrlichman, once again in a "sporting" mood, busily directed his home movie camera at the protesters. The helicopter was forced to set down on the south lawn of the White House because its usual landing site, the Ellipse, was "crisscrossed with demonstrators . . . blue-uniformed police giving chase." At 10:40 A.M., Ehrlichman was again training his home movie camera on the protesters, this time in the street five blocks from the White House. To his displeasure, he was spotted by reporters. Ehrlichman later explained to other officials that his activity in the field "enabled him to become properly assessed of situation; interested in deployment of troops and how they were being used."[91]

Around the same time as Dean and Ehrlichman were embarking on their flight, Chief of Police Jerry Wilson, in communication with the Justice Department, abandoned the policy of dispersing the demonstrators and opted for mass arrests. The protesters' hit-and-run tactics—in part a result of the dispersal policy—had created "a problem for the police because they were spread so thin," Ehrlichman told other officials afterward. "It became obvious to Chief Wilson that the policy of dispersing was counter productive because it was right in line with the kids' tactics." The decision to make mass arrests "was partly dictated by the fact that it was possible to make peaceful arrests," Ehrlichman said. "The kids gave up cheerfully. It became the MO of the morning."[92]

By 8 A.M., when the Washington rush hour was peaking, more than two thousand protesters, prematurely committed to the battle, were already in the clutches of police. Before the morning was over, more than seven thousand—the most for any single event or on any single day in U.S. history—would be arrested. Scores of innocent bystanders were swept up in the dragnet. Among them were a couple on their way to get married and six mental patients and their attendants. A high school senior from New Jersey who was in Washington to visit a cousin and speak to George Washington University admissions officials asked a policemen how to get away from the protest. "I'll show you where you'll be safe," the officer replied. He then grabbed the youth and placed him under arrest. At Wilson's order, formulated in collaboration with Justice, police dispensed with their standard arrest procedures, not bothering even to charge the protesters with any offense; on field arrest forms, under "arresting officer," they belatedly filled in the names and badge numbers of seven officers "on a rotating basis." Martial law might not have been declared, but it was in effect. (A subsequent class action suit by the ACLU won $12 million in damages for wrongfully arrested persons.) Officials acted to "keep those arrested out of circulation" for at least twelve hours; consequently, "extreme delays" marked their processing. The flood of arrests wreaked "chaos" in Washington's judicial system, straining it "to the bursting point"; the Justice Department had only been prepared for 1,600–2,500 busts. The D.C. Superior Court clerk's office was swamped with phone calls from worried parents: one woman from New York, who had just received a call from the city jail saying her son was there, tearfully said she thought he was in college in Florida.[93]

The protesters were crammed into city lockups and a detention camp hur-

riedly set up on a football field near RFK stadium ringed by an eight-foot cy-
clone fence. For many hours, prisoners in the makeshift compound had no food
or sanitary facilities, and scant protection against a chilly wind. "Calling this a
concentration camp would be a very apt description," Benjamin Spock, one of
the detainees, commented. The protesters managed to keep their senses of humor, however. Leaning against the fence toward police and troops, they chanted,
"Push 'em back, push 'em back, way back," and "We want Bob Hope." Black
Washington residents brought the overwhelmingly white prisoners carloads of
beans, soup, and sandwiches. "We gave them food so that they can put their
bodies on the line and disrupt the government," a veteran of the civil rights
movement said. "Anything that does that can help our people." Brad Lyttle
remembered, "The black community in Washington was just *amazed* by the
whole thing [May Day]. I never saw black people so friendly to movement
people. Everywhere you went, as soon as they found out you were associated
with the peace movement, they were just *effusive* in their warmth. They
thought it was tremendous. . . . Here The Man was getting it."[94]

In San Clemente, Nixon and Haldeman were receiving frequent reports on
the protest from Ehrlichman and Dean. Both Ehrlichman and Dean later said
Nixon wanted reports every half hour. "My staff would call each command post
for its latest word," Dean wrote. "We would write a hurried report, fire it off to
the President and begin immediately on the next one." Haldeman said Ehrlichman and Dean were overstating their contact with the president, however. "It
wasn't that frequent," he recalled, somewhat irritatedly. "John [Ehrlichman] and
I kept in touch," though. "Running loose—arresting fast," Haldeman's notes of
one meeting with Nixon that morning read. "Lots of film of arrests etc." Haldeman relayed to the president that Ehrlichman felt the makeshift prison was a
"bad situation." As Ehrlichman subsequently said, it was the "public relations
aspect" of that situation that "concerned" him. However, "let them out and
[they'll] disrupt traffic," one of the three officials warned. Haldeman and Nixon
decided to prod conservative—but not moderate—senators to denounce the
demonstrators. "Leave Muskie etc. stuck out with them," they proposed. "Keep
them tied to peace demonstration. . . . *Must* blame the Democrats. As the
worm turns—hit 'em." Also, "Don't let them [the protesters] come out looking
like nice kids. Get some." Ehrlichman suggested they "get someone to identify
[the] VC flag" the protesters had hoisted over the prison compound "and get
someone to tear it down."[95]

Charles Colson, who kept barging into Dean's office throughout the morning
with questions about the demonstration, annoying both Dean and his assistant
Fred Fielding, sent the prisoners a crate of oranges in Muskie's name. He informed the press of Muskie's generosity. "Heh-heh. Damn Colson thing,"
Haldeman chuckled to Nixon two days later. "He do something else?" asked the

president, who felt Colson had "the balls of a brass monkey." After Haldeman explained what Colson had done, provoking laughter from Nixon, he remarked, "I don't know how the hell he does that stuff, but he—it's good, you know, he's been around the District here so long, he has a lot of contacts and . . . he can get stuff done here, but . . . he's . . . gonna get caught at some of these things. . . . But he's [also] . . . got a lot done that he hasn't been caught at." Haldeman added, darkly, "We got some stuff that he doesn't know anything about too."[96]

Worried about harmful political fallout from the mass roundup and imprisonment of protesters, Ehrlichman and other officials gathered in Attorney General John Mitchell's office at 2 P.M. to discuss "detention and due process." Afterward, his thirst for activity in the field not yet quenched, Ehrlichman drove out to the prison compound with Colson's aide Richard Moore to get a firsthand look at it. Their experiences "confirmed their belief that the kids should be moved indoors," Ehrlichman recalled. "It looked like a concentration camp," he said, echoing Spock. "It was bad. I got on the Justice Department to do something about it." He added, "Those were the kinds of things that concerned me the most [about antiwar demonstrations]. I thought the early demonstrations were well in hand: we had pretty good liaison with the marshals and the people that were leading them, and I thought we handled it with some finesse. But [that] one I thought we did *not* handle well, and something had to be done rather quickly . . . about it." Following further official consultations, and after darkness had fallen, the protesters were bused to the Washington Coliseum, where they plopped their weary bodies on a bare stone floor. The Department of Justice reportedly delayed the distribution of army blankets to them.[97]

At 3:30 P.M., Rennie Davis held a press conference. "We want to make clear that we failed this morning to stop the U.S. government," Davis announced. Although protesters had made tactical mistakes, "our biggest problem was not appreciating the extent to which the government would go to put people on the skids." PCPJ leader Sidney Peck was appalled at Davis's declaration. "It was ridiculous, really ridiculous," he remarked. The protest hadn't *failed*, Peck waxed peeved. "It was a major political statement, a victory." Shutting down the government had never been a realistic objective anyway. David McReynolds agreed; he had seen enough of "mobile tactics" already to know better. "It was a miserable failure—again," he said. "It was an exciting concept, [but] it didn't work." White House officials and members of Congress also proclaimed the protest's failure. Senator Hugh Scott (R-Pa.) said it "deserved to fail, as it was fated to fail. These nasties are achieving their purpose. They came here to get arrested and they're getting arrested. This is a floating mob."[98]

That night, many PCPJ leaders felt a sense of relief. The May Day Tribe had gone for broke, leaving the remaining two days of the protest to clearer heads, some of whom had purposely laid low during the morning's battle so that they would still be around to lead the rest of the offensive. "We were all relieved," McReynolds remembered. "Because it was clear after the first day that it was back in our hands—out of Rennie's hands—back in the hands of . . . people who were much more stable in my view."⁹⁹

Hours earlier, in Saigon, two thousand people gathered in tribute to a young South Vietnamese student who had immolated herself in protest over the war four years earlier. Don Luce, only days from being expelled from Vietnam for publicizing the tiger cages and the building of new ones by the United States, had communicated with Rennie Davis to synchronize the protest with May Day. Luce helped mobilize students and Buddhists—"the usual suspects"—for the memorial ceremony.¹⁰⁰

At 1 P.M. on May 4, following morning clashes with police, leading to 685 arrests, several thousand protesters marched without a permit to the Justice Department. "Mass arrests expected, without violence," Dean apprised Nixon at noon. Dean also reported that a "live bomb" had been "found suspended underneath Taft Street Bridge," but, as he later conveyed, it turned out to be "a bogus, harmless device." The demonstrators rallied under the office window of Attorney General Mitchell, who periodically appeared on his balcony, scowling and smoking a pipe and "looking for all the world like Stalin," McReynolds recalled. Among the rally speakers was the Chicago Seven defendant John Froines, who had been sought by the FBI since the previous day on the same federal conspiracy charges Davis faced. The FBI code-named Froines "Echo" and "the package." "Echo is saying he came here not to surrender but to be protected by his people," an FBI agent radioed the bureau's Washington field office a block away. "Well, we want him!" replied the bureau. Agents watched Froines's every move as he stepped from the microphone. "The package is now moving east toward the flagpole," one radioed. "He's standing south of the flagpole talking to a man with a bald head." Moments later, "We have him! We have him!" "Good. Let's keep him!" came the response. Haldeman told Nixon the next morning that he didn't think Froines "amounts to anybody, but they got him."¹⁰¹

At around 2:30 P.M., McReynolds, an avowed alcoholic on the wagon, left the rally to purchase cigarettes and chocolate in preparation for an evening or more in jail. "I didn't have any cigarettes or chocolate, so I said to friends, 'I'll be right back,'" McReynolds recounted. "I went up to the PCPJ office, which is about five blocks away. When I got there, they said they'd busted everybody at the Justice Department. I said, 'No . . . they're going to do that at four o'clock. . . .' And they said, 'No, the reports are it just happened.'" "I was lucky that day." The police moved methodically into the crowd, "making individual arrests of all demonstrators in an effort to avoid the problems arising with yesterday's mass arrests," Dean told Nixon. "Offenders are dancing and singing and offering no resistance." But, Dean added, "the activities . . . have been covered extensively by news and the media." Clubbings were infrequent, despite Police Chief Wilson's concern that, after being "provoked, abused" and "harangued" since Sunday morning, his men "might lose their cool." Two thousand protesters in all were busted. "Wilson feels that the demonstrators have been broken in strength and spirit," Dean told Nixon at 7 P.M. Many were again stuffed into city lockups. "They packed seventeen of us in one small holding-cell for forty-eight hours," one recalled. "It was dirty, no water in the toilet. We had to organize rotation to lie down. It was so tight one person at all times had to stand on the toilet, or sit on it if they could bear it." The protesters were fed day-old sandwiches "loaded with mayonnaise. A lot of us got very sick from it."[102]

As the arrests were getting under way, Nixon discussed Dean's latest "riot report" with Ehrlichman. In addition, Haldeman and the president continued to scheme at getting political mileage out of the protesters. "Smear the liberals with the left—and keep at it," Haldeman's meeting notes read. Haldeman wrote Colson that afternoon or evening:

> I'm sure you've already thought of this, but it's imperative that we have a highly efficient system set up to log all of the quotes of the various Democratic candidates regarding the demonstrations of the last two weeks—also, all of the failures to make statements at critical times by each of these candidates.
>
> The point here, of course is, that as time goes on, the April/May demonstrations of 1971 will tend to run together as one event including the Veterans, the Saturday march, and the May Day tribe. Looking at it this way, we have the spectacle of Muskie on the platform with Rennie Davis, Teddy Kennedy in the Mall with the demonstrators and their marihuana, etc. We should have a very careful log of this and verbatim quotes of all their statements. They will obviously be very useful in the future.[103]

That night, protesters met at St. Stephen's Episcopal Church to plan a demonstration the next day at the Capitol. They were unable to agree on tactics. In the eyes of the White House, however, "trouble" was "very likely," Dean apprised Haldeman and Ehrlichman, since the protest would "follow the pattern established this week." Dean also reported other antiwar activity scheduled for May.[104]

The next morning, shortly after 9, Nixon and Haldeman discussed the impending demonstration. Haldeman related that the protesters would demand that Congress ratify the People's Peace Treaty. "This is this peace treaty that they've signed with North Vietnam," he laughed. When Haldeman repeated Dean's forecast that "trouble" was "very likely," Nixon replied, "Good." He later mused, "I wonder if the Congress today will really get a bellyful of these people." However, the president seemed to be struggling to see the silver lining in May Day and growing public criticism of Monday's mass arrests:

> We may have more going for us than we think here, Bob. Yeah. We shouldn't be frightened about it. . . . You're gonna run into people that—the overreaction thing and all that sort of thing. My point [is], you're gonna get accustomed to that. No way you're gonna avoid it. . . . So therefore, play it hard. Play it responsibly but play it hard and don't back off from it. . . . Stay firm and get credit for it. That's my point. See, I don't want to make an accident out of it. I don't want to be doing on the basis, well, we're sort of sitting here embattled and doing the best we can. . . . It may be that we're setting an example, Bob, for . . . universities, for other cities, and so forth and so on, right? . . . Let 'em look here. These people try something, bust 'em.

Haldeman suggested there was political mileage in TV footage of the "big mob" at the Justice Department the day before. "Fortunately, they're all just really bad-lookin' people," he told Nixon. "There's no semblance of respectability." Haldeman further opined that Rennie Davis, who was "a convicted conspirator and . . . discredited," was "good for us." He meant "good in the sense that it's bad for them," Haldeman later explained; Davis hurt the movement's public image, he believed, although the overall effect of his actions was harmful to the administration.[105]

The president and Haldeman also discussed a Federal Employees for Peace rally scheduled for that afternoon in Lafayette Park. Nixon wanted close surveillance of the traitors. "Can we get in there with those Government employees? Is there any way to?" he wondered. "I'd sure get a lot of pictures and everything. . . . You know, just get guys with . . . news things." Nixon crowed over his administration's monitoring of the demonstrators' plans: "We sure have good intelligence, don't we?" "Heh, heh," chortled Haldeman.[106]

Nixon and Haldeman went on to talk about the previously mentioned White House "stuff" against protesters that Colson knew nothing about. This stuff was undertaken by a "plant" that "Chapin's crew and . . . Ron Walker and the advance men" directed, Haldeman told Nixon. "What we've got is . . . a guy that nobody, none of us knows except Dwight . . . who is just completely removed. There's no contact at all. Who has mobilized a crew. . . . He's starting to build it now. We're gonna use it for the campaign next year." The president asked, "Are they really any good?" Responded Haldeman, "In fact this guy's a real conspirator . . . thug-type guy. . . . This is the kinda guy [who] can get out and tear things up." Haldeman reported that the crew had engaged in undercover work against Senator Muskie during a campaign stop in New Hampshire. Now, he said, "they're gonna stir up some of this Vietcong flag business as Colson's gonna do it through hard hats and Legionnaires. What Colson's gonna do on it, and what I suggested he do, and I think that they can get away with this, do it with the teamsters. Just ask them to dig up those, their eight thugs." After Nixon knowingly replied, "Yeah," Haldeman advised that they work through Teamsters president Frank Fitzsimmons, who was "trying to . . . play our game anyway." Submitted Nixon, "They've got guys who'll go in and knock their heads off." "Sure," Haldeman responded. "Murderers. Guys that really, you know, that's what they really do. . . . The regular strikebusters-types and all that . . . and then they're gonna beat the [obscenity] out of some of these people. . . . And hope they really hurt 'em. You know, I mean go in . . . and smash some noses." Years later, Haldeman said he didn't know whether this "was a serious discussion or whether it was facetious, playing back to the construction workers' [attack on protesters in 1970]—you know, saying, 'Well, maybe just the thing to do is to get the Teamsters, get some big guys out, and have them beat up on them.' . . . It may have been . . . out of frustration, possibly seriously. . . . 'Let's meet Goliath in his own field, send David out and let him throw a few rocks at him and see what happens.'"[107]

Shortly after noon, inside a police cordon, and facing another cordon around the White House, five hundred Federal Employees for Peace—the maximum number of protesters allowed in Lafayette Park—began their rally. "Majority of crowd not 'long-hair' types," Dean reported to Nixon. He also passed the president a flyer on the demonstration, which, unfortunately, "had extensive media coverage." At 2:30, those federal employees still present and other protesters marched to the Capitol. The marchers were "almost exclusively 'long hair' types" now, Dean told Nixon, "but they carry the banners of the Federal Employees for Peace group."[108]

Meanwhile two thousand demonstrators had gathered on the Mall for a "people's press conference." After the conference, "which appeared to be more of a rally" (as the *Post* wryly observed), the demonstrators surged toward the Capitol. Police sealed entrances to the building and lined several hallways. The protesters exuberantly sang, danced and whooped on the Capitol steps. One took all his clothes off, "to a chorus of cheers." At another point, Congressman G. V. "Sonny" Montgomery (D-Miss.) stormed up the steps to seize what he thought was an NLF flag. It turned out to be a copy of the People's Peace Treaty. Four members of Congress—three blacks and one woman—addressed the crowd. "Arrests appear imminent," Dean transmitted to Nixon at 3:15. Also, "demonstrators appear to be well organized tactically, e.g., use of radio equipment, contingency plans and post-demonstration arrangements." Fifteen minutes later, police began hauling the protesters away, again being careful to make "individual arrests," Dean reported. Some 1,450, largely youthful, demonstrators were busted. Many, including David McReynolds, were taken to the Coliseum. "I looked so ancient that the kids . . . all assumed I was a lawyer," McReynolds, then forty-one, remembered. "And it wasn't until after I'd been there twenty-four hours that I began to get irritated with being considered a lawyer."[109]

Inside the White House, with media and congressional criticism of Monday's mass roundup of protesters mushrooming (among other things, Senator Edward Kennedy announced he was planning hearings on the government's actions), officials continued to circle the wagons. "No one gives an inch regarding constitutionality of arrest procedure—absolute united front," Nixon directed in a 5 P.M. meeting with Ehrlichman and Haldeman. His own line would be: "I don't regret anyone's violation of constitutional rights. . . . Competent job—police, troops, officials." Ziegler delivered this line at an afternoon press briefing. In another meeting, either the president or Dean urged, "Be sure no leak out of White House regarding any concern regarding arrests." The White House political operative Jack Caulfield suggested to Dean that they publicize "detailed" police accounts of the arrests "as the criticism mounts—and all signs indicate that it will." And Dean informed Nixon that the May Day Tribe "now calls itself the DC 7000."[110]

Early that evening, three thousand demonstrators blocked traffic on a highway near the University of Maryland. Dean told the president that Rennie Davis was behind the disruption. After police and dogs routed the protesters, Maryland's governor imposed a dusk-to-dawn curfew in the area. University students were told of the curfew by announcements over loudspeakers on two helicopters that hovered eerily overhead.[111]

The same day, nationwide protests were held to commemorate the Kent State and Jackson State killings one year earlier. Thirty thousand gathered on the Boston Common, where they "passed bottles of wine and beer, smoked marijuana and generally ignored the speakers." Ten thousand turned out in New York, five thousand in Madison. In Seattle, without warning, police brutally broke up a downtown march and yanked bystanders out of stores. "Anybody that didn't have a necktie, they went after," a store manager angrily testified.[112]

The following day in Washington, scattered bands of May Day protesters marched on the South Vietnamese Embassy and the D.C. jail. They also posted copies of the People's Peace Treaty on the doors of federal buildings. As Dean informed Nixon, these remaining May Day Tribesmen were plagued by "internal dissension and confusion." Members of the American Association of Psychiatrists marched to the Justice Department that afternoon. "They have picked up a few demonstrator-types along the route," Dean reported. Overall, however, "city is very calm; streets are virtually devoid of 'long hair' types."[113]

The same day in Boston, several thousand demonstrators attempted to choke the Federal Building. "The cops stepped forward—we were just sitting there— and they kept saying, 'Move, move move,'" Daniel Ellsberg, who was once again on the pavement, recounted. "I put my hands over my head, [although] some people felt it was not nonviolent to put your hands over your head, that it was provocative or something—'Oh, screw that.' And I never agreed with that again, because . . . this four-foot baton smashed my Rolex watch, smashed the crystal. . . . It also drove glass into my wrist, and the watch into my wrist. So my wrist was rather badly cut, and I was bleeding a lot and had to go have it bandaged." Ellsberg amusedly discovered, however, that just as in the TV commercials that showed watches emerging unscathed from sharks' stomachs and surviving other forms of "punishment," his watch kept ticking. Several days later, he participated in a Harvard/MIT arms control seminar attended by Establishment notables with a large bandage conspicuously on his wrist. [114]

In the White House that morning, officials continued to plot their public relations counteroffensive to the criticism of Monday's mass arrests. "Emphasize grave danger to citizens," Colson suggested. When Ziegler expressed concern that the "constitutionality question will come up" at press briefings, Ehrlichman responded that "newspapermen are the least competent men to judge constitutionality. Most are amateur lawyers." And "no one is free from the jeopardy of arrest if he happens to be in or near the transaction of the crime." Ehrlichman added, "After the war in Germany, you couldn't find a Nazi anywhere—none were guilty. You can never find a man who did anything wrong after the fact." Apparently just trying to be helpful, Richard Moore chimed in, "Being arrested is not a violation of constitutional rights." Ziegler remained worried: was the White House's position that "no constitutional rights were violated?" "Don't take the question," Ehrlichman instructed. He further advised that the D.C. police spokesman Paul Fuqua "should talk about the miserable, filthy, dangerous, etc. who are the hard core." At the end of the meeting, Moore advocated stressing that Chief Wilson, not Nixon, ordered the mass arrests, then offered, "There were no mass arrests." [115]

At 3 p.m., the president and Ehrlichman discussed the results of public opinion polls on the antiwar movement's spring offensive. While 32 percent of Americans approved of VVAW's Operation Dewey Canyon III and 42 percent disapproved, they noted, the corresponding figures for May Day were 18 and 71 percent. Also, 56 percent approved of the police's methods during May Day, and 76 percent felt the mass arrests were justified. Only 11 percent believed the police had employed too much force against the protesters, 40 percent felt the police had used the right amount of force, and 23 percent felt they had been too lenient. Thus, reasoned Nixon, the White House should "push EMK's [Edward M. Kennedy's] 'courageous support of the demonstrators'" as exemplified in his public statements: "Distribute widely." [116]

Ehrlichman recalled that White House officials chalked up May Day as something of a victory for their side. "We felt we came out of it pretty good," he said. "May Day was considered by us to have been a failure. The protesters did not succeed in their goal of shutting down Washington." Colson felt the police's tactics had been "very successful." So did the White House aide Depray Muir: they "have certainly proved to be an effective stick," he wrote Dean. Officials were well aware that May Day received overwhelmingly hostile media coverage, perhaps typified by Eric Sevareid's comment, "It was Halloween to the 10th power." Ray Price said the protest "in a sense played into our hands by showing the other side of [the antiwar movement]"—that is, "the vicious side."[117]

But May Day was nonetheless a troubling experience for officials. It had taken an immense mobilization of armed might and twelve thousand arrests to keep Washington open. "If [the protesters] hadn't paralyzed the nation's capitol they had at least sent shivers down its spine," the editors of *Ramparts* wrote. Jeb Magruder recalled that the White House was "shaken" by May Day. The protest had certainly not helped the administration's image among black Washington residents. "In Washington it had a *real* effect on people," McReynolds remembered, echoing other accounts. "In Washington, by the third day, everybody was on our side. . . . The city was angry at the government, angry about the tear gas, angry at the troops. . . . The war had come home to people within that one city. That part had succeeded." May Day also impressed upon some Americans a sense of urgency about stopping the war. It reenergized some peace activists, too. But most important, May Day was a particularly stark sign to the administration that prolongation of the war meant continued social strife at home. CIA Director Richard Helms: "It was obviously viewed by everybody in the administration, particularly with all of the arrests and the howling about civil rights and human rights and all the rest of it, . . . as a very damaging kind of event. I don't think there was any doubt about that." "All the hullabaloo about the arrests," Helms said, would be "hard for any administration to handle." And May Day "was one of the things that was putting increasing pressure on the administration to try and find some way to get out of the war, some way to make a deal with the North Vietnamese."[118]

May Day's political impact can ultimately only be assessed in tandem with that of the peace movement's spring offensive as a whole, though. Haldeman was right: in the eyes of many Americans—including administration officials—the spring protests tended to "run together as one event." And as an event that dramatically brought the war to the attention of the nation for eighteen days in a row, helping keep debate over the issue alive, the offensive was an undeniable political success for the movement. To the vexation of the White House, "public protest—our nightmare, our challenge, and, in a weird way, our spur," as Henry Kissinger writes—would simply not go away. Plans for the offensive may have influenced Nixon's decision to announce the withdrawal of another one hundred thousand U.S. troops from Vietnam on April 7. The offensive was probably also a consideration in the administration's suggestion to the North Vietnamese later in May that they could keep their troops in the South as part of a peace settlement. Members of Congress, the targets of much of the spring dissent, clearly noticed it. As Richard Strout of the *Christian Science Monitor* observed, "the tumult that filled headlines and TV emphasized the new stage of the drama" to legislators, nourishing support for end-the-war and antidraft legislation. Sidney Peck, not a political Pollyanna by any means, perceived that the offensive had exerted "really a major impact on Congress."[119]

During the rest of the spring and summer, the Nixon administration took other steps to counteract the offensive and criticism of the mass arrests. Before press photographers, the president praised D.C. officials and U.S. military officers for their "successful handling" of the protests. "If the demonstrators had been able to run wild in the city, it might have resulted in untold injury and destruction," his recommended "talking points" for the meeting read. Nixon told his guests that "the city of Washington had set an example for the entire nation in dealing with demonstrations of this type," another memo records. The administration also announced that $3.9 million of Washington taxpayers' money had had to be spent to cope with the demonstrations. To publicize this price tag, it asked Congress to appropriate federal funds to reimburse the city. (Haldeman told Dean, who apparently proposed the request, that both he and the president "*strongly* favor[ed]" it "from a PR viewpoint.") White House aides advised Nixon not to issue a formal public statement on the request, however, as that would stimulate additional scrutiny of the mass arrests, a topic that had already attracted enough discussion. "Further comment would be useful only to the critical press," Dean counseled. Cautioned Muir, "In my judgment, it does not appear to be fully understood how broad and deep the feeling is against the tactics utilized by the Metropolitan Police. . . . My experience has indicated that this is a highly sensitive issue. No reason appears why the White House should continue to play up its support for these tactics." They "should be kept ready" for future use "with somewhat less fanfare," Muir advised. Senator Strom Thurmond (D-S.C.) introduced legislation requiring protesters to pay for any damage to public property inflicted by their demonstrations. "*Good!*" Nixon scrawled in the margin of one of his daily news summaries. "E [Ehrlichman]—I suggested this as you will recall."[120]

Haldeman ordered his right-hand man Lawrence Higby to widely distribute the results of a private poll showing public displeasure with the protests. A cover letter "from an appropriate person" should state "that the recipient will be pleased to note that the American people had the good judgment to disapprove strongly of the recent demonstration fiascos here in Washington," Haldeman instructed. Key congressmen should be personally apprised of the data. "Ziegler should give this a big play—working it with the friendly columnists," Haldeman directed. And White House propagandists should ponder "other means of getting maximum mileage" from the poll. Similarly, Colson sent fifteen thousand copies of press denunciations of the demonstrations and their congressional apologists to a variety of officials around the country.[121]

The administration made sure the public understood the sinister character of May Day. John Mitchell called the protesters "rights robbers" and likened them to "Hitler's brownshirts" (a comparison the *New York Times* quickly called "absurd"). Richard Kleindienst declared, "Make no mistake, this was a calculated attempt by organized disrupters, led by people who met repeatedly with Viet Cong and North Vietnamese leaders. It was not a group of frolicking picknickers." The "anarchistic mob" that fomented this "deadly serious program to halt the U.S. government" engaged in "widespread and unremitting acts of violence," Kleindienst charged, including "rolling boulders into streets," "stringing barbed wire and ropes across streets," "throwing rocks and bottles at passing motorists," and "slashing at motorists with wooden poles." This "vicious and wanton mob attack on Washington" made "life unsafe for hours at a time at key points on the streets" of the city, Kleindienst alleged.[122]

Government operatives stepped up their surveillance and harassment of VVAW. "They went into high gear after Dewey Canyon III," Jan Barry commented, based on released FBI documents. "It was full court press. . . . Hardball. . . . We started hearing reports of people being harassed on their jobs. I lost my job [as a researcher] with CBS News under tremendously strange and powerful circumstances that nobody would talk about." The orders "had to have come from Washington," Barry maintained.[123]

Colson orchestrated a covert campaign to smear the VVAW leader John Kerry. "I think we have Kerry on the run, he is beginning to take a tremendous beating in the press, but let's not let him up, let's destroy this young demagogue before he becomes another Ralph Nader," Colson exhorted another official. The administration initiated a "Jobs for Vets" campaign to appease unhappy veterans. After prompting the director of the VA to hold a press conference claiming that the campaign and VA were responsible for declining unemployment among Vietnam vets, Colson wrote an aide, "This is a classic illustration of what we can do when we use a little imagination."[124]

The White House dug for communist financing of the spring offensive. On June 4, through Fred Fielding, Dean transmitted to Haldeman, Ehrlichman, and "possibly the President" currently classified memos on funding of the protests and the New Left, noting, "This question has been posed several times and I have been asked where do these people get their money. This is the best information that we have come up with to date." And Nixon directed Colson to "note" reporters' comments on the protests and mass arrests so that the White House could better determine its friends and enemies and proceed accordingly.[125]

The Pentagon Papers

The evening of May 6, following the protest at Boston's Federal Building, Daniel Ellsberg, aged forty, former Marine officer, fellow at MIT (where he was office neighbor to William Bundy, with whom he had "cool" relations), sat before a typewriter and reflected on the spring offensive. "We are willing to violate traffic laws to try to end the war; the Government is willing to violate the Constitution to keep the war going," Ellsberg typed, his injured wrist wrapped in a medical dressing. "The demonstrators are determined to act non-violently. . . . But the U.S. government, and city and state governments, are willing to . . . visit the official violence that is commonplace to Vietnamese upon wives, sons, grandmothers in American cities. . . . In this effort, city police use clubs and boots on humans in the mob frenzy with which soldiers in Vietnam . . . [use] rifles and grenades, artillery and napalm on helpless civilians." Three days earlier in Washington, Ellsberg vexedly recalled, the government had "made it a crime to be young, with long hair . . . just as it is a capital crime to be Vietnamese in a rice paddy, within sight of an armed helicopter, and particularly to run." Ellsberg expressed his respect for other antiwar activists, whose principled moral action increasingly inspired him: "I have met, now, thousands of people who can oppose the war without hate, without anger. . . . People—some with fragile heads covered with white hair—who could regroup and sit again a few yards beyond the police and wait, singing, for the next attack: without bravado, without false emotion. . . . They set, above all, the example of responsible action . . . , of personal courage, of dignity, that . . . alone can end this war without further massive tragedies."[126]

When I interviewed him many years later, Ellsberg was one of America's most renowned peace activists and much in demand as a speaker; he traveled often to participate in antiwar events far from home. During the 1991 Gulf War, Ellsberg's was a prominent and impassioned voice for peace. An intense, driven man with receding, wavy white hair, a lean face, and an angular body, he had by then been arrested countless times protesting U.S. foreign and military policies. To Dan Ellsberg, getting arrested was nearly as old hat as taking the garbage out. I found him working in a cluttered basement office in his white, two-story house in the wooded hills above Berkeley, California.

Days after the spring antiwar offensive, Ellsberg gave a copy of the Pentagon Papers to Neil Sheehan, a "dour" *New York Times* reporter dissatisfied with the progress of his journalistic career whom he had first spoken to about getting the *Times* to publish the papers in late February, at the prompting of the antiwar activist Marcus Raskin. Ellsberg was still hoping for distribution through a splashy Senate hearing, TV lights and all, but his hope was waning; indeed, so frustrated was Ellsberg with his inability to persuade a prominent senator to publicize the papers that he even considered raining them down on Washington from a helicopter. Since their initial discussion, Ellsberg had given Sheehan a key to the Boston flat where he stored the papers. He was "nervous as a cat" over the arrangement; not only were the papers now passing through the fingers of someone he had only recently met and did not yet fully trust, but the *Times* might ultimately refuse to publish them. Sheehan was also nervous: he feared that someone else would break the explosive story before he did, and that personal glory would thus elude him. His nerves were "close to break-point." The underlying tone of the two men's relationship was "paranoid, almost psychopathic." Had Ellsberg known during their mid-May meeting that Sheehan had already made copies of the papers several weeks earlier, reneging on a previous promise not to, and had taken them over to hotel suites occupied by *Times* staffers for examination, the tone of their relationship might have been hostile. [127]

On June 10, following several weeks of internal debate and anxious perusal of the Pentagon Papers by its personnel, the *Times* resolved to publish them. This formerly Top Secret study of U.S. decision making in Vietnam would begin hitting the newstands in three days' time.

On the afternoon of June 12, Tricia Nixon was married in the White House Rose Garden. Police ringed a two-block area and a fence encircled the Ellipse to ward off protesters (whose plans John Dean had been reporting to Haldeman). Tricia's father, Richard, was in an uncharacteristically carefree mood. In the White House basement, however, shortly after the wedding ended, Kissinger's aide Alexander Haig was less relaxed. Advance warning had arrived of the *Times*'s decision to publish a "Vietnam study" the next day, and Haig was busily trying to find out everything he could about it. As Haig told the Johnson administration's Walt Rostow, whom he reached over the phone in Austin, Texas, the White House suspected "a guy named Ellsberg" was behind release of the study. [128]

In Cambridge, Ellsberg was agitated. He was pleased that the papers were finally coming out, but annoyed that Sheehan had not bothered to inform him (engendering "a long coolness" between the two men). That evening Ellsberg and his wife had dinner with Howard Zinn and his spouse, also an antiwar activist. After smoking some marijuana, the two couples went out for a movie. Before going home, Ellsberg asked the Zinns if they would mind keeping something for him for a couple of days. The Zinns agreed, and Ellsberg drove to his apartment, where he had recently brought a copy of the papers. His downstairs neighbors subsequently recalled being awakened "by the noise of boxes thumping down the stairs," then looking out the window and seeing the Ellsbergs loading the boxes into a car. Half an hour later, the neighbors heard the Ellsbergs returning home, laughing and singing reveille. It was somewhat odd behavior for a man still expecting to go to prison forever.[129]

The next morning, a Sunday, the *Times* published over six pages of the papers and explanatory articles. Initial reaction in the White House was muted. True, Nixon was irritated over the publication of classified documents, but the study focused on the Johnson administration's policies, not his own. He had no reason to fear embarrassment. Soon, however, "there was panic in the White House," Colson remembered. Henry Kissinger, worried that his links with Ellsberg would hurt his standing with Nixon and concerned that the leak might damage the secret negotiations he was then undertaking with the Chinese and North Vietnamese, flew into a fist-pounding rage, lighting a "white-hot" fire under Nixon's behind. Release of the documents could "destroy" U.S. foreign policy by suggesting to other nations that the United States could not negotiate confidentially, Kissinger contended. "It shows you're a weakling, Mr. President," he cunningly told Nixon. In a series of "panic sessions," Kissinger vehemently condemned Ellsberg in front of Nixon and other officials. Ellsberg was an "unbalanced" "genius" whose heavy drug use and bizarre sexual habits had turned him against the war, Kissinger alleged. Not only that, Ellsberg had other—more recent—Top Secret documents in his possession, including some focusing on U.S. nuclear targeting.[130] Kissinger "was quite agitated at times," Ehrlichman recalled. Said another official, "He was jumping up and down." One day, after Nixon had invited him into the Oval Office to meet two prowar veterans (including John O'Neill of "Vietnam Veterans for a Just Peace"), Kissinger went into "one of his most passionate tirades," Colson recounted. "He described Ellsberg as a sexual pervert, said he shot Vietnamese from helicopters in Vietnam, used drugs, had sexual relations with his wife in front of their children. Henry said he was the most dangerous man in America today. He said he 'must be stopped at all costs.'"[131]

Aroused, Nixon came to conclude that Ellsberg was part of a conspiracy. Two former Pentagon officials then at the Brookings Institution, Leslie Gelb and Morton Halperin, both of whom were also advisers to Senator Muskie, had additional Top Secret documents secreted away at Brookings, Nixon believed. Some of Kissinger's liberal staffers might be in cahoots with them. Moreover, Ellsberg reportedly had foreign communist connections.[132]

The Nixon administration moved swiftly to counter this latest political threat. On June 15, Justice obtained a temporary injunction in federal court ordering the *Times* to cease publication of the papers. Presidential Counsel John Dean and his aides simultaneously "dove into constitutional law" to assess the legality of the action. Their conclusions were pessimistic. "I had poor Fred Fielding talking to lawyers all over the country about . . . the little First Amendment problem here," recalled the balding, deep-voiced Dean, who when I met him was a Beverly Hills investment banker. Dean himself couldn't understand what Nixon and Kissinger were up in arms about. "Just a *tremendous* overreaction," he said over a hamburger and fries in a Marriott Hotel restaurant. "I could never figure it out. I'd read those issues of the *New York Times* when they came out, and I said, 'What's everybody so upset about? This doesn't reflect badly on Nixon.' . . . They should have just let it go, and then it would have been a non-issue. Let the *New York Times* run it all out—put them on the front page. You know, it's pretty dull reading."[133] On June 30, the Supreme Court ruled against the administration, permitting the *Times* to resume publication.

Also through the courts, Nixon moved to "get" Ellsberg (as he put it).[134] A federal grand jury in Los Angeles indicted Ellsberg for violating the Espionage Act and stealing government property. Ellsberg, who had gone underground after the papers came out, surrendered in Boston.

The White House asked Lyndon Johnson to condemn publication of the documents. The former president refused, saying that the *Times* and *Washington Post* (which had also begun publishing the papers) would assail him for it. Those newspapers, he bitterly charged from his ranch in Texas, were trying to "re-execute" him.[135]

Nixon directed Haldeman to "brutally chew . . . out" all heads of government departments and agencies and threaten to fire them if they didn't prevent future leaks. He told Haldeman to organize lie detector tests for "those bastards" in the State Department. The president also ordered that other measures be taken to undermine "the counter-government." "I don't give a damn how it is done," he railed. "I want to know who is behind this and I want the most complete investigation that can be conducted. . . . Whatever the cost."[136]

The president ordered penetration of the Brookings Institution to retrieve the classified documents Gelb and Halperin were apparently keeping there. This was not the first time Nixon had called for a break-in at Brookings. Two years earlier, informed that Gelb had taken Pentagon files there on events leading up to President Johnson's October 1968 bombing halt—files Nixon wanted for waging political war against former officials who had turned dove—the president "slammed a pencil on his desk, and said, 'I want that Goddamn Gelb material and I don't care how you get it,'" Haldeman recounted. Over the following months, Haldeman discussed "various James Bond-type techniques" for obtaining the material with Alexander Haig, "but nothing was done," Haldeman said. Tom Huston was urging Haldeman on. "If we reach the point that we really want to start playing the game tough, you might wish to consider my suggestion of some months ago that we consider going into Brookings," he wrote Haldeman in July 1970. "There are a number of ways we could handle this. There are risks in all of them, of course; but there are also risks in allowing this government-in-exile to grow increasingly arrogant and powerful as each day goes by." Ellsberg's release of the Pentagon Papers "rekindled" Nixon's desire to get the Gelb material. "I was furious and frustrated," the president later admitted. "I saw absolutely no reason for that report to be at Brookings, and I said I wanted it back right now—even if it meant having to get it surreptitiously." Nixon's appetite for the material was further whetted when Colson informed him that a Brookings study was then under way on U.S. policy in Vietnam utilizing more recent classified documents. Gelb, Ellsberg, and Halperin were working on it. Colson recalled that Nixon "blew up at Haldeman" when informed, saying: "God damn it, Bob, haven't we got that capability in place? . . . Get 'em back." Other officials were also aroused by the new study. "We were all climbing the walls about it," Dean writes.[137]

Colson was eager to begin playing the game tough. "Mr. Slime" (as Kissinger called him behind his back) proposed to Jack Caulfield a plan—approved by Ehrlichman and Nixon—to firebomb Brookings. As eventually developed by White House operatives Howard Hunt and G. Gordon Liddy, the scheme involved purchasing a used fire engine and firemen's uniforms for use by a team of right-wing Cubans trained in fire fighting "so their performance would be believable," Liddy remembered. After the Cubans fire-bombed Brookings, they would "hit the vault" containing Gelb's documents, then slip away "in the confusion." Caulfield, not usually one to shy away from black bag jobs, judged the scheme "insane." "There are so many holes in this thing we'd never get away with it," he flusteredly told his boss John Dean. Dean was also unnerved by the plan and flew out to San Clemente on a courier flight to ask Ehrlichman to call it off. After listening silently to Dean criticize the scheme, Ehrlichman picked up the phone and, while glaring at Dean "like he was a traitor," called Colson back at the White House: "Chuck, the Brookings thing. We don't want it anymore. I'm telling Dean to turn Caulfield off." Liddy said the plan was canceled because it was too expensive.[138]

The president ordered that a secret unit be set up inside the White House to investigate Ellsberg and his co-conspirators. Ehrlichman selected Egil Krogh and David Young to head it. In one meeting with Krogh and Ehrlichman, Nixon made it clear that the "Plumbers" (as the unit became known) would be going after some bad people: "I've studied these cases long enough, and it's always a son-of-a-bitch that leaks," the president said. He suggested that the Plumbers' first job should be to investigate "communist ties to Ellsberg."[139]

Enamored of political intrigue, Colson swiftly involved himself with the Plumbers. He steered their work in the direction of discrediting Ellsberg and his collaborators. Colson desired to "go down the line to nail the guy cold," as he told Hunt. Colson wrote Haldeman: "He is a natural villain to the extent that he can be painted evil. . . . We can discredit the peace movement and have the

Democrats on a marvelous hook because thus far most of them have defended the release of the documents." Colson speculated to Hunt, "This thing could go one of two ways. Ellsberg could be turned into a martyr of the New Left" or he could be "exposed" as part of a conspiracy. "We might be able to put this bastard into a hell of a situation and discredit the New Left." Hunt woodenly referred to his project as the "neutralization of Ellsberg." Nixon agreed that the conspiracy should be "smoked out through the papers." The Plumbers would leak rather than plug leaks. As in the 1970 campaign, the White House's strategy was to slander the left and link it to Democrats. But this time the effort would be carried out clandestinely.[140]

To secure damaging material on Ellsberg, the Plumbers planned a bag job on the office of his psychiatrist, Dr. Lewis Fielding, in Beverly Hills. Ehrlichman gave them the green light for the operation; he cautiously stipulated that it be "done under your assurance that it is not traceable." Nixon encouraged it. (Ehrlichman, who spent eighteen months in prison for his part in the break-in, later denied approving it and said he believed he took a bum rap for Nixon.) Colson wrung $10,000 out of the Associated Milk Producers to pay for the operation; he laundered half of the money through the "People United for Good Government." At the White House's request, Hunt rounded up some of his old CIA contacts, three right-wing Cubans, to help with the break-in. After Hunt and Liddy cased Fielding's office wearing wigs provided by the CIA (Liddy also wore a device in his shoe to make him limp), and talked their way past the cleaning woman to snap pictures of the office using a photographic tobacco pouch (Liddy with a corncob pipe in his mouth), they sent the Cubans inside. The burglars rifled Fielding's "Ellsberg" file, but found little of interest.[141]

The illegal covert activities of the Plumbers were among the abuses of power later cited by the House Judiciary Committee in its inquiry into the impeachment of Nixon. By leaking the Pentagon Papers, Daniel Ellsberg had thus promoted the downfall of the Nixon administration, a downfall that, as we shall see, played a pivotal role in ending the war.

In July the *New York Times* published key portions of the Pentagon Papers and commentary in book form. Americans rushed to buy the book in droves, but "almost nobody read it," Ellsberg granted. Still, the media devoted extensive attention to the papers and the evidence they provided of official duplicity on Vietnam, advancing still further public questioning of the war. With all of the press he was receiving, Ellsberg knew he was having an impact. He subsequently compared the media crush around him with that which engulfed Gary Hart during his 1988 run for the presidency after his secret liaison with the model Donna Rice was discovered. "Hart knew what was hitting him when he got this ferocious mob of people in New Hampshire—I had that every day, everywhere I turned around, every time I turned around," Ellsberg recalled.

"We lived with that. It was astounding." And whereas the Hart story sizzled for a week, "this took thirty days." Ellsberg remembered:

> Twice in Broadway shows, during the show, in curtain time, they announced the fact for this audience that Daniel Ellsberg was in the audience, and the audience gave a standing ovation. . . . On one occasion they *stopped* the performance. The performance for the show stopped, and they said, "We've just been informed that Daniel Ellsberg is in the audience." And the *cast* applauded. And the audience rose and applauded.[142]

The Pentagon Papers also greased the skids for public and congressional questioning of Nixon during the subsequent Watergate hearings. "Nixon was exposed much sooner, and paid a much higher price for Watergate, because of the Pentagon Papers," Ellsberg argued. "Because it focused on the question of presidential lying. Otherwise he would have been given so much benefit of the doubt that they just wouldn't have pressed that hard, they wouldn't have kept poking at it."[143]

One person affected by the release of the documents was Ellsberg's father-in-law, the toy magnate Louis Marx. "He never talked to me again after the Pentagon Papers," Ellsberg recalled. "I was never allowed in his presence."[144]

In July the espionage trial of Ellsberg and Anthony Russo, his accomplice and RAND colleague, began in Los Angeles. Ellsberg and his lawyers were girding for the worst. Not only did prison look certain, but the White House was surely concocting a smear campaign. "It was always very puzzling why it didn't seem to be happening at any given moment," Ellsberg said later. "We knew they were collecting as much as they could on my sexual life, associations, and personal things, but they didn't seem to be using it. We were always waiting for that shoe to drop."[145]

The White House took other measures that summer to counter its opponents. John Dean began compiling a new and improved digest of incoming "domestic intelligence," which he knew was "of great interest and importance to the President." Unlike the previous fall, White House advance men acted to keep demonstrators away from Nixon during his public speeches. Before a talk at an Air Force base in Ohio, as Dwight Chapin informed Nixon afterward, they "screened all vehicles and individuals entering the base and looked for: (1) Youth with long hair and sloppy dress, wearing sandals or barefooted, displaying any buttons or signs against the President or America, (2) Any large group making noise or disrupting other guests moving into the dedication area, (3) Any individual or group of individuals attempting to give the military or police officers a rough time regarding their uniforms, (4) Any individual or group of individuals heckling." Chapin added: "Needless to say, the set up was good and it kept the demonstrators out of the hangar." Chapin remained dissatisfied with the advance men's preparations for protests on the road, however. "Someone must . . . flag us when we are expecting demonstrations," he reproved Ron Walker on another occasion. Chapin also apparently worried that Colson was becoming a bit of a loose cannon when it came to engineering supportive demonstrations. Colson assured Chapin, however, that he only "cranked up" such displays after receiving approval through him or Walker. The White House also initiated a campaign to mobilize friendly youth for the 1972 election, which Nixon considered "a fight to the death for the big prize." Colson told a White House aide that he wanted this campaign "off and charging at 90 miles an hour."[146]

The administration was meanwhile engaged in secret peace talks with the Vietnamese enemy in Paris. In June Hanoi offered the same peace terms many members of Congress, the media, and antiwar movement were proposing: total U.S. withdrawal in exchange for the release of America's POWs. But, Hanoi stipulated, the United States could not interfere with the upcoming election in South Vietnam required by Vietnam's 1967 constitution. Barring American "tricks" with the election, Hanoi recognized, it would rid the South Vietnamese people of their repressive president, Nguyen Van Thieu. For the White House, however, keeping Thieu in power had become "the *raison d'être* of the war." The CIA thus fixed the election.[147]

The White House was also engaged in secret negotiations with China that summer. The war was no small factor in the policy. Rapprochement with China would help Nixon recover domestic support eroded by the war, and the Chinese could lean on Hanoi to settle the conflict. As Marshall Green said of Nixon's initiative, "This was designed to propitiate his opponents. . . . I don't think that the president would ever have gone as far and as fast as he did unless he'd had domestic political considerations in mind." On July 15, when Nixon announced that Kissinger had just returned from secret talks in China and that he himself would be visiting China before May 1972, his popularity shot upward. Stewing over the publicity his emissary had received for the diplomatic breakthrough, however, Nixon directed his aides to spy on Kissinger, who was forced to deplane out of the reach of reporters and photographers when he returned from another trip to China in October.[148]

"Evicting" Nixon

Following the spring offensive, the People's Coalition for Peace and Justice and National Peace Action Coalition discussed uniting on summer and fall antiwar activity. Mediators were called in to aid the talks, as relations between the two groups remained rife with tension. PCPJ organizers had more reason than ever to distrust the SWPers who controlled NPAC. "There was a lot of question about working with them," PCPJ's Sidney Peck remembered. "They used to say that they were opposed to civil disobedience because it was like an individual action, and here you had seventeen thousand or more people [participating] in civil disobedience in [the spring of] 1971. Where were they? Why didn't they organize political support for us? It was a mass action." PCPJers were still steamed about NPAC's attempts to control the April 24 demonstration too. "They had really irked me," Brad Lyttle recalled. "I had never seen such dishonesty in my life."[149]

Generally a forgiving sort, Lyttle began plotting an act of revenge that he "will never forget" and that was "indicative of my darker nature." "After that demonstration, I went to bed one night, and I got up in the morning and I said, 'These people need to be taught a lesson,'" he recounted. "My Gandhianism was beginning to erode a bit by that time. And I said, 'Where are they going next?' And I knew exactly what they were going to do." Lyttle figured that NPAC would be calling for a mass peace demonstration in New York in the fall, as the spring mobilization had been in Washington. It would surely include a march down Fifth Avenue, the veteran political organizer calculated. On what date? An examination of the calendar, with an eye on holidays and the academic schedule—standard considerations for a nuts-and-bolts organizer—yielded November 6. It "seemed just right," Lyttle recalled. "It just seemed to me that that was the date they were going to go for." The PCPJ co-coordinator then "went up to the permit office in New York City and I took out a permit in my name for Fifth Avenue. Not under any organization, just 'Brad Lyttle wants Fifth Avenue for this weekend for a parade.' . . . So they gave me the permit. And then I just waited. And, sure enough, they called their demonstration in New York City with a parade down Fifth Avenue exactly as I had calculated."[150]

Despite their mutual dislike, NPAC and PCPJ agreed to co-sponsor the demonstration and other regional mobilizations the same day, as well as a nationwide moratorium against the war on October 13. PCPJ and NPAC activists met to plan the New York demonstration. Lyttle remembered:

> One day they said, "You know, we've got something that's rather peculiar that's developed." They said, "Brad, we went down to get the permit for this demonstration the other day, and we found that you have a permit for Fifth Avenue on that day." And I said, "Well, that's true." And they said, 'Well, I certainly hope that we can work this out." And I said, "I'm sure that we will." And then the whole thing went along, and finally about a week or ten days before the demonstration they said, "You know, we still haven't worked this thing out on the permit." And I said, "Well, what's to be worked out?" And

they said, "Well, it should be a joint permit." And I said, "Why?" And they said, "Well, because we're co-sponsors." And I said, "But we got it first. I have the permit." And they said, "Well, what does that mean?" And I said, "It means that we'll *push you out* if you don't follow our policies, that's what it means." "Ooooohhhhh!" . . . They just hit the roof. And even the Communists, Gil Green and others, and Norma [Becker], [who] were in that meeting . . . were just *aghast* that I would tell them that. They'd never seen anything like that before. And they got to me afterwards, and they said, "Brad, you can't do this to them. We've got to go in with them col- lectively, we've got to get a joint permit." So I naturally agreed even- tually to have the joint permit. But ever since then the Trotskyists treated me with the *highest* respect, *just the highest respect!*[151]

PCPJ was also planning intensified civil disobedience against the war, pov- erty, and political repression in the fall. Its planning ultimately centered on an October 22–26 "Evict Nixon" campaign developed by Rennie Davis. "The crimes of this government must be exposed and those who are responsible driven from positions of power," Davis declared. "Richard Nixon can be endured no longer." Following a "historic" "People's Grand Jury" and a mass rally in Washington, he announced, demonstrators would choke the White House. The tireless Davis had not given up on the notion of shutting down the government. "The offices of the Presidency will be stopped for a· national memorial service that will surround and close the White House. We will serve an eviction notice on Richard Nixon." In his typically apocalyptic style, Davis proclaimed, "The fall program is perhaps the most serious, political project ever undertaken by the anti-war movement."[152]

In August, May Day clans gathered in Atlanta. Gay liberation and feminism were the dominant topics of discussion. Activists debated how to best express "the gayness in all of us." Those heterosexuals who claimed they didn't have any gayness that needed expressing were condemned as "sexist." (Earlier a gay transvestite May Dayer had exhorted male protesters to "put on the dress" to understand their sexism: "You recognized your own femininity when you started to grow your hair long. You've gone half the way, but now you've got to go all the way—start wearing a dress.") Carl Davidson, who covered the conference for the *Guardian* newspaper, was a bit unsettled by "all this touchy- feely shit." "At one point they had all the debates stopped while everybody hugged each other," he laughed. "I just remember going away from that meet- ing thinking, 'This is a trip. This is really *strange*.'" The conferees failed to agree on future activity.[153]

The following week, Clergy and Laymen Concerned (CALC)[154] had a very different kind of meeting in Ann Arbor. It brought five hundred religious activists together to systematically consider new antiwar approaches. "We feel that we need to take a more disciplined look at the way in which we work . . . so that we can develop a long-range strategy and the appropriate tactics to help us be more effective agents for change," the call for the conference stated. "We want to spend time having long discussions about strategy . . . and . . . about how strategy and tactics fit together in our day-to-day work. We feel this has not been discussed in previous religious or antiwar conferences and that it is a crucial discussion to have." Richard Fernandez and other CALC leaders were aware that perceptions of impotence were hampering effective organizing. "Most of us are frustrated," they wrote. "After several years of lobbying, letter campaigns and protest demonstrations . . . 73% of the American people want the war to end this year. . . . BUT IT'S NOT ENDING. Our frustration has at least three sources: President Nixon is telling us that the war *is* ending. . . . Because Americans want the war to end and because the people think they should be able to believe their President, many do believe that the war is winding down." Second, much of the public was critical of protests. Third, if "voting for peace, millions of Americans demonstrating in the streets, letters and public opinion polls haven't stopped the war . . . what else can we do?"[155]

Among CALC's decisions was to target the U.S. bombing of Indochina. With Vietnamization causing public interest in the war to wane, CALC activists determined, a focus on the air war was necessary.[156]

Simultaneously, in Camden, New Jersey, twenty-eight Catholic war resisters raided a draft board. As was later revealed at their trial, an FBI informer, Robert Hardy, was the primary organizer of the raid. With the bureau's assistance, he had devised a plan for the break-in; he had also purchased tools and walkie-talkies with FBI money. Approximately eighty FBI agents were conveniently on hand the night of the raid to make arrests; the indictment against the raiders had been drawn up by the Justice Department the day before. Hardy testified at the trial that he had become involved with the original group of protesters (which included his parish priest) in the hope of keeping them from going too far, and that the FBI promised him they would be stopped before actually undertaking the break-in. But, Hardy disclosed, an FBI agent told him that "someone in the little White House" in San Clemente wanted the crime to actually take place.[157]

The same month, a group of antiwar leaders traveled to Hanoi. As VVAW's representative on the trip and the first Vietnam veteran ever to visit Hanoi, Joe Urgo felt enormous responsibility. "So my attitude toward the Vietnamese was, 'I will tell them anything, I will work with them on any level that they want,'" he recalled. The Americans were given a tour of the Museum of the Revolution, which chronicled Vietnam's long history of fighting colonialism. "That was a shock," Urgo said. "I realized in a graphic way that . . . of all the countries in the world to pick . . . we picked these people who spent their *entire existence* fighting against invaders!" The museum contained antiwar posters from all over the world. "The first poster that you see is the one that says 'FUCK THE DRAFT!' with the [middle] finger up," Urgo remembered. The veteran was provided with a copy of an order to North Vietnamese troops not to shoot U.S. soldiers wearing antiwar symbols or carrying their rifles pointed down. The trip "had an enormous impact on me," Urgo reflected, "in convincing me that I was on the side of the Vietnamese *now*."[158]

In Vietnam, the discipline and morale of U.S. troops was continuing to slip. Over a thousand soldiers signed an antiwar petition organized by VVAW. "The morale, discipline and battleworthiness of the U.S. Armed Forces are, with a few salient exceptions, lower and worse than at any time in this century and possibly in the history of the United States," a retired Marine colonel wrote in the June 7 issue of *Armed Forces Journal*. "By every conceivable indicator, our army that now remains in Vietnam is in a state approaching collapse, with individual units avoiding or having refused combat, murdering their officers and noncommissioned officers, drug-ridden, and dispirited where not near-mutinous." In the United States and other countries, "the situation is nearly as serious," the colonel observed. Promoting the disobedience were civilian antiwar activists. Jane Fonda was holding FTA (Fuck the Army) shows near military bases: "Fonda was on the rampage," William Westmoreland irritatedly recalled. In San Diego, David Harris joined with members of the Concerned Officers Movement and others to mobilize opposition to the departure of the carrier USS *Constellation* for Vietnam. The protesters organized a local referendum on whether the ship should set sail. Most voters said no. Other "Stop Our Ship" (SOS) campaigns to prevent Navy vessels from sailing for Vietnam swiftly followed. On the USS *Coral Sea*, sailors defused bombs and attached stickers to them reading, "Repaired by SOS."[159]

Still keenly alert to its political enemies, the Nixon administration was meanwhile tracking protesters' plans for the fall demonstrations. On September 6, Dwight Chapin directed an aide to put October's "big moratorium . . . on our calendar." One month later, speaking for Haldeman, Lawrence Higby scolded John Dean for his failure to keep the White House fully informed of the demonstrators' designs. "It's kind of disappointing when the only way you can find out about these things is in the newspaper," he acidly wrote. Dean quickly sent Haldeman a three-page description of the protests. "In view of the lack of preparation and publicity, a large number of participants would appear unlikely," Dean reported. "As a result of the lessening U.S. involvement in Southeast Asia, the antiwar groups are shifting their attention and focus to other issues. . . . From the lessons learned in May, the organizers are also now keeping any specific plans for civil disobedience closely held. If such tactics are attempted again, a small number of demonstrators could still possibly cause major disruptions to occur." Dean passed Haldeman a flyer on the October 13 moratorium.[160]

The White House was most concerned about the "Evict Nixon" demonstrations. Not only were they being "billed as the principal fall anti-war demonstrations," Dean told the president, but they were targeting the Executive Mansion. Officials were pleased with waning talk by Davis of strangling the mansion. Dean reasoned that the increasingly "moderate" posture of Davis and other PCPJ organizers "could reflect either fears that there will only be a small turn out for their rallies or may be a cover for secret plans involving civil disturbance tactics." Since there was "still no hard intelligence on any other plans of the demonstrators which differ from what Davis has openly stated" and "little publicity and promotional activity" had been observed, he told Haldeman, the first explanation was "the most likely." Several days later, after some PCPJ organizers stated that they no longer envisioned a mass mobilization but rather an assembly for launching "a year long campaign to evict you from the White House," as Dean informed Nixon, the White House counsel crowed louder over PCPJ's problems. Its "abrupt about-face" on tactics stemmed "from the dismal failure of the PCPJ to create any interest in these demonstrations," Dean wrote the president. No more than two thousand people would turn out. "Virtually no buses have been chartered and no publicity attempted outside of Washington by the organizers. Informants have also not uncovered any plans for violent civil disobedience. Furthermore, the organizers are very disturbed by the fact that . . . they have few funds for promotional activities." However, "as a caveat," added Dean, "it should be noted that after the May Day fiasco Rennie Davis vowed never again to disclose publicly his plans for civil disobedience." And "our close coverage of Davis is not good."[161]

To contain any unruliness, the administration placed nine thousand troops and policemen on alert. City officials would conduct live television surveillance of the protesters, including the one thousand "hard-core 'Rennie Davis types'" expected. Those busted would be processed legally this time, and there would be "improved detention facilities from those available last May," Dean apprised Haldeman. Participants in a scheduled candlelight march past the White House would be "kept moving at all times." "Efforts will also be made to arrange parking on the mall for the demonstrators so that they will be certain to head in that direction at the termination of the procession," Dean noted. A high-intensity lamp would illuminate the front of the White House. White House staffers who parked their cars on the Ellipse on October 26 "should do so at your own risk," one Nixon aide warned. "You should be aware that if the demonstration gets out of hand something could happen to your automobile." (Dean considered such advice "alarmist.") The administration rejected a proposal by PCPJ that it have a representative accept a symbolic eviction notice from a delegation of protesters. Such receipt would "dignify" the act, Dean wrote.[162]

Dean anticipated "no problems" during the demonstration scheduled for November 6 in Washington. It "has not generated much interest," he told Haldeman. The "more militant" PCPJ was "ignoring this rally. Similarly, local schools have evidenced very little interest and only limited out-of-town participation appears likely. Therefore, the rally can be expected to draw an older, well-behaved crowd and should not be able to sustain itself longer than several hours." Nonetheless, Dean provided Haldeman with detailed descriptions of the protesters' plans.[163]

As the White House anticipated, the fall demonstrations were generally unimpressive. With U.S. casualties down and troops coming home, the war did seem to be ending to many Americans. Activists were tired, and it was unclear what good another demonstration or two would do. Draft calls were decreasing. Some activists' eyes were already on the 1972 elections. PCPJ's organizing was uninspired: "pretty bad," Sidney Peck said of its effort to mobilize support for the Evict Nixon actions. Not only was the group indeed strapped for cash, but many PCPJers were unenthusiastic about another Rennie Davis scheme for closing down the government. The movement remained hampered by bitter political divisions. NPAC would have nothing to do with Evict Nixon, PCPJ little to do with November 6. The largest of the October 13 moratorium demonstrations was in New York, where several thousand rallied. In other cities, turnouts were in the hundreds.[164]

On October 22–24, the People's Grand Jury was held in a Washington church. Among the "witnesses" was Fred Branfman, a free-lance journalist who had recently returned from four years in Laos and was then starting up "Project Air War," an educational campaign to focus public attention on the massive— and largely unreported—U.S. bombing of Laos. Branfman testified that the bombing was killing more civilians than soldiers. The proceedings ended, predictably, with an "indictment" of the Nixon administration: the "organs of the American government are unfit to govern," the jury ruled.[165]

The rally scheduled for October 25, which Davis now said "should be the most important gathering of people in twenty-five years," was rained out, as was the candlelight march. The next day, only seven hundred demonstrators showed up. At the cost of $800, North Vietnamese and NLF representatives at the Paris peace talks spoke to the crowd via transatlantic telephone. Reverend James Groppi urged the protesters to vote in 1972 "to get that madman out of the White House." Half of the crowd launched an abortive march to the White House; three hundred were arrested. Groppi called the poor turnout for the protest a "down."[166]

The November 6 demonstrations were an improvement. Some twenty-five thousand protested in New York; Benjamin Spock exhorted the largely youthful crowd to work to erase "that smirky, slick, oily smile of Nixon, who thinks he has conned us." Thirty thousand demonstrated in San Francisco, over five thousand in Boston and Denver. The Washington rally attracted three thousand.[167]

Two days earlier, Dean informed Haldeman that "sketchy reports" indicated that "militant" antiwar groups intended to "create civil disturbances" at fundraising dinners for Nixon's reelection campaign on November 9. The "prime target" would be Chicago, where the president would be speaking. Dean updated his report on the protests at least once in the days ahead, but Haldeman was dissatisfied with his intelligence, particularly for Chicago and New York, where Nixon would also be appearing. "Now that we are in the heart of the demonstration season it is terribly important that up to the minute information is continually being brought to Bob's attention," Lawrence Higby chided Dean in a HIGH PRIORITY memo on November 8. "What is the status on [New York and Chicago]?" Dean promptly relayed the "latest intelligence" on the protesters' plans. The demonstrations turned out to be relatively uneventful.[168]

To dramatize the continuing bloodshed in Vietnam, activists from CALC, the Fellowship of Reconciliation, and other peace groups were then launching "Project Daily Death Toll" in Washington. Every afternoon through Thanksgiving, contingents of protesters from different American cities lay down on the sidewalk in front of the White House. Many wore conical, wide-brimmed Vietnamese hats and the names of dead Vietnamese. "We count ourselves among the dead and are unable to move our bodies," one told a White House guard. Some also deposited their bodies in front of the Washington home of Senator Hugh Scott, a supporter of the war; they asked the permission of Scott's wife beforehand, however. Dean kept Haldeman abreast of the action outside the Executive Mansion, even providing him with a breakdown of the number of busts per day and the areas of the country from which the arrestees came. The White House tried unsuccessfully to obtain an injunction against the demonstrations. It also adopted a "firm policy" to quickly arrest any Death Toll protesters who infiltrated the public White House tour, and to immediately shut down the tour itself after any demonstration began. Dean told Haldeman in proposing the policy that "this problem occurred once during the Johnson Administration resulting in a day long negotiation before the protesters left." A month later Dean solicited the assistance of other officials in developing "imaginative legislation" that would allow Americans to view "this national monument [the White House] without the paraphernalia of the demonstrators all about it"; while Joe Protester should be able to "do his own thing," Dean felt, he should "not subject the rest of us to it unwillingly."[169]

On November 14, some fifteen hundred miles away, CALC activists demonstrated in the Protestant and Catholic chapels at the Air Force Academy in

Colorado. "We'd asked to be able to teach a class in the ethics of bombing, from fifty thousand feet off a map, people you'd never seen before, and they wouldn't let us," Richard Fernandez remembered. So "we just stood up in church . . . [during] a period of silence, and this wonderful old Brethren pastor from some place in Colorado, in the middle of the silence, in this room that you could hear a pin drop in—I mean, it probably held two thousand people and I could whisper to you and you could hear it twenty rows down—he just stood up and started to sing 'Kumbaya': 'Stop the war, O Lord . . .' And everybody kind of looked up: 'Uuuuhhhh? What is this?' And then people got up and began to testify. The MPs moved in after awhile." "We were all thrown out," Fernandez recalled.[170]

The next day, in Washington, Dean directed Robert Mardian to conduct an "in-depth study" of demonstrations and racial unrest, "two of the most critical problems of the last decade." The study, Dean instructed, should "analyze the major trends in these two areas over the past ten years" with "special emphasis" on the Nixon years. He hoped the research would help the White House "place in better perspective current incidents" and provide "guidance for the handling of these problems in the future." Dean told Mardian his research on demonstrations

> should focus on the size, frequency and intensity of these events. The changing leadership patterns should be analyzed with concentration on the relationships between militants and moderates; New Left and Old Left; and professional activists and part-time participants. A discussion of what has happened to some of the former leaders of the movement such as Mark Rudd, Sam Brown, or Mario Salvio [sic] would be interesting. Changes in the objectives of the demonstrations . . . should be examined as the goals sought are achieved. The tactics employed to gain these objectives from mass rallies to bombings should be discussed as well as the impact these have had on the political structure of the country. The composition of the majority of participants should also be investigated to determine the extent to which it consists of hard-core types, students, drop-outs, labor, church connected individuals, etc. Finally, an analysis of the present status of such demonstrations should be made to determine to what extent the present relative calm reflects real change or merely is a pause while the underlying forces regroup and reorganize.

Dean informed Mardian that these areas of study "are not intended to be exhaustive" and conceded that the project "will require a fair amount of time and energy."[171]

Don Luce was then embarking on another project for drawing public attention to the continuing killing in Southeast Asia. The 37-year-old agriculturalist, who was "to the South Vietnamese government what Ralph Nader is to General

Motors" (as *Time* commented), traveled in a van from community to community across the United States setting up a photographic exhibit, showing films, and speaking on "the culture, history and everyday life of the Indochinese" people. "The idea was to get into smaller communities that people weren't generally getting to," Luce remembered. Through his "Indochina Mobile Education Project," Luce strove to make the Vietnamese "look like us—as people with the same kinds of problems that we have"—rather than statistics. Luce believed that once Americans came to appreciate the culture of Vietnam, "then it became much easier to understand that when you bombed villages and created strategic hamlets, moved people off their farms, that they were going to get angry, and that that whole process was counterproductive." Luce toured with his Mobile Education Project for nearly three years. He recalled that though the receptions he received around the country were generally favorable,

> we would also run into crazy people. . . . Down in Augusta, Georgia, this guy grabbed me by the throat and said he was going to kill me. And I asked him why—I thought that was a reasonable question. He said, "Because you're a gook." I said, "Well, I'm not a gook." He said, "Well, if you were an American, you'd be showing pictures of Americans." A whole crowd of people gathered around to watch; they'd never seen anyone killed before, I guess. . . . And I just sort of stood there, kind of limp-like. And I guess he realized I was getting the sympathy vote, so he let go.[172]

On Thanksgiving, members of VVAW fasted and held memorial services at state capitols across the nation "because they could not see anything to be thankful for." The veterans and other activists also began laying plans for demonstrations during the Christmas period. Dean kept Haldeman apprised of their designs: "With the Yuletide Season now beginning, you should be aware that we have not been forgotten by our old friends," he wrote at the top of one report.[173]

In mid November President Nixon announced the withdrawal of another forty-five thousand U.S. troops from Vietnam, which would leave one hundred and thirty-nine thousand there by early 1972. The bombing, however, would continue. Nixon also ordered stepped-up air raids over southern sections of North Vietnam under the cover of "protective reaction." In December, the administration expanded the bombing of North Vietnam further, with five days of massive strikes on airfields, fuel depots, and air defense sites up to seventy miles south of Hanoi. It was the fiercest air assault on North Vietnam since 1968.[174]

The madman theory of war was being put into practice again.

Peace activists organized emergency demonstrations in response. VVAWers launched "protective reaction strikes" of their own. In San Francisco, they commandeered the South Vietnamese Consulate. "We have 'arrested' all members of the embassy," the fatigue-clad veterans declared. They used the teletype machine to send antiwar messages to the South Vietnamese government. Some occupied an Air Force recruiting station; they asked to enlist en masse but with a written guarantee that they would not have to commit war crimes. VVAWers occupied the historic Betsy Ross House in Philadelphia, the Lincoln Memorial in Washington, and the LBJ Library in Austin, Texas. Fifteen took over the Statue of Liberty in New York. "It was a really stoned out idea," one said afterward. "The original plan was to take over the island . . . secede from the Union, declare ourselves a sovereign state and recognize North Vietnam." The veterans hung an upside down American flag—a symbol of distress—from the crown of the statue; television news crews in helicopters hovered close by. The veterans also released an "Open Letter to President Nixon" that stated:

> Each Vietnam vet who has barricaded himself within this international symbol of liberty has for many years rationalized his attitude toward the war. When we were in Vietnam we excused our actions because we thought that we had no choice. After coming home we excused our bitterness because we thought that we were entitled to it. . . .
>
> Now, as we sit inside the Statue of Liberty . . . we have run out of excuses. . . . We can no longer tolerate the war. . . .
>
> Mr. Nixon, you set the date, we'll evacuate.

After two days the veterans left under an agreement that no criminal charges would be pressed. Their protest attracted worldwide media attention. "Tourists were asking, 'Where was the spot where the veterans stood?'" Jan Barry amusedly recalled. In other cities, veterans "napalmed" Christmas trees decorated with war toys and medals.[175]

As U.S. air attacks against North Vietnam continued in January, with antipersonnel bombs striking populated areas, the elation that many VVAWers felt over their protective reaction strikes dissipated. "Once again we overestimated the ability of these [protests] to really reach everyone to change policies," Barry remembered. "The policy didn't change—Nixon just got trickier." Joe Urgo observed, "The level of anger and frustration was . . . intensifying because it seemed like people were just going about and didn't care."[176]

TEN

1972–75

"The Bastards Have Never Been Bombed Like They're
Going to Be Bombed This Time"

On January 13, President Nixon announced the withdrawal of another seventy thousand U.S. troops from Vietnam by May 1. Only sixty-nine thousand would then remain. Melvin Laird declared that "the combat responsibility" in Vietnam had been "turned over completely" to the South Vietnamese. American air power would remain virtually unaltered, however. Nixon ordered the troop reductions despite an impending enemy offensive, given the "necessities of our domestic situation," Henry Kissinger writes. The American "appetite for withdrawals" had become "insatiable," he laments.[1]

Two weeks later, also to defuse the war issue in America, the President revealed the secret peace talks in Paris. He claimed that the United States had been offering Hanoi the same peace terms antiwar critics were proposing: total U.S. withdrawal in exchange for the return of the POWs. Nixon was lying, as the White House was also demanding a cease-fire throughout Indochina. The president knew the media would be so fascinated by the details of Kissinger's clandestine encounters in Paris that they would pay little heed to the fine points of the talks. "There's good cops and robbers stuff here," he told an aide. The media did indeed lap up the revelations. Buoyed, the administration stepped up its attacks on critics of its peace proposals. Nixon sent Charles Colson and H. R. Haldeman a memo outlining a "massive" assault on those "who continue to badger us." Colson later remembered the memo as one of many the president would compose late at night, often when drinking alone in his hideaway office.[2]

John Dean was keeping Haldeman informed of the protesters' latest designs. On January 31, he reported that the People's Coalition for Peace and Justice was planning demonstrations at the Republican convention in San Diego, still seven months away. "The picture," however, "is still too undefined to draw sound conclusions" about the demonstrations, Dean relayed. PCPJ "has developed serious splits with one faction urging that PCPJ engage in violent disruptive activities . . . and another faction arguing that such tactics would cause loss of support." Other protesters had additional plans. Nevertheless, "from past experience, it can be expected that the convention will serve as a magnet to attract numerous 'street people' and veterans of past demonstrations," Dean wrote. Also, "though most of the leaders are now stressing non-violent tactics, the inherent momentum of these demonstrations has proven time and time again that such activity can rapidly escalate into violence." Dean noted that, "significantly," the National Peace Action Coalition—"the group which has staged the largest and most successful demonstrations in Washington—has made no definite plans for San Diego." He promised Haldeman that he would be "in close touch with" developments and relay additional intelligence "as a clearer picture of the magnitude and proportions of this problem emerge."[3]

Apprehensive of a repeat of Chicago 1968, the White House began laying plans to counteract the protests. Haldeman and John Mitchell, the head of the Committee to Re-elect the President (CREEP), considered such planning a top priority. "Antiwar demonstrators would love to destroy our convention, but we're not going to let it happen," Haldeman told Dean. Dean later remembered that intelligence reports indicated that the protesters were going to try to shut down the convention "much like they had tried to close down Washington" during May Day. On January 27, G. Gordon Liddy, who had been hired as CREEP's general counsel three months after carrying out the bag job on the office of Daniel Ellsberg's psychiatrist, proposed a plan code-named "Operation Diamond." Liddy expected as many as half a million demonstrators at the convention, including "skilled and determined urban guerrillas," and seemed worried about the hazards they posed. Operation Diamond called for paid informants to infiltrate antiwar groups planning protests. "Highly trained demonstration squads, men who have worked successfully as street-fighting teams at the CIA," would "break up demonstrations *before* they reach the television cameras," Liddy suggested to Mitchell, Dean, and CREEP's assistant director, Jeb Magruder. Other teams "experienced in surgical relocation activities" would "kidnap" protest leaders. They would then "drug" these leaders and whisk them "across the border into Mexico until the convention is over," Liddy proposed. "They'd never even know who had them or where they were." The abductions would "strike fear into the hearts of the leftist guerrillas" and "throw them into confusion at a critical moment," he argued. Their "attack would be further disrupted by faked assembly orders and messages." To underscore his "seriousness of purpose," Liddy related that the men carrying out the abductions would "include professional killers who have accounted between them for twenty-two dead so far, including two hanged from a beam in a garage." Operation Diamond was one component of an overall campaign intelligence scheme concocted by Liddy code-named "Operation Gemstone"; among the plan's other features were blackmailing prominent Democrats through the use of prostitutes. Although Mitchell rejected Operation Gemstone as too farfetched and expensive, he and other officials agreed a week later that "we should have the capacity to break up hostile demonstrations" at the convention and infiltrate antiwar groups. Mitchell, Magruder, and Dean also agreed with Liddy that wiretaps on Democrats were desirable; top priority would be given to the office of Lawrence O'Brien, the Democratic National Committee chairman, in the Watergate apartment complex.[4]

On February 17, Nixon and Kissinger embarked for the China summit. Much to Kissinger's irritation, Haldeman had turned the event into a television extravaganza. "He was very disturbed about my involvement in the China trip planning," Haldeman smiled. "He kept saying I was going to destroy the whole trip." The media strategy worked, however, as live television images of Nixon's historic visit enthralled the nation, boosting the president's popularity. Afterward, he and Kissinger bickered over who should receive the most credit for the summit.[5]

The same month, Nixon authorized two days of concentrated air strikes over southern North Vietnam. In March he ordered a "massive blow" of one day's duration. The specter of renewed sharp protest was inhibiting the administration, however. "Everybody dreaded the public outcry sure to be unleashed" by sustained resumption of the bombing of the North, Kissinger writes.[6]

Americans voiced opposition nonetheless. In Honolulu, Catholic radicals poured blood on military maps of Indochina at an Air Force base. During Holy Week between Palm Sunday and Easter, Clergy and Laymen Concerned held protests against the air war across the United States. The CALC chapter in Ann Arbor, Michigan, dug a huge crater in the middle of town—"This is what it would be like if a bomb was dropped here." Several weeks later CALCers in Houston held a worship in a simulated bomb crater as several jets flew dramatically overhead. CALC also spoke out against the bombing on its own six-day-a-week radio program (carried on more than three hundred stations) and through an "Unsell the War" advertising campaign. Produced by advertising professionals, the ads were placed free of charge on hundreds of TV and radio stations and in magazines. "Our ads were better than many ads [the stations] had," Richard Fernandez boasted. "I mean, they were class pieces."[7]

PCPJ and other antiwar groups organized Holy Week activities in Harrisburg, Pennsylvania, site of the trial of Philip Berrigan and six others accused of conspiring to kidnap Henry Kissinger and blow up underground steam tunnels in Washington. The "Harrisburg Seven" were represented by Ramsey Clark, who told the judge they were "the gentlest of people." Caravans of antiwar pilgrims traveled to Harrisburg from around the country for workshops, rallies, and civil disobedience. The day after Easter, over ten thousand demonstrated against the air war, corporate war profits, racism, and political repression on the state capitol grounds. Among the speakers was Daniel Ellsberg, who received a "hero's welcome."[8]

In York, Pennsylvania, near Harrisburg, the American Machine and Foundry Company, producer of 500-pound bombs, announced on March 27 that "sabotage" had been taking place in its factory. A group called the "Citizens Committee to Demilitarize Industry" took credit for disarming the missiles. It mailed their nonexplosive plastic tops to several public figures.[9]

The Stop Our Ship movement was growing. In San Diego, nine crew members of the USS *Kitty Hawk* refused to sail for Vietnam and took sanctuary in churches. Peace activists on board the ship circulated copies of their antiwar newspaper, *Kitty Litter*.[10]

Internal political divisions continued to hamper the antiwar movement. PCPJ refused to endorse national demonstrations NPAC had called for April 22 in New York and Los Angeles. "It's just impossible to work with them," one PCPJer said. The radical *Guardian* newspaper lamented the "new low" in relations between the two antiwar coalitions. "What is of concern is that with imperialism at its most vulnerable so far and the opportunity to strike a major blow against it at hand, the organized antiwar movement in this country seems to have accelerated the divisions that have blunted its effectiveness over the past year-and-a-half," the *Guardian* fretted. "The reluctance of PCPJ to support (let alone initiate) concentrated mass demonstrations in the streets reflects a disastrously inappropriate weariness with methods of political mobilization and struggle that, in the past, have proved to be remarkably potent in their effect on U.S. policy."[11]

On March 30, the North Vietnamese and NLF launched their expected offensive. Three NVA divisions poured across the South Vietnamese border, routing ARVN forces. Air Force General John Vogt recalled seeing undamaged South Vietnamese tanks "abandoned by these little guys who ran. . . . These little guys knew they were up against something they couldn't handle and they just fled." The exact timing and size of the invasion startled U.S. officials. Nixon was enraged at Hanoi's apparent attempt to thwart his reelection. He accused Secretary of Defense Melvin Laird of deliberately withholding advance knowledge of the offensive; Laird was up to his old games, Nixon perceived. He decided to give Hanoi "a bloody nose." "The bastards have never been bombed like they're going to be bombed this time," the president told Haldeman and Mitchell on April 4. Nixon was "conducting the war by temper tantrum," as Seymour Hersh writes. The president ordered 105 additional B-52s sent to Southeast Asia—so many that an entire runway in Guam had to be closed down and converted into a parking lot. More aircraft carriers were dispatched to the area. Nixon called for unrelenting air strikes over South Vietnam. The bombing of the North was also intensified. General Vogt remembered a "wild-eyed" Nixon telling him that previous Air Force commanders had failed to act aggressively enough. "He wanted somebody to use some imagination—like Patton," Vogt said. [12]

Peace activists were informed of the massive military mobilization through contacts on military bases. A GI in Hawaii reported to Vietnam Veterans Against the War that nuclear weapons were targeted on Hanoi. Protesters responded with leaflets, rallies, traffic stoppages, building occupations, and student strikes in scores of cities. PCPJ called for an "emergency action" in Washington on April 15. The National Student Association planned a nationwide student strike on April 21. Associates of the Institute for Policy Studies called for noontime "emergency moratorium" protests at government offices on May 4, the second anniversary of the Kent State killings. Interest in the April 22 demonstrations mushroomed; PCPJ now expressed its "vigorous" and "full support" for them. [13]

On April 15, a thousand people demonstrated in Washington. Three hundred were arrested for congregating in Lafayette Park without a permit. John Dean had earlier apprised Haldeman of the plans of these "hardcore" demonstrators. That weekend, wave after wave of B-52s deposited their payloads on the Hanoi and Haiphong areas. It was the first time since 1968 that those two cities had come under heavy aerial bombardment. The bombs struck densely populated areas, killing hundreds of innocent civilians. "We really left them our calling card this weekend," Nixon told Haldeman. A Vietnamese spokesman in Paris had a different reaction to the bombing: "We consider Nixon the greatest criminal the world has ever known. He is even worse than Hitler." According to senior Pentagon officials, the strikes on Hanoi and Haiphong had initially been targeted to hit south of the cities, but were redirected by Nixon "some time between Friday night and Saturday morning." [14]

Antiwar activists quickly responded. Spontaneous protests erupted in numerous cities over the weekend. On Monday, April 17, three thousand students in Madison marched on their school's ROTC building and smeared blood on its walls. Protesters in California shut down the Alameda Naval Air Station for three hours and occupied an Air Force recruiting station. Noam Chomsky and others were arrested for blocking the entrance to an aircraft plant in Connecticut. Early the next evening, in Cambridge, five hundred students broke away from a march and stormed Harvard's Center for International Affairs, which they accused of training CIA agents. Two hundred broke into the building and tossed office equipment out windows, spraypainted antiwar slogans on walls, and ignited a small fire. Police sealed off Harvard Square and imposed a 9 P.M.

to 5 A.M. curfew. Other protesters headed to Cambridge's business district, where they shattered windows. Students at many schools voted to go on strike.[15]

Protest against the bombing mounted during the rest of the week. On April 20, following three days of unrest at the University of Maryland, including a sit-down on a major highway, the state's governor declared a state of emergency and dispatched National Guard troops onto the campus. Columbia University's president, William McGill, apparently decided he'd had enough of student disturbances by then. He ordered all classes canceled the next day. "Given what we have been through during the last several days," McGill said, "I feel that we should take a day off and see where we are going as a university." Students at Princeton occupied a dean's office and refused to leave until they had been provided a copy of the university's contract with Army ROTC. Seven draft resisters incarcerated at Danbury federal prison in Connecticut climbed a 175-foot water tower on the prison grounds and perched themselves on its catwalk. They unfurled a large bed sheet bearing a crudely inscribed antiwar slogan, clearly visible from a nearby highway. The inmates remained on the water tower for two days and nights despite rain.[16]

On April 21, students at over a hundred and fifty colleges and universities participated in the nationwide student strike, shutting down many campuses. Students occupied administration buildings at Northeastern University and Boston University. Students at Stanford laid siege to an electronics laboratory and snarled traffic, resulting in a hundred and fifty arrests. Michigan students ransacked the ROTC building, exuberantly tossing chairs and typewriters out windows and shredding documents. Three hundred and fifty students at Princeton commandeered the Woodrow Wilson School for Public and International Affairs and demanded that the university identify the donor who had earlier given $35 million to establish it. More than two hundred and fifty youths were arrested for civil disobedience at military bases. The strike activities fell far short of those that had followed Cambodia and Kent State two years earlier, however. Many students did not participate in them "because of cynicism and depression at the failure of previous campus struggles," the *Guardian* observed. "In some areas, minimal press coverage of antiwar struggles has served as a demoralizing factor."[17]

That week CALC announced a new antiwar campaign. The group would pressure Honeywell Inc., the number one producer of anti-personnel weapons, to cease production of them before its 1973 stockholders meeting. "We have come to see that generalized protest alone will not affect the systems that make war," CALC stated, "but that concentrated effort on a single arm of the war-making machine can yield results." Protesters needed to engage in activity that aimed at "specific clear objectives which, whether achieved or not, can be measured," CALC argued. While "mass demonstrations certainly continue to have a place in the antiwar movement . . . they will probably never again be seen . . . as that which will bring the war in Southeast Asia to an end." CALC activists met with Honeywell officials in Minneapolis. "We went out and had these negotiations like you're supposed to," Richard Fernandez recounted:

> We talked to them a little bit about the [ethical] responsibility of corporations. . . . And they said, "In a democracy, when the government asks you to help in an effort like this, we help." And they said, "That doesn't even mean that we believe in the war, but we do believe in our form of government." So we had a guy with us that day, Fred Branfman [of Project Air War]. Nice Long Island Jewish boy. And in the middle of this discussion . . . he said, "I'm wondering. You're making these antipersonnel weapons." He said, "If you had a visit from Washington, would you make gas ovens?" That ended the meeting. They didn't know what to say. Like, where would you stop? What weapon would be bad enough to say, "No, no, in a democracy we don't do that one?"[18]

Daniel Ellsberg responded to the bombing of Hanoi and Haiphong by leaking another classified document—the paper on U.S. options in Vietnam he had prepared for Kissinger in December 1968. Portions of the document were published in *Newsweek* and by the syndicated columnist Jack Anderson in late April.[19] Ellsberg's act and previous treachery would stimulate another White House attack on him within days.

On April 22, upwards of fifty thousand people braved pouring rain and bitter cold to demonstrate in New York. Many of the protesters fashioned rain gear out of plastic garbage bags, punching holes in the sides for their arms and heads. A high school band from New Jersey played "Hello, Dolly!" during the march down Seventh Avenue. The actor Ossie Davis, the former baseball star Jim Bouton, Ellsberg, Dave Dellinger, and others addressed the crowd. Most of the speakers conveyed a sense of urgency about the surging air war and suggested greater brutality might lie ahead. "Nothing is impossible," one said, including "the unthinkable, nuclear weapons." Bouton related that when his young children recently asked him who he wanted to win the war, "the 'Vietnams' or the Americans," he told them, "I want the 'Vietnams' to win." Twenty thousand demonstrated in Los Angeles that day, thirty thousand in San Francisco. Many of those in San Francisco paid twenty-five cents to throw darts at pictures of Richard Nixon and J. Edgar Hoover.[20]

Through the rest of April and early May, protests against the bombing continued. Quakers and veterans in aluminum canoes and rowboats paddled out into a bay off New Jersey to prevent the munitions ship USS *Nitro* from sailing for Vietnam. "We decided that we had to somehow put our bodies between the

U.S. bombs and the people of North Vietnam," David Hartsough, one member of the "People's Blockade," recalled:

> When we started paddling the police came over and threatened us with criminal conspiracy—twenty years in prison—if we didn't leave the area. You'd look up at these docks, and all these cartons had [anti]personnel bombs, napalm, just everything [in them]. . . . So I looked up at that, and then I looked back at this guy, and I said, "Thank you for warning us, but if these bombs leave for their destination, it's going to be much worse than twenty years in prison."
>   . . . We were up there paddling to try to get right in front of the ship as they were loosening the ropes and all of that. And the Coast Guard got orders to pull us out of the way. So they grabbed hold of the edge of our canoes, gunned the engines for maybe fifteen feet, and then let go. And we'd paddle so we were right back in front. . . .
>   As the ship approached us, [seven] of the sailors jumped overboard into the ocean and then started swimming toward us. It was speaking with their lives. And the national network news and the *New York Times* were all there in their helicopters taking all this in. By that night it was all around the world.

The seven sailors were plucked from the icy water and placed in the brig. Other "People's Blockades" of Navy ships followed.[21]

Students at Cornell occupied the engineering building for nearly a week. In Austin, Texas, students stoned the LBJ Library. Columbia students occupied five buildings. Veterans blocked the main entrance to the Groton, Connecticut, submarine base. Nuns wearing white sheets lay down on the ground during church services at St. Patrick's Cathedral in New York. A contingent of women blockaded the entrance to the Westover Air Force Base in Massachusetts. Some fifteen thousand people turned out for NPAC-sponsored demonstrations on April 29. More participated in May 4 moratorium protests, but the actions were small; the largest was at Kent State, where four thousand marched and tolled bells: four for the dead Kent students, two for those killed at Jackson State, and one "for all oppressed people." The antiwar upsurge sparked by the bombing of Hanoi and Haiphong was losing momentum. As the *Guardian* noted, "'battle fatigue' among the militants and a widespread sense of futility in the face of Nixon's refusal to end the war" were key factors.[22]

The White House was keeping a close watch on the protests, however. Dean sent Haldeman's aides Lawrence Higby and Gordon Strachan an average of two reports per day on them. At Haldeman's request, Dean also apprised Strachan of the activities of the "Majority Coalition," a politically diverse group at Columbia opposed to the building occupations there; the coalition threw protesters out of two buildings and threatened to sue the university if it didn't reopen the others. Haldeman apparently suggested that Nixon consider publicly commending the coalition, but Dean advised against it. "Due to the amorphous nature of the Coalition and its strong component of leftist antiwar members (practically all students at Columbia are opposed to the war), any Presidential recognition might undermine its effectiveness and cause internal dissention," Dean wrote Strachan. "It is also doubtful if a leader could be found who would be receptive to a Presidential communication."[23]

Contributing to the wane in the antiwar upsurge was an announcement by Nixon on April 26 that twenty thousand more U.S. troops would be withdrawn from Vietnam over the next two months, leaving only forty-nine thousand there. To some people, the war seemed to be inexorably on its way out despite the bombing. By ordering more troops home in the midst of the North Vietnamese offensive, however, Nixon was "paying extraordinary homage to the American peace movement," as Seymour Hersh points out. He was also paying homage to his Democratic opponents in the upcoming election. As the president told Kissinger, he worried that if he wasn't able to announce the departure of all U.S. combat forces before the Democratic Convention in July, "we will be in very serious trouble."[24]

Preventing World War III

Nixon remained intent on bloodying Hanoi, however. In fact, he was considering a roundhouse punch. During a cruise on the *Sequoia* the evening of May 2, the president, Kissinger, and Kissinger's aide Alexander Haig discussed a number of severe escalations, including bombing North Vietnam's dikes, a ground invasion of the North, and the use of nuclear weapons. Nixon rejected these options but agreed that "a major military move was called for." Two days later, meeting with Kissinger in his hideaway office, pacing back and forth, smoking a pipe ("yet one more from my chief's inexhaustible store of surprises," Kissinger wryly writes), playing General MacArthur, the president decided to mine North Vietnam's ports. Nixon also decided to renew the B-52 strikes on Hanoi and bomb the North's rail lines to China. It was time to put the Duck Hook plans into effect.[25]

Kissinger passed the decision on to JCS Chairman Thomas Moorer. Nixon made "Admiral Mormon" (as he often called Moorer) promise that advance word of the mining, which he planned to announce on May 8, would not reach the press. "I said, 'I'll guarantee you it won't leak, because I know what ship I'll use, and if any reporters are aboard I won't let them go ashore,'" recalled Moorer, who was ecstatic over the operation. Nixon also instructed Moorer not to inform Melvin Laird of the plan. It didn't leak.[26]

The May 2 cruise on the *Sequoia* also elicited talk of Daniel Ellsberg, some Watergate prosecutors concluded. Angered by Ellsberg's latest leak, the White

House was then recruiting a team of Cubans (including the three who had broken into his psychiatrist's office) to assault the renegade former official at an antiwar rally in Washington the next evening. "Our mission is to hit him—to call him a traitor and punch him in the nose," the team's leader, Bernard "Macho" Barker, instructed his comrades. "Hit him and run." Ellsberg later said that Nixon sent the Cubans "to incapacitate me, at least to beat me up, perhaps to kill me." Through Charles Colson, Nixon also directed the thugs to attack demonstrators waving NLF flags. "It would be fine if a couple of heads are knocked," Colson told aides. In a memo to Magruder he hoped they could "get . . . one or two scalps." Colson wanted to present the president with one of the liberated NLF flags. While Ellsberg was addressing the rally, the Cubans shouted "Traitor!" from the back of the crowd. They were unable to get their hands on their quarry, but did punch at least two other demonstrators (hard enough that one of the Cubans injured his hands). "I was aware that there were people fighting at the fringe of the crowd, after I had spoken," Ellsberg remembered. "I went over and watched that. . . . I saw some guys were yelling at us." Police grabbed two of the Cubans, but "a man in a gray suit" (probably Howard Hunt) "gave a signal" to the cops, who then released the pair. After the rally, Hunt and G. Gordon Liddy "debriefed" Barker while driving around Washington. Passing the Watergate apartment complex, Liddy said, "That's our next job, Macho."[27]

The next day, speaking at the funeral of J. Edgar Hoover (who had died two days earlier), Nixon declared, with supreme irony, "The American people today are tired of disorder, disruption, and disrespect for law. America wants to come back to the law as a way of life."[28]

On May 8, the president announced the mining of North Vietnam's ports and the intensified bombing, code-named "Operation Linebacker." Hanoi immediately claimed that U.S. warplanes "deliberately struck" a dike system. Media commentators and Democratic members of Congress strongly denounced Nixon's escalation. The *Washington Post* charged that the president had "lost touch with the real world" and was recklessly risking cancellation of the upcoming Moscow summit. Again, protests spontaneously broke out across the country. "The coast-to-coast outburst of demonstrations was the most turbulent since May, 1970," the *New York Times* observed. The tactic of choice was blockading major traffic arteries. In Boulder, Colorado, students obstructed intersections, a highway bridge, and the main Denver-Boulder turnpike with burning logs and automobiles; an irate driver who got out of his car brandishing a shotgun was disarmed by police. Protesters in Santa Barbara, California, closed off a three-mile stretch of U.S. 101 for two hours; they poured gasoline on the highway and set it on fire. Some occupied the city airport's runway. In Chicago the next morning, during rush hour, demonstrators abandoned cars on the

Eisenhower Expressway: "Nixon Blockades Haiphong: Peace Group Blockades Eisenhower," the headlines of one local newspaper declared. Police used high-pressure hoses to expel students from a highway in Gainesville, Florida. At UCLA, police chased a horde of students back and forth across campus all day; among the many arrestees was the All-American basketball player Bill Walton. In midtown Manhattan, protesters simulated a "saturation bombing," complete with recorded sounds of air raids, after which they "dropped dead" in the street. Demonstrators in Washington played a recording of heavy aircraft from the gallery in the House of Representatives. In other cities, students trashed corporate offices, fire-bombed ROTC buildings and engaged in "pitched battles" with police, particularly after nightfall. Police fired birdshot and buckshot, wounding many youths. Three cops were shot by a protester in Madison. Berkeley was on the brink of "anarchy," with protesters roaming through the streets breaking bank windows, overturning cars, and starting small fires.[29]

Stoking the outpouring were fears of World War III. "I thought the shit was going to come down," the draft resister Bruce Dancis remembered. "We thought we were very close to major catastrophe. We thought that at this point 'no business as usual' could be our only strategy." Dancis believed that "we could prevent the disaster if [disruptive actions] happened all over the country on a scale that was unprecedented."[30]

The White House was nervously tracking the protests. Dean sent Higby and Strachan several reports per day on them. On May 9, he fired off no fewer than six reports (more than one per hour in the late afternoon). Dean noted that the demonstrations were "of a much smaller size and intensity than those that took place following the thrust into Cambodia," however. Haldeman wanted to be sure the White House was maximizing its intelligence on the protests. His aides asked Dean how he assembled his reports. "Primary reliance" was placed on the FBI, Dean responded on May 11. The bureau's

> 59 field offices telephone information as soon as it is received from local police and other sources to the Washington headquarters. This is then followed by teletypes with more detail. The volume of the flow of information received by the Bureau is very large, *e.g.*, last night some 135 teletypes were received from the field. These reports are then telephoned to us immediately. . . . [They] come in approximately every 20–30 minutes during the day. At night we are also notified immediately of all major disturbances.
>
> . . . All information received is also double-checked against wire service reports which are delivered to us as they come in. . . .
>
> We are still basically not able to compete with the news media in the speed of our reporting. . . . This is due to the fact that, contrary to popular opinion, the FBI is not a monolithic organization with its

tentacles into every city and campus in the country. It must rely on local police reports or wait for its informants to report in whenever they can.

Solid advance intelligence on the protests was hard to come by, Dean relayed:

The vast majority of the demonstrations that have occurred so far are basically spontaneous demonstrations with no more than several hours warning. There is no conspiracy or vast organizational structure underlying these numerous outbreaks throughout the country. A great many plans have been formulated by various activists and groups, but the resulting demonstrations correlate only slightly with the plans. . . .

Some major demonstrations are currently being organized, but due to the quickness with which this entire situation arose, the persons planning the demonstrations are totally disorganized.

Dean passed along available intelligence on these upcoming demonstrations, including, presumably, on an "emergency" march on Washington on May 21 initiated the day before by both PCPJ and NPAC—the first such joint initiative in over two years—and a mass civil disobedience action in Washington on May 22.[31]

Peace activists were then roaming through the halls of Congress and cramming into reception rooms to lobby for an end to the war. Nineteen legislators joined them for a rally on the Capitol steps. Jane Hart, wife of Senator Philip Hart (D-Mich.), proclaimed her refusal to pay income taxes in objection to the bombing. Hundreds of protesters were arrested during a CALC-sponsored "witness and fast" in congressional offices, corridors, and the Capitol rotunda. Some demonstrators met with White House officials.[32]

The White House was bothered by the lobbying. Nixon realized that "the opposition, the peaceniks, the radicals, etc." were "sending delegations in [to legislators' offices] who insist on seeing the victim and then proceed to work him over and get a commitment from him," he wrote Colson. Not only was it hard for anyone to "turn one of these groups off" without throwing a bone their way, Nixon perceived, but "there are very, very few people with any backbone in the Senate or House anymore, and . . . they are really patsies for a group that comes in and puts it to them hard on an issue." At Dean's suggestion, Haldeman ordered White House officials to coordinate all of their future contacts with protesters with Dean's office so that adequate police arrangements could be made to prevent "sit-ins" and other "possible problems." Colson wrote Dean after receiving Haldeman's directive: "This is to advise you that I am planning tomorrow night to drive my Pontiac Station Wagon up onto the curb of Pennsylvania Avenue in front of the White House and run over all of the hippies who are lying there. My plan is to do this while they are asleep some-time between 2 and 3 A.M. Would you please let me know what coordination you would like to arrange?"[33]

The White House was meanwhile moving to surface public support for the mining and bombing. Once again it barraged itself with congratulatory tele-grams, supposedly from private citizens. It also applauded itself in a bogus *New York Times* ad. Officials flooded a Washington television station and newspaper conducting polls on the escalation with phony supportive votes. White House political undercover operatives of all stripes were involved in the administration's PR effort. "When all the instructions had gone out, just about every spy, sabo-teur, con man, extortionist, forger, impostor, informer, burglar, mugger, and bagman—for that, astonishingly, is what they were—in the employ of the White House was at work manufacturing the appearance of public support for the President," Jonathan Schell writes. Propaganda on the escalation was passed to the press. "We need some good strike pictures. We need to see ammunition and weapon dumps being blown up," a May 9 White House memo exhorted. "*Right!*" Haldeman scrawled in the margin. The memo also advised that "we need to personalize the villain . . . get some background information on the fact that they are killers, they are brutal men, they are war lords, etc." "*Excellent,*" Haldeman wrote. He also agreed that "we should radiate calmness." In an EYES ONLY memo six days later, Haldeman told Colson that the White House's PR men should "hammer hard on" Nixon's "courage, coolness in crisis, and [his] putting country above political and partisan and personal considerations." They would thereby, it might be hoped, "leave some residue of personal respect [for Nixon] in the public mind after what has happened has long been forgotten," a task at which "we have usually failed" in the past, largely owing to the animos-ity of the media. Nixon was vexed when the *Times* columnist Anthony Lewis claimed from Hanoi that the mining of Haiphong harbor was ineffective. "Ob-viously intoxicated," the president directed Ken Clawson, a White House aide, to attack the paper. "I got a call from Al Haig at Camp David and I hear the President in the background saying, 'Give 'em hell, give 'em hell,'" Clawson recalled. Clawson promptly released a White House statement charging that the *Times* was "a conduit of enemy propaganda to the American people."[34]

On May 13, Louis Harris reported that 59 percent of Americans supported the mining of North Vietnam's ports; only 24 percent opposed it. Nixon's ap-proval rating darted upward. Although sick of the war, most Americans felt North Vietnam's invasion justified the mining, and as always they backed sharp escalation in the short term.[35]

Two days later, the White House hatched an unusual plan for smearing its antagonists. The Democratic presidential hopeful George Wallace had just been shot, and Nixon and Colson wanted Howard Hunt to search the Milwaukee apartment of Wallace's assailant, Arthur Bremer, for evidence of left-wing leanings and other potentially useful information. Hunt might even plant literature from Senator George McGovern's presidential campaign in the apartment. FBI sealing of Bremer's apartment forced the White House to call the operation off, but Clawson told the *Washington Post* that literature found in it clearly linked Bremer to leftist causes.[36]

On May 17, seven presidents of Ivy League universities met with Henry Kissinger. The dons were unsettled by the latest campus disorders and restive about the future. "I don't see how we can continue to run our universities if the war escalates," one said. "What will we face in September?" When Kissinger suggested they try to "raise the level of the debate" over the war on campuses, one replied, "We try to introduce fairness and reason to the debate—but only at risk to our own lives. That is a fact."[37]

The next day Nixon directed Haldeman to cease recruiting White House officials "from any of the Ivy League schools or any other universities where either the university president or the university faculties have taken action condemning our efforts to bring the war to an end. . . . In filling our needs I want you to give first priority to those schools who have presidents or faculty members who have wired us or written us their support of what we have done in Vietnam."[38]

The worries of the Ivy League presidents notwithstanding, the campus turbulence over the mining and bombing was then on the ebb. It was hard to sustain an antiwar offensive in the best of times, but the numbers now had been somewhat low to begin with compared to the past, and many antiwar stalwarts had themselves grown tired of banging their heads against a wall. "I think a lot of people at that point had become sort of . . . dispirited," Bruce Dancis reflected. "They couldn't change U.S. policy." Many students' attention was turning to final exams. Word that Moscow planned to hold the scheduled summit with Nixon despite the escalation also took steam out of the outpouring. With the threat of World War III dissipating, protest seemed less pressing.[39]

Nonetheless, the White House continued to track the protests. Dean provided Haldeman's top lieutenants with at least two reports a day on them.[40]

On May 21, a cold, dank day, only fifteen thousand turned out for the "emergency" march in Washington. Again NPAC tried to control the demonstration. Militants led several breakaway raids on government buildings, smashing windows and provoking tear gas attacks on other protesters. The sage civil rights and antiwar leader Julius Hobson, then dying of cancer, welcomed the demonstrators to Washington "for the one thousandth damn time." The next day, several thousand held a "People's Blockade" of the Pentagon. Waves of protesters slowly advanced on a phalanx of police defending the building. The invaders were easily repulsed; more than five hundred were busted. Those protesters who wanted no part of this particular brand of direct action sat on the pavement nearby. The demonstration "wasn't too successful," Dave Dellinger recalled. "Not enough people came. Not enough people were sure that it made a difference."[41]

The same day, Nixon and Kissinger arrived in Moscow for the summit. They returned a week later with the first SALT agreement and Nixon's reputation as a peacemaker enhanced. And the Soviet Union, too, would pressure Hanoi to settle the war.

In Vietnam, U.S. bombing raids were then reaching unprecedented intensity. "We must *punish* the enemy in ways that he will really hurt," Nixon wrote Kissinger. "I intend to stop at nothing to bring the enemy to his knees." North Vietnamese and NLF forces suffered massive casualties. Civilians were maimed and killed in untold numbers. Although the enemy offensive stalled and President Nguyen Van Thieu remained in power in the South, the NVA had moved substantial troops and matériel into the countryside there, well positioned for another offensive when the time was ripe.[42]

Angered by the media's failure to fully appreciate the success of its escalation and reports that U.S. bombers were killing civilians, the White House counterattacked. Sensing a communist conspiracy was behind the bad press, Haldeman wrote Colson in an EYES ONLY memo on June 6:

> The tactics of the left-wing on Southeast Asia are becoming clear in the last few days. They are petrified at the thought that our diplomatic and military initiatives may succeed. Consequently, they have made a decision at the highest level to attempt to destroy American confidence in the South Vietnamese and Cambodians through articles by left-wing reporters. . . .
>
> . . . It is no accident that after Tony Lewis wrote those shocking Communist-line pieces from Hanoi for the TIMES, Selig Harrison now is on the scene in Hanoi writing about how nice the little 12-year-old boys and girls are who are attending school in Hanoi.
>
> This propaganda offensive is extremely subtle . . . and we need some effective action to combat it. . . . We must continue to discredit people like Harrison and Tony Lewis who obviously would never be let in to Hanoi unless they had a prior commitment to write the Communist party line while they were there. Clawson's crack at Lewis in the TIMES, while it disturbed some of our house liberals, was a master stroke and a similar analysis of Harrison's background might well be in order.[43]

Break-in

That evening George McGovern won the California Democratic presidential primary. He was now a shoe-in for the Democratic nomination, Nixon recognized. The president undoubtedly knew that White House dirty tricks against Edmund Muskie were partially responsible for McGovern's triumph. During the early primaries, Donald Segretti and other White House saboteurs had derailed Muskie's campaign through theft, espionage, forged schedules, sophomoric pranks, poison-pen letters, poison phone calls, and the like. Nixon was delighted that McGovern was his opponent, given the senator's liberal views. He moved to make them appear even more liberal. That day Nixon instructed Mitchell, Haldeman, and Colson to develop propaganda "nailing" McGovern "to his left-wing supporters" such as Abbie Hoffman and Jerry Rubin. The "media blackout" on the senator's extremist friends had to be broken, the president commanded: "I consider this a top priority objective." Colson, who didn't have to be convinced of McGovern's extremism ("Instead of running for President," he wrote his friend Jay Lovestone, the "traitor" "should be running from the gallows"), began collecting photos showing him "with his raunchiest-looking supporters." Pat Buchanan, for his part, put together an "Assault Book" that advocated portraying McGovern as the candidate of "snot-nosed demonstrators."[44]

On the early morning of June 17, police arrested five men in the Democratic National Committee headquarters at the Watergate apartment complex. The intruders, who included two veterans of the break-in at Daniel Ellsberg's psychiatrist's office and four veterans of the attempted attack on him, wore blue surgical gloves and were carrying lock picks, door jimmies, camera equipment, bugging devices, gas guns, and $2,400 in cash. This was the second penetration of the Watergate offices the Gemstone squad had undertaken; a few weeks earlier, it had installed phone taps and photographed documents. Its mission this time had apparently been to fix and rearrange the taps. Howard Hunt and G. Gordon Liddy had monitored the burglars' activity from a hotel room across the street.

DNC chairman Lawrence O'Brien swiftly charged that the break-in had "a clear line to the White House." So did other Democrats. The FBI also detected White House connections. Nixon consequently ordered the CIA to call the FBI off the case. He told Colson that he himself would "just stonewall it." White House aides shredded and hid incriminating documents. Liddy told Dean that he would be willing to stand on a street corner and take a bullet in the head to protect the White House. Prodded by Nixon, Mitchell resigned as head of CREEP. His good friend might have to take the fall for the break-in, the president contemplated. Soon hush money was going out to the burglars. By attempting to cover up the break-in, Nixon was trying not only to avoid being linked to it personally but to keep a lid on what Mitchell later called the other "White House horrors"—the Huston Plan, Ellsberg break-in, wiretaps, Brookings fire-bombing plot, and other Colson projects that "had brought such a gleam to his eye when they were happening," in Haldeman's words.[45]

Whatever the precise motives for the break-in, it was a political intelligence operation spawned by the White House's obsession with political enemies. And promoting that obsession, in no small part, was the antiwar movement. As Dean told the Senate Watergate committee, Watergate was "an inevitable outgrowth" of "excessive concern over the political impact of demonstrators" and leaks, and "an insatiable appetite for political intelligence." Many years later, Dean, who came to believe the White House was "just fishing" in the Watergate offices, commented, "I think there's a *tremendous* relationship [between] what happened to Nixon in Watergate . . . and the antiwar movement. I think the seeds of Watergate were sown in the way he was dealing with it. And I think that the repercussions, and his ultimate departure from office, was really the aftermath of that, really the final winding down and the last chapter of the antiwar movement." Roger Morris agreed, saying, "Watergate—the whole generic beast—is a product of the administration's insecurity and paranoia fed by the war in Southeast Asia and by an inability to cope with that dissent, and [by] these perceptions of dissent widening around it in an almost conspiratorial way." No war, no antiwar movement. No antiwar movement, no Watergate.[46]

Miami

Over that spring and summer the Nixon administration was continuing its efforts to counteract the demonstrations scheduled for the Republican convention in August. Dean funneled additional intelligence on the protesters' plans to Haldeman. In accordance with Liddy's Gemstone plan, informants were placed in antiwar groups. An ex-informer for the CIA and FBI remembered that a man calling himself "Eduardo" (probably Howard Hunt) offered him $1,500 a week to infiltrate VVAW and disrupt the group. "Basically, we had to expose the VVAW [as] being pink and Communist and all this stuff," he said. The White House moved the convention from San Diego to Miami because San Diego seemed "particularly vulnerable" to "massive demonstrations," given "the thousands of indigenous antiwar activists in Southern California," Magruder recalled. If Liddy was right that up to a half a million protesters would show up, violence "on an even greater scale than Chicago [1968]" was "almost certain," officials believed. "And the hotel that would be our convention headquarters seemed vulnerable, because it was located on an island just offshore that was easily reached from the mainland," Magruder writes. "We had a vision of an armada of thousands of wild-eyed hippies swimming across the inlet and overrunning our defenses."[47]

A federal grand jury indicted seven members of VVAW and a supporter for conspiring to disrupt the convention using "fried marbles," ball bearings, cherry bombs, slingshots, crossbows, automatic weapons, and other violent means. Government witnesses at the veterans' trial extended the list of armaments to include antitank weapons such as bazookas. It turned out that government infiltrators inside VVAW were the primary advocates of violence at the convention. One of these infiltrators had participated in the attempted attack on Daniel Ellsberg. The government's case against the veterans was further damaged by revelations about its star witness, an FBI informer. The informer had serious psychological imbalances: not only had he been threatened with psychiatric discharge by the U.S. Army, but his wife had recently successfully requested that he be held for a sanity hearing (a letter he had written her blaming VVAW for the collapse of their marriage and saying that if he chose to "get" the defendants he would do so silently "in tennis shoes" with a "length of piano wire" apparently influenced her request). The witness had also reportedly assisted in the attempted bombing of a campus building in 1971. The veterans were declared innocent of all charges in August 1973. "They had nothing on those boys," one juror commented.[48]

On June 22, five days after the Watergate break-in, twenty-five hundred women and children linked hands around the Capitol, encircling the building. The "Ring Around Congress" antiwar demonstration was the brainchild of the folk singer Joan Baez. It was hampered by attacks by black Washington political leaders, who demanded that it be canceled. They charged the peace movement with racism and argued that white demonstrators coming into Washington should pay a head tax since the cost of protests there was borne by the city's predominately black taxpayers. Baez and the WSP leader Cora Weiss, another organizer of the protest, concluded that the charges were government-inspired. "That demonstration was the target of the heaviest government interference of any demonstration that was ever held—anywhere," Weiss claimed. "And it caused an enormous amount of disruption in the planning of the demonstration." Baez remembered that planning as "the most difficult, demoralizing, battering, discouraging task I have ever taken on in my life." The protest was also hampered by freakish weather. "There was a terribly dangerous storm the night [before] that demonstration, which literally closed off access to Washington from Virginia, and it became quite dangerous—physically dangerous—to come in," Weiss recounted. "And the TV and radio were blaring warnings to passengers not to come to town. And we were convinced . . . that this was hand in glove, the government finding a convenient excuse to try to keep the demonstration from being effective."[49]

Another project geared toward compelling Congress to end the war was then getting off the ground. The "Indochina Peace Campaign" (IPC) was led by Tom Hayden, recently kicked out of a Berkeley commune for male chauvinism and manipulative behavior, and by his new lover, Jane Fonda. Hayden thought that with most Americans now against the war, a powerful grass-roots movement targeting Congress was possible. Seven years of antiwar protest had opened the

American political system up; protesters should now step into the opening. "It was the most clearly conceived notion in politics that I think I've ever participated in," the IPC organizer Jack Nicholl recalled. "It was very simple." It was also daunting to some. IPCers in Santa Barbara were "feeling discouraged by the apparent enormity of the task before us: on the one hand, an apparent widespread cynicism among movement people about the usefulness of action against the war, and on the other hand the continuing mystification of most of the population about the real meaning of the war," they wrote. "We were also awed by the task of finding ways to reach those not previously directly touched by the ideas of the anti-war movement." The campaign took off in earnest in September with a whirlwind speaking tour by Hayden and Fonda through states considered crucial to a McGovern presidential victory. IPCers presented films, slide shows, and exhibits on Indochinese history and the war. "We found that when people actually came to understand the history of Vietnam . . . it was a big leap forward in their understanding of why the war had to end," Nicholl said. IPCers also distributed a hundred thousand copies of a digest of the Pentagon Papers and a pamphlet on the war's human toll under Nixon entitled *Six Million Victims.*[50]

In July, George McGovern received the Democratic presidential nomination in Miami. Yippies, Zippies, gays, vets, blacks, and others demonstrated for their causes outside the convention hall, ringed by a chain-link fence topped by barbed wire. Some constructed a 60-foot symbolic dike out of sand. Ron Walker reported to Haldeman on the protests. "The smell in the area was bad," Walker relayed after visiting Flamingo Park, where many of the demonstrators were camped. "Obviously a lot of pot, obviously very few baths. . . . There seemed to be an awful lot of young people either loaded or sick. The sun had apparently taken a lot out of them."[51]

On the first day of the convention, meeting with John Ehrlichman in San Clemente, President Nixon "rambled" about possible disturbances there and at the Republican convention. If he was in any danger in Miami, Nixon said, he wanted the Secret Service to bust the protesters. Then, after the November election, he would pardon them. In return, the president fantasized, the Watergate burglars would also receive pardons.[52]

In late July Ramsey Clark journeyed to North Vietnam. Clark wanted to see the damage U.S. bombs were inflicting firsthand. He was distressed by what he observed. Clark said afterward that he had seen "more apartments, villages, dikes and sluices destroyed than I ever want to see again." North Vietnam "has now been bombed back into the 17th century," he stated. Seeing the stunned survivors of bombed villages was "almost unbearable," Clark reported. He predicted that American POWs would never be released until the bombing was stopped. Former Attorney General John Mitchell was angered by Clark's trip and comments. He charged that his predecessor had been "unwittingly duped into playing Hanoi's wretched game" of using the POWs as bargaining chips. Clark, said Mitchell, was "a megaphone for Communist propaganda."[53]

Days later the Republican Convention was held in Miami. White House fears of huge rampaging mobs turned out to be unwarranted. Fewer than ten thousand protesters showed up. Again they were a motley group: Yippies, veterans, SDSers, troops in the Attica Brigade, pacifists, PCPJers. "The leadership is fragmented and no single group seems to be in command," John Dean reported to Haldeman early in the week. The demonstrators also "tend to decide upon plans at the last minute," he noted. However, they were "more serious than at the Democratic Convention." Many young militants were bent on a repeat of Chicago 1968. They trashed vehicles and windows, and taunted the police and convention delegates, roughing up some delegates. During a protest at the Fontainebleau Hotel (the Republican headquarters) on convention eve, the militants "showed no fear of police," Dean told Haldeman; most would "probably be arrested before the Convention adjourns," he predicted. In fact, approximately thirteen hundred protesters were busted during the week. Most of the arrests took place on Wednesday, August 23, when protesters blocked entrances to the convention hall. Police fired "heavy barrages" of tear gas, creating a thick mist that hung in the air and stung the eyes of delegates and officials, including President Nixon, as they entered the arena. Jeb Magruder's wife and two of his children arrived in the hall "choking, crying, and terrified."[54]

PCPJ's Rennie Davis, who had predicted a million people would turn out for the protests, was a leader to many of the young militants in Miami. The PCPJ co-coordinator Brad Lyttle said that Davis, then nearing the end of a 40-day fast, was "at his worst down there":

> Here were all these people . . . having these meetings in Flamingo Park all the time to discuss strategy. And they were deeply committed movement-types and very serious about their discussion. They developed this elaborate organization and this elaborate demonstration. Which I thought was really very good; it was a good example of participatory democracy. And they had it all laid out. And Rennie went around and listened to all of these discussions. . . . Then he walks out on that platform, just before the demonstration was to take place, and he says, "Well, we hear this is going to be happening over here, and the police are going to do this, so we'll have to completely discard all of the plans we've made and do this." And then he told us what he was going to do. Which was to just take a crowd of people and walk along one of the highways until they came to the police and were blocked. . . . He was completely contemptuous, as far as I could see, of all the plans that these people had

made, and just imposed his own tactics on people because he controlled the microphone. . . . Rennie just totally disregarded days of planning.

Davis was hit by a tear-gas canister on the march. In addition to being weakened by his fast and "temporarily poisoned" by the gas, Davis was psychologically exhausted and wondering what else could possibly be done to end the war. Wounded by charges of male chauvinism and manipulation like his friend Tom Hayden, he began talking increasingly about the need for "a deeper lifestyle" and spiritual matters. His psychological bearings were beginning to slip: Davis mirthfully told Hayden not long after the convention that "the Vietcong were Jesus Christ."[55]

The VVAWers in Miami were uncomfortable with the political currents around them. "We arrived—the usual chaos is going on," Jan Barry said. "People are asking us to support sixteen thousand different causes. . . . The usual crazies are doing their crazy things, trying to drag VVAW into their crazy things." Among the crazies were agents provocateurs, the veterans detected. Some were pushing violence, others drugs. The veterans set up a perimeter around their campsite in Flamingo Park to keep the infiltrators out. "We had people on guard with walkie-talkies during the night," one recalled. The veterans also organized their own separate protests, including a dramatic silent march on the Fontainebleau Hotel. "There's nothing more to say," another vet commented.[56]

Peace or Politics?

During the late summer President Nixon was continuing to shore up his peace credentials. On August 12, the White House announced (later than hoped) that the last American ground combat troops had left South Vietnam. Two and a half weeks later, Nixon declared that only twenty-seven thousand U.S. troops would be in Vietnam by the end of the year. Prodded by Haldeman, the president also proclaimed the end of the draft as of July 1973. Polls showed him well ahead of McGovern.[57]

Privately, Nixon was wavering on the war. Alexander Haig told a senior U.S. military officer on August 2 that the president "vacillated between a strong impulse to get out of Vietnam as fast as possible at almost any price and an equally strong impulse to 'bomb North Vietnam back to the Stone Age.'"[58]

By the early fall, the Paris peace negotiations were bearing fruit. Pressured by Peking and Moscow, hurting from U.S. bombing, facing a military stalemate, and spurred by U.S. willingness to accept a tripartite electoral commission and NVA troops in the South, Hanoi dropped its previous insistence that South Vietnamese President Nguyen Van Thieu's ouster be part of a settlement. Within sixty days of a cease-fire in the South, the two sides agreed, the United

States would withdraw the rest of its troops, and Hanoi would release the POWs. The Provisional Revolutionary Government (i.e., the NLF) would have legal political status in the South. The electoral commission would oversee elections. And the United States would provide Hanoi with money for postwar reconstruction.[59]

Kissinger arranged to fly to Hanoi in late October to initial the agreement. But Thieu refused to accept it, bitterly accusing the United States of selling him out. Nixon also had doubts about the agreement and, more significant, believed a settlement now might hurt him in the November election. The president suspected that Kissinger wanted an agreement partly to ensure his indispensability to him after the election. He accused Kissinger—"that son-of-a-bitch"—of "wanting me to be in his debt for winning this election." Nixon knew that Kissinger's desire for personal acclaim was also fueling his peace efforts. "Henry wanted an agreement because he wanted the plaudits," Marshall Green said. "He was playing to an enormous gallery." Nixon acted to delay a settlement.[60]

Relations between the president and Kissinger grew increasingly strained. On two occasions, Nixon spoke with Kissinger only by phone, although they were in close physical proximity. Kissinger complained to a journalist about his plight, "You can't believe how hard it is, especially for a Jew. You can't begin to imagine how much anti-Semitism there is at the top of this government—and I mean at the top." The president opined to Haldeman and Ehrlichman that Kissinger was emotionally unstable. (This was not the first time that Nixon had offered this opinion: a year earlier he had asked Ehrlichman to persuade Kissinger to see a psychiatrist.) When Hanoi broadcast the terms of the peace agreement, thereby revealing that the White House had acted to settle the conflict without conferring with Thieu, Kissinger seemed "on the verge of a breakdown." "We almost lost Henry last night," Haldeman told Colson the morning after the broadcast. Six weeks later, Haldeman apprised Ehrlichman of Kissinger, "He's been under care."[61]

On October 31, Kissinger disingenuously announced to the world that "peace is at hand." Nixon was irate. The president's anger rose another notch when his private pollster Alfred Sindlinger told him that Kissinger's pronouncement had cost him the election. An hour later, Nixon phoned Sindlinger and asked him, "What would be the public reaction if we bombed Hanoi?"[62]

Amid these intrigues, Watergate was taking large portions of Nixon's time. He was keeping close tabs on the Justice Department's investigation of the break-in. His worries over the scandal deepened on October 15 when the *Washington Post* reported that a White House campaign of political sabotage linked to the burglary and led by Donald Segretti was monitored by his aide Dwight Chapin. Ten days later, the *Post* reported that Haldeman had exercised control over a slush fund that had financed the break-in and sabotage. Meanwhile the White House continued to raise money to buy the burglars' silence and coached officials in perjury. Nixon praised John Dean for his efforts to contain the scandal by "putting your fingers in the dikes every time that leaks have sprung here and sprung there." Most newspapers refused to take Watergate seriously, however. The public couldn't care less about it: an October poll found that only half of the public had even heard of the burglary. [63]

The antiwar movement was relatively quiet that fall. The Indochina Peace Campaign was the most prominent antiwar activity. In November the IPC launched a grass-roots crusade to pressure Nixon to sign the Paris peace agreement. IPC also protested U.S. funding of the corrupt and repressive Thieu regime in Saigon. Some activists raised money to send medical aid to "liberated" areas of Vietnam, Cambodia, and Laos. Don Luce publicized the continuing plight of South Vietnamese political prisoners and U.S. responsibility for them. Aware that members of Congress had direct telephone lines to the U.S. Embassy in Saigon, Luce also led a campaign whereby each legislator was lobbied on behalf of a particular prisoner. After the legislator had been barraged with phone calls and letters about the prisoner, Luce recalled, he would often pay him or her a visit, give the legislator additional information on the prisoner, then provide the phone number of U.S. Ambassador to South Vietnam Ellsworth Bunker. "So I would just sit there—and then they would call Ambassador Bunker," Luce said. The campaign did not exactly endear Luce to Bunker:

> One reason that he hated me was that . . . it's exactly twelve hours difference between Vietnam and the U.S. So I would visit [the legislators], of course, in the daytime, some time between eleven and, say, five . . . in the afternoon. So poor Ambassador Bunker would get calls like two or three times a day when I was in Washington, beginning at about eleven [P.M.] and going on until five in the morning, from senators and congresspeople, about [various political prisoners]. And these would just be like crazy names to him. And he would say, "Well, I don't think they're in prison," or something. And then they'd say, "Well, Don Luce here . . ." And then they'd start fighting . . . [64]

A jury in Seattle protested the war by acquitting ten activists charged with trying to stop a train loaded with bombs. "They were all guilty of violating the law," one juror remarked. "But, you know, this war is a nasty situation. If it weren't so nasty, we probably wouldn't have made the decision we did." Said another juror, "In my own mind I was protesting as much as they were."[65]

Many peace activists campaigned for George McGovern. PCPJ urged protesters to organize "the most massive vote" possible for the senator "to ensure either the defeat of Nixon or to avert what Nixon is driving for: a landslide vote which could be interpreted as a popular mandate for the war and repression." PCPJ also exhorted activists to "confront" Nixon wherever he campaigned.[66]

Although his campaigning was limited, the president did encounter demonstrations at most stops. Ten thousand greeted him in Los Angeles. Nixon could not resist taunting "all the nutheads in the nasty crowd" that turned out during a stop in Ohio. He raised his arms in the V sign. "This really knocks them for a loop, because they think this is their sign," the president wrote in his diary. Protesters taunted Vice President Spiro Agnew unmercifully. Some apparently vandalized and burned several Nixon campaign headquarters. "The demonstrators and arsonists detracted heavily from the spirit of this last campaign," Nixon writes.[67]

A series of black uprisings broke out aboard U.S. Navy ships. In Subic Bay, informed they were returning for combat in Indochina rather than to the United States as expected, crew members of the USS *Kitty Hawk*, already on edge over racial tensions, clashed violently. It was later revealed that the ship's return to Indochina had been compelled by sabotage aboard two other carriers. On one, a huge fire had roared through the admiral's quarters and crippled the ship's radar center. On the other, a sailor had stuck a paint scraper and two twelve-inch bolts into one of the engine's gears, causing extensive damage. Acts of sabotage took place aboard other ships as well. A November Justice Department memo recorded the government's "concern over an increasing number of suspected sabotage incidents aboard Naval vessels since the spring of 1972. The rise in sabotage . . . is considered to be the worst in U.S. Naval history."[68]

In early November the first mass mutiny in that history erupted. Blacks aboard the USS *Constellation* off the southern California coast embarked on a sit-down strike, prompting senior officers to curtail the ship's sea operations and take the rebellious sailors back to port. When the *Constellation* returned several days later to pick the 144 sailors up, they refused to reboard, raising clenched fists and launching a dramatic dockside strike. The dissidents laughed at officers who tried to round them up. Network camera crews captured their defiance on TV. President Nixon was enraged by the rebellion, which he caught on the evening news. At the Florida White House, Nixon had Kissinger call Chief of U.S. Naval Operations Admiral Elmo Zumwalt and order him to give the rebels dishonorable discharges "immediately if not sooner." "Kissinger all but shrieked at me," Zumwalt remembered. The admiral was "shocked" by what he heard. Nixon's order was patently illegal, he realized. It "grievously eroded my confidence in and respect for my Commander in Chief," Zumwalt writes, adding, "I did not yet know Mr. Nixon."[69]

JCS Chairman Thomas Moorer was in Melvin Laird's office that day. He later recalled overhearing Nixon angrily tell Laird over the telephone that he wanted all the rebels "court-martialed before dark." Moorer realized that that order was also problematic. (The admiral felt the dissidents just needed "a kick in the ass.") Intrigued, Moorer edged closer to the phone to catch more of Nixon's fumings. All of sudden, Moorer recounted, the mischievous Laird "says to the President, 'Admiral Moorer can tell you all about it'—and he hands me the phone!" Nixon told Moorer, "I'm not going to have a mod navy." The president was "very upset," Moorer said. His order was not carried out.⁷⁰

On November 7, Nixon defeated George McGovern in a landslide, 60.7 to 37.5 percent. He carried every state except Massachusetts. The returns depressed many antiwar activists. Ironically, Nixon was also feeling down. The war continued to nag; Congress remained controlled by Democrats; his last political campaign was over. Perhaps most troubling, the political land mines of Watergate might explode. The next morning, a "grim and remote" president perfunctorily thanked hungover White House staffers assembled in the Roosevelt Room, then quickly turned the meeting over to Haldeman. Haldeman ordered wholesale resignations. Apparently victory had released Nixon's hostility to his enemies, real and imagined. Kissinger calls these hours "the strangest period in Nixon's Presidency." "I was struck that triumph seemed to bring no surcease to this tortured man," he writes. "Isolation had become almost a spiritual necessity to this withdrawn, lonely, and tormented man who insisted so on his loneliness and created so much of his own torment."⁷¹

During the late fall, PCPJ and NPAC were bickering again. The bone of contention now was whether to demand that Nixon sign the October peace agreement or to call for immediate U.S. withdrawal from Vietnam. PCPJ supported the agreement; NPAC condemned it as a product of brute U.S. military force. The quarreling between the two coalitions was fed by frustration over the waning peace movement and public disinterest in the war. National demonstrations called by NPAC on November 18 ran only in the hundreds in most cities, although they had been planned since July. And few Americans seemed to care about which group had the correct demand. The Justice Department's Internal Security Division accurately perceived that "mounting" "tension" between the youth groups of the SWP and CP was also "due in part to the decline of the Vietnam War as a volatile issue, and the resultant difficulty in arousing the public to political activism." PCPJers were further frustrated by fading hope of a "permanent people's movement" capable of ending racism and domestic repression. According to Justice's intelligence sources, PCPJ leaders were "gravely concerned about possible post-war apathy."⁷²

For the first time since the war began, peace groups failed to call for spring demonstrations. The numbers would undoubtedly be low, they reasoned, and

peace might well be near. Some groups planned protests at the inaugural ceremonies for President Nixon in January, however. Of those plotting to disrupt
the ceremony in Washington, John Dean reported to Haldeman, "the most
militant and dangerous is the Attica Brigade, which participated in much of the
trashing and May Day type activity at the Republican Convention." Dean noted
that, "significantly," neither NPAC nor PCPJ were as yet planning protests.[73]

"New Madness"

On November 20, peace negotiations resumed in Paris. Kissinger proposed numerous changes in the October agreement and threatened Hanoi with reesca-
lation if it didn't yield. Feeling conned and betrayed, North Vietnam's leaders
vexedly rebuffed Kissinger and made new demands of their own. Nixon simultaneously pressured Thieu to soften his stance now that the election was over
and an agreement was politically beneficial. The president conveyed to Thieu
that he was prepared to sign a separate peace without him. But if Thieu got on
board, Nixon secretly promised, the United States would view any agreement
as meaningless and continue to support his regime, including with bombers.[74]

By early December the Paris negotiations were stalemated. To prepare for
military imposition of a settlement, the United States poured military hardware
into South Vietnam; "Operation Enhance" provided Thieu with the fourth largest air force in the world. Infuriated at the "tawdry, filthy shits" on the other
side of the negotiating table and mindful that advocacy of the madman theory
of war would help bring him back into Nixon's good graces, Kissinger urged the
president to resume massive bombing of North Vietnam. North Vietnam, for
its part, installed hundreds of additional antiaircraft batteries around Hanoi and
Haiphong. It also began evacuating children from Hanoi.[75]

Worried that heavy bombing would incite a domestic uproar, Nixon ordered
Kissinger to continue the negotiations. Other officials were also urging major
escalation, however. Alexander Haig, Haldeman, and Ehrlichman advocated B-
52 strikes on Hanoi and Haiphong. So did Admiral Moorer: he would recall
telling Nixon that there was "'only one way'" to force Hanoi's leaders to release
the POWs and end the war "'and that's to scare the hell out of them.' I said,
'These people are just little professional revolutionaries. They don't understand
but one thing and that's brute force.'"[76]

On December 14, Nixon ordered the reseeding of mines in Haiphong harbor
and concentrated B-52 bombing of Hanoi and Haiphong. "Operation Linebacker
II" would commence in three days. Its main purpose: to convince Thieu that
Nixon's promise of continued support was credible and thus to get him on the
team. The president told Moorer, "I don't want any more of this crap about the
fact that we couldn't hit this target or that one. This is your chance to use
military power effectively." It was time to "hit and hit hard," Nixon stressed.
Over a twelve-day period, U.S. warplanes unleashed the heaviest attacks of the

entire war. B-52s engaged in around-the-clock bombing, turning factories, train stations, and homes into rubble. "Immense incandescent mushrooms" rose up into the air "one after the other." Several thousand civilians were killed or injured. Hanoi's Bach Mai Hospital, the city's largest, was demolished, killing doctors, nurses, and patients; one doctor recalled amputating the limbs of victims in order to free them from the wreckage. A POW camp was also hit, injuring American prisoners. (Press reports on the strike on the POW camp infuriated Moorer, who told reporters they were ruining Christmas for the POWs' relatives. "Why does one American want to inflict such pain on another American?" he bitterly asked. "I can't understand you people.") Nearly a hundred American airmen were killed or captured during the bombing, victims of what one U.S. Air Force spokesman called "the greatest air-defense system in history"; the B-52s were "going down like flies," General John Vogt said.[77]

Joan Baez was in Hanoi during the "Christmas bombing." She had come to deliver Christmas mail to American POWs. As the bombs starting falling the first night, Baez, her heart "slamming," her ears "fluttering and popping," raced into an air raid shelter, "desperately afraid." The bunker was only twelve feet long and several feet wide; a single light bulb dimly illuminated the cold, damp room, filled with some ten other people. Following one particularly thunderous explosion, the shaking and sweating Baez "felt like vomiting." Ten times during that terrifying night, Baez scrambled into the shelter, not knowing whether she would die en route. By dawn she had managed to calm her nerves enough to sing to her companions. The next eleven days and nights brought more air raid sirens and more hasty trips into the shelter. "We rested as much as possible in between," Baez writes. "The mercury that measured fear and anxiety soared up and down totally out of my control." Walking around Hanoi when bombs weren't falling, Baez encountered huge craters, demolished homes, and "the smell of burnt flesh." Everywhere, Vietnamese were walking around in a daze, wearing white headbands, symbols of mourning for relatives. One woman was "sitting on a small heap of rubble, pounding her fists on her thighs and crying with a despair that was ferocious. She would go from a wail to a moan to almost a growl, then sob wretchedly." Another hobbled back and forth across a small section of ground, singing, "My son, my son. Where are you now, my son?"[78]

In the United States, antiwar activists were beyond fury. Didn't Nixon and Kissinger have any limits at all, they wondered? Norma Becker said her anguish and frustration over the war "reached a high point" during the bombings. "I was at my mother's in Florida for Christmas vacation," Becker recounted:

> The temperature went below 40 degrees . . . and we were indoors
> watching television. And I was just overwhelmed with this horror,
> and was feeling powerlessness—this utter, total, unbelievable horror
> that human beings could do this. . . . It was such barbarity, and such

dehumanization that was taking place. . . . The whole thing was a
horror show. And these politicians, in their privileged comfort and
safety, talking their *shit*, and just totally callous to the enormity of
the human suffering that they were inflicting upon people.

"One morning when I woke up and went to shower and looked at my hair,"
Becker added, "I had [a] gray streak." The streak literally appeared "overnight,"
she claimed. "It's one of those things that you read about in literature when
someone's hair turns white."[79]

Daniel Ellsberg was also feeling depressed. The bombing "was what I'd been
trying to avoid all this time" by leaking the Pentagon Papers, he remembered.
"People asked me, 'What effect . . . is the Pentagon Papers having?' . . . And I
said, 'No effect. . . . It's what we had to do, worth going to jail to try it. [But]
in terms of effect—zero. *Zero.*'" Ellsberg remained convinced that the papers
had influenced public opinion, though.[80]

Despite their despair, peace activists organized small protests in dozens of
cities around the country. Many gathered signatures on "sign-the-peace-treaty"
petitions. Thousands held vigils in front of shopping centers, churches, and
other public places. In New York, activists handed out leaflets soaked in their
own blood in front of St. Patrick's Cathedral. In numerous cities, protesters
marched through downtown areas and picketed federal buildings. More than a
thousand demonstrators blocked midtown Manhattan traffic for several hours.
Some engaged in civil disobedience at armed forces and corporate offices. Five
religious activists from New Jersey tried to throw another monkey wrench into
the bomb making of the American Machine and Foundry Company in York,
Pennsylvania; the protesters were arrested for pouring concrete into a railroad
switch alongside the factory. They inserted a message into the concrete declaring
that they had "no illusion that this small act will stop—or even delay—the daily
reign of death" in Vietnam but that they felt it "vital that we not allow ourselves
to be mesmerized by the magicians who cruelly tease a world with false hopes
of peace." Militants detonated four incendiary devices in New York department
stores; a table tennis ball packed with a delayed-action chemical mixture and
hidden among pillows in the home furnishings department of Gimbels wreaked
extensive damage. On Christmas Eve a group of women climbed a ladder to
occupy the stage of Radio City Music Hall in New York; they unfurled a banner
reading, "There's No Silent Night in Vietnam." The audience reportedly
cheered. Scholars attending academic conventions held rallies. Many protesters
raised money for newspaper ads. Some solicited funds to rebuild Bach Mai
Hospital; Ramsey Clark announced his support for the drive. Forty-one religious leaders issued a pastoral letter condemning the bombing and lies by Kissinger about the reasons for the breakdown in negotiations. On Christmas day,

a tree was delivered to the White House; its branches were broken, its orna-ments smashed.[81]

Resistance to the bombing broke out among the bombers themselves. Many pilots and crew members refused to take to the skies. "A man has to answer to himself first," explained one recalcitrant B-52 pilot, who found himself in "moral shock" over the strikes on civilian targets. Members of flight crews sabotaged electronic equipment aboard B-52s and neglected to arm bombs. Air-men flying intelligence missions for the bombers staged a work stoppage. Ac-cording to some, "cheers" arose from their ranks "every time a B-52 was shot down." Not coincidentally, many of the airmen had earlier been stationed at Westover Air Force Base (WAF) in Massachusetts, scene of intensive organizing of GIs by antiwar activists, including the former SDS leader Greg Calvert. "We reached a lot of people on base [and] developed a real community of resistance among airmen at WAF," Calvert recalled.[82]

As Dean had predicted to Haldeman, the Christmas bombing spurred orga-nizing for protests at the inaugural ceremonies in January. NPAC called for a mass demonstration at the ceremony in Washington on January 20. PCPJ ini-tially refused to co-sponsor the demonstration, citing, among other obstacles, NPAC's refusal to allow any favorable mention of the October peace agreement in publicity. Following heated squabbling, a compromise was reached. PCPJ ultimately shouldered most of the organizing of the demonstration.[83]

Foreign leaders and publics widely condemned the bombing. "One should call things by their proper name," Premier Olof Palme of Sweden remarked. "What is happening today in Vietnam is a form of torture." Palme likened the bombing to Nazi atrocities. (Washington promptly told Stockholm not to bother replacing its departing ambassador to the United States.) Britain's moderate *Guardian* newspaper angrily asked whether "Mr. Nixon wants to go down in history as one of the most murderous and bloodthirsty of American Presi-dents." Pope Paul VI expressed his "painful emotion" and "daily grief" over the bombing. Demonstrations erupted in Western Europe. Danish and Italian dock-workers boycotted U.S. ships.[84]

American media also assailed the bombing. "New madness," the *St. Louis Post-Dispatch* called it. "The rain of death continues," bewailed the *Boston Globe*. The *Washington Post* said the bombing was leading millions of Ameri-cans "to wonder at their President's very sanity." "Are *we* now the enemy—the new barbarians?" asked the *New York Times*. The *Times* darkly wondered "how we will be marked on the Day of Judgment." (The editorial upset the *Times*'s publisher, Arthur Ochs Sulzberger, who fired off "a rocket" at the editorial page editor, John Oakes. "He thought . . . that we'd gone too far, that we were too emotional and so on," divulged Oakes, who was out of town when the blast was written and agreed that it was too emotional.) The *Times* columnist Anthony

Lewis observed that the bombing was the work of "a man so overwhelmed by his sense of inadequacy and frustration that he had to strike out, punish, destroy." "It is a Christmas of horrors," Lewis lamented on December 25. Christmas was considered "a time of forgiveness," Lewis wrote, but "only saints can forgive mass murder."[85]

Although tempered, congressional reproval of the bombing surfaced as well. Both the House and Senate Democratic Caucuses passed resolutions calling for an immediate end to U.S. military action in Indochina pending the return of America's POWs. Senator William Saxbe (R-Ohio) said Nixon appeared to have "left his senses." White House officials had "no doubt anymore that Congress would move rapidly toward a cutoff in aid," Kissinger writes. Nixon's public approval rating plunged.[86]

"As the criticism outside mounted," the president recalls, "the pressure inside the White House became intense. I could feel the tension in the people I passed and greeted as I walked back and forth to the EOB. . . . I understood how difficult the bombing made it for many of them to face their friends and even their families during what should have been a happy holiday season." Suffering from insomnia, Nixon reached a state of "total exhaustion," Charles Colson remembered. "Many days his speech was not entirely clear." Faced with not only antagonistic negotiations and "the hysteria of domestic critics" but also the continuing "painful rift" with Nixon, Kissinger felt "in the eye of a hurricane." Most senior administration officials ducked for cover. Nixon flew to Key Biscayne, where he spent "the loneliest and saddest Christmas I can ever remember," he recalled. There were protesters in Florida too; the house seemed empty with his two daughters away in Europe; the bombing might not do the job, Nixon worried; and his wife Pat was "very upset" (Admiral Moorer revealed) over the strikes on Bach Mai Hospital. Aware that rallying the public would be impossible and "still seized by the withdrawn and sullen hostility that had dominated his mood since his electoral triumph," Kissinger records, Nixon was silent on the reasons for the bombing. Moorer remembered with some annoyance that Kissinger, William Rogers, and Melvin Laird had also left town during the strikes, leaving him to face flak from legislators and the media. Asked whether he thought they took off to get out of the line of fire, Moorer spat, "I wouldn't put it past them. I mean, they left me with the thing."[87]

On December 29, after "what seemed an eternity," given the domestic outcry, Nixon stopped the bombing north of the 20th parallel. Thieu had withdrawn some of his objections to the October peace agreement, allowing the White House to resume negotiations with Hanoi on the basis of that document. Also, there was "a real question" whether further heavy bombing would move Hanoi, Haldeman remembered, and "major dissension within the NSC staff." Perhaps most compelling was the domestic and international uproar over the strikes. "War-weariness" in the United States had reached the point where indefinitely continuing the bombing was infeasible, the president noted in his diary. Domestic censure of the strikes was "certainly a factor" in the decision to stop them, Haldeman said. Nixon was probably most concerned about the congressional dissent. If the bombing wasn't stopped before Congress reconvened in early January, he knew, legislators would vote to cut off funding.[88]

Admiral Moorer and other U.S. military men were sorely disappointed by the bombing halt. "What we should have done was to keep bombing them until they did everything that we wanted them to do," Moorer said firmly. "We could bomb them to doomsday."[89]

The Paris Accords

Despite the bombing halt, small demonstrations and acts of civil disobedience continued around the country. CALC and the AFSC sponsored a "Religious Convocation and Congressional Visitation" in Washington; on January 4, 1973, upward of two thousand peace activists, including national religious leaders, swarmed over Capitol Hill. They demanded that members of Congress pressure Nixon to sign the peace accords, secure the release of South Vietnam's political prisoners, and cut off aid to Thieu. Professional groups, labor unions, and notables also issued statements demanding that Nixon sign the accords. (Henry Kissinger's thirteen-year-old daughter was apparently among those citizens asked to sign a petition to that end, a request Kissinger considered "a terribly vicious thing.") Planning for the inaugural protests was moving forward. "All the ingredients now exist for a major anti-war demonstration on January 20th" in Washington, Dean reported to Haldeman on January 15. The turnout "could easily reach 20–30,000 persons." Dean also related that young militants planned to "engage in confrontation tactics" and incite "disturbances along the parade route." He predicted that the disruptions would be "serious" and "violent" if the Paris peace negotiations broke down. Dean maintained a detailed schedule of antiwar activities across the nation in January.[90]

On the eve of Nixon's inauguration, nearly twenty thousand people attended a "Plea for Peace" concert at the Washington Cathedral. Leonard Bernstein, a longtime opponent of the war, conducted Haydn's "Mass in a Time of War." Most of the overflow crowd stood outside in the cold and rain. At the official inauguration concert that evening, however, many seats were empty. Eleven members of the orchestra there had objected to participating in the event, leading the conductor, Eugene Ormandy, to denounce them as "left-wing sons of bitches." Ormandy's stance struck a responsive chord in Nixon. "What a man he is," the president wrote in his diary. The next morning, twenty-five hundred VVAWers marched from Arlington National Cemetery to the Lincoln Memorial. The afternoon rally drew eighty thousand, considerably more than either antiwar organizers or officials had predicted. The PCPJ leader Sidney Peck urged the crowd to join the "national emergency network" that would be activated if Nixon failed to sign the agreement or later violated it. Along the inauguration route, protesters chanted and held signs: "Nixon's secret plan killed my son and 25,300 GIs in Vietnam," the placard of one elderly man read. As Nixon was riding from the White House to the inauguration that morning, clusters of protesters hurled invective at him; they were "a pretty vicious lot," he recalled. More than a hundred thousand people protested the war in other cities that day; in several, activists held two separate marches: one for those who supported the "Sign the Treaty" demand, the other for those who didn't.[91]

Two days later, Lyndon Baines Johnson died in Texas. The ex-president was another casualty of Vietnam. As Nixon writes, "The combination of war abroad and at home proved too much for him."[92]

On January 23, Henry Kissinger and the North Vietnamese leader Le Duc Tho initialed a peace agreement in Paris that differed only cosmetically from the October treaty. A cease-fire would begin in Vietnam in four days' time, when the treaty would be formally signed. Within sixty days, the remaining twenty-seven thousand U.S. troops in Vietnam would be withdrawn and all American POWs would be released. The Provisional Revolutionary Government and Saigon government would have equal political status in the South. After the two parties peacefully settled their differences, North and South Vietnam would be reunited. The only significant concessions induced by the grisly Christmas bombing had thus been those of Nguyen Van Thieu.

Before the agreement was concluded, President Nixon reassured Thieu that it was only a piece of paper and that his regime would have continued U.S. support. Treaty or no treaty, Nixon schemed, South Vietnam would remain non-communist. The agreement would be ignored.[93]

Thieu wasted little time showing his own attitude toward the treaty. On January 24, he told the people of South Vietnam that "if Communists come into your village, you should immediately shoot them in the head." Also, fellow citizens who "begin talking in a Communist tone . . . should be immediately killed."[94]

Antiwar activists' reactions to the signing of the Paris peace treaty ran the gamut of emotions. Some were elated that the war was apparently over at last. From underground, the Weathermen expressed their "great joy" and said that the signing was "a moment to savour." Many protesters suspected Kissinger and Nixon were up to their old tricks. "Our attitude was skeptical—that we had to keep the antiwar movement together and not trust them," Fred Halstead remembered. "We knew what their game was," WSP's Alice Hamburg said. "We were not under any illusions." More than a few activists were too numb from years of mass killing to feel much of anything. Any relief they experienced was pleasureless.[95]

The North Vietnamese and NLF recognized that the peace treaty was a victory if adhered to. They invited Dave Dellinger and Rennie Davis to Paris to celebrate. Dellinger was unable to make the trip, as a decade of arduous political activism had taken a serious toll on his body. "I had a ruptured appendix and then a series of operations afterwards," Dellinger recalled. "And I think that came about because my body was just completely exhausted." Dellinger "almost died" in the hospital. He was too weak to travel to Paris. Davis did make the trip, though.[96]

Davis's companions on the flight to Paris reflected his growing fascination with "a deeper lifestyle." They were adherents of the Guru Maharaj Ji, a rich, fat, fifteen-year-old "Perfect Master" whose teachings Davis had recently taken an interest in. "Rennie called me up from Paris and told me about these people he'd met, and about how wonderful they were, and would I fly directly to India and meet him there—he was going to go there with them after the celebrations," Dellinger remembered. "And I said no." When Davis returned to the United States, "he told me all these things about what had happened to him," Dellinger said. Davis also spilled his guts to Tom Hayden. He told his friend that "at first" the guru's act "turned me off." But then, Davis said,

> I went through this initiation ritual. It blew out every socket in my head. I saw light. I could only see light for two whole weeks. It scared the shit out of me, because I lost my identity in it. It was so total and ecstatic, though, I couldn't believe it.
>
> Then one day I was at this little stream washing my clothes. All of a sudden this giant black bird, with huge wings, is hovering right above me, coming closer and closer. He was beating the air with his wings, and I just knelt there. I couldn't move or get away.
>
> It was like he was entering me, opening me up, and all of a sudden I felt helpless, prostrate. I saw myself from outside myself, and all I saw was ego. That's why I was hung up, because of ego. And that's why I dismissed the guru, because I looked only at his appearance. He was wearing all the symbols of ego to throw me off. I felt that I was in the presence of a larger force than myself. I was blissed out, man.

Listening to Davis, Hayden recalled, "I thought I was in the presence of a character from *Invasion of the Body Snatchers*." Hayden felt he "was going to be ill." His best friend's mind had "gone somewhere else." Davis also told Hayden that he was on a mission to convert other activists to the guru's faith.[97]

Hayden was not the only activist to question Davis's mental health. Brad Lyttle approached Dellinger about it. "I said, 'Look, Dave, good grief, Rennie for the past three or four years has been an advocate virtually of Maoism and various forms of Marxism-Leninism, and the Guru Maharaj Ji is *not* that,'" Lyttle remembered. "'This is something quite different.' And Dave looked at me and he said, 'Brad, I've got my eye on the situation.'" Dellinger recalled, "I just said that I really could get through to Rennie. And it was true." Lyttle added, "The guru exploited people—it was just nonsense to me. [But] I could see that it brought certain things that the peace movement was no longer giving Rennie. . . . There were no longer big rallies that Rennie could go to and speak to. But he could do that with the guru. . . . The guru was then able to have big rallies of ten, twenty thousand people—huge meetings. . . . And the guru had a lot of money, and Rennie had access to that." PCPJ's David McReynolds thought Davis's apocalyptic approach to politics explained "why he ended up where he did—he went this far and it didn't change the world, and so he went to his form of god." One well-known antiwar leader with whom Davis worked quite closely in the movement and who sadly observed his conversion to the guru avowed:

> If you want to know, on a personal level, for a while I wondered if I should kick myself because I didn't respond enough to Rennie. . . . Afterwards I stopped kicking myself, because I figured he was on a trajectory, and nobody else can take responsibility. But I think there were so many deep contradictions in his life that he needed to make a kind of break. . . . I got several beautiful letters from him [later]. He wrote me about what a special person I was, and about how much of a difference it would make if I came in, is what it amounted to. And I just couldn't take it, I just couldn't take it. Because he was still talking about [how] they were going to save the world, and the guru was going to go to China and they were going to convert the Chinese, and I think he wanted me to go with him. . . . After I got some of those letters from Rennie, which in a sense were like love letters, but they were also like "I've-got-the-truth" letters, I didn't even answer them, because I knew that this was not something that we could do lightly. . . . Having been through what we'd been through together, I should have done it, but . . . it would [have been] like a major invest-ment of time, energy, blood, sweat, and tears to go into all the mat-ters with him. I mean, all the inconsistencies and possible dishonesties.

Davis eventually left the guru's flock, "feeling bad about his involvement." He started up a similar spiritual enterprise of his own. Davis later owned an invest-ment company in Colorado.[98]

Unfinished Business

Rennie Davis's departure from the peace movement was part of a broader trend. The signing of the Paris peace treaty substantially reduced the number of protesters. Many returned to neglected families and work; some took up other political concerns. Most local antiwar coalitions closed their doors and shut down their phones lines. The factionalized PCPJ would fold within a year. NPAC maintained merely a "skeletal" structure. The inaugural protest was the last mass peace demonstration of the war.[99]

But a large and dedicated army of activists realized there was more work to do. The main tasks: forcing Nixon to honor the peace treaty, pressuring Congress to sever U.S. aid to Thieu and Cambodia's President Lon Nol, securing the release of South Vietnam's political prisoners, and stopping the accelerating bombing of Cambodia. Other tasks included raising humanitarian aid for Vietnam and securing amnesty for American war resisters. The Indochina Peace Campaign played a major role in carrying the ball for the antiwar movement during this post-treaty period. "Our goal from 1973 on was to concentrate like a laser" public antiwar sentiment on Congress, the IPC's Jack Nicholl recalled.[100] No less active in the crusade were religious and pacifist groups like the AFSC, CALC, WSP, WILPF, and WRL. The work of Don Luce and his Mobile Education Project and that of the informational Indochina Resource Center directed by Luce, David Marr, and Fred Branfman was equally important to the movement.

The decline in the size of the movement in one sense made the work of these stalwarts easier. The AFSC leader John McAuliff noted:

> As the political, sectarian groups dropped away, because they no longer saw [the war] as a key issue, it made it much easier to have productive discussions over what we needed to do in *x* time, and there was no longer this big controversy between whether you did public activity and educational work or congressional work. The two things were seen as meshing very closely together. So you had less of a mass movement, but you probably had a more effectively targeted movement. You had good networks of people in a large number of congressional districts that would be taking the principles of opposition to the war and coming down to very specific [issues]: "How are you going to vote the day after tomorrow?"[101]

During the winter and spring of 1973, activists publicized the terms of the peace treaty. This was important not only for keeping Nixon honest, Tom Hayden told IPCers, but to show other protesters that they had won a significant victory. Some activists campaigned to legitimize the Provisional Revolutionary Government. "Kissinger and Nixon won't speak of the PRG or the NLF," Hayden pointed out. "One million allied troops . . . could not discover who they are. No one knows who they are." Don Luce toured the country with his Mobile Education Project speaking out on the plight of South Vietnamese political prisoners. Some activists held protests alongside mock tiger cages, including in downtown areas, forcing people to pass the instruments of torture on their way to work in the morning. Tiger cages and NLF banners greeted Thieu at stops during a visit to the United States in April. IPCers distributed tens of thousands of plastic bracelets like those worn by South Vietnamese political prisoners, each with the name of a prisoner on it.[102]

Also to build public pressure on Congress, activists continued to present slide shows, distribute pamphlets, hold community meetings, rent billboards, and write letters to the editor. They generated a steady stream of telegrams, letters, and phone calls to legislators. Many activists paid personal visits to legislators; some demonstrated outside their offices and homes. A few testified at congressional committee hearings. The hearings were "very depressing affairs," the IPCer Dan Hirsch reported to his co-workers in July. "Very few members are present; the questions asked are immaterial or insane." Nevertheless, "grassroots pressure and Washington lobbying can both have a positive effect," Hirsch observed in Washington. "Congressional offices spend nearly all their time answering letters from constitutents, responding to pressure from wherever it comes (not equally, of course). They count each letter, each phone call, each personal visit; they are quite paranoid of losing the next election. Their ambition and fear of losing power create a kind of crazed democracy: the Representative or Senator is a pawn of political forces, and we can be one of those forces." "There is nothing you can teach a dog that you cannot teach a Congressman," Hirsch exhorted other activists. Protesters set up the Coalition to Stop Funding the War in Washington to strengthen lobbying of Congress.[103]

By late June their work was having some effect. Congress passed an amendment calling for the immediate termination of all U.S. military activity in and over Indochina. The bombing of Cambodia thus had to stop. The deadline was subsequently extended to August 15. Peace activists had mobilized their networks in support of the legislation, bombarding legislators with communications and invading Capitol Hill. Their activity undoubtedly shaped some legislators' votes. Hirsch perceived that they had "had an important effect in changing and maintaining votes by former hawks." An aide to Congressman Alphonzo Bell (R-Calif.) told him that Bell's office had been "a mad-house" at the time, "that it became more and more difficult to continue war votes under such pressure."[104]

Antiwar activists were, of course, hardly the only factor behind Congress's decision to stop the bombing of Cambodia. It was already readily apparent to numerous legislators that their constituents wanted U.S. military operations in Indochina to end, and most were themselves sick of the whole stinking mess.

Many questioned Nixon's right to bomb now that U.S. troops were coming out. Perhaps most important, the latest Watergate revelations were undermining the president's authority. [105]

"You Could Get a Million Dollars. And You Could Get It in Cash."

In March the Watergate cover-up had begun to unravel. Acting FBI Director L. Patrick Gray unguardedly divulged to the Senate that he had regularly turned over information on the FBI's Watergate investigation to John Dean. Dean's conduct was now suspect. Nixon rebuffed requests that Dean testify in the hearings, citing executive privilege. The president also invoked executive privilege as cause for keeping aides from testifying at upcoming Senate Select Committee hearings on the administration's 1972 campaign abuses, including the Watergate break-in. White House Press Secretary Ronald Ziegler often "seemed on the verge of tears or hysteria" in answering mushrooming press queries about Watergate. [106]

In mid March Howard Hunt threatened to reveal the "seamy things" he had done for the White House and thereby "bring John Ehrlichman down to his knees" if $122,000 more in hush money wasn't forthcoming. Fearful that the cover-up was going to blow, Dean warned Nixon on March 21 that "we have a cancer . . . close to the Presidency, that's growing." Dean predicted that the silence of the Watergate burglars was "going to cost a million dollars over the next two years." What's more, "people around here are not pros at this sort of thing," Dean said, "because we're . . . not criminals." The president acted unfazed by Hunt's demand. "You could get a million dollars," he told Dean. "And you could get it in cash. I know where it could be gotten." Nixon also told Dean, "Don't you have to handle Hunt's financial situation damn soon? You've got to keep the cap on the bottle." That evening $75,000 went out to Hunt in a manila envelope. It was the last of the Watergate hush money, totaling $429,500. [107]

The same day, the Watergate burglar James McCord defected. McCord delivered a letter to John Sirica, judge at the trial of the Watergate burglars, disclosing what he knew of the cover-up. News leaks indicated that, in testimony to Senate investigators, McCord had implicated Dean, John Mitchell, Jeb Magruder, and Charles Colson in the break-in.

Petrified of going to jail and unraveling, Dean went to the federal prosecutors to try to cut a deal. "This is an evil man, you know," Nixon remarked to Haldeman and Ehrlichman of their newest enemy. Dean told the prosecutors about the break-in at Daniel Ellsberg's psychiatrist's office. Also petrified of losing his hide and becoming unglued, Magruder—"that son-of-a-bitch," Nixon called him—went to the prosecutors as well. [108] The press reported his statements tying Mitchell and Dean to the Watergate break-in and hush money payments.[109]

Worried that the Ellsberg break-in might surface at Ellsberg's trial, Nixon had Ehrlichman offer the judge at that trial, Matthew Byrne, the job of FBI director. Byrne was interested. Three weeks later, however, federal Watergate prosecutors informed him of the break-in. Byrne publicly disclosed it on April 27. Also, the press reported that Ehrlichman had met with him about a senior government post. On May 11, concerned about his reputation, and after learning that phone conversations between Ellsberg and the former NSC staffer Morton Halperin had been wiretapped by the government, Byrne, "his face flushed," declared a mistrial. A jubilant Ellsberg vowed to "make love in every climate on earth." Ellsberg came to believe that disclosure of the break-in saved him from prison. "That judge wasn't going to let me get off 100 percent or he couldn't have been the head of the FBI," he said.[110]

To contain the mounting scandal, Nixon directed Ehrlichman in mid April to persuade Mitchell to assume responsibility for the Watergate break-in. "Give 'em an hors d'oeuvre and maybe they won't come back for the main course," the president strategized. However, "Brother Mitchell" (as Ehrlichman called the former attorney general, whom he disliked) refused to walk the plank for "Brother Dick" (as Mitchell called Nixon). Yet there were other hors d'oeuvres that could be served, Nixon realized. On April 29, he tearfully fired Ehrlichman and Haldeman, both of whom had also been publicly implicated in the cover-up and probably faced criminal indictments.[111] Nixon offered them between $200,000 and $300,000 in the hope that they would stay silent on sensitive matters (they refused the money). He told them that the previous night he had wished he would not wake up in the morning. The president also fired Dean and Attorney General Richard Kleindienst, who sobbed at the news. "It's all over," Nixon morbidly mused to Ziegler after the firings. A Gallup poll conducted shortly thereafter indicated that half of Americans believed Nixon had participated in the cover-up.[112]

May and June witnessed a torrent of disclosures on the White House's horrors, including the wiretapping, bag jobs, domestic spying, attacks on protesters, dirty tricks, hush money payments, Huston Plan, and the like. Dean testified on the horrors for five days on national television before the Senate Select Committee. Other former White House aides also testified on official illegalities. Daniel Ellsberg watched the hearings "with a feeling of tension and alertness, like being hunted."[113] To take more heat off himself, Nixon agreed to the appointment of a Watergate special prosecutor in May.

By the early summer, most of Congress and the public realized that Watergate went far beyond a break-in and that Nixon was being less than candid about his own role in events. His ability to lead was rapidly deteriorating. The war in Indochina, Nixon fretted, might be a lost cause. His plan to renew air strikes over Vietnam in support of Thieu was now politically unthinkable.[114]

Meanwhile, in Vietnam, the last American troops had left as scheduled. The United States employed a variety of schemes to maintain its substantial military aid to Thieu without obviously violating the Paris peace treaty. It dispatched huge quantities of "replacement" equipment, established a team of from ten to twenty thousand "civilian" advisers (many freshly plucked from the military) and fattened its military staff at the U.S. Embassy. It pointedly maintained enough air and naval power in the region to blow North Vietnam off the face of the earth.[115]

Hanoi released the POWs. At a White House gala for the POWs and their families, Nixon, his body dramatically bathed in floodlights and shadows, chiaroscuro-style, saluted "the brave men that took those B-52s in and did the job." Nixon also told the POWs that it was "time in this country to quit making national heroes out of those who steal secrets and publish them in the news-papers." Watching TV footage of Nixon's statement, Daniel Ellsberg felt an "eerie" sensation. After midnight, sitting alone in the Lincoln Sitting Room, Nixon waxed joyful over the gala, then suddenly was overcome by dread: Watergate would not leave him alone. "Do you think I should resign?" he asked his two daughters when they stopped by the room to visit. "It was almost painful for us to see how sad Daddy's face looked," Tricia Nixon wrote in her diary.[116]

Earlier one of the returned POWs had passed the president some gratifying news, however. The POW reported that the North Vietnamese "really thought that the President was off his rocker—was totally irrational."[117] The madman theory of war had received support.

Over the summer, peace activists launched a campaign to impeach Nixon for Watergate crimes. Although the president had told his family that "one wel-come personal benefit" of the Paris peace treaty was that "we would no longer be harassed by sign-carrying hecklers," the signs "had reappeared," he records. "Now they were Watergate signs." They even greeted him at church. The In-dochina Peace Campaign, which viewed Watergate as a major opportunity for pressuring Congress to change U.S. policy in Indochina, resolved to "*emphasize the Watergate crisis* in all our work."[118] Congressman Robert Drinan (D-Mass.) introduced a resolution to impeach Nixon for the illegal bombing of Cambodia and lying to Congress about it.

On July 13, the former presidential aide Alexander Butterfield revealed the existence of the White House taping system. His disclosure sent shockwaves across the country and into the Oval Office. Nixon, who was rumored to be mentally collapsing and drinking heavily, refused to turn over subpoenaed tapes to the Senate Select Committee or to Watergate Special Prosecutor Archibald Cox and his staff (referred to as "Cox-suckers" by certain presidential aides).[119]

Two other developments were eroding Nixon's authority late that summer and early fall. Vice President Spiro Agnew was forced out of office in disgrace after his systematic bribery while governor of Maryland became known. And reports surfaced that Nixon had enriched himself through tax evasion and shady financial transactions.

Turning Off the Tap

Antiwar activists were then continuing their work to force Nixon to honor the Paris peace treaty, cut off U.S. war funding and free South Vietnam's political prisoners. In July and August, some one hundred and fifty people were arrested inside the White House for breaking away from the public tour to kneel and pray for peace. "The antiwar movement is not dead," Cora Weiss proclaimed during picketing outside the Executive Mansion on August 14, the eve of the Cambodia bombing cutoff, when sixty-three worshippers were busted. Activists held small demonstrations in many cities across the United States and overseas during "International Days of Concern with Saigon's Political Prisoners" on September 16–23. Twenty congressional representatives endorsed the Days. Tom Hayden, Jane Fonda, and Jean-Pierre Debris, a French peace activist held for two years in a Saigon prison, conducted a month-long speaking tour of the United States. They decried the existence of an estimated two hundred thousand political prisoners in South Vietnam, many of whom suffered torture. Debris graphically described the tortures he had seen while in jail.[120]

At a "unity conference" in Germantown, Ohio, on October 26–28 instigated by the IPC, peace activists formed the United Campaign to End the War. The United Campaign was a broad coalition comprising most everyone still protesting U.S. policy. "We had a network of literally millions of activists out there," Jack Nicholl remembered. "And the network was incredible, and effective." The United Campaign called upon members of Congress, political candidates, and other Americans to sign an "Indochina Peace Pledge" to support congressional legislation designed to prohibit direct U.S. military involvement in Indochina, encourage a political settlement in Vietnam based on the Paris peace treaty, and end U.S. aid for Thieu's police and prison system. United Campaign activists also agreed to "wholeheartedly" participate in impeachment coalitions.[121]

In South Vietnam, proclaiming the start of the "Third Indochina War," Thieu launched thousands of attacks on enemy bases and territory that fall using his most reliable forces and heavy aerial bombardment. The North Vietnamese and PRG counterattacked, ravaging ARVN units and capturing additional territory. The Paris peace treaty had become "a dead letter."[122]

On October 20, President Nixon fired Archibald Cox for demanding access to White House tapes and documents. Washington was deluged with telegrams protesting the dismissal. A spontaneous wave of protests calling for Nixon's impeachment broke out across the country. "Nixon's the One," demonstrators in Berkeley waggishly chanted. Members of Congress introduced over twenty impeachment resolutions; the House Judiciary Committee announced it was organizing an impeachment inquiry. Media editorials called for Nixon's resignation. The president, who was "taken by surprise" by the "firestorm" of protest, replaced Cox with Leon Jaworski, a millionaire Houston corporate lawyer. The White House also announced to a skeptical nation that two of nine subpoenaed tapes did not exist, inciting more demands that Nixon step down. [123]

On November 7, over Nixon's veto, Congress passed the War Powers Act, which required that the president notify Congress within forty-eight hours of the deployment of U.S. troops overseas and that he withdraw those troops within sixty days in the absence of congressional approval. Once again Nixon's power to make war was being curtailed. And once again Watergate was substantially responsible. [124]

The president's political standing eroded further two weeks later when it was revealed that there was a suspicious eighteen-and-a-half-minute gap on a key subpoenaed tape. A panel of experts subsequently concluded that the gap was caused by between five and nine separate erasures. [125]

Public speculation about Nixon's mental health was growing. At daily White House press briefings, reporters began asking whether he was under psychiatric care and using drugs. Anonymous presidential aides spoke guardedly to reporters about his worsening insomnia, disjointed monologues, and impetuous urges to "drive somewhere, anywhere," often with his pal Bebe Rebozo behind the wheel. During a visit with Nixon, Clarence Kelley, the new FBI director, perceived that the haggard and rambling president was "breaking down under enormous strain." "Anyone would be troubled, really, if he couldn't go out anywhere without attracting hostile pickets and impeachment signs," one White House aide commented. Nixon's son-in-law, David Eisenhower, worried that the president might "go bananas," even commit suicide. [126]

In December, Congress voted to halt U.S. police training in South Vietnam and other foreign countries. It also voted to stop U.S. funding of Thieu's police and prison system through economic aid. The United Campaign had lobbied hard for the legislation; peace activists had earlier induced several congressmen to introduce it. "Clearly, the peace and social justice movements in the United States have won a substantial victory," the antiwar journalist Michael Klare asserted. [127]

On January 27, 1974, the first anniversary of the signing of the Paris peace treaty, the United Campaign launched a national "Honor the Peace" campaign.

In many cities, protesters held activities to commemorate the signing. Ramsey Clark spoke at a rally in New York.[128]

In March, the Nixon administration requested $474 million in additional military aid for South Vietnam. During the previous year, Congress had cut such aid by virtually the same amount, from $1.6 billion to $1.1 billion. The United Campaign mobilized its network in earnest to defeat the request. Activists leafleted, canvassed, and activated their phone lists, beseeching citizens to telegram their legislators. They also lobbied local media. The Coalition to Stop Funding the War secured the opposition of major religious denominations, the U.S. Conference of Mayors, the UAW, and Common Cause. Hayden, Fonda, and thousands of other activists met with members of Congress in Washington. Hayden taught a course on Indochina to congressional staffers.[129]

In early April, the House of Representatives voted down the administration's request. The *Washington Post* called it "a stunning defeat for the Nixon administration." Hayden remembered the vote as "a turning point for me in working through the system."[130] On April 27, nearly ten thousand people turned out in Washington for the first major impeachment demonstration. "It's just like the marches of the antiwar days," one remarked, reflecting widespread sentiment.[131]

Three days later, Nixon turned over heavily edited and sanitized transcripts of forty-two White House tapes subpoenaed by the House Judiciary Committee (he had already relinquished nineteen tapes). The release was a disaster for the president. Most Americans were appalled by the flavor and content of the tapes, which were widely reprinted. They engendered "sheer flesh-crawling repulsion," the columnist Joseph Alsop wrote. Nixon and the House Judiciary Committee struggled over tapes and documents into the early summer. By then it was nearly certain that the committee would recommend impeachment.[132]

In late June, a broad coalition of antiwar groups established a tiger cage vigil at the entrance to the Capitol. Protesters sat in the cage, shackled, while others leafleted passersby. Philip Berrigan was arrested while engaged in a mobile display of the cage. The vigil continued for seven weeks.[133]

Nixon suffered another blow on July 24 when the Supreme Court unanimously ruled that he had to turn over sixty-four tapes subpoenaed by Leon Jaworski. The same day, on national television, the House Judiciary Committee began formally debating articles of impeachment. Within a week the committee had voted in favor of three articles charging Nixon with obstruction of justice; abuse of presidential power by using the FBI, CIA, IRS, and other federal agencies to violate citizens' constitutional rights, and by creating the Plumbers to engage in illegal acts; and failing to provide material subpoenaed by the committee. Nixon was in San Clemente during the first three days of the proceedings; an aide remembered seeing him periodically "gazing out the window at the ocean with this haunted look in his eyes, the look of a man who knew he was going to die."[134]

On August 6, the House voted to limit U.S. military aid to Thieu to $700 million for the next fiscal year. The White House had requested $1.6 billion. Antiwar activists were elated. Once again their lobbying had paid off. "We saw dollars coming out of Saigon," Jack Nicholl recalled. "I mean, we could actually measure [our] impact." The aid cut, approved by the Senate in September, greatly hampered South Vietnam's fighting ability. Air operations were restricted, ammunition was rationed, morale plummeted. The reduction also worsened Thieu's economic and political problems. "We weakened Saigon," Nicholl argued. "We cut the heart out of Nixon's Vietnamization policy. And the North Vietnamese and the NLF did the rest."[135]

By the day of the House vote, rumors were rife that the president would resign. A large crowd began gathering outside the White House gates in a deathwatch. Nixon, who had been up the previous night pacing the mansion's halls, talking to pictures of ex-presidents on the walls, giving speeches, was indeed ruminating about death. "You fellows, in your business, you have a way of handling problems like this," he remarked to General Alexander Haig, now the White House Chief of Staff. "Somebody leaves a pistol in the drawer. I don't have a pistol," Nixon said gloomily, almost as if asking for one. Haig promptly called the president's doctors and ordered that all pills be taken away.[136]

The next evening, Nixon poured out his anguish to Henry Kissinger. Drinking and sobbing, the wrought-up president wondered aloud how it had come to this, then asked Kissinger to get down on the floor and pray with him. Kissinger complied. After praying, the still weeping Nixon banged his fist on the carpet and cried, "What have I done? What has happened?" Kissinger held the broken president.[137]

The following night, Nixon announced his resignation. Earlier that day he had mused that some politicians had done their best writing in jail. He mentioned Gandhi and Lenin.[138]

Nixon's resignation did not, of course, spell the end of the war. Shortly after assuming office, the new president, Gerald Ford, made it clear that he planned to continue Nixon's policy of support for Thieu and Cambodian President Lon Nol. Antiwar activists, in turn, made it clear that they planned to continue protesting until all U.S. war funding was cut off and South Vietnam's political prisoners were released. During an "International Week of Concern," September 29–October 6, they organized demonstrations, cultural events, educational programs, and displays of mock tiger cages. Many continued lobbying Congress. The Indochina Resource Center churned out more bulletins on the state of the war and U.S. policy, distributing many to congressional staffers.[139]

In December, North Vietnamese and NLF forces attacked Phuoc Long province some sixty miles north of Saigon. Three weeks later, they captured the province capital, shocking officials in Saigon. President Ford asked Congress for

$300 million in supplemental military aid for Thieu and $200 million for Lon Nol, who was also on shaky ground.

Shortly before Christmas, thirty-six American religious leaders issued a pastoral letter declaring that "we have not been seduced by leaders who tell us that peace has come to Southeast Asia. It has not. . . . The war goes on. American bombs are still dropped from American airplanes on Vietnamese targets. . . . American funds and American prestige support a dictatorship in South Vietnam that arrests and tortures dissidents. . . . We supply the dollars, the guns, the tanks, the planes, the bombs, everything but the corpses. The corpses are Vietnamese." The letter detailed numerous U.S. violations of the Paris peace treaty. It called for members of the American religious community to attend a national "Assembly to Save the Peace Agreement" in Washington the following month.[140]

Alarmed by the letter, U.S. Ambassador to South Vietnam Graham Martin cabled the State Department in Washington to urge "corrective action." Martin denounced the letter as "a tissue of lies from beginning to end" with "distortions so gross that they approach the dimension of caricature." The religious leaders had committed "the prostitution of the principal tenets of their faith in an attempt to insure the victory of Hanoi," the ambassador charged. Martin exhorted the State Department to fulfill its "clear moral responsibility" to "present the whole truth to the American people."[141]

On January 25–27, 1975, the second anniversary of the signing of the Paris peace treaty, some three thousand people gathered in Washington to attend the Assembly to Save the Peace Agreement. They held strategy sessions and a candlelight march past the White House. Many vigorously lobbied their congressional representatives. The president of the Senate of South Vietnam was in Washington at the time; the Assembly and the general mood on Capitol Hill led him to report to Saigon that Congress was "extraordinarily opposed to reason" (as Ambassador Martin put it), and that an end to U.S. military aid was thus near. When the State Department failed to heed his advice to counter the "incredibly efficient propaganda exercise" in Washington, Martin also concluded that "the game was up."[142]

On January 29, the Weathermen detonated a "powerful explosive device" at the State Department. The blast destroyed several offices of the Agency for International Development. In a communiqué, the Weathermen called for an end to U.S. support for Thieu and Lon Nol and implementation of the Paris treaty.[143]

In March, Congress rejected President Ford's earlier request for supplemental military aid for Thieu and Lon Nol. Martin credited the antiwar movement with inducing Congress's action. "The negative decision was made inevitable by one of the best propaganda and pressure organizations the world has ever seen,"

Martin asserted in later testimony to Congress. It was "the constancy of the drumming in day after day after day after day of certain particular themes" by peace activists that made the difference, he contended. "It's the building of the pressure from the constituencies, the use of . . . the humanitarian concerns, of most American people, good, wholly healthful concerns, but which are twisted and distorted by the flood of propaganda." Martin complained that the withdrawal of U.S. troops from Vietnam "seemed only to encourage the use of these organizations that had their roots in the constituencies" and the "letters about political prisoners." The Assembly to Save the Peace Agreement was "very effective," the ambassador opined. Martin singled out the Indochina Resource Center and "the multi-faceted activities of Mr. Don Luce" for special credit. "I must say I have watched these operations over the world for a long period of time, [and] those individuals deserve enormous credit for a very effective performance," he stated. The "beautifully orchestrated campaign" of the IRC was "enormously effective," Martin said. "I have enormous respect for the capabilities of Mr. [Fred] Branfman and Mr. Luce." Told by one congressional representative that he seemed to be paying IRC activists a "great compliment," the ambassador responded, "I meant it to be that. They deserve it."[144]

On March 11, North Vietnamese and NLF forces seized the provincial capital of Ban Me Thuot in the Central Highlands of South Vietnam. As they moved north against other highland towns, a frightened Thieu withdrew his troops from the region. The ARVN soldiers and departing civilians were mauled in a "Convoy of Tears."[145] South Vietnam's major northern coastal towns of Hue and Danang fell by the end of the month.

In early April, the Ford administration asked Congress for $700 million in supplemental military aid for South Vietnam. From Saigon, Martin called supporters on Capitol Hill, "begging for the money." Once again the administration was rebuffed. The State Department's Lawrence Eagleburger remembered the "contempt" he felt for Congress when it was "unwilling to provide even artillery shells." "There was literally nothing we could do but stand there and watch South Vietnam go down the tube," he said. That "got a little bit much for me."[146]

On April 17, Cambodia fell to the Khmer Rouge.

Several days later, Nguyen Van Thieu tearfully fled Saigon for Taiwan. He bitterly denounced the United States for deserting him.

On April 30, North Vietnamese and NLF troops rolled into Saigon. They renamed it Ho Chi Minh City. One victoriously unfurled the red-blue-and-gold flag of the Provisional Revolutionary Government from the balcony of the presidential palace.

In the United States, antiwar activists shed tears of joy and relief. "It was a moment that many thought would never come," the radical *Guardian* newspaper observed. "Vietnam has won. And so have we." More than fifty thousand people filled Sheep Meadow in Central Park on May 11 to celebrate the war's end. Colorful streamers and gigantic balloons reflected the festive mood of the crowd, bathed by spring sunshine. A large banner on the speakers' platform proclaiming THE WAR IS OVER was flanked by huge pictures of the 1970 Kent State killings. Many of the celebrants hugged each other. Some reflected on the countless meetings and demonstrations of the past ten years. "There's lots of lumps in lots of throats," one said. "It's unbelievable."[147]

But it was true.

Afterword

The American movement against the Vietnam War was perhaps the most successful antiwar movement in history. The movement did not exert its influence in any neat way, but its impact was clearly considerable. As the cutting edge of domestic antiwar sentiment as a whole, it played a major role in restricting, deescalating, and ending the war. As Admiral Thomas Moorer, chairman of the JCS during the Nixon administration, asserted, "The reaction of the noisy radical groups was considered all the time. And it served to inhibit and restrain the decision makers." The movement, Moorer accurately added, "had a major impact . . . both in the executive and legislative branches of the government."[1]

For those who took part in the movement, their success was intertwined with great frustration and pain. Many were unaware of the full extent of their impact on their government during the war, and those who recognized their power anguished over whether they were doing enough, grieved over the war's horrendous human toll. They were victors in the end, but emotionally bloodied victors. The pall of sadness at the end of their story reflects a sadness widely felt. They had indeed, in a very real sense, won, and there was much joy along the way, but their pain and torment had been great. In that sense, there were really no winners in this contest.

The protesters' victory over the war makers was not, of course, absolute. And that it was not fueled their pain. They had not prevented the war's steady upward climb during the Johnson years, nor had they prevented Nixon's assorted escalations of the conflict. They had not prevented some two million Vietnamese deaths and more than fifty-eight thousand American ones. Nor had they prevented many millions of injuries on both sides. And although they could never have accomplished all that they wanted, their shortcomings were partly of their own making: through factionalism and failure to appreciate their power, they had weakened themselves. Nonetheless, their influence on their government had been profound. Had they not acted, the death and destruction they mourned would have been immensely greater.

Following the war, Americans expressed disenchantment with U.S. military intervention overseas. America's enormous failure in Vietnam had left many uneasy about the use of force in foreign lands, particularly the sending of U.S. troops. The slogan "No more Vietnams" captured widespread sentiment. Even shortly before the war's end, a majority of citizens expressed support for foreign military intervention only in defense of Canada.[2] The public's disillusionment with U.S. military intervention was even given a name—"the Vietnam syndrome"—suggesting it was a type of disease.

Although the syndrome would weaken over time, it remained palpable for years, deterring Washington from undertaking other military ventures. The specter of Vietnam undoubtedly shaped the Reagan administration's decision not to send U.S. troops to Central America, including El Salvador and Nicaragua. Polls showed Americans leery of "another Vietnam." The Reagan administration's Robert McFarlane later recalled how the media's evocation of the memory of Vietnam in 1981 exposed "the reality of difficulty you will have in sustaining popular support for" U.S. troop deployments to Central America. The top Reagan aide Michael Deaver remembered that Secretary of State Alexander Haig "wanted to go in there and clean house." But Deaver and White House Chief of Staff James Baker "constantly cautioned the President" not only that "you cannot win" but that "the American people will not stand still for a war in Central America."[3] Aware of the public's sentiment, Congress restricted U.S. military aid to the region. The specter of Vietnam may also have influenced President Jimmy Carter's decision not to intervene against revolutionary movements in Angola and Iran, and restrained Reagan in Lebanon in 1983 following the suicide bombing of a Marine barracks. It may have shaped Reagan's decision not to try to roll back socialism in Cuba as well.

Many U.S. political and military leaders came to conclude that, to exorcise the Vietnam syndrome, the United States should apply its military firepower massively, overwhelmingly, and decisively in any intervention overseas. That way it could win swiftly, with minimal U.S. casualties, before domestic support for the operation eroded. If the United States wasn't prepared to act decisively, many argued, it shouldn't intervene at all. The gradualist approach in Vietnam, they observed, had been a loser. "As soon as they tell me it is limited, it means they do not care whether you achieve a result or not," the Bush administration's JCS Chairman General Colin Powell, who had been wounded in Vietnam, said in 1992 of suggestions to undertake limited air raids in the former Yugoslavia to protect Muslims from Serbs. "As soon as they tell me 'surgical,' I head for the bunker."[4]

American leaders know that the weaker their opponent, of course, the more likely a quick victory can be achieved. Although bungled, President Reagan's

1983 invasion of the tiny Caribbean island of Grenada predictably resulted in a swift, relatively inexpensive (to Americans), and therefore politically popular triumph. With few American casualties and U.S. military strength reasserted, most Americans applauded. They also largely applauded President George Bush's 1989 invasion of Panama, another quick and cheap flexing of the muscles. In both operations, public support was fostered by government press censorship of U.S. actions. For another lesson of Vietnam to many American leaders was that the government should control as much as possible what the public sees, hears and reads of such interventions. To those concerned with democracy, that is a very frightening lesson indeed.

During the 1990 U.S. military buildup in the Persian Gulf in response to Iraq's invasion of Kuwait, the ghost of Vietnam continued to haunt America, however. Despite Bush's effort to mobilize the country for war by declaring a national emergency and activating military reserve units, skepticism about the wisdom of war was widespread. In a *New York Times* poll that August, 40 percent of the public said they thought Bush was "too quick to send troops." A *Los Angeles Times* poll published in November found that 53 percent favored continuing economic sanctions against Iraq "no matter how long it takes" rather than going to war. (Perhaps not coincidentally, the Gallup poll in 1990 showed 72 percent agreeing with the statement that the Vietnam War was "more than a mistake; it was fundamentally wrong and immoral." A majority of them "strongly" agreed.)[5] The media's many analogies to Vietnam and predictions of numerous U.S. casualties in a war fed the public's disquiet.

Yet George Bush, eager to "kick some ass" (just as the Weathermen had been two decades earlier) and deflect attention from the country's domestic problems, thereby improving his reelection chances, readied a gargantuan military force. Over half a million Americans were dispatched to the Persian Gulf, virtually the same number as were in Vietnam at the height of U.S. involvement there; some were part of the largest reserve mobilization since the Korean War. Bush and his advisers knew that their chances of subduing Iraq with minimal U.S. casualties before public support for the war faded would be enhanced by the open desert terrain; in contrast to Vietnam's jungles, it was ideal for heavy bombing and the conventional ground tactics that the United States had long been preparing to utilize in Europe against the Soviet Union. And while economically undeveloped North Vietnam had offered few juicy bombing targets, Iraq was loaded with them. What's more, although the Vietnamese could be continually resupplied, Iraq could be cut off.

In January 1991, the United States unleashed an unprecedented barrage of military firepower against Iraq. Some six weeks of massive aerial bombardment was followed by a short mopping-up operation misleadingly called a ground war. "This will not be another Vietnam," Bush had declared as the blitzkrieg started. "Our troops . . . will not be asked to fight with one hand tied behind their back." The disgrace of Vietnam would now be expunged. "I measure everything in my life from Vietnam," General H. "Stormin' Norman" Schwarzkopf, who had also fought in Vietnam, would state in March.[6]

Although anxious, Americans overwhelmingly backed the Gulf War. Their anticipation of far higher U.S. fatalities than the one hundred and forty-eight that occurred undoubtedly contributed to their enthusiasm. When the blitzkrieg was over, President Bush stood at the pinnacle of his popularity. "By God," he gushed, "we've kicked the Vietnam syndrome once and for all."[7]

But had "we"? As Bush and other U.S. officials were undoubtedly aware, public support for the war would likely have steadily eroded if the conflict had dragged on, at far greater cost in American lives and resources. Before the start of the U.S. ground offensive, the public, fearful of another Vietnam and its horrendous toll in American lives, had overwhelmingly expressed hope that the air assault against Iraq be given more time.[8] Still haunted by the ghost of Vietnam, Americans remained averse to a lengthy military involvement and dreaded seeing another endless stream of body bags coming home. At the time of this writing, in May 1993, the specter of Vietnam was also a factor in the Clinton administration's reluctance to intervene in the former Yugoslavia, then bloodied by ethnic strife.

Nonetheless, there is truth in Bush's remark. America's easy victory over Iraq in some sense changed the nation's view of the military option. Although sustained military intervention in Third World jungles or in deep-seated ethnic conflicts remains politically forbidding to Washington, the concentrated application of decisive military force (particularly from the air) in favorable situations seems more tenable. Emerging, well-armed Third World powers like Iraq (especially those with a nuclear capacity) that are judged a threat to Washington's global interests may be the most likely targets of such action. The resulting engagements are likely to be "high-speed, high-tech affairs," as Michael Klare observes, "entailing the unrestrained use of America's most capable and sophisticated weapons." The demise of the Soviet Union as a countervailing force has given the United States even greater freedom to undertake such operations— indeed, it may have made the Gulf War possible.[9]

So while the public remains opposed to the spilling of American blood overseas, it seems prepared to accept—even cheer—the swift, concentrated use of American force. The Vietnam syndrome continues to give Washington pause. But whether it will prevent other unnecessary conflicts is, sadly, open to doubt.

Which is not to suggest that future antiwar protest will be inconsequential. It can nourish public and congressional doubts about the wisdom of resorting to war, thereby giving the executive branch cause for restraint; it can also exert pressure to restrict the fighting once it has begun. But the times do suggest that those opposed to aggressive U.S. military interventions should keep their marching shoes ready.

Chronology

1964

Tonkin Gulf episode, early August.

Congress passes Southeast Asia Resolution, August 7.

SDS begins planning first national antiwar demonstration, late December.

1965

President Johnson orders Operation Rolling Thunder, February 13.

Two Marine battalions land at Danang, March 8.

First "teach-in" on war held in Ann Arbor, March 24.

SDS-sponsored national antiwar demonstration in Washington, April 17.

Johnson administration sends speakers to campuses, takes other steps to counter growing antiwar movement, spring and summer.

Johnson approves deployment of 100,000 additional U.S. troops to Vietnam, July. Total U.S. troop strength now at 175,000.

Congress of Unrepresented People in Washington, August. National Coordinating Committee to End the War in Vietnam formed.

First International Days of Protest, October 15–16.

Norman Morrison immolates himself, early November.

SANE-sponsored antiwar demonstration in Washington, November 27.

General William Westmoreland requests 443,000 U.S. troops by the end of 1966, December. Johnson subsequently approves his request.

Johnson orders bombing halt over North Vietnam, December 24.

1966

Johnson resumes bombing of North Vietnam, January 31.

Fulbright hearings, January 28–February 18.

FCNL launches project to pressure Congress to end war, February.

Second International Days of Protest, March 25–26.

Clergy and Laymen Concerned About Vietnam born, spring.

SDS "counter-exam" to SSS exam, anti-class ranking protests, spring.

Four California housewives block shipment of napalm bombs, late May.

Quakers establish refugee-assistance project in Quang Ngai, summer.

Johnson administration begins bombing POL storage facilities in Hanoi and Haiphong, June 29.

First national antiwar "Mobilization" committee initiated, July.

Mobilization committee–sponsored protests, November 5–8.

Protest against Robert McNamara at Harvard, November 7.

Johnson administration bombs Hanoi, protesters blockade Whitehall induction center in New York, Harrison Salisbury begins reports from Hanoi, December.

Student Mobilization Committee formed, late December.

1967

Dean Rusk meets with student leaders, January 31.

First CALCAV mobilization in Washington, January 31–February 1.

Eugene McCarthy comes out against war, February 1.

Rev. Martin Luther King, Jr., comes out against war, winter and spring.

Resistance formed, March.

Spring Mobe demonstrations in New York and San Francisco, draft-card burning in Central Park, April 15.

Negotiations Now and Vietnam Summer launched, April.

International War Crimes Tribunal hearings in Sweden, May and November.

Johnson administration takes steps to counteract peace movement, spring and summer.

U.S. military leaders advocate major escalation, senior civilian officials urge stabilization or deescalation, Johnson chooses middle course, spring and summer.

Vietnam Veterans Against the War formed, June 1.

Quakers establish rehabilitation center in Quang Ngai, summer.

Johnson administration acts to counter upcoming National Mobe–sponsored demonstration at Pentagon, summer and fall.

National draft-card turn-in, October 16.

Oakland Stop the Draft Week, October 16–20.

Resist leaders present draft cards to Justice Department, October 20.

National Mobe demonstration at Pentagon, October 21.

Customshouse raid in Baltimore, October 27.

Protest against Dean Rusk in New York, November 14.

CIA submits first of several reports to White House on antiwar movement's "international connections," November 15.

Johnson administration continues slow escalation of war, attempts to rally public, fall.

Eugene McCarthy announces presidential candidacy, November 30.

National draft-card turn-in, December 4.

New York Stop the Draft Week, December 4–8.

1968

Johnson administration indicts five prominent advocates of draft resistance on conspiracy charges, January 5.

Tet offensive begins in South Vietnam, January 31.

General Westmoreland and JCS Chairman Earl Wheeler request 206,000 more troops, February 28.

New Defense Secretary Clark Clifford directs study of U.S. policy, turns against war, pushes for deescalation, winter and spring.

Eugene McCarthy almost beats Johnson in New Hampshire primary, March 12.

Robert Kennedy enters presidential race, March 16.

Wise Men meet in Washington, advocate deescalation, March 25–26.

Johnson announces partial bombing halt over North Vietnam and decision not to run for reelection, March 31.

National draft-card turn-in, April 3.

Rev. Martin Luther King, Jr., assassinated, April 4.

Student Mobe–sponsored national student strike, demonstrations in New York and San Francisco, late April.

FBI launches COINTELPRO campaign against New Left, May.

Catonsville draft board office raid in Maryland, May 17.

Robert Kennedy assassinated, June 5.

Student Mobe ruptures, late June.

Demonstrations at Democratic convention in Chicago, late August.

Johnson stops all bombing of North Vietnam, October 31.

Richard Nixon defeats Hubert Humphrey in presidential election, November 5.

National draft-card turn-in, November 14.

1969

Counterinaugural protests, January 19–20.

CALCAV leaders meet with Henry Kissinger, early February.

Major campus protests across country, winter, spring, and fall.

Nixon administration begins secret bombing of Cambodia, March.

Nixon administration attempts to counteract "youth problem," winter and spring.

Justice Department indicts eight Democratic convention protesters on conspiracy charges, March 29.

GI–Civilian demonstrations, civil disobedience, readings of names of war dead, early April.

Student leaders meet with Kissinger and John Ehrlichman, April 29.

Nixon administration begins illegal wiretaps, May.

Readings of names of war dead at Capitol, May and June.

Nixon announces withdrawal of 25,000 U.S. troops from Vietnam, June 8.

SDS disintegrates, mid June.

National antiwar conference in Cleveland, New Mobe born, July 4–5.

Nixon administration threatens Hanoi with major escalation, plans Operation Duck Hook, summer and fall.

Nixon administration continues to attempt to counteract protesters, including upcoming Mobe and Vietnam Moratorium protests, summer and fall.

Nixon announces withdrawal of 35,000 more U.S. troops from Vietnam, September 16.

Daniel Ellsberg begins copying Pentagon Papers, early fall.

Weatherman's Days of Rage in Chicago, October 8–11.

Vietnam Moratorium protests across country, October 15.

Nixon backs down from threat to Hanoi, fall.

Nixon gives "silent majority" speech, November 3.

My Lai massacre revealed, November 13.

March Against Death in Washington, November 13–15.

New Mobe demonstrations in Washington and San Francisco, November 15.

Nixon signs draft lottery bill, November 26.

Nixon announces withdrawal of another 50,000 U.S. troops from Vietnam, December 15.

1970

CALCAV Lent-Passover Fast, February–April.

SMC conference in Cleveland, February.

Wave of bombings in the United States, February and March.

Weatherman townhouse explosion, March 6.

Antidraft protests across country, March.

Nixon administration continues efforts to blunt antiwar movement, winter and spring.

New Mobe, Moratorium, and SMC protests across country, April.

Moratorium announces disbanding, April 19.

Nixon announces withdrawal of another 150,000 U.S. troops from Vietnam, April 20.

Three Kissinger aides resign over impending invasion of Cambodia, late April.

Nixon announces invasion of Cambodia, April 30.

Major protests, including student strike, across country, May.

Kent State killings, May 4.

White House attempts to rally public support for invasion, contain domestic uproar over invasion and Kent State, spring.

Construction workers assault demonstrators in New York, May 8.

Nixon announces all U.S. troops will be withdrawn from Cambodia by end of June, May 8.

Nixon has early-morning talk with demonstrators at Lincoln Memorial, May 9.

Mobe demonstration in Washington, May 9.

Jackson State killings, May 14.

Mobe splits, June.

Huston Plan submitted to Nixon, who approves it, early summer.

Senate approves Cooper-Church amendment, June 30.

Exposé of "tiger cages" in South Vietnamese prison, early July.

White House begins organizing "Americans for Winning the Peace," July.

McGovern-Hatfield amendment defeated, September 1.

VVAW's Operation RAW, September 4–7.

NCAWRR formed, September.

Another wave of bombings, fall.

Nixon administration takes steps to prevent terrorism against officials, fall.

Confrontation between Nixon and demonstrators in San Jose, California, October 29.

NPAC demonstrations, October 31.

Intensified bombing of North Vietnam, Son Tay prison raid, November.

J. Edgar Hoover warns of terrorist plot by Berrigans and others, November 27.

Nixon announces withdrawal of another 40,000 U.S. troops from Vietnam, December.

1971

Americans for Winning the Peace conference in Washington, January.

VVAW's Winter Soldier Investigation in Detroit, January 31–February 2.

NCAWRR disbands, PCPJ formed, winter.

Invasion of Laos begins, February 8.

Protests against invasion, February.

Tape recording systems installed in White House, EOB office, and at Camp David, February.

White House moves to counteract upcoming spring antiwar offensive, winter and spring.

Weatherman bombing of Capitol building, March 1.

Nixon announces withdrawal of another 100,000 U.S. troops from Vietnam, April 7, leaving 184,000 there by December.

VVAW's Operation Dewey Canyon III in Washington, April 19–23.

NPAC/PCPJ demonstrations in Washington and San Francisco, April 24.

People's Lobby in Washington, April 25–30.

May Day protests in Washington, May 1–6.

New York Times begins publishing Pentagon Papers, June 13.

Plumbers formed, summer.

White House plot to fire-bomb Brookings Institution, summer.

CALCAV conference in Ann Arbor, Camden draft-board raid, August.

Stop Our Ship campaigns, summer and fall.

Break-in at Daniel Ellsberg's psychiatrist's office, early September.

"Evict Nixon" activities, October 22–26.

NPAC demonstrations, November 6.

Project Daily Death Toll in Washington, November 8–25.

CALCAV protest at Air Force Academy, November 14.

Nixon announces withdrawal of another 45,000 U.S. troops from Vietnam, intensifies bombing of North, November and December.

VVAW protests around country, December.

1972

Nixon announces withdrawal of another 70,000 U.S. troops from Vietnam, January 13, leaving 69,000 there by May.

G. Gordon Liddy proposes Operation Gemstone, January 27.

North Vietnamese and NLF launch offensive, March 30.

Nixon administration intensifies bombing of Vietnam, April.

Protests against U.S. air war around country, April and May.

CALC begins Honeywell campaign, April.

Nixon announces withdrawal of another 20,000 U.S. troops from Vietnam, April 26.

Attempted attack on Daniel Ellsberg, May 3.

Nixon announces mining of North Vietnam's ports and intensified bombing, May 8.

Protests of mining and bombing across country, May.

Watergate break-in, June 17.

Ring Around Congress demonstration in Washington, June 22.

Indochina Peace Campaign begins, summer.

White House announces last U.S. ground combat troops have left Vietnam, August 12.

Protests at Republican convention in Miami, late August.

Peace agreement reached in Paris, Thieu refuses to sign, Kissinger announces that "peace is at hand," fall.

Antiwar activity in support of Paris peace agreement and against U.S. funding of repressive Thieu regime, including its holding of political prisoners, black uprisings on U.S. Navy ships, fall.

Nixon defeats George McGovern in presidential election, November 7.

"Christmas bombing" of Hanoi and Haiphong, protests of bombing, December.

1973

Nixon inauguration protests, January 20.

Paris peace agreement initialed, January 23.

Antiwar activity demanding Nixon honor peace treaty, pressuring Congress to sever aid to Thieu and Lon Nol, demanding release of South Vietnam's political prisoners and calling for stop to bombing of Cambodia, winter–fall.

John Dean warns Nixon of Watergate "cancer," March 21.

Congress passes amendment calling for halt to bombing of Cambodia, late June. Deadline subsequently extended to August 15.

United Campaign to End the War formed, October 26–28.

Congress passes War Powers Act, November 7.

Congress halts U.S. police training in South Vietnam and U.S. funding of Thieu's police and prison system through economic aid, December.

1974

House votes down Nixon administration request for $474 million in additional military aid for South Vietnam, early April.

Protesters establish tiger cage vigil at Capitol, late June.

House Judiciary Committee votes in favor of three articles of impeachment of Nixon, late July.

House votes to limit U.S. military aid to Thieu to $700 million for next fiscal year, August 6.

Nixon announces resignation, August 8.

Religious leaders issue pastoral letter against war, December.

1975

Assembly to Save the Peace Agreement in Washington, January 25–27.

Congress rejects President Gerald Ford's request for $500 million in supplemental military aid for Thieu and Lon Nol, March.

Congress rejects Ford's request for $700 million in supplemental military aid for South Vietnam, April.

North Vietnamese and NLF troops enter Saigon, April 30.

Abbreviations

ACLU	American Civil Liberties Union
AFL-CIO	American Federation of Labor and Congress of Industrial Organizations
AFSC	American Friends Service Committee
AFV	American Friends of Vietnam
ARVN	Army of the Republic of South Vietnam
ASG	Association of Student Governments
AUP	Assembly of Unrepresented People
AWP	Americans for Winning the Peace
BLUCB	Bancroft Library, University of California, Berkeley (Social Protest Project)
CALC	Clergy and Laymen Concerned
CALCAV	Clergy and Laymen Concerned About Vietnam
CAPAC	Cleveland Area Peace Action Council
CCD	Conference of Concerned Democrats
CCPFV	Citizens Committee for Peace with Freedom in Vietnam
CFSC	Canadian Friends Service Committee
CIA	Central Intelligence Agency
CINCPAC	Commander in Chief, Pacific
CNVA	Committee for Nonviolent Action
CO	conscientious objector
COR	Committee of Responsibility for Treatment in the United States of War-Burned Vietnamese Children
COSVN	Central Office for South Vietnam

COUP	Congress of Unrepresented People
CP	Communist Party
CREEP	Committee to Re-elect the President
DNC	Democratic National Committee
DPM	Draft Presidential Memorandum
EOB	Executive Office Building
FBI	Federal Bureau of Investigation
FCNL	Friends Committee on National Legislation
G	*Guardian* (New York)
GVN	Government of South Vietnam
HEW	Department of Health, Education and Welfare
IEC	Intelligence Evaluation Committee
IPC	Indochina Peace Campaign
IRC	Indochina Resource Center
IRS	Internal Revenue Service
ISA	International Security Affairs
IUCDFP	Inter-University Committee for Debate on Foreign Policy
IUCPHV	Inter-University Committee for a Public Hearing on Vietnam
IVS	International Voluntary Services
JCS	Joint Chiefs of Staff
LAT	*Los Angeles Times*
LBJL	Lyndon Baines Johnson Library
MNF	Meeting Notes File
NC	National Council
NCAWRR	National Coalition Against War, Racism and Repression
NCC	National Coordinating Committee to End the War in Vietnam
NCNP	National Conference for New Politics
NCRP	National Committee for Responsible Patriotism
NG	*National Guardian* (New York)
NLF	National Liberation Front
NP	Nixon Project
NPAC	National Peace Action Coalition
NSC	National Security Council
NSFB	National Security File, Files of McGeorge Bundy

NSFCFV	National Security File, Country File, Vietnam
NSFIF	National Security File, Intelligence File
NSFNF	National Security File, Name File
NSFNSCH	National Security File, National Security Council Histories
NSFSF	National Security File, Subject File
NVA	North Vietnamese Army
NYT	*New York Times*
PAPCV	Public Affairs Policy Committee for Vietnam
PC	New York Fifth Avenue Peace Parade Committee
PCPJ	People's Coalition for Peace and Justice
PL	Progressive Labor Party
POL	petroleum, oil, and lubricant
POW	prisoner of war
PP (NYT)	*The Pentagon Papers as Published by the New York Times*
PP	*The Pentagon Papers.* Senator Gravel edition.
PPRC	Personal Papers of Ramsey Clark
PPWC	Personal Papers of Warren Christopher
PRG	Provisional Revolutionary Government
QAG	Quaker Action Group
RAW	Rapid American Withdrawal
RN	Richard Nixon
ROTC	Reserve Officers Training Corps
RYM	Revolutionary Youth Movement
SANE	Committee for a Sane Nuclear Policy
SCLC	Southern Christian Leadership Conference
SDS	Students for a Democratic Society
SFC	*San Francisco Chronicle*
SHSW	State Historical Society of Wisconsin (Social Action Collection)
SMC	Student Mobilization Committee
SNCC	Student Nonviolent Coordinating Committee
SOS	Stop Our Ship
SS	Secret Service
SSS	Selective Service System
STDW	Stop the Draft Week

SWP	Socialist Workers Party
UAW	United Automobile Workers
USA	United Student Alliance
USIA	United States Information Agency
VA	Veterans Administration
VC	Viet Cong
VDC	Vietnam Day Committee
VFW	Veterans of Foreign Wars
VIG	Vietnam Information Group
VISTA	Volunteers in Service to America
VMC	Vietnam Moratorium Committee
VRF	Vietnam Reference File
VS	Vietnam Summer
VVAW	Vietnam Veterans Against the War
WAF	Westover Air Force Base
WHCF	White House Central Files
WHCFAF	White House Central Files, Aides Files
WHCFCF	White House Central Files, Confidential File
WHCFCFNF	White House Central Files, Confidential File, Name File
WHSF	White House Special Files
WHSFCF	White House Special Files, Confidential Files
WHSFPOF	White House Special Files, President's Office Files
WHSFPPF	White House Special Files, President's Personal Files
WILPF	Women's International League for Peace and Freedom
WP	*Washington Post*
WRL	War Resisters League
WSP	Women Strike for Peace
YAF	Young Americans for Freedom
YR	Young Republicans
YSA	Young Socialist Alliance

Notes

CHAPTER 1. 1965

1. Marshall Green interviews.
2. *PP* 3: 174, 177; *PP(NYT)*, 251–52.
3. Herring, 120.
4. Goulden, *Truth*, 11–12.
5. Ibid., 12.
6. Herring, 120.
7. Goulden, *Truth*, 160.
8. Herring, 123; Louis Harris, 56.
9. *Sunday Oregonian*, July 17, 1988; David Hartsough interview.
10. Eric Sevareid interview.
11. *PP(NYT)*, 307, 310, 311; *PP* 3: 110–11.
12. *PP(NYT)*, 338; William Westmoreland interview; *PP* 3: 593–94.
13. Halstead, 33; Lew Jones interview.
14. Sale, 170; Todd Gitlin interview.
15. Sale, 170–71; Carl Oglesby interview; Martin Roysher and Charles Capper, "The March as a Political Tactic," March or April 1965 (SDS papers, SHSW); Clark Kissinger interview.
16. The proposal had been narrowly defeated on a first vote.
17. Gitlin, *Sixties*, 181.
18. Oglesby interview; Morrison and Morrison, 297.
19. Morrison and Morrison, 301; Oglesby interview.
20. Oglesby interview.
21. Ibid.; Miller, 190.
22. Oglesby interview.
23. Ibid.
24. Sale, 136–37, 142.
25. Kissinger interview; Sale, 172; Gitlin interview.

26. "Report from the Editors: The SDS March on Washington," *Studies on the Left*, Spring 1965; Schlesinger, *Bitter Heritage*, 67; Gil Green interview.

27. Peter Camejo interviews.

28. Ibid.; Kissinger interview.

29. David McReynolds interview.

30. Camejo interview; Don Gurewitz interview.

31. Camejo interview.

32. Ibid.

33. *PP* 3: 269, 293.

34. Ibid., 296–97, 687; Berman, 38–39.

35. Halberstam, *Best and Brightest*, 195.

36. *PP* 3: 308–15.

37. Halberstam, *Best and Brightest*, 631–32.

38. Operation Rolling Thunder did not actually get under way until March 2, owing to turbulence in Saigon, a U.S.-Soviet diplomatic initiative and poor weather. For Bundy's remark about Pleiku, see Herring, 129.

39. Louis Harris, 58; Halstead, 34; Zaroulis and Sullivan, 34; Sale, 173; SDS press release, February 18, 1965 (SDS papers, SHSW); Small, *Johnson, Nixon and Doves*, 33; *NYT*, March 2, 1965.

40. Small, *Johnson, Nixon and Doves*, 33, 36.

41. Halstead, 35.

42. *WP*, February 28, 1965.

43. *WP*, March 1, 2, 1965; Powers, *War at Home*, 58; Cooper, 266; William Bundy interview.

44. *PP* 3: 418–19.

45. Caputo, 50.

46. *PP* 3: 417, 430; Westmoreland, 125.

47. *PP* 3: 703; Maclear, 117.

48. Thomas Moorer interview.

49. McGeorge Bundy interview; Harry McPherson interview.

50. McPherson interview; Paul Warnke interview; Dean Rusk interview; William Bundy interview; Clark Clifford to Lyndon Johnson, May 17, 1965 (VRF, box 1, LBJL); Jack Valenti's notes of July 25, 1965, Camp David meeting (VRF, box 1, LBJL); Ball, 400.

51. Halberstam, *Best and Brightest*, 712.

52. Menashe and Radosh, 3–5.

53. Ibid., 9–10.

54. Ibid., 5–6, 10, 11; Oglesby interview.

55. Menashe and Radosh, 11; Oglesby interview.

56. Oglesby interview.

57. Stephen Smale interview; Marilyn Milligan interview.

58. Sale, 174; "Report from the Editors," *Studies on the Left*, Spring 1965.

59. McGeorge Bundy to Johnson, April 14, 1965 (NSFCFV, box 16, LBJL).

60. *WP*, April 18, 1965; Gil Green interview; Sale, 185–89; Miller, 233.

61. Daniel Ellsberg interview.

62. Sale, 189–90.

63. Marvin Watson to Johnson, April 14, 1965 (WHCF, HU, box 59, LBJL).

64. Menashe and Radosh, 111–13, 274–81.

65. Valenti added, "When I later began to read more of his prose, I found it indistinguishable from his breath" (Valenti oral history, tape 5, 34, LBJL).

66. Menashe and Radosh, 126; Zaroulis and Sullivan, 43; Goldman, 429, 447, 501; Valenti oral history, tape 5, 33–34 (LBJL); Goodwin, 399–403.

67. Menashe and Radosh, 142, 143; Bundy to Donald Graham, April 20, 1965 (NSFB, box 18, LBJL).

68. Kissinger, *White House Years*, 295; McGeorge Bundy remark following March 18, 1992, speech at University of California, Berkeley; Talbot, 33; McGeorge Bundy interview.

69. William Bundy interview.

70. Bundy to Johnson, June 30, 1965 (NSFNSCH, box 43, LBJL); Rusk interviews; Valenti to Johnson, April 23, 1965 (WHCF, ND, box 215, LBJL).

71. Chester Cooper to Valenti, April 24, 1965 (WHCF, ND, box 215, LBJL); Valenti to Johnson, April 24, 1965 (WHCF, ND, box 215, LBJL); Menashe and Radosh, 119, 135.

72. Menashe and Radosh, 133–34, 137.

73. Valenti to Johnson, April 24, 1965 (WHCF, ND, box 215, LBJL); Ellsberg interview.

74. Menashe and Radosh, 173–75.

75. Ibid., 176; Cooper to Bundy, May 14, 1965 (NSFB, box 18, LBJL); Cooper to Bundy, May 14, 1965 (second of two) (NSFB, box 18, LBJL).

76. State Department Historical Office study, May 1965 (NSFB, box 18, LBJL); State Department Policy Planning Council study, May 1965 (NSFB, box 18, LBJL); Cooper to Bundy, May 14, 1965 (NSFB, box 18, LBJL); Cooper to Bundy, May 14, 1965 (second of two) (NSFB, box 18, LBJL); Powers, *War at Home*, 61.

77. James Thomson to Bundy, May 14, 1965 (NSFB, box 18, LBJL).

78. McGeorge Bundy interview; Goodwin, 400; Halstead, 52.

79. Arthur Schlesinger interview; Menashe and Radosh, 165–71, 183; Halstead, 52–53.

80. Walt Rostow to Dean Rusk, May 17, 1965 (NSFB, box 18, LBJL); Halberstam, *Best and Brightest*, 197.

81. Cooper to Bundy, June 4, 1965 (NSFB, box 18, LBJL).

82. Powers, *War at Home*, 67–68; Halberstam, *Best and Brightest*, 753–54; Zaroulis and Sullivan, 46.

83. Gentry, 604; Donner, 154n; Churchill and Vander Wall, 172; Cooper to Valenti, April 24, 1965 (WHCF, ND, box 215, LBJL); Gordon Chase memo on "August 3 Dinner Meeting on the Information Problem," August 4, 1965 (NSFCFV, box 197, LBJL); Valenti to Johnson, April 23, 1965 (WHCF, ND, box 215, LBJL); Herring, 134; Cooper memo on September 22, 1965, meeting of

PAPCV (NSFCFV, box 197, LBJL); David Cortright interview; Small, *Johnson, Nixon and Doves*, 254; Cooper memo on December 20, 1965, meeting of PAPCV (NSFCFV, box 197, LBJL).

84. Herring, 134; Small, *Johnson, Nixon and Doves*, 40; *PP* 3: 363.

85. Cooper to Valenti, April 24, 1965 (WHCF, ND, box 215, LBJL); Valenti to Johnson, April 24, 1965 (WHCF, ND, box 215, LBJL); Chase memo on "August 3 Dinner Meeting," August 4, 1965 (NSFCFV, box 197, LBJL); Cooper to Valenti, May 17, 1965 (NSFB, box 18, LBJL); Valenti to Johnson, May 27, 1965 (WHCF, "American Friends" name file, LBJL); Rusk interview.

86. Cooper to Valenti, April 24, 1965 (WHCF, ND, box 215, LBJL); Chase memo on "August 3 Dinner Meeting," August 4, 1965 (NSFCFV, box 197, LBJL); Charles Colson's handwritten notes, 1970 (WHSF, Colson, box 33, NP); Chase memo on "August 4 Luncheon Meeting on the Information Problem," August 4, 1965 (NSFCFV, box 197, LBJL); Small, *Johnson, Nixon and Doves*, 47.

87. Cooper to Valenti, April 24, 1965 (WHCF, ND, box 215, LBJL); Cooper memo on August 23, 1965, meeting of PAPCV (NSFCFV, box 197, LBJL); Bundy to Johnson, September 3, 1965 (NSFCFV, box 195, LBJL).

88. Chase memo on "August 3 Dinner Meeting," August 4, 1965 (NSFCFV, box 197, LBJL). Remarks in quotes are taken from this memo recording this meeting. They probably do not represent verbatim statements.

89. Chase to Douglass Cater, August 23, 1965 (NSFCFV, box 197, LBJL); Cooper to Bundy, August 18, 1965 (NSFCFV, box 197, LBJL); Cooper memo on August 23, 1965, meeting of PAPCV (NSFCFV, box 197, LBJL).

90. Milligan interview; Smale interview; Doug Dowd interview; Paul Booth, "Working Papers on Summer Projects," May 1965 (SDS papers, SHSW).

91. Milligan interview; Dowd interview.

92. Bruce Dancis interview; phone conversation with Doug Dowd; Dowd interview.

93. Dowd interview.

94. Ibid.

95. Menashe and Radosh, 333.

96. Gitlin interview; Booth, "Working Papers," May 1965 (SDS papers, SHSW); Carl Davidson interview.

97. "This is really war," President Johnson observed at a press conference on July 28, 1965 (*NYT*, July 29, 1965).

98. *PP* 3: 434–38, 456–57.

99. Ibid., 438.

100. Ibid., 438–41.

101. Ibid., 440.

102. Herring, 136–37.

103. *PP* 3: 462.

104. Berman, 73–75.

105. Ibid., 80.

106. Ibid., 82–83, 94.

107. *PP* 3: 381–83.

108. *PP* 4: 610–15; Berman, 89–91.

109. William Bundy interview.

110. *PP* 4: 299; Ellsberg interview; Stanley Resor interview.

111. Rusk interview.

112. Walt Rostow interview; Richard Helms interview; William Westmoreland interview; Warnke interview.

113. Eugene McCarthy interview; Herring (1979 Wiley edition for this citation only), 141–42, 144; McGeorge Bundy interview.

114. Ellsberg interview.

115. Rusk interview; Berman, 122, 125.

116. Herring, 140; Ellsberg interview; Cooper memo on August 23, 1965, meeting of PAPCV (NSFCFV, box 197, LBJL); Rusk interview.

117. Berman, 127; *NYT*, July 29, 1965; John Oakes interview.

118. Paul Booth interview.

119. Booth, "Working Papers," May 1965 (SDS papers, SHSW); minutes of April 18–20, 1965, SDS NC meeting (SDS papers, SHSW).

120. Kissinger interview.

121. Ibid.

122. Ibid.

123. Sale, 204–8, 214; Gitlin interview.

124. Booth interview.

125. Oglesby interview.

126. Todd Gitlin and Carl Oglesby, "Notes for National Convention Foreign Policy Workshop," June 1965 (SDS papers, SHSW); Booth interview. A prominent view at SDS's National Council meeting in early September was that "our actions are not going to affect the war" (minutes of this meeting, SDS papers, SHSW).

127. Booth and Lee Webb, "The Anti-War Movement: From Protest to Radical Politics," October 1965 (SDS papers, SHSW); Booth interview.

128. Oglesby interview.

129. Gitlin interview; Booth, "For Immediate Release," Fall 1965 (SDS papers, SHSW); Booth interview.

130. Assorted *MEMO* issues, 1965 (WSP papers, SHSW); Alice Hamburg interview.

131. Donna Allen interview; Dagmar Wilson interview.

132. Assorted *MEMO* issues, 1965 (WSP papers, SHSW); Cooper memo on September 16, 1965, meeting of PAPCV (NSFCFV, box 197, LBJL); Cooper to New York WSP activists, July 2, 1965 (WHCF, "Women, S" name file, LBJL).

133. Cora Weiss interview.

134. Wilson interview. Wilson did not go on the trip herself but received firsthand reports on it. See also Gitlin, *Sixties*, 265.

135. *NG*, May 22, June 26, 1965; *WP*, May 13, 1965; *NYT*, June 9, 1965.
136. Milligan interview; Taylor, 358–59; Halstead, 85.
137. VDC, "Stop the Troop Train!" August 1965 (VDC papers, BLUCB); *SFC*, August 6, 1965; Milligan interview.
138. VDC, "News from the Vietnam Day Committee," summer 1965 (VDC papers, BLUCB).
139. *WP*, August 9, 10, 1965; *NG*, August 14, 1965; DeBenedetti, *American Ordeal*, 121.
140. Halstead, 74–75; Lew Jones interview.
141. Norma Becker interview; phone conversation with Norma Becker.
142. Becker interview; Halstead, 78–79.
143. Lew Jones interview.
144. Bettina Aptheker interview.
145. Aptheker interviews.
146. Camejo interview; Lew Jones interview.
147. Camejo interview; Donner, 196–97.
148. Memo on August 30, 1965, meeting of PAPCV (NSFCFV, box 197, LBJL); Cooper memo on September 16, 1965, meeting of PAPCV (NSFCFV, box 197, LBJL); memo on September 29, 1965, White House luncheon meeting (MNF, box 1, LBJL); Small, *Johnson, Nixon and Doves*, 66.
149. Office of the Secretary of the Air Force to the Armed Forces Aide to the President, October 13, 1965 (WHCFCFNF, box 7, LBJL); Joseph Califano to Johnson, October 14, 1965 (WHCF, HU, box 59, LBJL); VDC, "International Days of Protest," October 1965 (VDC papers, BLUCB).
150. Thomas Lynch to James Rowley, October 1, 1965 (WHCF, HU, box 59, LBJL).
151. *NYT*, October 31, 1965; Warnke interview. On the administration's assistance with later prowar parades, see pp. 144 and 187. On its consideration of aid for prowar demonstrations in November, see p. 61.
152. Halstead, 89; Morrison and Morrison, 107–10; Milligan interview; DeBenedetti, *American Ordeal*, 125; *New Republic* commentary, "Jail's Too Good for Them," October 8, 1966; George Reedy to Johnson, December 1965 (WHCF, HU, box 59, LBJL); Larry Levinson memo, December 1965 (WHCF, HU, box 59, LBJL).
153. Sale, 229; Lang, 235; October 8, 1965 UPI story (copy in WHCF, HU, box 59, LBJL); November 30, 1965 UPI story (copy in WHCF, HU, box 59, LBJL); October 14, 1965 syndicated column by Rowland Evans and Robert Novak (copy in SDS papers, BLUCB); SDS *Bulletin*, October 21, 1965 (SDS papers, BLUCB); Clifford Alexander, Jr., to Nicholas Katzenbach, November 30, 1965 (WHCF, "Vietnam" name file, LBJL); Small, *Johnson, Nixon and Doves*, 69.
154. *WP*, December 2, 1985; Woode, 47; Shapley, 353–55; *WP*, May 10, 1984; Lynd and Ferber, 26, DeBenedetti, *American Ordeal*, 130.
155. McReynolds interview.
156. Lew Jones interview; Dave Dellinger interview; Fred Halstead interview.

157. Milligan interview.

158. Lew Jones interview; Halstead interview.

159. Dellinger interview.

160. "Workshop Reports and Plenary Decisions—NCCEWV Convention, Nov. 25–28," 1965 (NCC papers, SHSW); Booth and Webb, "The Anti-War Movement," October 1965 (SDS papers, SHSW); DeBenedetti, *American Ordeal*, 137; Booth interview.

161. Sale, 240n; "Workshop Reports and Plenary Decisions," 1965 (NCC papers, SHSW); Oglesby interview.

162. D. W. Ropa memo on November 1, 1965, meeting of PAPCV (NSFCFV, box 197, LBJL); Ropa memo on November 8, 1965, meeting of PAPCV (NSFCFV, box 197, LBJL); Freedom House, "For Peace . . . With Freedom: A Call for Public Action," November 29, 1965 (copy in NSFCFV, box 197, LBJL); Charles Sither to Watson, November 20, 1965 (WHCF, HU, box 59, LBJL).

163. Oglesby interview; Zaroulis and Sullivan, 65–66.

164. "Workshop Reports and Plenary Decisions," 1965 (NCC papers, SHSW); *PP* 4: 57, 303.

165. *PP* 4: 304.

166. Ibid., 305–10; *PP(NYT)*, 466–67.

167. Berkowitz, 6; Hayes Redman to Bill Moyers, November or December 1965 (WHCF, HU, box 59, LBJL); Goulden, *Meany*, 353–54; George Christian interview.

168. McPherson interview; Cooper to Bundy et al., December 14, 1965 (WHCFCF, ND, box 71, LBJL); Louis Harris, 59.

169. Craig McNamara interview; phone conversation with Craig McNamara.

170. *PP* 4: 33.

171. Ibid., 39–40.

172. Lynd and Hayden, 103.

CHAPTER 2. 1966

1. *PP* 4: 39; SANE, "The Voters' Pledge," January 1966 (WSP papers, SHSW); McCarthy, 21–24.

2. Richard Fernandez interview; Coffin, 217; *MEMO*, January 1966 (WSP papers, SHSW); Allen interview; Wilson interview.

3. Correspondence with J. William Fulbright; *Vietnam Hearings*, 32, 33.

4. *Vietnam Hearings*, 108, 110, 199, 222; Sevareid interview.

5. Anthony Lake interview.

6. Sevareid, 24; Gentry, 605; Donner, 253; *Sunday Oregonian*, July 17, 1988.

7. Harry McPherson to Moyers, Feburary 1966 (WHCFAF, McPherson, box 28, LBJL). Moyers jotted his response in the margin of this memo.

8. Verba et al., 317–33; Lynd and Ferber, 29–30, 33.

9. DeBenedetti, *American Ordeal*, 152.

10. Ropa to Moyers, March 25, 1966 (WHCF, HU, box 59, LBJL); Zaroulis and Sullivan, 79; Halstead, 143; Small, *Johnson, Nixon and Doves*, 256.

11. Schlesinger interview; *PP* 4: 46–47, 50–51; Maclear, 156.

12. *PP* 4: 78; Herring, 156.

13. *PP* 4: 84; Herring, 157.

14. Trewhitt, 231; McNamara interview.

15. Camejo interview.

16. *WP*, April 11, 1966.

17. Brad Lyttle interview; Lyttle, "Peace Action," ii, 16–21.

18. Sam Brown interview; Fernandez interview.

19. Fernandez interview. See also Hall, 28–29.

20. Fernandez interview.

21. Ibid.

22. Ibid.

23. CALCAV, "Clergy and Laymen Concerned About Vietnam," 1969 (CALCAV papers, SHSW).

24. Dan Hirsch, "Notes on Congressional Pressure," July 31, 1973 (IPC papers, SHSW); SANE, "The Voters' Pledge," January 1966 (WSP papers, SHSW); *MEMO*, May, September 1966 (WSP papers, SHSW); Wilson interview.

25. Hartsough interview.

26. Ibid.

27. Ibid.

28. Ibid.

29. Ibid.

30. Michael Ferber interview; Dowd interview.

31. Sidney Peck interview.

32. Camejo interview; Halstead interview.

33. Hartsough interview.

34. Camejo interview; Greg Calvert interview.

35. VDC International Committee, "Statement on the Scheer Campaign," January 19, 1966 (VDC papers, BLUCB).

36. Smale interview; Milligan interview.

37. Milligan interview.

38. Barbara Gullahorn et al., "Statement on Scheer Campaign," January 19, 1966 (VDC papers, BLUCB); Halstead, 157; Stein and Wellman, 63–68; Milligan interview.

39. Michael Delacour interview; Camejo interview.

40. Milligan interview.

41. Lang, 94, 103, 106, 173.

42. Ibid., 173, 179; Powers, *War at Home*, 126.

43. Lang, 115, 173.

44. Dowd interview; John Roche to Johnson, September 28, 1966 (WHCFAF, Watson, box 29, LBJL); Halstead, 161.

45. Baskin and Strauss, 23.

46. SDS, "SDS Vietnam Exam Program," April 1966 (SDS papers, SHSW); San Francisco Regional SDS Newsletter, June 1, 1966 (SDS papers, BLUCB).

47. Booth interview.

48. San Francisco Regional SDS Newsletter, June 1, 1966 (SDS papers, BLUCB); SDS, "National Vietnam Examination," 1966 (SDS papers, BLUCB).

49. Theodore Hesburgh interview.

50. Califano to Johnson, May 13, 1966 (WHCF, HU, box 59, LBJL); Small, *Johnson, Nixon and Doves*, 82.

51. Sale, 260–63.

52. Gellhorn, 109; Karnow, 22.

53. One antiwar activist wanted to carry more than *photos* of napalm victims on marches. The author of a position paper for a September antiwar conference wrote: "Carry South Vietnamese victims of napalm and strafing—dead or alive—through white suburbs. If they cannot be smuggled into the country, obtain napalm in sufficient quantities to roast unquenchable pigs and cows in suburban streets. Or drop it from small airplanes on white suburban schoolyards on the opening day of school." The activist exhibited a faint sign of sanity, though. "Whether this would raise *anti*-war sentiment would have to be considered," he added (Reickert, "Position Paper," 1966, NCC papers, SHSW).

54. Allen interview; Weiss interview.

55. Joyce McLean interview.

56. Ibid.

57. Tom Wicker interview; McLean interview.

58. Wicker interview; Wicker, 153.

59. Pepper, 58, 68; Madeline Duckles interview.

60. Duckles interview.

61. Valenti to Robert McNamara, January 14, 1966 (WHCFCF, FG, box 27, LBJL).

62. AFSC, "The AFSC Opens a New Front in Vietnam," 1967 (AFSC papers, BLUCB); AFSC, "Vietnam Programs," 1967 (AFSC papers, BLUCB).

63. *Vietnam Summer News* 1, no. 1, 1967 (VS papers, BLUCB).

64. Dave Elder interview; Hartsough interview.

65. Hartsough interview.

66. Joseph Barr to Johnson, April 23, 1966 (WHCFAF, McPherson, box 28, LBJL); *Vietnam Summer News* 1, no. 2, 1967 (VS papers, BLUCB).

67. Barr to McPherson, April 23, 1966 (WHCFAF, McPherson, box 28, LBJL); Barr to Johnson, April 23, 1966 (WHCFAF, McPherson, box 28, LBJL).

68. Earl Reynolds interview.

69. Bronson Clark interview; Colin Bell, "To members of the AFSC Corporation," April 3, 1967 (AFSC papers, BLUCB).

70. Fernandez interview; Hartsough interview.

71. Dowd interview.

72. Ibid.

73. Peck interview.

74. Sidney Peck to Frank Emspak, July 15, 1966 (NCC papers, SHSW); Peck interview.

75. Menashe and Radosh, 342, 345–46; A. J. Muste, Norma Becker, and Dave Dellinger, "Dear Friend," July 1966 (PC papers, SHSW); Peck to Emspak, July 15, 1966 (NCC papers, SHSW).

76. Halstead, 190; Dowd interview.

77. *NYT*, May 13, 1967. See also Lyndon Johnson, 432.

78. Dowd interview.

79. Minutes of July 22, 1966, Cleveland antiwar conference (NCC papers, SHSW).

80. Peck interview; NCC staff, "Dear Friend," October 1, 1966 (NCC papers, SHSW).

81. Halstead interview.

82. Davidson interview; Sale, 291.

83. Davidson interview.

84. Ibid.

85. Sale, 309; Calvert interview.

86. Booth interview; Kissinger interview.

87. *PP* 4: 107–12.

88. Maclear, 181, 182, 184; *PP* 4: 120–24, 126, 130, 135.

89. *PP* 4: 325, 326, 346.

90. Ibid., 348–54; Halberstam, *Best and Brightest*, 769; Westmoreland interview; Rusk interview.

91. *PP* 4: 350, 369.

92. McPherson to Moyers, August 4, 1966 (WHCFAF, McPherson, box 28, LBJL); Louis Harris, 59–60.

93. Alice Lynd, 181–82, 186; Heath, 150–53; Halstead, 179, 184; Rinaldi, 21.

94. Becker interview; Dellinger interview.

95. Lady Bird Johnson, 430; Halstead, 199.

96. Sale, 303–4; Zaroulis and Sullivan, 95; Trewhitt, 235; Shapley, 378; *WP*, May 10, 1984.

97. Christian, 159; Halberstam, *Best and Brightest*, 778; Christian interview; Califano to Johnson, November 15, 1967 (WHCF, HU, box 60, LBJL); CIA, "International Connections of the U.S. Peace Movement," November 1967 (NSFIF, box 3, LBJL).

98. Small, *Johnson, Nixon and Doves*, 150; Talbot, 33; Shapley, 463, 496; McNamara interview; Skolnick, 61.

99. Rusk interview; Rostow interview.

100. McPherson interview; Warnke interview; Morton Halperin interview.

101. William Bundy interview.

102. Christian interview.

103. James Reston interview; Christian interview; McPherson interview; Christian, 159; Warnke interview; Linda Morse interview; Trewhitt, 234; Shapley, 378; McNamara interview; Helms interview. Even Dean Rusk, who was extremely reluctant to give the peace movement credit for much of any-

thing other than fortifying Hanoi, suspected the harassment got to some officials (Rusk interview).

104. William Bundy interview; Trewhitt, 234; McNamara interview.

105. Small, "Impact of the Antiwar Movement," 9; William Bundy interview; Small, *Johnson, Nixon and Doves*, 11; McNamara interview; Shapley, 581; Westmoreland, 225.

106. Small, *Johnson, Nixon and Doves*, 11; Christian interview; Rusk interview; Rusk, 419–20, 624; Rostow interview; Ellsberg interview; Paul Nitze interviews; Warnke interview; Resor interview; Steve Weissman interview; Lake interview; *WP*, September 15, 1971; Schlesinger interview; Talbot, 32–33; William Bundy interview.

107. Resor interview.

108. McNamara interview; Morrison and Morrison, 169.

109. McNamara interview; phone conversation with McNamara; Shapley, 482.

110. McNamara interview; phone conversation with McNamara.

111. McNamara interview.

112. Ibid; Talbot, 47; correspondence with Robert McNamara; Ellsberg interview; Shapley, 490. Robert McNamara has said that he had hoped to release the Pentagon Papers to the public immediately after completion (Salisbury, 283).

113. McNamara interview; Shapley, 379.

114. McNamara interview; Shapley, 483; Morrison and Morrison, 163; H. R. Haldeman interview.

115. McNamara interview; Morrison and Morrison, 166–67; Talbot, 47.

116. McNamara interview.

117. Ibid; Warnke interview. See also Salisbury, 58. Walt Rostow writes that antiwar protesters "had a disproportionate and unsettling impact" on some officials. Rostow said he was referring to the influence of officials' antiwar children, but adamantly refused to name names. When read Rostow's passage, Warnke and Morton Halperin immediately advanced that he was referring to the McNamaras (Rostow, 499; Rostow interview; Warnke interview; Halperin interview).

118. Nitze interviews; Rusk interview; William Bundy interview.

119. Warnke interview.

120. See p. 63.

121. Hahn, 1189–91.

122. Morse interview; Zaroulis and Sullivan, 94; Halstead, 205–7; Muste et al., "Dear Fellow Peace Worker," November 14, 1966 (PC papers, SHSW); DeBenedetti, *American Ordeal*, 164; Dellinger interview.

123. Halstead, 224; Dellinger interview; Duckles interview; Halstead interview.

124. Becker interview; Muste et al., "Dear Fellow Peace Worker," November 14, 1966 (PC papers, SHSW).

125. Halstead, 213; Muste, "Preliminary Mobilization Memorandum," 1966

(Spring Mobe papers, SHSW); "Motions Passed (as amended) At Evaluation Conference, Cleveland, November 26, 1966" (Spring Mobe papers, SHSW).

126. Becker interview.

127. *PP* 4: 135–36; *PP(NYT)*, 523; Halberstam, *Best and Brightest*, 768; Trewhitt, 233.

CHAPTER 3. 1967: PART ONE

1. Aptheker interview; SMC, "Join the Mobilization," March 1967 (SMC papers, BLUCB).

2. Aptheker interviews; Peck interview.

3. SMC, "Join the Mobilization," March 1967 (SMC papers, BLUCB); Aptheker interview; Gurewitz interview.

4. Halstead, 262–63; New York WSP Steering Committee to James Bevel, February 24, 1967 (Spring Mobe papers, SHSW); Dellinger interview.

5. Dellinger interview.

6. Garrow, 543.

7. Ibid., 543, 545, 549.

8. Dellinger interview; Dellinger, *More Power*, 115.

9. Powers, *War at Home*, 179; *NYT*, March 6, 1967; John McAuliff interview.

10. Small, "Impact of the Antiwar Movement," 11; Rusk interview.

11. See pp. 147–48.

12. Roche to Johnson, January 4, 1967 (NSFNF, box 7, LBJL).

13. David Harris, 165–66; *Citizen: The Political Life of Allard K. Lowenstein* (the director of this film, Julie Thompson, provided me with a partial transcript of it).

14. Rusk interviews.

15. CALCAV, "Education-Action Mobilization," January 1967 (CALCAV papers, SHSW); *WP*, February 1, 1967; Fernandez interview; Hall, 36–37, 38; Hartsough interview.

16. Fernandez interview; McCarthy interview; *WP*, February 2, 1967.

17. McCarthy interview; McCarthy, 45.

18. Fernandez interview; *WP*, February 2, 1967.

19. Ibid.; Hall, 39.

20. Fernandez interview; CALCAV, "Lent-Passover Fast," February 1970 (CALCAV papers, SHSW).

21. *WP*, February 16, 1967, June 20, 1968; Wilson interview; Weiss interview; Allen interview.

22. Christian interview.

23. Louis Harris, 60; Berkowitz, 6; Verba and Brody, 329.

24. Schandler, 300; Berkowitz, 6.

25. Lynd and Ferber, 21–27, 33, 63; DeBenedetti, *American Ordeal*, 158.

26. Davidson interview. See also Sale, 313–15.

27. Dancis interview; Lynd and Ferber, 71–72.

28. Lynd and Ferber, 89; Steve Hamilton interview; Aptheker interview.

29. *NYT*, December 30, 1966; Goodman, 444–45; Lynd and Ferber, 72–73; Davidson interview.

30. Dancis interview; Ferber interview; Lynd and Ferber, 72.

31. David Harris interview.

32. Ibid.; Resistance, "The Resistance," 1967 (Resistance papers, BLUCB).

33. Resistance, "THE RESISTANCE," 1967 (Resistance papers, BLUCB); Ferber interview.

34. Ferber interview.

35. Ibid.; Resistance, "THE RESISTANCE," 1967 (Resistance papers, BLUCB).

36. Harris interview.

37. *NYT*, April 5, 1967; King, 32–37; Garrow, 553.

38. *WP*, April 6, 1967; *NYT*, April 7, 1967.

39. Wicker interview.

40. Roche to Johnson, April 5, 1967 (WHCFCF, OS, box 75, LBJL); McPherson interview; Garrow, 554–55.

41. Dellinger, *More Power*, 115; Dellinger interview.

42. Dancis interview; McReynolds interview; Dellinger interview.

43. Dancis interview.

44. Ramsey Clark interview.

45. Halstead interview.

46. *NYT*, April 16, 1967; *WP*, April 16, 1967; Powers, *War at Home*, 182; Jan Barry interview.

47. *WP*, April 16, 1967; Alan Levy and Harvey Thomson to Johnson, April 1967 (WHCF, HU, box 61, LBJL); *Cleveland Plain Dealer*, April 23, 1967 (copy in WHCF, HU, box 61, LBJL).

48. *WP*, April 16, 1967.

49. *NYT*, April 16, 1967; Dancis interview; Lynd and Ferber, 75.

50. *NYT*, April 16, 1967.

51. Powers, *War At Home*, 195.

52. *NYT*, April 16, 1967; Halstead interview.

53. Peck, 45.

54. *NYT*, April 16, 17, 1967.

55. *NYT*, April 15, 1967; *WP*, April 16, 1967.

56. Lyttle interview.

57. Schlesinger interview; Schlesinger, *Bitter Heritage*, 105–19; *WP*, February 1, 1967.

58. Schlesinger interview; Schlesinger, *Bitter Heritage*, 60–61.

59. Schlesinger interview; Schlesinger, *Bitter Heritage*, 63, 68–69.

60. Schlesinger interview.

61. Ibid.

62. Oakes interview.

63. *NYT*, May 28, September 19, 1967.

64. Halberstam, *Best and Brightest*, 739.

65. *WP*, April 24, 1967; VS, "Vietnam Summer," 1967 (VS papers, BLUCB).

66. Gar Alperovitz interview.

67. Ibid.

68. Ibid.

69. Ibid.; Fernandez and Webb, "Vietnam Summer 1967," August 1967 (VS papers, BLUCB).

70. Watson to Johnson, May 1967 (NSFCFV, box 191, LBJL); J. Edgar Hoover to White House et al., May 18, 1967 (NSFCFV, box 191, LBJL).

71. Barry interview; Chevigny, "Worst Years," 14.

72. Barry interview.

73. Ibid.

74. Ibid.; VVAW, "Rough History of VVAW," 1971 (VVAW papers, SHSW).

75. Barry interview; Chevigny, "Farewell to Arms," 22.

76. Gentry, 602.

77. Duffett, 9; Morrison and Morrison, 304.

78. Duffett, 36–37.

79. Ibid., 653.

80. U.S. Embassy (Stockholm) telegram to secretary of state, May 6, 1967 (NSFCFV, box 191, LBJL); USIA, "Media Reaction Analysis—The Russell Tribunal," May 5, 1967 (NSFCFV, box 191, LBJL); copy of February 19, 1967, *New York Times Magazine* article (NSFCFV, box 191, LBJL).

81. State Department telegram, May 8, 1967 (NSFCFV, box 191, LBJL); Rostow to Johnson, May 1967 (NSFCFV, box 191, LBJL).

82. State Department telegram, May 8, 1967 (NSFCFV, box 191, LBJL); U.S. Embassy (Stockholm) telegram to secretary of state, May 7, 1967 (NSFCFV, box 191, LBJL).

83. Rowe is alluding to a prowar parade held four days earlier. See p. 144.

84. James Rowe to Johnson, May 17, 1967 (WHCFCF, ND, box 73, LBJL).

85. McPherson to Johnson, April 20, 1967 (WHCFAF, McPherson, box 28, LBJL).

86. *NYT*, April 30, May 14, 1967; Charles Wiley to McPherson, May 25, 1967 (WHCFAF, McPherson, box 28, LBJL). See also other documents on organization of the parade in WHCFAF, McPherson, box 28, LBJL.

87. Nitze interviews.

88. Ibid.

89. *NYT*, May 5, 1967; Resor interview.

90. Roche to Johnson, April 27, 1967 (WHCFAF, Watson, box 29, LBJL).

91. Roche to Johnson, March 21, 1967 (WHCFCF, ND, box 73, LBJL); Roche to Rostow, August 9, 1967 (NSFNF, box 7, LBJL).

92. *NYT*, December 20, 1967; Roche to Watson, December 14, 1967 (WHCFAF, McPherson, box 29, LBJL).

93. John Schnittker to McPherson, June 9, 1967 (WHCFAF, McPherson, box 28, LBJL).

94. Rowe to Johnson, May 17, 1967 (WHCFCF, ND, box 73, LBJL). See also Abbott Washburn, "Thoughts on Complexion of Committee," September 29, 1967 (NSFNF, box 7, LBJL).

95. Roche to Johnson, May 19, 1967 (WHCFAF, Watson, box 29, LBJL). For earlier White House discussions on organizing the committee, see assorted documents in WHCFAF, McPherson, box 28, and WHCFCF, ND, box 73, LBJL.

96. Roche to Johnson, May 26, 1967 (WHCFCF, ND, box 73, LBJL). White House Counsel Joseph Califano was apparently less apprehensive. He deemed the committee "a great idea" (Califano to McPherson, May 27, 1967, WHCFCF, ND, box 73, LBJL).

97. Roche to Paul Douglas, July 31, 1967 (WHCFCF, ND, box 73, LBJL); Roche to Johnson, June 26, 1967 (WHCFAF, Watson, box 29, LBJL); Roche to Johnson, September 5, 1967 (WHCFCF, ND, box 73, LBJL). See also many other relevant memos in the WHCFCF, ND, box 73, LBJL.

98. Roche to Johnson, October 7, 1967 (WHCFCF, ND, box 73, LBJL); Roche to Johnson, October 19, 1967 (WHCFCF, ND, box 73, LBJL); Roche to George Christian, October 24, 1967 (WHCFCF, ND, box 73, LBJL); State Department telegram "to all diplomatic posts," October 30, 1967 (NSFCFV, box 99, LBJL); *NYT*, October 26, 1967.

99. The Vietnam propaganda committee the administration had formed in 1965 had apparently not worked out.

100. *PP* 4: 393; Tom Johnson to Christian, August 15, 1967 (WHCFCFNF, box 10, LBJL); Christian to Johnson, August 22, 1967 (WHCFAF, Panzer, box 427, LBJL); unidentified author (probably Rostow), "Vietnam Information Group—Personnel and Organization," August 1967 (WHCFAF, Panzer, box 427, LBJL).

101. Christian to Johnson, August 22, 1967 (WHCFAF, Panzer, box 427, LBJL); Roche to Johnson, May 2, 1967 (NSFNF, box 7, LBJL); Roche to Johnson, June 6, 1967 (NSFNF, box 7, LBJL); Small, *Johnson, Nixon and Doves*, 18.

102. McPherson to Moyers, August 4, 1966 (WHCFAF, McPherson, box 28, LBJL); McPherson to Johnson, August 25, 1967 (WHCFAF, McPherson, box 29, LBJL).

103. Rufus Youngblood, Charles Sither and DeVier Pierson to Watson, July 25, 1967 (WHCF, HU, box 59, LBJL); *WP*, August 25, 1967.

104. *PP* 4: 124, 139, 144, 402–6, 415, 427–38.

105. Rostow, 513; Rostow interview; correspondence with Rostow.

106. *PP* 4: 154. See also Westmoreland, 227.

107. *PP* 4: 138–39, 148–54, 187, 196, 527.

108. Ibid., 456–60; Sheehan, 683–84.

109. *PP* 4: 463–66.

110. Ibid., 468–69, 477–78, 482–83, 486, 489.

111. Ibid., 478–79, 482.

112. Ibid., 478, 527–28; Warnke interview; Halperin interview; Helms interview.

113. Nitze interviews.

114. Halperin interview; Rostow interview; *PP* 4: 188, 444, 469, 483, 503–4, 507, 510.

115. Helms interview; Christian interview; William Bundy interview; Rusk interview.

116. McPherson interviews; *PP* 4: 482; Lawrence Eagleburger interview.

117. *PP* 4: 444, 485, 486.

118. Ibid., 444–45, 482, 485–86; William Bundy interview. The administration was sending small teams into Laos and Cambodia beginning in May 1967, however. See Shawcross, 24.

119. Kolko, 190; Rusk interview.

120. *PP* 4: 147, 155, 156, 157–58, 161, 166, 167, 168–69, 172–73, 184, 185, 191, 469; Rusk interview; Nitze interview; William Bundy interview; Rostow interview.

121. Christian interview; McPherson interview; *PP* 4: 158, 166, 171–72, 191; Westmoreland interview; William Bundy interview.

122. Ellsberg interview; William Bundy interview.

123. Eagleburger interview.

124. Halberstam, *Best and Brightest*, 779.

125. Helms interview (emphasis added).

126. Christian interview; Warnke interview; *PP* 4: 167, 171; Ronnie Duger, *The Politician: The Life and Times of Lyndon Johnson* (quoted in *SFC*, April 23, 1989).

127. Dancis interview; Goodman, 476; Ferber interview.

128. Aptheker interview; McAuliff interview; Camejo interview.

129. Lynd and Ferber, 92–93; SDS, "N.C. Resolution on the Following Vietnam Memorandum," April 1967 (SDS papers, SHSW).

130. Booth interview.

131. Duckles interview.

132. Harris interview.

133. Lew Jones interview; Muste, Becker and Dellinger, "Dear Friend," January 1967 (PC papers, SHSW); Muste, Becker and Dellinger, "Dear Friend," March 4, 1966 (PC papers, SHSW); Dellinger interview; Allen interview; "Workshop Reports and Plenary Decisions," 1965 (NCC papers, SHSW).

134. Lyttle interview.

135. Camejo interview.

136. Oglesby interview; Dowd interview.

137. Dellinger interview; Morse interview.

138. Dowd interview; Allen interview.

139. Hamburg interview; Wilson interview.

140. Morse interview.

141. Hamburg interview; Aptheker interview; Brown interview.

CHAPTER 4. 1967: PART TWO

1. AFSC, "The AFSC Opens a New Front in Vietnam," 1967 (AFSC papers, BLUCB); Bell, "To Members of the AFSC Corporation," April 3, 1967 (AFSC papers, BLUCB).

2. Dot Weller interview. Weller was witnessing the brutal toll of a spring offensive by the U.S. Army in Quang Ngai, a pro-NLF province. The offensive had wiped out 70 percent of the province's estimated 450 hamlets (Sheehan, 686–87).

3. The AFSCers eventually ceased flying on military planes.

4. Weller interview; "Mail from Quang Ngai," *Friends Journal*, December 1, 1967 (AFSC papers, BLUCB).

5. AFSC, ". . . Looking through a Hole into Hell . . . ," 1969 (AFSC papers, BLUCB); "Mail from Quang Ngai," *Friends Journal*, December 1, 1967 (AFSC papers, BLUCB).

6. Weller interview.

7. McAuliff interview; Weller interview.

8. Fernandez and Webb, "Vietnam Summer 1967," August 1967 (VS papers, BLUCB).

9. *Vietnam Summer News* 1, no. 1, 1967 (VS papers, BLUCB); Alperovitz interview; Allen interview.

10. Brown interview; Alperovitz interview.

11. Fernandez interview. See also Hall, 69.

12. Keniston, 6; Alperovitz interview.

13. Alperovitz interview; Keniston, 7; Hall, 45–46.

14. Ferber interview; Staughton Lynd, 15.

15. Ferber interview.

16. Harris interview; Staughton Lynd, 16.

17. David Harris, 188–89, 204; Resistance, "THE RESISTANCE," 1967 (Resistance papers, BLUCB).

18. Ferber interview.

19. Ibid.; Harris interview.

20. Ferber interview.

21. Lynd and Ferber, 127–28; Hamilton interview.

22. Kissinger interview.

23. Baskir and Strauss, 25–26, 42–43; Hamilton interview.

24. Harris interview.

25. Hamilton interview; Lynd and Ferber, 140–41.

26. David Harris, 190.

27. Harris interview.

28. Goodman, 476–79; Lynd and Ferber, 141–42; Hamilton interview.

29. Harris interview; Hamilton interview.

30. Harris interview; David Harris, 197.

31. "Motions and Resolutions Approved, National Workshop Conference, May 20–21, 1967" (Spring Mobe papers, SHSW); Mailer, 247.

32. Mailer, 250–51; Halstead, 311.

33. Halstead, 312.

34. Ibid., 313.

35. Ibid., 314.

36. Mailer, 260–61.

37. Dellinger interview.

38. Dellinger interviews; G, April 17, 1985; Dellinger, *More Power,* 117.

39. Dellinger interviews; Dellinger, *More Power,* 117; G, April 17, 1985.

40. Dowd interview.

41. Lyttle interview.

42. Morse interview; Peck interview; Dowd interview.

43. Lyttle interview.

44. Lew Jones interview; Halstead interview.

45. Gurewitz interview; Dowd interview.

46. Dellinger interview.

47. Dellinger interviews; Dellinger, *Revolutionary Nonviolence,* 361, 365; Dellinger, *More Power,* 119.

48. McReynolds interview.

49. Dowd interview.

50. Halstead interview; Lyttle interview.

51. McReynolds interview.

52. Gwen Patton interview; McReynolds interview.

53. Abbie Hoffman interview.

54. Dellinger interview.

55. Dellinger, *More Power,* 112.

56. *PP* 4: 198, 206–7.

57. Oberdorfer, "'Wobble' on the War," 31; *PP* 4: 197–203; Moorer interview.

58. *PP* 4: 158; Herring, 181–82.

59. *PP* 4: 206–8, 531–32.

60. Oberdorfer, "'Wobble' on the War," 30–31, 98–107.

61. Oberdorfer, *TET!* 86–92; Schlesinger, "Vietnam and the 1968 Elections," 5; Joseph, 192.

62. Luce interview; *NYT,* September 20, 1967.

63. Lukas, 27–28; *NYT,* January 18, 1971.

64. Woode, 47–48; *NYT,* January 18, 1971.

65. Minutes of September 20, 1967, White House meeting (MNF, box 2, LBJL); Johnson to Ramsey Clark, October 3, 1967 (Diary Backup, box 80, LBJL); assorted other Johnson administration documents in PPWC, box 8; WHCFCF, HU, box 57; WHCFAF, Nimetz, box 14; WHCF, HU, box 60 (LBJL).

66. Minutes of September 20, 1967, White House meeting (MNF, box 2, LBJL); Tom Johnson to Christian, October 21, 1967 (WHCF, HU, box 60, LBJL); Halstead, 323–24; minutes of October 18, 1967, cabinet meeting (Cabinet Papers, box 11, LBJL). See also other memos on the protest in PPWC, box 8, and WHCFAF, Nimetz, box 14 (LBJL). On October 4, Ramsey Clark said that the overall turnout could "conceivably" run "as high as 100,000" (minutes of October 4, 1967, cabinet meeting, Cabinet Papers, box 10, LBJL). But this figure is inconsistent with others tossed about by officials.

67. Clark to Johnson, October 4, 1967 (PPWC, box 8, LBJL); Justice Department "Information Memorandum" on Pentagon protest, October 3, 1967 (WHCFCF, HU, box 57, LBJL); David McGiffert to Harold Johnson, October 20, 1967 (PPWC, box 8, LBJL); Charles Maguire to Roche, October 20, 1967 (WHCF, HU, box 60, LBJL).

68. Nitze interview.

69. Justice Department Information Memorandum on Pentagon protest, October 5, 1967 (WHCFCF, HU, box 57, LBJL).

70. Maguire to Roche, October 20, 1967 (WHCF, HU, box 60, LBJL).

71. Justice Department, "Recent Developments—October 21 Pentagon Demonstration," October 19, 1967 (WHCFAF, Nimetz, box 14, LBJL); Justice Department Information Memorandum on Pentagon protest, October 3, 1967 (WHCFCF, HU, box 57, LBJL); Tom Johnson to Christian, October 21, 1967 (WHCF, HU, box 60, LBJL); minutes of October 4, 1967, cabinet meeting (Cabinet Papers, box 10, LBJL); Nitze interview; Justice Department Information Memorandum on Pentagon protest, October 20, 1967 (PPWC, box 8, LBJL); Matthew Nimetz to Levinson, 1967 (WHCFAF, Gaither, box 50, LBJL).

72. Resor interview; *Time*, October 27, 1967.

73. Harry Van Cleve to Warren Christopher, October 30, 1967 (PPRC, box 29, LBJL).

74. Minutes of October 4, 1967, cabinet meeting (Cabinet Papers, box 10, LBJL); Califano to Johnson, October 16, 1967 (WHCF, HU, box 59, LBJL).

75. Clark to Johnson, October 6, 1967 (PPWC, box 8, LBJL); Christian interview. McNamara and Katzenbach also suggested to Johnson that he consider leaving the White House during the protest (minutes of September 20, 1967, White House meeting, MNF, box 2, LBJL).

76. Minutes of October 4, 1967, cabinet meeting (Cabinet Papers, box 10, LBJL).

77. Califano to Johnson, October 16, 1967 (WHCF, HU, box 59, LBJL).

78. Maguire to Roche, October 20, 1967 (WHCF, HU, box 60, LBJL).

79. Minutes of October 18, 1967, cabinet meeting (Cabinet Papers, box 11, LBJL).

80. *NYT*, October 23, 1967.

81. On official concern for violence, see minutes of October 4, 1967, cabinet meeting (Cabinet Papers, box 10, LBJL) and Van Cleve to Christopher, October 30, 1967 (PPRC, box 29, LBJL).

82. Helms interview.

83. Halstead, 332; minutes of October 4, 1967, cabinet meeting (Cabinet Papers, box 10, LBJL); minutes of September 20, 1967, White House meeting (MNF, box 2, LBJL); NYT, October 23, 1967.

84. Mailer, 265–66; Lynd and Ferber, 135–36.

85. Halstead, 331.

86. Mailer, 269; Woode, 47; Halstead, 332–33.

87. Mailer, 268–69; Nimetz notes, October 18, 1967 (WHCFAF, Nimetz, box 14, LBJL).

88. Justice Department memo, October 1967 (PPWC, box 8, LBJL); Califano to Johnson, October 16, 1967 (WHCF, HU, box 59, LBJL); Tom Johnson to Christian, October 21, 1967 (WHCF, HU, box 60, LBJL).

89. WP, October 21, 1967; Oberdorfer, "'Wobble' on the War," 104.

90. Roger Wilkins to Clark, October 5, 1967 (PPWC, box 8, LBJL); minutes of October 4, 1967, cabinet meeting (Cabinet Papers, box 10, LBJL).

91. Unidentified author, "Forces Available in the Area," October 19, 1967 (WHCFAF, Nimetz, box 14, LBJL); Fred Vinson to Califano, October 17, 1967 (WHCF, HU, box 59, LBJL); Califano to Johnson, October 16, 1967 (WHCF, HU, box 59, LBJL); Tom Johnson to Christian, October 21, 1967 (WHCF, HU, box 60, LBJL); Woode, 48.

92. Woode, 47.

93. McGiffert to Harold Johnson, October 20, 1967 (PPWC, box 8, LBJL); Nitze interview; Ramsey Clark interview.

94. Woode, 49; Maguire to Roche, October 20, 1967 (WHCF, HU, box 60, LBJL).

95. McGiffert to Harold Johnson, October 20, 1967 (PPWC, box 8, LBJL). See also minutes of October 4, 1967, cabinet meeting (Cabinet Papers, box 10, LBJL).

96. Halstead, 333.

97. Time, October 27, 1967; Woode, 48.

98. Lady Bird Johnson, 584.

99. David Harris, 208.

100. "Homefront USA," PBS television program ("Vietnam: A Television History" series); David Harris, 208.

101. Lynd and Ferber, 112, 222; Coffin, 244.

102. Fernandez interview; Ferber interview.

103. David Harris, 209; Goodman, 479–80; Halstead, 344; Powers, War at Home, 236.

104. Califano to Johnson, October 17, 1967, 12:40 P.M. (WHCF, HU, box 59, LBJL); "For the President's Night Reading," October 14, 1967 (WHCF, HU, box 59, LBJL).

105. Goodman, 478; Harris interview; David Harris, 210.

106. NG, October 28, 1967; Sale, 370–73.

107. Goodman, 478; Hamilton interview.

108. *NG*, October 28, 1967; *SFC*, October 21, 1967; Sale, 375–76; Hamilton interview.

109. *WP*, October 21, 1967; Morrison and Morrison, 102; Ramsey Clark interview; Powers, *War at Home*, 193–94.

110. Johnson to Clark, October 20, 1967 (WHCF, HU, box 60, LBJL). Johnson sent the same memo to J. Edgar Hoover and Lewis Hershey, with the added message, "I want you to be personally responsible for keeping me fully informed on this" (notation in bottom margin).

111. *Time*, October 27, 1967.

112. Lyttle interview.

113. Ibid.; *WP*, October 22, 1967.

114. Calvert interview.

115. Mailer, 281; *Time*, October 27, 1967.

116. Calvert interview; *NG*, October 28, 1967

117. Dellinger interview; Calvert interview; Dellinger, *Revolutionary Nonviolence*, 361–62, 364.

118. Hoffman, *Revolution*, 46–47; Hoffman interview; Califano to Johnson, October 26, 1967 (WHCFCF, HU, box 57, LBJL).

119. *Time*, October 27, 1967; Helms interview; Resor interview; Rostow interview; Ellsberg interview; Halperin interview.

120. *WP*, May 10, 1984; Nitze, 269.

121. Hoopes, 84; Isaacson and Thomas, 676; Sheehan, 692; Shapley, 444; Warnke interview; *PP* 4: 201–2; Clifford, *Counsel*, 485; Trewhitt, 228, 233; Nitze interview; "LBJ," PBS television program ("The American Experience" series).

122. Sevareid interview; Halberstam, *Best and Brightest*, 769.

123. McNamara to Johnson, November 1, 1967 (NSFCFV, box 127, LBJL); Abe Fortas to Johnson, November 5, 1967 (NSFCFV, box 127, LBJL); McPherson to Johnson, October 10, 1967 (WHCFAF, McPherson, box 29, LBJL). McPherson agreed with McNamara that he and Rusk had both lost their public credibility on Vietnam.

124. Trewhitt, 240; McNamara interview.

125. Trewhitt, 238, 244–45; Warnke interview; Halberstam, *Best and Brightest*, 783.

126. Ellsberg interviews; Ellsberg, 15–18; *WP*, May 10, 1984.

127. Ellsberg interviews.

128. Califano to Johnson, October 21, 1967, multiple times (WHCFAF, Nimetz, box 14, LBJL); *WP*, October 22, 1967; *Time*, October 27, 1967; Rostow interview.

129. *NG*, October 28, 1967; Goodman, 471–75; Califano to Johnson, October 26, 1967 (WHCFCF, HU, box 57, LBJL); Woode, 50.

130. *WP*, October 22, 1967; Califano to Johnson, October 26, 1967 (WHCFCF, HU, box 57, LBJL).

131. *NG*, October 28, 1967; Powers, *War at Home*, 240; Sale, 385; Stephen

Pollack to Clark, October 22, 1967 (PPRC, box 29, LBJL); Ramsey Clark interview.

132. Dowd interview.

133. Calvert interview; *NG*, October 28, 1967.

134. Califano to Johnson, October 26, 1967 (WHCFCF, HU, box 57, LBJL).

135. Justice Department press release, November 13, 1967 (PPRC, box 29, LBJL).

136. *WP*, October 22, 1967; *NYT*, October 23, 1967; *Time*, October 27, 1967.

137. *Time*, October 27, 1967; *WP*, October 22, 1967; *U.S. News and World Report*, November 6, 1967.

138. *NYT*, October 23, 1967, January 18, 1971.

139. Fred Panzer to Johnson, October 26, 1967 (WHCF, HU, box 60, LBJL). Some friendly columnists may already have received the message. *Time* pointed out on October 27 that the militants' attempt to bust into the Pentagon occurred "after 90-odd minutes of steadily rising invective and roiling around in the north parking lot."

140. *U.S. News and World Report*, December 4, 1967; Rostow to Johnson, October 23, 1967 (NSFCFV, box 143, LBJL); Gerald Ford press release, November 22, 1967 (WHCFAF, Nimetz, box 14, LBJL); DeBenedetti, "CIA Analysis," 33; Gerald Ford press release, November 22, 1967 (WHCFAF, Nimetz, box 14, LBJL).

141. Ramsey Clark interview; Donner, 258–59.

142. Helms interview; Donner, 259.

143. Small, *Johnson, Nixon and Doves*, 46; Goodwin, 401, 402–3, 404.

144. Goodwin, 401, 406; Halberstam, *Powers That Be*, 489–90.

145. Halberstam, *Best and Brightest*, 757–58.

146. Helms interview; FBI reports, 1967 (WHCFCF, HU, box 57, WHCFCFNF, boxes 9, 10, LBJL); Clark to Johnson, October 19, 1967 (WHCFAF, Nimetz, box 14, LBJL); Goodwin, 387, 404.

147. Dellinger interview; Rostow interview.

148. Rostow interviews; correspondence with Rostow.

149. Rostow to Johnson, July 27, 1967 (NSFSF, box 5, LBJL); U.S. intelligence reports on black unrest, July 1967 (NSFSF, box 5, LBJL); Resor interview. An August State Department report also found no Cuban involvement in the black power and civil rights movements (NSFSF, box 5, LBJL).

150. Ramsey Clark interview.

151. Jim Jones to Johnson, October 31, 1967 (MNF, box 2, LBJL); Jones to Johnson, November 4, 1967 (MNF, box 2, LBJL).

152. CIA, "International Connections of the U.S. Peace Movement," November 15, 1967 (NSFIF, box 3, LBJL).

153. CIA, "International Connections of U.S. Peace Groups—III," February 28, 1968 (NSFIF, box 3, LBJL).

154. Minutes of September 18, 1968, cabinet meeting (Cabinet Papers, box 15, LBJL); CIA, "Restless Youth," September 1968 (NSFIF, box 3, LBJL).

155. Helms interview; Ramsey Clark interview; Richard Helms to Johnson, September 4, 1968 (NSFIF, box 3, LBJL). Helms also reminded Johnson of the "peculiar sensitivity" of the CIA's research on domestic dissidence (i.e., its illegality).

156. McGeorge Bundy interview; Christian interview.

157. Christian interview.

158. Ibid.; Moorer interview.

159. Rusk interview; DeBenedetti, "CIA Analysis," 34.

160. Warnke interview; Nitze interview.

161. Moorer interview; Reston interview.

162. Warnke interview; Ramsey Clark interview.

163. Rostow interviews. Rostow seemed particularly fixated on Dellinger's links to foreign communists. Both times the issue of communist subversion came up, he immediately mentioned Dellinger.

164. Jones to Johnson, October 31, 1967 (MNF, box 2, LBJL); Lady Bird Johnson, 714; Moorer interview.

165. Rostow interview; minutes of September 18, 1968, cabinet meeting (Cabinet Papers, box 15, LBJL).

166. Small, *Johnson, Nixon and Doves*, 115; Califano to Johnson, October 26, 1967 (WHCFCF, HU, box 57, LBJL).

167. *PP* 4: 208, 215, 216, 532; Jones to Johnson, November 4, 1967 (MNF, box 2, LBJL).

168. Dowd interview; Dellinger interviews.

169. Morrison and Morrison, 145; Philip Berrigan interview.

170. Morrison and Morrison, 147; Byrne, 14; Berrigan interview.

171. Halstead, 350–52; Becker interview; *NYT*, November 15, 1967; Sale, 377–78; Hoffman, *Revolution*, 52–53, 57.

172. Sale, 380–81.

173. Ibid., 400–2; Davidson interview.

174. Harris interview; Becker interview; Goodman, 470.

175. Peck, 47–48; Peck interview.

176. Calvert interview.

177. Dellinger, *More Power*, 94; Dellinger interview.

178. Hamilton interview; Halstead, 349; Powers, *War at Home*, 250.

179. Minutes of November 4, 1967, SMC Continuations Committee meeting (SMC papers, SHSW); Morse interview.

180. Minutes of November 4, 1967, SMC Continuations Committee meeting (SMC papers, SHSW); Linda Morse, "Action Proposal—'Stop the Draft Week,'" November 1967 (SMC papers, SHSW); McReynolds interview.

181. Lynd and Ferber, 222; Powers, *War at Home*, 246–47; McReynolds interview.

182. Goodman, 470; Morse interview; Powers, *War at Home*, 248.

183. Powers, *War at Home*, 248–49; Halstead, 355.

184. Morse interview; McReynolds interview.

185. Oberdorfer, *TET!* 91; Converse and Schuman, 20; Berkowitz, 6; Hahn,

1189–90; Foner, 49–53; Bundy to Johnson, November 10, 1967 (VRF, box 1, LBJL).

186. Jones to Johnson, November 4, 1967 (MNF, box 2, LBJL); Isaacson and Thomas, 676; Oberdorfer, *TET!* 99; Hoopes, 90.

187. Lady Bird Johnson, 620–24; Kitt, 232–42; "60 Minutes" television program, December 3, 1989.

188. Bundy to Johnson, November 10, 1967 (VRF, box 1, LBJL); Oberdorfer, *TET!* 98.

189. McPherson to Johnson, October 27, 1967 (NSFCFV, box 127, LBJL); McPherson oral history, tape 5, 7 (LBJL); Rostow, 516; Rostow interview.

190. Rusk to J. William Fulbright, December 8, 1967 (NSFCFV, box 102, LBJL).

191. Hoopes, 93–94, 95–96; Warnke interviews.

192. Oberdorfer, *TET!* 99–102; Oberdorfer, "'Wobble' on the War," 104; Jones to Johnson, November 4, 1967 (MNF, box 2, LBJL); Hallin, 165; Defense Department memo, early 1968 (NSFCFV, box 100, LBJL).

193. Oberdorfer, *TET!* 102. See also Westmoreland, 231.

194. Westmoreland interview.

195. Westmoreland, 225, 234; Oberdorfer, *TET!* 104–5; Westmoreland interview. In his speech to the National Press Club, Westmoreland divided U.S. involvement in Vietnam into four historical phases. Perhaps coincidentally, perhaps not, McGeorge Bundy had written Johnson eleven days earlier that the administration should "explain—really for the first time—that this war has had a number of phases which are sharply different from each other" (Bundy to Johnson, November 10, 1967, VRF, box 1, LBJL).

196. Westmoreland interview.

CHAPTER 5.   1968

1. McCarthy interview; McCarthy, 36–50.

2. David Hawk interview.

3. David Harris, 213.

4. McCarthy, 58–59; McCarthy interview; David Harris, 218–9; Larner, 35–36.

5. David Harris, 221; McCarthy interview.

6. David Harris, 221–22. See also Powers, *War at Home*, 285–87.

7. McCarthy interview.

8. Morrison and Morrison, 132; Hawk interview; Brown interview.

9. Powers, *War at Home*, 281; Oglesby interview; McCarthy interview.

10. Camejo interview; Davidson interview.

11. Oglesby interview.

12. Ibid.

13. Ibid.

14. Correspondence with Carl Oglesby; Oglesby interview.

15. Dellinger, *More Power*, 89–94.

16. Fernandez interview; CALCAV, "Clergy and Laymen Concerned About Vietnam," 1968 (CALCAV papers, SHSW).

17. CALCAV, "Clergy and Laymen Concerned About Vietnam," 1968 (CALCAV papers, SHSW); Fernandez interview.

18. *MEMO*, November 1967 (WSP papers, SHSW).

19. Wilson interview; *WP*, January 16, 1968; Duckles interview.

20. Untitled WSP leaflet, 1968 (WSP papers, SHSW); Duckles interview; *Sacramento Bee*, March 30, 1967; Hamburg interview; phone conversation with Alice Hamburg.

21. McPherson interview; Sale, 406–7; Donner, 272; *NYT*, April 17, 1971; Califano to Johnson, November 14, 1967 (WHCFAF, Gaither, box 50, LBJL); Ramsey Clark interview; Baskir and Strauss, 25, 72.

22. Califano to Johnson, November 17, 1967 (WHCF, ND, box 7, LBJL); Nimetz to Califano, November 17, 1967 (WHCF, ND, box 7, LBJL); Califano to Johnson, November 15, 1967 (WHCF, HU, box 60, LBJL); *NYT*, April 17, 1971.

23. *NYT*, April 17, 1971.

24. Several months later, the Alameda County District Attorney indicted seven leaders of Oakland Stop the Draft Week on three conspiracy counts. Some activists regarded the action as federally inspired and part of the administration's escalating war against the peace movement. Ramsey Clark said that he "would be quite surprised" if federal pressure was exerted in the case, however. The U.S. attorney in Oakland, Cecil Poole, just plain "wouldn't have been interested" in prosecutions, Clark believed (Ramsey Clark interview). The Oakland Seven's trial ended in acquittals.

25. Ferber interview.

26. Ibid.

27. Ibid.

28. Ibid. See also Coffin, 263.

29. Ferber interview.

30. Ibid.

31. Lynd and Ferber, 124; Coffin, 268–69; Ferber interview.

32. Ferber interview; Morrison and Morrison, 104.

33. Ramsey Clark interview.

34. Ibid.

35. Ibid.

36. The Justice Department would ultimately prosecute over 1,500 draft cases by the end of 1968, however (Richard Harris, 62).

37. Ramsey Clark interview.

38. Ibid. See also Richard Harris, 63.

39. Ramsey Clark interview.

40. Ibid.

41. Ibid.

42. Ibid.

43. Dellinger interviews; Halstead, 357.

44. Dellinger interview; Dowd interview.

45. Gitlin, *Sixties*, 322; Lyttle interview; Dellinger, *More Power*, 122.

46. Dellinger, *More Power*, 121; Dellinger interviews; Dowd interview.

47. Zaroulis and Sullivan, 176; Dowd interview; Gitlin, *Sixties*, 321.

48. Halstead, 406; Calvert interview.

49. Walker, 46.

50. Davidson interview; Wilson interview; Walker, 38; Dellinger, *More Power*, 116.

51. Oberdorfer, *TET!* 4–8, 11–13.

52. Hoopes, 141–42.

53. Oberdorfer, *TET!* 33–34.

54. Ibid., 167, 171; Warnke interviews.

55. Sheehan, 707; Schandler, 75; Hoopes, 146; Halberstam, *Best and Brightest*, 786.

56. Isaacson and Thomas, 685; Oberdorfer, *TET!* 273; Hoopes, 158.

57. Interview with a Johnson administration official desiring anonymity; Oberdorfer, *TET!* 251; Halberstam, *Powers That Be*, 514; William Bundy interview.

58. Oberdorfer, *TET!* 366–67.

59. Eugene Rostow to Johnson, March 28, 1968 (NSFCFV, box 100, LBJL); Joseph, 166.

60. Jeff Jones interview; Ferber interview.

61. Isaacson and Thomas, 686.

62. Westmoreland interview; Schandler, 97.

63. Westmoreland interview; Westmoreland, 353–55.

64. *PP* 4: 546–49; Westmoreland, 356.

65. Cooper, 390; *PP(NYT)*, 593.

66. Goulding, 309.

67. Clifford to Johnson, May 17, 1965 (VRF, box 1, LBJL); Valenti's notes of July 25, 1965, Camp David meeting (VRF, box 1, LBJL); Berman, 121n; Clifford to Johnson, November 1967 (NSFCFV, box 127, LBJL); Cooper, 391.

68. Clifford, "Viet Nam Reappraisal," 606–7; Clark Clifford interview.

69. Schandler, 139–41; Clifford interview.

70. Helms interview; Joseph, 107.

71. Warnke interview.

72. Ibid.

73. Ibid.

74. Halperin interview; Schandler, 151–52, 156.

75. Clifford, *Counsel*, 493–94; Clifford interview; Clifford, "Viet Nam Reappraisal," 612; *PP* 4: 559–61; Hoopes, 180.

76. William Bundy interview; Rusk interview; Halperin interview; Schandler, 311–12.

77. Nitze interviews. See also Nitze, 258–60, 263, 268.

78. Nitze interviews.

79. Nitze interview.

80. Ibid. See also Nitze, 278; Clifford, *Counsel*, 506.

81. Hoopes, 200; Schandler, 215; Nitze interview.

82. Schandler, 245–47.

83. McPherson interviews; McPherson, 294–95, 443, 447; McPherson oral history, tape 5, 38 (LBJL).

84. *PP* 4: 262; Lyndon Johnson, 402.

85. Christian interview; Converse et al., 1092.

86. Christian interview; Kearns, 343.

87. Halperin interview.

88. Schandler, 255.

89. Hoopes, 215–16; Isaacson and Thomas, 685, 700; Helms interview; Lyndon Johnson, 422.

90. Oberdorfer, *TET!* 295, 310, 312–13, 314; Wicker interview; McPherson, 433; *Winston-Salem Journal*, March 17, 1968; Isaacson and Thomas, 696–97; William Bundy interview.

91. McPherson interview; Lyndon Johnson, 418; Isaacson and Thomas, 703.

92. McPherson interviews. The previous month Rostow had advised Johnson it was "time for a war leader speech . . . time to say plainly that hard fighting and heavy casualties lie ahead" (Rostow to Johnson, February 8, 1968, NSFCFV, box 100, LBJL).

93. Lyndon Johnson, 418; William Bundy interview; Schandler, 249.

94. Schandler, 242, 251–52.

95. Halberstam, *Best and Brightest*, 758; Oberdorfer, *TET!* 293; Kolko, 317; Isaacson and Thomas, 695.

96. Lyndon Johnson, 398, 422; Westmoreland, 358–59; Westmoreland interview; Halperin interview; Clifford interview; Warnke interview; *PP* 4: 594–96.

97. *PP* 4: 596–602.

98. Hallin, 170.

99. Goulding, 329–30, 333; Clifford interview; William Bundy interview; Warnke interview.

100. Halperin interview.

101. Helms interview.

102. Christian interview; Eagleburger interview; William Bundy interview; McPherson, 443–48; Warnke interview.

103. Christian interview; Warnke interview; McPherson interview; Clifford interview; Powers, *War at Home*, 72; Helms interview.

104. Bundy to Johnson, November 10, 1967 (VRF, box 1, LBJL); Helms interview; Rostow interview; correspondence with Rostow; Rusk interview.

105. Christian interview; Christian, 193.

106. Christian, 6; McGeorge Bundy interview; Nitze interview; Rusk interview.

107. McPherson interviews; Christian interview; Small, *Johnson, Nixon and Doves*, 9–12.

108. Helms interview; McGeorge Bundy interview; McPherson interview; Halperin interview; William Bundy interview.

109. State Department, "American Opinion Summary," January 20–26, 1966 (NSFB, box 17, LBJL); Rusk interview; McGeorge Bundy interview.

110. Rusk interviews.

111. Helms interview; McGeorge Bundy interview; Lyndon Johnson, 431, 530–31; Nitze interview; Clifford interview; transcript of McGeorge Bundy speech at DePauw University, October 12, 1968 (NSFCFV, box 103, LBJL).

112. Fernandez interview; *WP*, December 18, 1967.

113. Christian interview; John Sherman Cooper interview; Mike Mansfield to Johnson, March 13, 1968 (MNF, box 2, LBJL); Oberdorfer, *TET!* 85.

114. Wicker, 16; Reston interview; Sevareid interview; Oakes interview.

115. Oberdorfer, *TET!* 89; Sevareid interview.

116. Hallin, 162; Sevareid interview.

117. Hallin, 201; Sevareid interview.

118. Braestrup, 501; *Winston-Salem Journal*, March 17, 1968; Oakes interview; Sevareid interview; Sheehan, 740; Reston interview.

119. Schlesinger interview; Goodwin, 366, 367.

120. Rostow interview; Rusk interview; McPherson interview; Clifford interview.

121. Joseph, 260–62; Halberstam, *Best and Brightest*, 795; Clifford, *Counsel*, 524–25.

122. Clifford interview.

123. Joseph, 262; Helms interview; William Bundy interview; Lyndon Johnson, 424.

124. Lynd and Ferber, 155; Hamburg interview; Bill Ayers interview; Sale, 421.

125. PC, "Dear Friend," April 1968 (PC papers, SHSW).

126. Brown interview.

127. Fernandez interview.

128. Berrigan interview; Morrison and Morrison, 148; Byrne, 16.

129. Dowd interview.

130. Hoffman interview; Walker, 14; Ramsey Clark interview; Hoffman, *Soon to Be*, 145.

131. Phyllis Kalb position paper on SMC, May 1968 (SMC papers, SHSW); Gitlin, *Sixties*, 309.

132. McReynolds interview; Dowd, 178.

133. Dancis interview; Ferber interview.

134. Thorne, 119; Lynd and Ferber, 232.

135. Ferber interview.

136. Dancis interview.

137. Harris interview.

138. Ibid.; Resistance, "On the Resistance," 1968 (Resistance papers, BLUCB).

139. Warnke interview; Resor interview; Baskir and Strauss, 67, 77, 80.

140. Baskir and Strauss, 68–82.

141. Ibid., 75, 80.

142. Ibid., 66, 77.

143. Ibid., 5, 67; Harris interview. Some 3,250 resisters went to prison.

144. Harris interview; Dancis interview.

145. Morse interview.

146. McReynolds interview.

147. Oglesby interview; Sale, 418–21.

148. Oglesby interview; Booth interview.

149. Gitlin, *Sixties*, 306; Sale, 443–45; assorted Johnson administration documents (WHCFAF, Gaither, box 2, "Civil Disorders on Campus" folder, LBJL); Ayers interview.

150. Gitlin, *Sixties*, 311; Oglesby interview.

151. Sale, 451, 455.

152. Lyttle interview; minutes of June 5, 1968, meeting of PC's Administrative Committee (PC papers, SHSW); Becker interview.

153. Minutes of June 12, 1968, meeting of PC's Administrative Committee (PC papers, SHSW).

154. Camejo interview; Lew Jones interview.

155. Patton interview.

156. Lyttle interview; Calvert, 24.

157. Duckles interview; Patton interview; Becker interview.

158. Morse interview.

159. Morse position paper on SMC, May 1968 (SMC papers, SHSW); Morse interview.

160. Morse position paper on SMC, May 1968 (SMC papers, SHSW); Halstead, 393.

161. Lew Jones interview; Gurewitz interview.

162. Morse interview.

163. Ibid.

164. Halstead, 421; Churchill and Vander Wall, 57–58; Donner, 200.

165. Morse interview; Lew Jones interview; Weiss interview.

166. Churchill and Vander Wall, 176–86.

167. Barry interview; Gitlin, *Sixties*, 318.

168. Weiss interview.

169. Walker, 138–39; *Ramparts* editorial report, "The Decline and Fall of the Democratic Party," September 28, 1968.

170. Walker, 142–59; *Ramparts* editorial report, "Decline and Fall," September 28, 1968.

171. Hayden, 304, 306–7; Walker, 163–83; Zaroulis and Sullivan, 189; Dowd interview; Gitlin, *Sixties*, 330.

172. Walker, 220–30; Schultz, 164–73; Hayden, 314–17.

173. Dellinger interview; Hayden, 317–18; Zaroulis and Sullivan, 191; Peck interview.

174. Walker, 231–65; Gitlin, *Sixties*, 332–33; Zaroulis and Sullivan, 193; Dowd interview.

175. Morse interview; *Ramparts* editorial report, "Decline and Fall," September 28, 1968.

176. Dowd interview.

177. McGiffert to Clifford, August 20, 1968 (PPRC, box 96, LBJL); Nitze interview; Ramsey Clark interview.

178. Christian interview; Rostow, 522.

179. Rostow interview; Warnke interview.

180. Christian interview; Rostow interview; correspondence with Rostow.

181. Cortright, 53–56; Barry interview; Rinaldi, passim.

182. Cortright, 53, 56, 57.

183. William Westmoreland to Johnson, August 25, 1968 (WHCFCF, ND, box 68, LBJL); Westmoreland interview.

184. Westmoreland to Johnson, September 9, 1968 (WHCFCF, ND, box 68, LBJL); Cortright, 57.

185. Westmoreland interview; Cortright, 40–41, 52, 56, 70–71; Kolko, 364.

186. Dowd interview.

187. Hoffman interview; Heath, 9; Halstead, 418; Hoffman, *Revolution*, 118.

188. Converse et al., 1087; Robinson, 1–9; Converse and Schuman, 24; Gitlin, *Sixties*, 304.

189. Bernardine Dohrn, John Jacobs, and Jeff Jones, "Boulder and Boulder," October 1968 (SDS papers, SHSW); Morse interview; Albert and Albert, 387; Dellinger, *More Power*, 130.

190. Dancis interview.

191. Sale, 476–77, 490; Ayers interview.

192. Ayers interview.

193. Ibid.; Jeff Jones interview.

194. Ayers interview; Jeff Jones interview.

195. Dohrn, Jacobs, and Jones, "Boulder and Boulder," October 1968 (SDS papers, SHSW); Sale, 484.

196. Melvin Laird interviews; *NYT*, September 10, 11, 12, 25, 26, 30, 1968; Clifford, *Counsel*, 549, 554; Page and Brody, 983–85.

197. McAuliff interview; Warnke interview.

198. Laird interview.

CHAPTER 6. 1969: PART ONE

1. Laird interview; Laurence Lynn interview; Hersh, *Price of Power*, 90.

2. Selin (no page numbers); *Time*, August 29, 1969; Laird interviews; Eagleburger interview.

3. Laird interview; Kolko, 347–48; Selin.

4. Nixon, *RN*, 392; Selin; Hersh, *Price of Power*, 112; Kissinger, *White House Years*, 271.

5. Lake interview; Selin; Hersh, *Price of Power*, 90.

6. Kissinger, *White House Years*, 271–72; Marshall Green interview; Hersh, *Price of Power*, 108, 113–14; Nixon, *RN*, 433; Lynn interview.

7. Haldeman interview; Roger Morris interview.

8. Nixon, *RN*, 347–48; Nixon, *No More Vietnams*, 102, 107–8; Haldeman, 99. See also Kissinger, *White House Years*, 239, 244.

9. Haldeman, 82–83.

10. Laird interview; William Watts interview.

11. Hersh, *Price of Power*, 63–64; Shawcross, 25–26.

12. Shawcross, 28; Moorer interview.

13. Laird interview; Halperin interview; Shawcross, 34–35, 105; Hersh, *Price of Power*, 87.

14. Marshall Green interview.

15. Lynn interview; Hersh, *Price of Power*, 84, 91–92.

16. Haldeman, 97.

17. Lukas, 60.

18. Halstead, 439, 440; Dancis interview; *MEMO*, November–December 1968, April–May 1969 (WSP papers, SHSW).

19. Minutes of December 9, 1968, meeting of PC (PC papers, SHSW); Peck interview; National Mobe, "Demonstrate against the War and Racism, January 18–20," January 1969 (National Mobe papers, BLUCB); National Mobe, "Inauguration, Chicago Indictments, Anti-War Directions: A Mobilization Report," February 25, 1969 (PC papers, SHSW); minutes of December 23, 1968, meeting of PC's Administrative Committee (PC papers, SHSW).

20. National Mobe, "Inauguration, Chicago Indictments, Anti-War Directions," February 25, 1969 (PC papers, SHSW); Dellinger, *More Power*, 67; Dellinger interview.

21. Dellinger interview; Nixon, *RN*, 366; Richard Harris, 140; Oudes, 8–11; "Watergate: The Secret Story," CBS television program.

22. National Mobe, "Inauguration, Chicago Indictments, Anti-War Directions," February 25, 1969 (PC papers, SHSW); Churchill and Vander Wall, 59–60; Halstead, 446–47; Peck, "Perspective and Proposal for the New Mobilization Committee to End the War in Vietnam," December 2, 1969 (New Mobe papers, SHSW).

23. CALCAV, "Clergy and Laymen Concerned About Vietnam," 1969 (CALCAV papers, SHSW); Fernandez interview.

24. *WP*, March 23, 27, 1969; CALCAV, "Clergy and Laymen Concerned About Vietnam," 1969 (CALCAV papers, SHSW); Action Memorandum to Herb Klein and John Ehrlichman, March 27, 1969 (WHCF, HU, box 23, NP).

25. Halstead, 451–52; Churchill and Vander Wall, 60; DeBenedetti, *American Ordeal*, 245–46.

26. Hawk interview; *Newsweek*, May 12, 1969.

27. *WP*, May 6, 1969; Hartsough interview.

28. CALCAV, "Clergy and Laymen Concerned About Vietnam," 1969 (CALCAV papers, SHSW); Fernandez interview.

29. Lynd and Ferber, 202; Hartsough interview; *WP*, June 4, 1969.

30. Gurewitz interview.

31. Cortright interview.

32. Halstead, 455–57.

33. Cortright, 44–45; Heinl, 4.

34. Sale, 511–12.

35. Ibid., 512–13; *MEMO*, April–May 1969 (WSP papers, SHSW); Aptheker interview; Becker interview; Camejo interview.

36. Brown interview; McReynolds interview; Halstead interview.

37. Sale, 545.

38. Schell, 35; Oakes interview.

39. *WP*, May 2, 1969; Sale, 546–47; Richard Harris, 186, 187–88, 191; Lamar Alexander to Bud Krogh, June 7, 1969 (WHCF, HU, box 23, NP); Alexander Butterfield to Ehrlichman, June 2, 1969 (WHSF, Krogh, box 60, NP); Butterfield to Ehrlichman, June 10, 1969 (WHSF, Krogh, box 69, NP); Ehrlichman to staff secretary, June 9, 1969 (WHSF, Krogh, box 69, NP).

40. Sale, 547–50; Zaroulis and Sullivan, 240.

41. Hesburgh, 162; Hechinger, 15.

42. Connelly and Dooley, xi, 73, 135, 169, 175, 209; Hesburgh interview.

43. Connelly and Dooley, 89; Hesburgh interview.

44. Connelly and Dooley, 5, 228; Hesburgh interview.

45. Hesburgh, 128; Hesburgh interview.

46. Hesburgh, 162–63; Connelly and Dooley, 239–42.

47. Connelly and Dooley, 3, 242–43; Richard Nixon to Theodore Hesburgh, February 22, 1969 (WHCF, HU, box 23, NP); Ray Price interview.

48. Connelly and Dooley, 4, 243–45.

49. Ibid., 246–47, 248, 251, 259–60.

50. Hesburgh interview.

51. Connelly and Dooley, 260, 261, 268, 284; Hechinger, 17.

52. Hesburgh interview.

53. Sale, 488–97, 500, 503, 564; Jacobs, 401.

54. Ayers interview; Davidson interview.

55. Sale, 533–34, 557–58; AFL-CIO report on June 1969 SDS convention (WHSF, Krogh, box 60, NP); Richard Harris, 135; Ayers interview; Jacobs, 51–90.

56. Sale, 563–67.

57. Ibid., 568–70.

58. Jeff Jones interview; Ayers interview; Sale, 570–74; Zaroulis and Sullivan, 254.

59. Jacobs, 400.

60. *NYT*, June 22, 1969; Kissinger interview.

61. Richard Cook to Alexander, September 17, 1969 (WHSFCF, HU, box 36, NP); Stephen Hess to Ehrlichman, July 28, 1969 (WHSF, Krogh, box 60, NP).

62. Price, 154; Haldeman interview; Eagleburger interview; Price interview; Kissinger, *White House Years*, 300. On official discussions on "the youth problem," see particularly boxes 57, 66 and 69 of Egil Krogh's files in the WHSF, NP.

63. Morris interview; John Ehrlichman interview.

64. Morris interview.

65. Haldeman interviews; Ronald Ziegler interview; Ehrlichman interview; Price interview.

66. Butterfield to Klein and Bud Wilkinson, March 17, 1969 (WHCF, HU, box 23, NP); Daniel Moynihan to Nixon, April 14, 1969 (WHCF, HU, box 23, NP); Stephen Bull to Nixon, April 1, 1969 (WHCF, HU, box 23, NP); Butterfield to John Mitchell, Robert Finch and Ehrlichman, June 2, 1969 (WHSF, Krogh, box 69, NP).

67. Krogh to Deke DeLoach, February 25, 1969 (WHSF, Krogh, box 69, NP); Nixon to Henry Kissinger, April 10, 1969 (WHCF, HU, box 23, NP); Paul Courant to Paul McCracken, June 12, 1969 (WHCF, HU, box 24, NP); McCracken to Nixon, July 1, 1969 (WHCF, HU, box 24, NP); Ehrlichman to Moynihan and McCracken, June 2, 1969 (WHSF, Krogh, box 69, NP). On Nixon's reading on student protest, see the WHCF, HU, box 24, NP.

68. Arthur Burns to Nixon, May 26, 1969 (WHSFPOF, box 2, NP); Burns to Ehrlichman, May 6, 1969 (WHSF, Krogh, box 66, NP).

69. Ehrlichman, 271; Ehrlichman interview; Ehrlichman to staff secretary, March 27, 1969 (WHCF, HU, box 23, NP).

70. Kissinger, *White House Years*, 227; John Dean interview.

71. Dean, 19; Haldeman interview; Dean interview.

72. Haldeman interview; Ehrlichman interviews.

73. Ehrlichman to John Caulfield, April 29, 1969 (WHSF, Krogh, box 66, NP); Moynihan to Nixon, April 14, 1969 (WHCF, HU, box 23, NP); Burns to Ehrlichman, May 6, 1969 (WHSF, Krogh, box 66, NP). On Nixon's solicitation of officials' views on the adequacy of the administration's intelligence, see the "Campus Disorders / Student Unrest" folder in box 66 of Krogh's files in the WHSF, NP.

74. Sale, 541–42, 543–44; Viorst, 10; Schell, 60, 61; Donner, 161–62; Richard Harris, 135; Halstead interview; *NYT*, May 5, 1969.

75. Ehrlichman to Caulfield, April 29, 1969 (WHSF, Krogh, box 66, NP); Caulfield to Ehrlichman, June 20, 1969 (WHSF, Krogh, box 66, NP); Krogh to Ehrlichman, June 26, 1969 (WHSF, Krogh, box 66, NP); Krogh to Hoover, July 19, 1969 (WHSF, Krogh, box 66, NP).

76. Helms interview; Laird interview; Ehrlichman interview; Lukas, 26–27; Powers, *Man Who Kept Secrets*, 202–3; Morris, 65.

77. Action Memorandum to Ehrlichman, June 2, 1969 (WHSFCF, HU, box

36, NP); Ehrlichman to Nixon, June 5, 1969 (WHSFPOF, box 2, NP); Butterfield to Ehrlichman, June 10, 1969 (WHSF, Krogh, box 69, NP).

78. Schell, 60; Haldeman, 107.

79. Haldeman interview.

80. Price interview; Watts interview; Ziegler interview.

81. Haldeman interviews; Haldeman, 106.

82. Dean interview; Ehrlichman interview.

83. Morris interview; Lynn interview; Eagleburger interview.

84. Magruder, 165–66.

85. Kissinger, *White House Years*, 510; Morris, 169; Morris interview; Lake interview; Nixon, *RN*, 685.

86. Kissinger, *White House Years*, 297, 299, 301–2.

87. Haldeman interviews.

88. Price interview; Price, 143, 151, 152, 153.

89. Price, 154–56; Ray Price, "Thoughts on Dealing with Youthful Unrest," October 2, 1969 (WHSF, Krogh, box 66, NP); Nixon, *RN*, 685.

90. Robert Brown to Nixon, March 17, 1969 (WHSF, Krogh, box 69, NP).

91. Nixon, *No More Vietnams*, 125; Curt Smith, 217; Moynihan to Nixon, August 19, 1969 (WHSF, Krogh, box 57, NP).

92. Lake interview; *WP*, August 26, 1969.

93. Price, 156; Robert Brown to Nixon, March 17, 1969 (WHSF, Krogh, box 69, NP).

94. Bull to H. R. Haldeman, April 22, 1969 (WHCF, HU, box 23, NP); *WP*, August 26, 1969; Haldeman to Wilkinson, April 22, 1969 (WHCF, HU, box 23, NP).

95. Bull to Haldeman, April 22, 1969 (WHCF, HU, box 23, NP); Tom Huston to Haldeman, May 20, 1969 (WHSF, Krogh, box 69, NP); Nixon to Price, February 17, 1969 (WHCF, HU, box 23, NP); Butterfield to Ehrlichman, June 16, 1969 (WHSF, Krogh, box 66, NP).

96. Huston to Haldeman, March 18, 1969 (WHCF, HU, box 23, NP); Huston to Haldeman, May 20, 1969 (WHSF, Krogh, box 69, NP).

97. Nixon to Haldeman, March 17, 1969 (WHCF, HU, box 23, NP); Patrick Buchanan to Nixon, March 21, 1969 (WHCF, HU, box 23, NP); Huston to Haldeman, March 18, 1969 (WHCF, HU, box 23, NP).

98. Ehrlichman to William Brock, May 29, 1969 (WHSF, Krogh, box 69, NP); Krogh to Alexander, June 5, 1969 (emphasis added) (WHSF, Krogh, box 60, NP); *WP*, August 26, 1969; Marshall Green interview; Price interview; interview with a Nixon administration official desiring anonymity.

99. Lake interview; Price interview.

100. Lake interview; Price interview; Marshall Green interview.

101. *WP*, March 23, 1969; Jim Keogh to Ken Cole, March 17, 1969 (WHSFPPF, box 6, NP); Robert Brown to Nixon, March 17, 1969 (WHSF, Krogh, box 69, NP).

102. *WP*, March 23, 1969; Schell, 36–37.

103. Haldeman to Keogh, April 28, 1969 (WHCF, HU, box 23, NP); *WP*, April 30, 1969.

104. *WP*, June 4, 5, 1969.

105. Burns to Nixon, May 26, 1969 (WHSFPOF, box 2, NP); Alexander to Krogh, June 7, 1969 (WHCF, HU, box 23, NP); Ehrlichman to staff secretary, June 9, 1969 (WHSF, Krogh, box 69, NP).

106. *NYT*, June 22, 1969; *WP*, March 23, May 21, June 13, August 26, 1969.

107. Robert Brown to Nixon, March 17, 1969 (WHSF, Krogh, box 69, NP).

108. Ibid.; Ehrlichman to staff secretary, March 27, 1969 (WHCF, HU, box 23, NP); Price interview; Westmoreland interview; Laird interview; *Time*, August 29, 1969; *WP*, August 26, 1969.

109. Richard Harris, 163–64, 170–71, 186; Drew, 8–12; Schell, 30.

110. *NYT*, May 5, 1969, April 21, 1977; McReynolds interview; Sale, 544; Ehrlichman, 50.

111. Huston to Nixon, June 18, 1969 (WHSFPOF, box 2, NP); Oudes, 147; Kutler, 105; Schell, 61; *G*, January 26, 1972.

112. Viorst, 10; Ramsey Clark interview; *NYT*, September 24, 1981.

113. *WP*, May 2, 1969.

114. Kissinger, *White House Years*, 272; Helms interview; Halperin interview.

115. Price interview.

116. Westmoreland interview; Selin; Nixon, *RN*, 392; Morris interview; Lynn interview.

117. Laird interview.

118. Kissinger, *White House Years*, 274.

119. Document listing responses to Grossman's proposal, 1969 (CALCAV papers, SHSW).

120. Brown interview; Brown, 34.

121. Brown interview.

122. Ibid.; Hurwitz, 17.

123. Hawk interview.

124. Brown interview; Hawk interview; "Moratorium Strategy," May or June 1969 (VMC papers, SHSW).

125. *NYT*, July 1, 1969; "Call for a Vietnam Moratorium," June 1969 (VMC papers, SHSW).

126. VMC, "Dear Friend," July 8, 1969 (VMC papers, SHSW); Fernandez interview; Brown, 35; Hawk interview.

127. Halstead, 459–60; Lew Jones interview.

128. Peck, "Perspective and Proposal for the New Mobilization Committee," December 2, 1969 (New Mobe papers, SHSW); Peck interview.

129. Peck interview; Becker interview; Gurewitz interview; Halstead, 461–63.

130. Halstead, 463; Peck interview.

131. *G*, July 12, 1969; Halstead interview; Dellinger interview; Dowd interview; Halstead, 468.

132. Becker interview; Gurewitz interview.

133. Peck interview; Halstead interview; Halstead, 470–71; "Fall Proposals Passed Unanimously by National Antiwar Conference, July 4 & 5," 1969 (New Mobe papers, SHSW).

134. "Fall Proposals Passed Unanimously," 1969 (New Mobe papers, SHSW); Halstead, 474, 494–95; Fernandez interview.

135. Zaroulis and Sullivan, 258.

136. Dowd interview; Hurwitz, 84–85; Peck interview.

137. McAuliff interview; Dowd interview; Hawk interview; Zaroulis and Sullivan, 279.

138. Jacobs, 152, 160, 176–77, 186, 193; Jeff Jones interview.

139. Ayers interview.

140. Sale, 580–83, 587–89; Dellinger, *More Power*, 163–64; Jacobs, 154, 161, 163–64, 189; Ayers interview.

141. Jacobs, 148, 190; Sale, 583–86; Jeff Jones interview.

142. Sale, 590–91, 602; Jacobs, 188, 191–92, 194; Ayers interview.

143. Ayers interview.

144. Cole to Mitchell, September 23, 1969 (WHSFCF, HU, box 36, NP); Mitchell to Cole, September 25, 1969 (WHSFCF, HU, box 36, NP).

145. CALCAV, "Speak-Out," June 1969 (CALCAV papers, SHSW); Kissinger, *White House Years*, 289; CALCAV, "Clergy and Laymen Concerned About Vietnam," 1969 (CALCAV papers, SHSW); Lynd and Ferber, 193, 196–99, 202–3; Weiss interview; Duckles interview.

146. Halstead, 476–77.

147. *LAT*, August 18, 1969; Curt Smith, 216; Laird interview.

148. Cole to Ehrlichman, September 23, 1969 (WHSF, Krogh, box 66, NP).

149. Cortright, 33, 35–36; Luce interview; Ferber interview.

CHAPTER 7. 1969: PART TWO

1. Krogh, "Memorandum for the Student / Young People File," August 22, 1969 (WHSF, Krogh, box 57, NP); Ehrlichman to Leonard Garment, October 1, 1969 (WHSF, Ehrlichman, box 50, NP).

2. Krogh to Bill Timmons, September 8, 1969 (WHSF, Krogh, box 57, NP); Klein to Nixon, September 3, 1969 (WHSF, Krogh, box 57, NP); Krogh, "Memorandum for the Student / Young People File," August 22, 1969 (WHSF, Krogh, box 57, NP).

3. Krogh to Ehrlichman, August 13, 1969 (WHSF, Krogh, box 57, NP); Chester Finn to Dick Blumenthal, John Campbell and Krogh, August 1969 (WHSF, Krogh, box 57, NP).

4. Huston to Haldeman, August 8, 1969 (WHSF, Krogh, box 66, NP); Krogh to Ehrlichman, September 12, 1969 (WHSF, Krogh, box 57, NP).

5. *NYT,* September 21, 1969.

6. White House intern to Krogh, August 23, 1969 (WHSF, Krogh, box 57, NP); Todd Hullin to Krogh, September 17, 1969 (WHSF, Krogh, box 57, NP); Bill Gavin to Krogh et al., September 15, 1969 (WHSF, Krogh, box 57, NP); Wilkinson to Cole, August 25, 1969 (WHSF, Krogh, box 57, NP); Campbell to Krogh, August 4, 1969 (WHSF, Krogh, box 57, NP); Keogh to staff secretary, August 26, 1969 (WHSF, Krogh, box 57, NP); Huston to Gavin, September 16, 1969 (WHSF, Krogh, box 57, NP).

7. Moynihan to Nixon, August 19, 1969 (WHSF, Krogh, box 57, NP).

8. Oudes, 56; Jonathan Rose to Krogh, September 22, 1969 (WHSF, Krogh, box 57, NP).

9. Moynihan to Nixon, August 19, 1969 (WHSF, Krogh, box 57, NP).

10. Price, 155–56.

11. Charles Rogovin to Mitchell, July 18, 1969 (WHSF, Dean, box 16, NP); Butterfield to Haldeman, July 1, 1969 (WHSF, Krogh, box 66, NP).

12. Gene Knorr to Krogh, October 13, 1969 (WHSF, Krogh, box 21, NP); Lukas, 10; Dean interview; Magruder, 66; Bernstein and Woodward, 290–92.

13. Moynihan to Nixon, August 19, 1969 (WHSF, Krogh, box 57, NP); Oudes, 56; *Time,* August 29, 1969; *Washington Star,* September 9, 1969; *NYT,* October 23, 1969.

14. *I. F. Stone's Weekly,* September 22, 1969; Price interview.

15. Peck interview; Schell, 60–62; Ehrlichman to Peter Flanigan, August 25, 1969 (WHSF, Krogh, box 59, NP).

16. Assorted Nixon administration documents (WHSF, Dean, box 16, "Campus Disorder (1)" folder, Krogh, box 57, "Youth" folders, NP).

17. *WP,* August 26, 1969.

18. Huston to Haldeman, August 8, 1969 (WHSF, Krogh, box 66, NP). See also Ehrlichman to Garment, October 1, 1969 (WHSF, Ehrlichman, box 50, NP); Finn, "Toward a National Youth Policy," September 15, 1969 (WHSF, Krogh, box 66, NP); *WP,* May 14, 1970.

19. Huston to Haldeman, August 8, 1969 (WHSF, Krogh, box 66, NP). Haldeman passed Huston's memo to Ehrlichman, commenting, "while perhaps a bit strong, [it] does make some valid points" (Haldeman to Ehrlichman, August 12, 1969, WHSF, Krogh, box 66, NP).

20. Huston to Nixon, August 18, 1969 (WHCF, HU, box 24, NP). Apparently aware of his growing stature with the president, Huston, the man of superior "toughness and brains" (as Nixon earlier wrote), signed the memo, simply, "Huston."

21. Krogh to Campbell, July 24, 1969 (WHSF, Krogh, box 57, NP); *WP,* May 14, 1970; Blumenthal to Krogh, October 1969 (WHSF, Krogh, box 57, NP).

22. *WP,* August 26, 1969; Cole to Ehrlichman, September 16, 1969 (WHSF, Krogh, box 66, NP).

23. Magruder, 73; Charlie McWhorter to Klein, September 26, 1969 (WHSF, Krogh, box 66, NP); Huston, "Intelligence Memorandum No. 3," No-

vember 3, 1969 (WHSF, Ehrlichman, box 20, NP); internal Department of Interior memo, October 2, 1969 (WHSF, Dean, box 81, NP); McWhorter to Klein, September 25, 1969 (WHSF, Krogh, box 66, NP); Ehrlichman interview.

24. Ehrlichman interviews; Marshall Green interview; Haldeman interviews; Huston to Nixon, August 18, 1969 (WHCF, HU, box 24, NP).

25. Wilkinson to Kissinger, July 7, 1969 (WHCF, HU, box 24, NP).

26. Price interview; Marshall Green interview; Ehrlichman interview.

27. Haldeman interviews; Lake interview; Lynn interview; Huston to Nixon, August 18, 1969 (WHCF, HU, box 24, NP). On the administration's perception that the Moratorium and Mobe protests were "part of the same cloth," see also Nixon, *RN*, 412; Dwight Chapin to Haldeman, July 4, 1970 (WHCF, HU, box 32, NP), where Chapin refers to November 15 as "Moratorium Day"; and note 30 below. Pat Buchanan did distinguish between the two protests, however. He called November 15 the "hard-core demonstration" (Buchanan to Cole, October 14, 1969, WHCF, HU, box 31, NP).

28. Action Memorandum to Ehrlichman, June 24, 1969 (WHSF, Krogh, box 57, NP); John Brown to Cole, August 19, 1969 (WHCF, HU, box 24, NP); Krogh to Clark Mollenhoff, September 25, 1969 (WHSF, Krogh, box 57, NP). On official discussions on the need for a game plan, see also Krogh to Campbell, July 23, July 24, 1969 (WHSF, Krogh, box 57, NP).

29. Wilkinson to Kissinger, July 7, 1969 (WHCF, HU, box 24, NP); Wilkinson to Cole, August 22, 1969 (WHSF, Krogh, box 57, NP).

30. Garment used the name "Mobilization" to refer to the Moratorium, another reflection of the administration's view that the two protests were cut from the same cloth.

31. Nixon to Ehrlichman, July 9, 1969 (WHSFCF, ND, box 42, NP); Ehrlichman memo, September 1969 (WHSF, Ehrlichman, box 50, NP); Oudes, 45, 53; "Talking Paper: Notes re October 15," September 30, 1969 (WHSF, Haldeman, box 121, NP); Garment to Haldeman, September 27, 1969 (WHSF, Krogh, box 66, NP). Garment decided upon reflection that his analysis of public opinion was "a trifle bullish," although he stood by "the basic idea" (note in bottom margin).

32. *NYT*, October 15, 1969; Action Memorandum to Bryce Harlow, Kissinger, and Ehrlichman, October 2, 1969 (WHSFCF, HU, box 36, NP); Lyn Nofziger to Harlow, September 29, 1969 (WHSF, Haldeman, box 121, NP).

33. Henry Kissinger, Pat Buchanan, and other officials fed propaganda to *Newsday*'s Nick Timmisch promoting the theme that a hasty U.S. withdrawal would lead to mass slaughter. Thus nourished, Timmisch wrote an article on the danger. Nixon ordered his aides to give the article "the widest possible distribution" (Kissinger to Haldeman, October 9, 1969, WHSFCF, HU, box 36, NP; Buchanan to Cole, October 14, 1969, WHCF, HU, box 31, NP; Cole to Jeb Magruder, October 20, 1969, WHCF, HU, box 31, NP).

34. Buchanan to Nixon, September 30, 1969 (WHSFCF, HU, box 36, NP); Haldeman to Harlow, Kissinger, and Ehrlichman, October 1, 1969 (WHSFCF,

HU, box 36, NP); Haldeman to Nofziger, October 10, 1969 (WHSFCF, HU, box 36, NP); Nofziger to Cole, October 9, 1969 (WHSFCF, HU, box 36, NP); *WP*, October 1, 1969; Oudes, 16; Magruder, 79–80, 84; Action Memorandum to Klein, September 30, 1969 (WHSFCF, HU, box 36, NP).

35. Oudes, 44–45. Nixon's memo to Haldeman was one of eight to him that day dealing with public relations. According to Magruder, they had all been "inspired by" the upcoming Moratorium and Mobe protests (Magruder, 73).

36. "Talking Paper: Notes re October 15," September 30, 1969 (WHSF, Haldeman, box 121, NP); Tom Whitehead to Flanigan, September 29, 1969 (WHSF, Haldeman, box 121, NP).

37. McWhorter to Klein, September 25, 1969 (WHSF, Krogh, box 66, NP); McWhorter to Klein, September 26, 1969 (WHSF, Krogh, box 66, NP).

38. Nofziger to Harlow, September 29, 1969 (WHSF, Haldeman, box 121, NP); Whitehead to Flanigan, September 29, 1969 (WHSF, Haldeman, box 121, NP).

39. *NYT*, September 27, 1969; Price interview; Hawk interview; Morrison and Morrison, 134; *WP*, September 28, 1969; Brown interview.

40. Price interview; Krogh to Ehrlichman, October 6, 1969 (WHSF, Krogh, box 57, NP); Knorr to Krogh, October 13, 1969 (WHSF, Krogh, box 21, NP); Ehrlichman's notes of October 1, 1969, meeting with Nixon (WHSF, Ehrlichman, box 3, NP); Ehrlichman to Nixon, October 10, 1969 (WHSF, Ehrlichman, box 51, NP).

41. *WP*, October 14, 1969; Price, 158; Lake interview; Price interview.

42. Hurwitz, 40; DeBenedetti, *American Ordeal*, 253; Paul Hoffman, 34; Halstead, 484; Huston to Nixon, August 18, 1969 (WHCF, HU, box 24, NP); Hullin to Caulfield, October 9, 1969 (WHSF, Ehrlichman, box 50, NP); Justice Department's "Daily Intelligence Summaries" on Moratorium and New Mobe, October 1969 (WHSF, Dean, box 81, NP); Huston's "Intelligence Memoranda," October–November 1969 (WHSF, Ehrlichman, box 20, NP); assorted Moratorium and Mobe leaflets (WHSF, Dean, box 82, Ehrlichman, box 20, NP). Not all of the administration's intelligence on the protests was on the mark, though. Jack Caulfield erroneously reported to Ehrlichman not only that initial planning of the Moratorium took place in July in New York, but that the "heaviest outlay of funds" came from the SWP (Caulfield to Ehrlichman, October 10, 1969, WHSFPOF, box 3, NP). In reality, the SWP considered the Moratorium a Democratic Party plot to derail the antiwar movement.

43. "Talking Paper: Notes re October 15," September 30, 1969 (WHSF, Haldeman, box 121, NP); Cole to Nofziger, October 10, 1969 (WHCF, HU, box 31, NP); Caulfield to Ehrlichman, October 10, 1969 (WHCF, HU, box 31, NP).

44. *WP*, October 14, 1969; Hersh, *Price of Power*, 127; *NYT*, September 14, 1969; Paul Hoffman, 125.

45. James Turner report on October 11, 1969, administration meeting (WHSF, Dean, box 81, NP); permit for October 15, 1969, protest in Washington (WHSF, Dean, box 81, NP); Gulley, 165–66; Ehrlichman interview.

46. Nixon, *RN*, 393–96, 399. According to Kissinger, "the train has left the station and is heading down the track" was "a favorite Nixon phrase" (Kissinger, *White House Years*, 304).

47. Hersh, *Price of Power*, 124.

48. Joe Urgo interview.

49. Hersh, *Price of Power*, 120, 126, 129; Morris, 164.

50. Hersh, *Price of Power*, 127; Morris, 164.

51. Watts interview; Hersh, *Price of Power*, 127.

52. Morris interview.

53. Morris, 165; Lynn interview.

54. Morris interview.

55. Lynn interview; Morris, 165–66; Nixon, *RN*, 398–99; "Homefront USA," PBS television program.

56. Hersh, *Price of Power*, 49.

57. Ellsberg interviews.

58. Salisbury, 70; Lukas, 93; Shanks, 122.

59. Wenner, 3–4; Salisbury, 71–72.

60. Ellsberg interview; Wenner, 5, 10–11; Ellsberg, 35.

61. Ellsberg, 28–35; Ellsberg interview.

62. Ellsberg interview; Ellsberg, 38–39.

63. Ellsberg interviews; Ellsberg, 38.

64. Ellsberg interviews; *NYT*, October 9, 1969; Daniel Ellsberg to Charles Bolté, September 23, 1969 (copy in author's files).

65. Wenner, 31–32; Hersh, *Price of Power*, 326; Shanks, 137; Salisbury, 73.

66. Ellsberg interviews.

67. Paul Hoffman, 35; *Life*, June 27, 1969; Halberstam, *Powers That Be*, 484–85.

68. Paul Hoffman, 39, 46–47.

69. Rosenberg, Verba and Converse, 41; *LAT*, August 23, 1969.

70. Paul Hoffman, 36–37; Hersh, *Price of Power*, 123; Peck interview.

71. Halstead, 480; Paul Hoffman, 36, 37, 63; *NYT*, October 11, 1969; Laird interview.

72. *NYT*, October 15, 1969; *WP*, October 16, 1969; Haldeman's notes of October 14, 1969, meeting with Nixon (WHSF, Haldeman, box 40, NP); Small, *Johnson, Nixon and Doves*, 184. In Haldeman's notes of meetings with Nixon, he sometimes abbreviated words. For the sake of clarity, I have used the complete words. I have also inserted commas and periods. The same editing has been applied to John Ehrlichman's notes of meetings with Nixon.

73. *Chicago Tribune*, October 7, 1969; Jacobs, 196.

74. Jacobs, 199–200, 254–55.

75. Ibid., 201; Morrison and Morrison, 306; Sale, 604.

76. Delgado was a Chicano boy who had once derailed a train with a piece of concrete and was now an offbeat Weatherman folk hero. Using his name

afforded the Weathermen a few smug laughs and would, it was hoped, help keep Jones from getting an "incitement to riot" charge (Ayers interview).

77. Sale, 605–6; Jeff Jones interview.

78. Jacobs, 201–2, 256; Dellinger, *More Power,* 150.

79. Jeff Jones interview; Sale, 607–8; Ayers interview.

80. Sale, 609.

81. Jacobs, 270; Sale, 610–11.

82. Ayers interview; Jacobs, 290; Sale, 604.

83. Sale, 612; Ayers interview; Jacobs, 213; Jeff Jones interview.

84. Jeff Jones interview; Ayers interview.

85. Jeff Jones interview; Morrison and Morrison, 313; Gavin to Haldeman, October 16, 1969 (WHSF, Haldeman, box 130, NP); Sale, 613–14; Dellinger, *More Power,* 129.

86. Gitlin, *Sixties,* 396; Calvert interview.

87. Ayers interview; Jeff Jones interview.

88. Sale, 624; Jeff Jones interview; Ayers interview.

89. *NYT,* October 15, 1969; Hartsough interview; *WP,* October 15, 1969; Haldeman's notes of October 15, 1969, meeting with Nixon (WHSF, Haldeman, box 40, NP).

90. *WP,* October 16, 1969; VMC, "Broad Cross Section of Moratorium Day Activities," October 1969 (VMC papers, SHSW); Paul Hoffman, 110, 122–23.

91. *WP,* October 16, 1969; Paul Hoffman, 86–87; Brown interview.

92. VMC, "Broad Cross Section," October 1969 (VMC papers, SHSW); Paul Hoffman, 107–8.

93. *WP,* October 16, 1969; Nicholas J. Oganovic to Heads of Departments and Independent Establishments, November 20, 1969 (WHSF, Dean, box 83, NP).

94. *WP,* October 16, 1969; Halstead, 488–89; Paul Hoffman, 86, 88–89.

95. Hurwitz, 143–44; Camejo interview.

96. *WP,* October 16, 1969; Paul Hoffman, 91–92; Dean memo, early November 1969 (WHSF, Dean, box 82, NP); Dean interview.

97. Watts interview; Hersh, *Price of Power,* 131.

98. Lake interview; Lake and Lake, 26–31.

99. Marshall Green interview; Price interview; Haldeman interview; *SFC,* October 16, 1969; Ehrlichman interviews; Small, *Johnson, Nixon and Doves,* 172; Ziegler interview; Paul Hoffman, 96.

100. Small, *Johnson, Nixon and Doves,* 185.

101. *SFC,* October 16, 1969; Ferber interview.

102. *WP,* October 16, 1969; "Homefront USA," PBS television program.

103. Hallin, 198; *WP,* October 15, 1969; Gitlin, *Whole World,* 219–21; Hawk interview; Paul Hoffman, 80–81.

104. Hawk interview; Brown interview.

105. *WP,* October 16, 1969; Paul Hoffman, 92.

106. The administration often provided walkie-talkies to protesters to aid

intelligence gathering and crowd control (Dean to Ehrlichman and Krogh, May 16, 1972, WHSF, Dean, box 84, NP; Ehrlichman interview).

107. Ehrlichman to Krogh, October 15, 1969 (WHSF, Ehrlichman, box 50, NP); Krogh to Campbell, July 23, 1969 (WHSF, Krogh, box 57, NP); Haldeman interview; Ehrlichman interview.

108. Ziegler interview.

109. Small, *Johnson, Nixon and Doves*, 185; Moynihan to Nixon, October 16, 1969 (WHSF, Haldeman, box 130, NP).

110. Buchanan to Nixon, October 17, 1969 (WHSF, Haldeman, box 130, NP).

111. Huston to Haldeman, October 16, 1969 (WHSF, Haldeman, box 130, NP); Ehrlichman to Krogh, April 21, 1970 (WHSF, Ehrlichman, box 52, NP).

112. Nixon, *RN*, 401–3. Nixon was apparently feeling better earlier in the day, however. "Participation in M-day—very low," Haldeman's notes of a meeting with the president read. "Not successful across country" (WHSF, Haldeman, box 40, NP). It seems unlikely that Nixon maintained this belief for very long, though, if at all.

113. Ellsberg interview; Morris interview; Laird interviews.

114. Morris interview; Lynn interview. See also Morris, 165–66.

115. Morris interview; Laird interview; Haldeman interviews; Price interview.

116. Lake interview.

117. Haldeman to William Rogers, October 16, 1969 (WHSF, Haldeman, box 130, NP); Moynihan to Nixon, October 16, 1969 (WHSF, Haldeman, box 130, NP); Kissinger, *White House Years*, 300.

118. Gavin to Haldeman, October 16, 1969 (WHSF, Haldeman, box 130, NP).

119. Huston to Haldeman, October 16, 1969 (WHSF, Haldeman, box 130, NP).

120. Chapin to Haldeman, October 16, 1969 (WHSFCF, HU, box 36, NP).

121. Magruder, 115; Morris, 168; Haldeman's notes of October 16, 1969, meeting with Nixon (WHSF, Haldeman, box 40, NP); Haldeman to Rogers, October 16, 1969 (WHSF, Haldeman, box 130, NP); Huston to Haldeman, October 16, 1969 (WHSF, Haldeman, box 130, NP). In John Ehrlichman's notes of a discussion he had with Nixon about "mobilization tactics" on October 21, he jotted, "separate the good, the bad" (WHSF, Ehrlichman, box 3, NP).

122. Ehrlichman, 265; Haldeman interview; Huston to Haldeman, October 16, 1969 (WHSF, Haldeman, box 130, NP); Klein to Nixon, October 17, 1969 (WHCF, HU, box 31, NP); Lawrence Higby to Magruder, October 21, 1969 (WHSF, Haldeman, box 208, NP). Magruder writes that Chapin's game plan, which emphasized leaning on Congress and the media, both directly and through public pressure orchestrated by the administration, was "largely followed" by the White House (Magruder, 83).

123. Schell, 56–57, 62. Dean Acheson was less proud of the vice president.

The elder statesman advised Nixon that "he would do well to bench Agnew" (Kissinger to Nixon, October 23, 1969, WHSFCF, HU, box 36, NP).

124. Cole to Harlow, October 24, 1969 (WHCF, HU, box 31, NP); *Congressional Record*, November 4, 1969 (copy in WHSF, Dean, box 82, NP). Ehrlichman's notes of a meeting with Nixon on November 6 contain the notation, "Reds in Mobe" (WHSF, Ehrlichman, box 3, NP).

125. *WP*, November 7, 1969; Dean press release, November 6, 1969 (WHSF, Dean, box 81, NP); Richard Harris, 162–63; Huston to Ehrlichman, November 20, 1969 (WHSF, Ehrlichman, box 20, NP).

126. Assorted Nixon administration documents (WHSF, Dean, box 82, "Demonstration—Nov. 1969 (2)" folder, NP); Dean interview; Moynihan to Nixon, October 16, 1969 (WHSF, Haldeman, box 130, NP); Huston to Ehrlichman, November 20, 1969 (WHSF, Ehrlichman, box 20, NP). Moynihan was apparently less than confident that White House officials would act to minimize, rather than fuel, the violence. He bluntly advised Nixon, "I would get some *smart* people working on this one" (Moynihan to Nixon, October 16, 1969).

127. Lyttle, "Washington Action," 1–14; Dean interview.

128. *WP*, November 12, 1969; Richard Harris, 163; Lyttle, "Washington Action," 14.

129. Higby to Magruder, October 21, 1969 (WHSF, Haldeman, box 208, NP); Chapin to Haldeman, October 16, 1969 (WHSFCF, HU, box 36, NP); Huston to Haldeman, October 16, 1969 (WHSF, Haldeman, box 130, NP); Haldeman interview; Paul Hoffman, 137.

130. Morris interview; *WP*, November 4, 1969.

131. Brown interview; Halstead, 494.

132. Haldeman interview; Haldeman's notes of November 3, 1969, meeting with Nixon (WHSF, Haldeman, box 40, NP); Kissinger, *White House Years*, 307; Magruder, 53–54; Hersh, *Price of Power*, 92–93n.

133. Lake interview.

134. *WP*, November 10, 12, 1969; Oudes, 65–68; Paul Hoffman, 146.

135. Schell, 67–69; Paul Hoffman, 145; minutes of October 31, 1969, meeting between Mobe organizers and Justice Department officials (WHSF, Dean, box 82, NP).

136. Brown, 36; Ellsberg interviews; Becker interview; phone conversation with Becker.

137. *WP*, November 12, 13, 1969; Paul Hoffman, 144; Ehrlichman interviews; Gulley, 165–66; Ehrlichman to Richard Kleindienst, November 8, 1969 (WHSF, Ehrlichman, box 50, NP); Huston to Ehrlichman, October 29, 1969 (WHSF, Krogh, box 66, NP).

138. Hersh, *My Lai*, 4, 135, 137–41, 151–58; Morris interview; Barry interview.

139. Watts interview; Chapin to Haldeman, December 2, 1969 (WHCF, HU, box 32, NP); Hersh, *Price of Power*, 135; Robert Brown to Butterfield, December 10, 1969 (WHSFCF, ND, box 43, NP).

140. Hawk interview.

141. Brown, 36; Brown interview; Halstead, 510.

142. Minutes of October 23, 1969, meeting between Mobe leaders and Justice Department officials (WHSF, Dean, box 82, NP); Lyttle, "Washington Action," 30–32; *WP*, November 14, 1969; Hartsough interview.

143. Zaroulis and Sullivan, 283; Brown interview.

144. Paul Hoffman, 156; *WP*, November 14, 1969; Lyttle, "Washington Action," 11.

145. Gitlin, *Sixties*, 394; Paul Hoffman, 166–69; Hawk interview; Jeff Jones interview; Jacobs, 276.

146. Paul Hoffman, 161.

147. *WP*, November 16, 1969; Halstead, 504; Cortright, 62.

148. Halstead, 516; *WP*, November 16, 1969; Hawk interview; "Nixon," PBS television program ("The American Experience" series).

149. *WP*, November 16, 1969; Gulley, 165–67; Donner, 307.

150. *WP*, November 16, 1969.

151. Ibid.

152. Morris interview; Watts interview; Lynn interview; Caulfield to Ehrlichman, November 19, 1969 (WHCF, HU, box 24, NP); Huston to Ehrlichman, November 20, 1969 (WHSF, Ehrlichman, box 20, NP). Official underestimation of the size of the demonstration was largely a result of relying on counts of buses and trains reserved by protesters. "We all learned something about the futility of this exercise," Huston noted, "but more importantly we learned that the peace movement has a built-in crowd mobilizer which cannot be quantified through traditional investigative means" (Huston to Ehrlichman, November 20, 1969).

153. Morris, 170; Morris interview.

154. Watts interview; Kissinger, *White House Years*, 302; Morris interview.

155. Marshall Green interview.

156. The official erroneously remembered the demonstration as taking place in October (Kutler, 78–79).

157. *WP*, November 16, 1969; Watts interview.

158. *WP*, November 16, 1969.

159. *WP*, November 17, 1969; Paul Hoffman, 199; Krogh to Dean, December 4, 1969 (WHSF, Dean, box 82, NP); Action Memorandum to Magruder, December 2, 1969 (WHCF, HU, box 24, NP); Magruder to John Brown, December 18, 1969 (WHCF, HU, box 24, NP).

160. Huston to Ehrlichman, November 20, 1969 (WHSF, Ehrlichman, box 20, NP).

161. *WP*, November 18, 1969.

162. Oudes, 68–69; Watts interview; Dean to Krogh, April 24, 1970 (WHSF, Dean, box 82, NP). Lyttle's report was the above-cited "Washington Action" pamphlet.

163. Hoover, "An Open Letter to the Youth of America," December 24, 1969 (WHSF, Krogh, box 18, NP).

164. Ken Smith to Krogh, fall 1969 (WHSF, Krogh, box 57, NP).

165. Dellinger, Stewart Meacham and Cora Weiss, "Dear Friend," November 15, 1969 (New Mobe papers, SHSW); Peck interview; Peck, "Perspective and Proposal for the New Mobilization Committee," December 2, 1969 (New Mobe papers, SHSW).

166. Halstead, 522; VMC, "Dear Friend," January 2, 1970 (VMC papers, SHSW); DeBenedetti, *American Ordeal*, 267; Brown, 38; Berkowitz, 6; Buchanan to Nixon, November 30, 1969 (WHSFPOF, box 3, NP); Hawk interview; Dowd interview.

167. Lyttle interview; Peck interview; Becker interview.

168. Halstead interview; Zaroulis and Sullivan, 298; Peck interview; minutes of December 13–14, 1969, New Mobe steering committee meeting (New Mobe papers, SHSW).

169. Halstead interview.

170. Dellinger interview; Churchill and Vander Wall, 60.

171. Dellinger interview; Butterfield to Nixon, December 19, 1969 (WHCF, HU, box 24, NP).

172. Brown interview; Brown, 36, 38–42; Hawk interview.

173. Brown interview; VMC, "Dear Friend," January 2, 1970 (VMC papers, SHSW); VMC, "Dear Friend," February 13, 1970 (VMC papers, SHSW); Hawk interview.

174. Sale, 618, 632–35; Clavir and Spitzer, xi.

175. Caulfield to Ehrlichman, November 19, 1969 (WHCF, HU, box 24, NP); Chapin to Haldeman, December 2, 1969 (WHCF, HU, box 32, NP).

176. Sale, 616–17, 622–23.

177. Ibid., 626–28; Jacobs, 341–50; Dellinger, *More Power*, 152–53; Gitlin, *Sixties*, 404.

178. Gitlin, *Sixties*, 400; Sale, 629; Jeff Jones interview.

CHAPTER 8. 1970

1. Brown, 38–39, 42; CALCAV, "Issues and Actions," January 26, 1970 (CALCAV papers, SHSW); Dancis interview; Dowd interview.

2. Peck interview; Hurwitz, 182–83; Halstead, 525.

3. CALCAV, "Lent-Passover Fast," February 1970 (CALCAV papers, SHSW); Hall, 98; CALCAV, "Local Organizing Project," November 1969 (CALCAV papers, SHSW); CALCAV document, early 1970 (CALCAV papers, SHSW).

4. AFSC document, March 1970 (AFSC papers, BLUCB); *NYT*, March 20, 1970; Heath, xxiii–xxiv (Heath mistakenly records that the antidraft protests took place in March 1969.); VMC, "Nationwide 'We Won't Go' Statement," February 1970 (VMC papers, SHSW); Brown interview.

5. VVAW, "VVAW History," 1972 (VVAW papers, SHSW); Barry interview.

6. Cortright, 17, 107–9; Heinl, 7; Urgo interview.

7. Luce interview; NYT, December 25, 1969; Cortright, 36, 39–40, 47.

8. Halstead, 527–31; Kissinger interview; unidentified author, "SDS Position Paper," February 1970 (SMC papers, SHSW); Gurewitz interview.

9. NYT, April 16, 1970; Hurwitz, 189; Zaroulis and Sullivan, 312; Halstead, 532.

10. Hersh, Price of Power, 196n; Nixon, RN, 447–48; Ehrlichman, 62; Oudes, 72; Ehrlichman's notes of June 18, 1970, meeting with Nixon (WHSF, Ehrlichman, box 3, NP).

11. Zaroulis and Sullivan, 301; NYT, February 22, March 12, 13, 1970.

12. Sale, 647; NYT, March 13, 1970; Ayers interview.

13. NYT, March 12, 1970; Sale, 3–5; Gitlin, Sixties, 401; Morrison and Morrison, 319.

14. NYT, March 12, 1970.

15. Ayers interview; Jeff Jones interview.

16. Berrigan interview; Lockwood, 122–23, 133; Lynd and Ferber, 218.

17. NYT, April 22, 1970; Berrigan interview; Lockwood, 117, 129.

18. NYT, April 20, 1970; Brown, 42; Sam Brown et al., "Dear Friend," April 20, 1970 (VMC papers, SHSW); Hawk interview; Brown interview.

19. Kissinger, White House Years, 437; Berkowitz, 6; Oudes, 98.

20. Haldeman to Colson, March 2, 1970 (WHSF, Colson, box 124, NP); Colson to Haldeman, March 12, 1970 (WHSF, Colson, box 124, NP); Magruder to Colson, March 17, 1970 (WHSF, Colson, box 124, NP); Robert Odle to Cole, April 3, 1970 (WHSF, Colson, box 124, NP); Magruder to Haldeman, April 9, 1970 (WHSF, Colson, box 124, NP); Haldeman to Colson et al., March 12, 1970 (WHSF, Colson, box 124, NP); Odle to Magruder, April 21, 1970 (WHSF, Colson, box 124, NP); Oudes, 104; Magruder to Haldeman, April 30, 1970 (WHSF, Colson, box 125, NP).

21. Magruder to Haldeman, April 9, 1970 (WHSF, Colson, box 124, NP).

22. Magruder, 97–100.

23. Colson to Haldeman, February 5, 1970 (WHSF, Colson, box 120, NP); Colson to David Bradshaw, February 9, 1970 (WHSF, Colson, box 120, NP).

24. Colson to Haldeman, February 5, 1970 (WHSF, Colson, box 120, NP); Odle to Colson and Magruder, April 29, 1970 (WHSF, Colson, box 120, NP); Colson to Bradshaw, February 9, 1970 (WHSF, Colson, box 120, NP); unidentified author (probably Colson), "Proposed Budget for Expanded Citizens Committee for Peace with Freedom in Vietnam," no date (WHSF, Colson, box 120, NP).

25. Colson to Frank Barnett, January 16, 1970 (WHSF, Colson, box 33, NP); Colson to William Henderson, April 3, 1970 (WHSF, Colson, box 33, NP); Henderson to Colson, March 17, 1970 (WHSF, Colson, box 33, NP).

26. Colson to Haldeman, February 5, 1970 (WHSF, Colson, box 120, NP); Lukas, 59–60.

27. Oudes, 103–4.

28. *NYT*, April 12, 1970.

29. Huston to Haldeman, March 12, 1970 (WHSF, Haldeman, box 152, NP).

30. Moynihan to Haldeman, March 12, 1970 (WHSF, Haldeman, box 152, NP).

31. *NYT*, April 12, 1970.

32. Haldeman, 107–8; Chapin to Haldeman, April 24, 1970 (WHSFCF, ND, box 41, NP).

33. Churchill and Vander Wall, 229; Kleindienst to Robert Mayo, no date (early 1970) (WHSF, Dean, box 16, NP); Oudes, 106; John Brown to Ehrlichman, February 18, 1970 (WHSFCF, ND, box 42, NP).

34. Nixon, *RN*, 448; Kissinger, *White House Years*, 477–81; Oudes, 97.

35. Hersh, *Price of Power*, 168–71.

36. Dowd interview; Chomsky, *At War With Asia*, 268n.

37. Kissinger, *White House Years*, 483, 495; Hersh, *Price of Power*, 187–88; Haldeman, 26; Moorer interview; Marshall Green interview.

38. Kissinger, *White House Years*, 489, 498; Marshall Green interview; Nixon, *No More Vietnams*, 149–50.

39. Hedrick Smith, 344, 347, 353; Nixon, *RN*, 450; Marshall Green interview.

40. Morris interview; Lake interview; Watts interview; Hersh, *Price of Power*, 108–10, 117, 188, 396; Lynn interview; Lukas, 47.

41. Kissinger, *White House Years*, 497; Morris interview; Watts interview; Hersh, *Price of Power*, 190–91; Moorer interview.

42. Oudes, 137–38.

43. Nixon, *RN*, 449–51; Kissinger, *White House Years*, 491, 503; Ehrlichman interview; Marshall Green interview; Morris interview.

44. Kissinger, *White House Years*, 498, 503; Morris, 147, 174.

45. Gurewitz interview; Halstead interview.

46. Gurewitz interview; Halstead, 536; Halstead interview.

47. Becker interview.

48. Nixon, *RN*, 451; *Public Papers*, 405–10; Hedrick Smith, 345.

49. Peterson and Bilorusky, 2, 5; *NYT*, May 2, 3, 4, 1970; Urgo interview; Morrison and Morrison, 163; DeBenedetti, *American Ordeal*, 284.

50. Laird interview; Kissinger, *White House Years*, 506; Marshall Green interviews.

51. Marshall Green interview.

52. Ehrlichman interview; Kissinger, *Years of Upheaval*, 93–94; Resor interview.

53. Nixon, *RN*, 453–54; Hersh, *Price of Power*, 192–93; Laird interview; Westmoreland, 388–89; *NYT*, May 2, 1970; Marshall Green interviews.

54. J. V. Brennan to Rose Woods, May 4, 1970 (WHSFPPF, box 11, NP); Oudes, 124–25; Haldeman's notes of May 1, 1970, meetings with Nixon (WHSF, Haldeman, box 41, NP).

55. So much so that Daniel Patrick Moynihan could bluntly apprise Nixon that years of public perceptions of presidential lying about Vietnam "seemed to culminate in your April 30 address. Support for the address was extremely weak by any normal standard. The problem . . . was not that the public objected to the Cambodian operation per se, but rather that *almost no one believed it would be no more than you said it would be*" (Moynihan to Nixon, June 1, 1970, WHSFCF, SP, box 60, NP).

56. George Bell to Haldeman, May 1, 1970 (WHSF, Colson, box 37, NP); Magruder, 113; Haldeman's notes of April 30, May 2, May 4, 1970, meetings with Nixon (WHSF, Haldeman, box 41, NP); Safire, 190; *NYT*, May 1, 2, 3, 1970; Rosenberg, Verba and Converse, 26–29; "The President" (talking paper), late April or early May 1970 (WHSFCF, SP, box 60, NP).

57. Asked about official reactions to the Kent State killings, Roger Morris offered: "I never saw anywhere in the government a particular human sensitivity to the loss of life. . . . On the contrary, I saw men sit around tables and strive mightily to avoid any kind of human reaction . . . as being unmanly" (Morris interview).

58. Haldeman's notes of May 4, 1970, meeting with Nixon (WHSF, Haldeman, box 41, NP); Nixon, *RN*, 456–57; Colson, 34–35; Price interview; Dean interview; *Public Papers*, 411; *WP*, May 5, 1970.

59. *WP*, May 6, 7, 8, 1970; Peterson and Bilorusky, 1, 7, 15–20; Halstead interview; Alexander Heard to Nixon, June 19, 1970 (WHSFCF, HU, box 36, NP).

60. Peterson and Bilorusky, xi, 1, 4, 15–20; Lynd and Ferber, 291–93; Connelly and Dooley, 270; Sale, 637; *WP*, May 6, 7, 1970.

61. See pp. 325, 344–45, 478, and 508–9.

62. *NYT*, May 9, 10, 12, 27, July 22, 1970, September 24, 1981; *WP*, May 10, 1970; Schell, 101; Foner, 88–91; Ehrlichman interview; Haldeman interviews; Moynihan to Nixon, June 1, 1970 (WHSFCF, SP, box 60, NP).

63. *WP*, May 8, 9, 10, 1970; *NYT*, May 9, 10, 1970; Cortright, 66–68; Hawk interview.

64. Foner, 84–87; Halstead, 545–46; *WP*, May 8, 1970. Blue-collar workers lacking a high school education were apparently strongly opposed to the invasion of Cambodia (Hahn, 1192n).

65. Kissinger, *White House Years*, 512–13; Marshall Green interview; Hartsough interview. The White House aide Tom Pauken also perceived that the post-Cambodia demonstrations had affected Congress (Pauken to Dean, February 8, 1971, WHSF, Dean, box 83, NP).

66. The White House obtained a list, and identification, of the malcontents (Oudes, 143–44).

67. *WP*, May 7, 9, 1970; Colson, 36; Schell, 99; Haldeman's notes of May–June 1970 meetings with Nixon (WHSF, Haldeman, box 41, NP); Ehrlichman's notes of May–June 1970 meetings with Nixon (WHSF, Ehrlichman, box 3, NP); Ehrlichman memo on Hickel conversation, May 12, 1970 (WHSF, Ehrlichman, box 52, NP); Ehrlichman, 98–101.

68. Foner, 83; *WP*, May 8, 1970; Schell, 98; *NYT*, May 17, 1970; Krogh, "Memorandum on College Visits," May 28, 1970 (WHSF, Krogh, box 11, NP).

69. Peterson and Bilorusky, 1, 100; Dowd interview; Lew Jones interview; Camejo interview.

70. *WP*, May 10, 1970.

71. *WP*, May 8, 1970; Urgo interview.

72. Ehrlichman interview; Colson to Haldeman, May 6, 1970 (WHSF, Haldeman, box 152, NP); Klein to Nixon, May 6, 1970 (WHSF, Haldeman, box 152, NP); Nixon, *RN*, 457; Kissinger, *White House Years*, 509–14; *WP*, May 8, 1970; Marshall Green interview; Shawcross, 154; Magruder, 113.

73. Helms interview; Haldeman interview; Price interview.

74. Moorer interview. At the end of this interview, the author handed Moorer a release statement that had the author's Berkeley affiliation listed on it. The admiral had been informed of this affiliation in an earlier letter, but had apparently forgotten about it. "You're from Berkeley!" he exclaimed, angrily, as if he'd just been duped by a subversive himself.

75. Lynn interview.

76. *WP*, May 7, 8, 1970; Haldeman's notes of May 6, 1970, meetings with Nixon (WHSF, Haldeman, box 41, NP); Warren Parker to Haldeman, May 6, 1970 (WHSF, Haldeman, box 152, NP); Hess to Ehrlichman and Garment, May 6, 1970 (WHSF, Haldeman, box 152, NP); Klein to Nixon, May 6, 1970 (WHSF, Haldeman, box 152, NP); *NYT*, May 9, 10, 1970.

77. Klein to Nixon, May 6, 1970 (WHSF, Haldeman, box 152, NP); *WP*, May 7, 1970; Alexander to Nixon, May 7, 1970 (WHSF, Haldeman, box 152, NP); Hullin to Haldeman, May 7, 1970 (WHSF, Haldeman, box 152, NP).

78. Ehrlichman interview; Ehrlichman, comment under photo.

79. Ehrlichman interview; Nixon, *RN*, 458; Hersh, *Price of Power*, 196; *WP*, May 7, 1970; Landau, 94–99.

80. Magruder, 101; *WP*, May 9, 14, 1970; Haldeman interview.

81. Colson to Haldeman, May 6, 1970 (WHSF, Haldeman, box 152, NP); Klein to Nixon, May 6, 1970 (WHSF, Haldeman, box 152, NP).

82. Nixon, *RN*, 458–59; Nixon to Ehrlichman, June 16, 1969 (WHSFPOF, box 2, NP).

83. At the earlier congressional briefings, Nixon also stated that American troops would penetrate no further than nineteen miles into Cambodia. This was news to U.S. military leaders. "We had never—at least I had never—discussed twenty miles," Moorer recalled. "That more or less put a stopper on how many supplies we were going to capture" (Moorer interview).

84. *WP*, May 6, 9, 1970; *Public Papers*, 413–23; Kissinger, *White House Years*, 507, 516; Laird interview; Haldeman interview; Marshall Green interview; Ziegler interview; Helms interview; Lynn interview; Watts interview; Morris interview; Eagleburger interview; Westmoreland interview.

85. Haldeman interview; Morris interview.

86. Klein to Nixon, May 6, 1970 (WHSF, Haldeman, box 152, NP); assorted Nixon administration documents (WHSF, Colson, boxes 20, 37, 49, 112, 114,

125, NP); Foner, 88; Haldeman's notes of May 6, 7, 1970, meetings with Nixon (WHSF, Haldeman, box 41, NP); WP, May 8, 1970; NYT, May 9, 1970; Ehrlichman interview; Ehrlichman to Jerris Leonard, May 8, 1970 (WHCF, HU, box 32, NP). Herb Klein advised Nixon to order an independent investigation of Kent State, arguing along with another official that "in the eyes of the students, sending in the FBI is like asking police to look at police" (Klein to Nixon, May 6, 1970).

87. Magruder, 113; "Department of Defense Participation in Federal Activities Pertaining to the May 9 1970 Demonstration in Washington, D.C.," May 1970 (WHSF, Dean, box 82, NP); WP, May 7, 8, 1970; Ehrlichman interview.

88. NYT, May 10, 1970; Watts interview; Colson, 36; WP, May 9, 1970; Ehrlichman interview; Thomas Kelley to Kleindienst, May 28, 1970 (WHSF, Dean, box 82, NP).

89. "Department of Defense Participation," May 1970 (WHSF, Dean, box 82, NP); Colson, 36; WP, May 8, 9, 1970.

90. Price interview; Magruder, 114; Chapin to Haldeman, May 8, 1970 (WHSFCF, HU, box 36, NP).

91. Chapin to Haldeman, May 8, 1970 (WHSFCF, HU, box 36, NP).

92. Halstead interview; WP, May 8, 1970; Lyttle, May Ninth, 4, 6–7, 10; Peck interview.

93. Halstead interview; Lyttle, May Ninth, 4, 7, 19; Peck interview; Zaroulis and Sullivan, 323.

94. Nixon, RN, 459–60; Safire, 203–5; NYT, May 10, 1970; Ziegler interview; Price interview; Small, Johnson, Nixon and Doves, 206.

95. Safire, 205; Ehrlichman interview; Oudes, 129; Gulley, 167.

96. Oudes, 128, 133; WP, May 10, 1970; "Nixon," PBS television program; Lake interview.

97. Safire, 209–10; Oudes, 134; Haldeman interview; Ziegler interview; Price interview.

98. Marshall Green interview; NYT, May 10, 1970; Kissinger, White House Years, 514; interview with a Nixon administration official desiring anonymity.

99. Safire, 210–11; Price interview; Ehrlichman interview; Nixon, RN, 460.

100. Lyttle, May Ninth, 14; Halstead interview; Peck interview.

101. WP, May 10, 1970; NYT, May 10, 1970; Wicker interview; Lake and Lake, 30.

102. Lyttle, May Ninth, 6–7, 13–14; Dellinger interview; Zaroulis and Sullivan, 325; Lyttle interview; Peck interview.

103. Lyttle, May Ninth, 14; WP, May 10, 1970.

104. Colson, 37; "Nixon," PBS television program; Dean interview; Haldeman's notes of May 9, 1970, meeting with Nixon (WHSF, Haldeman, box 41, NP); Lyttle, May Ninth, 2; WP, May 10, 1970; Ehrlichman's notes of May 9, 1970, meeting with Nixon (WHSF, Ehrlichman, box 3, NP).

105. Dellinger, More Power, 142; Dellinger interview; Lyttle, May Ninth, 7, 13; Halstead interview; McAuliff interview; Peck interview; WP, May 10,

1970; *NYT*, May 10, 1970; Colson, 37; "Department of Defense Participation," May 1970 (WHSF, Dean, box 82, NP).

106. Lyttle, *May Ninth*, 6; Becker interview.

107. Peck interview.

108. Dellinger, *More Power*, 142–43; Lyttle, *May Ninth*, 19; Peck interview.

109. Peck interview; Halstead interview; Lyttle interview.

110. McReynolds interview.

111. Colson, 38.

112. Klein to Nixon, May 6, 1970 (WHSF, Haldeman, box 152, NP); Chapin to Haldeman, May 8, 1970 (WHSFCF, HU, box 36, NP); Magruder to Haldeman, June 4, 1970 (WHSFCF, HU, box 36, NP); Magruder to Haldeman and Klein, July 24, 1970 (WHSF, Haldeman, box 158, NP); Krogh, "Memorandum on College Visits," May 28, 1970 (WHSF, Krogh, box 11, NP); unidentified author, "Summary Report on Campus Visits," May 1970 (WHSFCF, HU, box 36, NP); Ehrlichman interview; Haldeman interview.

113. Ken BeLieu to Colson, June 4, 1970 (WHSF, Colson, box 114, NP); Colson to William Shockley, June 15, 1970 (WHSF, Colson, box 114, NP); Hullin to Magruder, May 27, 1970 (WHCF, HU, box 32, NP); action memorandum to Magruder, June 2, 1970 (WHSFCF, HU, box 36, NP); Colson to Magruder, May 20, 1970 (WHSF, Colson, box 120, NP); Odle to Colson, May 18, 1970 (WHSF, Colson, box 114, NP); Colson to Magruder, May 26, 1970 (WHSF, Colson, box 114, NP); Colson to Barnett, May 28, 1970 (WHSF, Colson, box 37, NP); Bell to Colson, May 13, 1970 (WHSF, Colson, box 125, NP); Foner, 89–91; *NYT*, May 21, July 22, 1970; Colson to Nixon, May 26, 1970 (WHSF, Colson, box 20, NP).

114. *NYT*, May 27, 1970; Colson to Bell, May 1970 (WHSF, Colson, box 95, NP); Colson, 38; Ehrlichman to Haldeman, May 23, 1970 (WHSF, Ehrlichman, box 52, NP); Colson to Nixon, May 26, 1970 (WHSF, Colson, box 20, NP). Haldeman's comments are on Colson's memo to Bell.

115. Magruder, 116; Moynihan to Nixon, June 1, 1970 (WHSFCF, SP, box 60, NP).

116. Ehrlichman's notes of May 21, June 18, 1970, meetings with Nixon (WHSF, Ehrlichman, box 3, NP); *WP*, June 19, 1970; *NYT*, June 15, 1970; Harry Dent to Nixon, June 17, 1970 (WHCF, FG 288, NP); Chapin to Haldeman, June 16, 1970 (WHCF, FG 288, NP).

117. Haldeman, 107–8; Lukas, 32–34; Gentry, 652–53.

118. Lukas, 33; Oudes, 125–26, 135.

119. Zaroulis and Sullivan, 336; Dellinger, *More Power*, 143; Dowd interview; New Mobe, "New Mobilization Committee Atlanta Resolutions, May 24, 1970" (New Mobe papers, SHSW).

120. Peck interview; Lyttle interview.

121. Lyttle interview.

122. McReynolds interview; Peck interview; Dowd interview.

123. Peck interview; New Mobe, "Atlanta Resolutions, May 24, 1970" (New Mobe papers, SHSW).

124. Dowd interview; Halstead, 568; Dellinger interview; Dellinger, *More Power*, 144; Halstead interview.

125. Peck interview.

126. New Mobe, "Atlanta Resolutions, May 24, 1970" (New Mobe papers, SHSW); *LAT*, August 28, 1970; Ron Walker to Haldeman, August 26, 1970 (WHCF, HU, box 32, NP); Halstead, 572; Heath, 194–204; DeBenedetti, *American Ordeal*, 286.

127. Three days earlier, Mitchell had announced that a federal grand jury in Detroit had indicted thirteen Weatherleaders on conspiracy charges.

128. Sale, 648; Jacobs, 376; Ayers interview.

129. Ayers interview; Hoffman, *Soon to Be*, 253; Hoffman interview.

130. Ehrlichman interview; Donner, 131, 160; Haldeman interview.

131. Urgo interview.

132. Ibid; Barry interview; VVAW, "Operation RAW," August 1970 (VVAW papers, SHSW).

133. VVAW, "History," 1972 (VVAW papers, SHSW); VVAW letter to peace groups, July 7, 1970 (VVAW papers, SHSW); VVAW, "A U.S. INFANTRY COMPANY JUST CAME THROUGH HERE!," September 1970 (VVAW papers, SHSW); Urgo interview; Barry interview.

134. Cortright, 68–69, 72–73; Cortright interview.

135. Cortright, 28, 29; Resor interview; *WP*, July 14, 1970; "Report of the Task Group Convened to Recommend Appropriate Revisions to DoD Policy on Drug Abuse," July 24, 1970 (Krogh note in margin) (WHSF, Krogh, box 43, NP).

136. Luce interview; Heath, 365–82.

137. Luce interview; *NYT*, July 7, 8, 9, 1970; *WP*, July 14, 1970. The same day that the South Vietnamese government announced the prisoner release, American peace activists led an antiwar demonstration in Saigon. Nixon saw a report of the demonstration on television and was not happy. He directed Kissinger to ferret out the identity of the agitators (Action Memorandum to Kissinger, July 14, 1970, WHCF, HU, box 32, NP).

138. Hersh, *Price of Power*, 328; Wenner, 5.

139. Wenner, 5–6.

140. Kissinger, *White House Years*, 968–69.

141. Klein, 285; Magruder to Haldeman and Klein, July 24, 1970 (WHSF, Haldeman, box 158, NP).

142. Magruder, 115; Nixon, *RN*, 490–91; Buchanan to Nixon, August 24, 1970 (WHSF, Haldeman, box 48, NP); Ehrlichman's notes of September 15, 1970, meeting with Nixon (WHSF, Ehrlichman, box 4, NP); Haldeman to Ehrlichman, September 11, 1970 (WHSFCF, HU, box 36, NP).

143. Magruder, 119–21.

144. Colson to Haldeman, August 12, 1970 (WHSF, Colson, box 123, NP);

Haldeman to Harlow et al., July 14, 1970 (WHSFCF, ND, box 42, NP); Gene Bradley to "Peter," August 18, 1970 (WHSF, Colson, box 36, NP); assorted other Nixon administration documents (WHSF, Colson, boxes 36, 37, 123, NP); *WP*, February 6, 1971.

145. Colson to Haldeman, August 12, 1970 (WHSF, Colson, box 123, NP); Klein, 123, 285–86; Colson to Timmons, May 6, 1971 (WHSF, Colson, box 129, NP).

146. Bradley to regional AWP chairmen, September 1, 1970 (WHSF, Colson, box 37, NP); Colson to Higby, September 8, 1970 (WHSF, Colson, box 36, NP); *WP*, February 6, 1971. Haldeman's "Damn Good" is in the margin of the memo from Colson to Higby. Colson also continued working with the American Friends of Vietnam over the summer. Though the group was "back to miniscule" and *"looking for funds,"* he wrote in his notes, it "has prestige as a hawk outfit" (WHSF, Colson, box 33, NP).

147. Hoover, "An Open Letter to College Students," September 21, 1970 (WHSF, Krogh, box 10, NP); Krogh to Magruder, Nofziger and Richard Moore, September 23, 1970 (WHSFCF, HU, box 36, NP); Krogh to Nofziger, September 23, 1970 (WHSF, Krogh, box 10, NP).

148. Gentry, 675; Donner, 178.

149. Heath, 180–93; Peck interview; Dellinger, *More Power*, 144; Dowd interview.

150. Walter Pietsch, "Dear Friends," September 1970 (PC papers, SHSW); Becker interview; Halstead, 582–83; Barry interview.

151. Halstead, 575; Peck interview; Lerner, 21.

152. Over half of the people on the FBI's list of fugitives were now youthful radicals (*NYT*, November 28, 1970).

153. *NYT*, October 9, 1970; Sale, 725; Ehrlichman's notes of October 9, 1970, meeting with Nixon (WHSF, Ehrlichman, box 4, NP); Dohrn, "Letter to the Movement: New Morning—Changing Weather," December 6, 1970 (*Liberation*, November 1970); unidentified author, "Analysis of Letter of Bernardine Dohrn," December 1970 (WHSF, Dean, box 83, NP); Dean to William Rehnquist, January 7, 1971 (WHSF, Dean, box 83, NP).

154. Peterson and Bilorusky, 80; Dellinger, "From Vietnam," 10; Schemmer, 164; Ellsberg interview.

155. Marshall Green interview.

156. Schell, 120; *WP*, September 17, October 31, 1970; *NYT*, September 27, 1970.

157. *NYT*, September 17, 1970; Colson memo, September 1970 (WHSF, Colson, box 36, NP).

158. Jeb Magruder apparently felt there were political dangers to harping on student unrest, however. "We were elected, in part, to put a stop to campus violence," he cautioned Krogh. "Therefore, such trouble is not necessarily beneficial to us now" (Magruder to Krogh, October 14, 1970, WHSF, Krogh, box 10, NP).

159. Krogh to Magruder, Nofziger and Moore, September 23, 1970 (WHSFCF, HU, box 36, NP); Haldeman to Ehrlichman, September 11, 1970 (WHSFCF, HU, box 36, NP); Magruder, 124; Haldeman to Keogh, November 10, 1970 (WHSFCF, HU, box 36, NP); Keogh to Cole, Colson and Odle, November 19, 1970 (WHSFCF, HU, box 36, NP).

160. Lukas, 3–4; Schell, 127–29, 130; *WP,* October 31, 1970; Gulley, 198; Ehrlichman interview; Chapin to Walker, October 13, 1970 (WHSFCF, HU, box 36, NP).

161. Schell, 130; *WP,* November 2, 1970; Ehrlichman interview; Haldeman interview; Gulley, 198.

162. Magruder, 128–29; *WP,* October 31, 1970; Ehrlichman to Nixon, October 30, 1970 (WHCF, HU, box 32, NP).

163. Klein to Republican senatorial candidates, October 31, 1970 (WHCF, HU, box 32, NP). This cable includes a transcript of Nixon's speech.

164. *WP,* October 31, November 2, 1970.

165. Colson to Keogh, September 22, 1970 (WHSF, Colson, box 44, NP); Magruder, 125–27.

166. Rogers to Haldeman, October 21, 1970 (WHSF, Haldeman, box 48, NP); Haldeman interview; Magruder to Haldeman, October 20, 1970 (WHSF, Haldeman, box 158, NP).

167. Action Memorandum to Magruder, September 14, 1970 (WHSF, Khachigian, box 2, NP); Haldeman to Colson, September 22, 1970 (WHSF, Colson, box 112, NP); Action Memorandum to Colson, September 30, 1970 (WHSF, Colson, box 112, NP); Bell to Colson, October 16, 1970 (WHSF, Colson, box 114, NP); Higby to Colson, October 23, 1970 (WHSF, Colson, box 114, NP); Colson to Higby, October 29, 1970 (WHSF, Colson, box 114, NP).

168. Colson to Chapin, November 27, 1970 (WHSF, Colson, box 36, NP); Colson to Chapin, December 24, 1970 (WHSF, Colson, box 36, NP); Colson to Haldeman, December 30, 1970 (WHSF, Colson, box 36, NP).

169. David Miller to Dean, October 26, 1970 (WHSF, Dean, box 44, NP); Geoff Shepard to Krogh, November 12, 1970 (WHSF, Krogh, box 18, NP); Krogh to Cole, November 16, 1970 (WHSF, Krogh, box 18, NP); Hoover, "Kidnappings and Assaults of United States Government Officials," October 23, 1970 (WHSF, Dean, box 44, NP).

170. *NYT,* November 28, 1970; Oudes, 183; Berrigan interview; *G,* March 1, 1972. Berrigan and Sister Elizabeth McAlister were found guilty, however, of smuggling contraband in and out of prison. The charges were later dropped.

171. Salisbury, 287–88; Dean interview; Lukas, 36–37.

172. Rehnquist to Dean, October 22, 1970 (WHSF, Dean, box 44, NP); Haldeman to Finch, December 2, 1970 (WHSF, Colson, box 124, NP).

173. Hersh, *Price of Power,* 301; Kissinger, *White House Years,* 984; Marshall Green interview; Butterfield to Chapin, December 29, 1970 (WHSFCF, ND, box 42, NP).

174. Haldeman to Nixon, December 1, 1970 (WHSF, Haldeman, box 48, NP).

175. Ibid.

CHAPTER 9. 1971

1. Dellinger interview; Dellinger, *More Power*, 52; Heath, 205–6; *G*, January 23, 1971.

2. Dellinger interview; Lyttle interview; McReynolds interview; Davidson interview.

3. Dellinger interviews; Dellinger, *Vietnam Revisited*, 121.

4. *G*, January 23, 1971; Halstead, 588; Peck interview.

5. Zaroulis and Sullivan, 344.

6. Halstead interview.

7. Dowd interview.

8. Lyttle interview.

9. Kerry and VVAW, 38, 42, 48, 54; Urgo interview.

10. Kerry and VVAW, 10; Barry interview; Urgo interview; VVAW, "History," 1972 (VVAW papers, SHSW).

11. *Newsweek*, December 7, 1970; *Time*, January 25, 1971; Heinl, 4, 9, 14; Cortright, 37–38, 41–43, 45–46.

12. *Time*, January 25, 1971; Westmoreland interview; Moorer interview.

13. Ziegler interview; Morris interview; Price interview; Helms interview; Haldeman interview; Resor interview; *Newsweek*, December 7, 1970.

14. *San Francisco Examiner*, January 17, 1971; Laird interviews.

15. Hersh, *Price of Power*, 310; Nixon, *RN*, 498; Marshall Green interview; Kissinger, *White House Years*, 994.

16. Schell, 144; *NYT*, February 1–8, 1971.

17. Hersh, *Price of Power*, 308, 311; Herring, 241.

18. Schell, 144–45.

19. Haldeman, 192, 194–96.

20. *NYT*, February 9, 10, 11, 1971; *G*, February 13, 20, 1971; Chomsky, "Mayday," 19.

21. *WP*, March 1, 2, 1971; *NYT*, March 2, 1971.

22. *WP*, March 2, 1971; *NYT*, March 2, 1971; Henry Cashen to Chapin, February 26, 1971 (WHCF, HU, box 26, NP); Cashen to Chapin, February 26, 1971 (second) (WHCF, HU, box 26, NP); Walker to Haldeman, March 4, 1971 (WHCF, HU, box 26, NP); Chapin to Walker, March 2, 1971 (WHCF, HU, box 26, NP).

23. Kissinger, *White House Years*, 1012.

24. Chomsky, "Mayday," 28.

25. Trudi Young and David McReynolds, "Reflections on Civil Disobedience," February or March 1971 (CALCAV papers, SHSW); Halstead, 592–96; Churchill and Vander Wall, 60.

26. *G*, February 20, 1971.

27. Lerner, 22; Lyttle interview; Peck interview.

28. PCPJ, "Let's Face It . . . Massive One-Day Demonstrations Aren't Enough . . . More's Needed to End the War," March or April 1971 (PCPJ papers, SHSW); PCPJ, "Time Is Running Out," April 1971 (PCPJ papers, BLUCB); Halstead interview; Lerner, 23; Peck interview.

29. Dellinger interview.

30. The Pentagon changed the code name of the 1971 invasion of Laos to "Lam Son 719," however, after VVAW, at its Winter Soldier Investigation, discovered the earlier incursion. It was apparently not good politics to call undue attention to the fact that this was the *second* invasion of Laos.

31. Al Hubbard, "The Winter Soldier Offensive (Phase-3)," March 1971 (VVAW papers, SHSW); Kerry and VVAW, 138.

32. Colson, "Questions re Americans for Winning the Peace," January 1971 (WHSF, Colson, box 36, NP); Bradley to Colson, January 19, 1971 (WHSF, Colson, box 36, NP); Colson to Butterfield, January 14, 1971 (WHSF, Colson, box 36, NP).

33. Assorted Nixon administration documents (WHSF, Colson, box 36, NP); Bradley to Colson, May 8, 1971 (WHSF, Colson, box 36, NP).

34. Magruder to Haldeman, January 14, 1971 (WHSF, Colson, box 125, NP); Haldeman to Finch, February 2, 1971 (emphasis added) (WHSF, Colson, box 114, NP).

35. Haldeman to Colson, February 20, 1971 (WHSF, Haldeman, box 74, NP); Colson to Haldeman, February 23, 1971 (WHSF, Haldeman, box 74, NP); Colson to Haldeman, March 3, 1971 (WHSF, Haldeman, box 74, NP).

36. Odle to Colson, March 11, 1971 (WHCF, HU, box 32, NP). Odle relayed Chapin's message to Colson.

37. Dean to Rehnquist, January 7, 1971 (WHSF, Dean, box 83, NP); Pauken to Dean, February 8, 1971 (WHSF, Dean, box 83, NP).

38. Ehrlichman to Robert Mardian, March 8, 1971 (WHSF, Dean, box 80, NP); Dean to Mardian, March 1971 (WHSF, Dean, box 83, NP).

39. Haldeman interview; Dean interview; Price interview.

40. Ehrlichman interview; Haldeman interview; Ziegler interview. Nixon had originally planned to stay in San Clemente until May 5 or 6, but decided to return early because of May Day (*WP*, April 28, 1971; Higby to Haldeman, late April 1971 (Haldeman note at bottom), WHSF, Haldeman, box 121, NP).

41. Schell, 150; assorted Nixon administration documents (WHSF, Dean, boxes 83, 84, "Demonstrations—May 1971" folders, NP); Dean, 33.

42. Dean to Haldeman and Ehrlichman, April 16, 1971 (WHSF, Dean, box 83, NP); Dean, 33; Price interview.

43. *WP*, April 25–May 6, 1971; Dean to Haldeman and Ehrlichman, April 15, 1971 (WHSF, Dean, box 83, NP); Ehrlichman interview.

44. Dean to Haldeman and Ehrlichman, April 27, 1971 (WHSF, Haldeman, box 121, NP); Robert Hampton, "Memorandum for Heads of Departments and

Agencies," late April 1971 (WHSF, Dean, box 83, NP); Higby to Haldeman, late April 1971 (WHSF, Haldeman, box 121, NP); Dean to John Nidecker, April 30, 1971 (WHSF, Dean, box 83, NP); Bill Hopkins to Dean, May 5, 1971 (WHSF, Dean, box 83, NP); Dean, "Minimum Work Force Personnel on May 3, 4 and 5," April 28, 1971 (WHSF, Dean, box 84, NP). Haldeman jotted his order in the top margin of this last memo.

45. Dean to Haldeman and Ehrlichman, April 27, 1971 (WHSF, Haldeman, box 121, NP); record of May 6, 1971, White House meeting (WHSF, Dean, box 84, NP); Mitchell to Melvin Laird, May 1, 1971 (WHSF, Dean, box 83, NP); Lukas, 10; Haldeman's notes of May 1, 1971, meeting with Nixon (WHSF, Haldeman, box 43, NP); Dean, "Meeting re Demonstrations—May 3–5th," late April 1971 (WHSF, Dean, box 83, NP); unidentified author, "Demonstrations—May Day 1971," late April 1971 (WHSF, Haldeman, box 121, NP). Mayor Washington reportedly refused to impose a curfew in Washington (*WP*, May 6, 1971).

46. *WP*, May 1, 1971.

47. Record of May 6, 1971, White House meeting (WHSF, Dean, box 84, NP); *WP*, May 3, 4, 1971; Ronald Ziegler and John Scali, "Public Information Suggestions From Ziegler/Scali," May 1, 1971 (WHSF, Dean, box 83, NP); Lerner, 25, 40; Dean to Nixon, May 7, 1971 (WHSF, Dean, box 83, NP).

48. Unidentified author, "Issues on Demonstration to Be Resolved," late April 1971 (WHSF, Haldeman, box 121, NP); Higby to Haldeman, late April 1971 (WHSF, Haldeman, box 121, NP); record of May 6, 1971, White House meeting (WHSF, Dean, box 84, NP); Ziegler and Scali, "Public Information Suggestions," May 1, 1971 (WHSF, Dean, box 83, NP); *WP*, April 30, May 4, 5, 1971.

49. Dean to Haldeman and Ehrlichman, April 15, 1971 (WHSF, Dean, box 83, NP); Dean to Haldeman and Ehrlichman, April 20, 1971 (WHSF, Dean, box 83, NP); staff secretary to White House staff, April 22, 1971 (WHSF, Dean, box 83, NP); Dean to Haldeman and Ehrlichman, April 21, 1971 (WHSF, Dean, box 83, NP).

50. Dean to Haldeman and Ehrlichman, April 28, 1971 (WHSF, Dean, box 83, NP); Hampton, "Memorandum for Heads of Departments and Agencies," late April 1971 (WHSF, Dean, box 83, NP); Oganovic to Heads of Departments and Independent Establishments, November 20, 1969 (WHSF, Dean, box 83, NP); Cole to Dean, April 23, 1971 (WHSF, Dean, box 83, NP); Dean to Haldeman and Ehrlichman, April 27, 1971 (WHSF, Haldeman, box 121, NP); acting IRS deputy director to IRS employees, late April 1971 (WHSF, Dean, box 83, NP).

51. Unidentified author (probably Dick Howard), "Tentative Plan—Vietnam Veterans," late March 1971 (WHSF, Haldeman, box 77, NP); Colson to Haldeman, April 2, 1971 (WHSF, Haldeman, box 77, NP); Colson to Haldeman, February 23, 1971 (WHSF, Haldeman, box 74, NP); unidentified author (probably Colson), "Plan to Counteract Viet Nam Veterans Against the War," April

1971 (WHSF, Colson, box 123, NP); "Ron" to "Chuck," April 1971 (WHSF, Colson, box 123, NP); Colson, "Telephone Call Recommendation," April 22, 1971 (WHSF, Colson, box 128, NP); copy of April 22, 1971, AP story on Rainwater press conference (WHSF, Colson, box 128, NP); Colson to Higby, April 22, 1971 (WHSF, Colson, box 128, NP); Colson to Haldeman, April 22, 1971 (WHSF, Colson, box 128, NP); Colson to Higby, April 28, 1971 (WHSF, Colson, box 128, NP).

52. Unidentified author (probably Howard), "Tentative Plan—Vietnam Veterans," late March 1971 (WHSF, Haldeman, box 77, NP); Colson to Haldeman, April 2, 1971 (WHSF, Haldeman, box 77, NP); Urgo interview.

53. Unidentified author (probably Colson), "Plan to Counteract Viet Nam Veterans Against the War," April 1971 (WHSF, Colson, box 123, NP); Howard, "Vietnam Veterans Against the War," April 1971 (WHSF, Haldeman, box 77, NP); Dean to Haldeman and Ehrlichman, April 16, 1971 (WHSF, Dean, box 83, NP); Howard, "Questions for John Kerry," April 1971 (WHSF, Haldeman, box 77, NP); Howard, "Questions for Al Hubbard," April 1971 (WHSF, Haldeman, box 77, NP); Howard, "Al Hubbard," April 1971 (WHSF, Haldeman, box 77, NP); Colson to Howard, May 4, 1971 (WHSF, Colson, box 129, NP); Colson to Ziegler, July 7, 1971 (WHSF, Haldeman, box 81, NP); Colson to Howard, May 3, 1971 (WHSF, Colson, box 129, NP).

54. Dean to Haldeman and Ehrlichman, April 15, 1971 (WHSF, Dean, box 83, NP); Dean to Haldeman and Ehrlichman, April 16, 1971 (WHSF, Dean, box 83, NP); Colson to Dean, April 19, 1971 (WHSF, Dean, box 84, NP); Dean to Haldeman and Ehrlichman, April 22, 1971 (WHSF, Dean, box 83, NP).

55. Goldberg, 13; Hubbard, "The Winter Soldier Offensive," March 1971 (VVAW papers, SHSW); VVAW document, 1971 (VVAW papers, SHSW).

56. Unidentified author (probably Colson), "Plan to Counteract Viet Nam Veterans Against the War," April 1971 (WHSF, Colson, box 123, NP).

57. *WP*, May 3, 1971; DeBenedetti, *American Ordeal*, 310.

58. Jon Huntsman to Colson et al., April 27, 1971 (WHSF, Colson, box 123, NP); Hersh, *Price of Power*, 315, 426.

59. *WP*, April 8, 1971; Colson, 43; Chomsky, "Mayday," 20.

60. Kerry and VVAW, 26–27, 35–37, 39–41; Goldberg, 12–13; Schell, 148–49.

61. Barry interview; Kerry and VVAW, 42–45; Goldberg, 11; Dean to Haldeman and Ehrlichman, April 20, 1971 (WHSF, Dean, box 83, NP).

62. Schell, 148; Kerry and VVAW, 64, 104–5; Urgo interview; Barry interview.

63. In 1932 President Herbert Hoover routed the World War I Bonus Marchers in Washington.

64. Dean to Haldeman and Ehrlichman, April 21, 1971 (WHSF, Dean, box 83, NP); Oudes, 240; Ehrlichman's notes of April 21, 1971, meeting with Nixon (WHSF, Ehrlichman, box 5, NP); *WP*, April 30, 1971.

65. Kerry and VVAW, 28–29, 72–77, 86–87; Barry interview.

66. Goldberg, 13; Dean to Haldeman and Ehrlichman, April 22, 1971 (WHSF, Dean, box 83, NP); Schell, 149.

67. Kerry and VVAW, 12, 18; Lifton, 185; Urgo interview; Barry interview.

68. Goldberg, 12; Barry interview; Kerry and VVAW, 58; Urgo interview.

69. Barry interview; Zaroulis and Sullivan, 356.

70. Kerry and VVAW, 123–43; Barry interview.

71. Peck interview.

72. Harris interview.

73. *WP*, April 25, 1971.

74. Bruce Kehrli to Haldeman, April 24, 1971, 9:30, 10:30 A.M. (WHSF, Haldeman, box 121, NP); Ehrlichman's notes of April 24, 1971, meeting with Nixon, 10:30 A.M. (WHSF, Ehrlichman, box 5, NP).

75. *WP*, April 25, 1971; Halstead, 608; Kehrli to Haldeman, April 24, 1971, 12:00 noon (WHSF, Haldeman, box 121, NP).

76. *WP*, April 25, 1971; Halstead, 611.

77. *WP*, April 25, 1971.

78. Colson to Haldeman, April 28, 1971 (WHSF, Colson, box 128, NP).

79. *WP*, April 26, 1971; Hartsough interview.

80. *WP*, April 27, 1971.

81. Ehrlichman's notes of April 26, 1971, meetings with Nixon, 5:00, 7:40 P.M. (WHSF, Ehrlichman, box 5, NP); *WP*, April 27, 1971.

82. *WP*, April 28, 29, 1971; McReynolds interview.

83. *WP*, April 29, 1971; Lerner, 24.

84. *WP*, April 30, 1971.

85. *WP*, May 1, 1971.

86. *WP*, May 4, 1971; *NYT*, May 5, 1971; record of May 6, 1971, White House meeting (WHSF, Dean, box 84, NP); Halstead, 618; Lerner, 19, 40.

87. Fernandez interview.

88. *WP*, May 4, 1971; Halstead, 618; Zaroulis and Sullivan, 361–62; Ellsberg interview.

89. Lyttle interview.

90. Price, 150–51; Price interview; Ziegler interview; Haldeman interview; Ehrlichman interview; Helms interview.

91. Record of May 6, 1971, White House meeting (WHSF, Dean, box 84, NP); Dean, 34; *WP*, May 4, 1971.

92. *WP*, May 5, 6, 1971; record of May 6, 1971, White House meeting (WHSF, Dean, box 84, NP).

93. *WP*, May 4, 5, 6, 1971; Halstead, 620; *NYT*, May 5, 1971; record of May 6, 1971, White House meeting (WHSF, Dean, box 84, NP).

94. *WP*, May 4, 6, 1971; Lyttle interview.

95. Ehrlichman interview; Dean, 33; Haldeman interview; Haldeman's notes of May 3, 1971, meetings with Nixon (WHSF, Haldeman, box 43, NP); record of May 6, 1971, White House meeting (WHSF, Dean, box 84, NP).

96. Dean, 33–34; *NYT*, September 24, 1981; Lukas, 12. Haldeman's ac-

count to Nixon had Colson sending the oranges to veterans participating in the protest.

97. Record of May 6, 1971, White House meeting (WHSF, Dean, box 84, NP); Ehrlichman interviews; *NYT*, May 5, 1971.

98. *WP*, May 4, 1971; Peck interview; McReynolds interview.

99. McReynolds interview.

100. *WP*, May 3, 1971; Luce interview.

101. Dean to Nixon, May 4, 1971, 12:00, 1:30, 5:00 P.M. (WHSF, Dean, box 83, NP); McReynolds interview; *NYT*, May 5, 1971, September 24, 1981.

102. McReynolds interview; Dean to Nixon, May 4, 1971, 3:30, 5:00, 7:00 P.M. (WHSF, Dean, box 83, NP); *NYT*, May 5, 1971; record of May 6, 1971, White House meeting (WHSF, Dean, box 84, NP); Halstead, 621.

103. Ehrlichman's notes of May 4, 1971, meeting with Nixon, 3:00 P.M. (WHSF, Ehrlichman, box 5, NP); Haldeman's notes of May 4, 1971, meeting with Nixon (WHSF, Haldeman, box 43, NP); Haldeman to Colson, May 4, 1971 (WHSF, Haldeman, box 196, NP).

104. *NYT*, May 5, 1971; Dean to Haldeman and Ehrlichman, May 4, 1971 (WHSF, Dean, box 83, NP).

105. Haldeman's notes of May 5, 1971, meeting with Nixon, 9:20 A.M. (WHSF, Haldeman, box 43, NP); *NYT*, September 24, 1981; Haldeman interview.

106. *NYT*, September 24, 1981.

107. Ibid; Haldeman interview. The "guy" who was "completely removed" from the White House was probably Donald Segretti, later convicted of distributing false campaign literature and sentenced to six months in prison (he served four). Segretti was not your stereotypical thug, however: he stood 5' 4" and weighed 135 pounds.

108. Dean to Nixon, May 5, 1971, 12:15, 1:30, 3:15 P.M. (WHSF, Dean, box 83, NP); *WP*, May 6, 1971.

109. *WP*, May 6, 1971; Dean to Nixon, May 5, 1971, 3:15, 4:45, 7:00 P.M. (WHSF, Dean, box 83, NP); McReynolds interview.

110. *WP*, May 6, 1971; Ehrlichman's notes of May 5, 1971, meeting with Nixon, 5:00 P.M. (WHSF, Ehrlichman, box 5, NP); Haldeman's notes of May 5, 1971, meeting with Nixon (WHSF, Haldeman, box 43, NP); Caulfield to Dean, May 5, 1971 (WHSF, Dean, box 83, NP); Dean to Nixon, May 5, 1971, 3:15, 4:45 P.M. (WHSF, Dean, box 83, NP).

111. *WP*, May 6, 1971; Dean to Nixon, May 5, 1971, 4:45, 7:00 P.M. (WHSF, Dean, box 83, NP).

112. *WP*, May 6, 1971.

113. Dean to Nixon, May 6, 1971, 11:00 A.M., 2:00 P.M. (WHSF, Dean, box 83, NP).

114. Ellsberg interview.

115. Record of May 6, 1971, White House meeting (WHSF, Dean, box 84, NP).

116. Ehrlichman's notes of May 6, 1971, meeting with Nixon, 3:00 P.M. (WHSF, Ehrlichman, box 5, NP).

117. Ehrlichman interview; Colson to Dean, May 11, 1971 (WHSF, Dean, box 81, NP); Depray Muir to Dean, July 2, 1971 (WHSF, Dean, box 81, NP); annotated news summary, May 1971 (WHSFPOF, box 33, NP); Price interview.

118. Price interview; Lerner, 20, 40, 41; Magruder, 197; McReynolds interview; Chomsky, "Mayday," 26; Helms interview.

119. Kissinger, *White House Years*, 1010; Hersh, *Price of Power*, 427n; *Christian Science Monitor*, May 8, 1971; Peck interview.

120. *WP*, May 9, 1971; Dean to Nixon, May 7, 1971 (WHSF, Dean, box 83, NP); record of May 8, 1971, White House meeting (WHSF, Dean, box 83, NP); Dean to Colson, Ehrlichman and George Schultz, May 13, 1971 (Haldeman note at top) (WHSF, Dean, box 84, NP); Dean to Ehrlichman, July 16, 1971 (WHSF, Dean, box 81, NP); Campbell memo, June 9, 1971 (WHSF, Dean, box 81, NP); Richard Nathan memo, June 1971 (WHSF, Dean, box 81, NP); Muir to Dean, July 2, 1971 (WHSF, Dean, box 81, NP); annotated news summary, May 1971 (WHSFPOF, box 33, NP).

121. Haldeman to Higby, May 11, 1971 (WHSF, Haldeman, box 196, NP); Colson to Haldeman, June 17, 1971 (WHSF, Haldeman, box 80, NP).

122. *WP*, May 11, 1971; *NYT*, May 12, 1971; copy of June 3, 1971, Cleveland speech by Kleindienst (WHSF, Dean, box 83, NP).

123. Barry interview.

124. Oudes, 275; Colson memo, July 1971 (WHSF, Haldeman, box 81, NP); *WP*, July 22, 1971; Colson to Desmond Barker, July 21, 1971 (WHSF, Barker, box 3, NP).

125. Dean to Fred Fielding, June 4, 1971 (WHSF, Dean, box 81, NP); annotated news summaries, May 1971 (WHSFPOF, box 33, NP).

126. Salisbury, 193n; untitled and unpublished essay by Ellsberg, May 6, 1971 (copy in author's files).

127. Salisbury, 79, 83–84, 87, 96–99, 119, 134–36, 165–68.

128. Ibid., 207–11; Dean to Haldeman, June 1971 (WHSF, Dean, box 84, NP).

129. Salisbury, 211–12, 214.

130. Ellsberg believes the White House perceived he also had documents on the planning of Operation Duck Hook (Ellsberg interview).

131. *NYT*, June 13, 1971; Haldeman, 110–11; "Nixon," PBS television program; Ehrlichman, 301; Lukas, 69; Hersh, *Price of Power*, 384–85; Salisbury, 267.

132. Nixon, *RN*, 512–13; Hersh, *Price of Power*, 383.

133. Dean, 35; Dean interview.

134. Salisbury, 262.

135. Nixon, *RN*, 510.

136. Haldeman, 111–12; Lukas, 71.

137. Haldeman, 220; Oudes, 148; Nixon, *RN*, 512; Hersh, *Price of Power*, 390; Dean, 35–36.

138. Salisbury, 268n; Ehrlichman, 403; Liddy, 171–72; Dean, 35–38; Bernstein and Woodward, 355.

139. Lukas, 75; Salisbury, 339–40.

140. Haldeman, 116; Schell, 163, 165; Salisbury, 339. Colson later served seven months of a one-to-three-year prison sentence for the effort.

141. Lukas, 92–101; Hersh, *Price of Power*, 395n; Ehrlichman, 399–405; Ehrlichman interview; Liddy, 162–68. Egil Krogh subsequently served six months of a two-to-six-year prison sentence for the break-in.

142. Ellsberg interview.

143. Ibid.

144. Shanks, 121.

145. Ellsberg interview; Wenner, 16.

146. Dean to Haldeman, August 2, 1971 (WHSF, Dean, box 87, NP); Haldeman memo drafted by Dean, August 2, 1971 (WHSF, Dean, box 87, NP); Chapin to Nixon, September 29, 1971 (WHCF, HU, box 32, NP); Chapin to Walker, August 20, 1971 (WHCF, HU, box 32, NP); Colson to Chapin, August 10, 1971 (WHSFCF, HU, box 36, NP); Oudes, 252; Colson to Jamie McLane, August 18, 1971 (WHSF, Colson, box 125, NP). On the White House's effort to keep demonstrators away from Nixon during his public speeches, see also Dewey Clower to Walker, March 4, 1971 (WHCF, HU, box 32, NP); Walker to Chapin, October 4, 1971 (WHCF, HU, box 32, NP); Schell, 179.

147. Hersh, *Price of Power*, 423–38.

148. Marshall Green interview; Hersh, *Price of Power*, 374, 379, 437.

149. Halstead, 646; Peck interview; Lyttle interview.

150. Lyttle interview.

151. Halstead, 646–47; Lyttle interview.

152. PCPJ, "Enough! Evict Nixon," 1971 (PCPJ papers, SHSW).

153. G, August 25, 1971; Lerner, 25; Davidson interview.

154. The group had recently dropped "About Vietnam" from its name.

155. CALC, "Come to Ann Arbor," June 1971 (CALCAV papers, SHSW); Fernandez interview; call for August 1971 CALC conference in Ann Arbor, June 1, 1971 (CALCAV papers, SHSW).

156. Fernandez interview. See also Hall, 118–19.

157. G, May 2, 30, 1973.

158. Urgo interview.

159. Cortright, 34, 111–13; Heinl, 3; Westmoreland interview; Harris interview.

160. Chapin to Parker, September 6, 1971 (WHCF, HU, box 32, NP); Higby to Dean, October 5, 1971 (WHSF, Dean, box 84, NP); Dean to Haldeman, October 8, 1971 (WHSF, Dean, box 84, NP); Dean to Haldeman, October 12, 1971 (WHSF, Dean, box 84, NP).

161. Dean to Nixon, October 23, 1971 (WHSF, Dean, box 84, NP); Dean to Haldeman, October 15, 1971 (WHSF, Dean, box 84, NP); Dean to Haldeman, October 19, 1971 (WHSF, Dean, box 84, NP); Dean to Nixon, October 25, 1971 (WHSF, Dean, box 84, NP).

162. *WP*, October 25, 27, 1971; Huntsman to White House staffers, October 21, 1971 (WHSF, Dean, box 84, NP); Dean to Haldeman, October 15, 1971 (WHSF, Dean, box 84, NP); Dean to Nixon, October 23, 1971 (WHSF, Dean, box 84, NP); Dean to Haldeman, October 19, 1971 (WHSF, Dean, box 84, NP); Treasury director to Butterfield, October 22, 1971 (WHSF, Dean, box 84, NP); Dean to Haldeman and Ehrlichman, October 19, 1971 (WHSF, Dean, box 84, NP).

163. Dean to Haldeman, November 4, 1971 (WHSF, Dean, box 84, NP); Dean to Haldeman, November 5, 1971 (WHSF, Dean, box 84, NP).

164. Halstead, 650; Peck interview; *NYT*, October 14, 1971.

165. *WP*, October 23, 24, 25, 1971.

166. Zaroulis and Sullivan, 371; *WP*, October 26, 27, 28, 1971.

167. *NYT*, November 7, 1971; Halstead, 651.

168. Dean to Haldeman, November 4, 1971 (WHSF, Dean, box 84, NP); Dean to Haldeman, November 5, 1971 (WHSF, Dean, box 84, NP); Higby to Dean, November 8, 1971 (WHSF, Dean, box 84, NP); Dean to Haldeman, November 9, 1971 (WHSF, Dean, box 84, NP); *NYT*, November 10, 1971.

169. *WP*, November 9, 10, 1971; *NYT*, November 10, 1971; Dean to Haldeman, November 11, 1971 (WHSF, Dean, box 84, NP); Dean to Haldeman, November 22, 1971 (WHSF, Dean, box 84, NP); Dean to Haldeman, November 5, 1971 (WHSF, Dean, box 84, NP); Dean to secretary of the Treasury, December 17, 1971 (WHSF, Dean, box 84, NP).

170. Fernandez interview. See also Fernandez editorial in *Christian Century*, December 1, 1971.

171. Dean to Mardian, November 15, 1971 (WHSF, Dean, box 85, NP).

172. "The Indochina Mobile Education Project," 1971 (CALCAV papers, SHSW); Luce interview.

173. VVAW, "Vietnam Veterans Against the War," early 1972 (VVAW papers, SHSW); Dean to Haldeman, December 4, 1971 (WHSF, Dean, box 84, NP).

174. Hersh, *Price of Power*, 441–43, 504–5; Halstead, 654.

175. VVAW, "History," 1972 (VVAW papers, SHSW); G, January 12, 1972; Jack McCloskey interview; VVAW, "Operation Peace on Earth," December 1971 (VVAW papers, SHSW); VVAW, "Vietnam Veterans Against the War," early 1972 (VVAW papers, SHSW); Figley and Leventman, 22; Tim MacCormick et al., "An Open Letter to President Nixon," December 1971 (VVAW papers, SHSW); Barry interview.

176. Barry interview; Urgo interview.

CHAPTER 10. 1972–75

1. *WP*, January 14, 1972; Kissinger, *White House Years*, 1101.

2. Hersh, *Price of Power*, 483, 485–86; Safire, 402.

3. Oudes, 360–62.

4. Dean, 63, 74–76; Dean interview; Lukas, 171–74; Liddy, 197–98; Magruder, 180.

5. Haldeman interview; Hersh, *Price of Power*, 500–2.

6. Kissinger, *White House Years*, 1100–2.

7. DeBenedetti, *American Ordeal*, 325; Fernandez interview; Hall, 138; Paul Moore and Fernandez, "Dear Friend," late April 1972 (CALCAV papers, SHSW).

8. *G*, March 1, 29, April 12, 1972.

9. *G*, April 5, 1972.

10. Cortright, 113.

11. *G*, February 9, March 8, 1972.

12. Hersh, *Price of Power*, 503–4, 506, 510, 511, 515; Zumwalt, 379.

13. *G*, April 12, 26, 1972; Urgo interview.

14. *G*, April 26, 1972; Dean to Haldeman, April 14, 1972 (WHSF, Dean, box 84, NP); *WP*, April 16, 1972; Nixon, *RN*, 590; *NYT*, April 18, 1972.

15. *G*, April 26, 1972.

16. *NYT*, April 21, 22, 1972; *G*, May 3, 1972.

17. *G*, May 3, 10, 1972; *NYT*, April 22, 1972.

18. Moore and Fernandez, "Dear Friend," late April 1972 (CALCAV papers, SHSW); CALC leaflet on Honeywell campaign, 1972 (CALCAV papers, SHSW); CALC, "Honeywell Campaign Organizing Manual," 1972 (CALCAV papers, SHSW); Fernandez interview.

19. Hersh, *Price of Power*, 520n.

20. *NYT*, April 23, 1972; *G*, May 3, 1972.

21. Hartsough interview; Cortright, 118.

22. *G*, May 10, 17, 1972.

23. Dean to Higby, Dean to Gordon Strachan, late April and early May 1972, numerous dates and times (WHSF, Dean, box 84, NP); Dean to Strachan, May 1, 1972 (WHSF, Dean, box 84, NP).

24. Hersh, *Price of Power*, 515; Oudes, 379.

25. Kalb and Kalb, 300; Kissinger, *White House Years*, 1176, 1179.

26. Morris interview; Moorer interview; Zumwalt, 385.

27. Hersh, *Price of Power*, 520–21n; Lukas, 194–96; Schell, 240; Ellsberg interview; Oudes, 435; Liddy, 220–21. See also Magruder, 206–7.

28. Lukas, 196.

29. *NYT*, May 9, 10, 11, 12, 1972; Kissinger, *White House Years*, 1191; *G*, May 17, 1972; Lyttle, *Chicago Anti–Vietnam War Movement*, 151; DeBenedetti, *American Ordeal*, 330.

30. Dancis interview.

31. Dean to Higby and Strachan, early and mid May 1972, numerous dates and times (WHSF, Dean, box 84, NP); Dean to Higby and Strachan, May 10, 1972, 8:30 A.M. (WHSF, Dean, box 84, NP); Dean to Higby and Strachan, May 11, 1972 (WHSF, Dean, box 84, NP).

32. *NYT*, May 12, 1972; DeBenedetti, *American Ordeal*, 331; CALC docu-

ments on May 1972 "emergency witness and fast" in Washington (CALCAV papers, SHSW).

33. Oudes, 451, 455; Dean to Haldeman, May 15, 1972 (WHSF, Dean, box 84, NP); Haldeman to White House staff, May 19, 1972 (WHSF, Dean, box 84, NP).

34. Magruder, 207–8; Schell, 242–43; unidentified author, "List of Follow-Up Items," May 9, 1972 (WHSFCF, SP, box 60, NP); Higby to Colson, May 9, 1972 (WHSFCF, SP, box 60, NP); Haldeman to Colson, May 15, 1972 (WHSFCF, SP, box 60, NP); Hersh, *Price of Power*, 528n.

35. *NYT*, May 14, 1972; Herring, 248–49.

36. Liddy, 224–25; Hersh, "Nixon's Last Cover-up," 76; Bernstein and Woodward, 357.

37. Kissinger, *White House Years*, 1198–99.

38. Oudes, 448–49.

39. *NYT*, May 14, 1972; Dancis interview; Peck interview.

40. Dean to Higby and Strachan, mid May 1972, multiple dates and times (WHSF, Dean, box 84, NP).

41. Halstead, 673–76; Peck interview; Zaroulis and Sullivan, 387; Dellinger, *More Power*, 178–79.

42. Herring, 249; Nixon, *RN*, 606; Hersh, *Price of Power*, 561.

43. Haldeman to Colson, June 6, 1972 (WHSF, Haldeman, box 100, NP).

44. Nixon, *RN*, 622; Oudes, 431, 462–74, 488.

45. Kutler, 190–91, 365–66; Schell, 261; Liddy, 257–58; Haldeman, 217–18.

46. Lukas, 341–42; Dean interview; Morris interview.

47. Dean to Haldeman, April 1972 (WHSF, Dean, box 90, NP); Lukas, 168; G, June 20, August 8, 1973; Magruder, 199–200, 250.

48. Churchill and Vander Wall, 190; G, June 20, 27, August 22, September 12, 1973.

49. Baez, 184–92; Halstead, 681–84; Weiss interview.

50. Jack Nicholl interview; Santa Barbara IPC, "IPC's Original, Continuing, and Current Goals," early 1973 (IPC papers, SHSW); G, October 11, 1972; unidentified author, "Indochina Peace Campaign: Action," 1972 (IPC papers, SHSW); Hayden, 448–52.

51. *WP*, July 10–14, 1972; Oudes, 516–20.

52. Kutler, 221–22.

53. *Life*, August 25, 1972; Mitchell press release, no date (WHSF, Colson, box 49, NP).

54. *WP*, August 22, 23, 24, 1972; Dean to Haldeman, August 22, 1972 (WHSF, Dean, box 86, NP); Dean to Haldeman, August 21, 1972 (WHSF, Dean, box 86, NP); Dellinger, *More Power*, 130; Nixon, *RN*, 678; Magruder, 263. Dean closely tracked the convention protests for Haldeman. See the "Disturbances During Republican National Convention" folder in box 86 of Dean's files in the WHSF, NP.

55. Halstead, 688–89; Lyttle interview; Hayden, 461; interview with a source desiring anonymity.

56. Barry interview; McCloskey interview; *WP*, August 23, 1972; De-Benedetti, *American Ordeal*, 339.

57. Hersh, *Price of Power*, 572; Zaroulis and Sullivan, 392; Oudes, 539.

58. Zumwalt, 399.

59. Hersh, *Price of Power*, 561–83; Marshall Green interview.

60. Hersh, *Price of Power*, 564–65, 568–600; Marshall Green interview.

61. John Osborne's "Nixon Watch" column, *New Republic*, December 16, 1972; Hersh, *Price of Power*, 603–5; Ehrlichman, 307–8, 314.

62. Hersh, *Price of Power*, 605–6.

63. Schell, 270, 287.

64. Unidentified IPCer, "Sign the Agreement Workshop," fall 1972 (IPC papers, SHSW); statement by Tom Hayden at Los Angeles Press Club, November 21, 1972 (IPC papers, SHSW); IPC Boston/Cambridge Resource Center to IPC state offices, December 15, 1972 (IPC papers, SHSW); Luce interview.

65. *G*, January 10, 1973.

66. PCPJ, "Vote No to Nixon and the War," early fall 1972 (PCPJ papers, SHSW).

67. *G*, October 11, 1972; Nixon, *RN*, 685–86, 711–13.

68. Cortright, 120–21, 123–25; Justice Department Civil Disturbance Information, November 17, 1972 (WHSF, Dean, box 80, NP).

69. Cortright, 121–22; Zumwalt, 221–41.

70. Moorer interview. Forty-six of the sailors received discharges, only ten of which were dishonorable. Most were simply reassigned to other duty.

71. Nixon, *RN*, 717; Kissinger, *White House Years*, 1406–8.

72. Halstead, 688, 691–92; Justice Department Civil Disturbance Information, January 26, 1973 (WHSF, Dean, box 80, NP); PCPJ, "Vote No to Nixon and the War," early fall 1972 (PCPJ papers, SHSW); Justice Department Civil Disturbance Information, December 8, 1972 (WHSF, Dean, box 80, NP).

73. Zaroulis and Sullivan, 395; Dean to Haldeman, December 20, 1972 (WHSF, Dean, box 85, NP).

74. Hersh, *Price of Power*, 613–17; Herring, 252.

75. Herring, 253; Maclear, 315; Nixon, *RN*, 733; Hersh, *Price of Power*, 619–20, 628n.

76. Nixon, *RN*, 722–33; Moorer interview.

77. Szulc, 61, 67; Nixon, *RN*, 734; Herring, 254; *NYT*, December 19, 30, 1972, January 8, 1973; Karnow, 668; Moorer interview; Hersh, *Price of Power*, 625n.

78. Baez, 193–221.

79. Becker interview.

80. Ellsberg interview.

81. *G*, December 27, 1972, January 3, 10, 17, 24, 1973; *NYT*, December 19, 23, 24, 25, 26, 1972; Hamburg interview; Baez, 219.

82. Hersh, *Price of Power*, 628n–29n; Cortright, 135–36; *NYT*, December 30, 1972; Calvert interview.

83. Dean to Haldeman, December 20, 1972 (WHSF, Dean, box 85, NP); *G*, December 27, 1972, January 3, 10, 17, 24, 1973; Peck interview.

84. *NYT*, December 21, 24, 1972; *G*, January 3, 10, 1973.

85. Kissinger, *White House Years*, 1453; Nixon, *RN*, 738; *NYT*, December 23, 24, 25, 1972; Oakes interview.

86. *G*, January 10, 17, 1973; Kissinger, *White House Years*, 1453; Herring, 254.

87. Nixon, *RN*, 736, 738–40; Colson, 82; Kissinger, *White House Years*, 1449, 1455; Frost, 126; *NYT*, December 25, 1972; Moorer interview.

88. Price interview; Hersh, *Price of Power*, 626–27; Haldeman interview; Nixon, *RN*, 743.

89. Moorer interview.

90. *G*, January 10, 17, 24, 1973; CALC leaflet on January 3–4, 1973, "Religious Convocation and Congressional Visitation" in Washington, D.C. (CALCAV papers, SHSW); Nixon, *RN*, 757; Dean to Haldeman, January 15, 1973 (WHSF, Dean, box 85, NP); schedule of January 1973 antiwar activities (WHSF, Dean, box 85, NP).

91. *G*, January 31, 1973; Nixon, *RN*, 752–53.

92. Nixon, *RN*, 754–55.

93. Hersh, *Price of Power*, 631–34.

94. Ibid, 634.

95. "Notes from IPC National Meeting, February 16–18, 1973, Detroit, Michigan" (IPC papers, SHSW); Halstead interview; Hamburg interview; Lifton, 445.

96. Dellinger interviews.

97. Dellinger interview; Hayden, 462–63; Miller, 318.

98. Lyttle interview; Dellinger interview; McReynolds interview; interview with a source desiring anonymity; Hayden, 463; phone conversation with Rennie Davis.

99. Dellinger, *More Power*, 13, 17–18; Halstead, 702–4.

100. Nicholl interview.

101. McAuliff interview.

102. "Notes from IPC National Meeting, February 16–18, 1973" (IPC papers, SHSW); Santa Barbara IPC, "IPC's Original, Continuing, and Current Goals," early 1973 (IPC papers, SHSW); IPC Boston/Cambridge Resource Center to IPC state offices, December 15, 1972 (IPC papers, SHSW); Duckles interview; *G*, April 18, 1973; Nicholl interview.

103. "Notes from IPC National Meeting, February 16–18, 1973" (IPC papers, SHSW); Santa Barbara IPC, "IPC's Original, Continuing, and Current Goals," early 1973 (IPC papers, SHSW); Duckles interview; Hirsch, "Notes on Congressional Pressure," July 31, 1973 (IPC papers, SHSW).

104. Hirsch, "Notes on Congressional Pressure," July 31, 1973 (IPC papers, SHSW).

105. Herring, 261; Bundy, 403–4; Kissinger, Years of Upheaval, 356.

106. Kutler, 271–72.

107. Ibid., 276; Lukas, 297–99.

108. Lukas, 334; Kutler, 283.

109. Dean ultimately pleaded guilty to obstruction of justice and defrauding the United States; he served four months of a one-to-four-year prison sentence. Magruder pleaded guilty to the same charges and wiretapping the Democratic Party headquarters; he spent seven months behind bars.

110. Lukas, 331–32; Ellsberg interview.

111. Haldeman was later convicted of conspiracy, obstruction of justice, and perjury in connection with the break-in and served eighteen months in prison.

112. Lukas, 313, 315, 336, 339; Kutler, 285, 295–96, 319; Nixon, RN, 847–48.

113. Wenner, 15.

114. Nixon, RN, 887–89; Hersh, Price of Power, 637–38.

115. Herring, 259–60; Halstead, 701; G, November 14, 1973.

116. Wenner, 15; Nixon, RN, 866–69.

117. Nixon, RN, 864.

118. Ibid., 838; "Notes on National IPC Meeting, Cleveland, June 8–10, 1973" (IPC papers, SHSW).

119. Kutler, 391; Nixon, RN, 961–62; Lukas, 422.

120. G, late August, October 3, 10, 1973.

121. Record of October 26–28, 1973, United Campaign conference (IPC papers, SHSW); Nicholl interview; "Indochina Peace Pledge," early 1974 (IPC papers, SHSW); "Germantown National IPC and United Campaign Conference: Oct. 26–28," 1973 (IPC papers, SHSW).

122. Herring, 262; G, October 10, November 14, late November, 1973.

123. G, November 7, 14, 1973; Kutler, 410, 412–13; Nixon, RN, 935, 945.

124. Kutler, 438–39.

125. Lukas, 462.

126. Nixon, RN, 962; WP, January 28, 1974; Kutler, 437; Woodward and Bernstein, 377.

127. IPC, "United Campaign to Cut Aid to Thieu," 1974 (IPC papers, SHSW); G, January 30, 1974.

128. Assorted United Campaign documents, 1974 (IPC papers, SHSW); G, February 6, 13, 1974.

129. Hayden, 459–60; IPC, "United Campaign to Cut Aid to Thieu," 1974 (IPC papers, SHSW).

130. WP, April 5, 1974; Hayden, 459–60. The Senate voted down the administration's request on May 6.

131. G, May 8, 1974.

132. Lukas, 490–91, 509.

133. *G*, July 3, August 14, 1974.

134. Lukas, 537.

135. *WP*, August 8, 1974; Nicholl interview; Herring, 263–64.

136. *WP*, August 7, 1974; Woodward and Bernstein, 438, 447–48.

137. Woodward and Bernstein, 470–72. Woodward and Bernstein's account of this episode was confirmed by a senior Nixon administration official in an interview with the author. The official, who requested anonymity (indeed, turned off the author's tape recorder), believed he was the primary source for the account. He regretted having spoken with Woodward and Bernstein. "I didn't mean to put President Nixon through that," he said, referring to the publicity over the episode. "I'll never talk to those two guys again."

138. Lukas, 565; Woodward and Bernstein, 483.

139. *G*, September 4, October 2, 1974.

140. AFSC reprint of excerpts from Ambassador Graham Martin's January 27, 1976, congressional testimony. Martin submitted the pastoral letter to Congress for the record.

141. Ibid. Martin submitted his cable to Congress for the record.

142. *WP*, January 26, 27, 1975; *G*, February 5, 1975; AFSC reprint of excerpts from Ambassador Graham Martin's January 27, 1976, congressional testimony.

143. *G*, February 12, 1975.

144. AFSC reprint of excerpts from Ambassador Graham Martin's January 27, 1976, congressional testimony.

145. Herring, 264–65.

146. Karnow, 681; Eagleburger interview.

147. *G*, May 7, 21, 1975; *NYT*, May 12, 1975.

AFTERWORD

1. Moorer interview.

2. Herring, 274.

3. Hertsgaard, 113–14.

4. SFC, September 28, 1992.

5. Bennet, 362; Karnow, 29. "American Public Opinion and U.S. Foreign Policy poll sponsored by Chicago Council on Foreign Relations, 1990.

6. Summers, 153; Arkin, 510.

7. Tucker and Hendrickson, 73, 152.

8. Ibid., 73–74.

9. Klare, 466; Tucker and Hendrickson, 1–2.

Interviews

The following people were interviewed for this book; an asterisk (*) following a name signifies that more than one interview was conducted.

ACTIVISTS

Donna Allen, Gar Alperovitz, Bettina Aptheker*, Bill Ayers, Jan Barry, Norma Becker*, Philip Berrigan, Paul Booth, Sam Brown, Greg Calvert, Peter Camejo*, Bronson Clark, David Cortright, Bruce Dancis, Carl Davidson, Michael Delacour, Dave Dellinger*, Doug Dowd, Madeline Duckles, Dave Elder, Michael Ferber, Richard Fernandez, Todd Gitlin, Gil Green, Don Gurewitz, Fred Halstead, Alice Hamburg, Steve Hamilton, David Harris, David Hartsough*, David Hawk, Abbie Hoffman, Jeff Jones, Lew Jones*, Clark Kissinger, Brad Lyttle, Don Luce, John McAuliff, Jack McCloskey*, Joyce McLean*, Craig McNamara*, David McReynolds, Marilyn Milligan, Linda Morse, Robert Musil, Jack Nicholl, Carl Oglesby, Gwen Patton, Sidney Peck, Earl Reynolds, Stephen Smale, Joe Urgo, Cora Weiss, Steve Weissman, Dot Weller, Dagmar Wilson.

OFFICIALS

McGeorge Bundy, William Bundy, George Christian, Ramsey Clark, Clark Clifford, John Dean, Lawrence Eagleburger, John Ehrlichman*, Daniel Ellsberg*, Marshall Green*, H. R. Haldeman*, Morton Halperin, Richard Helms, Melvin Laird*, Anthony Lake, Laurence Lynn, Harry McPherson*, Thomas Moorer, Roger Morris, Paul Nitze*, Ray Price, Stanley Resor, Walt Rostow*, Dean Rusk*, Paul Warnke*, William Watts, William Westmoreland, Ronald Ziegler.

OTHERS

John Sherman Cooper, J. William Fulbright (written correspondence), Theodore Hesburgh, Eugene McCarthy, John Oakes, James Reston, Arthur Schlesinger, Jr., Eric Sevareid, Tom Wicker.

Select Bibliography

Albert, Judith Clavir, and Stewart Edward Albert, eds. *The Sixties Papers: Documents of a Rebellious Decade.* New York: Praeger, 1984.

Arkin, William M. "The Teddy Bear's Picnic." *Nation,* November 2, 1992.

Baez, Joan. *And a Voice to Sing With: A Memoir.* New York: Summit Books, 1987.

Ball, George W. *The Past Has Another Pattern: Memoirs.* New York: Norton, 1982.

Baskir, Lawrence M., and William A. Strauss. *Chance and Circumstance: The Draft, the War and the Vietnam Generation.* New York: Vintage Books, 1978.

Bennet, James. "How the Media Missed the Story." In Micah L. Sifrey and Christopher Cerf, eds., *The Gulf War Reader: History, Documents, Opinions.* New York: Times Books, 1991.

Berkowitz, William R. "The Impact of Anti-Vietnam Demonstrations upon National Public Opinion and Military Indicators." *Social Science Research* 2 (March 1973).

Berman, Larry. *Planning a Tragedy: The Americanization of the War in Vietnam.* New York: Norton, 1982.

Bernstein, Carl, and Bob Woodward. *All the President's Men.* New York: Warner Books, 1976.

Braestrup, Peter. *Big Story: How the American Press and Television Reported and Interpreted the Crisis of Tet 1968 in Vietnam and Washington.* Garden City, N.Y.: Anchor Press/Doubleday, 1978.

Brown, Sam. "The Politics of Peace." *Washington Monthly,* August 1970.

Bundy, McGeorge. "Vietnam, Watergate and Presidential Powers." *Foreign Affairs* (Winter 1979/80). Reprint.

Byrne, Richard, Jr. "Revolution 9." *City Paper,* January 29, 1993.

Calvert, Greg. "A Left Wing Alternative." *Liberation* 14 (May 1969).

Caputo, Philip. *A Rumor of War.* New York: Ballantine Books, 1984.

Chevigny, Bell Gale. "Vietnam: The Worst Years of Our Lives." *Village Voice,* February 15, 1968.

———. "A Farewell to Arms: 'Over There' Is Here." *Village Voice,* March 14, 1968.

Chomsky, Noam. *At War with Asia.* New York: Vintage Books, 1970.

———. "Mayday: The Case for Civil Disobedience." *New York Review of Books,* June 17, 1971.

Christian, George. *The President Steps Down: A Personal Memoir of the Transfer of Power.* New York: Macmillan, 1970.

Churchill, Ward, and Jim Vander Wall. *The COINTELPRO Papers: Documents from the FBI's Secret Wars against Domestic Dissent.* Boston: South End Press, 1990.

Clavir, Judy, and John Spitzer, eds. *The Conspiracy Trial.* Indianapolis: Bobbs-Merrill, 1970.

Clifford, Clark. "A Viet Nam Reappraisal: The Personal History of One Man's View and How It Evolved." *Foreign Affairs* 47 (July 1969).

Clifford, Clark, with Richard Holbrooke. *Counsel to the President: A Memoir.* New York: Random House, 1991.

Coffin, William Sloane, Jr. *Once to Every Man: A Memoir.* New York: Atheneum, 1977.

Colson, Charles. *Born Again.* New York: Bantam, 1977.

Connelly, Joel R., and Howard J. Dooley. *Hesburgh's Notre Dame: Triumph in Transition.* New York: Hawthorn Books, 1972.

Converse, Philip E., Warren E. Miller, Jerrold G. Rusk, and Arthur C. Wolfe. "Continuity and Change in American Politics: Parties and Issues in the 1968 Election." *American Political Science Review* 63 (December 1969).

Converse, Philip E., and Howard Schuman. "'Silent Majorities' and the Vietnam War." *Scientific American* 222 (June 1970).

Cooper, Chester L. *The Lost Crusade: America in Vietnam.* New York: Dodd, Mead, 1970.

Cortright, David. *Soldiers in Revolt: The American Military Today.* Garden City, N.Y.: Anchor Press/Doubleday, 1975.

Dean, John. *Blind Ambition: The White House Years.* New York: Pocket Books, 1977.

DeBenedetti, Charles. "A CIA Analysis of the Anti-Vietnam War Movement: October 1967." *Peace and Change* 9 (Spring 1983).

DeBenedetti, Charles, with Charles Chatfield. *An American Ordeal: The Antiwar Movement of the Vietnam Era.* Syracuse, N.Y.: Syracuse University Press, 1990.

Dellinger, Dave. "From Vietnam . . . to Cambodia . . . to Laos . . . to?" *Liberation* 15 (January 1971).

————. *Revolutionary Nonviolence.* New York: Anchor Books, 1971.

————. *More Power Than We Know: The People's Movement toward Democracy.* Garden City, N.Y.: Anchor Press/Doubleday, 1975.

————. *Vietnam Revisited: From Covert Action to Invasion to Reconstruction.* Boston: South End Press, 1986.

Donner, Frank J. *The Age of Surveillance: The Aims and Methods of America's Political Intelligence System.* New York: Vintage Books, 1981.

Dowd, Douglas. "The Strength and Limitations of Resistance." In Stephen Halpert and Tom Murray, eds., *Witness of the Berrigans.* Garden City, N.Y.: Doubleday, 1972.

Drew, Elizabeth B. "Reports: Washington." *Atlantic,* May 1969.

Duffet, John, ed. *Against the Crime of Silence: Proceedings of the Russell International War Crimes Tribunal.* Flanders, N.J.: O'Hare Books, 1968.

Ehrlichman, John. *Witness to Power: The Nixon Years.* New York: Simon & Schuster, 1982.

Ellsberg, Daniel. *Papers on the War.* New York: Simon & Schuster, 1972.

Figley, Charles R., and Seymour Leventman, eds. *Strangers at Home*. New York: Praeger, 1980.

Foner, Philip. *American Labor and the Indochina War*. New York: International Publishers, 1971.

Fox, Douglas M., ed. *The Politics of U.S. Foreign Policy Making*. Pacific Palisades, Calif.: Goodyear, 1971.

Frost, David. *"I gave them a sword": Behind the Scenes of the Nixon Interviews*. New York: Ballantine Books, 1978.

Garrow, David J. *Bearing the Cross: Martin Luther King, Jr., and the Southern Christian Leadership Conference*. New York: Morrow, 1986.

Gellhorn, Martha. "Suffer the Little Children." *Ladies' Home Journal*, January 1967.

Gentry, Curt. *J. Edgar Hoover: The Man and the Secrets*. New York: Norton, 1991.

Gitlin, Todd. *The Whole World Is Watching: Mass Media in the Making and Unmaking of the New Left*. Berkeley and Los Angeles: University of California Press, 1980.

———. *The Sixties: Years of Hope, Days of Rage*. New York: Bantam Books, 1987.

Goldberg, Art. "Vietnam Vets: The Anti-War Army." *Ramparts*, July 1971.

Goldman, Eric F. *The Tragedy of Lyndon Johnson*. New York: Knopf, 1969.

Goodman, Mitchell, ed. *The Movement toward a New America: The Beginnings of a Long Revolution*. New York: Knopf, 1970.

Goodwin, Richard. *Remembering America*. Boston: Little, Brown, 1988.

Goulden, Joseph C. *Truth Is the First Casualty: The Gulf of Tonkin Affair—Illusion and Reality*. New York: Rand McNally, 1969.

———. *Meany*. New York: Atheneum, 1972.

Goulding, Phil G. *Confirm or Deny: Informing the People on National Security*. New York: Harper & Row, 1970.

Gulley, Bill, with Mary Ellen Reese. *Breaking Cover*. New York: Simon & Schuster, 1980.

Hahn, Harlan. "Correlates of Public Sentiments about War: Local Referenda on the Vietnam Issue." *American Political Science Review* 64 (December 1970).

Halberstam, David. *The Best and the Brightest*. Greenwich, Conn.: Fawcett Crest, 1972.

———. *The Powers That Be*. New York: Knopf, 1979.

Haldeman, H. R., with Joseph DiMona. *The Ends of Power*. New York: Times Books, 1978.

Hall, Mitchell K. *Because of Their Faith: CALCAV and Religious Opposition to the Vietnam War*. New York: Columbia University Press, 1990.

Hallin, Daniel C. *The "Uncensored War": The Media and Vietnam*. New York: Oxford University Press, 1986.

Halperin, Morton H. "The Lessons Nixon Learned." In W. Anthony Lake, ed., *The Vietnam Legacy*. New York: New York University Press, 1976.

Halpert, Stephen, and Tom Murray, eds. *Witness of the Berrigans*. Garden City, N.Y.: Doubleday, 1972.

Halstead, Fred. *Out Now! A Participant's Account of the American Movement Against the Vietnam War*. New York: Monad Press, 1978.

Harris, David. *Dreams Die Hard*. New York: St. Martin's / Marek, 1982.

Harris, Louis. *The Anguish of Change*. New York: Norton, 1973.

Harris, Richard. *Justice: The Crisis of Law, Order, and Freedom in America*. New York: Dutton, 1970.

Hayden, Tom. *Reunion: A Memoir*. New York: Random House, 1988.

Heath, Louis G., ed. *Mutiny Does Not Happen Lightly: The Literature of the American Resistance to the Vietnam War*. Metuchen, N.J.: Scarecrow Press, 1976.

Hechinger, Fred. "A Servant of Church and Academe." *Notre Dame*, Spring 1987.

Heinl, Col. Robert D., Jr. "The Collapse of the Armed Forces." *Armed Forces Journal* (June 7, 1971). AFSC reprint.

Herring, George C. *America's Longest War: The United States and Vietnam, 1950–1975*. Philadelphia: Temple University Press, 1986.

Hersh, Seymour M. *My Lai 4: A Report on the Massacre and Its Aftermath*. New York: Random House, 1970.

———. *The Price of Power: Kissinger in the Nixon White House*. New York: Summit Books, 1983.

———. "Nixon's Last Cover-up: The Tapes He Wants the Archives to Suppress." *New Yorker*, December 14, 1992.

Hertsgaard, Mark. *On Bended Knee: The Press and the Reagan Presidency*. New York: Schocken Books, 1989.

Hesburgh, Theodore M. *The Hesburgh Papers: Higher Values in Higher Education*. Kansas City: Andrews & McMeel, 1979.

Hoffman, Abbie. *Revolution for the Hell of It*. New York: Pocket Books, 1970.

———. *Soon to Be a Major Motion Picture*. New York: Putnam, 1980.

Hoffman, Paul. *Moratorium: An American Protest*. New York: Tower Publications, 1970.

Hoopes, Townsend. *The Limits of Intervention: An Inside Account of How the Johnson Policy of Escalation in Vietnam Was Reversed*. New York: David McKay, 1973.

Hurwitz, Ken. *Marching Nowhere*. New York: Norton, 1971.

Isaacson, Walter, and Evan Thomas. *The Wise Men: Six Men and the World They Made*. New York: Simon & Schuster, 1986.

Jacobs, Harold, ed. *Weatherman*. San Francisco: Ramparts Press, 1970.

Johnson, Lady Bird. *A White House Diary*. New York: Holt, Rinehart & Winston, 1970.

Johnson, Lyndon Baines. *The Vantage Point: Perspectives of the Presidency 1963–1969*. New York: Holt, Rinehart & Winston, 1971.

Joseph, Paul. *Cracks in the Empire: State Politics in the Vietnam War*. Boston: South End Press, 1981.

Kalb, Marvin, and Bernard Kalb. *Kissinger*. Boston: Little, Brown, 1974.

Karnow, Stanley. *Vietnam: A History*. New York: Penguin Books, 1991.

Kearns, Doris. *Lyndon Johnson and the American Dream*. New York: Harper & Row, 1976.

Keniston, Kenneth. *Young Radicals: Notes on Committed Youth*. New York: Harcourt, Brace & World, 1968.

Kerry, John, and Vietnam Veterans Against the War. *The New Soldier*. New York: Macmillan, 1971.

King, Martin Luther, Jr. "Declaration of Independence from the War in Vietnam." *Ramparts*, May 1967.

Kissinger, Henry. *White House Years*. Boston: Little, Brown, 1979.

————. *Years of Upheaval.* Boston: Little, Brown, 1982.

Kitt, Eartha. *Confessions of a Sex Kitten.* Fort Lee, N.J.: Barricade Books, 1989.

Klare, Michael T. "The Pentagon's New Paradigm." In Micah L. Sifrey and Christopher Cerf, eds., *The Gulf War Reader: History, Documents, Opinions.* New York: Times Books, 1991.

Klein, Herbert G. *Making It Perfectly Clear.* Garden City, N.Y.: Doubleday, 1980.

Kolko, Gabriel. *Anatomy of a War: Vietnam, the United States and the Modern Historical Experience.* New York: Pantheon Books, 1985.

Kutler, Stanley I. *The Wars of Watergate: The Last Crisis of Richard Nixon.* New York: Knopf, 1990.

Lake, Antonia, and Anthony Lake. "Coming of Age through Vietnam." *New York Times Magazine,* July 20, 1975.

Lake, W. Anthony, ed. *The Vietnam Legacy.* New York: New York University Press, 1976.

Landau, David. *Kissinger: The Uses of Power.* Boston: Houghton Mifflin, 1972.

Lang, Serge. *The Scheer Campaign.* New York: W. A. Benjamin, 1967.

Larner, Jeremy. *Nobody Knows: Reflections on the McCarthy Campaign of 1968.* New York: Macmillan, 1970.

Lerner, Michael P. "May Day: Anatomy of the Movement." *Ramparts,* July 1971.

Liddy, G. Gordon. *Will: The Autobiography of G. Gordon Liddy.* New York: St. Martin's Press, 1980.

Lifton, Robert Jay. *Home from the War.* New York: Simon & Schuster, 1973.

Lockwood, Lee. "Berrigan at Large." In Stephen Halpert and Tom Murray, eds., *Witness of the Berrigans.* Garden City, N.Y.: Doubleday, 1972.

Lukas, J. Anthony. *Nightmare: The Underside of the Nixon Years.* New York: Viking, 1976.

Lynd, Alice, ed. *We Won't Go: Personal Accounts of War Objectors.* Boston: Beacon Press, 1968.

Lynd, Staughton. "The Movement: A New Beginning." *Liberation* 14 (May 1969).

Lynd, Staughton, and Michael Ferber. *The Resistance.* Boston: Beacon Press, 1970.

Lynd, Staughton, and Thomas Hayden. *The Other Side.* New York: Signet Books, 1967.

Lyttle, Bradford. "Peace Action in Saigon." Unpublished. 1966.

————. "Washington Action Nov. 13–15, 1969." Unpublished. 1970.

————. *The Chicago Anti–Vietnam War Movement.* Chicago: Midwest Pacifist Center, 1988.

Lyttle, Bradford, ed. "May Ninth." Unpublished. 1970.

Maclear, Michael. *Vietnam: The Ten Thousand Day War.* London: Thames Methuen, 1981.

Magruder, Jeb Stuart. *An American Life: One Man's Road to Watergate.* New York: Atheneum, 1974.

Mailer, Norman. *The Armies of the Night.* New York: New American Library, 1968.

McCarthy, Eugene. *The Year of the People.* Garden City, N.Y.: Doubleday, 1969.

McPherson, Harry. *A Political Education.* Boston: Little, Brown, 1972.

Menashe, Louis, and Ronald Radosh, eds. *Teach-ins: U.S.A.* New York: Praeger, 1967.

Miller, James. *"Democracy is in the streets": From Port Huron to the Siege of Chicago.* New York: Touchstone, 1987.

Morris, Roger. *Uncertain Greatness: Henry Kissinger and American Foreign Policy.* New York: Harper & Row, 1977.

Morrison, Joan, and Robert K. Morrison, eds. *From Camelot to Kent State: The Sixties Experience in the Words of Those Who Lived It.* New York: Times Books, 1987.

Nitze, Paul H., with Ann M. Smith and Steven L. Rearden. *From Hiroshima to Glasnost: At the Center of Decision.* New York: Grove Weidenfeld, 1989.

Nixon, Richard M. *RN: The Memoirs of Richard Nixon.* New York: Grosset & Dunlap, 1978.

———. *No More Vietnams.* New York: Arbor House, 1985.

Oberdorfer, Don. "The 'Wobble' on the War on Capitol Hill." *New York Times Magazine*, December 17, 1967.

———. *TET!* Garden City, N.Y.: Doubleday, 1971.

Oudes, Bruce, ed. *From: The President; Richard Nixon's Secret Files.* New York: Harper & Row, 1989.

Page, Benjamin, and Richard Brody. "Policy Voting and the Electoral Process: The Vietnam War Issue." *American Political Science Review* 66 (September 1972).

Peck, Sidney. "Notes on Strategy and Tactics: The Movement Against the War." *New Politics*, August 1968.

The Pentagon Papers. Senator Gravel Edition. Vols. 3, 4. Boston: Beacon Press, 1971.

The Pentagon Papers as Published by the New York Times. New York: Bantam Books, 1971.

Pepper, William. "The Children of Vietnam." *Ramparts*, January 1967.

Peterson, Richard E., and John A. Bilorusky. *May 1970: The Campus Aftermath of Cambodia and Kent State.* Carnegie Commission on Higher Education, 1971.

Powers, Thomas. *Vietnam: The War at Home.* New York: Grossman, 1973.

———. *The Man Who Kept the Secrets: Richard Helms and the CIA.* New York: Knopf, 1979.

Price, Raymond. *With Nixon.* New York: Viking, 1977.

Public Papers of the Presidents: Richard Nixon, 1970. Washington, D.C.: Government Printing Office, 1971.

Rinaldi, Matthew. "The Olive-Drab Rebels: Military Organizing during the Vietnam Era." *Radical America*, May–June 1974.

Robinson, John P. "Public Reaction to Political Protest: Chicago 1968." *Public Opinion Quarterly* 34 (Spring 1970).

Rosenberg, Milton J., Sidney Verba, and Philip E. Converse. *Vietnam and the Silent Majority: The Dove's Guide.* New York: Harper & Row, 1970.

Rostow, Walt W. *The Diffusion of Power: An Essay in Recent History.* New York: Macmillan, 1972.

Rusk, Dean, as told to Richard Rusk. *As I Saw It.* New York: Norton, 1990.

Safire, William. *Before the Fall: An Inside View of the Pre-Watergate White House.* Garden City, N.Y.: Doubleday, 1975.

Sale, Kirkpatrick. *SDS.* New York: Vintage Books, 1973.

Salisbury, Harrison E. *Without Fear or Favor: The New York Times and Its Times.* New York: Times Books, 1980.

Schandler, Herbert Y. *The Unmaking of a President: Lyndon Johnson and Vietnam.* Princeton, N.J.: Princeton University Press, 1977.

Schell, Jonathan. *The Time of Illusion.* New York: Vintage Books, 1976.

Schemmer, Benjamin F. *The Raid*. New York: Harper & Row, 1976.

Schlesinger, Arthur M., Jr. "Vietnam and the 1968 Elections." *New Leader*, November 6, 1967.

———. *The Bitter Heritage: Vietnam and American Democracy, 1941–1968*. Greenwich, Conn.: Fawcett Premier Books, 1968.

Schultz, John. *No One Was Killed: Documentation and Meditation: Convention Week, Chicago, August 1968*. Chicago: Big Table, 1969.

Schuman, Howard. "Two Sources of Antiwar Sentiment in America." *American Journal of Sociology* 78 (November 1972).

Selin, Douglas. "Vietnamization: January to September 1969." Unpublished. 1984.

Sevareid, Eric. "Why Our Foreign Policy Is Failing." *Look*, May 3, 1966.

Shanks, Bob. "The Middle Age of Daniel Ellsberg." *California*, November 1985.

Shapley, Deborah. *Promise and Power: The Life and Times of Robert McNamara*. Boston: Little, Brown, 1993.

Shawcross, William. *Sideshow: Kissinger, Nixon and the Destruction of Cambodia*. New York: Pocket Books, 1979.

Sheehan, Neil. *A Bright Shining Lie: John Paul Vann and America in Vietnam*. New York: Random House, 1988.

Sifry, Micah L., and Christopher Cerf, eds. *The Gulf War Reader: History, Documents, Opinions*. New York: Times Books, 1991.

Skolnick, Jerome. *The Politics of Protest*. New York: Ballantine Books, 1969.

Small, Melvin. "The Impact of the Antiwar Movement on Lyndon Johnson, 1965–1968: A Preliminary Report." *Peace and Change* 10 (Spring 1984).

———. *Johnson, Nixon and the Doves*. New Brunswick, N.J.: Rutgers University Press, 1988.

Smith, Curt. *Long Time Gone: The Years of Turmoil Remembered*. South Bend, Ind.: Icarus Press, 1982.

Smith, Hedrick. "Nixon's Decision to Invade Cambodia." In Douglas M. Fox, ed., *The Politics of U.S. Foreign Policy Making*. Pacific Palisades, Calif.: Goodyear, 1971.

Stein, Buddy and David Wellman. "The Scheer Campaign." *Studies on the Left*, January–February 1967.

Summers, Harry G. *On Strategy II: A Critical Analysis of the Gulf War*. New York: Dell, 1972.

Szulc, Tad. "Behind the Vietnam Cease-Fire Agreement." *Foreign Policy*, no. 15 (Summer 1974).

Talbot, David. "And Now They Are Doves." *Mother Jones*, May 1984.

Taylor, Maxwell D. *Swords and Plowshares*. New York: Norton, 1972.

Thorne, Barrie. "Protest and the Problem of Credibility: Uses of Knowledge and Risk-Taking in the Draft Resistance Movement of the 1960's." *Social Problems*, December 1975.

Trewhitt, Henry L. *McNamara*. New York: Harper & Row, 1971.

Tucker, Robert W., and David C. Hendrickson. *The Imperial Temptation: The New World Order and America's Purpose*. New York: Council on Foreign Relations Press, 1992.

Verba, Sidney, and Richard A. Brody. "Participation, Policy Preferences, and the War in Vietnam." *Public Opinion Quarterly* 34 (Fall 1970).

Verba, Sidney, Richard A. Brody, Edwin B. Parker, Norman H. Nie, Nelson W.

Polsby, Paul Ekman, and Gordon S. Black. "Public Opinion and the War in Vietnam." *American Political Science Review* 61 (June 1967).

The Vietnam Hearings. New York: Vintage Books, 1966.

Viorst, Milton. "Attorney General Mitchell: 'The Justice Department Is an Institution for Law Enforcement, Not Social Improvement.'" *New York Times Magazine*, August 10, 1969.

Walker, Daniel. *Rights in Conflict: The Violent Confrontation of Demonstrators and Police in the Parks and Streets of Chicago during the Week of the Democratic National Convention of 1968.* New York: Bantam Books, 1968.

Wenner, Jann. *The Rolling Stone Interview: Dan Ellsberg.* San Francisco: Straight Arrow Publishers, 1973. Reprint.

Westmoreland, General William C. *A Soldier Reports.* Garden City, N.Y.: Doubleday, 1976.

Wicker, Tom. *On Press.* New York: Viking, 1978.

Woode, Allen. "How the Pentagon Stopped Worrying and Learned to Love Peace Marchers." *Ramparts*, February 1968.

Woodward, Bob, and Carl Bernstein. *The Final Days.* New York: Avon Books, 1977.

Zaroulis, Nancy, and Gerald Sullivan. *Who Spoke Up? American Protest Against the War in Vietnam, 1963–1975.* Garden City, N.Y.: Doubleday, 1984.

Zumwalt, Elmo R., Jr. *On Watch: A Memoir.* New York: Quadrangle, 1976.

Index

Indochina Peace Campaign (IPC), 550–51, 555, 567, 568, 571, 572
Indochina Resource Center (IRC), 567, 575, 577
Institute for Policy Studies, 146, 537
Intelligence Evaluation Committee (IEC), 469, 483–84
Internal Revenue Service (IRS), 325, 345, 405, 489, 499, 574
International Days of Protest (1965), 51, 52, 53, 55–57, 79
International Days of Protest (1966), 60, 70
International Voluntary Services (IVS), 183, 405
Interreligious Committee on Vietnam, 50
Inter-University Committee for a Public Hearing on Vietnam (IUCPHV), 30–31, 32, 33
Inter-University Committee for Debate on Foreign Policy (IUCDFP), 91
In the Name of America, 228
Iraq, 1991 Gulf War with, 328, 515, 581–82
Isla Vista, Calif., 406
Israel, Jared, 101

Jackson, Henry, 119
Jackson State College, 426, 510, 540
Jaworski, Leon, 573, 574
Jeannette Rankin Brigade, 228–29
Jezer, Marty, 215
Johns Hopkins University, 33–34, 406
Johnson, Don, 483, 489
Johnson, Harold, 22, 190, 191, 207
Johnson, Lady Bird, 252, 457; and antiwar movement, 100, 191, 211, 212; and Eartha Kitt, 219–20; and husband's abdication, 222, 261, 262
Johnson, Luci, 94, 222
Johnson, Lynda, 212, 222
Johnson, Lyndon: and AWP, 460; and black riots, 206–7; and Clifford, 244, 246, 249; and Congress, 22, 42, 43, 63, 67, 68, 112, 153, 256, 261; death of, 564; and Dominican Republic, 30, 32; and draft, 57, 145; and Eartha Kitt, 220; and economic costs of war, 43, 137, 250; and Eu-

gene McCarthy, 250; and February 1968 troop request, 243, 249; and Fulbright hearings, 68, 69; and "Great Society," 22, 42; and Humphrey's 1968 presidential candidacy, 279, 281, 286; and Khe Sanh, 243; and leaks, 149, 249; and McGeorge Bundy, 20, 32; and McNamara, 71, 198, 199, 219, 248–49; March 1968 partial bombing halt of, 105, 252–53; and media, 12, 205, 256; and Nitze, 248; paranoia of, 27, 205; and Pentagon Papers, 518; and public opinion, 10, 22–23, 41–42, 63, 75, 99, 123–24, 149, 182, 219, 220, 221, 222, 252, 256–57; relations with Ramsey Clark of, 236; and reserve mobilization, 40–42, 151, 153; and Robert Kennedy, 123, 250; swearing of, 417; and Tet offensive, 241; and Tonkin Gulf, 10, 11; and traitors, 219, 249; and U.S. bombing of North Vietnam, 11, 20, 34, 64, 67, 68, 94, 113, 114, 151, 155, 156, 157, 158, 181, 182, 212, 253; and U.S. troop deployments to Vietnam, 21, 22, 40, 43, 63, 151, 152, 253; and war strategy, 12, 19, 22, 38, 39, 71, 150, 151, 154, 198, 252, 253–54 (*see also specific topics*); and Wise Men, 250, 251–52; withdrawal from 1968 presidential race of, 105, 222, 253, 254, 261–62, 285
——and antiwar movement, 4, 49, 56, 70, 81, 82, 139, 142, 255; antidraft protests, 83, 193, 195, 211, 230, 615; effect of, on abdication by, 105, 261–62; and effects on policy of, 105, 154, 155, 157, 252, 254, 255–56, 257; efforts to counteract, 33–34, 35, 90, 143–44, 146, 147–48, 149, 183, 184 (*see also particular protests*); and foreign communism, 4, 33, 69, 204–10, 617; letters of, to, 117, 118, 137, 183; and Martin Luther King, 130, 131; October 1967 Pentagon demonstration, 184–89 passim, 201, 202, 203, 204, 212, 613; organizing